ANNUAL EDITIONS

Urban Society
Thirteenth Edition

EDITORS

Fred Siegel
The Cooper Union

Fred Siegel, the author most recently of *The Prince of the City: Giuiliani, New York and the Genius of American Life* from Encounter Books, is a professor of history at The Cooper Union for Science and Art in New York.

Harry Siegel
New Partisan.com

Harry Siegel, editor of New Partisan.com, has written extensively on cities for publications including the *New York Sun,* where he was the chief urban affairs editorial writer, *Commentary, The Public Interest,* and the *New York Post.* He is writing a book on gentrification in New York for Ivan R. Dee, publisher.

Contemporary Learning Series

2460 Kerper Blvd., Dubuque, IA 52001

Visit us on the Internet
http://www.mhcls.com

Credits

1. **The Urban Frame**
   Unit photo—Photodisc/PunchStock
2. **The Inner Life: City Stories**
   Unit photo—Dynamic Graphics/PictureQuest
3. **Selling the New City: The Fight to Attract the Young and the Restless**
   Unit photo—Ryan McVay/Getty Images
4. **Urban Revival, Gentrification and the Changing Face of the City**
   Unit photo—The McGraw-Hill Companies, Inc./Andrew Resek, photographer
5. **Urban Economies, Politics and Policies**
   Unit photo—1997 IMS Communications Ltd./Capstone Design. All Rights Reserved.
6. **Sprawl: Challenges to the Metropolitan Landscape**
   Unit photo—Royalty-Free/CORBIS
7. **Urban Problems: Crime, Education, and Poverty**
   Unit photo—Getty Images/PhotoLink/S. Meltzer
8. **Cities and Disasters: Viewing 9/11 and Katrina, and Preparing for What's Next**
   Unit photo—FlatEarth Images

Copyright

Cataloging in Publication Data
Main entry under title: Annual Editions: Urban Society 13/e.
1. Urban Society—Periodicals. I. Siegel, Fred, comp. II Title: Siegel, Harry, comp. III. Title: Urban Society.
ISBN-13: 978–0–07–339743–6   MHID 10: 0–07–339743–1   658'.05   ISSN 0735–2425

Thirteenth Edition

Cover image: PhotoLink/Getty Images and Arthur S. Aubry/Getty Images
Composition: Laserwords

Printed in the United States of America   1234567890QPDQPD987   Printed on Recycled Paper

Editors/Advisory Board

Members of the Advisory Board are instrumental in the final selection of articles for each edition of ANNUAL EDITIONS. Their review of articles for content, level, currency, and appropriateness provides critical direction to the editor and staff. We think that you will find their careful consideration well reflected in this volume.

Preface

In publishing ANNUAL EDITIONS we recognize the enormous role played by the magazines, newspapers, and journals of the public press in providing current, first-rate educational information in a broad spectrum of interest areas. Many of these articles are appropriate for students, researchers, and professionals seeking accurate, current material to help bridge the gap between principles and theories and the real world. These articles, however, become more useful for study when those of lasting value are carefully collected, organized, indexed, and reproduced in a low-cost format, which provides easy and permanent access when the material is needed. That is the role played by ANNUAL EDITIONS.

Fifteen years ago, crime, poverty and their attendant economic costs were overwhelming America's big cities. The middle class was fleeing for safer and more affordable climes, leaving behind only pockets of immense wealth amid sprawling ghettoes. Movies like *Blade Runner* and *Escape from New York* depicted cities as post-apocalyptic nightmares that seemed all too familiar to those still living in them, while books like *American Psycho* and *The Bonfire of the Vanities* depicted a wealthy urban class cut off from American morals and mores. There was a prevailing sense that the nation's cities were lost—that their failed schools meant the next generation of inner city youth were already doomed to lives of poverty, crime and despair, that the problems of crime and the costs of social services were demographic certainties beyond the control of any mayor, and that the city as the pulse and lure of American life was a thing of the past.

The new mayors of the 1990s changed much of that. They brought crime under control, balanced budgets, and restored a sense of hope and promise to urban life. For some cities the problems of crime and poverty are still central. But for many of our post-industrial cities, sprawl and gentrification have pushed their way onto center stage. Both are the inevitable result of economic prosperity, and while serious challenges, certainly beat the alternatives of depopulation and poverty. Sprawl draws life from the central city and means less people need the physical density of cities for their jobs. Without fear of crime, new urbanites will move into areas where they can purchase more space for less money as surely as water flows downhill. In the process, gentrification revives neighborhoods, but at the price of generating social resentments and at times displacing longtime residents.

Cities have responded to the growth of the exurbs by competing to attract—and retain—highly educated and highly mobile members of the "knowledge economy." The continued decline of manufacturing and industrial jobs has reduced the urban dependence on highly cyclical industries in favor of more stable service sector work. But the loss of such jobs has left the cities with a social structure resembling an hourglass. Cities are attracting young single professionals and immigrants.

Population decentralization, an inevitable and continued result of first the electric grid and the automobile, and later the internet, has contributed to the urban sprawl that eats up farmland and creates competing corridors of power and influence that threaten both the central cities and those smaller cities that fail to retain and attract a middle-class population. A number of articles deal with alternatives to decentralization; they elaborate the core ideas of the "new urbanism," such as the virtues of density and the elements of urban design that encourage civic life. These ideas, along with the competition to attract citizens, have lead cities to rebuild their downtowns. A renewed desire for densely trafficked public spaces—parks, commercial and residential centers, and downtowns—in cities as diverse as Newark and Cincinnati, Kansas City and Denver heralds a new national affection for the urban life. But, the still unresolved problems of failing schools continue to push middle class families with young children to suburbia.

Without immigrants continuing to flood into cities—especially New York, Los Angeles, Miami and Chicago—over the past two decades, filling jobs and neighborhoods that many others had fled, the urban revival of the 1990s would have been far more limited. They have rebuilt down-and-out city neighborhoods building by building, and reshaped and revived local economies. Without the demographic renewal these immigrants provided, entire urban neighborhoods would now be largely depopulated. But immigrants bring to our cities and our country problems as well as benefits. Post-9/11 security issues, notably INS screening and the tension between police and communities of illegal immigrants, remain unresolved.

The attacks on New York City and Washington D.C. on September 11, 2001, vividly illustrated the dangers of density. Hurricane Katrina exposed the failings of disaster planning, even after 9/11. It is still too early to discern the full long-term economic and demographic fallout of the terror attacks, let alone what the effect of additional attacks might be.

For those cities where crime is no longer an overriding concern, mayors are no longer forced to dedicate themselves entirely to social services and policing. They are tempted to bypass the crucial work-a-day tasks of education, trash collection, policing, and the like to focus instead on visionary projects—without ensuring that the foundation is solid.

Urban America, then, is at a crucial junction. Having made major gains in the war on crime, the cities are in many ways on the front lines of the war on terror. The funding for first responders in case of a terror attack, however, is deeply skewed by the structure of the United States Senate which gives sparsely populated states far more of a say than heavily populated urban areas. This means that the cities most at risk like New York and Los Angeles are receiving a fraction of what unlikely targets like Wyoming are receiving on a per capita basis.

This thirteenth edition of *Annual Editions: Urban Society* looks at all these challenges, with sections on topics including the creative class, the new downtown, suburbs, exurbs and sprawl, and 9/11 and Katrina. It also has a new section of essays and stories about various cities, to offer a different perspective on the urban experience.

As of late 2006, it remains unclear whether America's cities will hold on to their hard-earned gains of the 1990s, or fall back into what had seemed the intractable decline of the previous 30 years. Hopefully, the 1990s will be remembered more as a turning point than passing phase in the longer trend of urban decline.

Fred Siegel

Fred Siegel
Editor

Harry Siegel

Harry Siegel
Editor

Contents

UNIT 1
The Urban Frame

UNIT 2
The Inner Life: City Stories

The concepts in bold italics are developed in the article. For further expansion, please refer to the Topic Guide and the Index.

UNIT 3
Selling the New City: The Fight to Attract the Young and the Restless

The concepts in bold italics are developed in the article. For further expansion, please refer to the Topic Guide and the Index.

UNIT 4
Urban Revival, Gentrification and the Changing Face of the City

The concepts in bold italics are developed in the article. For further expansion, please refer to the Topic Guide and the Index.

UNIT 5
Urban Economies, Politics and Policies

The concepts in bold italics are developed in the article. For further expansion, please refer to the Topic Guide and the Index.

UNIT 6
Sprawl: Challenges to the Metropolitan Landscape

UNIT 7
Urban Problems: Crime, Education, and Poverty

The concepts in bold italics are developed in the article. For further expansion, please refer to the Topic Guide and the Index.

The concepts in bold italics are developed in the article. For further expansion, please refer to the Topic Guide and the Index.

UNIT 8
Cities and Disasters: Viewing 9/11 and Katrina, and Preparing for What's Next

The concepts in bold italics are developed in the article. For further expansion, please refer to the Topic Guide and the Index.

Topic Guide

This topic guide suggests how the selections in this book relate to the subjects covered in your course. You may want to use the topics listed on these pages to search the Web more easily.

On the following pages a number of Web sites have been gathered specifically for this book. They are arranged to reflect the units of this *Annual Edition*. You can link to these sites by going to the student online support site at *http://www.mhcls.com/online/.*

ALL THE ARTICLES THAT RELATE TO EACH TOPIC ARE LISTED BELOW THE BOLD-FACED TERM.

Internet References

The following Internet sites have been carefully researched and selected to support the articles found in this reader. The easiest way to access these selected sites is to go to our student online support site at *http://www.mhcls.com/online/*.

AE: Urban Society 07/08

The following sites were available at the time of publication. Visit our Web site—we update our student online support site regularly to reflect any changes.

General Sources

Library of Congress
http://www.loc.gov

Examine this extensive Web site to learn about the wonderful resource tools, library services/resources, exhibitions, and databases in many different subfields of urban studies.

National Geographic Society
http://www.nationalgeographic.com

This site provides links to National Geographic's huge archive of maps, articles, and other documents. There is a great deal of material of interest to students of urban society.

UNIT 1: The Urban Frame

Manchester, N.H., Open Urban Space Website
http://www.mv.com/ipusers/env

At this site, read about the "urban open space philosophy" and explore specific initiatives in various communities.

WNET/Tenement Museum
http://www.wnet.org/archive/tenement/eagle.html

The Tenement Museum in New York City's Lower East Side is a unique place. Visit this Public Broadcasting Service site to learn the history of a tenement building as housing during subsequent waves of immigration.

UNIT 2: The Inner Life: City Stories

UNIT 3: Selling the New City: The Fight to Attract the Young and the Restless

Center for Democracy and Citizenship
http://www.publicwork.org

This site from the Center for Democracy and Citizenship, associated with the Hubert H. Humphrey Institute of Public Affairs, provides information on current projects and research aimed at strengthening citizenship and civic education. Click on the links to stories describing various such endeavors.

Civnet/CIVITAS
http://www.civnet.org/index.htm

CIVITAS is an international, nongovernmental organization dedicated to promoting civic education and civil society. Find news from around the world related to civic education and civil society, a journal, and Web links here. Resources include a number of great historical documents.

The Gallup Organization
http://www.gallup.com

Open this Gallup Organization home page for links to an extensive archive of public opinion poll results and reports on a variety of topics related to urban life.

UNIT 4: Urban Revival, Gentrification and the Changing Face of the City

Connect for Kids/Workplace
http://www.connectforkids.org/info-url1564/info-url_list. htm?section= Workplace

Browse here to learn about how employees, employees' families, society in general, and management can help a company and a community become more family-friendly. It provides useful hints and guidelines.

WWW Virtual Library: Demography & Population Studies
http://demography.anu.edu.au/VirtualLibrary

This is a definitive guide to demography and population studies with important links to information about the urban environment and the quality of life worldwide.

UNIT 5: Urban Economies, Politics and Policies

IISDnet
http://iisd1.iisd.ca

This site of the International Institute for Sustainable Development, a Canadian organization, presents links on business and sustainable development, developing ideas, and Hot Topics. Linkages is its multimedia resource for environment and development policymakers.

The International Center for Migration, Ethnicity, and Citizenship
http://www.newschool.edu/icmec

The Center is engaged in scholarly research and public policy analysis bearing on international migration, refugees, and the incorporation of newcomers in host countries. Explore this site for current news and to learn of resources for research.

National Immigration Forum
http://www.immigrationforum.org/index.htm

This pro-immigrant organization examines the effects of immigration on the U.S. economy and society. Examine the links for discussion of underground economies, immigrant economies, and other topics.

School of Labor and Industrial Relations
http://www.lir.msu.edu

This MSU/SLIR Hot Links page takes you to sites regarding industrial relations throughout the world. It has links from U.S. government and statistics, to newspapers and libraries, to international intergovernmental organizations.

U.S. Equal Employment Opportunity Commission
http://www.eeoc.gov

The EEOC's mission "is to ensure equality of opportunity by vigorously enforcing federal legislation prohibiting discrimination in employment." Consult this site for small business information, facts about employment discrimination, and enforcement and litigation.

Munisource.org
http://www.munisource.org

Hundreds of links to government bodies and agencies at all levels and from countries all over the world may be accessed here.

U.S. Department of Housing and Urban Development
http://www.hud.gov

Explore this government site for information on public housing, community development, and other topics. Click on Communities for links to state and local government sites.

Virtual Seminar in Global Political Economy/Global Cities & Social Movements
http://csf.colorado.edu/gpe/gpe95b/resources.html

This site of Internet resources is rich in links to subjects of interest in urban studies, covering topics such as sustainable cities, megacities, and urban planning. Links to many international nongovernmental organizations are included.

UNIT 6: Sprawl: Challenges to the Metropolitan Landscape

American Studies Web
http://www.georgetown.edu/crossroads/asw

This eclectic site provides links to a wealth of Internet resources for research in American studies, from rural and urban development, to federalism, to race and ethnic relations.

Sprawl Guide
http://www.plannersweb.com/sprawl/home.html

The online Sprawl Guide is designed to explain the key issues associated with sprawl: housing density, urban sprawl, and growth management. See the Sprawl Resource Guide to link to the wealth of information that is available on the Web.

Yahoo/Social Science/Urban Studies
http://www.yahoo.com/Social_Science/Urban_Studies

Yahoo's page provides many valuable links to resources on various topics in urban studies and development, such as urban planning and urban sprawl.

UNIT 7: Urban Problems: Crime, Education, and Poverty

The Center for Innovation in Education, Inc.
http://www.center.edu

This is the home page of the Center for Innovation in Education, self-described as a "not-for-profit, non-partisan research organization" focusing on K–12 education reform strategies. Click on its links for information about and varying perspectives on various reform initiatives such as the voucher system.

Justice Information Center
http://www.ncjrs.org

Provided by the National Criminal Justice Reference Service, this JIC site connects to information about corrections, courts, crime prevention, criminal justice, statistics, drugs and crime, law enforcement, and victims—among other topics—and presents news and current highlights.

National Institute on the Education of At-Risk Students
http://www.ed.gov/offices/OERI/At-Risk

The At-Risk Institute supports a range of research and development activities designed to improve the education of students at risk of educational failure due to limited English proficiency, race, geographic location, or economic disadvantage. Access its work and links at this site.

The Urban Institute
http://www.urban.org

Visit this home page of the Urban Institute, an organization that investigates social and economic problems and analyzes efforts to solve these problems. Click on the links provided to access information on such topics as welfare reform and health care financing.

UNIT 8 Cities and Disasters: Viewing 9/11 and Katrina, and Preparing for What's Next

Department of State International Information Programs
http://usinfo.state.gov

A wide-ranging page, which is prepared by the Department of State, this site leads to discussions of topics of global concern such as urbanization. The site addresses today's Hot Topics as well as ongoing issues that form the foundation of the field. Many Web links are provided.

Metropolis Archives: Sustainability
http://www.metropolismag.com/html/content_1001/sup/index_b.html

At this site find many articles from the *Metropolis* journal's archives, which discuss issues of sustainability worldwide.

SocioSite: University of Amsterdam
http://www.pscw.uva.nl/sociosite/TOPICS

This huge sociological site provides access to many discussions and references of interest to students of urban studies, such as links to information on inner cities and the effects of rapid urbanization.

United Nations
http://www.unsystem.org

Visit this Official Web Site Locator for the UN to learn about programs and plans related to urban development and urbanization around the world.

Urban Education Web
http://iume.tc.columbia.edu

Dedicated to urban students, their families, and the educators who serve them, this site is a clearing house on urban education.

We highly recommend that you review our Web site for expanded information and our other product lines. We are continually updating and adding links to our Web site in order to offer you the most usable and useful information that will support and expand the value of your Annual Editions. You can reach us at: *http://www.mhcls.com/annualeditions/*.

UNIT 1
The Urban Frame

Unit Selections

1. **Fear of the City, 1783 to 1983,** Alfred Kazin
2. **The Death and Life of America's Cities,** Fred Siegel
3. **Interview with Jane Jacobs,** Bill Steigerwald
4. **Broken Windows,** James Q. Wilson and George L. Kelling

Key Points to Consider

- Why have Americans traditionally feared big cities? Are these fears well founded?

- What are the different ways to define a city? To define urban life?

- Which is the best definition, and why?

- What is the role of the city in America? What should it be?

- What are the best-designed public spaces in your city or town? What makes a well-designed public space?

- In what ways and to what extent can local politicians have an effect on their cities? How much effect does the federal government have? What goals should they pursue? How and why are Americans re-sorting themselves geographically? What effect will these population shifts have on social tensions and political life?

Student Web Site
www.mhcls.com/online

Internet References
Further information regarding these Web sites may be found in this book's preface or online.

Manchester, N.H., Open Urban Space Web Site
   http://www.mv.com/ipusers/env
WNET/Tenement Museum
   http://www.wnet.org/archive/tenement/eagle.html

Scholars agree that cities have existed for many centuries and in most parts of the world, but before 1800 only about three percent of the world's population lived in towns of more than 5,000 inhabitants. Even today, less than 30 percent of the world's population lives in cities larger than 20,000 people. Nevertheless, urbanization has profoundly influenced the course of global development.

Urbanization is a complex and continuous process. It involves the movement of people from rural to urban areas, generates new patterns of living, and communicates these new patterns to both urban and rural populations.

The rapid growth of modern American cities was largely a consequence of the development of agricultural surpluses and factory systems. When farms produced surpluses, they needed a center for exchange. When factories were developed, the need for a concentrated labor supply and services became apparent. Thus, the city came into existence and became not only a center of trade and culture, but of factory production as well.

Social scientists have been fascinated with the process and consequences of urbanization. For the historian, the dynamics of urban growth illustrate the ways in which entire cultures and nations change over time. Sociologists saw urbanization as a means of studying the effect of new living arrangements on traditional institutions such as the extended family. The psychologist saw urbanization as a force in the ways that individuals learned to cope with new challenges. Economists saw cities, and more recently techno-burbs, as important units for generating wealth and for allocating resources. Political scientists, too, studied urbanization in order to gain a better understanding of the ways in which order and change were managed in these dynamic units. Anthropologists were given a new view of the nature and operation of subcultures.

Opening a new chapter in American urban history, the relative decline of big cities has been a central feature of American political and economic life since the 1960s. Alfred Kazin examines the anti-urban threads that weave through American culture and literature, and looks at how the city has been seen by those outside of its gates. Jane Jacobs sees the city as the engine of creativity, and considers how cities need to change and evolve to continue in that essential role. James Q. Wilson and George Kelling's "Broken Windows" introduced a new theory of policing, based on maintaining order instead of responding once a crime is committed, that proved a central part of the historic drop in crime in the 1990s. Fred Siegel's "The Death and Life of America's Cities" reviews the misguided perspectives and policy choices that drove cities down, and the new generation of reformist mayors in the 1990s who debunked the conventional wisdom and seized control of local taxes, quality of life issues, police strategies, and even improved local public schools in some instances. Now that these reformist mayors have left office, it remains to be seen whether cities can consolidate these gains, or if the 1990s will prove a fleeting recovery in the midst of a longer decline.

Fear of the City 1783 to 1983

The city has been a lure for millions, but most of the great American minds have been appalled by its excesses. Here an eminent observer, who knows firsthand the city's threat, surveys the subject.

ALFRED KAZIN

Every Thursday, when I leave my apartment in a vast housing complex on Columbus Avenue to conduct a university seminar on the American city, I reflect on a double life—mine. Most of the people I pass on my way to the subway look as imprisoned by the city as my parents and relatives used to look in the Brooklyn ghetto where I spent my first twenty years. Yet no matter where else I have traveled and taught, I always seem to return to streets and scenes like those on New York's Upper West Side.

Two blocks away on Broadway there is daily carnage. Drunks outside the single-room-occupancy hotel dazedly eye me, a professor laden with books and notes trudging past mounds of broken glass, hills of garbage. Even at eight in the morning a craps game is going on in front of the hydrant that now gives off only a trickle. It has been left open for so many weeks that even the cover has vanished. On the benches lining that poor polluted sliver of green that runs down the center of Broadway, each drunk has his and her bottle in the regulation brown paper bag. A woman on crutches, so battered looking that I can't understand how she stands up, is whooping it up—totally ignored by the cars, trucks, and bicycles impatiently waiting at the red light. None of the proper people absorbed in their schedules has time to give the vagrants more than a glance. Anyway, it's too dangerous. No eye contact is the current rule of the game.

I left all this many times, but the city has never left me. At many universities abroad—there was even one improbable afternoon lecturing in Moscow—I have found myself explaining the American city, tracing its history, reviewing its literature—and with a heavy heart, more and more having to defend it. The American city has a bad reputation now, though there was a time, as the violinist Yehudi Menuhin said during World War II, when one of the great war aims was to get to New York.

There is no general fear of the city. While sharing it, I resent it, for I have never ceased feeling myself to be one of the city's people, even as I have labored in libraries to seize the full background to my life in the city. But when in American history has

there not been fear of the city—and especially on the part of those who did not have to live in it?

Before there were American cities of any significance, the best American minds were either uninterested in cities or were suspicious of them. The Puritans thought of Boston as another Jerusalem, "a city upon a hill," but even their first and deepest impression was of the forest around it. This sense of unlimited space was bewitching until the end of the nineteenth century. In his first inaugural address in 1801, Thomas Jefferson pronounced, as if in a dream, that Americans possessed "a chosen country, with room enough for our descendants to the hundredth and thousandth generation." What was "chosen" was not just an endless frontier but the right people to go with it. This, as a matter of course to a great country squire like Jefferson, surveying the future from his mountaintop at Monticello, meant excluding the mobs he associated with European cities. Jefferson's attitude may have been influenced by the European Philosophes whom Louis XVI blamed for the French Revolution. Jefferson was a Philosophe himself; he would have agreed with a leader of the revolution, Saint-Just, that oppressed people "are a power on the earth." But he did not want to see any oppressed people here at all—they usually lived to become the kind of mob he detested and feared. "The mobs of great cities," he wrote in *Notes on Virginia,* "add just so much to the support of pure government, as sores do to the strength of the human body."

Jefferson knew what the city mob had done to break down ancient Rome as well as feudal France. America was a fresh start, "the world's best hope," and must therefore start without great cities. As a universal savant of sorts, as well as a classicist and scientist, Jefferson knew that Athens and Rome, Florence and Venice, Paris and London, had created the culture that was his proudest possession. And since he was an eighteenth-century skeptic, this cosmopolitan world culture was his religion. But anticipating the damage that "manufactures" could inflict on the individual, he insisted that on an unsettled continent only the proudly self-sustaining American "cultivator" could retain his dignity in the face of the Industrial Revolution.

It is not easy now to appreciate all Jefferson's claims for the rural life, and his ideas were not altogether popular with other great landowners and certainly not with such promoters of industry as Hamilton. Jefferson was a great traveler and world statesman who hardly limited himself to his country estate. Monticello, with its magnificent architecture, its great library, its array of inventions and musical and scientific instruments, more resembled a modern think tank (but imagine one this beautiful!) than the simple American farm he praised as a bastion of virtue.

But "virtue" was just what Jefferson sought for America. Whatever else they did, cities corrupted. The special virtue of rural folk rested on self-reliance, a quality unobtainable in "manufactures and handicraft arts" because these depended "on casualties and caprice of customers. Dependence begets subservience and venality, suffocates the germ of virtue, and prepares fit tools for the designs of ambition."

A few years later Emerson had a more complicated view of his society. The Sage of Concord was no farmer (Thoreau was his handyman) and did not particularly think the farmers in his neighborhood were the seat of all virtue. They were just of the earth, earthy. But believing in nothing so much as solitude, *his* right to solitude, his freedom only when alone to commune with Nature and his own soul ("Alone is wisdom. Alone is happiness."), Emerson found the slightest group to be an obstruction to the perfect life.

There is an unintentionally funny account in Emerson's journal for 1840 of just how irritating he found his fellow idealists. There was a gathering in some hotel—presumably in Boston, but one Emerson likened to New York's Astor House—to discuss the "new Social Plans" for the Brook Farm commune: "And not once could I be inflamed, but sat aloof and thoughtless; my voice faltered and fell. It was not the cave of persecution which is the palace of spiritual power, but only a room in the Astor House hired for the Transcendentalists. . . . To join this body would be to traverse all my long trumpeted theory, and the instinct which spoke from it, that one man is a counterpoise to a city—that a man is stronger than a city, that his solitude is more prevalent and beneficent than the concert of crowds."

Emerson finally agreed to help found Brook Farm but he could not have lived there. Hawthorne tried it for a while and turned his experiences into the wry novel *The Blithedale Romance*. Hawthorne was another Yankee grumpily insisting on his right to be alone but he did not take himself so seriously; he was a novelist and fascinated by the human comedy. A twentieth-century admirer of Emerson, John Jay Chapman, admitted that you can learn more from an Italian opera than from all the works of Emerson; in Italian opera there are always two sexes.

But Emerson is certainly impressive, bringing us back to the now forgotten meaning of "self-reliance" when he trumpets that "one man is a counterpoise to a city—that a man is stronger than a city. . . ." This was primary to many Americans in the nineteenth century and helped produce those great testaments to

the individual spirit still found on the walls of American schoolrooms and libraries. Power is in the individual, not in numbers; in "soul," not in matter or material conglomeration. And "soul" is found not in organized religion, which is an obedience to the past, but in the self-sufficient individual whose "reliance" is on his inborn connection, through Nature, with any God it pleases him to find in himself.

Certainly it was easier then to avoid the "crowd." Thoreau, who went back many an evening to his family's boardinghouse for meals when he was at Walden Pond writing a book, said that the road back to Concord was so empty he could see a chicken crossing it half a mile off. Like Thoreau's superiority to sex and—most of the time—to politics, there is something truly awesome in the assurance with which he derogates such social facts as the city of New York: "I don't like the city better, the more I see it, but worse. I am ashamed of my eyes that behold it. It is a thousand times meaner than I could have imagined. . . . The pigs in the street are the most respectable part of the population. When will the world learn that a million men are of no importance compared with *one* man?"

To which Edgar Allan Poe, born in Boston and fated to die in Baltimore, could have replied that Thoreau had nothing to look at but his reflection in Walden Pond. Poe would have agreed with his European disciple Baudelaire on the cultural sacredness of great cities. He would have enjoyed Karl Marx's contempt for "rural idiocy." Poe was a great imagination and our greatest critic; as an inventor of the detective story and a storyteller, he was as dependent on the violence and scandal of New York in the 1840s as a police reporter. "The Mystery of Marie Roget," based on the actual murder of a New York shop assistant named Mary Rogers who was found dead in the Hudson after what is now believed to have been a botched abortion, was the first detective story in which an attempt was made to solve a real crime. Even the more than usual drunkeness that led to his death in Baltimore on Election Day of 1849 was typical of his connection with "low" urban life. He was found in a delirious condition near a saloon that had been used for a voting place. He seems to have been captured by a political gang that voted him around the town, after which he collapsed and died.

Yet just as Abraham Lincoln was proud of having a slow, careful countryman's mind, so Poe would have denied that *his* extraordinary mind owed anything to the cities in which he found his material. In the same spirit, John Adams from once rural Quincy, his gifted son John Quincy, and his even more gifted great-grandson Henry, all hated Boston and thought of the financial district on State Street as their antithesis. Herman Melville, born in New York, and forced to spend the last twenty-five years of his life as a customs inspector on the docks, hated New York as a symbol of his merchant father's bankruptcy and of his own worldly failure as an author. In a poem about the Civil War, when the worst insurrection in American history broke out in New York as a protest against the Draft Act, Melville imagined himself standing on the rooftop of his house on East Twenty-sixth Street listening to the roar of the mob and despising it:

Figure 1 A victorious James Buchanan (center) is shown calmly observing his opponent, Millard Fillmore, descending from the national stage.

Source: Library of Congress Rare Book and Special Collections.

> *... Balefully glares red Arson—there—and there.*
> *The Town is taken by its rats—ship-rats*
> *And rats of the wharves. All civil charms*
> *And priestly spells which late held hearts in awe—*
> *Fear-bound, subjected to a better sway*
> *Than sway of self; these like a dream dissolve,*
> *And man rebounds whole aeons back in nature.*

Before the Civil War there was just one exception among the great American writers to the general fear and resentment of the city. Whitman was to be prophetic of the importance of New York as a capital of many races and peoples and of the city as a prime subject in modern American writing. Whitman found himself as man and poet by identifying with New York. None of the gifted writers born and bred in New York—not Melville or Henry James or Edith Wharton—was to make of the city such an expression of personal liberation, such a glowing and extended fable of the possibilities released by democracy. "Old New York," as Edith Wharton called it (a patriciate that Melville could have belonged to among the Rhinelanders and Schuylers if his father had not failed in

business), still speaks in Melville's rage against the largely Irish mob burning and looting in 1863. But Whitman, his exact contemporary, did not despair of the city's often lawless democracy when he helped put the first edition of *Leaves of Grass* into type in a shop off Brooklyn's Fulton Street.

Whitman found himself by finding the city to be the great human stage. Unlike earlier and later antagonists of the city, who feared the masses, Whitman saw them as a boundless human fellowship, a wonderful spectacle, *the* great school of ambition. The masses, already visible in New York's population of over a million, were the prime evidence Whitman needed to ground his gospel of American democracy as "comradeship." Formerly a schoolteacher, printer, carpenter, a failure at many occupations who was born into a family of failures and psychic cripples, Whitman felt that the big anonymous city crowd had made it possible for *him* to rise out of it.

> *One's self I sing, a simple separate person, Yet utter*
> *the word Democratic, the word En-Masse.*

Whitman found the model and form of *Leaves of Grass,* the one book he wrote all his life, in the flux and mass of the city—he even compared his book *to* a city. He never reached his countrymen during his lifetime, and the Gilded Age took the foam off his enthusiasm for democracy, but in decline he could still write, "I can hardly tell why, but feel very positively that if anything can justify my revolutionary attempts & utterances, it is such *ensemble*—like a great city to modern civilization & a whole combined clustering paradoxical unity, a man, a woman."

Whitman was that "paradoxical unity, a man, a woman." His powerful and many-sided sexuality gave him friends that only a great city can provide; his constant expectation of love from some stranger in the street, on the ferryboat, even his future reader—"I stop somewhere waiting for you"—made stray intimacies in the city as sweet to him as they were repellent to most Americans.

The trouble with the city, said Henry James, Henry Adams, and Edith Wharton, *is* democracy, the influx of ignorant masses, their lack of manners, their lack of standards. The trouble with the city, said the angry Populist farmers and their free-silver standard-bearer Bryan in 1896, is Wall Street, the "moneyed East," the concentration of capital, the banking system that keeps honest, simple farmers in debt. Before modern Los Angeles, before Dallas, Phoenix, and Houston, it was understood that "the terrible town," as Henry James called New York, could exist only in the crowded East. The West, "wild" or not, was land of heart's ease, nature itself. The East was the marketplace that corrupted Westerners who came East. There was corruption at the ballet box, behind the bank counter, in the "purlieus of vice." The city was ugly by definition because it lacked the elemental harmony of nature. It lacked stability and relentlessly wrecked every monument of the past. It was dirt, slums, gangsters, violence.

Above all it was "dark." The reporter and pioneer photographer Jacob Riis invaded the East Side for his book *How the Other Half Lives* (1890) because he was "bent on letting in the light where it was much needed."

Look at Riis's photograph "Bandit's Roost," 59 Mulberry Street, taken February 12, 1888. "Bandit's Roost" did not get its name for nothing, and you can still feel threatened as your eye travels down the narrow alley paved with grimy, irregularly paved stone blocks that glisten with wet and dirt. Tough-looking characters in derbies and slouch hats are lining both sides of the alley, staring straight at you; one of them presses a stick at the ground, and his left knee is bent as if he were ready, with that stick, to go into action at a moment's notice. The women at the open windows are staring just as unhelpfully as the derbied young fellow in the right foreground, whose chin looks as aggressive as the long, stiff lines of his derby.

Consider New York just a century ago: the rooftops above the business district downtown are thick with a confusion of the first telephone lines crossing the existing telegraph wires. The immigrant John Augustus Roebling has built a suspension bridge of unprecedented length over the East River, thanks to the wire rope he has invented. This wire makes for a rooted strength and airy elegance as Roebling ties his ropes across one another in great squares. Brooklyn Bridge will be considered stronger as well as infinitely more beautiful than the

other bridges to be built across the East River. But a week after opening day in 1883, the crowd panics as vast numbers cross the bridge, crushing several people to death—and exposing a fear of numbers, of great bridges, of the city itself, that even city dwellers still feel. What they thought of New York in the prairie West and the cotton South may easily be imagined.

But here is Central Park, the first great public park in the New World, finally completed after decades of struggle to reclaim a horrid waste. Unlike the European parks that were once feudal estates, Central Park has been carved, landscaped, gardened, built, and ornamented from scratch and specifically for the people. And this by a Connecticut Yankee, Frederick Law Olmsted, the most far-seeing of democratic visionaries, who saw in the 1850s that New York would soon run out of places in which city dwellers could escape the city. Though he will never cease complaining that the width of his park is confined to the narrow space between Fifth Avenue and what is now Central Park West, he will create a wonderland of walks, "rambles," lakes, gardens, meadows. All this is designed not for sport, political demonstrations, concerts, the imperial Metropolitan Museum, but for the contemplative walker. As early as 1858, before he was chosen superintendent but after having submitted the winning design, "Greensward," in a competition, Olmsted wrote of his park: "The main object and justification is simply to produce a certain influence in the minds of the people and through this to make life in the city healthier and happier. The character of this influence is a poetic one, and it is to be produced by means of scenes, through observation of which the mind may be more or less lifted out of moods and habits in which it is, under the ordinary conditions of life in the city, likely to fall. . . . "

Alas, Central Park is not enough to lift some of us out of the "moods and habits" into which we are likely to fall. Even Walt Whitman, who truly loved New York, acidly let it drop in *Democratic Vistas* (1871) that "the United States are destined either to surmount the gorgeous history of feudalism, or else prove the most tremendous failure of time." The "great experiment," as some English sardonically call the democratic Republic, may very well depend on the city into which nearly a million immigrants a year were to pour at the beginning of the next century. Whitman was not prepared to estimate the effect on America of the greatest volunteer migration recorded in history. It was the eclipse of virtue that surprised him at the end of the century. As if he were Jefferson, he wrote: "The great cities reek with respectable as much as nonrespectable robbery and scoundrelism. In fashionable life, flippancy, tepid amours, weak infidelism, small aims, or no aims at all, only to kill time. In business (this all-devouring modern word business), the one sole object is, by any means, pecuniary gain. The magician's serpent in the fable ate up all the other serpents; and money-making is our magician's serpent, remaining today sole master of the field."

Are cities all that important as an index of American health and hope? The French sociologist Raymond Aron thinks that American intellectuals are too much preoccupied with cities. He neglects to say that most Americans now have no other life but the life in those cities. Paris has been

Figure 2   "Mullen's Alley," by Jacob Riis (c.1888). Riis later found that five of nine children who lived in one of these houses were dead by the end of the year.

Source: Library of Congress Prints and Photographic Division.

the absolute center of France—intellectually, administratively, educationally—for many centuries. America has no center that so fuses government and intellect. Although Americans are more than ever an urban people, many Americans still think of the city as something it is necessary to escape from.

In the nineteenth century slums were the savage places Jacob Riis documented in his photographs, but on the whole the savagery was confined to the slums. The political scientist Andrew Hacker has shown that "there was actually little crime of the kind we know today and in hardly any cases were its victims middle class. The groups that had been violent—most notably the Irish—had by 1900 turned respectable. The next wave of immigrants, largely from Eastern Europe and southern Italy, were more passive to begin with and accepted the conditions they found on their arrival. . . . they did not inflict their resentments on the rest of society. . . . "

What has finally happened is that fear of the city on the part of those who live in it has caught up with the fear on the part of those who did not have to live in it.

American fear of the city may seem ungrateful, since so much of our social intelligence depends on it. But the tradition of fear persists, and added to it nowadays—since all concern with the city is concern with class—has been fear of the "underclass," of blacks, of the youth gangs that first emerged in the mid-fifties. Vast housing projects have become worse than the slums they replaced and regularly produce situations of extreme peril for the inhabitants themselves. To the hosts of the uprooted and disordered in the city, hypnotized by the images of violence increasingly favored by the media, the city is nothing but a state of war. There is mounting vandalism, blood lust, and indiscriminate aggressiveness.

The mind reels, is soon exhausted, and turns indifferent to the hourly report of still another killing. In Brooklyn's 77th precinct a minister is arrested for keeping a sawed-off shotgun under his pulpit. On Easter Sunday uniformed police officers are assigned to protect churchgoers from muggers and purse snatchers. In parts of Crown Heights and Bedford-Stuyvesant, the *Times* reports that "there, among the boarded-up tenements, the gaudy little stores and the residential neighborhoods of old brownstones and small row houses, 88 people were killed in one year—16 in one three-block area." A hundred thousand people live and work in this precinct, but a local minister intones that "Life has become a mean and frightening struggle." Gunshots are heard all the time.

I was born and brought up alongside that neighborhood; the tenement in which my parents lived for half a century does not exist and nothing has replaced it. The whole block is a mass of rubble; the neighborhood has seen so much arson that the tops of the remaining structures are streaked with black. Alongside them whole buildings are boarded up but have been broken into; they look worse than London did after the blitz.

Democracy has been wonderful to me and for me, and in the teeth of the police state creeping up elsewhere in the world, I welcome every kind of freedom that leaves others free in the city. The endless conflict of races, classes, sexes, is raucous but educational. No other society on earth tolerates so many interest groups, all on the stage at once and all clamoring for attention.

Still, the subway car I take every day to the city university definitely contains a threat. Is it the young black outstretched across the aisle? The misplaced hilarity proceeding from the drinking group beating time to the ya-ya-ya that thumps out of their ghetto blaster? The sweetish marijuana fumes when the train halts too long in this inky tunnel and that make me laugh when I think that once there was no more absolute commandment in the subway than NO SMOKING?

Definitely, there is a threat. Does it proceed from the unhelpful, unsmiling, unseeing strangers around me? The graffiti and aggressive smears of paint on which I have to sit, and which so thickly cover every partition, wall, and window that I cannot make out the stations? Can it be the New York *Post*—"Post-Mortem" as a friend calls it—every edition of which carries the news MOM KILLS SELF AND FIVE KIDS? The battle police of the transit force rushing through one car after another as the motorman in his booth sounds the wailing alarm that signifies trouble?

What a way to live! It is apartness that rules us here, and the apartness makes the threat. Still, there is no other place for me to work and live. Because sitting in the subway, holding the book on which I have to conduct a university seminar this afternoon, I have to laugh again. It is *Uncle Tom's Cabin, or Life Among the Lowly.*

ALFRED KAZIN was Distinguished Professor of English at the City University of New York Graduate Center. He was the author of several books, including *An American Procession,* a book about American writers from Emerson to T. S. Eliot.

The Death and Life of America's Cities

FRED SIEGEL

In the wake of the events of September 11, American cities are basking in the reflected glory of New York and its courageous mayor, Rudolph Giuliani. Giuliani's ascent to the status of a national hero, "America's mayor," has eclipsed not only his own accomplishments but the mixed if hopeful condition of big-city America.

America's larger cities are on the upswing after a wave of reformist mayors in the 1990s. Even before the economic boom of that decade took hold, Cleveland's mayor Mike White, Chicago's Richard Daley, Milwaukee's John Norquist, Indianapolis's Steven Goldsmith, Denver's Wellington Webb, and Philadelphia's Ed Rendell had begun to turn their cities around. While the federal government was locked in a decade of trench warfare, reform currents flowed through city halls. Innovations in school, welfare, and crime policy all had a local address. When George Bush described himself as a "compassionate conservative" during the 2000 presidential campaign, he was following in the path of Los Angeles's highly effective Republican mayor, Richard Riordan, who called himself "a bleeding heart conservative." Bush's rival, Al Gore, wrapped himself in the success of Democratic mayors such as Daley, Webb, and Detroit's Dennis Archer.

But for all the accomplishments associated with these men, most cities will need several more successful administrations to repair the damage done over the past 40 years. For the revival to be sustained, it must transform the big cities' dysfunctional political culture. The danger, in the words of a world-weary veteran of Philadelphia politics, is that "Rendell improved things here just enough to make it safe to go back to the policies that produced the problems in the first place."

Unlike the crusading mayors of the Progressive era, none of these recent reformers were part of a broad social movement to institutionalize reform. Thus few of the reformers groomed successors. The new-wave chief executives who left office in Philadelphia, Los Angeles, Jersey City, and Cleveland have been replaced by back-to-business-as usual mayors, though in the first two cities reform currents haven't been entirely stilled. Reform continues in Indianapolis and to a lesser extent in New York while the situation in Detroit is ambiguous.

Big-City Revival

Before we consider the problem of sustaining the urban revival, let's consider the nature of the revival itself. The prosperity of the 1990s was different from earlier expansions. The

1960s boom had been accompanied by riots, rapidly rising crime rates, and social breakdown. In the 1980s, many major cities, including Detroit and Baltimore, never caught the economic wave, while those that did still suffered from increasing crime and welfare dependency. In the 1990s, by contrast, urban home ownership achieved historic highs, and poverty dropped sharply to its lowest rate since 1979. This trend was particularly pronounced in New York, where the greatest gains occurred in poor outer-borough neighborhoods.

New Orleans mayor Marc Morial captured the spirit of the urban renewal when he announced last year that the city was reviving the streetcar route along the Desire corridor. "People," he exulted, will once again "be able to ride a streetcar named Desire." "We're returning to the future." The 2000 Census suggests that cities all across America have been "returning to the future" as incubators of new businesses and catalysts of upward mobility for immigrants. Fueled by immigration, New York, Los Angeles, and Miami reached record population levels. Prosperity hit not only these and other fast-growing cities like Denver, Charlotte, and Columbus, but also so-called "dinosaurs" like Chicago, Boston, and Kansas City, all once given up for dead. Eight of the ten largest cities posted growth, and even those that continued to shrink, including Detroit, Philadelphia, and Cleveland, did so at much slower rates or in some cases nearly held even.

It would be a mistake to assume that the big cities can ever again achieve the dominant position they once held. America continues to become more suburban, as city populations continue to decline relative to their surrounding areas. For every three households that "returned" to the city, notes demographer Bill Frey, five households departed for the suburbs. Growth was fastest in overwhelmingly white exurbia, but minorities joined the move out of the cities as well. Still, as recently as the early 1990s, rising crime, welfare, and unemployment rates as well as riots in Los Angeles and New York led many to assume that central cities were dying if not already dead. What happened to turn things around? Some of the credit goes to the surging economy, some to immigration. But both of those elements were present in the 1980s and failed to spur an urban revival at that time.

Three broad social changes made an enormous difference. First, the storm created by the rise of black political power in the 1960s has largely passed. Day-to-day racial tensions have eased, and African-American leaders have been incorporated into the political classes of all the major cities. Race remains a major factor in local politics, but after three decades of black mayors, whites are far less fearful of blacks in power, and blacks have, for the most part, come to recognize that black mayors are fully capable of failing their own core constituency.

Secondly, the decline of manufacturing finally began to pay off in many cities. The reduction of manufacturing production in the past half-century occurred almost entirely within city boundaries, as nonurban manufacturing has held steady. Deindustrialization, a disaster for some cities, has been an opportunity for others to upgrade their quality of life by turning manufacturing lofts into living spaces and once-polluted waterways into recreation areas. Old manufacturing districts, like Soho in New York and Lodo in Denver, are now hip places to live. College graduates have flocked back to the center cities, which have become the place to meet other young, single twenty-somethings. Refurbished lofts and a newly developed nightlife like that of Baltimore's intriguing harbor neighborhood, Fell's Point, attract young professionals, while empty-nesters are drawn to the city's museums, restaurants, and theaters.

Many of those who work in Fell's Point are part of the software and graphics industry. The first phase of the high-tech revolution occurred largely in exurbia, but the second phase, involving designing software content, has found a natural home in the creative quarters of our older cities. Even famously conservative Cincinnati, a city torn apart by recent riots, is home to a thriving software sector.

Thirdly, retailers have discovered the untapped buying power of the underserved inner-city market. Cities have benefited from the saturation of suburban markets. One developer explained that he was looking at Brooklyn locations because "if we put up one more shopping center on the [New Jersey] Route 1 corridor, the whole place is going to sink into the ground, if it isn't killed off by traffic congestion first." Insurance companies have similarly awakened to the potential of what the *Wall Street Journal* has called "the last untapped insurance market in the U.S."

Policies That Made a Difference

But these structural changes would not have brought about the resurgence of the big city in the 1990s without a concurrent reconceptualization of urban issues. Washington, D.C., mayor Marion Barry captured the essence of many 1980s mayoralties when he insisted that he should not be held accountable for the mayhem in his city. He blamed the federal government for not giving the District enough money and exclaimed, "I'm not going to let murder be the gauge, since we're not responsible for murders, we can't stop the murders." Barry's portrait of a victim mayor presiding over a victimized population was challenged in the Reagan years, but to little effect. In the summer of 1982, the Reagan administration created a firestorm with a report written by Housing and Urban Development staffer Steven Savas. Savas, a veteran of the disastrous mayoral administration of John Lindsay, used

his New York experience to challenge every major assumption of 1960s urban liberalism. Guarantees of federal support, Savas wrote, have created "crippling dependency rather than initiative and independence." Federal programs, he argued, have transformed local officials "from leaders of self-reliant cities to wily stalkers of federal funds." But Savas insisted that "cities can learn to become masters of their own destinies—regardless of the level of federal support."

The Savas argument was received with hostility, but it slowly gained currency. By the early 1990s, a group dubbed "the new mayors" had embraced his approach to city governance. Over the course of the 1990s, the federal government's involvement in cities declined while the cities, newly skeptical of Washington, have revived. If Barry depicted himself as a cork on the ocean, the reform mayors of the 1990s, beginning with Milwaukee's John Norquist, assumed responsibility for the condition of their cities. Denver mayor Wellington Webb encapsulated their approach when he described mayors as "CEOs," fully accountable for the performance of city government. He argued that mayors "need to bury forever the old image of mayors with a tin cup and an extended palm asking for handouts to sustain and expand cumbersome bureaucracies." Providence's roguish but enormously effective mayor Buddy Cianci summed up the change in attitude: "I've been a mayor in the 70s, 80s, and 90s, and it used to be that being a big city mayor meant being a social worker. . . . Now mayors are entrepreneurs."

All the new mayors recognized that the central cities would continue to lose population and jobs to their suburbs unless steps were taken to bring taxes under control and improve the quality of life. This conclusion has led to a new concern with the details of daily existence. Daley planted trees throughout the city, even on the roof of City Hall, and Cleveland's mayor Mike White attacked graffiti and potholes. John Norquist has encouraged excellence in the architectural design for new projects in Milwaukee, arguing that cities' strong suit is their public spaces. Cities offer pleasures of public life unavailable in suburbs, he notes, where "life is filtered through a two screen experience—the TV and the windshield."

Less dramatic, but almost as significant, has been the new attention paid to neighborhood vitality by mayors like Thomas Menino of Boston, Norquist, Daley, and Webb. Menino recognizes that retail is crucial to a neighborhood's revival. "You can't just do housing," he argues. "Commerce isn't the last step in a community's comeback; more often, it has to be the first." Many mayors speak of new convention centers or stadiums, but Menino endorses a different strategy. He proudly told *Governing Magazine* that "in the eight years I've been in office, Boston has built 12 new supermarkets." He explained that "a supermarket is the focal point of a community; you need it to get the foot traffic."

But the greatest achievement of the last decade was bringing crime under control. New York led the way through a combination of the "broken windows" policing strategy and the Comstat crime-mapping program. Broken-windows policing takes seriously small crimes, such as public drinking and urination, that can make a neighborhood seem threatening to residents and inviting to would-be felons. In the most famous example of the broken-windows approach, the New York City Transit Police began arresting turnstile jumpers in the early 1990s and found that one in seven was wanted on outstanding felony warrants. Before Comstat, a method of charting crime trends, the information that police used was sometimes weeks or even months old. Now crime patterns are tracked daily so that problems can be quickly addressed and precinct commanders held responsible for the crime rates in their districts.

Baltimore's innovative mayor Martin O'Malley has taken the Comstat principles and applied them to a range of services. In the case of sanitation, he has used the Comstat mapping principles to target emerging problems and hold district managers accountable. O'Malley's innovations have introduced an unaccustomed transparency to government agencies, whose operations were once understood only by a few insiders. Baltimore's success has led mayors and other officials from more than one hundred cities to visit and learn how it was done.

How much of the legacy of the new mayors will endure? How much of their success has been institutionalized? After a decade of strong, successful mayors, cities such as Los Angeles, Oakland, Spokane, and Cincinnati have enhanced the power of the executive office relative to city councils and school boards. The experience of recent years suggests that mayors need the authority to override the parochial interests that dominate city councils and boards of education. In Chicago, Detroit, and Philadelphia, mayors now have more power over the educational system, and New York is also likely to move in that direction. But a strong mayor doesn't guarantee a strong city: Detroit's Coleman Young ruled virtually without opposition but sent his city deeper and deeper into failure.

George Musgrove, Oakland's deputy city manager, not too long ago took an optimistic view of the future, claiming that "a movement of good government for cities has swept the country, and all good mayors—African-American, white, Latino—are governing that way." New Orleans mayor Marc Morial sounded a more cautious note: "The last few years have been tremendous for most of the mayors." But looking at the mayoral campaigns then underway in Atlanta, Cincinnati, Cleveland, Detroit, Hartford, Houston, New York, and Seattle, Morial mused that there was no guarantee that the sort of people and policies that had made for the 1990s revival would continue to hold sway. Morial was right to worry. The recent rounds of elections suggest, at best, a range of possibilities for continued urban revitalization.

The Good and the Bad

Indianapolis and Philadelphia represent the best- and worst-case scenarios, respectively. With a string of four consecutive effective mayors, Indianapolis is the envy not only of misbegotten neighbor Cincinnati but of much of the country. In the 1990s, Steve Goldsmith transformed Indianapolis government by opening up city services to competition with private-sector vendors. The result has been a more efficient government, as union workers now have the opportunity to compete to perform city services. But despite his successes on services ranging from bus routes to waste-water management to the upkeep of the parks, Goldsmith had scant luck in reforming the hidebound police department and the schools, which are under an independent board of education. Democrat Bart Peterson, picking up where Goldsmith left off, is trying to circumvent the board of education by supporting charter schools. He is the first mayor in the country to be given state authorization to approve charter schools on his own.

Following the record levels of homicide of the Goldsmith era, Peterson has also promised to hire 200 more police officers over four years. But his reform efforts are likely to be hampered by a system that allows a new administration to appoint only the chief and deputy chief of police, while everyone else in the department, officers and patrolmen alike, belong to the same strong union.

In Philadelphia, by contrast, the reform impetus of the 1990s, already fading during the second term of Mayor Ed Rendell, has been replaced by a return to patronage and process-driven politics. Rendell saved Philadelphia from collapse, but whether he permanently altered the city's self-defeating political culture is not yet clear.

In the early 1990s, Mayor Rendell made a reputation for himself as an urban reformer by rescuing Philadelphia—which was losing jobs and population—from near bankruptcy. This was a city that had raised taxes 19 times in 11 years, and in which municipal workers could take off one workday in five. Rendell knew that Philadelphia's traditional patronage politics had come to a dead end. He faced down the city's powerful unions, which he said hadn't "had a bad day in 30 years," by trimming paid holidays and eliminating work rules that required, for example, three workers to change a light bulb at the city-owned airport.

But successor John Street, who was elected in 1999 with the support of those same unions and interest groups, has shown little inclination to buck the city's permanent political class. Street, the city's second African-American mayor, was elected by the same racially mixed public-sector coalition that former tough-guy mayor Frank Rizzo tried to put together just before his death in 1991. Mayor Street is a brilliant tactician and negotiator. But while his allies and donors are doing well, Philadelphia as a whole has very little to show for the first two years of his administration.

Philadelphia lost 68,000 people—4 percent of its population—in the 1990s. Ten percent of the city's land is unoccupied, and about 14,000 abandoned buildings blight the landscape. The obstacles to redeveloping abandoned land for new uses are numerous. Before confronting the city's rococo zoning rules and permit processes, a prospective builder must get legal possession of the abandoned lots. According to the *Philadelphia Daily News,* "Anyone wanting to take over a tax-delinquent vacant lot in Philadelphia must go through 54 steps at 12 agencies, a process that takes at least two years and often many more. The job is only slightly easier if the city already owns the lot: 30 steps at nine agencies." If persistent enough to acquire the land, builders will then face labor costs that make construction 60 to 80 percent more expensive than in the suburbs. And after overcoming all those hurdles, they will find that the building-trades member of the zoning board—an ally of Mayor Street and a representative of the sheet-metal workers—requires that all new homes, no matter how modest in price, have central air-conditioning.

But instead of acknowledging the obvious fact that the city's permit and zoning system is designed to produce public-sector jobs rather than new construction, Street and the city council got bogged down in a lengthy fight over control of the money set aside for cleaning abandoned lots and buildings. Street wanted council permission to float $250 million worth of bonds before receiving public or city-council sanction. But the council, well aware of Street's history on this matter, balked. As Rendell's council president, Street had controlled Philadelphia's empowerment-zone monies. He produced consulting contracts and several large holes in the ground, but virtually no new development. In fact, the population inside Philadelphia's empowerment zone dropped 17 percent in the 1990s, or four times the city's overall rate of decline, despite an infusion of $79 million in federal funds. Suspicions were therefore aroused that the blight money was intended largely for Street's friends and donors. The mayor himself, never bashful on this point, has explained that "the people who support me in the general election have a greater chance of getting business from my administration."

Mayor Street appears to view all policy choices through a special-interest lens. This year the state threatened a takeover of the city's violence-ridden, financially bankrupt school system, in which fewer than half of the students graduate and the teachers' workday is among the shortest in the country. Street initially welcomed the takeover as a chance for reform. But when the NAACP, the strike-prone teachers, and the contractors and suppliers objected, Street changed his tune. His staff and allies devised a secret plan to subvert reform. The 67-page plan explained how Street could undermine the state by shifting key educators to the city payroll to "cripple" school operations. But the report warned that the city must "avoid the public perception that the mayor does not care about improving education and is using the city's schoolchildren as pawns in a political power struggle."

Street largely succeeded in derailing major school reform. The new school commission run by the city and the state quickly moved to divide the spoils by awarding $675,000 worth of consulting and legal contracts to Pennsylvania Republicans and Street's Democratic backers. But Street's "victory" so aroused the ire of the state legislature that limited change in the form of several new charter schools will now go ahead. In the words of one Philadelphia insider, "School reform has gone from promising to fraudulent to weak."

After Street's early manipulation of school-reform politics, a local political insider claimed that "John Street has just removed the last obstacle to his reelection in two years." But in March, 2002 the overconfident mayor provoked an unexpected civic storm by announcing that he was suspending the small scheduled reductions in the city's onerous wage tax. This levy gives Philadelphia the highest family-tax burden in the country. Economists at the Federal Reserve estimate that Philadelphia has lost more than 200,000 jobs to the wage tax since 1970. During the 1990s, when other cities were enjoying an employment boom, Philadelphia lost 33,662 private-sector jobs.

With his announcement, Street ignited a very public fight with the usually moribund business leadership. Philadelphia politics is defined by an exquisite cynicism: Columnists brag that the city is a model of democracy because everyone can afford the $10 bribes necessary to buy off city plumbing inspectors. But when the mayor insisted that even a small tax cut would lead to library and recreation-center closings and possibly even a shortage of police bullets, he tapped an unexpected wellspring of anger in a city where the population has shrunk even as the city workforce continues to grow. The city chamber of commerce, its members shod in wing-tipped loafers, led a march on city hall that was joined by Teamsters and a bevy of black ministers. Loudspeakers blared the Beatles' "Taxman" and "Revolution" and, of course, the theme from *Rocky*. Conceding that the wage tax "has become symbolic of something that is fundamentally wrong with our city and its tax structure," Street backed off and allowed the tax cut to go through.

To Street's surprise, it wasn't possible to go all the way back to business as usual. The rising expectations produced by the Rendell years had become a factor to be reckoned with. But even with the tiny cuts in the wage tax restored, Philadelphia is still uncompetitive. And it remains uncertain whether this will be the end of tax relief or the beginning of a more promising future.

Los Angeles

Richard Riordan, who became mayor of Los Angeles in 1992, restored the confidence of his riot-torn city. In the early 1990s, Los Angeles was struck by a series of blows. The city was particularly hard hit by the 1991 recession, which coincided with the end of the Cold War and a sharp decline in the area's defense employment. The administration of Tom Bradley, mayor since 1973, was shaken by scandals. Additionally, in a city where the two-party system usually refers to the mayor's party and the police chief's party, Bradley and his police chief—the imperious Daryl Gates—were not on good terms. They hadn't spoken for a year when the 1992 Los Angeles riots broke out, and their feud left the city government paralyzed.

Riordan, a businessman with a long history of civil involvement, inherited a dispirited city and an office with sharply limited powers. Los Angeles had a uniquely organized city government—a strong council, a commission system that ran the port and the water and power systems, and a police chief who was virtually independent. But Riordan used his limited powers to calm and reassure the city. He recognized that the loss of military contractors, as well as other major corporations, meant the city was going to have to pay a great deal more attention to small and medium-sized businesses. He was particularly effective at restoring business confidence by reducing the red tape that had built up during Bradley's long reign.

Despite his campaign promises, Riordan was never able to bring the LAPD up to full strength. Demoralized by the 1992 Rodney King riots, rogue cops, threats of a federal consent decree, and intense hostility between the chief and the police union, the force was perennially short-staffed. Los Angeles has roughly 40 percent of New York's population, but only about 21 percent of the Big Apple's police officers. Riordan spoke with admiration of New York's broken-windows and Comstat policing but was never able to push through similar reforms in Los Angeles. Riordan was successful, however, in using his own considerable fortune to win public approval of a new charter that expanded the powers of the mayoralty. The 1999 city charter limited the executive power of the city council and gave the mayor the ability to replace department heads, subject to a council veto. It represented, asserted the *Los Angeles Times,* "the most profound change in the structure of government since the 1920s." Furthermore, the office of the police chief was stripped of its right to tenure and was made subject to oversight by a police commission, which now can terminate the chief's contract after a five-year term.

By restructuring the institutions of city government, the new charter held out the promise of continued reform. But Riordan's chosen heir, Republican businessman Steve Soboroff, was eliminated in the first round of the 2001 nonpartisan primary. Neither of two leading candidates, Democrat James Hahn, a cautious career politician whose father had been a great favorite of African-American voters, nor the charismatic Antonio Villaraigosa, a former state assembly speaker bidding to be the city's first Latino mayor, campaigned on the continuation of Riordan's policies. Instead, both invoked the memory of the late Tom Bradley.

The year 2001 was an important one for Los Angeles. The city was to elect a new mayor, a new controller, and new city attorney, and, due to term limits, six of eleven council members. Furthermore, the city had gone through an unprecedented demographic change. Over the course of 40 years, Los Angeles had been transformed from the whitest major city in the United States to a city with a Latino majority.

After the first round of voting, it appeared that Villaraigosa would be the victor. Backed by a labor-Latino alliance, the candidate spoke of using the mayor's enhanced powers to remake the city. "Villaraigosa," explained influential journalist Harold Meyerson, promised to turn "Los Angeles into the next great proving ground for American progressivism, the place where the great wave of new immigrants stakes its claim on the nation's conscience, bounty and future." But it was a false denouement. Villaraigosa was defeated in the runoff by Hahn, who assembled a *mesalliance* of black voters from South Los Angeles and white moderates from the San Fernando Valley.

Hahn, who grew up as a part of the political class of this apolitical city, has continued and even enhanced policies designed by Riordan that aimed at supporting small businesses. But Hahn's tenuous electoral coalition has fractured. The perennial contest for control over the police department has roiled his relationship with blacks, even as a strong secession movement suggests that much of the city assumes that Los Angeles is unreformable.

Los Angeles, with its 466 square miles, is *de facto* a regional city. The downtown area, where city government is located, is only one of a half-dozen business centers and is remote from the lives of most people. Like Riordan, Hahn was elected with the support of the San Fernando Valley, which is separated from the rest of the city by a low-lying mountain chain. The Valley sees itself as forever shortchanged when it comes to city services, comparing unfavorably the services it receives with those in the nearby small cities of Burbank, Glendale, and Pasadena, where city government is accessible and responsive. Like Riordan, Hahn has paid lip service to Valley concerns, and in the campaign, he implied that he would stay neutral in the secession fight. But as mayor, Hahn has aligned himself with the city's public-sector unions, which bitterly oppose a divorce, eliciting cries of betrayal. As of mid-March of this year, polls show that support for secession has grown by 10 percent and now leads 55 to 36 percent in the Valley and 46 to 38 percent in the city as a whole. There is even a growing secession movement in Hahn's home territory, the port neighborhood of San Pedro.

Secessionists are not the only ones crying foul. The crime rate, driven by a revival of gang activity, is rising rapidly. But this has been overshadowed by the hostilities between two of Hahn's core constituencies, African Americans and the Police Protective League (PPL). Hahn, who seems unaware of, and uninterested in, the methods that have made other cities more successful in reducing crime, promised both to retain African-American Bernard Parks as police chief and to grant the PPL a three-day work week. But the PPL has been at war with Parks, who has cited 6,000 of the 9,000 officers for one infraction or another. Hahn has had personal difficulties with Parks, who often overshadows him, and ultimately sided with the PPL, agreeing not to reappoint Parks. His once-loyal black supporters were angered, seeing his decision as a dangerous erosion of their political power.

In other cities these two developments might produce enormous turmoil. Hahn supporters fear that an alliance between anti-Hahn secessionists and blacks angry over Parks's dismissal might allow the secessionists to break away. But government tends to be at best a secondary matter in this sunshine city where politics is derided as a profession for people without the good looks to make it in the movies. Hahn, who to date has made but limited use of his enhanced powers, seems to have little in the way of an agenda other than hanging on. If he falters, he may be replaced in the next election by the new city attorney Rocky Delgadillo, a Latino centrist. Delgadillo, who appeals to African Americans, has a strong probusiness agenda and has promoted New York-style police practices.

Detroit

In Detroit, the successor administration has been slow to reveal its character. It remains to be seen whether the reforms of former mayor Dennis Archer will be sustained, let alone advanced. Detroit's population had declined from 2 million in 1950 to a little under 1 million in 2000, but like Philadelphia, the city caught a bit of the 1990s rising tide. The city Archer inherited from five-term mayor Coleman Young in 1993 was near collapse. The government barely functioned: "When I walked into the city hall," Archer has commented, "I didn't even have a computer. We still had rotary dial phones in some departments." But that was hardly the worst of it. Coleman Young, who liked to think of himself as a "badass," had taken pleasure in cursing at the suburbanites beyond Eight Mile road, whom he accused of "pillaging the city." They returned the sentiment in kind, leaving Detroit economically isolated. Young was similarly hostile to the police, arguing that "crime is a problem but not the problem. The police are the major threat . . . to the minority community." Murder and arson soared. As one observer put it, "It is as if the [1967] riot never ended, but goes on in slow motion."

Young created a cult of personality, but he was never able to deliver basic services—the city didn't even plow residential streets after snowstorms. The subject of numerous federal investigations, Young was never found guilty of anything, though his former police chief, the chief's top deputy, and a Young business partner were convicted of embezzling about $2.5 million each from a Detroit Police Department fund. Detroit's downtown was so vacant that it was proposed that the empty skyscapers be turned into a necropolis, a monument to urban failure. When the city cut back on power for lighting to save money, people joked that the "last one to leave should turn off the lights."

Unlike Young, Archer consistently maintained a high standard of conduct and kept his administration largely free of scandals. He reduced Detroit's growth-stunting business and income taxes and balanced its budgets. He put the city's fiscal house in order, rescuing it from near junk-bond status. Archer's most important accomplishment was to reconnect Detroit to the surrounding region. He enticed General Motors and the Compuware Corporation to move their headquarters into downtown Detroit, bringing back more than 10,000 jobs. The city's baseball team, the Tigers, has returned to the downtown, and its football team, the Lions, is soon to follow. Archer also repaired relations with both the state government, which responded with "brownfields" legislation, making it easier to clean up polluted industrial sites, and with the local county governments, which pitched in to help Detroit when it was unable to cope with a major snowstorm.

But for all this progress, Detroit still can't plow its streets. Having foresworn competitive bidding to appease the city's powerful unions, Archer struggled to improve city services. He pushed through a $10 million modernization of the streetlight system, boosting the number of working lights from 60 percent to 95 percent. But when he left office, more than a third of the city's traffic signals were still out of commission. Archer was also unable to reform a police department that leads the country in fatal shootings, in a city that is near the top in homicides. Detroit's crime statistics are so unreliable that the FBI has refused to include them in its uniform crime surveys. And in June of 2000, Detroit suffered a two-day blackout when the city-owned power system failed.

Like Philadelphia, Detroit has a massive government of 44 departments, built up when the city's population was far larger. Archer has made some progress in straightening out the land titles for the city's 44,000 abandoned lots. But as in Philadelphia, getting a title is only the start of a builder's problems, as some 350 different permits, issued by 11 different city agencies, are required. In addition, 5 separate agencies issue 83 different licenses, and responsibility for environmental inspections is split among 13 operations across 6 departments. In short, as Archer's successor Kwame Kilpatrick enters office, Detroit still hasn't decided whether city government exists to provide jobs for organized interests or services to citizens.

Kilpatrick won the mayoralty this past November in an election dominated not by Archer's incremental achievements but by the long shadow of Coleman Young. Archer, a Catholic in a city of Baptists, was dogged by charges that he "wasn't black enough," and was always more popular in the suburbs than at home. He was even subject to a failed recall effort in 1999. Neither Kilpatrick nor his rival, former police officer Gil Hill, talked about building on what he had achieved. The public, explained Bill Johnson of the *Detroit News,* "still buys Coleman Young's argument that the psychic benefits of a black autonomy outweigh the material gains of rejoining the region." To underscore that point in the midst of the mayoral election, the city council unanimously voted to create a holiday honoring Coleman Young.

The 31-year-old Kilpatrick, the country's youngest big-city mayor, is a former star football player who comes from the city's leading political family. His mother is a congresswoman, his father a key advisor to the Wayne County executive. He worked well with Republicans when he was House minority leader in Lansing, earning a reputation as a moderate. But running for mayor in Detroit, Kilpatrick found it necessary to establish his Coleman Young credentials by blasting his home state as "the Mississippi of the north."

Kilpatrick enjoys the backing of the business community, but with the auto economy slumping and Ford laying off workers, he has a formidable task ahead. He enters office with a growing budget deficit and a host of union contracts up for renewal. In his inaugural address, the crowd responded with enthusiasm when Kilpatrick promised to root out city workers with a "quit-and-stay mentality"—those who, as he put it, "quit a long time ago, but they come to work every single day." But it's not clear how he can accomplish this, having won office with the backing of public-sector unions and having all but promised never to submit city services to managed competition.

If the new mayor sticks to his campaign platform, it is likely that Detroit will revert once again to being Coleman Young's city. But there are some indications that Kilpatrick, a man with higher ambitions, might surprise. Jerry Oliver, his choice to head the dysfunctional police force, told the press that public-sector "unions are about maintaining the status quo and mediocrity." Kilpatrick himself has made a point of firing very publicly city workers caught on camera goofing off on the job. To date, notes George Canto of the *Detroit News,* Kilpatrick "has been successful at symbolism," but the city is "waiting to see what the substance of the administration will be like."

New York

The mayor who most inspired these others was New York's Rudy Giuliani. Giuliani exerted an enormous influence on American cities through New York's broken-windows policing and its Comstat computer-tracking model, which has been adapted by other cities for a wide range of services. But these successes were only the precondition for his greatest achievement, the restoration of upward mobility as the social norm in New York. Before Giuliani, New York politics was mostly about striking caring poses. Giuliani's predecessors, from John Lindsay to David Dinkins, spoke endlessly of what the city owed the poor but delivered instead rising rates of crime and welfare.

Dinkins' New York was organized around the unspoken assumption that poverty was a permanent condition, and that the best that could be done was to make it bearable. In Giuliani's words, "We blocked the genius of America for the poorest people in New York." Under Giuliani, the city restored the ideal of upward mobility. Giuliani spoke not only of the rights of the poor but also of their obligations to society. As mayor, he delivered greater safety and a rising standard of living in the city's most blighted areas, from Mott Haven in the South Bronx to Brooklyn's East New York. New York's poorest neighborhoods experienced the sharpest drop in crime and the biggest rises in income and property values. None of this was predestined. No other city has made comparable gains, let alone sustained them. New York's crime rates continue to decline even as they have been rising in other big cities. Turning the tables on those who would substitute intentions for outcomes, writer James Traub has asked of Giuliani's critics, "Isn't preserving people's lives, well-being, and property the most compassionate policy of all?"

But Giuliani cultivated no heir. Near the end of a mayoral campaign overshadowed by the terrorist attacks and the war in Afghanistan, he endorsed the eventual victor, billionaire Michael Bloomberg. A lifelong Democrat and a self-proclaimed liberal, Bloomberg spent his way to the Republican nomination and went on to burn through a record-shattering $75 million (plus untold dollars in the form of charitable donations) in the course of defeating the favorite, Democrat Mark Green. Insulated from criticism and scrutiny by a wall of money and advisors, Bloomberg put together a *mesalliance*

easily as strange as that which elected Hahn in Los Angeles. He won the votes both of Giuliani's most fervent admirers and his angriest detractors. One of these partners is likely to be disappointed.

The new mayor, who has brought a gentler style to City Hall, has made a point of stressing cooperation and partnership whenever he speaks. To date, this emphasis on teamwork seems to be paying off. His efforts to cut the $4.8 billion budget deficit produced by the stock-market slowdown, the destruction of the World Trade Center, and the cost of new hires brought on in Giuliani's second term, have brought what for New York is a relatively minor reaction. Bloomberg's pledge to impose no new broad-based taxes has drawn uncharacteristically mild criticism from the city council, which is dominated by representatives of public-sector unions and social-service agencies funded by the city.

Bloomberg has reached out to interests shut out of City Hall during the Giuliani years, and he has, for the most part, continued Giuliani's policing practices. The mayor will no doubt use his personal fortune, estimated at $4 billion, to keep many of the city's often ferocious interest groups in his corner, through ongoing "charitable" donations. Like Nelson Rockefeller, he has his own system of rewards and punishment independent of the public treasury.

The new mayor's first big policy initiative and the first major test of his consensual style has been his continuation of Giuliani's fight to abolish the dysfunctional board of education. The board, which has seen its funding rise from $8 to $12 billion annually over the past four years to little educational effect, has been described by Bloomberg as a "rinky-dink operation." But in order to assume mayoral control, Bloomberg needs the cooperation of the state legislature, traditionally a handmaiden to the city's powerful teachers' union. His effort is also complicated by the fact that the teachers' contract is up for renegotiation. Bloomberg declares that his administration should be judged in large measure by its educational achievements. It's a fair measure, and his commitment partially undercuts those critics who worry that by softening the hard edges of "Rudyism," Bloomberg may revert to treating the poor with the paternalism and condescension associated with Nelson Rockefeller and John Lindsay in the 1960s. But if Bloomberg's cooperative approach fails, he may have little choice but to return to a Rudy-style politics.

No Turning Back?

The reform mayors of the 1990s made a sharp break with the past. Once-standard arguments that poverty was the root cause of urban problems, and that therefore crime could not be reduced until poverty was eliminated, largely fell by the wayside. With the declining crime rates and the broad national prosperity of the 1990s, poverty became less a proof of oppression than evidence of failed social and economic policies.

While reform currents have been slowed in some cities, they are unlikely to be entirely displaced. The new urban reformism has no ideological competition. Some of the policy successes of the 1990s in the areas of taxes, policing, and welfare reform have come under attack, but the critics have offered little in the way of alternatives. Furthermore, as in Philadelphia, the 1990s awakening created a change in expectations, an updraft, that makes citizens less likely to accept ongoing failure. Cincinnati, for instance, looks with envy at the success of nearby Indianapolis, while Detroiters talk about how it's done in Cleveland.

Still, some mayors and cities will continue to fail. It is hard to be optimistic about the future of Philadelphia and Detroit, where the gravitational pull of a patronage-driven parochialism—more intent on preserving old jobs than creating new ones—may be too strong for mayors to escape from its orbit. It may be that the reforms of the 1990s will turn out to be merely an Indian summer in those cities where failed political cultures undermine the self-correcting mechanisms of democracy. But failure now exacts a political price. In both Philadelphia and Detroit, state governments have shown an increasing willingness to take over city institutions such as schools, parking authorities, and the courts.

For nearly 70 years—from roughly 1920 to 1990—the broad trends of American life ran against the country's big cities. Federal efforts to bolster urban areas in the 1960s tended to make matters worse, as cities waited passively for the federal government to rescue them. In the 1990s, the tides shifted and urban America, once stranded, rejoined the rest of the country. A new generation of mayors stopped relying on Washington and broke out of old orthodoxies. In those cities that remain on the path of self-reliance and economic growth, progress will continue.

Reprinted with permission from *The Public Interest,* (148) Summer 2002, pp. 3–22.

An Interview with Jane Jacobs

Urban studies legend Jane Jacobs on gentrification, the New Urbanism, and her legacy

BILL STEIGERWALD

Today, Jane Jacobs is revered as North America's great expert on cities and the way they work. But 40 years ago, when her masterpiece *The Death and Life of Great American Cities* was first published, she was assaulting—and shattering—the fundamental tenets of urban planning.

That book was part literature, part journalism, and part sociology; it looked at cities from the sidewalks and street-corners up, not from the Ivory Tower down. Healthy cities, Jacobs argued, are organic, messy, spontaneous, and serendipitous. They thrive on economic, architectural, and human diversity, on dense populations and mixed land uses—not on orderly redevelopment plans that replaced whole neighborhoods with concrete office parks and plazas in the name of slum clearance or city beautification.

Jacobs has no professional training and only a high school diploma. But in the years since *Death and Life* was published, her "radical" ideas about what makes cities livable have become popular—in some quarters, near gospel. To some extent, this was driven by Jacobs' own civic activism, fighting to protect her New York neighborhood against the city planners' designs.

Jacobs' subsequent books have been just as revolutionary, if not always as widely read. *The Economy of Cities* (1969) and *Cities and the Wealth of Nations* (1984) laid out new ideas about urban economics, stressing the importance of dynamic, open-ended growth. *Systems of Survival* (1992) delved into political philosophy, while last year's *The Nature of Economies* showed some of the ways economics follows the same principles that govern nature. She has also written a children's book and a book on Quebeçois separatism, and has edited the memoirs of her great-aunt, a schoolteacher in early 20th century Alaska.

Jacobs, who turns 85 this year, is as sharp as ever. She has lived in Toronto's bustling Annex neighborhood since 1968, when she and her late husband moved there from New York City so their sons wouldn't be drafted during the Vietnam War. She's a Canadian citizen, but she was born in the hard-coal town of Scranton, Pennsylvania. Bill Steigerwald, an associate editor and columnist for the *Pittsburgh Tribune-Review,* interviewed her in mid-March by phone.

Reason: What should a city be like?

Jane Jacobs: It should be like itself. Every city has differences, from its history, from its site, and so on. These are important. One of the most dismal things is when you go to a city and it's like 12 others you've seen. That's not interesting, and it's not really truthful.

Reason: Unlike American cities, Canadian cities have not been destroyed by the experts and the planners, have they?

Jacobs: Well, they've had some bad things happen to them. They had some terrible housing projects built in Toronto, although we learned later how to do it right.

That's mostly true about Canadian cities, but it's not all peaches and cream. It's really surprising how few creative, important cities Canada has for its size, its population, and its great human potential and attributes. There's a whole region of Canada, the Atlantic Provinces, that has a lot of pleasant little places but doesn't have one single really significant creative city. And the whole area is very poor as a consequence. It would be like a Third World country, that whole area, if it wasn't getting transfer payments and grants of various kinds from the rest of Canada.

Reason: But Canada didn't have the urban renewal problem that America did?

Jacobs: It had a little of it. It also had what Marshall McLuhan called "an early warning system." Urban renewal came to America earlier, so Canada had the advantage of seeing what the mistakes were and could be cautious. Canada had an urban renewal agency for a while, and it did just as badly as the one in the U.S. But it didn't last long, because as soon as the Canadian government saw what a mess it was making, how many fights it was causing, and how much opposition was arising, it just demolished the whole department.

That was the difference. All these troubles were becoming recognized in the U.S., but the government there didn't seem to be able to think, "This is a mistake. Out with it."

Reason: I know some businesspeople begged you to come to Pittsburgh and help fight a big City Hall redevelopment project that would have wiped out two city streets downtown. [See "Death by Wrecking Ball," June 2000.] The huge project has ended, so it's sort of a happy ending. But I'm wondering if, in a general sense, you think the people who control cities have learned the lessons of the '60s?

Jacobs: In that case, they certainly hadn't. That attitude—that you can sacrifice small things, young things, and a diversity of things for some great big success—is sad. That's the kind of attitude that killed Pittsburgh as an innovator.

Reason: And it comes from people who either have the power or the money or both to have their way?

Jacobs: Well, they have their way with the powers of eminent domain, government powers that were intended for things like schools and roads and public things, and are used instead for the benefit of private organizations and individuals.

That's one of the worst things about urban renewal. It introduced that idea that you could use those government powers to benefit private organizations. The courts never have given the kind of overview to this that they should. The time it went to the Supreme Court, back in the 1950s, the decision was that to make a place beautiful or more orderly or helpful, government could do what it pleased with eminent domain. That just left the door open. As one New York state official said at the time, "If Macy's wants to condemn Gimbel's, it can do it if Moses gives the word."

Reason: Robert Moses, the New York City planner and infamous power broker.

Jacobs: Yes. He's an extreme example, but in effect that's what the shift in eminent domain law did. But even before that, it was being done unofficially when what had grown big and successful was used to eat up, or wipe away, or starve what was not. You might as well have no birth rate and then wonder why there aren't people. If you don't have an entrepreneurial birth rate, you don't have new industries and new chances for other successes.

Reason: It seems virtually impossible for the biggest, clumsiest, most unenlightened government to squelch innovation and new growth. It might not come up in the middle of downtown Pittsburgh, but it will come up somewhere else, whether they like it or not.

Jacobs: Sure. Look at the big automobile companies in America and how they didn't make smaller cars, more economical ones that would run farther on gasoline. It took Japanese cars coming in, and German cars coming in. There was a market for them. But they were not being produced and designed by the big, rich, much more successful American companies. Then, when they saw what competition they had, the U.S. auto makers began to produce compact cars. But it sure was innovation from a long way off.

Reason: Do you think that the people who run American cities have learned what to do and what not to do?

Jacobs: I think some of them have learned a lot. There are quite a few cities that are more vigorous and more attractive than they were 10 or 20 years ago. A lot of good things are being done, but it's not universal.

Reason: Can you give me an example?

Jacobs: In Portland, a lot of good things are being done. Same with Seattle. San Francisco has done many attractive things.

Reason: What is it that you like about Portland?

Jacobs: People in Portland love Portland. That's the most important thing. They really like to see it improved. The waterfront is getting improved, and not with a lot of gimmicks, but with good, intelligent reuses of the old buildings. They're good at rehabilitation. As far as their parks are concerned, they've got some wonderful parks with water flows in them. It's fascinating. People enjoy it and paddle in it. They're unusual parks. The amount of space they take and what they deliver is just terrific.

They're pretty good on their transit too. It's not any one splashy thing. It's the ensemble that I think is so pleasant.

Reason: You are against regional planning and metropolitanism, yet isn't an important part of what's going on in Portland the pretty strong powers given to a regional planning authority?

Jacobs: I don't know. You're probably better informed than I am on that. I'm talking about the city of Portland itself.

Reason: The criticisms of Portland are these: By fixing boundaries and limiting growth by government fiat, they are guaranteeing that prices of housing will go up higher within the boundaries of Portland and that traffic will get worse. And this has happened.

Jacobs: Well, my goodness. Portland is not a dense city and never was. Whoever made that prediction, that densifying the city itself would have all those bad consequences, they don't know anything about it.

Reason: I lived in Los Angeles for 12 years. When I moved there in 1977, I just loved it immediately. It was so open and free and full of life and vitality. Not only the people, but there seemed to be a lot fewer rules and regulations about what you could do and couldn't do. Peter Hall says in *Cities in Civilization* that L.A. was built on freedom, and when I read that, I thought, "That makes sense to me."

Jacobs: Well, it does if you are able to drive a car and have enough money. But only in those cases.

Reason: Los Angeles wasn't too bad for money. My daughter is a lawyer and she had to leave San Francisco because she couldn't afford living there.

Jacobs: It's gotten so popular . . . .

Reason: I remember interviewing the head of regional planning in Los Angeles. He shocked me, because I had grown up thinking Los Angeles was the best example of bad city planning. That it was sprawled all over the place, and it was just a mess, and nobody was in charge or anything. This was 1984, and this guy told me, "Now I have people coming from around the world to Los Angeles to see how we did it, how we established a city that had so many city centers—and not just two or three big centers, but 18." The answer was that no one planned it, obviously. It just happened that way and there is not any way to arrange it to happen in this way.

Jacobs: That's what I say: Every city is different. But don't think that because Los Angeles can do that, and it turned out that way, that every city can be a Los Angeles.

Reason: Some people say cities are destined to become workplaces by day and entertainment centers by night and weekend. Do you think that's true?

Jacobs: To a certain extent. Cities have always had a lot of leisure things that people use after work hours. But there are a lot of people who don't work during the day. Children have short working hours, you might' say. There are seniors who don't have a lot of work during the day. I think it's important that there be recreational places during the day, too. Places where people can swim. Community centers. Places where they can bicycle.

Reason: In the city center area?

Jacobs: All over the city. The idea of this strict segregation of hours is fairly ridiculous. There are also more and more people who are working at night. Especially people who work at home.

Reason: A couple of years ago, Jesse Walker, an associate editor of REASON, wrote that your ideas are being seized by the sustainability crowd and are being abused. He wrote, "To the extent that they have digested Jacobs, they have romanticized her vision, bastardizing her empirical observations of how cities work into a formula they want to impose not just on cities but on suburbs and small towns as well."

Jacobs: I think there's a lot of truth to that. For example, the New Urbanists want to have lively centers in the places that they develop, where people run into each other doing errands and that sort of thing. And yet, from what I've seen of their plans and the places they have built, they don't seem to have a sense of the anatomy of these hearts, these centers. They've placed them as if they were shopping centers. They don't connect. In a real city or a real town, the lively heart always has two or more well-used pedestrian thoroughfares that meet. In traditional towns, often it's a triangular piece of land. Sometimes it's made into a park.

Reason: What kind of traditional towns?

Jacobs: You can see it in old Irish towns. You can also see it in towns in Illinois. The reason for it is that the action so often was where three well-traveled routes came together and made a Y. There are also T-intersections and also X-intersections. But they're always intersections that are well-traveled on foot. People speak about the local hangout, the corner bar. The important word there is *corner.*

Reason: Corner store, corner bar. They're illegal in most places today—certainly in the suburbs.

Jacobs: Yes. The corner is important. It's of all different scales. For instance, big cities have a lot of main squares where the action is, and which will be the most valuable for stores and that kind of thing. They're often good places for a public building—a landmark. But they're always where there's a crossing or a convergence. You can't stop a hub from developing in such a place. You can't make it develop if you don't have such a place. And I don't think the New Urbanists understand this kind of thing. They think you just put it where you want.

Reason: And that people will go there, as opposed to what's really happening—that people are already going there? You're just giving them a place to stop and congregate?

Jacobs: That's right. It occurs naturally. Now it also has the advantage that it can expand or contract without destroying the rest of the place. Because the natural place for such a heart to expand is along those well-used thoroughfares.

Reason: What do the people who run cities have to do now to make their cities into more livable, more interesting places? Is it to remove some of the things they've done in the last 50 years, or just keep their hands off completely?

Jacobs: It's much less a matter of removing things than adding things, I think. For instance, here in Toronto there were two areas of the downtown that were dying. They were in very good locations but they were old industrial buildings that were becoming vacant. Manufacturing was moving out to where they had more room and where it wasn't as expensive. There were a lot of small developers who saw that these nice old buildings were just ideal for converting into apartments. They were lofts, mostly, and you know how popular they've become. But they were blocked from doing anything about it because of use zoning that said it should be industrial. So you can change that use zoning and allow residential.

Reason: But aren't you then just removing an impediment? Some people say zoning is the big problem.

Jacobs: Wait a minute, I haven't finished. It didn't help to change that use because, again, there were so many impediments that went with it. There were rules and regulations about dwellings—especially parking places. And the ground coverage in these areas was high, and you couldn't make basements under these nice old buildings. You couldn't satisfy the parking requirements without fairly well destroying what was really nice about the areas and also making it just too expensive. So no matter what happened, they were blocked.

We had a very intelligent mayor at that time, and she listened to what they were saying. And she wanted to remove those impediments. She talked to everybody who had an interest in the area and they agreed that these buildings should be put to the additional use. But they were all so stymied in their thinking about, How do you make it practical?

Well, you're smart. You've already jumped to the conclusion of what makes it practical—you remove the impediments. The mayor's hardest job was re-educating the planning department, but she did it. They added one new rule, and you might not like this. But it was a very important rule to add: None of the sound old buildings could be destroyed. That was to prevent environmental and aesthetic waste. Otherwise, except for the safety and fire codes, which apply to all the buildings, just about all the old regulations were removed.

Reason: And what happened?

Jacobs: It's magical, it's wondrous, how fast those areas have been blossoming and coming to life again.

It wasn't just removing impediments. It was a use that was missing in the mixture. It didn't replace all the working places. A lot of the working places hadn't disappeared yet, and new ones have come in and been allowed to be added. Also, there are other things that the people who now live there, in combination with the people who work there, can support. The main thing missing in the mixture was added. The same principle you can apply to languishing bedroom communities. What's missing there is workplaces. Here's why I don't like segregation into night things and day things: You don't get the additional things that the workers and the people living there support jointly.

Reason: Such as?

Jacobs: Parking is one of them. No parking lot was built for the big baseball stadium here in Toronto, the one with the retractable roof, because it was figured that there were enough parking places for workers that weren't being used while the games were on. So why build more parking places?

Reason: You would agree that that is a smart way to do it?

Jacobs: Yes. The same thing applies to eating places. People who want to eat out in the evening can use the same places as working people who eat at lunchtime.

Reason: People complain that suburbanites are too dependent on cars. Yet the newest suburbs—the car suburbs, not the trolley suburbs—are so heavily zoned and so carefully laid out. The uses are segregated so much—you live here, you work there, you shop here, you play there, you go to school over here. If you didn't have a car, you couldn't possibly live in the suburbs— because of the way they're laid out.

Jacobs: That's right. Your children couldn't get to school. And they couldn't get to their dancing lessons or whatever else they do. You're absolutely dependent on a car. It's very expensive for people, especially if they need a couple of cars. It's a terrific burden. It costs about—somebody figured it out fairly recently—it costs about $7,000 a year for one car. That's a lot of money, you know.

Reason: I'm a five-minute drive from all the shopping I need, but I couldn't walk it.

Jacobs: Sure, you want to defend the car in those cases. It's a lifeline. It's as important as your water tap.

Reason: You aren't anti-car, are you?

Jacobs: No. I do think that we need to have a lot more public transit. But you can't have public transit in the situation you're talking about.

Reason: You don't literally mean publicly owned transit?

Jacobs: No. All forms of transit. It can be taxis, privately run jitneys, whatever. Things that people don't have to own themselves and can pay a fare for.

Reason: You're not an enemy of free-market transportation.

Jacobs: No. I wish we had more of it. I wish we didn't have the notion that you had to have monopoly franchise transit. I wish it were competitive—in the kinds of vehicles that it uses, in the fares that it charges, in the routes that it goes, in the times of day that it goes. I've seen this on poor little Caribbean islands. They have good jitney service, because it's dictated by the users.

I wish we could do more of that. But we have so much history against it, and so many institutional things already in place against it. The idea that you have to use great big behemoths of vehicles, when the service actually would be better in station-wagon size. It shows how unnatural and foolish monopolies are. The only thing that saves the situation is when illegal things begin to break the monopoly.

Reason: You've said it's a fallacy that jobs are coming out to the suburbs. What about the edge cities that Joel Garreau talks about? Hasn't it changed somewhat?

Jacobs: It has, but it's very uneven as to where the people live who go to that work. The old Garden City idea was that the jobs would be there in the suburbs, in the Garden City. That very seldom happened. For one thing, if you have two breadwinners or more in the same family, they aren't likely to work in the same place. People change their jobs in the course of their life. If they're confined geographically to just the selection there is in their little town, it's tough. It's one reason people move to cities or move to suburbs where they can commute into cities.

It's a fallacy to think that you can eliminate travel by putting people close to their work. In a few cases, they will be. But all the accounts I've ever seen, especially after a lapse of time, they aren't working and living in the same place.

Reason: I remember reading that the hub-and-spoke kind of movement of commuters is not as common in cities. People live in one suburb and work in another, not downtown.

Jacobs: That's right, they can work in another suburb. Exactly.

Reason: Is it a straw man to say that if you live in a suburb, you should work in that suburb? Is that what they really wanted people to do?

Jacobs: That's how they were justified, often, especially the ones that were considered model towns. You really can cut down the need to travel and the dependency on a car, or on public transit, in suburbs. But it's not by trying to hope, much less dictate, that people will work close to where they live. It's by their errands. There's an awful lot of unnecessary travel. If people want to get a quart of milk, they have to get in the car and get it. This is especially hard on children, too, who don't have freedom, even when they are old enough to go on foot to this place and that. It

could easily be arranged that you could do almost all your errands on foot. But not so, if—again the question of monopoly comes up—you have to have these monopolies called shopping malls.

Reason: And they are monopolies that are protected by zoning in many cases, right?

Jacobs: Yes, and also at the behest of their developers.

Reason: The fix is in between the developers and the local government?

Jacobs: Yeah, and people have gotten afraid to have commerce get outside of these monopoly prisons.

Reason: Do you think suburbs will evolve into cities?

Jacobs: They'll evolve into something, but I don't know what you'll call them and I don't know exactly how they'll resolve. But they'll thicken up, get denser.

Reason: That solves a lot of problems, I guess.

Jacobs: Sure it does. And that's why those people are crazy when they said what would happen to Portland. It was an argument. They were trying to stop it and they said any kind of baloney.

Reason: There are suburbs in Pittsburgh where the people who run the township, the zoning officers, despise commerce. It's virtually 100 percent residential use—big homes, mostly. And of course there are no granny flats, no corner stores, no duplexes. I don't know if people want to change that. People are happy to be living there. They are some of the wealthiest people in Pittsburgh.

Jacobs: Yes, but now consider what happens with the change of generations. Remember how people despised Victorian buildings earlier in this century? They were just ruthless with them. They were just thought to be automatically ugly and disgusting. Many wonderful, wonderful buildings were destroyed. Well, that was a big rejection of Victorianism. Not just the buildings. There was the feeling that it was stuffy, it was repressive.

There'll come a time when the standard suburbs that you're talking about—even the wealthiest ones—will change. Look at what has happened to very wealthy areas within cities where great mansions turned into funeral parlors, and so on. It'll happen. Just when, I don't know. I'm very suspicious of prophesizing, because life is full of surprises, but I think we are seeing the precursors of the very beginning of the change in the suburbs.

Reason: My parents are still in a 1950s suburban tract home. When we were growing up, we didn't want to live in an old house. Now you'd have to pay me to live in my parents' house, which is just a suburban box.

Jacobs: Exactly. And when this happens, people get absolutely ruthless with the old stuff. Too ruthless, I think, because I don't like waste, and I don't like thoughtlessness.

Reason: When the change comes, if it is an incremental, slowly evolving, uncontrolled sort of natural change, it's easy for society to accommodate that, isn't it?

Jacobs: Yes it is. But if all that zoning is kept, that can't happen.

Reason: This is why I'm one of the few people you've met who likes Houston, because it has no zoning.

Jacobs: It has no zoning. But all the same, it looks like all the places that do have zoning. Because the same developers and bankers who deal with places that do have zoning carry their same ideas when they finance or build something in Houston.

Reason: There are not enough Houstons to change the way things are built or developed?

Jacobs: Right. In fact, places where change does happen are where people face it and really start to overhaul and rethink these things. That's what holds back change—when people don't overhaul and rethink. People are awfully scared of changes in zoning, because they think the neighborhood will go to the dogs and it will ruin their property values.

I mentioned before about this anatomy of the streets, and how if you have the streets that are good pedestrian thoroughfares as part of the anatomy of the heart, those are the logical places to convert from residences, say, to businesses. If the place is really an economic success, that's going to happen. That's not a bad thing to happen, the expansion of the commerce and the working places.

Reason: It's a good sign, right?

Jacobs: It's a very good sign. But you see, if it's in places where that hasn't been thought of, the commerce begins to intrude on the parts of the community that were just meant for residences. Sometimes these conversions are very charming, but usually not. They are ugly and they are like a smear that begins to spread. People look at it and say the neighborhood is going to the dogs. And they're scared of this. But actually, if you have these busy streets that have the kind of buildings on them that can easily be converted back and forth to different uses. . .the place doesn't go to the dogs.

Reason: The problem is when you lock yourself into one use and never allow it to change, or make it so impossible to change that it'll never happen.

Jacobs: Yes, or that it'll just be an ugly smear if it does happen. I don't think the New Urbanists are thinking of those things.

Reason: Have you been to any of these new towns they're building, like Disney's Celebration in Florida?

Jacobs: I've been to one outside Toronto.

Reason: What did you think?

Jacobs: I was disappointed. The town center is very much a constricted thing unto itself, located as if it were a shopping center. It doesn't have this anatomy. Instead of having parking lots around it, it has a good-sized park, but all the residential streets that impinge upon it are very residential and not at all part of the anatomy of the center.

Reason: The perfect towns we think of, the kind of towns that New Urbanists are trying to reproduce from on high, were developed 100 years ago all across America with very little official kind of planning. How is it people seemed to be more sensible about how towns were not made, but allowed to grow, 100 or 150 years ago, then lost it? What is the secret they knew then that we have forgotten? Or am I romanticizing?

Jacobs: No, that's a very interesting question. They weren't being as ruthless, for one thing. A lot of these towns were ruined, you know. You can see these just awful strip developments.

Reason: I don't know if you think of yourself in these terms, but when they list the 100 most important American intellectuals of this century, your name is on that list.

Jacobs: (Laughs.) It's a little early to say. Usually those things don't mean much until a couple centuries have passed.

Reason: What do you think you'll be remembered for most? You were the one who stood up to the federal bulldozers and the urban renewal people and said they were destroying the lifeblood of these cities. Is that what it will be?

Jacobs: No. If I were to be remembered as a really important thinker of the century, the most important thing I've contributed is my discussion of what makes economic expansion happen. This is something that has puzzled people always. I think I've figured out what it is.

Expansion and development are two different things. Development is differentiation of what already existed. Practically every new thing that happens is a differentiation of a previous thing, from a new shoe sole to changes in legal codes. Expansion is an actual growth in size or volume of activity. That is a different thing.

I've gone at it two different ways. Way back when I wrote *The Economy of Cities,* I wrote about import replacing and how that expands, not just the economy of the place where it occurs, but economic life altogether. As a city replaces imports, it shifts its imports. It doesn't import less. And yet it has everything it had before.

Reason: It's not a zero-sum game. It's a bigger, growing pie.

Jacobs: That's the actual mechanism of it. The theory of it is what I explain in *The Nature of Economies.* I equate it to what happens with biomass, the sum total of all flora and fauna in an area. The energy, the material that's involved in this, doesn't just escape the community as an export. It continues being used in a community, just as in a rainforest the waste from certain organisms and various plants and animals gets used by other ones in the place.

Reason: It becomes denser and more diverse.

Jacobs: That's right, and it is linked with new development, because the new kinds of things that are being contrived are able to feed off of each other. The trouble is, people have always been trying to put development and expansion together as one thing. They're very closely related. They need each other. But they aren't the same thing and they aren't caused by the same thing. I think that's the most important thing I've worked out. And if I am thought of as a great thinker, that will be why.

The Police and Neighborhood Safety

Broken Windows

JAMES Q. WILSON AND GEORGE L. KELLING

In the mid-1970s, the state of New Jersey announced a "Safe and Clean Neighborhoods Program," designed to improve the quality of community life in twenty-eight cities. As part of that program, the state provided money to help cities take police officers out of their patrol cars and assign them to walking beats. The governor and other state officials were enthusiastic about using foot patrol as a way of cutting crime, but many police chiefs were skeptical. Foot patrol, in their eyes, had been pretty much discredited. It reduced the mobility of the police, who thus had difficulty responding to citizen calls for service, and it weakened headquarter's control over patrol officers.

Many police officers also disliked foot patrol, but for different reasons: it was hard work, it kept them outside on cold, rainy nights, and it reduced their chances for making a "good pinch." In some departments, assigning officers to foot patrol had been used as a form of punishment. And academic experts on policing doubted that foot patrol would have any impact on crime rates; it was, in the opinion of most, little more than a sop to public opinion. But since the state was paying for it, the local authorities were willing to go along.

Five years after the program started, the Police Foundation, in Washington, D.C., published an evaluation of the foot-patrol project. Based on its analysis of a carefully controlled experiment carried out chiefly in Newark, the foundation concluded, to the surprise of hardly anyone, that foot patrol had not reduced crime rates. But residents of the foot-patrolled neighborhoods seemed to feel more secure than persons in other areas, tended to believe that crime had been reduced, and seemed to take fewer steps to protect themselves from crime (staying at home with the doors locked, for example). Moreover, citizens in the foot-patrol areas had a more favorable opinion of the police than did those living elsewhere. And officers walking beats had higher morale, greater job satisfaction, and a more favorable attitude toward citizens in their neighborhoods than did officers assigned to patrol cars.

These findings may be taken as evidence that the skeptics were right—foot patrol has no effect on crime; it merely fools the citizens into thinking that they are safer. But in our view, and in the view of the authors of the Police Foundation study (of whom Kelling was one), the citizens of Newark were not fooled at all. They knew what the foot-patrol officers were doing, they knew it was different from what motorized officers do, and they knew that having officers walk beats did in fact make their neighborhoods safer.

But how can a neighborhood be "safer" when the crime rate has not gone down—in fact, may have gone up? Finding the answer requires first that we understand what most often frightens people in public places. Many citizens, of course, are primarily frightened by crime, especially crime involving a sudden, violent attack by a stranger. This risk is very real, in Newark as in many large cities. But we tend to overlook or forget another source of fear—the fear of being bothered by disorderly people. Not violent people, nor, necessarily, criminals, but disreputable or obstreperous or unpredictable people: panhandlers, drunks, addicts, rowdy teenagers, prostitutes, loiterers, the mentally disturbed.

What foot-patrol officers did was to elevate, to the extent they could, the level of public order in these neighborhoods. Though the neighborhoods were predominantly black and the foot patrolmen were mostly white, this "order-maintenance" function of the police was performed to the general satisfaction of both parties.

One of us (Kelling) spent many hours walking with Newark foot-patrol officers to see how they defined "order" and what they did to maintain it. One beat was typical: a busy but dilapidated area in the heart of Newark, with many abandoned buildings, marginal shops (several of which prominently displayed knives and straight-edged razors in their windows), one large department store, and, most important, a train station and several major bus stops. Though the area was run-down, its streets were filled with people, because it was a major transportation center. The good order of this area was important not only to those who lived and worked there but also to many others, who had to move through it on their way home, to supermarkets, or to factories.

The people on the street were primarily black; the officer who walked the street was white. The people were made up of "regulars" and "strangers." Regulars included both "decent folk" and some drunks and derelicts who were always there but who "knew their place." Strangers were, well, strangers, and viewed suspiciously, sometimes apprehensively. The officer—call him Kelly—knew who the regulars were, and they knew him. As he saw his job, he was to keep an eye on strangers, and make certain that the disreputable regulars observed some informal but widely understood rules. Drunks and addicts could sit on the stoops, but could not lie down. People could drink on side streets, but not at the main intersection. Bottles had to be in paper bags. Talking to, bothering, or begging from people waiting at the bus stop was strictly forbidden. If a dispute erupted between a businessman and a customer, the businessman was assumed to be right, especially if the customer was a stranger. If a stranger loitered, Kelly would ask him if he had any means of support and what his business was; if he gave unsatisfactory answers, he was sent on his way. Persons who broke the informal rules, especially those who bothered people waiting at bus stops, were arrested for vagrancy. Noisy teenagers were told to keep quiet.

These rules were defined and enforced in collaboration with the "regulars" on the street. Another neighborhood might have different rules, but these, everybody understood, were the rules for *this* neighborhood. If someone violated them, the regulars not only turned to Kelly for help but also ridiculed the violator. Sometimes what Kelly did could be described as "enforcing the law," but just as often it involved taking informal or extralegal steps to help protect what the neighborhood had decided was the appropriate level of public order. Some of the things he did probably would not withstand a legal challenge.

A determined skeptic might acknowledge that a skilled foot-patrol officer can maintain order but still insist that this sort of "order" has little to do with the real sources of community fear—that is, with violent crime. To a degree, that is true. But two things must be borne in mind. First, outside observers should not assume that they know how much of the anxiety now endemic in many big-city neighborhoods stems from a fear of "real" crime and how much from a sense that the street is disorderly, a source of distasteful, worrisome encounters. The people of Newark, to judge from their behavior and their remarks to interviewers, apparently assign a high value to public order, and feel relieved and reassured when the police help them maintain that order.

S econd, at the community level, disorder and crime are usually inextricably linked, in a kind of developmental sequence. Social psychologists and police officers tend to agree that if a window in a building is broken *and is left unrepaired,* all the rest of the windows will soon be broken. This is as true in nice neighborhoods as in run-down ones. Window-breaking does not necessarily occur on a large scale because some areas are inhabited by determined window-breakers whereas others are populated by window-lovers; rather, one unrepaired broken window is a signal that no one cares, and so breaking more windows costs nothing. (It has always been fun.)

Philip Zimbardo, a Stanford psychologist, reported in 1969 on some experiments testing the broken-window theory. He arranged to have an automobile without license plates parked with its hood up on a street in the Bronx and a comparable automobile on a street in Palo Alto, California. The car in the Bronx was attacked by "vandals" within ten minutes of its "abandonment." The first to arrive were a family—father, mother, and young son—who removed the radiator and battery. Within twenty-four hours, virtually everything of value had been removed. Then random destruction began—windows were smashed, parts torn off, upholstery ripped. Children began to use the car as a playground. Most of the adult "vandals" were well-dressed, apparently clean-cut whites. The car in Palo Alto sat untouched for more than a week. Then Zimbardo smashed part of it with a sledgehammer. Soon, passersby were joining in. Within a few hours, the car had been turned upside down and utterly destroyed. Again, the "vandals" appeared to be primarily respectable whites.

Untended property becomes fair game for people out for fun or plunder, and even for people who ordinarily would not dream of doing such things and who probably consider themselves law-abiding. Because of the nature of community life in the Bronx—its anonymity, the frequency with which cars are abandoned and things are stolen or broken, the past experience of "no one caring"—vandalism begins much more quickly than it does in staid Palo Alto, where people have come to believe that private possessions are cared for, and that mischievous behavior is costly. But vandalism can occur anywhere once communal barriers—the sense of mutual regard and the obligations of civility—are lowered by actions that seem to signal that "no one cares."

We suggest that "untended" behavior also leads to the breakdown of community controls. A stable neighborhood of families who care for their homes, mind each other's children, and confidently frown on unwanted intruders can change, in a few years or even a few months, to an inhospitable and frightening jungle. A piece of property is abandoned, weeds grow up, a window is smashed. Adults stop scolding rowdy children; the children, emboldened, become more rowdy. Families move out, unattached adults move in. Teenagers gather in front of the corner store. The merchant asks them to move; they refuse. Fights occur. Litter accumulates. People start drinking in front of the grocery; in time, an inebriate slumps to the sidewalk and is allowed to sleep it off. Pedestrians are approached by panhandlers.

At this point it is not inevitable that serious crime will flourish or violent attacks on strangers will occur. But many residents will think that crime, especially violent crime, is on the rise, and they will modify their behavior accordingly. They will use the streets less often, and when on the streets will stay apart from their fellows, moving with averted eyes, silent lips, and hurried steps. "Don't get involved." For some residents, this growing atomization will matter little, because the neighborhood is not their "home" but "the place where they live." Their interests are elsewhere; they are cosmopolitans. But it will matter greatly to other people, whose lives derive meaning and satisfaction from local attachments rather than worldly involvement; for them, the neighborhood will cease to exist except for a few reliable friends whom they arrange to meet.

Such an area is vulnerable to criminal invasion. Though it is not inevitable, it is more likely that here, rather than in places where people are confident they can regulate public behavior by informal controls, drugs will change hands, prostitutes will solicit, and cars will be stripped. That the drunks will be robbed by boys who do it as a lark, and the prostitutes' customers will be robbed by men who do it purposefully and perhaps violently. That muggings will occur.

Among those who often find it difficult to move away from this are the elderly. Surveys of citizens suggest that the elderly are much less likely to be the victims of crime than younger persons, and some have inferred from this that the well-known fear of crime voiced by the elderly is an exaggeration: perhaps we ought not to design special programs to protect older persons; perhaps we should even try to talk them out of their mistaken fears. This argument misses the point. The prospect of a confrontation with an obstreperous teenager or a drunken panhandler can be as fear-inducing for defenseless persons as the prospect of meeting an actual robber; indeed, to a defenseless person, the two kinds of confrontation are often indistinguishable. Moreover, the lower rate at which the elderly are victimized is a measure of the steps they have already taken—chiefly, staying behind locked doors—to minimize the risks they face. Young men are more frequently attacked than older women, not because they are easier or more lucrative targets but because they are on the streets more.

Nor is the connection between disorderliness and fear made only by the elderly. Susan Estrich, of the Harvard Law School, has recently gathered together a number of surveys on the sources of public fear. One, done in Portland, Oregon, indicated that three fourths of the adults interviewed cross to the other side of a street when they see a gang of teenagers; another survey, in Baltimore, discovered that nearly half would cross the street to avoid even a single strange youth. When an interviewer asked people in a housing project where the most dangerous spot was, they mentioned a place where young persons gathered to drink and play music, despite the fact that not a single crime had occurred there. In Boston public housing projects, the greatest fear was expressed by persons living in the buildings where disorderliness and incivility, not crime, were the greatest. Knowing this helps one understand the significance of such otherwise harmless displays as subway graffiti. As Nathan Glazer has written, the proliferation of graffiti, even when not obscene, confronts the subway rider with the "inescapable knowledge that the environment he must endure for an hour or more a day is uncontrolled and uncontrollable, and that anyone can invade it to do whatever damage and mischief the mind suggests."

In response to fear, people avoid one another, weakening controls. Sometimes they call the police. Patrol cars arrive, an occasional arrest occurs, but crime continues and disorder is not abated. Citizens complain to the police chief, but he explains that his department is low on personnel and that the courts do not punish petty or first-time offenders. To the residents, the police who arrive in squad cars are either ineffective or uncaring; to the police, the residents are animals who deserve each other. The citizens may soon stop calling the police, because "they can't do anything."

The process we call urban decay has occurred for centuries in every city. But what is happening today is different in at least two important respects. First, in the period before, say World War II, city dwellers—because of money costs, transportation difficulties, familial and church connections—could rarely move away from neighborhood problems. When movement did occur, it tended to be along public-transit routes. Now mobility has become exceptionally easy for all but the poorest or those who are blocked by racial prejudice. Earlier crime waves had a kind of built-in self-correcting mechanism: the determination of a neighborhood or community to reassert control over its turf. Areas in Chicago, New York, and Boston would experience crime and gang wars, and then normalcy would return, as the families for whom no alternative residences were possible reclaimed their authority over the streets.

Second, the police in this earlier period assisted in that reassertion of authority by acting, sometimes violently, on behalf of the community. Young toughs were roughed up, people were arrested "on suspicion" or for vagrancy, and prostitutes and petty thieves were routed. "Rights" were something enjoyed by decent folk, and perhaps also by the serious professional criminal, who avoided violence and could afford a lawyer.

This pattern of policing was not an aberration or the result of occasional excess. From the earliest days of the nation, the police function was seen primarily as that of a night watchman: to maintain order against the chief threats to order—fire, wild animals, and disreputable behavior. Solving crimes was viewed not as a police responsibility but as a private one. In the March, 1969, *Atlantic,* one of us (Wilson) wrote a brief account of how the police role had slowly changed from maintaining order to fighting crimes. The change began with the creation of private detectives (often ex-criminals), who worked on a contingency-fee basis for individuals who had suffered losses. In time, the detectives were absorbed into municipal police agencies and paid a regular salary; simultaneously, the responsibility for prosecuting thieves was shifted from the aggrieved private citizen to the professional prosecutor. This process was not complete in most places until the twentieth century.

In the 1960s, when urban riots were a major problem, social scientists began to explore carefully the order-maintenance function of the police, and to suggest ways of improving it—not to make streets safer (its original function) but to reduce the incidence of mass violence. Order-maintenance became, to a degree, coterminous with "community relations." But, as the crime wave that began in the early 1960s continued without abatement throughout the decade and into the 1970s, attention shifted to the role of the police as crime-fighters. Studies of police behavior ceased, by and large, to be accounts of the order-maintenance function and became, instead, efforts to propose and test ways whereby the police could solve more crimes, make more arrests, and gather better evidence. If these things could be done, social scientists assumed, citizens would be less fearful.

A great deal was accomplished during this transition, as both police chiefs and outside experts emphasized the crime-fighting function in their plans, in the allocation of resources, and in deployment of personnel. The police may well have become better crime-fighters as a result. And doubtless they remained aware of their responsibility for order. But the link between order-maintenance and crime-prevention, so obvious to earlier generations, was forgotten.

That link is similar to the process whereby one broken window becomes many. The citizen who fears the ill-smelling drunk, the rowdy teenager, or the importuning beggar is not merely expressing his distaste for unseemly behavior; he is also giving voice to a bit of folk wisdom that happens to be a correct generalization—namely, that serious street crime flourishes in areas in which disorderly behavior goes unchecked. The unchecked panhandler is, in effect, the first broken window. Muggers and robbers, whether opportunistic or professional, believe they reduce their chances of being caught or even identified if they operate on streets where potential victims are already intimated by prevailing conditions. If the neighborhood cannot keep a bothersome panhandler from annoying passersby, the thief may reason, it is even less likely to call the police to identify a potential mugger or to interfere if the mugging actually takes place.

Some police administrators concede that this process occurs, but argue that motorized-patrol officers can deal with it as effectively as foot-patrol officers. We are not so sure. In theory, an officer in a squad car can observe as much as an officer on foot; in theory, the former can talk to as many people as the latter. But the reality of police–citizen encounters is powerfully altered by the automobile. An officer on foot cannot separate himself from the street people; if he is approached, only his uniform and his personality can help him manage whatever is about to happen. And he can never be certain what that will be—a request for directions, a plea for help, an angry denunciation, a teasing remark, a confused babble, a threatening gesture.

In a car, an officer is more likely to deal with street people by rolling down the window and looking at them. The door and the window exclude the approaching citizen; they are a barrier. Some officers take advantage of this barrier, perhaps unconsciously, by acting differently if in the car than they would on foot. We have seen this countless times. The police car pulls up to a corner where teenagers are gathered. The window is rolled down. The officer stares at the youths. They stare back. The officer says to one, "C'mere." He saunters over, conveying to his friends by his elaborately casual style the idea that he is not intimidated by authority. "What's your name?" "Chuck." "Chuck who?" "Chuck Jones." "What you doing, "Chuck?" "Nothin." "Got a P.O. [parole officer]?" "Nah." "Sure?" "Yeah." "Stay out of trouble, Chuckie." Meanwhile, the other boys laugh and exchange comments among themselves, probably at the officer's expense. The officer stares harder. He cannot be certain what is being said, nor can he join in and, by displaying his own skill at street banter, prove that he cannot be "put down." In the process, the officer has learned almost nothing, and the boys have decided the officer is an alien force who can safely be disregarded, even mocked.

Our experience is that most citizens like to talk to a police officer. Such exchanges give them a sense of importance, provide them with the basis for gossip, and allow them to explain to the authorities what is worrying them (whereby they gain a modest but significant sense of having "done something" about the problem). You approach a person on foot more easily, and talk to him more readily, than you do a person in a car. Moreover, you can more easily retain some anonymity if you draw an officer aside for a private chat. Suppose you want to pass on a tip about who is stealing handbags, or who offered to sell you a stolen TV. In the inner city, the culprit, in all likelihood, lives nearby. To walk up to a marked patrol car and lean in the window is to convey a visible signal that you are a "fink."

The essence of the police role in maintaining order is to reinforce the informal control mechanisms of the community itself. The police cannot, without committing extraordinary resources, provide a substitute for that informal control, on the other hand, to reinforce those natural forces the police must accommodate them. And therein lies the problem.

Should police activity on the street be shaped, in important ways, by the standards of the neighborhood rather than by the rules of the state? Over the past two decades, the shift of police from order-maintenance to law-enforcement has brought them increasingly under the influence of legal restrictions, provoked by media complaints and enforced by court decisions and departmental orders. As a consequence, the order-maintenance functions of the police are now governed by rules developed to control police relations with suspected criminals. This is, we think, an entirely new development. For centuries, the role of the police as watchmen was judged primarily not in terms of its compliance with appropriate procedures but rather in terms of its attaining a desired objective. The objective was order, an inherently ambiguous term but a condition that people in a given community recognized when they saw it. The means were the same as those the community itself would employ, if its members were sufficiently determined, courageous, and authoritative. Detecting and apprehending criminals, by contrast, was a means to an end, not an end in itself; a judicial determination of guilt or innocence was the hoped-for result of the law-enforcement mode. From the first, the police were expected to follow rules defining that process, though states differed in how stringent the rules should be. The criminal-apprehension process was always understood to involve individual rights, the violation of which was unacceptable because it meant that the violating officer would be acting as a judge and jury—and that was not his job. Guilt or innocence was to be determined by universal standards under special procedures.

Ordinarily, no judge or jury ever sees the persons caught up in a dispute over the appropriate level of neighborhood order. That is true not only because most cases are handled informally on the street but also because no universal standards are available to settle arguments over disorder, and thus a judge may not be any wiser or more effective than a police officer. Until quite recently in many states, and even today in some places, the police make arrests on such charges as "suspicious person" or "vagrancy" or "public drunkenness"—charges with scarcely any legal meaning. These charges exist not because society wants judges to punish vagrants or drunks but because it wants an officer to have the legal tools to remove undesirable persons from a neighborhood when informal efforts to preserve order in the streets have failed.

Once we begin to think of all aspects of police work as involving the application of universal rules under special procedures, we inevitably ask what constitutes an "undesirable person" and why we should "criminalize" vagrancy or drunkenness. A strong and commendable desire to see that people are treated fairly makes us worry about allowing the police to rout persons who are undesirable by some vague or parochial standard. A growing and not-so-commendable utilitarianism leads us to doubt that any behavior that does not "hurt" another person should be made illegal. And thus many of us who watch over the police are reluctant to allow them to perform, in the only way they can, a function that every neighborhood desperately wants them to perform.

This wish to "decriminalize" disreputable behavior that "harms no one"—and thus remove the ultimate sanction the police can employ to maintain neighborhood order—is, we think, a mistake. Arresting a single drunk or a single vagrant who has harmed no identifiable person seems unjust, and in a sense it is. But failing to do anything about a score of drunks or a hundred vagrants may destroy an entire community. A particular rule that seems to make sense in the individual case makes no sense when it is made a universal rule and applied to all cases. It makes no sense because it fails to take into account the connection between one broken window left untended and a thousand broken windows. Of course, agencies other than the police could attend to the problems posed by drunks or the mentally ill, but in most communities—especially where the "deinstitutionalization" movement has been strong—they do not.

The concern about equity is more serious. We might agree that certain behavior makes one person more undesirable than another, but how do we ensure that age or skin color or national origin or harmless mannerisms will not also become the basis for distinguishing the undesirable from the desirable? How do we ensure, in short, that the police do not become the agents of neighborhood bigotry?

We can offer no wholly satisfactory answer to this important question. We are not confident that there *is* a satisfactory answer, except to hope that by their selection, training, and supervision, the police will be inculcated with a clear sense of the outer limit of their discretionary authority. That limit, roughly, is this—the police exist to help regular behavior, not to maintain the racial or ethnic purity of a neighborhood.

Consider the case of the Robert Taylor Homes in Chicago, one of the largest public-housing projects in the country. It is home for nearly 20,000 people, all black, and extends over ninety-two acres along South State Street. It was named after a distinguished black who had been, during the 1940s, chairman of the Chicago Housing Authority. Not long after it opened, in 1962, relations between project residents and the police deteriorated badly. The citizens felt that the police were insensitive

or brutal; the police, in turn, complained of unprovoked attacks on them. Some Chicago officers tell of times when they were afraid to enter the Homes. Crime rates soared.

Today, the atmosphere has changed. Police–citizen relations have improved—apparently, both sides learned something from the earlier experience. Recently, a boy stole a purse and ran off. Several young persons who saw the theft voluntarily passed along to the police information on the identity and residence of the thief, and they did this publicly, with friends and neighbors looking on. But problems persist, chief among them the presence of youth gangs that terrorize residents and recruit members in the project. The people expect the police to "do something" about this, and the police are determined to do just that.

But do what? Though the police can obviously make arrests whenever a gang member breaks the law, a gang can form, recruit, and congregate without breaking the law. And only a tiny fraction of gang-related crimes can be solved by an arrest; thus, if an arrest is the only recourse for the police, the residents' fears will go unassuaged. The police will soon feel helpless, and the residents will again believe that the police "do nothing." What the police in fact do is to chase known gang members out of the project. In the words of one officer, "We kick ass." Project residents both know and approve of this. The tacit police–citizen alliance in the project is reinforced by the police view that the cops and the gangs are the two rival sources of power in the area, and that the gangs are not going to win.

None of this is easily reconciled with any conception of due process or fair treatment. Since both residents and gang members are black, race is not a factor. But it could be. Suppose a white project confronted a black gang, or vice versa. We would be apprehensive about the police taking sides. But the substantive problem remains the same: how can the police strengthen the informal social-control mechanisms of natural communities in order to minimize fear in public places? Law enforcement, per se, is no answer. A gang can weaken or destroy a community by standing about in a menacing fashion and speaking rudely to passersby without the law.

We have difficulty thinking such matters, not simply because the ethical and legal issues are so complex but because we have become accustomed to thinking of the law in essentially individualistic terms. The law defines *my* rights, punishes *his* behavior, and is applied by *that* officer because of *this* harm. We assume, in thinking this way, that what is good for the individual will be good for the community, and what doesn't matter when it happens to one person won't matter if it happens to many. Ordinarily, those are plausible assumptions. But in cases where behavior that is tolerable to one person is intolerable to many others, the reactions of the others—fear, withdrawal, flight—may ultimately make matters worse for everyone, including the individual who first professed his indifference.

It may be their greater sensitivity to communal as opposed to individual needs that helps explain why the residents of small communities are more satisfied with their police than are the residents of similar neighborhoods in big cities. Elinor

Ostrom and her co-workers at Indiana University compared the perception of police services in two poor, all-black Illinois towns—Phoenix and East Chicago Heights—with those of three comparable all-black neighborhoods in Chicago. The level of criminal victimization and the quality of police–community relations appeared to be about the same in the towns and the Chicago neighborhoods. But the citizens living in their own villages were much more likely than those living in the Chicago neighborhoods to say that they do not stay at home for fear of crime, to agree that the local police have "the right to take an action necessary" to deal with problems, and to agree that the police "look out for the needs of the average citizen." It is possible that the residents and the police of the small towns saw themselves as engaged in a collaborative effort to maintain a certain standard of communal life, whereas those of the big city felt themselves to be simply requesting and supplying particular services on an individual basis.

If this is true, how should a wise police chief deploy his meager forces? The first answer is that nobody knows for certain, and the most prudent course of action would be to try further variations on the Newark experiment, to see more precisely what works in what kinds of neighborhoods. The second answer is also a hedge—many aspects of order-maintenance in neighborhoods can probably best be handled in ways that involve the police minimally, if at all. A busy, bustling shopping center and a quiet, well-tended suburb may need almost no visible police presence. In both cases, the ratio of respectable to disreputable people is ordinarily so high as to make informal social control effective.

Even in areas that are in jeopardy from disorderly elements, citizen action without substantial police involvement may be sufficient. Meetings between teenagers who like to hang out on a particular corner and adults who want to use that corner might well lead to an amicable agreement on a set of rules about how many people can be allowed to congregate, where, and when.

Where no understanding is possible—or if possible, not observed—citizen patrols may be a sufficient response. There are two traditions of communal involvement in maintaining order. One, that of the "community watchmen," is as old as the first settlement of the New World. Until well into the nineteenth century, volunteer watchmen, not policemen, patrolled their communities to keep order. They did so, by and large, without taking the law into their own hands—without, that is, punishing persons or using force. Their presence deterred disorder or alerted the community to disorder that could not be deterred. There are hundreds of such efforts today in communities all across the nation. Perhaps the best known is that of the Guardian Angels, a group of unarmed young persons in distinctive berets and T-shirts, who first came to public attention when they began patrolling the New York City subways but who claim now to have chapters in more than thirty American cities. Unfortunately, we have little information about the effect of these groups on crime. It is possible, however, that whatever their effect on crime, citizens find their presence reassuring, and that they thus contribute to maintaining a sense of order and civility.

The second tradition is that of the "vigilante." Rarely a feature of the settled communities of the East, it was primarily to be found in those frontier towns that grew up in advance of the reach of government. More than 350 vigilante groups are known to have existed; their distinctive feature was that their members did take the law into their own hands, by acting as judge, jury, and often executioner as well as policeman. Today, the vigilante movement is conspicuous by its rarity, despite the great fear expressed by citizens that the older cities are becoming "urban frontiers." But some community-watchmen groups have skirted the line, and others may cross it in the future. An ambiguous case, reported in *the Wall Street Journal,* involved a citizens' patrol in the Silver Lake area of Belleville, New Jersey. A leader told the reporter, "We look for outsiders." If a few teenagers from outside the neighborhood enter it, "we ask them their business," he said. "If they say they're going down the street to see Mrs. Jones, fine, we let them pass. But then we follow them down the block to make sure they're really going to see Mrs. Jones."

Though citizens can do a great deal, the police are plainly the key to order-maintenance. For one thing, many communities, such as the Robert Taylor Homes, cannot do the job by themselves. For another, no citizen in a neighborhood, even an organized one, is likely to feel the sense of responsibility that wearing a badge confers. Psychologists have done many studies on why people fail to go to the aid of persons being attacked or seeking help, and they have learned that the cause is not "apathy" or "selfishness" but the absence of some plausible grounds for feeling that one must personally accept responsibility. Ironically, avoiding responsibility is easier when a lot of people are standing about. On streets and in public places, where order is so important, many people are likely to be "around," a fact that reduces the chance of any one person acting as the agent of the community. The police officer's uniform singles him out as a person who must accept responsibility if asked. In addition, officers, more easily than their fellow citizens, can be expected to distinguish between what is necessary to protect the safety of the street and what merely protects its ethnic purity.

But the police forces of America are losing, not gaining, members. Some cities have suffered substantial cuts in the number of officers available for duty. These cuts are not likely to be reversed in the near future. Therefore, each department must assign its existing officers with great care. Some neighborhoods are so demoralized and crime-ridden as to make foot patrol useless; the best the police can do with limited resources is respond to the enormous number of calls for service. Other neighborhoods are so stable and serene as to make foot patrol unnecessary. The key is to identify neighborhoods at the tipping point—where the public order is deteriorating but not unreclaimable, where the streets are used frequently but by apprehensive people, where a window is likely to be broken at any time, and must quickly be fixed if all are not to be shattered.

Most police departments do not have ways of systematically identifying such areas and assigning officers to them. Officers are assigned on the basis of crime rates (meaning that marginally threatened areas are often stripped so that police can investigate crimes in areas where the situation is hopeless) or on the basis of calls for service (despite the fact that most citizens do not call the police when they are merely frightened or annoyed). To allocate patrol wisely, the department must look at the neighborhoods and decide, from first-hand evidence, where an additional officer will make the greatest difference in promoting a sense of safety.

One way to stretch limited police resources is being tried in some public-housing projects. Tenant organizations hire off-duty police officers for patrol work in their buildings. The costs are not high (at least not per resident), the officer likes the additional income, and the residents feel safer. Such arrangements are probably more successful than hiring private watchmen, and the Newark experiment helps us understand why. A private security guard may deter crime or misconduct by his presence, and he may go to the aid of persons needing help, but he may well not intervene—that is, control or drive away—someone challenging community standards. Being a sworn officer—a "real cop"—seems to give one the confidence, the sense of duty, and the aura of authority necessary to perform this difficult task.

Patrol officers might be encouraged to go to and from duty stations on public transportation and, while on the bus or subway car, enforce rules about smoking, drinking, disorderly conduct, and the like. The enforcement need involve nothing more than ejecting the offender (the offense, after all, is not one with which a booking officer or a judge wishes to be bothered). Perhaps the random but relentless maintenance of standards on buses would lead to conditions on buses that approximate the level of civility we now take for granted on airplanes.

But the most important requirement is to think that to maintain order in precarious situations is a vital job. The police know this is one of their functions, and they also believe, correctly, that it cannot be done to the exclusion of criminal investigation and responding to calls. We may have encouraged them to suppose, however, on the basis of our oft-repeated concerns about serious, violent crime, that they will be judged exclusively on their capacity as crime-fighters. To the extent that this is the case, police administrators will continue to concentrate police personnel in the highest-crime areas (though not necessarily in the areas most vulnerable to criminal invasion), emphasize their training in the law and criminal apprehension (and not their training in managing street life), and join too quickly in campaigns to decriminalize "harmless" behavior (though public drunkenness, street prostitution, and pornographic displays can destroy a community more quickly than any team of professional burglars).

Above all, we must return to our long-abandoned view that the police ought to protect communities as well as individuals. Our crime statistics and victimization surveys measure individual losses, but they do not measure communal losses. Just as physicians now recognize the importance of fostering health rather than simply treating illness, so the police—and the rest of us—ought to recognize the importance of maintaining, intact, communities without broken windows.

James Q. Wilson is Shattuck Professor of Government at Harvard and author of *Thinking About Crime*. **George L. Kelling,** formerly director of the evaluation field staff of the Police Foundation, is currently a research fellow at the John F. Kennedy School of Government at Harvard.

UNIT 2
The Inner Life: City Stories

Unit Selections

Key Points to Consider

- What can literature teach us about the city?

- How have cities changed over the past 50 years? How are they the same?

- Does proximity breed tolerance?

Student Web Site

www.mhcls.com/online

Internet References

Further information regarding these Web sites may be found in this book's preface or online.

Cities and city life have long played a central role in our literature and culture. Because of their density, they are a place where different classes and cultures interact, not always voluntarily. By nature, American cities are dynamic, democratic and sometimes violent.

Jacob Siegel, writing about Jonathan Lethem, compares race relations now to the 1970s, and Lethem to Ellison. John Fante conjures up the sprawling, diverse Los Angeles outside of Hollywood, made up of hard-scrabble working class Italians and Mexicans. Saul Bellow's Chicago is a place where an old, gay professor can walk a block from his university to the ghetto, and speak on an equal footing about sartorial decisions with young men from a different place, race, culture and age. Adam Chimera relates a very different sort of exchange between two very different men in the midst of bustling anonymity.

Back to the Fortress of Brooklyn and the Millions of Destroyed Men Who Are My Brothers

Jacob Seigel

More than a year has passed since the publication of Jonathan Lethem's eighth novel, The *Fortress of Solitude.* The book was touted as the first major work of an important young author, and treated as such by most of its many reviewers. Yet of all the essays and reviews I've read, none has confronted the book's central theme. The soul of the story, both its bravery and perniciousness, is an exceptionally candid obsession with blackness in the white mind. Mingus, the central black character, is the story's only true love, blackness its only beating heart.

The failure of the critical establishment to seize on this theme illuminates those dark racial corners where both critics and the culture at large still fear to tread. Melanie Rehak's review in *The Nation,* in which the word "race" appears only once outside of quotes, is typical of the book's reception. To mention that the book dealt with race was enough—no need for the critic to endanger themselves or their readers by engaging just what Lethem had to say about the matter. And what Lethem did say was indeed dangerous.

The Fortress of Solitude is an exploration into the much charted but still murky racial grounds where the arch iden- tities of Black and White duel, romance, and hide their essential condition. Lethem, to his credit, shuns sociology, and creates enough vital truth in his fiction to penetrate and immerse us in the lives of his characters so that when race breathes into them and their environment we too feel it breathe into our individual and collective selves.

My own Brooklyn upbringing shares much with that of both Lethem and his protagonist Dylan, and this probably affords me greater insight into the more coded and provincial facets of his work. But background alone can't account for the blindness of so many reviewers to the book's overarching racial element. And this is no personal or esoteric theme—the obsession with race is visible everywhere across the cultural landscape, written with the bold imprint of a graffiti burner. To ignore it can only be a willful act. When Lethem writes, "under oblivious eyes the invisible autographed the world," he describes his own endeavor.

Dylan Ebdus, the novel's hero, is borne by bohemian parents—an artist father and a former Brooklyn street kid-turned-radical mother—into Dean street, a one block stretch in 1970s Brooklyn. During his early years Dylan's neighborhood Gowanus, a black and Puerto Rican enclave is fitfully gentrifying and being remade into Boerum Hill. Though Boerum lacks a hill, the title links it to places like Park Slope and Brooklyn Heights, as a community for the bourgeois whites of newly revitalizing Brooklyn. Dylan's mother protests this gentrification, whereby refurbished boarding houses become townhouses, street life gives way to parlor culture, and dark faces disappear so lighter ones can feel comfortable, even as her family's presence portends and encourages its coming. The first half of the book—its crucial arc—is the story of Dylan's childhood, the reinventions of his home and himself, and his entry into the world where pools of black and white spill into each other in patterns of mystery, cruelty and empathy.

Rachel, Dylan's socially conscious mother, tries to mold him in her own image—at ease in any situation, unburdened by racial and class anxieties. Her advice to Dylan in dealing with Brooklyn's rougher elements is to be "wilder than they are, wear flames in your hair, that's my recommendation." To this end she ushers him as the sole white kid into his block's black scene, and brags to her friends that he is one of only three whites at the local public school. Initially pining for the blonde girls in roller skates that he feels are his birthright, Dylan stays on the margins of his block's activities. Inept at the various games and rituals of his peers, he is not an outsider but an outlier.

Dylan's induction into Brooklyn and its rites is not accomplished by gaining the acceptance of local kids or, as his mother wishes, by becoming tough enough to walk his own way. He earns his entry by resigning himself to the role of whiteboy, given to him personally by his peers and anonymously by his circumstances. The whiteboy is not only a perpetual mark to be taken by tougher kids, but the familiar imposition of a generic type on a rough edged individual. By prescribing behavior without regard for a persons inner content the role breeds dissonance and double consciousness.

Dylan accepts the part both from weakness and from a sense that he deserves it for the privilege and sins of his color. Only by rehearsing his own victimhood to the point where he can act out his part can he be integrated into Gowanus' drama with some degree of safety. Robert Woolfolk, a black kid from the projects who arrives on Dean Street without notice bearing an omen of violence, is the crucial figure in Dylan's inauguration as a white-boy. Unlike the other black and Puerto Rican kids on Dylan's relatively peaceful block, Robert is not just poor but ghetto. He lacks the guiding constraints of family and community that keep the other kids in check and afford some of them promising futures.

Describing Robert's entrance into a round of stoopball Lethem's narrator observes that "another kid could ask to join a ball game, Robert Woolfolk had to hustle in. His basic premise was criminal. It wasn't something he could leave behind when it happened to be unnecessary." It is Robert who first introduces Dylan to the "yoke", a sort of racial mugging that still existed as recently as my own youth unchanged in practice but renamed "herbing". A yoke is a demand made by black kids for a white kid's things, enforced by the threat of violence and the deeper threat of exposing the white kid as a racist. Here is Lethem's account of how yoking figures in Dylan's youth:

He might be yoked low, bent over, hugged to someone's hip then spun on release like a human top, legs buckling, crossing at the ankles. Or from behind, never sure by who once the headlock popped loose and three or four guys stood around, witnesses with hard eyes, shaking their heads at the sheer dumb luck of being white. It was routine as laughter. . . . He was dismissed from it as from an episode of light street theater. "Nobody hurt you man. It ain't for real. You know we was just fooling with you, right?" They'd spring away, leave him tottering, hyperventilating, while they highfived, more like amazed spectators than perpetrators. If Dylan choked or whined they were perplexed and slightly disappointed at the white boy's too-ready hysteria. Dylan didn't quite get it, hadn't learned his role. On those occasions they'd pick

up his books or hat and press them on him, tuck him back together. A ghost of fondness lived in a headlock's shadow.

Dylan is yoked by any number of kids during his childhood and its premise burrows deep within his psyche, becoming the existential emblem of his youth and the specter that haunts his later years.

In his review of *The Fortress of Solitude* in *The New Republic,* James Wood cites the passage above as an example of Lethem's weakness for "over-articulate explanation". Wood goes on to assert that crucial point to be taken from the yoking episode is Lethem's "ability to seize at once the knowingness and the inexperience of children." He finally reproves Lethem for "insisting on telling us what we might divine anyway—that this is light street theater."

This is comically misguided. Wood takes the novel's central, recurring metaphor, which ought to shock with it's distillation of the violent racial energy that powers the entire story, and dismisses it with hardly a mention of race. Considering Wood's reproach of Lethem it is ironic that he still missed the point even as it was "over-explained" in this line where the motivations of the yokers is spelled out: "We yoke you for thinking that we might: in your eyes we see that you come pre-yoked."

It's depressing to see one of our greatest literary critics explicate only the most formalist, literary aspects of a passage that offers real humanity, pathos and social resonance. I use Wood as an example not because his review is particularly unique or egregious in its failings—it is not—but to show how even our best critics seemed unable to face the book's racial themes head-on. Lethem has stared so unflinchingly at race that critics ought to have been able to return his gaze.

The power of the yoke lies not in what it shares with the rote mechanics of robbery, but in the dynamics of its racial blackmail, which corrupt all involved. A simple mugging becomes a yoke only when black boys make a whiteboy complicit in his own victimization with an unspoken threat, the tortured logic of which is that they are the real victims of his fear that they will mug him. Despite the idealism of Dylan's parents they could not convince their neighbors that they were trying to join the community, ideological credentials never distinguish Dylan on the street. He is just a dumb kid who deserves to get yoked, according to his yokers, for encroaching on Gowanus when he has the whole white world that he can lay claim to.

When Lethem compares yoking to theater or writes that "the whole event [was] a quotation of itself," he is invoking not only the drama of the actions but the tentative choreography of the actors. Just as Dylan was being taught his role by the black kids robbing him, they were trying on their own roles. Dylan's inclusion was necessary partly for the benefits of rehearsing with all the leads present. By assenting to the yoke he tightened its future performance. Similarly, when Dylan was casually dismissed at the incident's conclusion, or warned from making too big a deal of it, the purpose was not only to intimidate him into silence, but to ease the conscience of his assailants, still unsure in their identity as aggrieved predators. They encourage Dylan to brush off the episode so that they can do the same, and demure from acknowledging that they were doing anything more than having a little fun.

To be a young black boy and one day discover that you wield a power over whiteboys, whether or not you choose to exercise it, is a sticky piece of knowledge to dislodge. It is not a far stretch from recognizing that a latent fear indicts you, a fear that you have done nothing to provoke, to deciding that this fear enables you—or even licenses you—to exploit it. At some point a black kid realizes the power of his blackness, and a white kid the yoke of his whiteness. What the pair does not yet see is that the hierarchy of their youth is both an historical inversion and also often an abjectly ironic projection of their respective futures. The crossing channels of race blurring who is owed what from whom, breeding a false determinism that fulfills its own invented prophecies—these are the sources of double consciousness that assail Dylan and his partners in the Brooklyn street.

Everything changes for Dylan with the arrival of Mingus Rude. One day in the summer of Dylan's youth, Barret Rude Jr., a famous black soul singer on the wane, moves in next door. Barret puts his royalties toward keeping his new brownstone full of cocaine and paranoia, which leaves little room for his son Mingus, a boy of Dylan's age. Seeing her chance to integrate Dylan into Brooklyn and blackness, Dylan's mother longingly predicts that he and Mingus will become best friends. And they do. The story of their friendship, its secrets, betrayals and resonance in Dylan's imagination, forms the story's Rosetta Stone, without which nothing else can be rightly understood.

Lethem's impressionistic portraits, rendering their subjects in lucid, beautiful passages, received their due praise from most reviewers. But his power to conjure images and evocations of even the most personal and seemingly inexpressible wonders of childhood and Brooklyn obscured for his critics the narrative ends for which these talents were applied. The breathy romance of much of the book's first half is not only a means to elicit a nostalgic picture of Brooklyn in the 70s, but a spell cast to make the reader see in Mingus what Dylan sees: A superhero's myth and lore with the key to all the secrets of the city.

Mingus, nicknamed "the million dollar kid" for the money his father paid to win custody from his now absent white mother, is—initially, at least—as much an outsider

and gentrifier as Dylan and his family. In the boys' first encounter, Mingus models the Boy Scout uniform that he has brought from the Philadelphia suburbs while Dylan silently wishes to warn him not to expose such enticingly vulnerable artifacts to their harsh environs:

> He wished to protect them both by commanding the new boy never to bring any of these madly fertile and irrelevant obsessions out on the block for any other kid to see. . . . Dylan wanted Mingus Rude and himself to build a fire and smother the uniforms in damp smoke until the plastic blackened and melted, until the numbers and names, the evidence, was destroyed.

But without any perceptible break, Dylan's role of protector becomes a farce as Mingus—due in part to his blackness or half-blackness—fast gains the acceptance of the other kids in the neighborhood and displays a native's ease with the esoteric practices that are the tests for inclusion. Drawn out of isolation by a growing fascination with the elusive character of Mingus, Dylan forgets his furtive yearning for the comforts of a white milieu and follows Mingus into the avenues of black Brooklyn. He becomes attuned to the enthralling, nascent world of hip hop and graffiti. The art of "tagging," or drawing an assumed moniker on public spaces, becomes the pivotal act of their friendship.

In Dylan's eyes, Mingus, despite his more recent arrival, owns New York in a way that he never can. And life in New York, especially for the young, is often a contest of ownership. My stoop, my block, my neighborhood, my subway car, my subway seat, my turn to speak, my right to stare at you and enter your conversation uninvited. This is petty territoriality, of course, but also the invention and inflation of identity. To know the city best is to take from it anything you wish, to conflate your own narrow individuality with its epic stature.

The underground worlds of New York, hip hop chief among them, are not built from nothing, but constructed by a set of abstract relations on the actual, physical city. Subcultures, as such, are really superstructures, inventions held aloft by the shared belief and active participation of their followers in grounding them to what readily exists. Only in Mingus' presence can Dylan navigate through the city's anonymous landmarks and understand, if not fully participate in, their existence. In one of the novel's most perfect and quoted passages Mingus leads Dylan from the edge of Brooklyn to the verge of Manhattan, over the bridge:

> They circled under the onramp to find stone stairs up into the sunlight of the bridge's walkway, then started across, over the river, traffic howling in the cages at their feet, the gray clotted sky clinging to the bridge's veins, Manhattan's dinosaur spine rotating into view as they mounted the

great curve above the river. . . . They halted two-thirds across. On the cast tower planted at Manhattan's mouth were two lavish word-paintings, red and white and green and yellow sprayed fantastically high in the rough stone, edges bled in geological texture. The first read MONO, the second LEE, syllables drained of meaning, like Mingus's Dose. Dylan understood what Mingus wanted him to see. The painted names had conquered the bridge, pinned it to the secret street, claimed it for Brooklyn.

To write on the bridge was to re-form its meaning and to read it was to be initiated into the culture of that meaning. To claim the Brooklyn Bridge for Brooklyn was a heroic feat, known only to the partisans who could recognize their conquering flag.

Paired with Mingus, Dylan gains some access to the avenues of black life in Brooklyn, and takes a few shaky steps toward adopting the speech and dress, but no amount of immersion makes him any less a whiteboy. It is a stigma he cannot shake and an immutable message, broadcast against his will, of where and with whom he belongs. Entering junior high Dylan's hopes that Mingus will protect him from being yoked are shattered. Mingus disappears, retreating further into himself and into the petty crime and delinquency of the neighborhood, in which Robert Woolfolk becomes his partner. Privately, Dylan feels that Mingus has abandoned him, breeding a resentment that festers for decades.

To make matters worse, Dylan becomes friends with Arthur Lomb, his school's other whiteboy, with whom he is paired against his will. Dylan's friendship with the bookish, implicitly Jewish Arthur, the only kid in his neighborhood who makes him seem tough by contrast, is not only a danger—two chumps make a more visible target than one—but an affront to his mother's egalitarianism and his own attempt to dissolve his differences with Mingus in a larger, shared belonging. In the cruelest turn, Dylan cannot avoid the fact that he and Arthur share not only race, but sensibility. Playing chess, making knowing references to comic books and pop culture, they affirm that their otherness is deeper than their skin. At the time Dylan still does not understand and thus takes no consolation from the fact that the difference between his new friend and his black friends has more to do with their parents' respective class, character and backgrounds than the gleaming salience of their whiteness.

Arthur, despite or because of his nerdiness, wishes to be cool and accepted. When Dylan, with secret, possessive pride, introduces Arthur to Mingus, it doesn't take long for Arthur to ingratiate himself with a buffoonish mimicry of blackness that eventually includes a friendship with Robert Woolfolk. Unwilling to join in Arthur's minstrelsy and incapable of reclaiming Mingus for himself Dylan follows along uneasily as an outsider among his own friends.

One of the book's most telling details, never commented on by Lethem or his reviewers, is Mingus' bi-racial identity. Mulatto Mingus becomes the balance point between Robert, Arthur and Dylan—the patois through which they can all communicate. It is Mingus, with his background in the Boy Scouts, and not Arthur, who first introduces Dylan to the hermetically cool world of comic books. It is Mingus again who is able to calmly talk Robert out of yoking Dylan. And it is the same Mingus, Dylan's best friend, from whom a white woman tries to save him when they wander into the wealthy precinct of Brooklyn Heights. When this young mother sees the two boys together, she can only assume that Dylan has strayed from the safety of one of the local private schools and is now being threatened by the borough's dark side. Her intrusion forces on Dylan the knowledge that he can't fully belong anywhere. He is too poor and marginal for white gentility, to weak and intellectual for white-ethnic toughness, and too brightly lit to pass unnoticed in black company. By trying to rescue him she has proven to both Mingus and himself that the anonymous eyes under which they pass will never see them as brothers, the way Dylan wishes them to be seen.

Far later in the book, his adolescent awkwardness behind him, it becomes clear that although he can never be convincingly black, it is no great feat for Dylan to be white and pass in that culture. For now though, while that revelation remains distant, its eventuality is begun by Dylan's retreat from his neighborhood and its people. The road out of Brooklyn leads him first into Manhattan, where he attends the city's most elite public school, later to the country's most expensive private college in the lily white preserve of Vermont, and finally to California.

It's fitting that a book about the recondite mysteries of Brooklyn and the underworlds of childhood is rife with coded allusions and clues for its own concealed insights. As with race, most reviewers merely mention these recurring symbols without probing them for meaning. Most significant among them, the nexus wherein Dylan's comic book fantasies collide with his neighborhood's realities, is a magical ring that grants its wearer superpowers that change not only with time and place, but according to its user. Bequeathed to Dylan by a homeless, gin-soaked black man, Aaron X. Doily, the ring is given with the cryptic admonition that Doily can no longer use it to fly because he "can't fight the airwaves."

Aeroman is the superhero Dylan invents to use the powers of the ring, an alter-ego that he allows Mingus to share just as Mingus had shared his graffiti identity with Dylan. When they are together, their identities merged, they have only one purpose for Aeroman, but apart they put the ring towards sharply divergent ends. The shared role for Aeroman involves Dylan luring toughs into confronting him so that Mingus can swoop down and scare them off. Despite their brazen use of the ring's superpowers Dylan and Mingus never fear being caught or revealed, they trust that in Brooklyn, "These streets always make room for two or three figures alone in struggle, as in a forest, unheard. The stoops lean away from the street, the distance between row houses widens to a mute canyon." On the same register that he had been yoked, too low to sound in adult society, Dylan is able to enact his vengeance undetected.

Alone, Mingus uses the ring to accomplish two crucial acts as Aeroman that illustrate the wrenching ambivalence of his condition. When he jumps a group of drug dealers outside the nearby projects we are left to wonder whether the motive of the robbery is to feed his growing addiction or to rage against it and its facilitators. In his ultimate use of the ring, Mingus burns his tag in towering characters on the side of the Brooklyn House of Detention. Autographing the emblem of his future imprisonment, he is, at once, defacing and claiming his fate.

Dylan's last act before first leaving Brooklyn for Vermont is to buy back the ring from Mingus, to whom he had entrusted it. Desperate for money to bankroll a drug venture with Arthur and Robert, Mingus sells the ring back. Both of them are bitterly aware that the transaction is Dylan's way of proving that he can buy out of Brooklyn and their friendship.

While for Mingus, the ring's sole attribute is flight, Dylan (who can only use it to fly only in the presence of other white people or when alone and outside of Brooklyn) can also use it at times to become invisible in a way that seems to change not so much his racial identity as his identity in relation to race. Mostly, Dylan flies while in Vermont, described by Mingus as "Ver-mont, where the girls go swimming without any clothes and niggers work in gas stations," and the only place in which Dylan makes an outward show of his Brooklyness. Parodying the street talk and hustle of Mingus, he plays a safe-to-the-touch nigger for the amusement of his rich, white college friends. Aeroman is a way for Dylan to play superman in solitude or to act out the racial grievances that he can't own up to without an alternate identity. Pretenses of heroism aside, Dylan initially uses the ring only to settle his personal scores.

When critics pondered Lethem's central conceit, a ring that can confer invisibility on its wearer, is it proper that only one thought to mention Ralph Ellison? Would that have been too obvious? Perhaps Henry Roth and Jonathan Franzen were more clever, more literary comparisons. Nor do the echoes of Ellison end with the ring. As the book's coda pined for "middle spaces," was there no reviewer who thought of "lower frequencies"? Whether or not Lethem intended these shades of "Invisible Man" is irrelevant. Had the novel been considered for what it was, a study of race and American identity, rather than a conventional bildungsroman about the pains of maturation, it is impossible to imagine that so few would have picked up on such clear parallels with Ellison. The fact that these analogies were ignored is evidence either that the book was universally misread or that its reviewers skimmed over the vast racial swamp that gives the story its mass to attend to the garden of lesser themes at its edges.

The novel loses its power and momentum once Dylan leaves Brooklyn, as Lethem wanders through superfluous plot lines that he affords too much attention and significance. In its final arc the book switches to the first person and Dylan, as an adult rock critic on the West Coast, treats us to a fight with his black girlfriend. But the girlfriend is less a character than a narrative device through which Lethem calls Dylan out on the interwoven strands of blackness and childhood that still bind him.

Haunted by their friendship and its loss, Dylan sees that Mingus is the key to understanding himself. All these years later, he is still kept in a headlock by his memories of being yoked, and the meaning of the yoke itself. To break out he goes to see Mingus, now being held in a Watertown prison that also houses Robert Woolfolk. Before Dylan arrives at the prison, the narrative is interrupted by a neutrally voiced chronicle of how Mingus wound up there. We learn of his descent into crack use with its mounting debasements and routinized jail time, and the purposeless survival that has become his existence.

Dylan brings the ring to Mingus so that its powers can be used to free him, but before he offers it he exhumes the two buried questions that he has spent all these years carrying in silence: Did Mingus know that he was getting yoked all the time? Did Mingus ever yoke a whiteboy? Which are Dylan's crude way of asking if they are brothers, and if so how could his brother have abandoned him to such cruelty. That Mingus answers yes to both questions does not stop Dylan from offering the ring, and in doing so he implicitly obviates the question of who was owed a reckoning by whom. Where was Dylan when Mingus needed him? In Vermont, degrading him for cheap laughs. Dylan's pain from his yokings and his shame at allowing them without a fight had crippled his empathy, which he was only now slowly regaining.

In defying one's image as a willing victim it is dangerously easy to become louder than necessary and brasher than appropriate, adopting a posture that is too aggressive to pass as a defensive measure—a false indifference to race based on staring at it past the point of decency. Dylan's tortured position is not quite like this: rather than becoming hostile, he's shrunken into a shell of callousness.

Earlier in the novel, just before Dylan retakes the ring and leaves Brooklyn, Dylan's father relates his own encounter with Mingus:

"He didn't look so well to me," said Abraham.

"When I asked he laughed it off, only suggested I give him a dollar."

"Did you do it?"

"Of course."

"You got yoked, dad."

Here is the moral dead end, when one day out of a specious bid at self-assertion you refuse a dollar to a black man who actually needs it because you can no longer parse the difference between a request and a demand—and worse, that black man is your best friend.

Trapped in a stunted mindset in which he still expected Mingus to protect him, Dylan ignored the reversal of their roles in the adult world where it was he who should have tried to protect Mingus. In the end Mingus, resigned to his condition, refuses the ring and it is Dylan who escapes the prison. But not before he obliges Mingus' request and sneaks the ring to Robert. When Robert tries to use the ring to break out, it fails to grant him flight, as it always had, and he is killed without ever breaching the prison's walls. The fact that Dylan on Mingus' behest gives Robert, his enemy the arch-yoker, the tool of his own demise—and the question of whether Mingus does so willfully—are left unresolved for the reader to consider. Although the book goes on for a few more pages, this is the real conclusion: Dylan finding Mingus and confronting the imbalance between their inseparable fates.

The Fortress of Solitude is a profound achievement, but it is not without considerable faults. First there is Lethem's penchant for wordiness and overdescription. This sin is real but inseparable from the book's overall style. Lethem's gift as a writer, and one of his themes, is naming things—particularly those that are left nameless out of fear of acknowledging their nature. The style is a detriment only when, having already crystallized an idea or image, Lethem persists in stringing on further, needless adjectives that shroud the subject's clarity. At its worst, this tendency reduces genuine reflection to flaccid paraphrase, but its strengths underpin the book's vivid expressiveness.

More significant than crowded prose is the abundance of secondary themes and storylines that threaten to obscure the thrust of the narrative. Distractions from the book's perilous guiding venture, they offer the comforts of conventionality and well marked escape routes along the curve of its plot. Forays into comic book conventions and screenplays, like the scattered allusions to Dylan's mother, are meaningless without relation to the overarching drama between Dylan and Mingus. It is partly Lethem's own fault that his reviewers could treat race as a single, if larger, point in a constellation of themes rather than the planetary center that holds even the smallest mote in its gravity.

Having made my point, let me step back and say that the book is not all about race. A mark of its worth as a novel is that it arranges disparate voices in a cacophony that evokes the sheer effusive variety of life. *Fortress* offers many pivotal story lines which I never address at all, some of these lines are powerful, others less so, none should be criticized for failing to hew to the racial themes if they could stand alone. But the story itself, the passion and conviction with which it is told and its impact on the reader, suffers when it strays from the racial core that is so clearly its animating force.

The novel's one betrayal of its ambitions is that while Dylan sometimes fails to stand out as fully realized, Mingus is often too dim even to emerge fully as his fraternal shadow. The offense is not unforgivable. Lethem never reduces Mingus to an icon of primitive or sexual energy, but he leaves the mystery of his person undisturbed until the very end. Preserving Mingus's enigmatic allure to Dylan is integral to the book's thematic conceit, but it would have been still more powerful had Lethem shown the power of an enigma exuded by a fully realized person. Instead he trains all his illumination on Dylan, the brother who already holds more light.

We never know: What does Mingus think of Brooklyn? What does Mingus think of Dylan? What does Mingus think of Mingus? We are never privy to the reasons why Mingus would want to belong to Dylan's world, expressing as it does the lure of whiteness to black people. Much could have been gained by looking past the easy trappings of wealth, comfort, or pride of place and into the hazy psychic stuff of whiteness that might offer the deeper appeal that we readily recognize blackness holds for whites.

Not until the penultimate section of the book's five hundred pages is the fortress of Mingus' enigma penetrated. All paths in the story lead to the coda, the unraveling of a mysterious being until the abstract rhythm fades to reveal the syncopated details of another sad, familiar, crack-ruined life. For all his elusive wonder, Mingus is alone among the millions of destroyed men who are not his brothers, no less alone for being Dylan's brother.

In Dylan's mind, which directly or indirectly voices much of the book, Mingus is a romantic paradox, a symbol of the racial other half. Intimately intertwined with Dylan, Mingus nonetheless exudes, both in his private art and his public degradation, the tragic illusion that he cannot be known. Lethem's essential riff is on the ability of race, a socially constructed idea, to hatch inside a person and manifest its presence from the inside out as if it naturally belonged.

An essential feature of being black, Lethem suggests through the magic ring, is simply to pass unnoticed among other blacks and to be a presence among whites. Thus Dylan could be assumed into the bourgeoisie, the gates of which, without his knowing it, had always been open to him. A breezy white entitlement that allowed for poverty as a backstory rather than a fate was the gift that Dylan could never share with Mingus. The ring that he could share bore the message of the privilege that he could not. Mingus, the million dollar kid with the famous father, had none of guiding forces, neither the bohemian father nor the surrogate mother from Brooklyn Heights, to usher him in to Dylan's stake in material comfort and emotional anguish.

Here is the book's perilous leap and a likely cause of its critical neglect. To have honestly probed its racial dimension one would have been forced to confront evidence that Lethem espouses a vision of essentialist racial difference. The novel can be read as the account of a white heart breaking when it learns that a qualitative difference in humanity separates it by an unbridgeable gap from its black love. Although the book is not racist, it is unfortunate that it was not decried as such. Had Lethem been so impugned his champions and detractors alike might have spent less time marveling at his wondrous depictions of stoopball and more time examining the substance of his work.

Race is the great gift of the American experience to the literature of identity. Nothing else is so tenuously real and yet so strenuously felt, so perfect a metaphor and yet such a suffering reality. The national culture hums with blithe chatter about it, most of it voicing either the cartoonish archetypes of opposed black and white evoked in music, film and most everything else—as if any American could be fully one or the other—or the complementary obverse, starry-eyed, disingenuous portraits of racial harmony. Meanwhile the real engine of our protean American identity, miscegenation, continues to work not only from above but most often as an invisible hand guided by individual interest, inquiry and self-expression.

With few exceptions, frank talk about race, if it is to be proper and acceptable, belongs only to the social sciences where it can be sheltered by graphs and appendices and presented for the public good rather than private understanding. This obscurantist demurral, aside from its obvious harm to the nation, helps explain why even the best literary critics, living in a time when many wonder whether our culture is even capable of producing great novels, missed the explicit point of a monumental book in which Lethem seized the torch of Twain, Faulkner, Ellison and Murray, and lit upon the dark secret of our identity that we hide in plain view.

My L.A.

JOHN FANTE

Mary Osaka, I Love You

It happened in Los Angeles, in the fall of that breathless year. It happened in the kitchen of the Yokohama Café, and it happened during the dinner hour, when Segu Osaka, her ferocious father, was up front minding the customers and the cash register. It happened very quickly. Mary Osaka, her arms full of dishes, came into the kitchen and laid the dishes on the sink board. Mingo Mateo was washing dishes at the sink. He was slushing out a batch of soup bowls.

Said he, "Mary Osaka, I love you very much."

Mary Osaka reached up with two firm brown hands and held the face of Mingo Mateo to the light. "And I love you, too, Mingo. Didn't you know?"

She kissed him. Mingo Mateo felt the blood and bones melting out of his shoes, and they were very expensive shoes, the very best, with square toes, made of pigskin, costing twelve dollars a pair, three days' wages. "I've loved you since you came here three months ago," she said. "But—oh, Mingo! we can't. We mustn't. It's impossible!"

Mingo dried his hands on a dish towel and got his breath. "Is possible," he said. "Is absolutely possible. Everything is possible!"

There wasn't time to answer. The swinging doors crashed open, and Segu Osaka rushed into the kitchen waving thick fingers and shouting: "Helly up, helly up. Bling 'em chop suey two times, bling 'em tea one time, alla same, helly up, yes!"

On the other side of the kitchen Vincente Toletano dug out two orders of chop suey from the big cauldron on the stove and threw them on the serving tray. Vincente Toletano was a proud Filipino, a somber, brooding man, who, but for the scarcity of work during those times, would have spat upon a Japanese rather than work for him. After Mary hurried away with the orders, Vincente Toletano was alone with his countryman, Mingo Mateo.

Said Vincente: "Mingo, my friend, I see you make passionate love with this Japanese girl. You are a crazy man, Mingo. Also, you are a disgrace to the whole Filipino nation."

Mingo Mateo turned around. He folded his arms and glared, chin jutting, at Vincente Toletano. Said he: "Toletano, thank you ever so much if you mind your own business. For why you peek like a sneak, if you see I make love with this wonderful girl?"

Said Vincente: "I have right to peek. This girl, she is Japanese woman. Is not good for you to make kiss with this kind of woman. Better for you to wash your mouth with soap."

Mingo smiled. "She is very beautiful, eh, Vincente? You are jealous little bit, maybe?"

Vincente turned his lips as though an evil taste fell upon them. "You are a fool, Mingo. You make sickness in my stomach. I make challenge. If you kiss some more with Mary Osaka, I quit this job."

"Quit," Mingo shrugged. "I no care when you quit. But me— ah, I never quit making kiss with Mary Osaka."

Vincente's voice changed. It was threatening now, soft and menacing, as he leaned forward with his hands gripping the table that separated them.

"How you like if I tell Filipino Federated Brotherhood? How you like that, Mingo? How you like when I stand before Brotherhood and point finger and say to Federated Brotherhood, 'This man, this Mingo Mateo, he is make love with Japanese girl!' How you like that, Mingo?"

"I no care," said Mingo. "Tell whole world. It only make me more happy."

Vincente Toletano had more to say, but Mary was back in the kitchen again. "Pork chow mein on two," she called, crossing to Mingo.

Vincente threw two platters on the table and spooned out the order. Mary was talking, and what she said made Vincente splash chow mein crazily.

"It can't happen, Mingo. You know how Papa feels about you. About Vincente. About all Filipinos." She was standing very close to Mingo, a small, snug girl, whose black hair reached, sleek and lovely, to his nostrils.

"Smell good," he said, sniffing the bright blackness. "It make no difference about your papa. I no love your papa. I love you, Mary Osaka."

"You don't know Papa," she smiled.

"I know," said Mingo. "We have little talk."

Here was his opportunity, for the swinging doors flew open and Segu Osaka charged into the kitchen waving his short arms. "Helly up, quick. Bling 'em chow mein two times, chasso, chasso!" His quick black eyes lashed at Mary, at Mingo, at Vincente. Popping himself on the forehead with his open palm, he rushed back to the dining room. They could hear him muttering in Japanese something about Filipinos.

Suddenly without shame Mingo Mateo dropped to his knees and threw his arms around the slim waist of Mary Osaka. He clung to her, his face tight against her.

"Oh, Mary Osaka," he panted, "please, you be my wife?"

"Mingo, be careful!"

She tore herself away, dragging him so that he walked a little on his knees after her before letting go. When she had disappeared with the two orders of chow mein, there was Mingo Mateo on his knees, sitting on his heels, and across the room with lips curled in disgust stood Vincente Toletano. His face said, "Finished." His cold eyes said much more than that.

Grabbing his high-crowned chef's hat, Toletano flung it to the floor. He stood upon it, wiped his feet upon it, while his fingers fought and burst the strings of his apron, which he ripped away.

"Already I am quit," he said. "Is too much for one Filipino to see."

But the eyes of Mingo Mateo were on the swinging doors. Half-kneeling, half-sitting, he watched them go thump-thump, thump-thump, before coming to a stop. His hands hung loosely at his sides. His chin lay like a heavy stone against his chest.

Vincente Toletano crossed to him. "My countryman!" he sneered, and he seized the head of Mingo Mateo by the hair, turning the face upward toward him. Deliberately he slapped Mingo first across one cheek, then the other. Now he held the face toward him again. Calmly he spat upon it.

"Fooey!" he said, pushing Mingo. "Disgrace to the good name of the Filipino people."

Mingo did not resist, did not speak. The tears fell from his eyes and slithered down his brown cheeks. Vincente was gone; the alley door slammed loudly behind him. Mingo staggered to his feet. He washed his face with cold water, pulling the flesh at his cheeks with long fingers, running his hands through his hair, clenching his teeth against a surge of grief that shook his body like a fit of coughing. When Mary Osaka returned to the kitchen, she found him that way, his head bent down and smothered in his hands, his sobs louder than the sound of the running water that was coming from the faucet.

She put down a trayful of dishes and took him in her arms. The curve of her neck fitted his forehead like a nest as he leaned heavily upon her. She stroked his wet hair with spread fingers; she smoothed his thin shoulders with small, eager palms.

"You mustn't. Mingo, you mustn't."

"Nothing good in this world but you," he choked. "Is better to die without my Mary. Make no difference what Vincente say, or your papa, or anybody."

Vincente? She looked about and realized the cook was gone. All at once Mingo was erect, tense, his eyes aflame, his two hands on her shoulders, the fingers hurting her flesh as he held her at arms' length.

"Mary! Why we care? Filipino, he say is disgrace to marry Japanese. Japanese, he say is disgrace to marry Filipino. Is lie, big lie, whole thing. For in the heart is what count, and the heart of Mingo Mateo say alla time, boom boom boom for Mary Osaka."

The face of Mary Osaka brightened, and the eyes of Mary Osaka were drenched with delight. "Oh, Mingo!"

Eagerly he spoke. "We marry, yes? No?"

"Yes!"

He caught his breath, held back a giddy laugh, and fell at her feet, his knees booming on the floor. He kissed her hands and pulled them across his lips. He was pecking quick kisses on the tips of her fingers when Segu Osaka bounced into the kitchen.

"Helly up, helly up!"

There was Mingo Mateo at his daughter's feet.

Said Mingo Mateo, "Mr. Osaka, if you please—"

Said Osaka; "No no no. Get 'em out. Fire. Go. Out!"

Not tall, Osaka, but squat and powerful. His fists were quickly inside Mingo's collar. There was a tearing of cloth, with Mingo's face a thickish blue as Osaka dragged him sacklike across the floor and out the kitchen door.

"But Mr. Osaka! Is love! Is marriage!"

"No no no. No no no."

Sprawled in the alley, Mingo saw the stumpy little man slam the door, heard it bolted. Inside, Osaka spluttered violent Japanese, and Mary answered with equal vehemence. Mingo jumped to his feet and rushed the door, kicking it, drumming it with knuckles.

"Don't hurt her," he shouted. "Don't touch!"

The voices inside grew louder. Desperately he flung himself against the door. The wood panel splintered, the bolt and hinges creaked. For a moment the voices were silent.

Then a piercing cry cut the night as Segu Osaka shrieked: "Help, police! Help!"

Mingo paused, glanced up and down the alley. The moonlight illuminated a canyon of fire escapes and garbage tins leading to a bright street fifty yards away. Osaka still screamed. Now there were other voices and the sound of running feet inside the kitchen.

Mary's voice rose above the noise. "Run, Mingo, run!"

Pulling off his apron, Mingo threw it into a garbage can. Upstairs a window howled, opened. The frail head and shoulders of Mary Osaka's mother peered out. She did not speak, only looked down at him nervously, her hands clutching her mouth. He backed into the darkness and ran toward the street, his feet filling the alley with tiny echoes.

He slowed to a walk when he reached the street. Little Tokyo was crowded with Saturday-night strollers. Coatless, he lost himself among the shoppers, making his way past the toy stores and cafés, the clean, bright shops. The windows always shone in Little Tokyo, there was less refuse in the gutters, the street lamps were brighter, and incense from a hundred doors filled the air with sweetness. Like the others, Mingo Mateo sauntered unhurried and at ease in the warm December night.

The brightness of the street gradually ended. Now there were blackened warehouses, and beyond them the Filipino Quarter began. Flophouses and wine shops, burned hamburgers and strong perfume, barbershops and massage parlors, jukebox music and chippies, and everywhere his countrymen, the little brown brothers, exquisitely tailored, exquisitely lonely, leaning against poolroom doorways, smoking cigars and staring alternately at the stars overhead and the clicking high heels passing by.

At the fountain of the Bataan Poolhall Mingo ordered a glass of orange juice. As he raised it to his lips, someone touched his shoulder and spoke his name. He gulped the drink and turned around.

Vincente Toletano stood there. The two men with him were Julio Gonzales and Aurelio Lazario. Without glancing at Toletano, Mingo understood why they were there. These men were officers of the Filipino Federated Brotherhood. Vincente Toletano had gone to them with the name of Mary Osaka on his lips.

Julio Gonzales spoke first. "Come into back room, Mateo. We wish to have little talk." He was the largest of the three, a middleweight prize fighter with mauled ears and a crushed nose.

"Talk with Toletano!" Mingo sneered. "He is stool pigeon. He tell everything."

Said Toletano: "You lie, Mingo. I do this for good of the Filipino Federated Brotherhood. You make the oath. You must keep."

Said Mingo: "Cannot keep the oath. I am in love with Mary Osaka. I resign from Brotherhood."

"Not so easy to resign," said Gonzales. "Better to come and have little talk."

Said Mingo: "I love Mary Osaka. Go to hell."

Said Gonzales, "How you like when I put best right on whole Pacific Coast inside your mouth, bust out the teeth?" He lifted a heavy brown fist into Mingo's view.

"Is make no difference. Still I love Mary Osaka."

Aurelio Lazario got between them. An educated man, Aurelio. Bachelor of Arts, Pomona College; Doctor of Law, University of California; now a dishwasher in Jason's cafeteria. Aurelio laid his thin, soap-softened hand on Mingo's shoulder, and friendship was in his voice. "Come with us, Mingo. There won't be any trouble. I promise you that."

Mingo looked into the warm eyes of Aurelio Lazario, and he knew that Lazario was his friend, the friend of all Pinoys. Twelve years he had known this man, twelve years in America, and the fame of Aurelio Lazario had spread to every Filipino community on the Pacific Coast. Lazario, the fighter for Filipino rights, a leader in the asparagus country, with gunshot wounds to prove it; Lazario, who got them better housing in the Imperial Valley. Aurelio Lazario, an old man of thirty-five, his head still high and unbroken despite the clubs of the vigilantes; prunes in Santa Clara, rice in Solano, salmon in Alaska, tuna in San Diego—side by side with his brother Filipinos, Lazario had worked and suffered; and though he had gone on to the university and become a great man among his people, yet his face, like Mingo's, was forever marked by the hot sunlight of the San Joaquin, and his brown eyes were soft and womanlike with compassion for all men.

"I come," said Mingo. "We talk."

He got off the stool and followed them past the pool tables to a door that led to the back room. Gonzales opened the door and switched on a plain light bulb hanging from the ceiling. The room was dusty, empty, with newspapers spread over the floor. Gonzales stood at the door, waiting for them to enter. After they filed in, he closed the door and stood before it with folded arms. Mingo crossed to the far corner, leaned against the wall, biting his lip, opening and closing his fists. Lazario stood directly under the light, Toletano beside him.

"So you're in love, Mingo," Lazario smiled.

"Whole lots," said Mingo. "I no care what happen."

Toletano spat on the floor. "Japanese girl! Ugh. Is terrible."

Said Mingo: "Not Japanese. American. Born in Los Angeles. American citizen."

Said Toletano: "And her papa, her mama?" He spat again. "Japanese."

Said Mingo: "I no love her papa, her mama. I love Mary Osaka. Crazy for her."

Abruptly Gonzales crossed from the door and pushed Mingo against the wall. He held him there with his right hand. Drawing back his left, he held it on a line with Mingo's nose. "Say one more time you love this Japanese woman, and I give you best left hook on whole Pacific Coast."

The eyes of Mingo bulged; his face turned bloated and purple; still he blubbered stubbornly, "Mary Osaka, I love you."

Lazario raised his hand. "Wait, Gonzales. Violence won't help matters. He has his rights like the rest of us."

Gonzales shook his right fist between Mingo's eyes. "I have right, too, best right on whole Pacific Coast. I think maybe I let him have it."

Lazario waved him away. "Let's get down to the facts. We founded the Federated Brotherhood of Filipinos in protest against the Japanese invasion of China. We've pledged ourselves to boycott Japanese goods, to have as little as possible to do with all Japanese elements. Unfortunately, some of us can't carry out this pledge. We need jobs. Sometimes we have to work for Japanese employers."

It was Lazario, the man of learning who spoke now, and they listened respectfully. Gonzales pulled a cigar from his checkered sports coat and bit off the end.

"Boycotting Japanese goods is one thing," Lazario went on, "but falling in love with a Japanese girl who isn't Japanese at all, but an American of Japanese descent—well, I don't know. The Federation perhaps might be overstepping itself here."

Gonzales lit his cigar and puffed contentedly. Aurelio Lazario, the smartest Filipino on the whole Pacific Coast, was talking, and what he said was gospel, even though he, Gonzales, understood not one word of it. Slumped in the corner, Mingo rubbed his bruised neck and stared at the floor. Toletano shoved his hands in his pockets. Plainly he had no patience with Lazario's argument.

Lazario turned to him. "Vincente, have you ever been in love?"

Toletano considered this. "Yah. Two times." Melancholy softened his face. "Two times," he repeated. "Is wonderful, sad. It hurt so—" he touched his heart—"here."

"Were you in love with American women?"

"Beautiful American girl. In Stockton. Blonde."

"And did you ask her to marry you?"

"Alla time. Every few minutes."

"And why wouldn't she?"

"She was American. I was Filipino."

Said Lazario: "You see, Vincente? The same is true of Mingo. She is of Japanese descent. He is Filipino. We mustn't be prejudiced. A man's heart knows nothing of race or creed or color."

Toletano shook his head doubtfully. "Good Filipino can always smell Japanese." He went on shaking his head. "Is different. American girl is one thing, Japanese something else."

But Lazario wouldn't have it. "Love is very democratic, Vincente. Nationality is an accident. You say you were in love twice. What about the other girl?"

Vincente sighed. "Was same blonde American girl. She move to San Francisco. I follow her. Fall in love in San Francisco, too."

Lazario gestured with both palms. "There. You see?"

Gonzales took the cigar from his mouth and flipped the ash. "Maybe better," he said, "if Mingo fall in love with American girl."

"Mary Osaka is American girl," said Mingo. "Hundred percent. Graduate, Manual Arts High School."

Lazario crossed to the prize fighter, laid a hand on his shoulder. "Look, my friend Gonzales. Put yourself in Mingo's place. We are all Filipinos. We all know the life of a Filipino in the United States is hard. How can we expect justice if we interfere in the life of one of our brothers? He loves this girl, this Mary Osaka. You, Julio. Have you ever been in love?"

Gonzales filled his great chest proudly. "Four times," he said. "All American girls, finest on whole Pacific Coast."

"And what happened?"

"Was wonderful. I marry with all of them. Then divorce."

Lazario blinked thoughtfully. He placed his arm around the pugilist's shoulder and turned him toward Mingo, slumped in the corner. "Look at him, Julio. There he is, a small, insignificant little Filipino. He's your countryman, Julio, brother of your brothers. But you're a strong man, Julio, a great middleweight, with a deadly left hook. You're successful, handsome, exciting. Women fall at your feet. You have to fight them off with your fists. But look at him! Timid, scared. He needs the support of a tiger like you. Why shouldn't he marry this girl? After all, she's probably the best he can find."

Gonzales pouted, the cigar in the middle of his mouth. He rolled it thoughtfully. "Sure," he said finally. "Is okay by Julio Gonzales."

In the corner Mingo hung limp and tear-sodden, his arms like broken branches at his sides.

Gonzales stepped forward. Said he, "Mingo, you want to marry this woman?"

"Mary Osaka," Mingo groaned, "I love you."

Gonzales pulled a bunch of keys from his pocket. "Here. I have Packard roadster, white tire, red leather upholster, go hundred-ten mile an hour. You take, Mingo. Go to Las Vegas. Get marry tonight."

Mingo lifted his sodden, grateful eyes. Slowly he sank to his knees. He took the hand that held the keys and kissed it, wet it considerably with his lips and his tears. Gonzales tried to pull his hand away.

Said Mingo: "God bless you, Julio."

Gonzales dropped the keys to the floor, jerked his hand free, and hurried from the room. Lazario and Toletano stood with dry mouths. Quietly they tiptoed away.

From ASK THE DUSK by John Fante (Harper Perennial, 2006), pp. 175–189. Copyright © 2000 by Joyce Fante. Reprinted by permission.

Chicago, City of Champions

SAUL BELLOW

I wonder what terms to apply to Ravelstein's large, handsome apartment—his Midwestern base. It wouldn't be right to describe it as a sanctuary: Abe was in no sense a fugitive. Nor a solitary. He was actually on good terms with his American surroundings. His windows gave him a huge view of the city. He seldom had to use public transportation in his latter years, but he knew his way around, he spoke the language of the city. Young blacks would stop him in the street to ask about his suit or his topcoat, his fedora. They were familiar with high fashion. They talked to him about Ferre, Lanvin, about his Jermyn Street shirtmaker. "These young dudes," he explained, "are lovers of high fashion. Zoot suits and such crudities are things of the past. They're extremely savvy about automobiles, too."

"And maybe about twenty-thousand-dollar wristwatches. And what about handguns?"

Ravelstein laughed. "Even black women stop me in the street to comment on the cut of my suits," he said. "They're intuitively responsive."

His heart warmed toward such connoisseurs—lovers of elegance.

The admiration of black adolescents helped Ravelstein to offset the hatred of his colleagues, the professors. The popular success of his book drove the academics mad. He exposed the failings of the system in which they were schooled, the shallowness of their historicism, their susceptibility to European nihilism. A summary of his argument was that while you could get an excellent technical training in the U.S., liberal education had shrunk to the vanishing point. We were in thrall to the high tech, which had transformed the modern world. The older generation saved toward the education of its children. The cost of a B.A. had risen to $150,000. Parents might as well flush these dollars down the toilet, Ravelstein believed. No real education was possible in American universities except for aeronautical engineers, computerists, and the like. The universities were excellent in biology and the physical sciences, but the liberal arts were a failure. The philosopher Sidney Hook had told Ravelstein that philosophy was finished. "We have to find jobs for our graduates as medical ethicists in hospitals," Hook had admitted.

Ravelstein's book was not at all wild. Had he been a noisy windbag he would have been easy to dismiss. No, he was sensible and well informed, his arguments were thoroughly documented. All the dunces were united against him (as Swift or maybe Pope expressed it long ago). If they had had the powers of the FBI, the professors would have put Ravelstein on "most wanted" posters like those in federal buildings.

He had gone over the heads of the profs and the learned societies to speak directly to the great public. There are, after all, millions of people waiting for a sign. Many of them are university graduates.

When Ravelstein's outraged colleagues attacked him, he said he felt like the American general besieged by the Nazis—was it at Remagen? When they demanded his surrender, his answer was "Nuts to you!" Ravelstein was upset, of course; who wouldn't have been? And he couldn't expect to be rescued by some academic Patton. He could rely on his friends, and of course he had generations of graduate students on his side as well as the support of truth and principle. His book was well received in Europe. The Brits were inclined to look down their noses at him. The universities found fault, some of them, with his Greek. But when Margaret Thatcher invited him to Chequers for a weekend, he was *"aux anges"* (Chequers was heavenly: Abe always preferred French expressions to American ones; he didn't say "a chaser" or "a womanizer" or "ladies' man"—he said *"un homme à femmes."*). Even bright young left-wingers were strongly for him.

A Play at Contrition

ADAM CHIMERA

The first thing I noticed when I set down my bag in front of Penn Station that morning was that the whole area was crawling with police.

I was Pennsylvania-bound and I had time before my train would arrive so I stood outside the station to relax and smoke. The weather was cold and the light was pale and harsh so I wore a long, double breasted coat and a gray tweed hat with the brim down to shield my eyes. My huge, overstuffed duffel lay at my heels, suggesting that I was a too-hip out-of-towner on my way back to the farm. Other than being male and reasonably large, I looked like the perfect mark. This would not discourage my assailant-to-be.

I noticed him walking toward me from about forty feet away, a short and scruffy man staring intently at me. He was wearing dark, shabby sweat pants and a blue varsity style jacket with white vinyl arms. His hands were in the belly pockets of the coat and as he drew close I noticed that he had a lazy eye. I don't like to categorize people on the basis of their looks, but this man was a perfect rendering of a pulp novel hustler, appearing dangerous not so much for what he could do physically but, rather, morally. He would attempt to sell me drugs. There would be a misunderstanding and I would be arrested. It was destiny.

As he closed the final ten feet, I shook my head to signify, "No crack, sir. No crack for me." He spoke quickly and quietly and I remember his words very clearly.

"Don't move. Don't scream. I got a gun on you."

Well. This was exciting. For an instant my mouth was filled with the cold, metallic zing of copious adrenaline. I was up against a building so I wasn't going anywhere. I looked at his coat pockets. I could see the outlines of every joint in both his hands. He had no gun.

If I had been thinking clearly, many options would have been open to me but, at this point, less than a second had passed since my assailant's declaration. I was still working on the panicked binary logic of adrenaline. What were my options? Run: Zero. Call for help: Zero. Stand and wait: Zero. Attack: One!

No fake-out mugger expects to get punched by his mark. Moreover, his hands were in his pockets; I could make this blow a good one. I stepped out to my left intending to use the rotation of my hips to whip my right hand into his head like a rock on a string. It would connect spectacularly and I would walk briskly out of there like nothing had happened.

As I stepped, however, my changing point of view revealed a police officer on the corner who had until now been obscured by my target. Before my foot landed, a new scenario flitted through my mind: I strike him. He does not fall. I tackle him and continue striking him until the police arrive.

"He threatened me with a gun," I say.

The police frisk him and find two dollars, a loose Kool, a razor blade wrapped in a cardboard safety band and a jolly rancher. The police frisk me and find the Mag-Lite that I had haphazardly stuffed into my belt that morning. I go to jail. One way or another I would get arrested today. Destiny.

My left foot hit the ground and my hips rotated but I held the momentum there. Sooner or later, I always reach this point of divergence at which justifying an attack requires a more convoluted manipulation of reason than simply standing down. Excluding the occasional imagined indulgence, I've never struck a man full force even when gloved for sport. The blood thrill's never seemed worth the while when weighed against the possible consequences: arrest, someone croaking unexpectedly and, most frighteningly, contracting a blood-born disease. Possibly all of the above.

But more paralyzing than the potential consequences is the feeling of imminent wrongdoing. My editor blames it on my peculiar West Village Catholic upbringing. I disagree.

But whatever the explanation, the qualms always win and years of erratic training and mental preparation are invariably wasted on a peaceful solution. The man misinterpreted my step.

"Don't try to run," he said, "I'll blow your thing away."

His alleged gun hand was in position to do it. For a moment I questioned my judgment. Was I sufficiently certain that he was bluffing? I reexamined the bulge in his pocket. He had nothing. I was sure.

Thus far my violent impulses had been more a matter of terror-warped logic than of vengeance. But until now I hadn't been absolutely certain he didn't have a gun. Still, the suggestion of explosive genital mutilation was another bomb in the debris-field of my shock-scattered thoughts.

Though his empty threat could not restrain me, I did not receive it flatly as I would have had I never been frightened. In visceral terms, I was still cornered and this man had become infinitely sinister. Maintaining an expression more neutral than my poker-face, I was no longer thinking in terms of a punch, but rather of something I could do to his tonsils. But the urge to commit elaborately contrived acts of violence hardly lends itself to swift action. Given time to operate, my paranoia overcame my anger and I returned my hips to their original orientation.

I'd like to say I picked up my bag and walked away but I could not think of anything to do but to reach in my pocket and assuage this harmless monster.

"Hurry up, man! Give me something!"

I was frozen by my distaste for this solution.

"Hold on!" I growled.

Perhaps the rasp of my voice conveyed the bleeding eye sockets in my imagination because he took on a pleading tone.

"You don't have to give me everything. I'm hungry, man. Just a few bucks."

With this, I was back in front of Penn Station, returned from the panic-dislocated anywhere of the past few seconds, the like of which I have never since experienced, even during the real stick-up that occurred years later. This man could not command me to give him anything. He wasn't a monster, nor even a mugger, but a short, unarmed beggar on whom I had at least forty pounds.

With a hand in my pocket, I could feel a few large bills I had neatly folded in a wad. Some ones and a five were floating free. I grabbed a loose bill and began to wriggle it out.

"Come on, man," he said, "I'm hungry."

I got the bill free. It was the five. I just handed it over. He took it and looked down at it for a long moment. When he brought his eyes back up they were filled with guilt. He took his empty hand from his pocket and said,

"I don't have a gun."

I nodded. He looked at the bill again and then back at me.

"Do you want it back?"

"No. Keep it," I said.

The rest of the encounter is something of a blur now. He talked a little bit about how life was hard and no one would help him unless he made threats. I couldn't help but wonder if this was part of the act: Loosen the wallet with a good shock, confess what everyone already knows about the imaginary status of your gun, and play at contrition. What man could bring himself to take the money back? Five dollars was probably a meager haul for this guy. I told him he shouldn't stick people up.

We parted with a handshake. Grateful as I am that I didn't wind up in jail that day, and that no foreign saliva got into my bloodstream, I still resent the guy's tactics. It took me the full four-hour train ride to wind back to my usual strenuous alertness, which was of course overkill in the boondocks of Pennsylvania.

UNIT 3

Selling the New City: The Fight to Attract the Young and the Restless

Unit Selections

Key Points to Consider

- Can cities prosper without manufacturing?

- Describe creative "knowledge workers." What draws this group to cities?

- What are the best ways for cities to attract this group?

- Why are their members drawn to cities? Should they be?

- What cities have succeeded in drawing this group, and what methods have they employed to attract them?

- What makes a cool city? What are the benefits of a cool city? What are the drawbacks? What makes for a successful city?

Student Web Site

www.mhcls.com/online

Internet References

Further information regarding these Web sites may be found in this book's preface or online.

Center for Democracy and Citizenship
 http://www.publicwork.org
Civnet/CIVITAS
 http://www.civnet.org/index.htm
The Gallup Organization
 http://www.gallup.com

America's cities have been in economic decline since the 1930s. The growth of new technologies such as the automobile and the telephone began to disperse the cities' functions over a wider and wider area. The changes were exacerbated in the 1960s, by not only crime, but by the painful dislocations brought by the shift from manufacturing to services and the accelerating loss of businesses as well as residents to the suburbs and smaller cities.

Cities are still readjusting, and in "The Rise of the Creative Class," Richard Florida trumpets the tendency of highly-educated young "knowledge workers" to seek out cities like Boston and Seattle that offer the best lifestyle amenities. Attracting highly mobile members of this new creative class, he argues, is the key to building the post-industrial city. In "Too Much Froth," Joel Kotkin and Fred Siegel argue that Florida's proposals ignore the key qualities that make for a livable and prosperous city: affordable taxes, flexible zoning and quality schools. The other articles and essays in the section look at how cities are attempting to attract these young and restless residents, and what happens when they succeed.

The Rise of the Creative Class

Why cities without gays and rock bands are losing the economic development race.

RICHARD FLORIDA

As I walked across the campus of Pittsburgh's Carnegie Mellon University one delightful spring day, I came upon a table filled with young people chatting and enjoying the spectacular weather. Several had identical blue T-shirts with "Trilogy@CMU" written across them—Trilogy being an Austin, Texas-based software company with a reputation for recruiting our top students. I walked over to the table. "Are you guys here to recruit?" I asked. "No, absolutely not," they replied adamantly. "We're not recruiters. We're just hangin' out, playing a little Frisbee with our friends." How interesting, I thought. They've come to campus on a workday, all the way from Austin, just to hang out with some new friends.

I noticed one member of the group sitting slouched over on the grass, dressed in a tank top. This young man had spiked multi-colored hair, full-body tattoos, and multiple piercings in his ears. An obvious slacker, I thought, probably in a band. "So what is your story?" I asked. "Hey man, I just signed on with these guys." In fact, as I would later learn, he was a gifted student who had inked the highest-paying deal of any graduating student in the history of his department, right at that table on the grass, with the recruiters who do not "recruit."

What a change from my own college days, just a little more than 20 years ago, when students would put on their dressiest clothes and carefully hide any counterculture tendencies to prove that they could fit in with the company. Today, apparently, it's the company trying to fit in with the students. In fact, Trilogy had wined and dined him over margarita parties in Pittsburgh and flown him to Austin for private parties in hip nightspots and aboard company boats. When I called the people who had recruited him to ask why, they answered, "That's easy. We wanted him because he's a rock star."

While I was interested in the change in corporate recruiting strategy, something even bigger struck me. Here was another example of a talented young person leaving Pittsburgh. Clearly, my adopted hometown has a huge number of assets. Carnegie Mellon is one of the world's leading centers for research in information technology. The University of Pittsburgh, right down the street from our campus, has a world-class medical center. Pittsburgh attracts hundreds of millions of dollars per year in university research funding and is the sixth-largest center for college and university students on a per capita basis in the country. Moreover, this is hardly a cultural backwater. The city is home to three major sports franchises, renowned museums and cultural venues, a spectacular network of urban parks, fantastic industrial-age architecture, and great urban neighborhoods with an abundance of charming yet affordable housing. It is a friendly city, defined by strong communities and a strong sense of pride. In the 1986 Rand McNally survey, Pittsburgh was ranked "America's Most Livable City," and has continued to score high on such lists ever since.

Yet Pittsburgh's economy continues to putter along in a middling flat-line pattern. Both the core city and the surrounding metropolitan area lost population in the 2000 census. And those bright young university people keep leaving. Most of Carnegie Mellon's prominent alumni of recent years—like Vinod Khosla, perhaps the best known of Silicon Valley's venture capitalists, and Rick Rashid, head of research and development at Microsoft—went elsewhere to make their marks. Pitt's vaunted medical center, where Jonas Salk created his polio vaccine and the world's premier organ-transplant program was started, has inspired only a handful of entrepreneurs to build biotech companies in Pittsburgh.

Over the years, I have seen the community try just about everything possible to remake itself so as to attract and retain talented young people, and I was personally involved in many of these efforts. Pittsburgh has launched a multitude of programs to diversify the region's economy away from heavy industry into high technology. It has rebuilt its downtown virtually from scratch, invested in a new airport, and developed a massive new sports complex for the Pirates and the Steelers. But nothing, it seemed, could stem the tide of people and new companies leaving the region.

I asked the young man with the spiked hair why he was going to a smaller city in the middle of Texas, a place with a small airport and no professional sports teams, without a major symphony, ballet, opera, or art museum comparable to Pittsburgh's. The company is excellent, he told me. There are also terrific people and the work is challenging. But the clincher, he said, is that, "It's in Austin!" There are lots of young people, he went on to explain, and a tremendous amount to do: a thriving music scene, ethnic and cultural diversity, fabulous outdoor recreation, and great nightlife. Though he had several good job offers from Pittsburgh high-tech firms and knew the city well, he said he felt the city lacked the lifestyle options, cultural diversity, and tolerant attitude that would make it attractive to him. As he summed it up: "How would I fit in here?"

This young man and his lifestyle proclivities represent a profound new force in the economy and life of America. He is a member of what I call the creative class: a fast-growing, highly educated, and well-paid segment of the workforce on whose efforts corporate profits and economic growth increasingly depend. Members of the creative class do a wide variety of work in a wide variety of industries—from technology to entertainment, journalism to finance, high-end manufacturing to the arts. They do not consciously think of themselves as a class. Yet they share a common ethos that values creativity, individuality, difference, and merit.

More and more businesses understand that ethos and are making the adaptations necessary to attract and retain creative class employees—everything from relaxed dress codes, flexible schedules, and new work rules in the office to hiring recruiters who throw Frisbees. Most civic leaders, however, have failed to understand that what is true for corporations is also true for cities and regions: Places that succeed in attracting and retaining creative class people prosper; those that fail don't.

Stuck in old paradigms of economic development, cities like Buffalo, New Orleans, and Louisville struggled in the 1980s

The Creativity Index

The key to economic growth lies not just in the ability to attract the creative class, but to translate that underlying advantage into creative economic outcomes in the form of new ideas, new high-tech businesses and regional growth. To better gauge these capabilities, I developed a new measure called the Creativity Index (column 1). The Creativity Index is a mix of four equally weighted factors: the creative class share of the workforce (column 2 shows the percentage; column 3 ranks cities accordingly); high-tech industry, using the Milken Institute's widely accepted Tech Pole Index, which I refer to as the High-Tech Index (column 4); innovation, measured as patents per capita (column 5); and diversity, measured by the Gay Index, a reasonable proxy for an area's openness to different kinds of people and ideas (column 6). This composite indicator is a better measure of a region's underlying creative capabilities than the simple measure of the creative class, because it reflects the joint effects of its concentration and of innovative economic outcomes. The Creativity Index is thus my baseline indicator of a region's overall standing in the creative economy and I offer it as a barometer of a region's longer run economic potential. The following tables present my creativity index ranking for the top 10 and bottom 10 metropolitan areas, grouped into three size categories (large, medium-sized and small cities/regions).

—Richard Florida

and 1990s to become the next "Silicon Somewhere" by building generic high-tech office parks or subsidizing professional sports teams. Yet they lost members of the creative class, and their economic dynamism, to places like Austin, Boston, Washington, D.C. and Seattle—places more tolerant, diverse, and open to creativity. Because of this migration of the creative class, a new social and economic geography is emerging in America, one that does not correspond to old categories like East Coast versus West Coast or Sunbelt versus Frostbelt. Rather, it is more like the class divisions that have increasingly separated Americans by income and neighborhood, extended into the realm of city and region.

The Creative Secretary

The distinguishing characteristic of the creative class is that its members engage in work whose function is to "create meaningful new forms." The super-creative core of this new class includes scientists and engineers, university professors, poets and novelists, artists, entertainers, actors, designers, and architects, as well as the "thought leadership" of modern society: nonfiction writers, editors, cultural figures, think-tank researchers, analysts, and other opinion-makers. Members of this super-creative core produce new forms or designs that are readily transferable and broadly useful—such as designing a product that can be widely made, sold and used; coming up with a theorem or strategy that can be applied in many cases; or composing music that can be performed again and again.

Beyond this core group, the creative class also includes "creative professionals" who work in a wide range of knowledge-intensive industries such as high-tech sectors, financial services, the legal and healthcare professions, and business management. These people engage in creative problem-solving, drawing on complex bodies of knowledge to solve specific problems. Doing so typically requires a high degree of formal education and thus a high level of human capital. People who do this kind of work may sometimes come up with methods or products that turn out to be widely useful, but it's not part of the basic job description. What they are required to do regularly is think on their own. They apply or combine standard approaches in unique ways to fit the situation, exercise a great deal of judgment, perhaps try something radically new from time to time.

Much the same is true of the growing number of technicians and others who apply complex bodies of knowledge to working with physical materials. In fields such as medicine and scientific research, technicians are taking on increased responsibility to interpret their work and make decisions, blurring the old distinction between white-collar work (done by decisionmakers) and blue-collar work (done by those who follow orders). They acquire their own arcane bodies of knowledge and develop their own unique ways of doing the job. Another example is the secretary in today's pared-down offices. In many cases this person not only takes on a host of tasks once performed by a large secretarial staff, but becomes a true office manager—channeling flows of information, devising and setting up new systems, often making key decisions on the fly. These people

Table 1 Large Cities Creativity Rankings

Rankings of 49 metro areas reporting populations over 1 million in the 2000 Census

The Top Ten Cities	Creativity Index	% Creative Workers	Creative Rank	High-Tech Rank	Innovation Rank	Diversity Rank
1. San Francisco	1057	34.8%	5	1	2	1
2. Austin	1028	36.4%	4	11	3	16
3. San Diego	1015	32.1%	15	12	7	3
3. Boston	1015	38.0%	3	2	6	22
5. Seattle	1008	32.7%	9	3	12	8
6. Raleigh–Durham–Chapel Hill	996	38.2%	2	14	4	28
7. Houston	980	32.5%	10	16	16	10
8. Washington–Baltimore	964	38.4%	1	5	30	12
9. New York	962	32.3%	12	13	24	14
10. Dallas	960	30.2%	23	6	17	9
10. Minneapolis	960	33.9%	7	21	5	29

The Bottom Ten Cities	Creativity Index	% Creative Workers	Creative Rank	High-Tech Rank	Innovation Rank	Diversity Rank
49. Memphis	530	24.8%	47	48	42	41
48. Norfolk–Virginia Beach, VA	555	28.4%	36	35	49	47
47. Las Vegas	561	18.5%	49	42	47	5
46. Buffalo	609	28.9%	33	40	27	49
45. Louisville	622	26.5%	46	46	39	36
44. Grand Rapids, MI	639	24.3%	48	43	23	38
43. Oklahoma City	668	29.4%	29	41	43	39
42. New Orleans	668	27.5%	42	45	48	13
41. Greensboro–Winston-Salem	697	27.3%	44	33	35	35
40. Providence, RI	698	27.6%	41	44	34	33

contribute more than intelligence or computer skills. They add creative value. Everywhere we look, creativity is increasingly valued. Firms and organizations value it for the results that it can produce and individuals value it as a route to self-expression and job satisfaction. Bottom line: As creativity becomes more valued, the creative class grows.

The creative class now includes some 38.3 million Americans, roughly 30 percent of the entire U.S. workforce—up from just 10 percent at the turn of the 20th century and less than 20 percent as recently as 1980. The creative class has considerable economic power. In 1999, the average salary for a member of the creative class was nearly $50,000 ($48,752), compared to roughly $28,000 for a working-class member and $22,000 for a service-class worker.

Not surprisingly, regions that have large numbers of creative class members are also some of the most affluent and growing.

The New Geography of Class

Different classes of people have long sorted themselves into neighborhoods within a city or region. But now we find a large-scale re-sorting of people among cities and regions nationwide, with some regions becoming centers of the creative class while others are composed of larger shares of working-class or service-class people. To some extent this has always been true. For instance, there have always been artistic and cultural communities like Greenwich Village, college towns like Madison and Boulder, and manufacturing centers like Pittsburgh and Detroit. The news is that such sorting is becoming even more widespread and pronounced.

In the leading centers of this new class geography, the creative class makes up more than 35 percent of the workforce. This is already the case in the greater Washington, D.C. region, the Raleigh-Durham area, Boston, and Austin—all areas undergoing tremendous economic growth. Despite their considerable advantages, large regions have not cornered the market as creative class locations. In fact, a number of smaller regions have some of the highest creative-class concentrations in the nation—notably college towns like East Lansing, Mich. and Madison, Wisc. (See chart, "Small-size Cities Creativity Rankings")

At the other end of the spectrum are regions that are being bypassed by the creative class. Among large regions, Las Vegas, Grand Rapids and Memphis harbor the smallest concentrations of the creative class. Members of this class have nearly abandoned a wide range of smaller regions in the outskirts of the South and Midwest. In small metropolitan areas like Victoria,

Texas and Jackson, Tenn., the creative class comprises less than 15 percent of the workforce. The leading centers for the working class among large regions are Greensboro, N.C. and Memphis, Tenn., where the working class makes up more than 30 percent of the workforce. Several smaller regions in the South and Midwest are veritable working class enclaves with 40 to 50 percent or more of their workforce in the traditional industrial occupations.

These places have some of the most minuscule concentrations of the creative class in the nation. They are symptomatic of a general lack of overlap between the major creative-class centers and those of the working class. Of the 26 large cities where the working class comprises more than one-quarter of the population, only one, Houston, ranks among the top 10 destinations for the creative class.

Chicago, a bastion of working-class people that still ranks among the top 20 large creative centers, is interesting because it shows how the creative class and the traditional working class can coexist. But Chicago has an advantage in that it is a big city, with more than a million members of the creative class. The University of Chicago sociologist Terry Clark likes to say Chicago developed an innovative political and cultural solution to this issue. Under the second Mayor Daley, the city integrated the members of the creative class into the city's culture and politics by treating them essentially as just another "ethnic group" that needed sufficient space to express its identity.

The plug-and-play community is one that somebody can move into and put together a life—or at least a facsimile of a life—in a week.

Las Vegas has the highest concentration of the service class among large cities, 58 percent, while West Palm Beach, Orlando, and Miami also have around half. These regions rank near the bottom of the list for the creative class. The service class makes up more than half the workforce in nearly 50 small and medium-size regions across the country. Few of them boast any significant concentrations of the creative class, save vacationers, and offer little prospect for upward mobility. They include resort towns like Honolulu and Cape Cod. But they also include places like Shreveport, Lou. and Pittsfield, Mass. For these places that are not tourist destinations, the economic and social future is troubling to contemplate.

Plug-and-Play Communities

Why do some places become destinations for the creative while others don't? Economists speak of the importance of industries having "low entry barriers," so that new firms can easily enter and keep the industry vital. Similarly, I think it's important for a

Table 2 Medium-Size Cities Creativity Rankings

Rankings of 32 metro areas reporting populations 500,000 to 1 million in the 2000 Census

The Top Ten Cities	Creativity Index	% Creative Workers	Creative Rank	High-Tech Rank	Innovation Rank	Diversity Rank
1. Albuquerque, NM	965	32.2%	2	1	7	1
2. Albany, NY	932	33.7%	1	12	2	4
3. Tuscon, AZ	853	28.4%	17	2	6	5
4. Allentown–Bethlehem, PA	801	28.7%	16	13	3	14
5. Dayton, OH	766	30.1%	8	8	5	24
6. Colorado Springs, CO	756	29.9%	10	5	1	30
7. Harrisburg, PA	751	29.8%	11	6	13	20
8. Little Rock, AR	740	30.8%	4	10	21	11
9. Birmingham, AL	722	30.7%	6	7	26	10
10. Tulsa, OK	721	28.7%	15	9	15	18
The Bottom Ten Cities	Creativity Index	% Creative Workers	Creative Rank	High-Tech Rank	Innovation Rank	Diversity Rank
32. Youngstown, OH	253	23.8%	32	32	24	32
31. Scranton–Wilkes-Barre, PA	400	24.7%	28	23	23	31
30. McAllen, TX	451	27.8%	18	31	32	9
29. Stockton–Lodi, CA	459	24.1%	30	29	28	7
28. El Paso, TX	464	27.0%	23	27	31	17
27. Fresno, CA	516	25.1%	27	24	30	2
26. Bakersfield, CA	531	27.8%	18	22	27	19
25. Fort Wayne, IN	569	25.4%	26	17	8	26
24. Springfield, MA	577	29.7%	13	30	20	22
23. Honolulu, HI	580	27.2%	21	14	29	6

place to have low entry barriers for people—that is, to be a place where newcomers are accepted quickly into all sorts of social and economic arrangements. All else being equal, they are likely to attract greater numbers of talented and creative people—the sort of people who power innovation and growth. Places that thrive in today's world tend to be plug-and-play communities where anyone can fit in quickly. These are places where people can find opportunity, build support structures, be themselves, and not get stuck in any one identity. The plug-and-play community is one that somebody can move into and put together a life—or at least a facsimile of a life—in a week.

The list of the country's high-tech hot spots looks an awful lot like the list of the places with highest concentrations of gay people.

Creative centers also tend to be places with thick labor markets that can fulfill the employment needs of members of the creative class, who, by and large, are not looking just for "a job" but for places that offer many employment opportunities.

Cities and regions that attract lots of creative talent are also those with greater diversity and higher levels of quality of place. That's because location choices of the creative class are based to a large degree on their lifestyle interests, and these go well beyond the standard "quality-of-life" amenities that most experts think are important.

For instance, in 1998, I met Gary Gates, then a doctoral student at Carnegie Mellon. While I had been studying the location choices of high-tech industries and talented people, Gates had been exploring the location patterns of gay people. My list of the country's high-tech hot spots looked an awful lot like his list of the places with highest concentrations of gay people. When we compared these two lists with more statistical rigor, his Gay Index turned out to correlate very strongly to my own measures of high-tech growth. Other measures I came up with, like the Bohemian Index—a measure of artists, writers, and performers—produced similar results.

Talented people seek an environment open to differences. Many highly creative people, regardless of ethnic background or sexual orientation, grew up feeling like outsiders, different in some way from most of their schoolmates. When they are sizing up a new company and community, acceptance of diversity and of gays in particular is a sign that reads "non-standard people welcome here."

The creative class people I study use the word "diversity" a lot, but not to press any political hot buttons. Diversity is simply something they value in all its manifestations. This is spoken of so often, and so matter-of-factly, that I take it to be a fundamental marker of creative class values. Creative-minded people enjoy a mix of influences. They want to hear different

Table 3   Small-Size Cities Creativity Rankings

Rankings of 63 metro areas reporting populations 250,000 to 500,000 in the 2000 Census

The Top Ten Cities	Creativity Index	% Creative Workers	Creative Rank	High-Tech Rank	Innovation Rank	Diversity Rank
1. Madison, WI	925	32.8%	6	16	4	9
2. Des Moines, IA	862	32.1%	8	2	16	20
3. Santa Barbara, CA	856	28.3%	19	8	8	7
4. Melbourne, FL	855	35.5%	1	6	9	32
5. Boise City, ID	854	35.2%	3	1	1	46
6. Huntsville, AL	799	35.3%	2	5	18	40
7. Lansing–East Lansing, MI	739	34.3%	4	27	29	18
8. Binghamton, NY	731	30.8%	12	7	3	60
9. Lexington, KY	717	27.0%	28	24	10	12
10. New London, CT–Norwich, RI	715	28.%1	23	11	13	33
The Bottom Ten Cities	Creativity Index	% Creative Workers	Creative Rank	High-Tech Rank	Innovation Rank	Diversity Rank
63. Shreveport, LA	233	22.1%	55	32	59	57
62. Ocala, FL	263	16.4%	63	61	52	24
61. Visalia, CA	289	22.9%	52	63	60	11
60. Killeen, TX	302	24.6%	47	47	51	53
59. Fayetteville, NC	309	29.0%	16	62	62	49
58. York, PA	360	22.3%	54	54	26	52
57. Fayetteville, AR	366	21.1%	57	57	42	17
56. Beaumont, TX	372	27.8%	25	37	56	55
55. Lakeland–Winter Haven, FL	385	20.9%	59	56	53	5
54. Hickory, NC	393	19.4%	61	48	32	30

kinds of music and try different kinds of food. They want to meet and socialize with people unlike themselves, trade views and spar over issues.

As with employers, visible diversity serves as a signal that a community embraces the open meritocratic values of the creative age. The people I talked to also desired nightlife with a wide mix of options. The most highly valued options were experiential ones—interesting music venues, neighborhood art galleries, performance spaces, and theaters. A vibrant, varied nightlife was viewed by many as another signal that a city "gets it," even by those who infrequently partake in nightlife. More than anything, the creative class craves real experiences in the real world.

They favor active, participatory recreation over passive, institutionalized forms. They prefer indigenous street-level culture—a teeming blend of cafes, sidewalk musicians, and small galleries and bistros, where it is hard to draw the line between performers and spectators. They crave stimulation, not escape. They want to pack their time full of dense, high-quality, multidimensional experiences. Seldom has one of my subjects expressed a desire to get away from it all. They want to get into it all, and do it with eyes wide open.

Creative class people value active outdoor recreation very highly. They are drawn to places and communities where many outdoor activities are prevalent—both because they enjoy these activities and because their presence is seen as a signal that the place is amenable to the broader creative lifestyle. The creative-class people in my studies are into a variety of active sports, from traditional ones like bicycling, jogging, and kayaking to newer, more extreme ones, like trail running and snowboarding.

Places are also valued for authenticity and uniqueness. Authenticity comes from several aspects of a community—historic buildings, established neighborhoods, a unique music scene, or specific cultural attributes. It comes from the mix—from urban grit alongside renovated buildings, from the commingling of young and old, long-time neighborhood characters and yuppies, fashion models and "bag ladies." An authentic place also offers unique and original experiences. Thus a place full of chain stores, chain restaurants, and nightclubs is not authentic. You could have the same experience anywhere.

Today, it seems, leading creative centers provide a solid mix of high-tech industry, plentiful outdoor amenities, and an older urban center whose rebirth has been fueled in part by a combination of creativity and innovative technology, as well as lifestyle amenities. These include places like the greater Boston area, which has the Route 128 suburban complex, Harvard and MIT, and several charming inner-city Boston neighborhoods. Seattle has suburban Bellevue and Redmond (where Microsoft is located), beautiful mountains and country, and a series of revitalized urban neighborhoods. The San Francisco Bay area has everything from posh inner-city neighborhoods to ultra-hip districts like SoMa (South of Market) and lifestyle enclaves like Marin County as well as the Silicon Valley. Even Austin includes traditional high-tech developments to the north, lifestyle centers for cycling and outdoor activities, and a revitalizing university/ downtown community centered on vibrant Sixth Street, the warehouse district and the music scene—a critical element of a thriving creative center.

Institutional Sclerosis

Even as places like Austin and Seattle are thriving, much of the country is failing to adapt to the demands of the creative age. It is not that struggling cities like Pittsburgh do not want to grow or encourage high-tech industries. In most cases, their leaders are doing everything they think they can to spur innovation and high-tech growth. But most of the time, they are either unwilling or unable to do the things required to create an environment or habitat attractive to the creative class. They pay lip service to the need to "attract talent," but continue to pour resources into recruiting call centers, underwriting big-box retailers, subsidizing downtown malls, and squandering precious taxpayer dollars on extravagant stadium complexes. Or they try to create facsimiles of neighborhoods or retail districts, replacing the old and authentic with the new and generic—and in doing so drive the creative class away.

It is a telling commentary on our age that at a time when political will seems difficult to muster for virtually anything, city after city can generate the political capital to underwrite hundreds of millions of dollars of investments in professional sports stadiums. And you know what? They don't matter to the creative class. Not once during any of my focus groups and interviews did the members of the creative class mention professional sports as playing a role of any sort in their choice of where to live and work. What makes most cities unable to even imagine devoting those kinds of resources or political will to do the things that people say really matter to them?

The answer is simple. These cities are trapped by their past. Despite the lip service they might pay, they are unwilling or unable to do what it takes to attract the creative class. The late economist Mancur Olson long ago noted that the decline of nations and regions is a product of an organizational and cultural hardening of the arteries he called "institutional sclerosis." Places that grow up and prosper in one era, Olson argued, find it difficult and often times impossible to adopt new organizational and cultural patterns, regardless of how beneficial they might be. Consequently, innovation and growth shift to new places, which can adapt to and harness these shifts for their benefit. This phenomenon, he contends, is how England got trapped and how the U.S. became the world's great economic power. It also accounts for the shift in economic activity from the old industrial cities to newer cities in the South and West, according to Olson.

Olson's analysis presciently identifies why so many cities across the nation remain trapped in the culture and attitudes of the bygone organizational age, unable or unwilling to adapt to current trends. Cities like Detroit, Cleveland, and my current hometown of Pittsburgh were at the forefront of the organizational age. The cultural and attitudinal norms of that age became so powerfully ingrained in these places that they did not allow the new norms and attitudes associated with the creative age to grow up, diffuse and become generally accepted. This process, in turn, stamped out much of the creative impulse, causing talented and creative people to seek out new places where they could more readily plug in and make a go of it.

Most experts and scholars have not even begun to think in terms of a creative community. Instead, they tend to try to emulate the Silicon Valley model which author Joel Kotkin has dubbed the "nerdistan." But the nerdistan is a limited economic development model, which misunderstands the role played by creativity in generating innovation and economic growth. Nerdistans are bland, uninteresting places with acre upon acre of identical office complexes, row after row of asphalt parking lots, freeways clogged with cars, cookie-cutter housing developments, and strip-malls sprawling in every direction. Many of these places have fallen victim to the very kinds of problems they were supposed to avoid. The comfort and security of places like Silicon Valley have gradually given way to sprawl, pollution, and paralyzing traffic jams. As one technology executive told *The Wall Street Journal,* "I really didn't want to live in San Jose. Every time I went up there, the concrete jungle got me down." His company eventually settled on a more urban Southern California location in downtown Pasadena close to the CalTech campus.

Kotkin finds that the lack of lifestyle amenities is causing significant problems in attracting top creative people to places like the North Carolina Research Triangle. He quotes a major real estate developer as saying, "Ask anyone where downtown is and nobody can tell you. There's not much of a sense of place here. . . . The people I am selling space to are screaming about cultural issues." The Research Triangle lacks the hip urban lifestyle found in places like San Francisco, Seattle, New York, and Chicago, laments a University of North Carolina researcher: "In Raleigh-Durham, we can always visit the hog farms."

The Kids Are All Right

How do you build a truly creative community—one that can survive and prosper in this emerging age? The key can no longer be found in the usual strategies. Recruiting more companies won't do it; neither will trying to become the next Silicon Valley. While it certainly remains important to have a solid business climate, having an effective people climate is even more essential. By this I mean a general strategy aimed at attracting and retaining people—especially, but not limited to, creative people. This entails remaining open to diversity and actively working to cultivate it, and investing in the lifestyle amenities that people really want and use often, as opposed to using financial incentives to attract companies, build professional sports stadiums, or develop retail complexes.

The benefits of this kind of strategy are obvious. Whereas companies—or sports teams, for that matter—that get financial incentives can pull up and leave at virtually a moment's notice, investments in amenities like urban parks, for example, last for generations. Other amenities—like bike lanes or off-road trails for running, cycling, rollerblading, or just walking your dog—benefit a wide swath of the population.

There is no one-size-fits-all model for a successful people climate. The members of the creative class are diverse across the dimensions of age, ethnicity and race, marital status, and sexual preference. An effective people climate needs to emphasize openness and diversity, and to help reinforce low barriers to entry. Thus, it cannot be restrictive or monolithic.

Openness to immigration is particularly important for smaller cities and regions, while the ability to attract so-called bohemians is key for larger cities and regions. For cities and regions to attract these groups, they need to develop the kinds of people climates that appeal to them and meet their needs.

Yet if you ask most community leaders what kinds of people they'd most want to attract, they'd likely say successful married couples in their 30s and 40s—people with good middle-to-upper-income jobs and stable family lives. I certainly think it is important for cities and communities to be good for children and families. But less than a quarter of all American households consist of traditional nuclear families, and focusing solely on their needs has been a losing strategy, one that neglects a critical engine of economic growth: young people.

Young workers have typically been thought of as transients who contribute little to a city's bottom line. But in the creative age, they matter for two reasons. First, they are workhorses. They are able to work longer and harder, and are more prone to take risks, precisely because they are young and childless. In rapidly changing industries, it's often the most recent graduates who have the most up-to-date skills. Second, people are staying single longer. The average age of marriage for both men and women has risen some five years over the past generation. College-educated people postpone marriage longer than the national averages. Among this group, one of the fastest growing categories is the never-been-married. To prosper in the creative age, regions have to offer a people climate that satisfies this group's social interests and lifestyle needs, as well as address those of other groups.

Furthermore, a climate oriented to young people is also attractive to the creative class more broadly. Creative-class people do not lose their lifestyle preferences as they age. They don't stop bicycling or running, for instance, just because they have children. When they put their children in child seats or jogging strollers, amenities like traffic-free bike paths become more important than ever. They also continue to value diversity and tolerance. The middle-aged and older people I speak with may no longer hang around in nightspots until 4 a.m., but they enjoy stimulating, dynamic places with high levels of cultural interplay. And if they have children, that's the kind of environment in which they want them to grow up.

My adopted hometown of Pittsburgh has been slow to realize this. City leaders continue to promote Pittsburgh as a place that is good for families, seemingly unaware of the demographic changes that have made young people, singles, new immigrants, and gays critical to the emerging social fabric. People in focus groups I have conducted feel that Pittsburgh is not open to minority groups, new immigrants, or gays. Young women feel there are substantial barriers to their advancement. Talented members of racial and ethnic minorities, as well as professional women, express their desire to leave the city at a rate far greater than their white male counterparts. So do creative people from all walks of life.

Is there hope for Pittsburgh? Of course there is. First, although the region's economy is not dynamic, neither is it the basket case it could easily have become. Twenty years ago there were no significant venture capital firms in the area; now there are many, and thriving high-tech firms continue to form and make their mark. There are signs of life in the social and cultural milieu as well. The region's immigrant population has begun to tick upward, fed by students and professors at the universities and employees in the medical and technology sectors. Major suburbs to the east of the city now have Hindu temples and a growing Indian-American population. The area's gay community, while not large, has become more active and visible. Pittsburgh's increasing status in the gay world is reflected in the fact that it is the "location" for Showtime's "Queer as Folk" series.

Many of Pittsburgh's creative class have proven to be relentless cultural builders. The Andy Warhol Museum and the Mattress Factory, a museum/workspace devoted to large-scale installation art, have achieved worldwide recognition. Street-level culture has a growing foothold in Pittsburgh, too, as main street corridors in several older working-class districts have been transformed. Political leaders are in some cases open to new models of development. Pittsburgh mayor Tom Murphy has been an ardent promoter of biking and foot trails, among other things. The city's absolutely first-rate architecture and urban design community has become much more vocal about the need to preserve historic buildings, invest in neighborhoods, and institute tough design standards. It would be very hard today (dare I say nearly impossible) to knock down historic buildings and dismember vibrant urban neighborhoods as was done in the past. As these new groups and efforts reach critical mass, the norms and attitudes that have long prevailed in the city are being challenged.

For what it's worth, I'll put my money—and a lot of my effort—into Pittsburgh's making it. If Pittsburgh, with all of its assets and its emerging human creativity, somehow can't make it in the creative age, I fear the future does not bode well for other older industrial communities and established cities, and the lamentable new class segregation among cities will continue to worsen.

RICHARD FLORIDA is a professor of regional economic development at Carnegie Mellon University and a columnist for *Information Week*. This article was adapted from his forthcoming book, *The Rise of the Creative Class: and How It's Transforming Work, Leisure, Community and Everyday Life* (Basic Books).

Too Much Froth

The latte quotient is a bad strategy for building middle-class cities.

JOEL KOTKIN AND FRED SIEGEL

Like smokers seeking a cure from their deadly habits, city politicians and economic development officials have a long history of grasping at fads to solve their persistent problems and rebuild middle class cities. In the 1960s and 1970s, the fad was for downtown malls. In the 1980s, it was convention centers and sports stadiums. But none of the fads came close to living up to their lofty billings.

Today, a new fad is bewitching urbanists and pols alike. Known as the "creativity craze," it promotes the notion that "young creatives" can drive an urban revival. It is a belated extension of the New Economy boom of the late 1990s. As with the idea of a New Economy, there is some merit to the focus on creativity. But as we learned from the dot-com bust that followed the boom, even the best ideas can be oversold.

Long before the current craze, Robert D. Atkinson of the Progressive Policy Institute wrote, "The ticket to faster and broader income growth is innovation." And one of the keys to innovation, he noted in describing his Metropolitan New Economy Indexes, is the ability to attract talented and innovative people. But he also emphasized the importance of school reform, infrastructure investments, work force development partnerships, public safety, and reinventing—and digitizing—city government. All these critical factors have been widely ignored by those who've discovered the magic bullet of "creative" urban development.

The new mantra advocates an urban strategy that focuses on being "hip" and "cool" rather than straightforward and practical. It is eagerly promoted by the Brookings Institution, by some urban development types, and by city pols from both parties in places like Cincinnati, Denver, Tampa, and San Diego. It seeks to displace the Progressive Policy Institute's New Economy Indexes with what might be called a "Latte Index"—the density of Starbucks—as a measure of urban success. Cities that will win the new competition, it's asserted, will be those that pour their resources into the arts and other cultural institutions that attract young, "with-it" people who constitute, for them, the contemporary version of the anointed. Call them latte cities.

But, like all the old bromides that were supposed to save America's cities, this one is almost certain to disappoint. Based partly on the ideas in Carnegie Mellon professor Richard Florida's book, *Rise of the Creative Class,* the notion of hip *uber alles* reminds one of the confectionary world of earlier gurus such as Charles Reich, author of *The Greening of America,* and John Naisbitt, author of *Megatrends.* Both promised a largely painless path to a brave new world, but both now are largely forgotten.

It's not surprising that after 50 years of almost uninterrupted middle class and job flight to the suburbs—even with the partial urban revival of the 1990s—urban officials might be tempted to clutch at straws. The appeal of such fads is plain to see. They seem to offer a way around the intractable problems of schools that fail to improve, despite continuous infusions of money; contentious zoning and regulatory policies that drive out business; and politically hyperactive public-sector unions and hectoring interest groups that make investment in cities something most entrepreneurs studiously avoid.

The "creative solution" pointedly avoids such hurdles, suggesting that the key to urban resurgence lies in attracting the diverse, the tolerant, and the gay. Having such a population is well and good, but unlikely by itself to produce a revival, let alone a diversified economy. Those most outspoken about such a culture- and lifestyle-based urban revival have all the heady passion of a religious movement; indeed, they've organized themselves into something called the Creative Class. One hundred of them—they called themselves the "Creative 100"—met in Memphis last spring to lay out their principles in a document called the Memphis Manifesto. Their mission, it reads, is to "remove barriers to creativity, such as mediocrity, intolerance, disconnectedness, sprawl, poverty, bad schools, exclusivity, and social and environmental degradation." The 1934 Soviet constitution couldn't have said it better.

This is an urban strategy for a frictionless universe. There is no mention of government or politics or interest groups. There's no recognition of the problems produced by outmoded regulations, runaway public spending, or high taxes. Instead we get the following froth: "Cultivate and reward creativity. Everyone is part of the value chain of creativity. Creativity can happen at any time, anywhere, and it's happening in your community right now."

Why do supposedly serious people embrace such ideas? After decades of decline and often fruitless political combat, mayors, city councils, and urban development officials seem ready to embrace any notion that holds out hope without offending the entrenched constituencies that resist real reform.

"The economic development people will buy anything that makes it seem easy," suggests Leslie Parks, former chairwoman of the California Economic Development Corp. "They see a schtick that requires few hard choices, and they bought it."

Parks traces much of the current enthusiasm for the "creative" strategy to the late 1990s dot-com boom. In this period, there was a palpable economic surge in certain cities—San Francisco; Portland, Ore.; Seattle; Austin, Texas; New York—that also attracted bright, "creative" young people, and, incidentally, many gays. These are the cities that Florida and his acolytes have held up as models for other towns.

Yet virtually all these places have been hemorrhaging jobs and people since the boom busted. San Francisco, according to economist David Friedman, has actually lost employment at a rate comparable to that of the Great Depression. Roughly 4 percent of the population has simply left town, often to go to more affordable, if boring, places, such as Sacramento. San Francisco is increasingly a city without a real private-sector economy. It's home to those on the government or nonprofit payroll and the idle rich—"a cross between Carmel and Calcutta," in the painful phrase of California state librarian Kevin Starr, a San Francisco native.

As for the others, they are no bargain either. Seattle has also lost jobs at a far faster rate than the rest of the country and has its own litany of social problems, including a sizable homeless population; the loss of its signature corporation, Boeing; and growing racial tensions.

Although Portland is often hailed as a new urban paradise, it is in a region suffering very high unemployment. "They made a cool place, but the economy sucks," notes Parks, who conducted a major study for the Oregon city. "They forgot all the things that matter, like economic diversification and affordability."

New York City has also suffered heavy job losses. Gotham's population outflows, which slowed in the late 1990s, have accelerated, including in Manhattan, the city's cool core. In contrast, New York's relatively unhip suburbs, particularly those in New Jersey, quietly weathered the Bush recession in fairly fine fettle.

Today, economic growth is shifting to less fashionable but more livable locales such as San Bernardino and Riverside Counties, Calif.; Rockland County, N.Y.; Des Moines, Iowa; Bismarck, N.D.; and Sioux Falls, S.D.

In many cases, this shift also encompasses technology-oriented and professional service firms, whose ranks ostensibly dominate the so-called "creative class." This trend actually predates the 2000 crash, but it has since accelerated. Since the 1990s, the growth in financial and other business services has taken place not in New York, San Francisco, or Seattle, but in lower-cost places like Phoenix; Charlotte, N.C.; Minneapolis; and Des Moines.

Perhaps more important, the outflow from decidedly unhip places like the Midwest has slowed, and even reversed. Employers report that workers are seeking more affordable housing, and, in many cases, less family-hostile environments.

To be sure, such cities are not without their share of Starbucks outlets, and they have put great stress on quality-of-life issues—like recreation and green space—that appeal to families and relocating firms. But the watchword is livability, not coolness. "It's gotten very easy to get workers to relocate here," notes Randy Schilling, founder and CEO of Quilogy, a St. Louis-area technology company. "You get a guy here from Chicago, New York, and San Francisco, and even if he gets a pay cut, he and his family lives better."

There is, fortunately, an alternative to a hollow urban politics that relies mainly on the hip and the cool. Such a politics lies not in trendy ideas that will be forgotten a decade from now, but in commonsense policies that stress basic services like police and firefighters, innovative public schools that are not beholden to teachers' unions, breaking down of barriers to new housing construction, and policies that lead local businesses to expand within the urban area. It's a politics that, to paraphrase the great urbanist Jane Jacobs, seeks not to "lure" a middle class with bars, bells, and whistles, but instead aims to create one at the grassroots level.

That's the kind of "creativity" that cities, and Democrats, really need to embrace.

JOEL KOTKIN is a senior fellow at the Davenport Institute for Public Policy at Pepperdine University. He is writing a history of cities for Modern Library. Fred Siegel is a professor at The Cooper Union and culture editor of *Blueprint*.

From *Blueprint*, January 8, 2004, published by the Democratic Leadership Council. Reprinted by permission.

Packaging Cities

How Lesser-Known Metro Areas Are Positioning Themselves As the Next Hot Brands

REBECCA GARDYN

Last year, Milwaukee's Chamber of Commerce, Visitors Bureau, Economic Development Office, and a variety of other local institutions pooled their resources to try to sell their city to the rest of the world in a cohesive way. Rather than continue individual marketing strategies with separate advertising themes, they hired Development Counsellors International (DCI), a Manhattan-based consulting firm specializing in regional marketing, to help them create the city's first integrated campaign. It is expected to be launched this May.

In the past, city tourism departments, economic development groups, and other government and civic organizations—each with different priorities and separate budgets—rarely combined their marketing efforts. Today, many municipal leaders, like those in Milwaukee, are sharing resources to come up with sharper, more professional strategies to sell their cities to diverse consumer audiences, among them business decision makers, conventioneers, and professionals. Whether making their market debuts, retooling their images, or repositioning themselves to reach new demographics, cities are beginning to regard themselves as the new brands, and everyone as their customer.

Choices of where to live, where to visit, and where to do business have expanded over the past decade, as advances in communications technology increasingly enable individuals and companies to operate efficiently pretty much anywhere, almost regardless of geography. Sensing the opportunity, some local leaders were beginning to take an integrated marketing approach even before September 11, promoting their communities as alternatives to big cities. But following the attacks, the apparent stability and quality of life offered by smaller and lesser-known cities well away from the national capitals of commerce and business have become even bigger selling points.

Mark Zandi, chief economist for Economy.com, an online provider of economic and financial research and analysis, says that now might be the perfect time for some oft-overlooked cities and regions to advertise. "Things that were weights on some economies two years ago are now assets, like the fact that they are more removed from the hustle and bustle of urban areas," he says. "Now that big urban areas are having major problems financially, and people are more wary about being there in general, it's probably a good time for many of these places to be aggressive in marketing and positioning themselves as alternative places to visit, do business, and live."

That's because smaller and lesser-known cities are expected to be less affected economically by the tragedies than are the larger, flashier ones. For example, according to Economy.com's forecast of economic growth by metro area, prior to September 11, Milwaukee's annual gross domestic product (GDP) was expected to grow 2.29 percent through the second quarter of 2002. After the attacks, the company reduced the city's growth projections by 2.6 percentage points. Meanwhile, Chicago, Milwaukee's bigger and better-known competitor, was expected to grow 2.86 percent through the second quarter of 2002, and after the attacks, its projected GDP was lowered by 3.13 percentage points.

As *American Demographics* found in our December 2001 special report, Americans are undergoing a subtle reality shift in almost every fundamental aspect of their lives. As a result, quality of life attributes such as better commute times, access to public parks, and clean air may play bigger roles in where people choose to live, says Steve Higdon, president of Greater Louisville, Inc., an organization created to promote Louisville, Kentucky, and its surrounding regions. "What has happened to this country has really underscored the importance of Middle America," he says. "Of course, we will never take advantage of this tragedy in our marketing directly, but I do think our target audiences will look at our product different."

If it worked for Crest toothpaste, why not Milwaukee, Indianapolis, or Philadelphia? The concept of branding—the idea that one product is more valuable, has more "equity," than an alternative because it is attached to a recognizable name and promise of authenticity—began about 200 years ago, when Josiah Wedgwood realized that stamping his name on his pottery and naming his dinnerware after English nobility made it more desirable. Fast forward to the 1930s when Procter & Gamble's Neil McElroy, the company's promotion department manager, developed the "P&G brand management system," an organizational structure that assigned groups of people to handle specific marketing strategies for competing brands.

By the 1970s and '80s, "brand manager" was a coveted job title for the typical business school graduate, and by the mid-1990s, branding began to be applied not just to products but to the retailers that sell them, with names like Victoria's Secret and Bath & Body Works. "What has happened since the turn of the millennium is that everyone else is discovering branding," says Roger Blackwell, a marketing professor at the Fisher College of Business at Ohio State University. "It was inevitable that the people who market cities would turn to a concept that has been so productive and successful for others."

This push to integrate a city's disparate parts into one cohesive branding approach comes as competition among regions for tourists, conventioneers, and skilled workers has increased dramatically over the past 50 years. Alastair Morrison, director of the Purdue University Tourism and Hospitality Research Center, estimates that the number of city or regional visitors bureaus has grown from about 250 to 1,600 since 1950. Among economic development agencies, which specialize in industrial recruitment, the competition is even greater. According to the International Economic Development Council, for any given business relation or expansion, an estimated 15,000 cities, regions, or communities are in contention, and that's only in the U.S. Says Ted Levine, chairman of consulting firm DCI: "If you think about the fact that there are only about a half-dozen car manufacturers, it puts things into perspective. This is an extremely competitive field."

Cities and regions are also vying for permanent bodies, especially those with professional heads on their shoulders. With an estimated 80 percent of jobs and wealth created by privately owned companies or entrepreneurs, there's pressure on cities to keep and attract more educated workers and young entrepreneurs. While only 16 percent of the total U.S. population moved house in 1999, better-educated people are more likely to move longer distances, presumably for better-paying jobs, according to the Census Bureau's 2000 Current Population Survey. Forty-seven percent of movers with a college degree moved to a new county, either within the same state or in another state, compared with 34 percent of those with less than a high school education who did so. And the younger folks are the most mobile: 34 percent of 20- to 29-year-olds and 22 percent of 30- to 34-year-olds moved, making these demographics the primary target for many cities and regions.

For those doing the moving, whether they are employees looking for new digs or CEOs expanding or relocating their companies, image has become an important deal-breaker. According to Arthur Andersen's "Best Cities 2000" survey of 1,433 senior executives worldwide, conducted June through November 2000, a city's suitability for business is no longer just about geographic location, tax incentives, or cheap land. Instead, the top three factors mentioned are: "pro-business attitudes" (20 percent), "local availability of professionals" (12 percent), and "entrepreneurial activity" (10 percent).

"Thirty or 40 years ago, you just needed green grass by a railroad to set up shop," says Shari Barnett, senior manager of global location strategies at PricewaterhouseCoopers. Now there are so many variables, and there is never just one city that's right for a business or employee. Barnett says she is working with several companies that nixed her recommendation of a city she thought perfect because decision makers had an impression that

its economy was failing or its quality of life was poor, even though the city was actually thriving. "Things like geography and tax incentives will get you on the short list, but at the end of the day, if the client doesn't perceive your city well, they'll move on."

Yet, lessons from the corporate boardroom extend only so far. Branding a city has its own set of challenges. The first is persuading city leaders, many of them with little or no marketing experience, that they need to do so. "You have to convince city councils that they need to spend money on something they know nothing about, and that's a tough sell," says Elizabeth Goodgold, CEO of The Nuancing® Group, a brand consultancy in San Diego.

Deborah Knudsen knows that dance. As president and CEO of the Traverse City, Michigan, Convention and Visitors Bureau, she spent 10 years trying to convince fellow civic leaders and small-business owners to participate in a branding effort before finally succeeding two years ago when she helped launch its brand—"A World Apart"—targeting affluent tourists. Raised in a family of restaurateurs, Knudsen grew up understanding the value of a brand maintaining consumer loyalty and ensuring repeat business. "I've followed what P&G and GM have been doing over the years and seen it work for them, so I knew we should be doing it too, at least at some level," she says. "But it's not easy when you're dealing with people from many different backgrounds."

Even when most leaders concur on the need for such activity, agreeing on strategy is another story. Unlike a corporation with one CEO calling the shots as to how to proceed, a city has multiple entities with very different, and often conflicting, priorities and target audiences. Indianapolis is struggling with this step in its current branding process, says Mike Lawson, president of the Indianapolis Regional Economic Development Partnership. In the past, the region was marketed as nine individual counties, with nine individual budgets. Now they've merged, but that has simply increased the number of cooks in the kitchen. What's more, there are a number of other private and nonprofit organizations in the area, all promoting the city differently to various consumers.

"The biggest challenge we face is coming to a consensus on an umbrella brand that will work for everyone's consumers," says Lawson. "It can be difficult to get people to see the big picture all the time, and there's a lot of 'protecting turf' going on." But they're working on it. Representatives of six entities, including Lawson's economic development group, the city's Arts Council, the Indiana Sports Corporation, and Indianapolis Downtown, Inc., met all through last summer, and have hired an independent facilitator, a marketing professor at Indiana University, to help.

Another obstacle to branding cities has to do with turnover in leadership, especially those in cities and counties with term limits for elected officials. "Often, you'll have political leaders who agree that someone should put the region on the map, but then say, 'It's not my job, I'm out of here in a few years,'" says Rod Underhill, chief executive of Spherical, Inc., the brand strategy consulting arm of The Richards Group, a Dallas-based advertising agency. That's why a good brand strategy has to be based and rigorously analyzed, he says. Otherwise, every mayoral election can bring a change in focus resulting in a stop-and-start marketing effort that is ineffective. "There has to be so much conviction among the other civic organizations and leaders that branding needs to get to withstand a turnover in leadership," he adds.

Underhill says that level of conviction exists in the Dallas-Fort Worth region—the Metroplex. The dual Chambers of Commerce hired Spherical to help brand the area. While details about their strategy are still under wraps, Underhill says that the biggest challenge has to do with reeling in and managing a brand that has been unmanaged for so long. "Most cities are a victim of their unmanaged reputations," he says. "In the absence of a brand strategy, Dallas-Fort Worth conjures images of J.R. Ewing and cheerleaders, but those cultural icons are not necessarily what the city would like to be known for."

And then there's the opposite problem. DCI's Levine estimates that 60 percent to 70 percent of all cities in the U.S. have no image at all in the public mind. Thus, finding a core distinguishable asset, or "unique selling proposition," as he terms it, becomes even more important. Nancy Koehn, marketing professor at Harvard and author of *Brand New: How Entrepreneurs Earned Consumers' Trust from Wedgwood to Dell* (Harvard Business School Press, 2001), recommends that decision makers turn to their city's unique histories. "Almost every city or region has some interesting piece of history that everyone can relate to," she says. "That can be your connection point with consumers. In any kind of branding, connecting on a personal level is always a very strong motivator."

But for some cities, history is double-edged. Leaders of nine public and private civic organizations in the Richmond, Virginia, region worked all through last summer, with Martin Branding Worldwide of "Virginia is for Lovers" fame, on an integrated branding effort. The region's rich ties to America's history were cited as a distinguishing asset in all its focus group sessions among all demographic groups, from tourists to business leaders to potential residents. Still, they debated as to whether or not that history was the best way to brand that area. Yes, the region is the birthplace of many U.S. presidents, but it was also once home to the country's largest slave port, notes Greg Wingfield, president of the Greater Richmond Partnership, the region's economic development organization. In the end, Richmond's leaders decided the positives about the area's five-century history outweighed any negatives, and in October 2001, its new brand was unveiled: "The Historic Richmond Region: Easy to Love."

Still, other cities continue to struggle with their identity crises. A nationwide study of 300 CEOs conducted by the Columbus, Ohio, Chamber of Commerce found that fewer than 10 percent of respondents knew anything about that city. And its municipal leaders are worried about the bigger picture. Columbus has consistently been a good place to live and work, with continuous growth, says Sally Jackson, president of the Greater Columbus Chamber of Commerce. But as business becomes more global and people become more mobile, that won't be enough if no one knows about it. "We need to get a lot better at projecting what we are all about," Jackson says. Because, for today's consumers, image is everything.

Urban Warfare

American cities compete for talent, and the winners take all

BLAINE HARDEN

In a Darwinian fight for survival, American cities are scheming to steal each other's young. They want ambitious young people with graduate degrees in such fields as genome science, bio-informatics and entrepreneurial management.

Sam Long was easy pickings. He was born, reared and very well educated in Cleveland. With a focus on early stage venture capital, he earned his MBA at Case Western Reserve University. Venture capital is in Long's blood. His great-great-grandfather invested in Standard Oil of Ohio, the company that John D. Rockefeller built in Cleveland in the late 19th century.

In the early 21st century, Cleveland desperately needs entrepreneurs, but it never had a shot at keeping Long. He wanted to sail in Puget Sound, ski in the Cascades and swim in Seattle's deep pool of money, ideas and risk-taking young investors.

He now runs a small venture capital company. It sniffs out software ideas, many of them incubated in the computer science department at the University of Washington. "Birds of a feather, you know," said Long, who arrived here in 1992, when he was 28. "There are more people like me in Seattle."

Long is part of an elite intercity migration that is rapidly remaking the way American cities rise and fall. In the 2000 Census, demographers found what they describe as a new, brain-driven, winner-take-all pattern in urban growth.

"A pack of cities is racing away from everybody else in terms of their ability to attract and retain an educated workforce," said Bruce Katz, director of the Center on Urban and Metropolitan Policy at the Brookings Institution. "It is a sobering trend for cities left behind."

The long economic downturn has stalled growth and increased unemployment in almost every U.S. city, and has brought a sense of near-desperation to the intercity fight for young talent. Mayors, business leaders and university presidents are scrambling to secure new technology companies and entice young people to live downtown.

"In our business, you have to cannibalize," said Ron Sims, the county executive of King County, which surrounds Seattle, and a Democratic candidate for governor of Washington state. "Many cities don't fight back very well."

In addition to Seattle, the largest brain-gain cities include Austin, Atlanta, Boston, Denver, Minneapolis, San Diego, San Francisco, Washington, and Raleigh and Durham, N.C.

The rising tide of well-schooled talent has created a self-reinforcing cycle. Newcomers such as Sam Long have made a handful of cities richer, more densely populated and more capable of squeezing wealth out of the next big thing that a knowledge-based economy might serve up.

Some of these cities are blessed with relatively young, home-grown billionaires. They understand technology and are making huge bets to lure more talent. Seattle, with Microsoft Corp. co-founders Paul G. Allen and Bill Gates fronting much of the money, is probably making the most expensive such bet in the country—on biotechnology.

"If you have the resources," said Allen, the world's fourth-richest man ($20.1 billion), "you try to do positive things. You help keep momentum going."

Brain-gain cities are hardly immune to the economic cycle. In the tech-driven recession, Seattle, like San Francisco and Austin, endured wrenching levels of business failure and unemployment. The Seattle area lost more than 60,000 jobs in the past four years, as average wages declined and population growth stagnated. But this city and those like it remain national leaders in the availability of venture capital, and demographers say they appear to have kept most of their educated young people, who hang on even without good jobs.

The winner-take-all pattern of the past decade differs substantially from the Rust Belt decline and Sun Belt growth of the 1970s and '80s. Then, manufacturing companies moved south in search of a low-wage, nonunion workforce. Now, talented individuals are voting with their feet to live in cities where the work is smart, the culture is cool and the environment is clean.

Migrants on the move to winner-take-all-cities are most accurately identified by education and ambition, rather than by skin color or country of birth. They are part of a striving class of young Americans for whom race, ethnicity and geographic origin tend to be less meaningful than professional achievement, business connections and income.

The Sun Belt is no sure winner in this migration. Such cities as Miami and El Paso are struggling to keep college graduates,

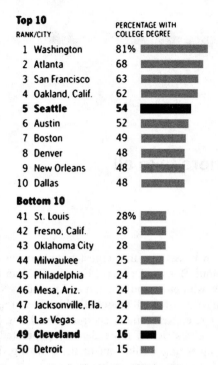

Top 10 RANK/CITY	PERCENTAGE WITH COLLEGE DEGREE
1 Washington	81%
2 Atlanta	68
3 San Francisco	63
4 Oakland, Calif.	62
5 Seattle	**54**
6 Austin	52
7 Boston	49
8 Denver	48
9 New Orleans	48
10 Dallas	48

Bottom 10	
41 St. Louis	28%
42 Fresno, Calif.	28
43 Oklahoma City	28
44 Milwaukee	25
45 Philadelphia	24
46 Mesa, Ariz.	24
47 Jacksonville, Fla.	24
48 Las Vegas	22
49 Cleveland	**16**
50 Detroit	15

Figure 1 College Graduates. Among the 50 largest U.S. cities, Seattle ranks fifth in percentage of residents with college degrees. Cleveland ranks 49th.

Source: Brookings Institution Center on Urban and Metropolitan Policy

who are flocking to such foul-weather havens as Minneapolis, Seattle and Ann Arbor, Mich.

Among the country's 100 largest metro areas, the 25 that entered the 1990s with the largest share of college graduates had, by the end of the decade, sponged up graduates at twice the rate of the other 75 cities, according to a Brookings analysis of the census.

Talent helps make these top-tier cities diverse, tolerant and rich with the cultural amenities that help them steal still more talent.

These cities tend to have a high percentage of residents who are artists, writers and musicians, as well as large and visible gay communities. They often have pedestrian neighborhoods, with good food, live music and theater. The percentage of foreign-born residents is also high in these cities, reflecting a significant population of college-educated imports.

"The great advantage of places like Seattle is that they have become the kind of place where young people want to freaking be," said Richard Florida, a professor of regional economic development at Carnegie Mellon University in Pittsburgh.

Florida is author of "The Rise of the Creative Class," an influential book among big-city politicians and urban planners. It tells them they can secure the future of their cities by tending to the care and feeding of smart young people.

Rapid population growth, by itself, does not guarantee that a city will experience a relative gain in college graduates. In most cases, extraordinary growth is a negative indicator.

With the exception of Austin, none of the 10 fastest-growing U.S. cities of the 1990s ranked among the top 25 cities for increases in the percentage of residents with college degrees. The fastest-growing city, Las Vegas, leads the nation in attracting more high school dropouts than college graduates.

"Really fast-growing places, like Las Vegas and Phoenix, have needs not associated with college education, like the construction industry and service workers for retirement communities," said William H. Frey, a demographer at the University of Michigan.

Another peculiarity of brain-gain cities is that they have a tendency to lose residents of lesser educational attainment, even as they vacuum up more college graduates.

In the second half of the 1990s, San Francisco experienced a 6.5 percent decline in residents who had only a high school degree, according to Frey's analysis of census data. At the same time, the number of college graduates rose by 2.8 percent. Driven mostly by housing costs, a similar trend exists in Seattle and other brain-gain cities.

Frey said this demographic crosscurrent appears to have continued through the high-tech recession. It helps explain why—even as the college-educated young continue to cluster in a handful of cities—broader demographic trends show a substantial movement of people from large metropolitan centers to outer suburbs, small cities and rural areas.

"Clearly, as the economy got bad, lesser-educated folks had a harder time staying in San Francisco," Frey said. "My guess is that the higher-educated folks found a way to stay, or they circulated to one of the other idea-opolises, like Seattle."

New York, Chicago and Los Angeles are perennial magnets of high-end talent, but their size and the constant churning of their population make it difficult for demographers to discern the winner-take-all pattern identified in mid-size cities.

What is easy—and depressing—to see in brain-drain cities is the extraordinary cost of losing talent. The departure of people such as Sam Long from these cities has stalled growth, lowered per-capita income and prevented the formation of a critical mass of risk-takers who can create high-paying jobs.

Besides Cleveland, these cities include Baltimore; Buffalo; Detroit; Hartford, Conn.; Milwaukee; Miami; Newark; Pittsburgh; St. Louis; and Stockton and Lodi, Calif.

Some of the damage to these cities is to their spirit, as they have lost the swagger of youth. "There is a pervasive inferiority complex in this town," said Mark A. Rosenberger, programming director of WVIZ, a public television station in Cleveland. "People are afraid to try new things. They fear they will fail."

It is a cultural weakness of the city, said Peter B. Lewis, the Cleveland-born billionaire who heads the Progressive Corp., an insurance company that is the largest private employer in the area. "People leave because they are not challenged and people leave because they feel different. There are better venues than Cleveland, if you are creative. Cleveland has never been particularly good in keeping its oddballs," he said.

For the past two years, Cleveland's daily newspaper, the Plain Dealer, has published a series of reports about the city's "Quiet Crisis" of disappearing talent and economic stagnation.

The graduates most likely to leave the Cleveland area have degrees linked to innovation. A recent series in the Plain Dealer found that the higher their degree, the more likely young people were to move. The newspaper found that about two-thirds of doctoral graduates in engineering, the sciences and the creative arts cleared out of Ohio between 1991 and 2001.

A recent Census Bureau report reinforced that finding of brain drain, saying the Cleveland region lost young, single college graduates to other parts of the country in the late 1990s. It was one of only three of the nation's 20 largest metropolitan areas to do so.

Cities such as Cleveland have become painfully aware of what they are losing, and their leaders have come to regard cities such as Seattle as mortal enemies.

"Are they a threat to the survival of Cleveland? Absolutely," said Manuel Glynias, a Cleveland-born scientist and entrepreneur. "Are they a threat that we haven't figured out how to answer yet? Absolutely."

His own story is not encouraging—unless you live in a winner-take-all city.

In 1996, he created a successful bio-informatics company called NetGenics, which employed 100 people in downtown Cleveland and won accolades in the local media as a harbinger of the city's high-tech future. His employees wrote software that allowed drug companies to make better use of vast amounts of research data.

But NetGenics did not grow as fast as its primary competitor, the German company Lion. Part of the problem, Glynias said, was that he could not find marketing people in Cleveland who understood high-tech. Lion bought NetGenics last year and has moved many of its jobs to San Diego, a major biotech center. The last jobs left Cleveland this summer.

"It was felt that there were better places to do business in a high-tech sort of way," Glynias said. "If Cleveland can't find a way to stop this, I will be visiting my children and grandchildren in San Diego or Austin or Seattle."

It might seem unfair to set up Cleveland as a foil for Seattle, like arranging a prizefight between a has-been and a cocky contender. But the comparison mirrors a national reality, as Austin, Minneapolis and Boston routinely poach talent—and steal the future—from cities such as San Antonio, St. Louis and Hartford.

"It is a totally unfair fight, and it is the way the market works now," said Michael Fogarty, director of the School of Urban Studies at Portland State University and former professor of economics at Case Western.

Cleveland and Seattle are about the same size, with about a half-million residents inside the city limits and 2 million-plus in the metro region. Both cities have a history of big money. Each produced the richest men of its era (Rockefeller and Gates). In an explosion of capitalistic energy, they became world-famous centers for technical innovation, entrepreneurial creativity and a bullying business style that pushed—and sometimes broke—the limits of the law.

These bursts of prosperity, of course, were separated by nearly a century. Cleveland flowered in the second half of the 19th century and peaked by 1930, when productivity started to slide in steelmaking and metalworking.

As with many cities in the Rust Belt, the population began to decline in the 1960s. Racial segregation played a chronically corrosive role, as poverty rose, public schools nose-dived and whites fled to the suburbs.

Sprawl was encouraged and hugely subsidized by Ohio's tax policy. It sucked gas taxes out of Cleveland and other cities, and the state spent the money on roads in rural areas that often blossomed into affluent suburbs. At the same time, Cleveland failed to become a "gateway city" for new immigrants. Large waves of Asian or Latin American immigrants did not pour into the city or its close-in suburbs (as occurred in Seattle and Washington) to replace those who had been vacuumed out by subsidized sprawl.

Cleveland's population in 1950 was 914,808, but it lost 30 percent of its residents in the 1970s, 15 percent in the '80s and 5 percent in the '90s. Rockefeller left early, moving to New York before the turn of the century.

Although Seattle is mired in its worst recession in three decades and hobbled by the loss of about 17,000 jobs at Boeing Co., it is an altogether different story.

The city has succeeded in shifting its economic base over the years—from lumber and fishing to airplane manufacturing to high-tech enterprises and specialty retail. Its school system, although far from perfect, never collapsed. It does not have intractable pockets of poverty. It does not have to clean up the festering environmental legacy of the industrial age. It is 70 percent white, 13 percent Asian, 5.4 percent black and 5 percent Hispanic. (Cleveland is 51 percent black, 41.5 percent white and 7.3 percent Hispanic.)

The success of U.S. cities, demographers agree, is not related to racial composition but rather to education levels. High levels of immigration by nonwhite college graduates in the 1990s to such cities as Seattle, Austin and San Francisco have been a major factor in their prosperity. At the same time, the relative dearth of college-educated immigrants of any race to cities such as Cleveland is viewed as a key reason for their decline.

Although Cleveland has sprawled without growth, Seattle has grown while winning a come-from-behind fight against sprawl. After losing population to the suburbs for 30 years, it turned a corner in the '90s, growing by 9 percent, with many newcomers moving to housing near the waterfront.

State law has forced more than 80 percent of new housing construction to occur inside designated urban zones in King County. Population growth continues in Seattle, although the recession slowed it to a crawl.

Thanks in large measure to the drawing power of such companies as Microsoft, Amazon.com Inc. and Starbucks Corp., Seattle ranks near the top on virtually every national index of knowledge-based urban muscle.

More than a half-million people moved to King County in the past two decades and about 10,000 millionaires were minted, mostly at Microsoft. Forty-seven percent of Seattleites have at least a bachelor's degree, about twice the national rate and four times higher than Cleveland's.

More households have access to the Internet (80.6 percent) than in any other U.S. city, and Seattle ranked second in the country (after Minneapolis) in a recent survey of literacy. The city also ranks among the top five high-tech cities in percentages of creative artists, foreign-born residents and gays.

The emergence of winner-take-all cities is usually linked to the presence of a dominating research university. Seattle is no exception. The University of Washington, which is in the city, has doubled its research budget in the past decade and is the country's leading public university as measured by federal funding.

Among urban scholars, business leaders and big-city politicians, there is a chicken-and-egg debate over what exactly makes a high-tech city grow. Does technology come first and lure talent? Or does the mere presence of talent, through some creative alchemy, hatch technology that spawns high-paying jobs? A look at a recent software startup in Seattle suggests the answer is both.

The new company, called Performant Inc., emerged from an idea that Seattle investors quickly grasped and bathed in a nourishing pot of money. One of them was Sam Long, the venture capitalist who moved here from Cleveland. Three years ago, Long got a call from Ashutosh Tiwary, an Indian immigrant and doctoral student at the University of Washington's School of Computer Science and Engineering.

Tiwary had an idea that came to him while he was working part time at Boeing, where he was troubleshooting design software for new aircraft. He found a way to diagnose why computer systems at major companies often slow to a crawl. His software could speed them up.

He took the idea back to the university, where a professor and a senior software researcher from Microsoft (an adjunct professor) saw its potential. They helped him refine, patent and market a product. They also hooked him up with a venture capital company run by wealthy Microsoft retirees. That company, in turn, gave him Long's phone number.

Long quickly invested $750,000, part of the $10 million that Tiwary and his partners raised during the teeth of Seattle's recession. This spring, they sold the company, doubling their investors' money. Thirty jobs created by the company are staying in Seattle.

Tiwary said he never would have come up with the idea—or made money from it so quickly—had he not been in Seattle. He moved there in the late 1990s, by way of India, Texas and California.

"There is a business ecosystem here that is both creative and technical," said Tiwary, now a vice president at *Mercury Interactive Corp.,* the company that bought him out. "It starts with people who understand technology, have built successful things before and want to do it again. It is a little bit of an addiction."

At the very top of the entrepreneurial food chain in Seattle, the addiction to risk-taking is being turned loose on biotech.

The city's two richest residents—with the backing of the University of Washington and enthusiastic help from the city and county governments—are bankrolling a bet that could supercharge the local economy for decades to come. Seattle is already a leader in biotech, but lags far behind Boston and San Francisco.

Paul Allen has spent $225 million of his own money to close the gap—fast. "You have to be ready to take advantage of the next big cycle," Allen said.

He said Seattle has strung together all the beads on that thread: a research university, a cooperative city government, lots of venture capital and "you have to be able to attract people . . . . That is just not a problem in Seattle."

In the past decade, Allen has bought 50 acres in downtown Seattle for a biotech research center. His company, Vulcan, is transforming a sterile stretch of parking lots, used-furniture stores and badly designed streets into what is expected to be the nation's largest urban life-science campus.

It will have the capacity to employ 20,000 scientists and technicians, according to Vulcan. If Allen's plan works, about 10,000 of them would live in a pedestrian neighborhood at the south end of the city's Lake Union, amid new restaurants, nightclubs and retail stores surmounted by apartments.

To help Seattle create a critical mass of biotech talent, Gates donated $70 million this spring to the University of Washington to build departments of genome science and bioengineering. For nearly a decade, Gates has used his money and his fame to recruit eminent biotech scientists from around the country.

"Gates and Allen are giving the city a real forward momentum," said Leroy Hood, whom Gates lured from the California Institute of Technology to start a biotechnology department at the University of Washington. "In 10 years, I think Boeing will be irrelevant to Seattle."

Scholars who study U.S. cities agree that Cleveland has probably tried harder—and achieved more—than any other major brain-drain city.

It has substantially rebuilt its downtown, winning national attention as a "comeback city" with the Rock and Roll Hall of Fame, as well as new complexes for professional baseball, basketball and football. The percentage of residents with high school degrees has increased and concentrated poverty has been reduced.

The fastest-growing neighborhood in Cleveland is the downtown core. There, city government has worked with developers to turn warehouses and abandoned department stores into apartments that appeal to young professionals. Cleveland's leading university, Case Western, is urging students and faculty to live in the city. It is spending hundreds of millions of dollars for new housing and for a retail neighborhood near the university. "You must position yourself as the place people want to move to, rather than from," said the school's new president, Edward M. Hundert.

He is demanding that the school's researchers work with, rather than compete against, other local research centers, such as the Cleveland Clinic and University Hospitals of Cleveland.

"This is a city that, against all odds, is getting its act together," said Katz, whose Urban Affairs Center at Brookings monitors most major U.S. cities. "I believe that if Cleveland had not tried so hard, it would look like St. Louis or Detroit."

And yet, in Cleveland—as in many other brain-drain cities that are trying to fight back—the loss of talent continues. Throughout the '90s, even as Cleveland made its highly publicized comeback, it continued to lose college graduates and income. It lost about $35 billion because it could not keep the people and maintain the per-capita income it had in 1990, according to an analysis in the Plain Dealer.

A critical mass of money, ideas and risk-taking has not coalesced in Cleveland, said David Morgenthaler, one of the country's most eminent venture capitalists. He manages $2 billion and lives in Cleveland. Morgenthaler said he would love to invest more money in his home town. But he does not do so because the city "does not breed enough good horses to bet on."

His judgment is echoed in Cleveland's dismal ranking among the 50 largest cities as measured by venture capital as a percentage of the metro economy. Cleveland ranks 42nd, while Seattle ranks second, behind San Francisco. "Cleveland lives off the past, and the executives from these old industries are still the community leaders," Morgenthaler said. "The city has made progress, but it is not close to where it has to be."

A decade after leaving Cleveland for Seattle, Sam Long wishes his hometown well, but says he cannot conceive of a reason he would live there. He just built a four-bedroom house near Lake Washington in one of Seattle's most expensive neighborhoods. At regular dinners with friends from the computer science department at the University of Washington, he schemes about turning ideas into money. "We talk of pie in the sky," he said.

In Seattle, unlike his home town and many other cities that keep losing young talent, pie in the sky has a way of turning into high-paying jobs and companies that own the future.

The Geography of Cool

What defines cool in a city, and why does the temperature change? We look at seasonal shifts in London, New York, Berlin, Paris and Tokyo

London never set out to be cool. Indeed, London never set out to be anything, which may be the secret of its success. The British capital is essentially a conservative city: communes belong in Paris, springs in Prague and revolutions in St Petersburg. London has never used its built environment to proclaim a sense of change. Even today, of the billions of pounds of lottery money being spent in the capital, most is going on fixing up existing structures, such as the Royal Opera House and the new Tate Bankside gallery. London will never get a pyramid in the forecourt of Buckingham Palace.

Then again London has never had a politician to carry out such a plan. Even the new mayor won't have the power of his counterparts in Paris, Barcelona or New York to push through grandiose schemes. Officially sanctioned modernising projects usually fall flat in London. And Londoners are often the first to deride projects like the hapless Millennium Dome. The Pompidou Centre (co-designed by a Briton) was built in Paris, not London.

No. Cool in London is a village affair. Uniquely, London is a haphazard conglomeration of villages. And the villages were shaped into a city more by the accidents of history than by the imperatives of town-planning. Sometimes a village manages to capture the spirit of the age, to reflect a wider social and cultural phenomenon. Chelsea did so in the "swinging sixties". In the mid-1990s, "Cool Britannia" was supposed to be spilling out on to the streets of Camden and Islington.

Thus creating "cool" in London is a uniquely organic and authentic process. It is this very authenticity which makes the city such a magnet for the youth of Europe. So how does a London village become trendy in the first place? Here is a step-by-step guide:

- To begin with the area has to be relatively seedy and poor, with a plentiful supply of cheap, but solid, housing. Fortunately, London's villages are well provided with an abundant stock of large Victorian and Georgian accommodation.

- This means that young, trend-setting bohemians— active agents from London's enormous number of art schools—can afford to move into the area when they are at their penniless but creative best. Since the 1960s, artists have been joined by rock musicians, fashion designers and the like.

- For real bohemia you also need immigrants. These are essential to create cultural diversity and to challenge the complacent mono-culture of the resident English. Two of the trendiest parts of London in recent years, affluent Notting Hill and upcoming Brixton, were both hosts to large numbers of West Indian immigrants in the 1950s, because they could afford the cheap rents in the areas.

- The ethnic mix of the areas have contributed to the sense of edginess and roughness that first attracted the trendsetters to the area. Since the late 1950s Brixton and Notting Hill have both seen violent riots.

- This sense of danger is a strong draw for the more adventurous members of the middle and upper classes, as long as the violence can be viewed from a safe distance. They bring money into the area, and institutionalise bohemia into shops and cafés. Most of the trendy areas have been spillovers from the smarter parts of town. Thus Notting Hill from Kensington, Islington from the City and Chelsea from Belgravia.

- All this has to be fuelled by a plentiful supply of drugs. Drugs were as essential to the 1960s as they were to creating the clubbing and dance scene of the 1990s. Though Britain has some of the harshest drug laws in Europe, its capital has one of the most flourishing drug economies.

Put these ingredients together, and a village will reach critical mass—but only for a while. Thus Chelsea was the trendiest part of town in the Victorian era, boasting painters such as James Whistler and writers such as Oscar Wilde amongst its residents. The Chelsea Arts Club survives to this day as a reminder of this vanished era.

Notting Hill started to take off in the late 1960s, when artists and designers like David Hockney and Ossie Clark moved in. Jimi Hendrix died there in 1970, and "The Clash" made it into a centre of punk rock in 1976. Islington began to move in the late 1970s, and the upwardly mobile middle classes (such as Tony Blair) arrived en masse in the late 1980s.

To be "cool", all these villages had to strike a delicate balance between holding on to enough of the danger, the seediness and the ethnic and cultural mix that made them chic in the first place, while surrendering enough of it to make it safe for incomers to enjoy. The moment it becomes too comfortable, trendification leads inexorably to gentrification, accompanied by rapid house-price inflation. At which point the party moves on.

By the time the film "Notting Hill" internationalised the appeal of that particular village, the game was up. Notting Hill's estate agents now trade on an ersatz trendiness. A two-bedroom maisonette in the All Saints Road, once London's dingiest drugs den, now sells for half a million. But then it is in the middle of a "very trendy" area.

So where is cool now? Hoxton, just east of the City of London, has been the centre of the "Britart" movement during the 1990s. White Cube, an offshoot of London's smartest art gallery, opens there this week. It looks set to start a stampede as the more avant-garde galleries migrate across town from Mayfair and St James's. But the arrival of so many dealers, let alone the imminent opening of the Prince of Wales's school of architecture, spells the end of the Hoxton scene. And for the future? Watch out for Brixton, which still has some way to go, and Hackney Downs.

The Best of Mates

According to the young Americans described by Ethan Watters in Urban Tribes, we don't need our families any longer. Andy Beckett looks at the new grouping

ANDY BECKETT

On weekday afternoons in San Francisco, the sunlit, airy cafés that seem to stand on every street corner are always puzzlingly full. Not with pensioners or parents with babies, but with single people in their 20s and 30s in well-cut casual clothes. Most Americans of that age and apparent level of wealth are stuck in offices, but in San Francisco and other liberal American cities a different form of young middle-class life seems to flourish.

Ethan Watters calls them "urban tribes", and describes them as "the fastest-growing demographic group in America". They have been to university, they have confidence and money, but they are uninterested in what comes next in the conventional middle-class life: a structured career, marriage, children. Instead, Watters's subjects form groups with like-minded peers, and spend the decades between early adulthood and middle age going out together, bonding and gossiping with their new extended family, earning money by freelance means, and drinking a great number of leisurely coffees.

A few of the many tribe members Watters interviews live in Britain and other nations besides the United States. The phenomenon he has identified, he implies, is becoming apparent in all wealthy countries. But essentially this is a book about America. Foreign readers are expected to understand its references to "Seinfeldian" situations and "Costco-sized" supermarket products and—as with all the other trendspotting American popular sociology books that have crossed the Atlantic in recent years, such as The Tipping Point by Malcolm Gladwell and John Seabrook's Nobrow—to consider the insights here about American society as relevant to non-American lives.

Watters, a freelance writer in his 30s, lives in San Francisco. Until recently, he was a member of exactly the kind of peer group he writes about here, and he cites his and his friends' experiences at length. But the whiff of narcissism about this book feels entirely appropriate. The world Watters describes is inward-looking, self-sufficient, cut off from the rest of society. "In certain hipster areas," he writes, "you could literally go days without seeing a child." Working and playing in their small peninsular city at the very edge of America, he and his fellow bohemians can ignore the traditional family values of

the Bush era: "I lived in a social microculture to such an extent that the national zeitgeist was felt only as a small shifting of the breeze."

Watters writes vividly about his tribe's existence: a perpetual present of parties, noisy dinners and group excursions, whole years passing in a pleasant blur in the seasonless San Francisco weather. The group share houses, collaborate on freelance writing and art projects. They drive to a festival in the desert to build a sculpture. For them, and their counterparts in Seattle and New York and elsewhere, money is not much of a worry. They have saleable skills and contacts—a hippyish-sounding artist mentioned here turns out to be making a chandelier for the architect Frank Gehry. They do each other favours—the writer Po Bronson, another member of Watters's group, provides a favourable cover quote for this book. And they know their actual families, with whom they remain in sporadic contact, may one day hand them substantial inheritances. The property and savings acquired by more conventional generations usefully underwrites the urban tribes' years of fun and experiments: as Watters says with commendable but slightly shocking directness, "Why worry about saving for retirement when your parents have done it for you?"

He is sufficiently self-aware to see that the lives he depicts can seem "comically selfish and self-absorbed". But he argues, quite convincingly, that urban tribes cannot simply be dismissed in those terms. The spirit of cooperation and mutual reliance also present in these gangs of friends is presented here as a throwback to the collective American traditions that existed before modern working patterns and consumer capitalism created a nation of office addicts and lonely shoppers.

All this material is presented in a conversational, informally researched way. At one point, he mentions "searching the web with words like 'friendship', 'loyalty, 'meaning of'." There is little of the erudition and sharp-elbowed argument that animates the older, non-American tradition of writing about city subcultures, exemplified by Peter York and Dick Hebdige in the 70s and 80s. They defined urban tribes in a more political and class-connected way—as skinheads, punks, Sloane Rangers—that fitted a more overtly political era; Watters's soft-edged portrait of a generation fits its time and its subject matter, but at times feels a bit unfocused and shallow by comparison.

There is not much here about ageing, or the biological difficulties of having children late. There is a long section speculating about why the author and his peers have delayed getting married that could be a vaguely argued women's magazine article. But the book regains its momentum in the final chapter, as Watters's train of thought heads off in an unexpected direction.

He has hinted already that being in a tight gang of friends well into your 30s might have a time-filling aspect. The relentless, heavily ritualised activities of the groups he describes—weekly group dinners, group parties held at the slightest excuse—do suggest a fear of being alone and thinking about the trajectory of your life. In the long term, he says, this has a cost: "[You] dam up certain desires, hopes, and plans. With each passing year, the pressure builds a little."

Yet close groups do not always let their members leave easily. Watters is good on the ways groups have of discouraging relationships with outsiders: the murmurs against "unsuitable" partners, the maintenance of an "ambient sexual charge" within the group itself, through "long-standing flirtations, unexpressed crushes, and glimmers of mutual attraction".

By the end of the book, Watters's urban tribes feel less free and appealing. Abruptly, he reveals he has left his and got married. Perhaps a conventional career awaits him after all, as a repenting bohemian in the Daily Mail. But he'll have to harden up his prose style.

UNIT 4

Urban Revival, Gentrification and the Changing Face of the City

Unit Selections

Key Points to Consider

- Define urban revival.

- Describe the factors that have made it possible for many cities to think in terms of urban revival.

- Can urban revival be sustained? What do you see as the pitfalls to continuing progress?

- What are some possible ways to invigorate urban centers? Do you think these plans would work in any urban center in America? Why or why not?

- Describe the effects of racial and class segregation at the neighborhood level.

- What does gentrification mean to the existing residents of a neighborhood?

- Can a city prosper without gentrification? If so, how?

- Can a neighborhood attract an affluent or upwardly mobile population without pushing out poorer residents? Can a city do the same? If you said "yes" to either question, how?

Student Web Site

www.mhcls.com/online

Internet References

Further information regarding these Web sites may be found in this book's preface or online.

Connect for Kids/Workplace
http://www.connectforkids.org/info-url1564/info-url_list.htm?section= Workplace

WWW Virtual Library: Demography & Population Studies
http://demography.anu.edu.au/VirtualLibrary

This section is divided into two subsections: Urban Revival and Gentrification. The first subsection focuses on the expanded role of downtowns in twenty-first century cities. Cities increasingly use cultural and educational institutions to attract the well-educated and well-heeled, and to market their lifestyle advantages. The economic benefits of hosting major cultural and educational institutions have been widely recognized and consciously used as levers of urban revitalization. Arts and educational institutions now calculate and publicize the economic benefits they bring to their home cities.

In New York, Julia Vitullo-Martin tells the remarkable story of how Bryant Park, once home to drug dealers and other criminals, became one of the most densely used parks in America, and details the symbolic and practical effects of this transformation for midtown Manhattan. Lou Winick, an astute urban analyst, once said immigration is our most successful urban policy. Joel Kotkin's essay highlights the role immigrants have played in revitalizing Los Angeles. The second subsection looks at gentrification, and the effect of new arrivals on their surroundings, for better and for worse, and at how "hot neighborhoods" change, and the effect on those already there.

Return to Center

States that moved offices and jobs out to the suburbs are moving them back downtown.

CHRISTOPHER D. RINGWALD

Last spring, New York's Department of Environmental Conservation moved back where it started out: downtown Albany. After 30 years in a headquarters just off Interstate 87, in the suburb of Colonie, the agency and its 1,900 employees packed up and relocated to 625 Broadway, a few blocks from the state capitol.

Not every employee is happy—most had grown accustomed to off-ramp freeway access, massive parking lots and other accoutrements of a suburban location. On the other hand, there are compensations. "I like having sidewalks to walk on," says Franz Litz, a DEC attorney, standing outside his new 14-story office building after strolling back from lunch at a nearby restaurant. "I can walk to some meetings," says one of his colleagues. "Before, I used to have to drive to all of them."

Whether they approve of it or not, however, the return to downtown Albany is a change that thousands of New York State employees will need to get used to. The DEC is only one of the agencies involved. The state's Dormitory Authority, which finances and constructs major public facilities, has moved to a five-story glass-and-granite box at 515 Broadway, down the street from DEC. The state Comptroller's office is consolidating its workforce a few blocks away. In the past five years, more than 4,500 state employees have relocated into the city's center.

None of this is a coincidence. New York's General Services Commissioner, Kenneth Ringler, puts it succinctly. "The governor," he says, "has a downtown policy."

This is not the first time that major efforts have been launched to rescue downtown Albany. During the 1960s and 1970s, Governor Nelson Rockefeller—with the strong support of Democratic Mayor Erastus Corning II—cleared 80 acres in the center of the city and built the Empire State Plaza, nine giant buildings arrayed on a marble mall with vast reflecting pools. Grandiose, windswept and impersonal, the project has always generated more critics than admirers. Still, it did serve the purpose of concentrating thousands of state workers in the vicinity of the capitol.

But as the workforce ballooned in the 1980s, little effort was made to accommodate the new growth in the center of the city. Many agencies located in the suburbs. By the early 1990s, downtown Albany was again forlorn, Empire State Plaza notwithstanding. The new governor, George Pataki, decided it was time to try again.

That in itself might seem a little surprising. Pataki did not come into office with a reputation as a urbanist—all of his prior experience had been in Peekskill, a small village in northern Westchester County, where he was mayor and served as a state legislator. But Peekskill underwent its own miniature revival in the 1990s as artists from New York were enticed by cheap studio space and old houses.

This hometown experience had its effect on Pataki. In 1998, he proposed and the legislature approved a $240 million "Albany plan," built around returning the central city to its former role as the nerve center of state government. "By moving state facilities into downtown areas and neighborhoods," Pataki said, "we can revitalize the cities that are so important to the state, and particularly the city of Albany. We are committed to Albany being not just the capital, but being a revitalized capital."

The Pataki administration is trying not to repeat the mistakes of the previous era. "It is important how we locate in downtowns," Ringler says, "and not just that we do so." Instead of bulldozing vast sections of town to build a massive complex, the state has built at modest scale at various locations within the existing downtown grid. The buildings line up along the sidewalk; the new architecture blends reasonably well with historic appearances.

No state government is currently attempting anything as ambitious as New York's, but a surprising number of them have a similar idea. In New Jersey, where much of the state workforce moved to leased suburban space during the 1980s, the departments of Human Services and Education have both moved back to downtown Trenton. Former Governor Christine Todd Whitman halted construction of a Revenue Division building in suburban Hamilton Township "because it was going to move jobs out of the city," according to Robert Runciano, the state's former director of Property Management and Construction.

Two years ago, Kentucky was ready to build a new office for its Transportation Cabinet. Many state legislators favored moving it out of the capital area in central Frankfort. The business community wanted to keep it there. Business won. Construction started last month on the new Transportation center, a five-story, $113 million downtown building that will house several hundred workers. "The construction of it has spurred a lot of other developments, new water and sewer lines and also private development," says Don Speer, commissioner of the state Department of Administration. Meanwhile, a nearby public-private project, the Sullivan Square Office Building, has consolidated state workers from scattered spots and attracted a graphics firm with 50 employees.

Alabama's capital, Montgomery, lost so many state offices to the suburbs that, as one visitor put it, the city presented the image "of these gleaming alabaster government buildings up on a hill and down below it was a desperate scene" of urban decay. It was the state pension fund for civil servants and teachers that turned the tide by building six prime office buildings, one of them 26 stories, to lease to state agencies along Commerce Street, in the heart of downtown, and on Dexter Avenue, which leads up to the capitol. "It stabilized a deteriorating and dying central business district," says Tommy Tyson, the city's director of planning. The influx of money and workers has generated new restaurants and led to the opening of two hotels.

The phenomenon exists in even the smallest state capitals. In Montpelier, Vermont (population 8,000), rented state offices on the outskirts are being moved to retrofitted state-owned buildings downtown. And a $10 million state office project is on the drawing board. "The policy is to invest in downtowns whenever renovating or building state office space," says Thomas Torti, Vermont's Building and General Services commissioner. "If you're coming to see the tax people, drop something off at motor vehicles and then check on personnel, those are all near each other now." The new facilities in Montpelier aim to stimulate other development through multi-use buildings with room for retail and commerce. A new state parking complex is slated to include offices and housing.

In New York's case, the Albany plan is more complicated than just a one-way return to the city. It is actually a game of musical buildings. While some agencies head back downtown, others are being shuffled around to take advantage of the space being vacated. The Transportation Department will occupy the offices that the Department of Environmental Protection has given up. The Depression-era Alfred E. Smith building, an ornate downtown landmark badly in need of renovation, is being fixed up to house workers coming in from the 350-acre Harriman campus, built in the 1960s on the outskirts of the city. The state has yet to decide whether the 16 Harriman buildings will be sold to private developers. By preliminary estimates, the plan could save at least $86 million in renovation costs and recoup millions more from sales.

Albany is not the only city in the area benefiting from the urban commitment. Across the Hudson, in tiny, blue-collar Rensselaer, the state's Office of Children and Family Services consolidated its workers, previously spread across various sites, into a renovated felt factory. Ten miles upriver in Troy, the state restored two historic structures and a defunct mall and moved in more than 1,000 workers from the Health, Labor and Law departments. About 20 miles west, Schenectady, already home to the headquarters of the state lottery, is gaining 450 Department of Transportation workers and a new office building. In distant Buffalo, an old windshield wiper factory was remodeled to create 60,000 square feet of space for the New York State Office of Temporary Disability Assistance and other tenants. "The local mayors are ecstatic," says Ringler, the General Services administrator.

Not everyone is on board. Critics trace the Troy moves to log-rolling, saying that these came at the behest of Joseph Bruno, the Senate majority leader who represents Troy. Others challenge the deal between Pataki and Jerry Jennings, the Democratic mayor of Albany, that led to the ongoing $11 million reconstruction of Pearl Street, the city's downtown backbone.

And there are those who complain that the Albany Plan relies too heavily on the buildings themselves, rather than on the less tangible investments needed for urban recovery. "State workers are downtown, and that's more people downtown," says Paul Bray, a local planning and environmental attorney and founder of a monthly civic forum, the Albany Roundtable. "But building a city is a much more nuanced, complex thing than moving offices."

Bray wants the state to provide incentives for its employees to live downtown, as well as work there, so that the city's core no longer will empty out after the work day. Critics also say the money spent on construction of bulky parking garages for each new building—a feature demanded by public employee unions—could have been used for improved bus lines or other alternatives to the automobile. "Cities make poor suburbs," Bray says. "You really need to concentrate on mass transit more than parking garages."

In truth, no one can guarantee that the return of state government to any downtown will generate a local economic revival. The sidewalks of downtown Troy, a treasure-trove of 19th-century buildings, are busier since the civil servants began arriving in 1995. But Mayor Mark Pattison warns his counterparts in New York and elsewhere not to expect new government offices to work miracles. "They are not causing the economic boom that people thought they might," Pattison told a local newspaper reporter earlier this year. "The myth of the state worker is that they don't work hard. In fact, they have just a half-hour for lunch, and when they're done working, they go back home to the family and kids just like we all do. They bring a little bit of additional business but not quite the amount we expected."

Meanwhile, at the Stagecoach coffee and sandwich shop in downtown Albany, just across the park from the new Environmental Conservation building, a longtime employee concedes it is taking a while for the relocated workers to reorient themselves to city life. "It's been good for business, but not as great as we expected," she said last fall. "They complain because there's no mall to go to, they don't have enough shops to go to. A lot of them get an hour for lunch, and they don't know what to do with themselves."

But some of the restaurant's employees have been working longer hours since the Environmental Conservation building opened. And a couple of blocks away, the owners of Lodge's, a small department store dating back to the 1800s, are renovating four long-empty storefronts for interested retail and commercial tenants.

Whatever the economic impact turns out to be, long-suffering downtown Albany seems convinced that the plan will have been worth the effort, and the cost—if only for reasons of simple logic. "It's the capital," says Chungchin Chen, executive director of the Capital District Regional Planning Commission. "The agencies are supposed to be there—instead of dispersed in the suburbs."

The Fall and Rise of Bryant Park

JULIA VITULLO-MARTIN

Shrewd developers often name their buildings for their neighborhood's most attractive asset. In this tradition, the Durst Organization recently announced that it was conferring the address of One Bryant Park on its flashy new Midtown tower, whose major tenant will be the Bank of America. On an average day in good weather, lovely, crime-free Bryant Park is wildly popular, drawing some 5,300 visitors at midday, or 900 people an acre. It is almost surely the most used urban open space in the world, exceeding even St. Mark's in Venice. The New York Times calls it "Manhattan's town square."

Yet associating any new building with Bryant Park would have been unthinkable just 20 years ago—akin to naming a building One Needle Park, which would pretty well summarize the drug den that was then Bryant Park. I remember this well because the Citizens Housing and Planning Council, my former employer, had offices on West 40th Street, Bryant Park's southern boundary. We had ringside seats for the sordid dealing and using that went on openly in the park, nestled behind the New York Public Library.

Entrepreneur Michael Fuchs, who was the first chairman of HBO, which was headquartered across the park on West 42nd Street, also remembers those days well. "It was the Wild West down there," he recalled recently. We had all come from uptown—Rockefeller Center, a good neighborhood. The Bryant Park area was so bad that people had no reason to go out. We developed a philosophy that we would make the HBO building self-sufficient, with a great cafeteria, gym, screenings, whatever people needed."

In retrospect, it may be hard to grasp that city government actually permitted the ongoing, daily degradation of such a magnificent asset. After all, the city-owned Bryant Park wasn't hidden in some obscure corner, far away from official eyes. It's been right there since the mid-19th century. It sits squarely in the middle of Midtown, surrounded by world-renowned landmarks. For example, the gorgeous Beaux-Arts New York Public Library, which opened in 1911 and uses two acres of Bryant Park, was designed by Carrère & Hastings. Raymond Hood's 1924 neo-Gothic American Radiator building, on West 40th Street, now the Bryant Park Hotel, is regarded by many architects as the finest building in New York.

The Beaux-Arts Bryant Park Studios Building, which opened in 1901, was built for a New York artist who had just returned from Paris, bringing with him the French emphasis on natural northern light. He commissioned lavish double-height workshop/residential studios with huge windows to capture the unobstructed light from Bryant Park. Yet in 1979, things were such a mess that the eminent urbanist, William Whyte, wrote about Bryant Park, "If you went out and hired the dope dealers, you couldn't get a more villainous crew to show the urgency of the situation."

Bryant Park had 150 reported robberies and 10 rapes annually, countless auto break-ins on the periphery, and a murder every other year. As a public park it was so mismanaged that it held down the property values of the surrounding neighborhood.

Today Bryant Park pumps up property values. Bank of America Senior Vice President John Saclarides says about the new tower, "Because of Bryant Park, we anticipate great employee happiness with our site. We think our employees will use the park for visitation, for reading, and for a remote office at lunch time." (The park now has free wireless fidelity Web access, known as "wi fi.") What happened?

In 1980 a group of civic-minded New Yorkers, property owners, and neighbors decided to rescue the park, and set up the Bryant Park Restoration Corporation. They spent seven years negotiating with the New York City Department of Parks and Recreation before they succeeded in getting a 15-year lease, which began in 1988. (The lease was subsequently renewed for another five years.) The BPRC immediately closed the park for five years of rebuilding.

The old design—a formal French garden—had dated from 1934, when Parks Commissioner Robert Moses, New York's master of public works, decided to elevate and isolate the park above the sidewalk. Instead of making Bryant Park an elegant respite from the congestion of midtown as intended, the isolationist design deterred desirable users while attracting undesirable users.

The new BPRC design aimed to re-people the park while raising revenues to pay for the expensive planned maintenance of several million dollars annually—far more than the city spent. The designers cut new entrances, tore down the iron fencing, ripped out high hedges, restored the fixtures, and added neoclassical kiosks for concessions.

Fixed benches were replaced with some 3,200 movable, pretty French chairs and 500 tables, providing what Mr. Biederman calls "freemarket seating." The park's Upper Terrace, which had been its most active drug market, was leased to the trendy Bryant Park Grill, which became an instant hot spot.

High standards of behavior are enforced by the security officers, whom Mr. Biederman calls "friendly but firm." They deter "little pieces of disorder," as Mr. Biederman calls misdemeanors. The old laissez-faire attitude toward disruptive behavior is gone. Neighboring business people and property owners are overjoyed.

The chairman of Mountain Development Corporation, which owns the now-landmarked Bryant Park Studios, Robert Lieb, recalled that crime was so bad in 1980 that his building could only be marketed by promising strong private security. "The park should have been a positive for us, but the drug dealing and crime made it a negative," he said.

Today, he says, his company doesn't even have to work to rent space. "Our tenants, boutique designers, and manufacturers who specialize in sales to stores like Barney's and Nordstrom's, want to be on the park." Tenants include hip designers like Theory and Angel Zimick.

"Bryant Park proves that if you build something beautiful that people can enjoy," Mr. Lieb said, "they will pay a premium price to be there." And, indeed, rents soared to the mid-50s today from $14 a square foot in 1980.

Perhaps best of all, taxpayers aren't footing the bill for the park's $4 million annual budget, which is all privately raised. While $5 million of the $18 million spent on capital improvements came from public funds, no public money has been spent on the park since 1996. It may well be the only urban park in the world supported by neither government nor charitable funds.

"Because this park is integral to the functioning of Midtown, we ask commercial interests and users to pay for it," Mr. Biederman said.

Bryant Park's successful privatization is a tribute to a selfless innovation by the public sector—permitting the private sector to step in with resources and operational skills to restore and manage a splendid public space. Most public officials wouldn't have had the courage to let the private sector take over.

New York taxpayers owe heartfelt thanks to the four mayors, beginning with Edward Koch, and the four parks commissioners, finishing with Adrian Benepe, who made this happen.

MS. VITULLO-MARTIN is a senior fellow at the Manhattan Institute.

Ground Zero in Urban Decline

Cincinnati isn't just a town down on its luck. It's the future of the American city.

SAM STALEY

Welcome to ground zero in inner-city decline: the Over-the-Rhine district in Cincinnati, Ohio. This is the neighborhood, settled a couple hundred years ago and named for the predominantly German immigrants who once populated it, that was at the center of America's most recent spasm of social turmoil. In April, after police shot an unarmed black man, hundreds of Cincinnati residents took to the streets to protest entrenched racism and economic inequities. Cincinnati—once renowned as the Queen City of the Ohio River, once dubbed "Porkopolis" for its dominance in pig processing, once famous as the home of baseball's legendary Big Red Machine—is now known for civil disorder and a sagging population. The 2000 Census underscores that Cincinnati's glory days were somewhere in the past: During the 1990s, the city lost over 30,000 residents, or about 9 percent of its population.

Any prospects for revival in this Midwestern city were dealt a staggering setback by images of smoldering fires in the streets, angry men hurling bricks through storefront windows, and shop owners holding vigil over their property with shotguns. In less than a week, more than 600 people were arrested for disorderly conduct, vandalism, and assault. Urban decay—vacant buildings, declining population, few jobs—provided the tinderbox for the riots that thrust this famously staid city into the national headlines.

If the nation was shocked—this was a town known for its conservatism, restraint, and bedrock Midwestern values—so were Cincinnati's city leaders. Prior to the riots, the business community had been cultivating the city's reputation as a bastion of middle-class values and the German work ethic, regardless of the current residents' cultural heritages. The unrest provided a dramatic counterpoint to other recent development efforts. Earlier this year, in a bid to win the 2012 Summer Olympic Games, local activists and leaders put together an 800-page document touting Cincinnati's competitive advantages. In 1996, voters in Hamilton County, of which Cincinnati is a part, approved a sales tax increase to underwrite the construction of two new professional sports stadiums—a baseball-only stadium for the Reds (the nation's oldest professional baseball team) and a separate football facility for the Bengals. The city and county have also invested substantial public funds in redirecting Port Washington Way, a freeway providing easy access to downtown from the outer edge of the metropolitan area.

All told, those recent investments in downtown and riverfront improvements have cost Hamilton County residents close to $1 billion, and that's not counting the interest on bonds. The city lists 34 projects on its downtown development plan; if everything on that wish list gets built, the total price tag would be something like $4 billion. And yet Cincinnati has little to show for the effort, other than some white-elephant public works projects and the wreckage—physical and emotional—from this spring's riots. "The problems of the city," notes city councilman Phil Heimlich, "are not so much that white and black people don't get along; it's that white and black people don't stick around. I think the most important fact is that the city has lost almost 10 percent of its population over the last 10 years."

Cincinnati is a very specific place: Well-known for its steep hills and riverfront location, it has been built into its landscape in a singular and striking way (Winston Churchill once called it "America's most beautiful inland city"). Yet Cincinnati is also a very generic place in today's America. It's a city smack dab in the middle of a long, slow decline—not just in population but in prospects for the future. Its story—a sad one, though not without some measure of hope—is one that is being played out in urban centers throughout the country. The reasons for Cincinnati's decline and the misguided attempts to reverse it are all too representative of what's happening throughout the U.S. today. For good and ill, what's happening in Cincinnati may well be coming to a city near you. If, in fact, it's not already there.

In 2001, the Fannie Mae Foundation studied three dozen of the nation's largest cities and found that most have been losing population since the 1970s. While some cities gained population during the '90s—including such long-bleeding cosmopolises as New York and Chicago—more lost ground: Cincinnati, Cleveland, Milwaukee, Rochester, Syracuse, Toledo, Baltimore, Buffalo, Detroit, Philadelphia, St. Louis, and the District of Columbia, among others, continued long traditions of population decline.

A closer look inside Cincinnati's city limits reveals a more troubling trend: Only three of its 48 neighborhoods added people between 1990 and 2000. One of those neighborhoods—Queensgate—only grew because the city built a new jail. Twenty-six neighborhoods lost more than 10 percent of their population. The Over-the-Rhine area saw its population shrink from 9,572 people to 7,638.

A Long Line of Spenders

Cincinnati's recent orgy of high-profile, publicly funded projects is hardly its first. At the turn of the 19th century, public works projects served mainly to line the pockets of political boss George B. Cox's friends, earning Cincinnati the reputation of a corrupt frontier burg. The excesses of corrupt city bosses helped inspire a series of reform groups, including the Taxpayers' League, in 1880. By the early 20th century, the same sort of public works projects were carried out in the name of social welfare—whether the project in question entailed constructing a 15-mile commuter rail and subway system or taking over the local utilities. Despite its public profligacy, Cincinnati ranked among the nation's largest cities at the turn of the 19th century—a gateway to the West and a thriving commercial center sustained by the Ohio River and the Miami-Erie canal. The city quickly became a center for industry, hosting the nation's largest concentration of factories making soap, cleaners, shortening, candles, oils, and chemicals. The legacy is symbolically embodied in the twin towers of Procter & Gamble's world headquarters in the heart of the city's downtown. Pork processing and beer brewing rounded out the list of major industries.

The city's German history reaches back nearly two centuries. An ethnic German was elected its first mayor in 1802, and by the 1840s, the city was printing bilingual ordinances. By the mid-19th century, one-fifth of Cincinnati's population spoke German, and Germans are largely credited with the expansion of savings and loans, called "bauvereins," that created a foundation of homeownership among the middle and working classes. Even in the mid-20th century, high-rise apartment buildings were scarce, an architectural legacy that benefits even the poorest neighborhoods, including Over-the-Rhine.

In the wake of the riots, city leaders created a task force—Cincinnati Can—and charged it with developing recommendations to address the simmering problems of urban decline. The effort is strikingly similar to Rebuild LA, the largely ineffective effort to revitalize South Central Los Angeles after its riots in 1992. Whether Cincinnati Can actually does anything to revitalize the city, this much seems certain: It will provide cover for dozens of other projects that elected officials and prominent business leaders have trumpeted in recent years to stimulate the city. For instance, city leaders are pushing hard to expand the money-losing, municipally owned and operated Dr. Albert A. Sabin Convention Center. The proposal would double the size of the current convention center to more than 600,000 square feet.

Citizens for Civic Renewal, a nonprofit local urban reform organization, commissioned "regional government" guru Myron Orfield to do a study of the region. Orfield, an elected representative in the Minnesota state legislature, is best known for *Metropolitics*, an influential 1997 book published by the Brookings Institution that argued that declining inner suburbs were as much a victim of sprawl as central cities. Orfield's preliminary report, released earlier this year, highlighted growing inequalities among the city, its inner suburbs, and the growing outer suburbs, and called for regional planning to minimize them.

> What seems to be missing in the mess of publicly financed projects is any rational—let alone balanced—debate on whether such endeavors have *any* positive effects, much less the pie-in-the-sky results proponents routinely claim.

If his past is any prologue, Orfield's final report, to be released later this year, will call for more regional government and revenue-sharing to redistribute income from relatively wealthy neighborhoods (and suburbs) to relatively poor inner-city neighborhoods (and suburbs). A multibillion-dollar light-rail project has also been proposed by the Ohio-Kentucky-Indiana council of governments (OKI), an organization that includes 105 representatives of government, business, social, and civic groups in an eight-county region. Proponents argue that the rail system will do just about everything—reduce regional congestion, promote economic development, revitalize inner-city neighborhoods, and constrain sprawl.

The Actual Effects

What seems to be missing in the mess of publicly financed projects is any rational—let alone balanced—debate on whether such endeavors have *any* positive effects, much less the pie-in-the-sky results proponents routinely claim. Sports stadiums have emerged as a classic case in point. "Adding professional sports teams and stadiums to a city's economy does not increase aggregate spending for the city," wrote Lake Forest College economist Robert Baade, a leading expert on the subject, in a 1996 study. In fact, according to Baade's research, adding teams "appears to realign leisure spending rather than adding to it and is, therefore, neutral with regard to job creation." Baade's conclusions are based on his analysis of economic growth in 48 cities between 1958 and 1987, some with and others without new professional sports stadiums. Other analysts go even further, arguing that public investment in a sports stadium might reduce economic growth by siphoning money away from other important projects, such as road improvements, or from lowering taxes.

Clemson political scientist David Swindell echoes Baade's concerns. Swindell has studied the general economic and neighborhood impacts of minor and major league professional sports stadiums in places as varied as Indianapolis; Fort Wayne, Indiana; Arlington, Texas; and Cincinnati. He stresses that stadiums and convention centers have a "marginal impact" and "might even be negative"; he has seen "no evidence to support subsidies for private companies" in this way.

"Part of the problem," says one frustrated elected official in Cincinnati who requested anonymity, is that "people in this city look around and ask what [nearby] Indianapolis has done and they want to do that better." There's no question that Indianapolis, just a couple of hours northwest of Cincinnati, has grown in a major way, adding more than 40,000 people to its population between 1990 and 2000. Although Indianapolis is more than four times larger than Cincinnati (362 square miles vs. 78 for Cincinnati), Cincinnatians still compare the cities since their respective metropolitan areas are about the same size: 1.5 million people. Between 1974 and 1992, the period of the most intense investment in its downtown, Indianapolis funneled $2.76 billion into various development projects, most of which were centered on sports.

The civic leaders who cite these cases fail to check the peer-reviewed academic research that shows that Indianapolis' downtown development has largely failed. One of the most extensive studies of Indianapolis comes from Clemson's Swindell, Indiana University political scientists Michael Przybylski and Daniel Mullins, and Mark Rosentraub, author of *Major League Losers* and director of Indiana University's Center for Urban Policy and the Environment. Published in the *Journal of Urban Affairs* in 1994, the study found that such investments in Indianapolis increased sports-related employment by 60 percent. But since these jobs accounted for just 0.32 percent of all jobs in the Indianapolis economy, the overall effect on economic development was negligible.

"Indianapolis' focus on its downtown area and sports as a development strategy was associated with a general trend of increased employment and economic growth," conclude the authors. "However, Indianapolis' strategy did not result in more growth than was experienced by other Midwestern communities and did not lead to a concentration of higher paying jobs in the region." In short, Indianapolis' growth was the result of larger regional economic trends and the expansion of existing businesses, including a dramatic increase in Indiana University-Purdue University's employment base from 3,000 full-time faculty and staff to 8,200. Moreover, although the city's raw population grew from 1990 to 2000, its share of the region's population fell from 52.9 percent to 48.8 percent.

And even if public-sector investments did fuel job growth downtown, nearby neighborhoods would still be unlikely to see benefits. Consider Cleveland, the notorious Rust Belt city that pumped millions of public dollars into revitalizing its downtown during the 1980s. The value of commercial properties downtown doubled in value during that decade, but commercial property values outside the downtown fell by 4 percent overall.

Ironically, while local leaders look to other cities for new programs and projects, few look to those cities whose citizens have rejected such measures. Just two hours up I-71 from Cincinnati, voters in Columbus, Ohio, turned down a 1997 measure to publicly finance a new soccer stadium and a new hockey arena. Both facilities were eventually built anyway—with mostly private money—and both now house professional sports teams, despite predictions that public funding would be crucial to land the franchises.

Studies by the Pound

Cincinnati's emphasis on large, visible downtown development projects is in part a reflection of the "expert" advice proffered by consultants who have "studied" their "feasibility" and "economic benefits." In the case of the city's convention center, consultants concluded that Cincy needed a bigger (and more expensive) facility to compete with other cities. More recently, OKI released the results of its study from a national consulting firm "quantifying" the benefits of the first leg of the proposed multibillion dollar rail system, a light-rail trolley line extending from Northern Kentucky through the downtown of Cincinnati and up to its northern suburbs.

The studies seem endless at times, and the intent of most is transparent. One, written by Vanderbilt management professor Richard W. Oliver, purported to show the economic benefits of having the NHL Predators in Nashville. It was titled: *They Shoot! They Score! NHL Nashville Predators Score Winning Goal for Middle Tennessee!* Convention center expansions fit the same mold. "The rhetoric of convention center investment is drawn from 'feasibility studies' often developed by a national accounting or economic research firm," explains Heywood Sanders, a professor of political science at the University of Texas at San Antonio. Sanders has researched convention centers and their economic impacts for almost two decades, reviewing dozens of feasibility studies and writing numerous professional articles and reports, including a highly regarded 1998 article in the policy journal *The Public Interest*. "These studies lay out an invariably positive market analysis, justifying more local convention space and lending visible, supposedly objective support to political pressures to spend more public money for convention centers."

The studies are little more than marketing tools for chambers of commerce pushing one project or another; despite popular local support, big and small cities across the nation are littered with failed economic development projects, almost all dramatically oversold by their proponents. What's too often missing is the bottom line.

In a study last year written for the Boston-based Pioneer Institute, a market-oriented think tank focusing on Massachusetts policy issues, Sanders documents the shrinking market for conventions, a harsh reality that is rarely acknowledged by gung-ho city big wigs and their consultants. Most forecasts during the 1990s for trade shows and conventions were "unreasonable and unreliable," Sanders writes. Total event counts declined from 1998 to 2001, and average trade-show attendance dropped by more than 24 percent. Large, money-making conventions are gravitating toward a select few locations—Atlanta, Orlando, Las Vegas, Chicago, and New York. Other traditional destination spots, such as Boston, haven't fared well, with events there slipping from 71 in 1996 to just 63 in 2001. Even large, vibrant, expanding metropolitan areas such as Houston or Dallas don't have what it takes to be competitive in the current convention market.

Along with stadiums and convention centers, consultants tout light-rail transit projects with reports that project fantastic benefits. Untold in these "studies" is the fact that the benefits are the product of computer models and have never been achieved in the real world. For example, in 1978, planners in Portland, Oregon, forecast that by 1990 the city's light-rail ridership would be 42,500. In reality, it was half that. In Sacramento, light-rail ridership was initially projected to be 50,000 on an average weekday. By 1998, average weekday boardings were 28,000 (slightly higher than a revised projection made once local officials had committed to the project). Studies typically highlight the congestion-relief benefits of rail transit, even as transportation planners refuse to argue that these benefits exist. Indeed, in his 1998 survey of rail transit investments built since 1980, Jonathan Richmond of Harvard's Taubman Center for Local Government concluded that none had appreciably reduced congestion in cities.

Nevertheless, OKI is pushing a 117-mile system of seven rail lines criss-crossing Cincinnati. The twin goals: to bring people back into the city and reduce road congestion. A 1998 estimate by OKI pegged the cost of the entire system at $1.8 billion. A single line running from Northern Kentucky through downtown Cincinnati to suburban Blue Ash might cost close to $900 million. And that's a conservative estimate: Large public investments are notorious for coming in over budget. A light-rail system being built in Jersey City, New Jersey, was supposed to cost $1 billion, but costs have exceeded the early estimates with just two-thirds of the track laid.

Real Development

This isn't the first time Cincinnati and Hamilton County have dabbled in rail—or been taken to the cleaners while doing so. In 1912, reformist mayor Henry Hunt proposed a 15-mile rapid rail transit system; ironically, he thought it would help relieve congestion in the inner city by letting people live farther apart from one another. By 1920, private contractors were digging tunnels in the drained Miami-Erie Canal bed. The project was abandoned in 1927, after the costs ramped up well beyond original estimates and the rampant corruption became public. The entrances to buried subway stations and rail lines are still visible for those who know where to look.

In the 1920s, when the reform-minded Charter Party was voted into office, Cincinnati became the first major city to adopt a comprehensive plan. "In this concept," notes Ohio State University professor Laurence Gerckens, one of the nation's leading authorities on the history of American planning, "legal control of community development is used as a tool for, and is subservient to, the realization of a set of long-range comprehensive community goals." Later, the city developed a freeway (the recently realigned Fort Washington Way) that was explicitly designed to bring people in from the edges of the city and dump them into the downtown.

Cincinnatians took this approach to heart. Throughout the 20th century, city leaders took on one scheme after another using public money. Urban renewal and federal dollars helped pave over and renovate the Union Terminal railroad station on the West Side of town in the 1970s. Cincinnati also poured millions into the perennially troubled convention center in the 1960s, giant Riverfront Stadium in the 1970s, and the Fountain Square and Fountain Square West developments in the 1980s. The '90s, of course, brought stadiums for the Reds and the Bengals.

It's tempting to blame such projects on the "edifice complex," well-known among elected officials who want to leave their mark on a landscape. But such projects aren't simply the brainchild of elected officials or faceless bureaucrats. The business community consistently provides very visible support. With corporate giants such as Procter & Gamble and Chiquita Banana headquartered downtown, the Cincinnati business community flexes its muscle for public largess, especially in the core city. "Cincinnati is one of the clearest cases of the 'Downtown will save us' approach," says one outside observer still advising local officials. "In any other context, the business community would be talking about the virtues of unfettered free markets. When it comes to protecting 'their' investments in the core city, they are unified in their belief the public sector should pay for it—anything goes."

> **There's always hope for down-on-their-heels urban areas. Even in Cincinnati, spontaneous economic development is happening right under the noses of local officials despite apparent "neglect" by the well-heeled big business sector.**

Such efforts are not only ineffective and wasteful. They stand in stark contrast to the bottom-up economic development efforts that pop up in neighborhood after neighborhood, often right under the noses of local development officials. One of the most dramatic examples is "Toy Town" near downtown Los Angeles. As city leaders were throwing around millions of dollars in post-riot Los Angeles through the high-profile but ineffective Republic LA, Charlie Woo was taking advantage of a market opportunity. Mr. Woo, a Hong Kong-born former graduate student in physics at UCLA, realized the depressed downtown real-estate market allowed him to buy or lease old warehouse space for $1 or $2 per square foot. He used those bargain-basement prices to get a foothold in the toy manufacturing and distribution industry. Over the ensuing decade, more and more toy distributors, manufacturers, and retailers took advantage of the accessible and affordable location, building the area into an economic juggernaut employing 5,000 people and generating half a billion dollars in sales annually. City officials were completely unaware of Toy Town until its presence was simply too large to ignore any longer (See "Movers & Shakers," December 2000.)

So there's always hope for down-on-their-heels urban areas. Indeed, even in Cincinnati, spontaneous economic development is happening right under the noses of local officials despite apparent "neglect" by the well-heeled big-business sector. About 80 technology-focused companies have located along a 10-block stretch of Main Street in Over-the-Rhine, making up what has become known as the "Digital Rhine" (digitalrhine. com). To some extent, the tech district is the product of Main

Street Ventures, a private development company that owns five buildings and provides space to 13 businesses.

The Digital Rhine

Created in 1999, Main Street Ventures is a private effort to promote tech companies in the Digital Rhine. It is also a response to a market trend in Cincinnati. Tech businesses were sprouting up all across the region, but a few local leaders thought that concentrating the budding industry in one area would give it the synergies necessary to grow. By attracting similar businesses to the Digital Rhine, investors also felt they could get more attention from venture capitalists, banks, consultants, and technology providers. Main Street Ventures grabbed the attention of some tech-sector heavy hitters: Taft, Stettinius & Hollister, Procter & Gamble, Oracle, Whittman-Hart, Compaq, Microsoft, Broadwing, Lucent, Deloitte & Touche, Fifth Third Bank, and the Greater Cincinnati Chamber of Commerce all provided substantial resources that allowed it to expand its services.

Why is this happening in Over-the-Rhine, one of the poorest neighborhoods in the city? Access to technology is one factor. Cincinnati Bell, the local telephone utility, laid fiber optic cables here and, based on proximity, it was the easiest, least costly access point.

But location isn't the whole story. The district also has a key amenity in abundance: historic architecture, with many buildings dating to the 1840s and 1860s. As urban renewal was bulldozing other parts of the city, the Over-the-Rhine district maintained its architectural integrity. Rents were also affordable, typically half the going rate in other parts of the city, Artists, bars, and restaurants had pioneered a commercial foothold on the first floors of many buildings. Main Street Ventures leased a floor in a building and advertised for resident companies. In 1991, the first two—PlanetFeedback, an on-line consumer empowerment firm, and ConnectMail, an electronic video messaging company—moved in.

The spontaneous establishment of a commercial district in a hot new market, however, didn't prompt a flood of public money and support from city council. Which isn't to say that the city council completely neglected the fledgling commercial center. "The city has done a super job with infrastructure improvements," notes George Molinsky, an attorney with Taft, Stettinius & Hollister who is widely credited with spearheading revitalization efforts in the district. The city has invested in new sidewalks, stepped up policing, buried wiring, provided decorative lighting, and created a façade program to spiff up several neglected buildings. "This helped create an environment conducive to additional investment by the private sector," notes Molinsky.

But in terms of public outlays, that's about it. While the Digital Rhine continues to get vocal and productive support from several city council members and local pols, the city has largely taken a hands-off approach, letting the private sector lead the way.

What of the riots? They were, after all, in Over-the-Rhine, though not in the high-tech end of the neighborhood. But Los Angeles has shown that riots do not have to be a death knell for neighborhoods. South Central's population climbed to almost 1 million in the 1990s. Almost 3,000 manufacturers are still located there, employing 80,000 people.

Similarly, the early signs after the Cincinnati riots are positive in the Digital Rhine. No companies left because of the unrest, and several have actually moved in. As long as the city provides the sort of minimal infrastructure it has in the past, there's no reason the Digital Rhine—and other entrepreneurial zones—can't flourish.

Yet cities such as Cincinnati make such development more difficult by continuing to focus on white elephants rather than the basic reforms that can help generate a broad economic base. Developers complain that many building inspectors are too narrowly focused on minimizing any risk when they should be letting the market innovate and diversify. Inspectors are focused on the narrowest interpretation of the law, and many rulings are arbitrary. Many developers in Cincinnati think of this as the cost of doing business, but it makes those areas less competitive than their suburban counterparts. Red tape shouldn't be considered simply another cost.

The city requires six complete documents to get a permit, and another week to process the permit once the documents are signed. On top of that, Hamilton County requires up to an additional two weeks. Obtaining a building permit takes only two days in nearby Clarmont County. Warren County, north of Cincinnati, requires one week. Developers expect four to six weeks in the city of Cincinnati. Builders also complain of not being able to find employees to start the permit application process in the city's Department of Public Works. Building standards sometimes double the costs of laying infrastructure on properties. "As a result," notes one large homebuilder, "we have made the decision to substantially limit our building in the city to projects that are financially feasible. Unfortunately, a project in the city rarely qualifies as being financially feasible. It simply isn't worth it for us."

Housing activists have also effectively created a moratorium on new construction in Over-the-Rhine. How? By passing ordinances that require developers to pony up the equivalent of $4 per square foot for low-income housing if they want to tear down an existing house. The unintended consequence is "demolition by neglect"—property owners let their properties deteriorate to the point where inspectors have to condemn the building, allowing them to circumvent the ordinance, tear down the building, and develop the property.

No Magic Bullets

Still, some key players are trying to improve the overall business climate and move away from the big-spending, big-ticket items that have historically plagued Cincinnati's development strategy. City Council member Pat DeWine pushed through legislation that eliminated entire classes of permits for minor repairs and renovations to homes. A bigger change, however, may come when the city reforms its 38-year-old zoning code. The city did little to overhaul the code before a comprehensive review process began in 2000. The goal, says Steven Kurtz, a planner in the city's land-use management division since 1991, is to create more certainty in the process by simplifying zoning and development review. Kurtz notes that the revised code should reduce the number of zoning districts, streamline the public hearing process, and allow more varied and mixed uses. Planners hope to send a draft ordinance to the planning commission by the end of the year. These are small steps, to be sure, but important ones.

The larger lesson for Cincinnati and other cities is to look beyond a single magic bullet—the one major project or set of projects that true believers think will pull a city into great times.

The larger lesson for Cincinnati and other cities is to look beyond a single magic bullet—the one major project or set of projects that true believers think will pull a city into great times. "I tell folks in Cincinnati the same thing I tell them in other medium-sized cities," says convention center expert Sanders. "You are pursuing a strategy that is essentially imitative; at the same time you're discussing expanding your convention center, so are all other cities."

David Swindell, the Clemson political scientist, reinforces the point. "Many politicians know full well that there are no magic bullets, but getting a new neighborhood grocery store is not front page news, and it takes a lot of work to create a climate so that one will locate in a given area." In the meantime, warns Swindell, politicians chase white elephants in their downtowns. The result is that a "lot of needs go unmet—streets are slow to be paved. More attention needs to be paid to the neighborhoods because they are important to providing a quality of life that can attract people to the inner city."

The best advice for urban renewal might come from the people actually investing in the Digital Rhine. "Do an exceptional job when it comes to the basic issues that cities are responsible for, such as infrastructure," says Molinsky. "Tax incentives are nice," he continues, but entrepreneurially minded people really want to live and work in neighborhoods that are "clean, safe, affordable, interesting, and eclectic, with valuable amenities."

Whether Cincinnati and other cities can learn this lesson is not clear. But their futures are riding on it.

SAM STALEY (sams@rppi.org) is director of the Urban Futures Program at the Reason Public Policy institute and co-founder of the Buckeye Institute for Public Policy Solutions, a think tank based in Columbus, Ohio. Staley has written widely on planning and land use. He recently co-edited, with Randall G. Holcombe, *Smarter Growth: Market-Based Strategies for Land Use Planning in the 21st Century* (Greenwood Press).

Saving Buffalo from Extinction

Refugees from war-torn countries could help revive a dying city—but first, they'll have to stop fleeing it.

David Blake

Soe Soe and Hla Ohn met in a Thai refugee camp. Both belonged to separate rebel forces battling Burma's ruling military junta, which had killed or enslaved 30,000 people in the last 10 years. They spent seven years in the camp, where they fell in love, married and had their first child, Khin Hsint. In the spring of 2000, they moved into an apartment on 14th Street, in the West Side, one of the poorest neighborhoods in one of America's most woebegone cities: Buffalo, New York.

The West Side is known for transvestite prostitution and other trades of the underground economy, conducted mostly after dark. But during fine-weather days like this one, the street buzzes with playing children—there's a bottomless metal milk crate nailed to a telephone pole—and dueling stereos, an amalgam of Latino and African-American pop rhythms. The old houses here are well built: Soe Soe and Hla's apartment is spacious, with high ceilings, hardwood floors, nice woodwork and relatively large rooms.

The refugee resettlement agency that found them the apartment, the International Institute, also helped Soe and Hla apply for social services and find work. One of their neighbors, Thein Lwin, who goes by his pen name of Thara, was another Burmese refugee who had been in Buffalo for more than five years and had recently landed a job with Radio Free America there. A writer and an intellectual with over 60 books to his credit, all banned in his homeland, Thera is an unofficial godfather to Buffalo's small but expanding expatriate Burmese community. He speaks English, a language neither Soe nor Hla know, and was able to help them with both translation and transition. Soe would get a job; the kids would go to school. Hla was pregnant again. "We were happy," says Soe, Thera translating. "We wanted to stay."

These are people who need a place, living in a place that needs people. At the turn of the 20th century, Buffalo was one of the largest cities in the world—a national icon of growth, prosperity and optimism. Buffalo's own heyday had everything to do with the arrival of outsiders, mainly German, Irish, Italian and Polish immigrants, as well as a few African-Americans—for escaped slaves, Buffalo was the last stop before Canada on the Underground Railroad.

Today, the symbols of the city's identity are snowstorms, chicken wings and an unrelenting economic deterioration. Buffalo entered a long, slow spiral of decline when traditional industries like steel and shipping began to erode. As its industrial base withered, the city's population began to slip away, declining to just over half its 1950 high of 580,132. The lost tax revenue sunk the city's economy even deeper into its already mortal regression. In 2000, the U.S. Census put Buffalo's population under 300,000 people—292,648, to be precise—for the first time since 1890. As it thus drops in rank from a second-tier to a third-tier city, Buffalo stands to lose $2.8 million in federal block grants, and possibly one or two congressional seats as well. This past December, after being forced to lay off 433 public school teachers, the city's government began to consider a drastic solution it had always rejected before: letting Erie County swallow it whole and dissolving its own city government, effectively committing civic suicide.

Yet Buffalo has one remarkable advantage, one that defies its status as a national weather joke: This flat, swampy, snowy, isolated city has world-class geography.

The city's proximity to Canada—less than an hour away by car—along with that country's more tolerant citizenship laws, makes Buffalo a natural way station for refugees. Since 1984, thousands of asylum-seekers have filtered through Buffalo, seeking refugee status in Canada. The wandering populations come from wherever the world's latest atrocities crop up: Last October, four Afghans managed to find their way here, and in November, the number of Pakistanis spiked to 32. In the 1990s, the number crept up steadily; last year alone, at least five thousand exiles came to Buffalo to wait, making the city the crucial last stage of a journey that begins with escape from torture, starvation or death, and ends with a new life in a new country.

Roughly a thousand more refugees come to Buffalo each year to be integrated into American life by the city's four resettlement agencies. The ones who seek status in Canada could conceivably do the same: Though they're more likely to get refugee status in Canada than in the U.S., it's not unheard of for refugees to be rejected in Canada and later apply to and be accepted by the Immigration and Naturalization Service.

But in Buffalo, almost as a rule, they don't. Of the five thousand refugees who passed through Buffalo last year seeking Canadian citizenship, most are like Nasrat Mohamed: A Tanzanian who fled both political persecution and domestic abuse, she found Buffalo a desperate place. She felt sorry, she said, for people who must live there, expressing her pity to a local photographer for having grown up and lived in Buffalo all his life. She was on her way back to Canada; the idea of living in Buffalo horrified her. Of the refugees who pass through Buffalo, less than 1 percent of them try to stay.

So this class of temporary citizens continues to pass through, getting by on whatever public money they can, but never becoming a permanent part of the city or its economy. "It's kind of like they're on a train, and we're the final stop before they reach their destination," says Chris Owens, who runs Vive la Casa, the shelter where refugees wait to get their tickets into Canada. "And there's not much point in getting off here. But I wish they would."

He's not the only one. Owens and a few other local visionaries are suggesting an innovative solution to Buffalo's population problem: fill it up with refugees. "We need these people to move into our area, fill up some empty houses, fill up some jobs, bring some vitality," urges Greg Olma, a local politician.

"Historically, immigrants have been a great source of energy for New York [City], as well as other places, and that's a great thing to bring to upstate cities," agrees Robert B. Ward, director of research for the Public Policy Institute, a business-backed Albany think tank that studies New York State's economy. Last June, Ward wrote an op-ed in the *Buffalo News* suggesting the city replenish itself with refugees.

Urban growth and vitality in the U.S. has always depended on the resettlement of people from other places. The people who run cities know this, and in the past decade, those losing population have looked to refugees for salvation. Louisville, Kentucky, which created a new city office to coordinate translation and community support services, gained 20,000 immigrants and refugees in the 1990s. Boston created an Office of New Bostonians, and gained 32,000 Latino and Asian immigrants. Pittsburgh, as bereft an old steel town as Buffalo—like Buffalo, it lost about 10 percent of its population in the 1990s alone—is trying to attract refugees and other immigrants as well. Last April, a private foundation awarded four local nonprofits $800,000 to help lure immigrants with the promise of jobs. The hope is that they'll settle in, help fill up a depleted labor market—especially those ubiquitous low-wage, unskilled labor positions—buy homes and use their various talents to rebuild communities.

In Buffalo, where good jobs are scarce but low-wage jobs go begging, Ward thinks refugees could help keep local businesses in town. "We have traditionally looked at the fact that every community needs employers. If you don't have employers, people are certainly going to leave, and we certainly saw that all across western New York," he says. "But the other side

of the coin is that if people move away, then employers can't make it either. You need to have workers."

Other upstate cities have done it: Ward cites Utica, an even smaller, struggling upstate city, which manages to successfully resettle over 700 refugees a year. A study conducted at Hamilton College in upstate's Mohawk Valley found that in the first years of resettlement, refugee households cost the local economy in resources—mainly education, public assistance and Medicaid. But once they stay a certain number of years—in the Mohawk Valley, it was 13—the net economic benefits to the workforce and to the tax base begin to accumulate, and add up for as long as they stay.

But in order for Buffalo to hit that point of increasing returns, it's going to have to convince refugees to remain. These days, even some of the refugees who come expressly to Buffalo to start new lives there leave. Thara, the venerated elder of the Burmese expats, is looking to move somewhere else; Texas, he's heard, is not bad.

Soe and Hla are also finding their lives in Buffalo supply more misery than other parts of America have to offer. Soe got a job working for a pallet company in Tonawanda, north of the city. But the job only pays minimum wage, and he has to leave daily at 11 for a two o'clock shift. Without a car, it's a trip that includes three changeovers and a three-mile walk from the last bus stop. When I ask Soe why he would take a job that pays so little and is so far away, Thara, interpreting, explains that when the agency finds you a job, you are obliged to take it, or else you're on your own.

What's more, he says, the weather is unbearably frigid, and the big apartment is expensive to heat in the winter. They received heating cost assistance last year, but by the time they figured out all the paperwork and got it processed, it was already March. "The weather here is too cold," says Thara, "even in the summer."

Mostly, though, Soe wants to make more money. Living in a larger Burmese community may take some of the edge off the family's loneliness as well. There's a Burmese refugee community in Fort Wayne, Indiana, he tells me, where a worker can get a better wage. Since neither Soe nor Thara can afford to move just yet, for now they're waiting it out. "They want to move someplace warmer, where they can make more money," Thara explains. "They can get welfare anywhere."

In the end, refugees flee this dying city for the same reasons natives do: poverty, hopelessness, poor housing, worse transportation. "Why are people leaving Buffalo like crazy?" asks one refugee from Vietnam who has stayed. "It's simple. Look at Buffalo."

Vive La Casa is located off a small side street on the East Side, in an abandoned Catholic school with bars on the windows, in a neighborhood visitors are usually warned to stay away from. The refugees who stay here are cautioned not to drift too far from the grounds, but there are always a few who get mugged.

Inside, long, poorly lit corridors lead to classrooms turned into dormitories, one for men and one for women and children. People here are dressed in the clothing of their cultures:

bright colored shirts and skirts, shawls, turbans, loose-fitting and light colored for warm-weather climates—whatever they showed up here with. (One African man walked the miles from the downtown Greyhound station in a blizzard, wearing nothing but his best dinner jacket and an elegant Ascot.) Some never remove their winter hats. Others, awkwardly outfitted in old suits from charity donations, look like they could be auditioning as extras for *Casablanca*. They are all waiting, coming or going to and from nowhere in particular, playing pool, talking in clusters according to language. In the basement cafeteria someone's written *Russia Rules* in red marker on one of the walls. Underneath it, someone else wrote *Russia Sucks.*

Within the exile community, these are the lowest of the low. Even Soe and Hla's helpful neighbor Thara, the Burmese political exile and novelist who wrote about "the common man," refers to Vive's residents as "dirty illegals" and "liars," although he has never met one of them.

Five thousand people come through Vive every year, more than all the refugee resettlement agencies in Buffalo combined. All are searching for some place and possibility, but with the clerical distinction that they don't have the proper documentation and are therefore considered illegal aliens. If they were not at Vive, they would be in an INS detention facility or on the streets.

Nearly all are seeking asylum in Canada because chances of acceptance are greater there (48 percent) than they are in the U.S. (23 percent, and that was before September 11). Besides providing food and shelter, Vive helps them with their residency applications, and provides those who have been denied on their first try in Canada—and therefore must leave the land of the maple leaf for 90 days before they can reapply—a place to sit it out and hope for better luck next time.

Owens would like to encourage more of them to stay, and he has reached out to both local foundations, hoping they would sponsor a Pittsburgh-style population effort, as well as to the city's resettlement agencies. (He's also seeking international funding, since Vive functions as a de facto nongovernmental intermediary between countries.) But it's slow going: These are tough times for both Buffalo and refugees, and funding a grand international urban experiment is not high on anyone's list of priorities. Only two schools in Buffalo have resources to serve children who don't speak English, and they're both filled to capacity. Buffalo's budget crisis means there's little hope that things will get better.

Vive also has its own problems to attend to. Since late September, the agency has been filled to double capacity with refugees desperately seeking to get into Canada before this June, when strict new immigration laws prompted by 9/11 take effect there. (Among them, asylum-seekers will now have just a single opportunity to apply for Canadian citizenship before they must go back home or into the limbo of detention.) And in 1996, federal welfare reform removed New York State's obligation to fund certain services for legal immigrants. The result, for Vive, was a $400,000 budget cut. Vive would have gone out of business entirely had Erie County not decided to channel funds from other sources to the organization.

"Refugees are the largest and most silent homeless population in Buffalo," says Alex Priebe, Vive's former development officer. "When you apply for asylum in the United States, you cannot work, you cannot receive benefits. You are dependent on the kindness of anyone who will give it to you. Unless you come with money in your pocket—a lot of these people come with only the clothes on their backs—you are an orphan in a system not set up to be kind."

On a run-down section of Broadway Street, among liquor stores, bars, tattoo shops and abandoned houses, you'll find the low-slung office of the last politician who set out to make Buffalo a refugee haven. Until he lost at the polls this November, burly maverick Greg Olma was a Democratic county legislator.

The walls of Olma's office are bare, with two exceptions. On one there are the police mug shots of the actor Hugh Grant and Divine Brown, the prostitute he was picked up with a few years back. On the other is a life-size, smiling cardboard cutout of Buffalo's Common Council President, James Pitts, the powerful Democrat and political leader of Buffalo's black East Side. He's also a well-known Olma nemesis. Next to the cutout a carefully positioned cartoon balloon reads, in neat block letters: GREG OLMA IS A VERY SMART MAN!

Olma has a reputation for being outspoken and controversial, which, along with allegations of corruption (he denies them), probably contributed to his election defeat. Breaking from the fulsome provincialism and sophistry standard among the city's elected officials, he may be the only local politician who'll speak candidly about the city's pattern of spiraling decline and realistically about its prospects for revival. As county legislator, he was certainly the only one considering immigrant and refugee recruitment as part of any redevelopment plan.

"Buffalo's a sad case. It's not as bad as Youngstown, Ohio, or Gary, Indiana, or Newark, but it's pretty damn close to that," he said in an interview conducted before his defeat. "Our only hope would be to encourage immigration of people from countries that will work and maintain a partisan and ethnic enclave."

But Olma's attempt to revive the glory years of the urban immigrant political machine ran into some hitches. For one thing, Buffalo's refugee agencies are not well coordinated: They operate independently and sometimes competitively, spending their limited resources on services—like English language classes and job placement programs—that often duplicate one another.

Olma's vision, for which he got some local support but ultimately too little funding, was to combine their efforts into one comprehensive community development initiative, making it easier for refugees to buy houses right away and begin building their new lives. "Essentially, what you got to have are people from poor countries without anything," says Olma. "There's a lot of those out there, and Buffalo's a good place to bring them, because they will help build us up again."

Olma's no stranger to the power of refugees in community revitalization. In the 1980s, the city built a low-rent housing project in the Broadway-Fillmore district, the Walentynowicz Apartments, designed for post-Solidarity refugees from Krakow. Noted for its strong ethnic ties, the district became a bustling Polish neighborhood, the symbol and center of which remains the Broadway Market—a large indoor bazaar with small kiosks selling everything from ethnic food to televisions. (Regularly mired in patronage scandals, Broadway Market also became a symbol of Buffalo's tradition of graft.)

But Broadway-Fillmore's comeback faded quickly when the immigrants headed for the suburbs. The way Olma sees it, that was because the refugees weren't poor enough or desperate enough. "What you have to have to build a community—to build an ethnic community in the inner city—you've got to have lower-income immigrants who come from a certain kind of poverty situation," he explains. "The problem with European immigrants, Eastern European, is that they watched Western TV. They think this country's like *Dynasty.* And so, you get good workers and stuff; it's good for the community; it's good for your restaurant selection—if you get enough immigrants you'll get some interesting food and things like that, parties to go to. But you don't get a real community from that kind of situation.

"A lot of it has got to do with education," he continues, oblivious that he's getting into sensitive territory. "A lot of these people from Poland had some college education, or they're more Westernized, so to speak."

There are, believe it or not, things Olma doesn't say. One of them is that one reason so many Polish residents were moving out was because African-Americans were moving in. At the same time, Broadway-Fillmore, like many other parts of the city, became run down with unemployment, declining property values and hard poverty. The tiny white enclave that remains is called the Iron Triangle, as much a reference to its siege mentality as its East European flavor. "I think that's the same thing that's going to happen with the Bosnians. There's some Bosnians moving in," says Olma. "But generally speaking, they're climbers and they're going to climb right out."

For Olma, a desire to settle, stay and build a life is what distinguishes the Vietnamese from some of the other immigrating populations. "Since the Polish dried up we've had a lot of Somalians, Bosnians, Vietnamese," he says. "And the Vietnamese," he declares, "were the ones that were the most durable."

It's this "Vietnamese-type of immigrant" that serves as the model for Olma's visions of refugee-fueled revival. He describes them as being "like the old immigrants," which is to say that they buy houses in his district and tend to bring over their extended families, which means more votes—preferably for him. "They're Catholics, most of them, which is good for the Catholic parishes," he points out. "They're savers, they're frugal, and they're not glory-seekers."

This is a point Olma stresses: that the earth's truly wretched will be grateful to live in Buffalo. "To me, the best thing for refugees is not doctors and lawyers," he says. "The best refugees are able-bodied workers who have some education but are not looking for the stylized American lifestyle. They just want to get ahead, you know . . . they don't pull themselves out and

live in [suburban] Amherst, like the doctors and lawyers do. They're not that enculturated. I don't know if this sounds bad or not, but it makes perfect sense to me: Not every immigrant is as good as the other one."

Minh Tran is Olma's dream personified. He lives in a pleasant two-story house on the Lower West Side. On the corner directly opposite the house is his family's store, a tiny building so overcrowded with products and advertising that stepping inside is enough to trigger a swarming disorientation.

Minh's family arrived here in 1981 via South Vietnam, after a year in a Hong Kong refugee camp. Minh's father, a former officer in the South Vietnamese army, died in the camp, leaving Minh, his mother, two sisters and a baby brother to carry on without him. "My mother never took social services; she refused," says Minh, in a tone about as humble as a statement like that can be.

The family came over with some savings, but not enough to save Minh, who at 19 was the oldest son, from having to take a sewing job in Buffalo's old garment district to help support them all while his younger sisters and brother went off to school and, later, college. When he wasn't working, Minh was busy helping his mother run the store; to this day, he himself has never taken a college class. As a result his English, while not quite broken, is still thick with accent.

That kind of experience can cause bitterness, but there's no sense of that in Minh. Confident and charismatic, he's become a leader in Buffalo's close-knit, small, yet relatively powerful Vietnamese community. He is also a case manager at the International Institute, the agency that helped resettle his family. He gets calls at all hours from his clients, refugees new to the area who get lost, don't know how to call a taxi or need to find the nearest hospital.

Minh's *querencia,* his place of strength, comes from a mixture of individual will and genuine compassion. His success and kindness make him a local legend, but he deflects individual credit. "A lot of people help me out," he says, and specifically mentions Greg Olma.

More than once, Olma has driven across town to sit at Minh's table and talk to the local Vietnamese leaders, asking them what services they need and checking to see how many of them have registered to vote.

It was Olma who helped arrange a deal with the city so they could purchase space for a Buddhist cultural center. For those who are Catholic, it was Olma who helped them find a priest for their church.

"Greg, he welcomes people. He wants to build community," Minh says, struggling to fit a tile around a tricky corner. We are sitting on plywood that for the moment is passing as Minh's dining room floor, drinking cans of beer, while Minh is carefully measuring and laying new floor tiles. Not liking the fit, he peels it up, frowning, and tosses it over his shoulder. "There goes 99 cents," he says with a light laugh.

There are lots of pictures on the walls: family portraits, a painting of Jesus and other religious artifacts, including a large cross. I ask Minh if he's Catholic. "Yeah," he laughs, "but what is Catholic anyway, you know."

Minh thinks the whole Buffalo population crisis is way overblown. "The Census got it wrong," he insists. "Refugees weren't counted, for one; they don't know what those Census forms are or how to fill them out. And when the people come to the door to ask they come during business hours when the refugee is at work."

I ask Minh if he's concerned that Buffalo has trouble attracting immigrants and refugees who are willing to stay, and what that ultimately means for the community. "What problem?" he says. "In my mind, they all stay."

Once Minh leaves to go pick up his son from day care, though, his younger brother, Thom, says he can see why people are leaving Buffalo. "I'm not complaining; Buffalo treated me well," he adds quickly. Thom, which is not his real name but

the only one he's willing to provide, went to SUNY-Buffalo and got a business degree. Now, he works at the Walentynowicz Apartments, a job Olma got him. For $7.50 an hour, he cleans apartments and collects rents from less fortunate, more recently arrived refugees. "I know it's hard for them. They only get the minimum wage jobs," he says. "But what am I supposed to do? I have to do my job."

Sitting on the porch, after a few beers, Thom begins talking about his life here, his childhood in Ho Chi Minh City, venal politicians. About trouble and the need, sometimes, for a new start. "I would like more, of course," he says, "but people have to accept reality."

DAVID BLAKE is a writer who used to live in Buffalo. BRENDAN BANNON, who provided additional reporting for this story, has been photographing refugees in Buffalo for over two years.

Movers & Shakers

How immigrants are reviving neighborhoods given up for dead

JOEL KOTKIN

For decades the industrial area just east of downtown Los Angeles was an economic wreck, a 15-square-block area inhabited largely by pre–World War II derelict buildings. Yet now the area comes to life every morning, full of talk of toys in various South China dialects, in Vietnamese, in Korean, in Farsi, in Spanish, and in the myriad other commercial languages of the central city.

The district now known as Toytown represents a remarkable turnaround of the kind of archaic industrial area that has fallen into disuse all across the country. A combination of largely immigrant entrepreneurship and the fostering of a specialized commercial district has created a bustling marketplace that employs over 4,000 people, boasts revenues estimated at roughly $500 million a year, and controls the distribution of roughly 60 percent of the $12 billion in toys sold to American retailers.

"In December we have about the worst traffic problem in downtown," proudly asserts Charlie Woo, a 47-year-old immigrant who arrived in 1968 from Hong Kong and is widely considered the district's founding father. During the holiday season, thousands of retail customers, mostly Latino, come down to the district seeking cut-rate toys, dolls, and action figures, including dubious knockoffs of better-known brands. For much of the rest of the year, the district sustains itself as a global wholesale center for customers from Latin America and Mexico, which represent nearly half the area's shipments, as well as buyers from throughout the United States.

Few in L.A.'s business world, City Hall, or the Community Redevelopment Agency paid much attention when Woo started his family's first toy wholesaling business in 1979. "When Toytown started, the CRA didn't even know about it," recalls Don Spivack, now the agency's deputy administrator. "It happened on its own. It was a dead warehouse district."

How dead? Dave Zoraster, an appraiser at CB Richard Ellis, estimates that in the mid-1970s land values in the area—then known only as Central City East—stood at $2.75 a square foot, a fraction of the over $100 a square foot the same property commands today. Vacancy rates, now in the single digits, then hovered at around 50 percent. For the most part, Spivack recalls, development officials saw the district as a convenient place to cluster the low-income, largely transient population a safe distance from the city's new sparkling high-rises nearby.

To Charlie Woo, then working on a Ph.D. in physics at UCLA, the low land costs in the area presented an enormous opportunity. Purchasing his first building for a mere $140,000, Woo saw the downtown location as a cheap central locale for wholesaling and distributing the billions of dollars in toys unpacked at the massive twin ports of Long Beach and Los Angeles, the nation's dominant hub for U.S.-Asia trade and the world's third-largest container port. Woo's *guanxi,* or connections, helped him establish close relationships with scores of toy manufacturers in Asia, where the vast majority of the nation's toys are produced. The large volume of toys he imported then allowed him to take a 20 percent margin, compared with the 40 to 50 percent margins sought by the traditional small toy wholesalers. Today Woo and his family own 10 buildings, with roughly 70 tenants, in the area; their distribution company, Megatoys, has annual sales in excess of $30 million.

> **"Immigrants are hungrier and more optimistic," says Harvard's William Apgar. "Their presence is the difference between New York and Detroit."**

Toytown's success also has contributed to a broader growth in toy-related activity in Southern California. The region—home to Mattel, the world's largest toy maker—has spawned hundreds of smaller toy-making firms, design firms, and distribution firms, some originally located in Toytown but now residing in sleek modern industrial parks just outside the central core. Other spin-offs, including a new toy design department at the Otis College of Art and Design in West Los Angeles and the Toy Association of Southern California, have worked to secure the region's role as a major industry hub.

Woo envisions Toytown as a retail center. But whatever its future, the district's continuing success stands as testament to the ability of immigrant entrepreneurs and specialized industrial districts to turn even the most destitute urban neighborhoods around. Woo notes: "The future of Toytown will be as a gathering point for anyone interested in toys. Designers and buyers will come to see what's selling, what the customer wants. The industry will grow all over, but this place will remain ground zero."

For much of the 19th and early 20th centuries, immigrants filled and often dominated American cities. With the curtailment of immigration in the 1920s, this flow was dramatically reduced, and urban areas began to suffer demographic stagnation, and in some places rapid decline. Only after 1965, when immigration laws were reformed, did newcomers return in large numbers, once again transforming many of the nation's cities.

This was critical, because despite the movement of young professionals and others into the urban core, native-born Americans continued, on balance, to flee the cities in the 1990s. Only two of the nation's 10 largest metropolitan areas, Houston and Dallas, gained domestic migrants in the decade. As over 2.5 million native-born Americans fled the nation's densest cities, over 2.3 million immigrants came in.

The impacts were greatest in five major cities: New York, Los Angeles, San Francisco, Miami, and Chicago. These cities received more than half of the estimated 20 million legal and 3 million to 5 million illegal immigrants who arrived over the past quarter century. Without these immigrants, probably all these cities would have suffered the sort of serious depopulation that has afflicted such cities as St. Louis, Baltimore, and Detroit, which until recently have attracted relatively few foreigners.

In this two-way population flow, America's major cities and their close suburbs have become ever more demographically distinct from the rest of the country. In 1930, one out of four residents of the top four "gateway" cities came from abroad, twice the national average; by the 1990s, one in three was foreign-born, five times the norm. Fully half of all new Hispanic residents in the country between 1990 and 1996 resided in the 10 largest cities. Asians are even more concentrated, with roughly two in five residing in just three areas: Los Angeles, New York, and San Francisco.

In places such as Southern California, immigration has transformed the economic landscape. Between 1992 and 1999, the number of Latino businesses in Los Angeles County more than doubled. Some of these businesses have grown in areas that previously had been considered fallow, such as Compton and South-Central Los Angeles. In these long-established "ghettos," both incomes and population have been on the rise largely because of Latino immigration, after decades of decline.

A similar immigrant-driven phenomenon has sparked recoveries in some of the nation's most distressed neighborhoods, from Washington, D.C., to Houston. Along Pitkin Avenue in Brooklyn's Brownsville section, Caribbean and African immigrants, who have a rate of self-employment 20 to 50 percent higher than that of native-born blacks, have propelled a modest but sustained economic expansion.

The recovery of such once forlorn places stems largely from the culture of these new immigrants. Certainly Brooklyn's

infrastructure and location remain the same as in its long decades of decline. Along with entrepreneurship, the newcomers from places such as the Caribbean have brought with them a strong family ethic, a system of mutual financial assistance called *susus,* and a more positive orientation to their new place. "Immigrants are hungrier and more optimistic," notes William Apgar of Harvard's Joint Center for Housing Studies. "Their upward mobility is a form of energy. Their presence is the difference between New York and Detroit."

It is possible that newcomers to America might even be able to revive those cities that have not yet fully felt the transformative power of immigration. A possible harbinger can be seen on the South Side of St. Louis, a city largely left out of the post-1970s immigrant wave. Once a thriving white working-class community, the area, like much of the rest of the city, had suffered massive depopulation and economic stagnation.

"Bosnians," says one immigrant, "don't care if they start by buying the smallest, ugliest house. At least they feel they have something."

This began to change, however, in the late 1990s, with the movement into the area of an estimated 10,000 Bosnian refugees, along with other newcomers, including Somalis, Vietnamese, and Mexicans. Southern Commercial Bank loan officer Steve Hrdlicka, himself a native of the district, recalls: "Eight years ago, when we opened this branch, we sat on our hands most of the time. We used to sleep quite a lot. Then this place became a rallying place for Bosnians. They would come in and ask for a loan for furniture. Then it was a car. Then it was a house, for themselves, their cousins."

In 1998, largely because of the Bosnians, Hrdlicka's branch, located in a South St. Louis neighborhood called Bevo, opened more new accounts than any of the 108-year-old Southern Commercial's other six branches. Over the last two years of the 1990s, the newcomers, who have developed a reputation for hard work and thrift, helped push the number of accounts at the branch up nearly 80 percent, while deposits have nearly doubled to $40 million.

A translator at the Bevo branch, 25-year-old Jasna Mruckovski, has even cashed in on the Bosnians' homebuying tendencies. Moonlighting as a real estate salesperson, she has helped sell 33 homes in the area over the past year, all but one to Bosnian buyers. In many cases, she notes, these homes were bought with wages pooled from several family members, including children. Mruckovski, a refugee from Banjo Luka who arrived in St. Louis in 1994, observes: "St. Louis is seen as a cheap place to live. People come from California, Chicago, and Florida, where it's more expensive. Bosnians don't care if they start by buying the smallest, ugliest house. At least they feel they have something. This feeling is what turns a place like this around."

Immigration also helps cities retain their preeminence in another traditional urban economic bastion: cross-cultural trade. Virtually all the great cities since antiquity derived much of their sustenance through the intense contact between differing peoples in various sorts of markets. As world economies have developed through the ages, exchanges between races and cultures have been critical to establishing the geographic importance of particular places. Historian Fernand Braudel suggests, "A world economy always has an urban center of gravity, a city, as the logistic heart of its activity. News, merchandise, capital, credit, people, instructions, correspondence all flow into and out of the city. Its powerful merchants lay down the law, sometimes becoming extraordinarily wealthy."

Repeatedly throughout history, it has been outsiders—immigrants—who have driven cross-cultural exchange. "Throughout the history of economics," observes social theorist Georg Simmel, "the stranger appears as the trader, or the trader as stranger." In ancient Greece, for example, it was *metics,* largely foreigners, who drove the marketplace economy disdained by most well-born Greeks. In Alexandria, Rome, Venice, and Amsterdam—as well as the Islamic Middle East—this pattern repeated itself, with "the stranger" serving the critical role as intermediary.

As in Renaissance Venice, the increasing ethnic diversity of America's cities plays a critical role in their domination of international trade.

As in Renaissance Venice and early modern Amsterdam or London, the increasing ethnic diversity of America's cities plays a critical role in their domination of international trade. Over the past 30 years, cities such as New York, Los Angeles, Houston, Chicago, and Miami have become ever more multiethnic, with many of the newcomers hailing from growing trade regions such as East Asia, the Caribbean, and Latin America. The large immigrant clusters in these cities help forge critical global economic ties, held together not only by commercial bonds but by the equally critical bonds of cultural exchange and kinship networks.

These newcomers have redefined some former backwaters into global trading centers. Miami's large Latino population—including 650,000 Cubans, 75,000 Nicaraguans, and 65,000 Colombians—has helped turn the one-time sun-and-fun capital into the dominant center for American trade and travel to South America and the Caribbean. Modesto Maidique, president of Florida International University, who is himself a Cuban émigré, observes: "If you take away international trade and cultural ties from Miami, we go back to being just a seasonal tourist destination. It's the imports, the exports, and the service trade that have catapulted us into the first rank of cities in the world."

Like the *souk* districts of the Middle East, diversified cities provide an ideal place for the creation of unique, globally oriented markets. These *souks,* which are fully operational to this day, are home mostly to small, specialized merchants. In most cases, the districts consisted of tiny unlighted shops raised two or three feet from street level. Stores are often grouped together by trade, allowing the consumer the widest selection and choice.

The emergence of the Western *souk* is perhaps most evident in Los Angeles, home to Toytown. Within a short distance of that bustling district are scores of other specialized districts—the downtown Fashion Mart, the Flower district, and the jewelry, food, and produce districts are crowded with shoppers, hustlers, and buyers of every possible description. These districts' vitality contrasts with the longstanding weakness of downtown L.A.'s office market, which has been losing companies and tenants to other parts of the city.

Similar trade-oriented districts have arisen in other cities, such as along Canal Street in New York, in the "Asia Trade District" along Dallas's Harry Hines Boulevard, and along the Harwin Corridor in the area outside the 610 Loop in Houston. Once a forlorn strip of office and warehouse buildings, the Harwin area has been transformed into a car-accessed *souk* for off-price goods for much of East Texas, featuring cut-rate furniture, novelties, luggage, car parts, and electronic goods.

These shops, owned largely by Chinese, Korean, and Indian merchants, have grown from roughly 40 a decade ago to more than 800, sparking a boom in a once-depressed real estate market. Over the decade, the value of commercial properties in the district has more than tripled, and vacancies have dropped from nearly 50 percent to single digits. "It's kind of an Asian frontier sprawl around here," comments David Wu, a prominent local store owner.

Indeed, few American cities have been more transformed by trade and immigration than Houston. With the collapse of energy prices in the early 1980s, the once booming Texas metropolis appeared to be on the road to economic oblivion. Yet the city has rebounded, in large part because of the very demographic and trade patterns seen in the other Sun Belt capitals. "The energy industry totally dominated Houston by the 1970s—after all, oil has been at the core of our economy since 1901," explains University of Houston economist Barton Smith. "Every boom leads people to forget other parts of the economy. After the bust, people saw the importance of the ports and trade."

Since 1986, tonnage through the 25-mile-long Port of Houston has grown by one-third, helping the city recover the jobs lost during the "oil bust" of the early 1980s. Today, Smith estimates, trade accounts for roughly 10 percent of regional employment and has played a critical role in the region's 1990s recovery: By 1999 a city once renowned for its plethora of "see-through" buildings ranked second in the nation in total office space absorption and third in rent increases.

Immigrants were the critical factor in this turnaround. Between 1985 and 1990, Houston, a traditional magnet for domestic migrants, suffered a net loss of over 140,000 native-born residents. But the immigrants kept coming—nearly 200,000 over the past decade, putting the Texas town among America's seven most popular immigrant destinations.

Among those coming to Houston during the 1970s boom was a Taiwan-born engineer named Don Wang, who in 1987 founded his own immigrant-oriented financial institution, Metrobank. Amid the hard times and demographic shifts, Wang and his clients—largely Asian, Latin, and African immigrants—saw an enormous opportunity to pick up real estate, buy homes, and start businesses. Minority-owned enterprises now account for nearly 30 percent of Houston's business community.

Says Wang: "In the 1980s everyone was giving up on Houston. But we stayed. It was cheap to start a business here and easy to find good labor. We considered this the best place to do business in the country, even if no one on the outside knows it.… When the oil crisis came, everything dropped, but it actually was our chance to become a new city again."

Increasingly, the focus of immigrants—and their enterprise—extends beyond the traditional *souk* economy to a broader part of the metropolitan geography. Most dramatic has been the movement to the older rings of suburbs, which are rapidly replacing the inner city as the predominant melting pots of American society. This trend can be seen across the nation, from the Chinese- and Latino-dominated suburbs east of Los Angeles to the new immigrant communities emerging in southern metropolitan areas such as Houston, Dallas, and Atlanta. This move marks a sharp contrast to the immediate postwar era, when these suburbs, like their high-tech workforces, remained highly segregated.

The demographic shift in the near suburbs started in the 1970s, when African-Americans began moving to them in large numbers. In the ensuing two decades, middle-class minorities and upwardly mobile recent immigrants have shown a marked tendency to replace whites in the suburbs, particularly in the inner ring, increasing their numbers far more rapidly than their Anglo counterparts. Today nearly 51 percent of Asians, 43 percent of Latinos, and 32 percent of African Americans live in the suburbs.

This development is particularly notable in those regions where immigration has been heaviest. Among the most heavily Asian counties in the nation are such places as Queens County in New York, Santa Clara and San Mateo counties in Northern California, and Orange County, south of Los Angeles. Queens and Fort Bend County, in suburban Houston, rank among the 10 most ethnically diverse counties in the nation.

The melting pot has spilled into the suburbs. About 51 percent of Asians, 43 percent of Latinos, and 32 percent of African Americans live in the suburbs.

Today these areas have become as ethnically distinctive as the traditional inner cities themselves, if not more so. Some, like Coral Gables, outside of Miami, have become both ethnic and global business centers. Coral Gables is home to the Latin American division headquarters of over 50 multinationals.

Other places, such as the San Gabriel Valley east of Los Angeles, have accommodated two distinct waves of ethnic settlement, Latino and Asian. Cities such as Monterey Park, Alhambra, and San Gabriel have become increasingly Asian in character; areas such as Whittier and La Puente have been transformed by Latino migration. Yet in both cases, the movement is predominantly by middle-class homeowners. "For us this isn't a dream, this is reality," notes Frank Corona, who moved to the area from East Los Angeles. "This is a quiet, nice, family-oriented community."

The reason the melting pot has spilled into the suburbs lies in the changing needs of immigrants. In contrast to the early 20th century, when proximity to inner-city services and infrastructure was critical, many of today's newcomers to a more dispersed, auto-oriented society find they need to stop only briefly, if at all, in the inner cities. Their immediate destination after arrival is as likely to be Fort Lee as Manhattan, the San Gabriel Valley as Chinatown or the East L.A. barrios. Notes Cal State Northridge demographer James Allen: "The immigrants often don't bother with the inner city anymore. Most Iranians don't ever go to the center city, and few Chinese ever touch Chinatown at all. Many of them want to get away from poor people as soon as possible."

As proof, Allen points to changes in his own community, the San Fernando Valley, which for a generation was seen as the epitome of the modern suburb. In the 1960s, the valley was roughly 90 percent white; three decades later it was already 44 percent minority, with Latinos representing nearly one-third the total population. By 1997, according to county estimates, Latinos were roughly 41 percent of the valley population, while Asians were another 9 percent.

Similarly dramatic changes have taken place outside of California. Twenty years ago, Queens County was New York's largest middle-class and working-class white bastion, the fictional locale of the small homeowner Archie Bunker. Today it is not Manhattan, the legendary immigrant center, but Queens that is easily the most diverse borough in New York, with thriving Asian, Latino, and middle-class African-American neighborhoods. Over 40 percent of the borough's businesses are now minority-owned, almost twice as high as the percentage in Manhattan.

This alteration in the suburban fabric is particularly marked in the American South, which largely lacks the infrastructure of established ethnic inner-city districts. Regions such as Atlanta experienced some of the most rapid growth in immigration in the last two decades of the millennium; between 1970 and 1990, for example, Georgia's immigrant population grew by 525 percent. By 1996, over 11.5 million Asians lived in the South. Yet since most Southern cities lacked the preexisting structure of an ethnic Asian or Latino community to embrace the newcomers, most new immigrants chose to cluster not in the central city but in the near suburbs.

"Well, we still have one fried-chicken place left somewhere around here," jokes Houston architect Chao-Chiung Lee over dim sum in one of the city's heavily Asian suburbs. "It's a kind of the last outpost of the native culture lost amid the new Chinatown."

Yet if the successes of immigrants represent the success of the melting pot, the demographic shift also presents some potential challenges. In addition to a swelling number of entrepreneurs and scientists, there has been a rapid expansion of a less-educated population. For example, Latinos, the fastest-growing group in Silicon Valley, account for 23 percent of that region's population but barely 7 percent of its high-tech work force. Part of the problem lies with education: Only 56 percent of Latinos graduate from high school, and less than one in five takes the classes necessary to get into college.

Indeed, as the economy becomes increasingly information-based, there are growing concerns among industry and political leaders that many of the new immigrants and, more important, their children may be unprepared for the kind of jobs that are opening up in the future. Immigrants may be willing to serve as bed changers, gardeners, and service workers for the digital elites, but there remains a serious question as to whether their children will accept long-term employment in such generally low-paid and low-status niches.

George Borjas, a leading critic of U.S. immigration policy and professor of public policy at Harvard's John F. Kennedy School of Government, suggests that recent immigration laws have tilted the pool of newcomers away from skilled workers toward those less skilled, seriously depleting the quality of the labor pool and perhaps threatening the social stability of the immigration centers. "The national economy is demanding more skilled workers," Borjas says, "and I don't see how bringing more unskilled workers is consistent with this trend. . . . When you have a very large group of unskilled workers, and children of unskilled workers, you risk the danger of creating a social underclass in the next [21st] century."

In the coming decades, this disconnect between the labor force and the economy in some areas could lead to an exodus of middle-class people and businesses to less troubled places, as happened previously in inner cities. Across the country, many aging suburbs, such as Upper Darby near Philadelphia and Harvey outside Chicago, are well on the way to becoming highly diverse suburban slums as businesses move farther out into the geographic periphery. Others—in regions including Boston, New Orleans, Cleveland, St. Louis, Dallas, and Indianapolis—now struggle to retain their attractiveness.

If unchecked, a broader ghettoization looms as a distinct possibility, particularly in some of the older areas filled with smaller houses and more mundane apartment buildings. These areas could become—as have some suburbs of Paris—dysfunctional, balkanized losers in the new digital geography. "It's a different place now. We can go either way," says Robert Scott, a former L.A. planning commissioner and leader of the San Fernando Valley's drive to secede from Los Angeles.

Scott grew up in the once all-white, now predominantly Latino community of Van Nuys. "The valley can become a storehouse of poverty and disenchantment," he says, "or it can become a series of neighborhoods with a sense of uniqueness and an investment in its future." As Scott suggests, for these new melting pots, the best course may be not so much to try clinging to their demographic past as to find a way to seize the advantages of their more diverse roles, both economically and demographically. No longer "lily white" enclaves, such communities increasingly must draw their strength, as the great cities before them did, from the energies, skills, and cultural offerings of their increasingly diverse populations.

No longer "lily white" enclaves, suburbs must draw their strength, as the great cities before them did, from their increasingly diverse populations.

JOEL KOTKIN (jkotkin@pacbell.net) is a senior fellow with the Pepperdine University Institute for Public Policy and a research fellow of the Reason Public Policy Institute. Excerpted from the book *The New Geography: How the Digital Revolution Is Reshaping the American Landscape* by Joel Kotkin. Copyright © 2000 by Joel Kotkin. Reprinted by arrangement with Random House Trade Publishing, a division of Random House Inc.

The Gentry, Misjudged As Neighbors

JOHN TIERNEY

We all think we know how gentrification works. Developers and yuppies discover charm in an old neighborhood, and soon the very people who created the neighborhood can't afford it anymore. Janitors and artists are forced out of their homes to make room for lawyers and bankers.

This process has been routinely denounced in neighborhoods like Harlem and Park Slope in Brooklyn. But when researchers recently looked for evidence of such turnover, the results were surprising.

Gentrification does not cause an exodus of the poor and the working class, according to a study in New York and another in Boston. Just the opposite happens: people with relatively little income and education become more likely to stick around. The rate of turnover declines, apparently because people don't like to leave a neighborhood when it's improving.

You may have a hard time believing these results, but you can't dismiss them as propaganda from developers. The New York study was done by Lance Freeman, a professor of planning at Columbia University, and Frank Braconi, an economist and the executive director of the Citizens Housing and Planning Council, a well-respected nonprofit research organization with a centrist position in New York's housing wars.

There are always, of course, some people who move out of gentrifying neighborhoods. But then, some people would move out even if the neighborhood didn't change. To see how gentrification affects turnover, Dr. Freeman and Dr. Braconi analyzed the city's Housing and Vacancy Survey, which is gathered by revisiting the same 15,000 housing units every three years.

According to the survey, only 5 percent of the New Yorkers who moved during the late 1990's reported being forced to move by high rents. That percentage was a little lower than during the real estate doldrums of the early 1990's, when there was less gentrification going on.

For a more precise measure, Dr. Freeman and Dr. Braconi looked at the survey data in seven gentrifying neighborhoods: the Lower East Side, Chelsea, Harlem and Morningside Heights in Manhattan, and Williamsburg, Fort Greene and Park Slope in Brooklyn. In those neighborhoods, the poor and working-class tenants—those who had low incomes or who lacked a college degree—were about 20 percent less likely to move during the

1990's than were socioeconomically similar tenants in the rest of the city.

"You've got two competing forces in a gentrifying neighborhood," Dr. Braconi said. "The prices are going up, which gives low-income people an incentive to leave. But the neighborhood's getting nicer, so people have more incentive to stay. There's been an assumption by community activists that the incentive to leave is stronger, but that turns out to be wrong. You don't displace the poor. You actually slow down the process of people moving out of the neighborhood."

In the past, Dr. Braconi has argued that rent regulation can be useful in preventing displacement, and he said that was borne out by the research. The tenants in rent-regulated apartments were especially likely to remain in place. But even tenants in unregulated apartments were more likely to remain in gentrifying neighborhoods than elsewhere, he said.

THESE results jibe with those of a new study by Jacob L. Vigdor, an economist at Duke University, who tracked changes at 3,000 houses and apartments in Boston and its suburbs from 1985 to 1993. Fewer than 10 percent of the apartments were covered by rent control, but the trend was the same as in New York: low-income and less-educated residents of gentrifying neighborhood were more likely to remain in place than were similar residents in other neighborhoods.

How did the poor manage to stay? "I didn't find much evidence of more people crowding into the homes," Dr. Vigdor said. "For the most part, people simply paid more." About 3 percent of the people, typically elderly tenants on fixed incomes, complained that the higher rents weren't accompanied by improvement in living conditions, but most people said they were benefiting from improvements to their dwellings and their neighborhood as well as better public services. Most people's income rose at least as fast as the rents, in some cases presumably because of new jobs that came into the neighborhood.

When you add up all these advantages, it may seem hard to imagine how the opponents of gentrification could keep up the fight. If the neighborhood's improving and old-timers aren't being displaced, what's not to like? But let's see what new complaints they come up with.

Red Hook—Wounded by Good Intentions

ZACH INTRATER

"The rest of the country gets her ass," says Frank, a long-time Red Hook resident. "Red Hook is the only place you can see her face." We're on the recently renovated Pier 39, now a fantastic pocket park, staring directly into the green eyes of the Statue of Liberty. It's true: except for some technicalities—like the north shore of Staten Island, which doesn't really count—Red Hook has, by virtue of its location, a singular view of Lady Liberty. But then, for Red Hook, location has always meant everything.

Red Hook is a peninsula, surrounded by the Gowanus Bay, the Erie Basin and the Buttermilk Channel. From the 1600s, when the Dutch first settled "Roode Hoek," until the 1960s, the waterfront was the whole of Red Hook's economy. The Brooklyn Navy Yard, founded in 1801, launched many of America's most famous fighting ships—the USS Monitor, the USS Maine and the USS Missouri among them. Normally an employer of about 6,000 during peacetime, the Yard boomed during WW II, putting over 70,000 Brooklynites to work. In 1840, the Atlantic Docks opened, and by the end of the 19th century more grain was shipped from there than from any other place in the world. The Grain Terminal, an incredible pile of cement, still hulks grey-black, enormous and desolate at the mouth of the Gowanus Inlet. During the first half of the 20th century, New York boasted the busiest piers in the country, and Red Hook's were among the busiest in New York.

All this seafaring action led to a rough-hewn, violent neighborhood, filled with bars and grills like Byrnes' Bar on Lorraine St., which sported a lovely nickname: "the Bucket of Blood." One bar owner from that period recalled that if he came in Sunday morning and there wasn't sawdust on the floor, soaking up Saturday night's bodily fluids, he knew there'd been a slow night.

All this ended in the 20 years after the war. The avarice of the mafia goons who controlled the docks didn't help, but mostly it was the new container-style shipping moving south to deeper piers in Charleston and Houston. The shuttering of the Navy Yard in 1966 dealt another serious blow to Red Hook's working-class ranks. But those two factors alone didn't kill the waterfront. What killed the waterfront was well-intentioned urban planning.

Looking at an MTA Subway map, the mad tangle of colored lines in downtown Manhattan gives way, just right of the East River, to a vast expanse of putty-hued blankness. It looks, in fact, as though all trains have been pushed north and east, up towards the Heights and downtown Brooklyn. The closest stop to Red Hook is Smith & 9th St., which at 91 feet above ground is the city's highest elevated station, due to navigation rules intended to allow the now long-departed tall-mast ships to pass along Gowanus Creek under the station. From the southbound side, the view west toward Red Hook is cut off by the Gowanus Expressway (known more generally as the Brooklyn-Queens Expressway), which, along with the Brooklyn Battery Tunnel, cuts Red Hook off from its residential, working- and middle-class neighbors. Both viaducts date to the Moses era.

The Smith & 9th stop is a good mile and change away from Red Hook. Its detachment from the city's arteries is shared in the borough only by such "tightly-knit communities" as Mill Basin and Marine Park, which have never wanted to be invaded by the subway. But Red Hook is not a residential neighborhood; it's a working one.

And here, again, location is key. When the neighborhood was flush with dock jobs, Navy Yard jobs and bar jobs, Red Hook residents could walk to work and walk home, or take a short trolley or bus ride. But when the jobs left, the residents who stayed had to go elsewhere for work, and were stuck with a long ride on the B77 bus down truck-choked Van Brunt St. to the F, itself one of the slowest trains in the system.

Further isolating Red Hook from the rest of Brooklyn—and from a fully-functioning future—are the Red Hook Houses, East and West, which are home to the vast majority of the neighborhood's remaining residents. Completed in 1938 as part of the first generation of government-built projects, the Houses now squat, low and wide, smack-dab in the center of the neighborhood. Their vast swathes of undifferentiated single-use housing hold mostly the dysfunctional and the disenfranchised, who are even more cut off from the life of the city than residents of the typical housing project by virtue of the neighborhood's isolation. Mostly because of the project residents, Red Hook is one of Brooklyn's poorest neighborhoods, with an unemployment rate of 21.6 percent, and with a 43.6 percent high school graduation rate. It's yet another factor that discourages outsiders from coming in.

This same isolation, though, has allowed Red Hook to house many of the small industrial businesses that keep New York running, and that have been zoned and priced out of much of the city. There is a road salt distributor, a large shop that makes sets for television shows and lots of bus and trucking concerns. There are woodworking shops, metalworking shops, construction companies and a plexiglass manufacturer. You can get your fire extinguisher fixed, you can get a footbridge built, you can buy a live chicken (or a *really* freshly slaughtered one) and you can find the best cabinet-makers in New York, all in Red Hook.

And now, of course, you can buy a cute handbag. Yes, the space pirates have invaded Red Hook, which means white folk with white belts and oversized sunglasses and tight pants bicycling around at odd hours. Several upscale stores have opened on Van Brunt St., the neighborhood's commercial hub, and many more have come to Columbia St., which, because it runs further north than the rest of the neighborhood's streets, has always been more connected to Brooklyn-at-large.

The hipoisie are attracted by the cheap rents, but also by the authenticity that Red Hook has in spades. It is hard to get to, it still has lots of cobblestone streets and it is still really fucked up. It remains to be seen, though, how far gentrification can proceed without better public transportation, and given rising interest rates.

Now, as always, the location of this neighborhood, so tantalizingly close to the city, but so very far away from just about everything, is the key.

The Essence of Uptown

Can the latest hot neighborhood move up without leaving itself behind?

A.T. PALMER
Special to the Tribune

When Eric Snyder moved to Chicago from Atlanta last spring and started scouting North Side neighborhoods for housing, he had absolutely no intention of buying in Uptown, he claims.

The 2.3-square-mile neighborhood, bounded by Lake Michigan, Irving Park Road, Clark Street and Montrose, Ravenswood and Foster Avenues, "looked like a dive," recalls the 34-year-old banker.

Yet, Snyder's purchase in August was a $214,000 two-bedroom, 1.5-bath condominium in southeast Uptown. And, it's already appreciated $56,000, the result of some bathroom and closet upgrades, he boasts.

Why Uptown?

"Where else in the city can I make a return of 20 percent? Plus have the lake, easy access to transportation and fewer crowds than Lincoln Park?" he says.

"There's a Starbucks, a gym, and hopefully a Fresh Fields [grocery] and Borders [bookstore] coming soon. This is becoming a middle-class neighborhood."

Latest figures from the Multiple Listing Service of Northern Illinois, which compiles a quarterly report of median sale prices of local housing listed with real estate agents, concurs. The median price of a home in Uptown rose to $215,000 in the third quarter from $192,000 in the year-earlier period. That exceeds median prices for such desirable suburbs as Palatine ($190,000) and Flossmoor ($195,000).

According to Mimi Slogar, Uptown Community Development Corp. chairman, Uptown is among the top five areas citywide in condo conversion volume—on a par with the West Loop.

"I couldn't even use the word 'Uptown' 6 to 12 months ago when I was marketing property there," says Scott Kruger, a Koenig & Strey GMAC broker, longtime Uptown resident and six-flat owner there.

"It had a connotation of poor housing stock and streets that weren't pretty," he says. "Now, people specifically ask to see Uptown properties. There's new construction and rehabbing attractively priced on almost every block. It's such a transformation."

This transformation isn't being greeted with the same enthusiasm by other long-time residents, such as State Rep. Larry McKeon (D-34th).

When he moved into his one-bedroom rental apartment at Ravenswood and Montrose Avenues 10 years ago, the monthly rent was $550. Now it's $1,000.

"As a renter, I'm being priced out of my own district," complains McKeon, looking for rental housing in areas to the north that were recently annexed to his district—North Andersonville (part of Edgewater) and Rogers Park.

"There's been little development in the mid-range for firefighters, social workers and government workers like me," he says. "There's been tremendous displacement of the most vulnerable people—seniors on fixed incomes and welfare-to-work people, who must live near work when they find jobs. I'm not against development and gentrification. But, balanced development must be protected."

Snyder and McKeon represent two sides of the multi-faceted debate over Uptown's dramatic changes.

Built as a luxury lakeside summer resort in the 1890s and which became one of the nation's feature film production headquarters after World War I, Uptown was hit hard by Great Depression economics. Many big homes were divided into rental apartments, priced cheaply.

Since then, Uptown has become Chicago's port of entry for newcomers—Southerners, immigrants from Vietnam, Cambodia, Ethiopia and Bosnia, plus deinstitutionalized patients from state psychiatric facilities, says Sarah Jane Knoy, executive director of Organization of the Northeast (ONE), a community action group.

State and not-for-profit social service agencies established offices in the neighborhood to serve this clientele. But, now Uptown's changing: 4,000 property parcels vacant in 1990 have dwindled to 1,000, according to latest census data.

One parcel, at 4848 N. Sheridan Rd., is the future home of The Alexa, a 70-unit condominium midrise. The one- to three-bedroom units, base-priced from $170,000, and up to $450,000 for the 1,700-square-foot penthouse, are more than 40 percent sold, reports Victor E. Cypher, president of Chicago-based ViCor Development Co.

"Eight years ago, $250,000 bought a lake view," says Chip Long, broker at Lakefront Group Realty Associates Inc. "Now two- and three-bedroom condos that sold for $150,000 are going for $200,000 to $350,000."

Commercially, this neighborhood of primarily small owner-operated shops and a vibrant Asian commercial strip on Argyle Street from Sheridan to Broadway is also changing.

Neighborhood residents have seen final plans to renovate the long-vacant Goldblatt's Department Store into a mixed retail/

residential building with a 25,000-square-foot Border's Books & Music, other retailers, and 37 condominiums.

The historic Uptown Theatre received a recent $1 million grant from the Albert Goodman Foundation to help rehab the theater, one of the country's largest.

But, growth has an underside, community leaders warn. Uptown has lost about 2,000 to 3,000 families since 1990, says McKeon. The number of children under age 18 is down more than 20 percent.

New census data about Uptown's 63,551 residents show population is down marginally (0.45 percent). Anglo-Caucasians increased to 42 percent of the population from 38 percent, while the number of African-Americans dropped to 21 percent from 24 percent, Hispanics, to 20 percent from 23 percent, and Asians, to 13 percent from 14 percent.

Gentrification and its impact on Uptown's property values, affordable housing and racial and ethnic diversity elicit a range of reactions from long-time residents, newcomers, community activists, real estate brokers and urban experts.

There's some excitement by homeowners about rising property values, an increasing middle class and plans for brand-name retail stores; some dismay over the changing look of some residential streets and loss of some local citizenry; and worry because there's no comprehensive, long-range neighborhood plan.

"I'm happy that gentrification has finally come," says Bob Peterson, president of the Gunnison Block Club in northeast Uptown. Bought 15 years ago for $115,000, his duplex condo has more than doubled in value.

"Diversity should include middle-class families," he says. "That's the biggest change gentrification has brought to Uptown. We have a stronger group of middle-class families committed to staying and sending their children to school here. That will strengthen the neighborhood."

Rae Mindock, a chemical engineer and Beacon Neighbors Block Club member, shares Peterson's happiness. Her two-bedroom condo in southwest Uptown appreciated to more than $250,000 from $100,000 in 10 years. But, she's worried about other aspects of gentrification.

"There are lots of affluent individuals who've moved in," she says. "That's not bad. What's difficult is their inability to accept the neighborhood they've moved into 'as is'—with homeless and other residents.

"I'm also worried too many condos will destabilize our neighborhood," she adds.

Neighborhood destabilization also concerns Syd Mohn, president of Heartland Alliance, a not-for-profit social service association serving the poor. Since 1996, Heartland's Uptown client list of 8,000 has dropped 15 to 20 percent.

Rising apartment rents have prompted about half of Uptown's 8,000 Cambodian residents to relocate, says Kompha Seth, executive director of the Cambodian Association of Illinois. The association itself moved to Albany Park from Uptown earlier this year. "It was heartbreaking leaving Uptown," says Seth. "I feel very isolated now."

This trend is troublesome to newcomers attracted by Uptown's racial and ethnic diversity.

"I picked Uptown over Lincoln Park or Andersonville," says 24 year-old Jackie Aicher, a supermarket retailer who moved from Evanston into a rental in Uptown in September.

"Uptown's more individual, more local and not corporate," she says. "This area won't be special if Border's comes in. They're everywhere. I'm also afraid that gentrification will displace the African-Americans, Hispanics and Asians that I came here to live with."

"I'm African-American and wanted a neighborhood where I'd see a black, white and Hispanic when I walk down the street," adds Andrew Stroth, 34. The sports and entertainment attorney moved from Lake View ("all yuppies," he says) into a three-bedroom condo near Truman College in May. "This neighborhood is vibrant."

Uptown's community leaders are dealing with gentrification issues with innovative programs.

The neighborhood is one of the first citywide to implement Chicago's Purchase Price Assistance Program. Developers voluntarily set aside 10 percent of their building's units for sale to low- and middle-income individuals. The city subsidizes down payments. The Alexa and proposed Goldblatt's development are participants.

Community leaders helped 10 federally subsidized apartment buildings convert to ownership by tenants, not-for-profits or for-profit companies that pledge to maintain affordable housing, says Knoy, ONE's executive director.

"Loyola University Chicago is preparing the first comprehensive set of baseline data on real estate in a Chicago community—Uptown," says Rep. McKeon, the project's catalyst. "Available next spring, this data will include all federal, state, county and municipal housing information and will be available for all stakeholders," he says. "Sometimes, this data is not readily available. When it is, it's for purchase only.

"Because there's been a lack of viable and reliable data on housing, Uptown has been divided into 'those that have' and 'those that don't' in this debate," he claims. "We've ended up with two political extremes. This lack of information increases the intensity and acrimony of arguments."

"It's easy to get emotional about gentrification with a few inflammatory sentences," says Cindi Anderson, president of the Uptown Chicago Commission, another citizen group, who also complains about the dearth of information. "Conversations about the 'big picture' don't occur here."

Will these solutions be enough to retain Uptown's uniqueness amid gentrification? It's unclear, but residents, real estate professionals and community activists are determined.

"Uptown can be strong in growth and diversity," says the Heartland Alliance's Mohn. "This community needs to come together to decide what to preserve and what to become."

"Uptown must learn how to stay Uptown," adds Mindock, the Beacon Street resident. "People are learning to have conversations with people who are different from themselves. This is a start."

In Parts of U.S. Northwest, a Changing Face

Economics drive white gentrification of core black neighborhoods of Seattle and Portland

BLAINE HARDEN
Washington Post Staff Writer

Already the whitest major city in America, Portland is rapidly becoming even whiter at its core.

"The heart of the black community is gone," said Charles Ford, 76, a black activist whose neighborhood in Portland has flipped in recent years from majority black to majority white. "There ain't no center anymore."

About 150 miles north in Seattle, the nation's second-whitest major city, the same process of downtown demographic bleaching is accelerating for the same reasons.

An invasion of young, well-educated and mostly white newcomers is buying up and remaking Seattle's Central District, the birthplace of Jimi Hendrix and the once-bluesy home of the young Ray Charles. What had been the largest black-majority community in the Pacific Northwest has become majority white.

"I am concerned and I am frustrated because I don't know what the alternatives are," said Norman Rice, who in the 1990s was Seattle's first and only black mayor. "It clearly isn't racist; it's economics. The real question you have to ask yourself is: Is this good or bad?"

White gentrification is hardly unique to Portland and Seattle. It is changing Harlem, the District of Columbia and many other cities. Demographers say it is especially noticeable in major California cities—a function of population density, the desire to escape long commutes and the relative housing bargains in black neighborhoods.

But as white gentrification accelerates in Portland and Seattle, where the percentage of black residents was already the lowest among the nation's largest cities, it is erasing the only historically black neighborhoods these cities have ever had.

In many cities with large black populations, gentrification has caused only marginal racial change. In the District, for example, the percentage of white non-Hispanic residents increased 2.7 percent between 1990 and 2004, according to William H. Frey, a demographer at the Brookings Institution.

Still, Washington remains less than one-third white and about 60 percent black.

In Seattle's Central District, though, racial change is anything but marginal. The non-Hispanic white population in the area jumped from 31 percent in 1990 to 50 percent in 2000, according to the census.

Local demographers say white growth since 2000 has gained momentum, while the percentage of black residents appears to have fallen to less than 40 percent. With real estate prices rollicking upward at about 25 percent a year, the Central District appears to be getting whiter and richer by the month.

As black residents leave the central areas of Portland and Seattle for the suburbs—either because they have sold their homes or been forced out by higher rents—their community is being splintered by geographic dispersal and racial integration.

"It's destroying us, socially and politically," said Ford, the neighborhood activist from Portland. "It is just a total inconvenience and disrespect to black folks."

Rice does not view the changes as nearly so dire, especially for people who have been able to sell their homes at a substantial profit and set aside money for retirement.

Census figures suggest that blacks in Seattle and Portland have not been displaced into homelessness and that they are not economically worse off in the suburbs than they were downtown. In many cases, housing in the suburbs is newer, schools are better and crime is lower.

But Rice said that newly suburbanized African Americans in Seattle and Portland are being isolated from one another and "will have to find new places to embrace our black heritage."

With attendance falling, some black churches in Seattle and Portland have moved or are opening second sanctuaries in the suburbs.

"I have begged our people not to sell their properties but to no avail," said the Rev. Reggie Witherspoon, pastor of Mount Calvary Christian Center, a church in the Central District that is trying to open a second location in Seattle's southern suburbs, where many parishioners have moved. "A good majority of them have decided they cannot afford to drive into the city, so they have joined suburban white churches."

Neither blacks nor whites, Rice said, appear to have found a way to stop or slow the disappearance of core black neighborhoods. "They are concerned, but they don't have an option or a plan," he said.

The pressures of growth, worsening traffic congestion and the rising price of gasoline seem certain to make the hunt for close-in, upscale housing even more obsessive in the next two decades.

"The location of the Central District is so superior to the suburbs—it has great views, it's close to downtown and to the University of Washington—that there's a tremendous incentive to buy, especially for people with no kids or the money to send them to private schools," said Richard Morrill, a demographer and professor emeritus at the University of Washington.

Over the next two decades, Seattle is predicting the creation of 50,000 jobs in the central city, which amounts to nearly a 25 percent increase in a job base that tends to be high-wage and highly skilled. Portland, too, is growing, largely by attracting young, well-educated newcomers from California and the East Coast.

In both Seattle and Portland, which take considerable pride in being green, liberal and tolerant, the fading away of black inner-city communities has occasioned considerable hand-wringing among the overwhelmingly white population. Portland is 75 percent white, and Seattle 68 percent white.

"Many of the white liberals who condemned white flight are just as angry at the white folks who are moving back into the cities," Dan Savage, editor of the *Stranger,* an alternative weekly in Seattle, wrote last month in his blog about movement from Seattle in the 1950s, '60s and '70s.

The dispersal of African Americans is also an embarrassing reminder of why they were concentrated in the first place—and of a time when neither Portland nor Seattle was especially tolerant.

In the '50s and '60s, when the black population was growing in the region, restrictive real estate covenants and racial prejudice kept most African Americans in selected central areas of the two cities.

"Finally, the African American community is able to make the same choice about where it's going to live as the white community," Rice said. "They are choosing to move. Is that bad or not? Stay tuned."

In northeast Portland, where Ford has been complaining for years about gentrification, he acknowledges that the tipping point has come and gone. White folks are taking over, he said, and blacks folks are all but gone.

Recently, Ford took a reporter on a tour of his gentrified neighborhood. En route, he discovered that a not-so-handsome house was for sale for $400,000. The price astonished him, especially because the house was considerably smaller than his own.

"When I see prices like that, I wonder who . . . of my race can continue to live here," he said.

Ford began ruminating about the price—and the profit—he might be able to get for his house, which he has owned since 1968 and which sits on a fine corner lot near a fixed-up city park.

"I have said I would never sell," Ford said. "But who can resist these prices?"

Rocking-Chair Revival

Nostalgic front porch makes a comeback in a new century

LESLIE MANN
Special to the Tribune

It was gone, but not forgotten, and now is back—in force.

The American front porch nearly disappeared during the second half of the 20th Century, except for a blip on the screen during the '70s and '80s when some builders attached pretend porches to the facades of faux-Victorians.

They looked good on paper, but, in real life, you couldn't cram a rocking chair into them with a crowbar.

Now, front porches seem to be enjoying a retro revival, along with comfort foods and Radio Flyer wagons.

Not just ornamental, pretend porches, but deep, roomy porches that invite passers-by to come on up, put their feet up and have a glass of lemonade.

Front porches and their backyard cousins are nothing new, of course. The word "porch" derives from the Latin word "porticus." Early American homes, including George Washington's Mount Vernon and Thomas Jefferson's Monticello, had porches.

From the start, they were decorative (dressing up Plain-Jane homes or embellishing the already ornate) and/or functional (adding square footage and offering free air conditioning).

"The late 1800s to WWI were the heydays of the front porch and the front stoop," says Emily Talen, professor of urban and regional planning at the University of Illinois. "Then our culture became a car culture and the garage went up front."

Builders trace the current front-porch craze back to the mid-1990s, when Walt Disney Co. built the much-publicized Celebration community outside Orlando. It was billed as the flagship for the neo-traditional housing trend, which pushed garages to the backs of lots, resurrected alleys and clustered homes closer together.

As backyards shrunk, front porches became the new gathering spots. According to the National Association of Home Builders (NAHB), the number of porches (front and back) on new homes grew from 42 percent in 1992 (the first year it tallied them) to 50 percent in 2000.

> ## 'The neighbors walk by and say hi. The porches give the neighborhood a Mayberry, small-town kind of feeling.'
>
> Homeowner Stacy Connor

"Whether you use the front porch or not, it makes for a better streetscape," says Talen. "The garage doors out front say, 'Cars live here.' Front porches say, 'People live here.'"

Builders say the front-porch passion crosses demographic lines.

"Front porches are appealing to all kinds of buyers—young families and older couples," reports Naperville-based builder John Schillerstrom, who has built dozens of custom and semi-custom homes with front porches in the last few years. "The common thread—they like to socialize with their neighbors."

"The front porch was pleasant, not exciting," recalls William Geist in his book, "Towards a Safe & Sane Halloween & Other Tales of Suburbia" (Random House).

"It was a place to sit. To sit and talk—something called visiting—about anything that came up.

"Sometimes nothing was said for several minutes, just sharing the silence, the sound of the crickets, the lawn sprinkler, or whatever. It was okay to be silent then, not a failure to communicate that you had to seek professional help for."

Then came TV, says Geist in his 1985 book. Then, the central air.

By the 1950s, recalls Geist sarcastically, "A body'd have to be a fool to sit out on the front porch talking with his next-door neighbor when he could be in his air-conditioned 'TV room' being talked at by the big stars from Hollywood and New York."

The trend started before 9–11, but now people are staying home even more. The front porch is a place they can relax.

Front porches are selling at all price points, too, from modest, subdivision homes to the over-$350,000 homes Schillerstrom builds.

Figure 1   Antique furniture and planters, as well as benches, rocking chairs and swings, are common fare on porches at HomeTown Aurora.
Photo for the Tribune by Steve Lasker.

Prices in a Wide Range

Like the houses they adorn, their prices run the gamut, he says, "from a $3,500, simple one with a concrete floor to a $10,000 to $15,000 one with a beadboard ceiling and canned lights. The sky's the limit."

Municipal land planners like front porches "because they help create safe, feel-good neighborhoods," says Mark Elliott, president of the Elliott Group in Morton Grove, which builds custom and semi-custom homes in the $500,000-and-up market.

"But it's not just the curb appeal they add," reports Elliott. "People are really using them." "We're out there spring, summer and fall, and eat out there in the summer," says Stacey Connor, of the porch that wraps around her two-story, four-bedroom home in HomeTown Aurora, built by Palatine-based Bigelow Homes.

"We [Connor and her husband, Keith] sit there and watch the kids play in the tot lot next door. The neighbors walk by and say hi. The porches give the neighborhood a Mayberry, small-town kind of feeling."

Furniture is Abundant

Surrounded by wooden railings, the Connors' porch is deep enough to accommodate plenty of patio furniture, she says.

"When the kids get older, I'll put a porch swing out there, too," she says.

Research showed that people "yearned for more connected, social neighborhoods, and front porches are part of this," says Bigelow's vice president of sales and marketing, Jamie Bigelow.

"They no longer want to be prisoners of their backyards like they were in the '70s, '80s and '90s."

Bigelow says about 70 percent of the buyers in his neo-traditional HomeTown communities in Aurora, Oswego and Romeoville choose the front-porch upgrade.

Bigelow offers several versions—wrap-around, two-thirds, full-front and double-decker (plantation-style).

The average cost of $7,000 includes cement floors, wooden columns and railings. The homes range in base prices from $121,900 to $180,000.

"Buyers are willing to forgo interior upgrades such as wooden floors, ceramic tile or oak [stairway] railings for front porches," says Bigelow.

Roger Mankedick, executive vice president of Concord Homes in Palatine, agrees.

"Buyers give up other amenities or just pay more for porches, which they say remind them of their grandmothers and of simpler times," he says.

Front porches are hot tickets at Concord's neo-traditional communities—Montgomery Crossing in Montgomery and Madrona Village in Round Lake, where base prices range from $177,990 to $245,990.

Although front porches seem especially popular in the new, neo-traditional neighborhoods, they are sprouting in new subdivisions with more traditional layouts, too.

Rolling Meadows-based Kimball Hill, for example, features two-story front porches at its Fisher Farms development in west suburban Geneva, where homes go for $235,900 to $430,000.

Distinctive Homes of Orland Park builds wrap-arounds on its Prairie Trail homes in Plainfield, priced from $159,000 to $225,000.

A notch up the price ladder, Joe Keim Builders of Geneva has full front porches on its Majestic Oaks homes in St. Charles, where pricetags range from $500,000 to more than $1 million.

Front porches help soften the look of new homes on teardown properties, says Schillerstrom. While neighbors and village boards don't always take kindly to garage-nosed monstrosities replacing teardowns in older neighborhoods, "houses with front porches are good fits," he says.

As the front porch trend saturates the single-family market, it is spilling into the multi-family market, too. A local case in point is the townhouse line-up at Sho-Deen Inc.'s Mill Creek in Geneva.

"Now we're even seeing them in public housing," reports Talen.

At least one family, Carla and Michael Perry of Palatine, are repeat buyers of front porches. Their last home, a townhouse, had one. So a front porch topped their list of amenities when they bought a single-family home recently in Concord's new Concord Estates.

"We even changed lots to make sure we had the right elevation for the porch," says Carla Perry.

This summer, she says, they plan to spend evenings on their new front porch, getting to know their new neighbors.

"We have two rocking chairs on order," she says. "I can't wait."

In New York City, Fewer Find They Can Make It

MICHAEL POWELL
Washington Post Staff Writer

Michael Bloomberg, this city's billionaire mayor, looks at Manhattan's glittering economy and all but chortles. "Jobs are coming back to the Big Apple," he said recently. "Our future has never looked brighter."

The Wall Street bull is snorting. Investment bankers arm-wrestle for a $18 million Park Avenue apartment. Slots at prestigious private kindergartens retail for $26,000. Lines trail out of the latest, hot restaurants, and black limos play bumper car in Tribeca.

"New York," a recent newspaper article proclaims, "it's HOT."

Except that a closer look at this largest of U.S. cities reveals much that's not so hot. New York's unemployment rate jumped in January from 8.0 to 8.4 percent, the worst performance among the nation's top 20 cities. It has lost 230,000 jobs in the past three years. Demand for emergency food has risen 46 percent over the past three years, and 900,000 New Yorkers receive food stamps. Inflation, foreclosures, evictions and personal bankruptcies are rising sharply. Fifty percent of the city's black males no longer are employed.

President Bush will journey here this August for the Republican convention, and he is expected to celebrate the revival of the nation's financial capital since the Sept. 11, 2001, terrorist attacks. But at this point, that recovery is characterized more by its weakness—and by the stark disparities between rich and poor.

In the third quarter of 2003, the nation's gross domestic product grew at a rate of 8.4 percent; the comparable rate in New York grew by 0.3 percent.

"Our economy is polarized; our population is polarized," said Kathryn S. Wylde, president of the Partnership for New York City, which represents the city's 200 top private-sector chief executives. "The bonuses of a relative handful of very wealthy people are driving our economy."

The Invisible Poor

Around the corner from City Hall in downtown Manhattan, Arthur Harvey considers his economic prospects, which happen to stink. He is one of a record number of 40,000 homeless New Yorkers.

"My landlord raised my rent from $125 a week to $200, so I began to sleep in my mom's back yard in Queens," said Harvey, 40, with a goatee and hollowed-out eyes. "I used to work as a messenger, but the company's gone out of business.

"I'm in trouble, y'know what I mean?"

Seen from the perspective of Manhattan and the ever-more-swank streets of brownstone Brooklyn, these are curiously invisible hard times. Home prices spiral upward 10 percent or more each year, midtown is crowded and retail sales are strong, and the Wall Street bonus is back, $10 billion worth this year. A half-dozen new restaurants open each week, and a survey found that New Yorkers plan to eat out more than they did last year.

Nor is the current downturn as deep as recessions past. In the early 1990s, New York lost 360,000 jobs and the three horsemen of urban decline—AIDS, crack and crime—left its streets mean and forbidding. The plagues have stabilized, and the crime rate has plummeted. Bloomberg preserved many city services during the recession by raising property taxes.

"I live in Greenwich Village, and if you walked around the past few years, you'd never guess that 300,000 New Yorkers don't have a job," said Patrick Markee, a senior policy analyst with Coalition for the Homeless. "But if you venture out of the 'hot' neighborhoods, you find a lot of people doing phenomenally badly."

That *other* New York can be found in Chinatown and in Upper Manhattan, and across the East and Harlem Rivers in the Bronx and Brooklyn, where the unemployment rates stand at 10.3 and 8.5 percent, respectively. Queens is a proudly middle-class borough with thriving immigrant communities. But last year, 210 homeowners defaulted on their mortgages each month. Forty-five percent of those homes were auctioned off, twice the national foreclosure rate, according to Foreclosures.com, which analyzes national trends.

There are more harbingers of hard times. There has been a 20 percent rise over the past three years in the number of tenants being sued for nonpayment of rent. About 300,000 New Yorkers—10 percent of the city's workforce—labor for less than $7 an hour.

"A lot of businesses have folded out here," said Al Titone, director of the Small Business Development Center at York College, which sits at the end of the E-subway line in lower middle-class Jamaica, Queens. "A lot of folks are in scary shape."

At the Yorkville Common Pantry, on the southern edge of East Harlem, director Jeffrey Ambers recently converted his food program for the poor into a 24-hour-a-day operation—and began serving 12,000 more meals. "We are serving more people, and some days we run out," Ambers said. "We're not seeing signs here of an improving economy."

New York's labor participation rate—the percentage of employed adults relative to population—fell from 65.6 percent in July 2002 to 57 percent now. The city comptroller's office recently framed that drop this way: "If the labor force participation rate had remained at the level of July 2002, the NYC unemployment rate [now] would . . . rise to 19.9 percent."

Harvey Robins served as a senior official in two mayoral administrations, and has analyzed the city economy for 20 years. "We talk on and on about the price of real estate, but the other city is ignored," Robins said. "The elites focus on the difficulty of getting a restaurant reservation but never hear about the restaurant worker who spends 50 percent of his salary on rent."

Worrisome Job Market

Juan Batista has arrived at his 62nd year without a job or health insurance. For decades, the East Harlem man threaded fabric through textile machines—until he was laid off in 2002. Now he leafs through the classified ads each morning and walks the streets. He sees rug stores but no longer the factories that make them.

His wife's salary is his sole support. "I don't want to retire, but I don't have the possibilities of youth," Batista said last week. "I'm worried. What can I do but wait for death?"

The talk of late on Wall Street is resurgent profits and young analysts hungry for their first Jaguar. But a survey of the job market finds worry in many corners. Manufacturing still employs 126,000 New Yorkers, but it has bled jobs for decades and lost another 1,100 jobs in January.

The private sector gained 20,600 jobs. But the Fiscal Policy Institute found that the sectors gaining jobs paid $34,000 less, on average, than the sectors that lost jobs. Health and education are the fast-growing sectors in Manhattan; the average salary for both is $42,000. But the cost of the average Manhattan co-op apartment is $983,000.

"It takes two of the jobs we've gained to make up for one that we've lost," said James Parrott, chief economist for the labor-funded Fiscal Policy Institute. "That does not bode well for the future."

Economic calamity has fallen with particular force on the shoulders of black males. The Community Service Society, a liberal social policy organization, discovered a sharp three-year decline in employment that has left 51.8 percent of black males holding jobs.

The city's core economic sector—securities trading and financial services—displays more strength. The Wall Street spigots are again running and profit margins are staggering. Securities firms recorded profits of $15 billion last year. This has fed a revival in advertising, legal work, catering, and restaurants and hotels.

Still, Wall Street remains a slender version of its Gilded Age self. Many firms retain corporate suites in New York but have placed back offices in Long Island and Jersey City, or farther afield. Last year, the nation gained 120,000 finance jobs; the city lost 1,500.

"We lag behind the rest of the nation in job creation in our key sectors," said Jonathan Bowles of the Center for an Urban Future, a think tank that examines the city economy. "The national economy is outperforming New York."

Hiding Behind Sept. 11

It is a matter of secular faith among many local politicians that New York owes the severity of its hard times not to structural economic problems but to the devastating effects of the 2001 terrorist attacks.

Several influential economists, however, offer a dissent. They note that the city pitched into recession in January 2001 and job losses were mounting rapidly before the attacks. They say the popping of the stock bubble and the city's economic dependence on Wall Street accounted, chiefly, for the severity of the downturn.

"The terror attack created sizeable job and income losses, but the city's current downturn appears to stem largely from the national economy and the financial markets," Jason Bram, an economist with the Federal Reserve Bank of New York, wrote last year.

The hangover from those attacks has stifled frank discussion. Analysts of various ideological stripes say the city needs to retool its taxes and fees—which are among the nation's highest—restructure labor contracts, raise the minimum wage and address its extreme reliance on Wall Street. But that conversation is rarely heard.

"September 11th came along, and there was all this talk of how it pulled us closer together," said Richard Murphy of the Community Food Resource Center. "But, economically, we are further apart than ever, and no one talks about it."

Partnership for New York City president Wylde added that nothing about the city's economic dominance can be taken for granted. "We had done a good job of restoring the middle class, but it's very transient, very fragile," she said. "We have an economy where a lot of job growth is epitomized by restaurant jobs and nannies."

As if to underline this point, Bloomberg News Service reported that there are 15 applications for every $26,000 seat at the most prestigious private kindergartens. And last month, the Time Warner twin towers opened at Columbus Circle, occasioning fleets of Lincoln Town Cars and apple martinis and gymnastics by Cirque du Soleil. Undercover cops came in tuxes, as did reporters.

"It's like a mecca for everything," wrote one local newspaper scribe.

That same evening, three miles to the north, Clinton Campbell, 47, walked into a Community Food Resource Center in Harlem to have his tax forms prepared for free. An African American and New York native, he managed a McDonald's until he was laid off a year ago. Now he collects unemployment more often than he works.

Afterward, he walked down Eighth Avenue to a food pantry for dinner.

"I worked at a grocery store last month, but I was too old to lug boxes upstairs," Campbell said as he stood in line with a tray. "They say if you make it here, you can make it anywhere. But I'm hurting real bad."

With that he excused himself, said a prayer, and lifted his knife and fork.

UNIT 5

Urban Economies, Politics and Policies

Unit Selections

Key Points to Consider

- What makes a successful mayoralty? What makes a successful city?

- How has Michael Bloomberg defined his mayoralty? What issues seem most important to him? Using John Lindsay and Richard Daley as examples, explain how differing mayoral on race can affect urban life.

Student Web Site

www.mhcls.com/online

Internet References

Further information regarding these Web sites may be found in this book's preface or online.

IISDnet
http://iisd1.iisd.ca
The International Center for Migration, Ethnicity, and Citizenship
http://www.newschool.edu/icmec
National Immigration Forum
http://www.immigrationforum.org/index.htm
School of Labor and Industrial Relations
http://www.lir.msu.edu
U.S. Equal Employment Opportunity Commission
http://www.eeoc.gov
Munisource.org
http://www.munisource.org
U.S. Department of Housing and Urban Development
http://www.hud.gov
Virtual Seminar in Global Political Economy/Global Cities & Social Movements
http://csf.colorado.edu/gpe/gpe95b/resources.html

The politics and policies of the 1960s helped accelerate the urban decline of the 1970s and 1980s. "Mayors and Mayorality: Daley and Lindsay Then and Now" provides a broad historical perspective that contrasts the different approaches and reputations of the past mayors of Chicago and New York. Their distinct approaches to race, public safety, quality of life, and neighborhoods help frame the urban experience in the second half of the twentieth century.

"Bloomberg So Far" looks at the first two years under Gotham's current mayor, and determines that the city has not slid back to the morass of the pre-Giuliani days, nor has it not made further progress. "Winds of Change," which implicitly compares Chicago to New York, shows through the history of one warehouse how and why Chicago has managed to steady itself by diversifying its economic base—even as other cities have created incentives to attract specialized industries.

Winds of Change

Tale of a Warehouse Shows How Chicago Weathers a Decline

After Montgomery Ward Exits, City's Diverse Industries Transform a Neighborhood Traders, Telecoms and Sushi

ILAN BRAT

To understand how Chicago has avoided the decline that has ravaged so many other Midwestern cities, take a look at a massive 98-year-old building in a crook of the Chicago River just outside the city's famed downtown Loop.

It began life as the warehouse at the heart of Montgomery Ward & Co.'s catalog business. It emptied out in 1980, as the building's catalog operation moved elsewhere. It housed some company offices and then shut altogether just before the retailer went out of business in 2000.

Today on the building's eighth floor, Paul Gavin and 50 fellow traders track stock and futures indexes on flat-screen monitors at Jump Trading LLC. Down the hall, a print-outsourcing company works on getting the lowest price to print brochures for companies such as agricultural-equipment maker Deere & Co. The iconic Chicago gum and candy maker Wm. Wrigley Jr. Co. recently has moved much of its U.S. marketing staff to the fifth floor. At Japonais Restaurant on the ground floor, waiters and waitresses in silver kimono shirts serve sushi to a room packed with well-heeled diners. "This building combines everything great about the city," says Mr. Gavin, 28 years old, who also lives on the seventh floor in a new condominium annex called Domain.

As other Midwestern cities have struggled with waning manufacturing employment, Chicago has survived by repeatedly reinventing itself. Once a monument to retail, banking, meat-packing and manufacturing, it now boasts a strong presence in accounting, computer-systems design, legal services and consulting, among others. In October, it cemented its place as derivatives market to the world when the Chicago Mercantile Exchange Holdings Inc. agreed to buy its neighbor and rival, CBOT Holdings Inc., for $8 billion.

Based on an economic measure called industrial diversity, Chicago has developed an economy that more closely reflects the broad national economy than almost any other city in the country. That means it is less exposed to the stumbles of any given industry than cities in the lower half of the rankings, such as Philadelphia, Houston, Los Angeles or New York, or those at the very bottom, including Boston and Gary, Ind.

The city's location in the middle of the country and at the confluence of every major freight railroad has long been an advantage. The city government over the past 20 years mostly has poured money into general beautification and infrastructure rather than wooing specific industries, says Glen Marker, director of research for World Business Chicago, a not-for-profit economic development corporation headed by Mayor Richard M. Daley.

With its lakefront parks, an extensive public-transit system and a thriving arts and culture community, Chicago attracts young professionals from around the country for jobs with relatively high incomes. Chicago's population grew by 4% between 1990 and 2000 while some other big Midwestern cities dropped by more than 5%. It has since slipped 2%, according to the U.S. Census Bureau, but that decline is smaller than in many other Midwest cities. Though families are moving into the suburbs, people in their 20s like Mr. Gavin continue to pour into the city proper, says Kenneth Johnson, a demographer at Loyola University Chicago.

The city's August unemployment rate of 5.2% was higher than the nation's 4.7%, but lower than Midwestern neighbors Detroit, Milwaukee, Kansas City, Kan., Cleveland and Cincinnati. For the wider Chicago metropolitan area, the rate of job creation surpassed the Midwest as a whole last year and is forecast to continue doing so through 2009, says Moody's Economy.com, a research firm in West Chester, Pa.

Like the fast-changing weather here, not all is sunny. Per capita income growth has been constrained, perhaps by the city's vast influx of Mexican immigrants, says William Testa, Midwest economist for the Federal Reserve Bank of Chicago. An Economy.com forecast predicts that Chicago and other Great Lakes cities could be hurt by the retirement of aging baby boomers after 2010. And diversification is no cure-all: Buffalo, N.Y., the only city that ranks ahead of Chicago on that measure, has been declining in population and job growth.

Chicago also remains challenged by poverty, crime and racial segregation, though by some measures they have stabilized or eased somewhat during the past decade. Hispanics have moved into both black and white neighborhoods, and a recent report by the Brookings Institution says several other Midwestern cities are more segregated. Chicago's reported crime came down by a third in the 10 years from 1995 to 2004, according to one measure, about twice the drop in comparable national figures.

For now at least, diversification has helped cushion Chicago from the economic woes of some other Midwestern cities, as a look at the former Montgomery Ward "Catalog House" shows.

The building opened in 1908 as demand for goods from the 1,000-page-plus Montgomery Ward catalog was booming. It was perfectly positioned on the river to take advantage of Chicago's industrial and transportation base. Three rail spurs, around 100 truck docks, miles of conveyor belts and dozens of forklifts helped shuttle everything from clothing to barbed wire to saddles. Montgomery Ward "pickers," who plucked items from shelves, used roller skates to traverse a concrete floor the length of 2½ football fields.

The eight-story warehouse, with more than 1.5 million square feet of space, forms a trapezoidal footprint that takes up most of a city block. When it opened, it was surrounded by companies that made Chicago an industrial powerhouse. Oil-tank makers, wagon works, faucet makers and underwear factories set up alongside lumber, coal and stone yards, tanneries and varnish companies.

Fifty years later, Montgomery Ward had opened stores across the country and passed $1 billion in annual sales. But Sears Roebuck & Co. was first to open suburban stores, helping send Montgomery Ward into a gradual decline. By 1980, the company's catalog business had shriveled, and the Catalog House was too old and too big for its distribution needs. Montgomery Ward transferred the building's shipping operations to Ohio and began remodeling the structure, which had been named a National Historic Landmark two years earlier.

The company decided to shut down its catalog business entirely in 1985. By then, most of the Catalog House was empty. Floors once occupied by rows of merchandise bins now housed a company print shop, other Montgomery Ward corporate services and a giant mainframe computer.

Likewise, Chicago was undergoing painful change. The recession of the early 1980s had hit hard. Foreign competition and productivity gains from new technologies buffeted the city's factory workers. Steel mills and other plants closed. Bank consolidation or closures robbed the city of several of its bank headquarters.

By the late 1980s, though, business services that had grown up around Chicago's Rust Belt industries were flourishing. As manufacturers streamlined their operations, they outsourced former in-house functions like human resources or marketing. In turn, those business-service firms needed their own business services. The number of Chicago metro-area jobs created in specialized professional services like legal advice, consulting and

accounting outpaced nearly every other U.S. metropolitan area between 1990 and 2000, according to a review of U.S. Bureau of Labor Statistics done by the city's economic development corporation.

At the end of the 1990s, Montgomery Ward was on its last legs and in bankruptcy proceedings. The Catalog House seemed destined to become a boarded-up eyesore, joining other vacant buildings in the neighborhood.

Instead, the warehouse was revived and transformed. In 1999, two real-estate development companies acquired the building from General Electric Co., Montgomery Ward's new owner. It was part of a $62 million deal that included 26 acres near the merchandiser's headquarters tower and other land GE was selling off. The developers hoped the warehouse and surrounding land could anchor a redevelopment of the area.

Big Obstacle

The revival faced a big obstacle from the outset: The neighborhood is dominated by the Cabrini-Green Homes, a huge public-housing development that was once one of the most notorious projects in the country for crime and violence. Though the city had begun tearing them down, a large number of the 10-story brick buildings still housed many poor families. Prostitutes walked the streets and break-ins were common, says Ron Shipka Sr., a principal in the Enterprise Cos., a real-estate development firm that's now based in the former warehouse and which developed one of the nearby properties. "This was a horrible neighborhood," he says. "It was a ghost town."

The owners—Chicago-based developer Centrum Properties Inc. and New York City-based investment firm Angelo, Gordon & Co.—christened the immediate area Kingsbury Park, after a street running through the land. They began a $250 million rehab on the aged building converting it to offices and spent another $150 million turning an extension into condos, hoping to bring in young professionals who were already swarming into nearby trendy neighborhoods, such as Wicker Park and Lincoln Park, says Sol Barket, a partner with Centrum.

The owners donated some of the land to the city for parks, and the city then spent $30 million in the area on extending roads, landscaping parks and building a riverside pedestrian and bicycle thoroughfare along the edge of the Montgomery Ward property.

The owners first tried a narrow-sector approach aimed at the booming dot-com industry. They brought in a third partner, the telecom development firm Taconic Investment Partners, which had converted the former Manhattan headquarters of the Port Authority of New York and New Jersey into a building for media and telecom tenants. The owners renamed the building "e-port" and poured hundreds of thousands of dollars into high-end wiring, power generators and fancy plasma TVs in the lobby.

They reopened the building in October 2001, and at first attracted large telecom and Internet tenants, including RCN Corp. and WorldCom Inc., as MCI was then called. But just as quickly, the telecom industry unraveled and the dotcom boom went bust. The e-port reached only a dismal 40% occupancy. Broadwing Corp. vacated, and fellow fiber-optics provider Level 3 Communications Inc. put up two-thirds of its 180,000 square feet for sublease.

Broader Appeal

By the next April, management zigged again, dropping the "e-port" name to broaden the appeal to Chicago's other industries. They renamed the warehouse 600 West Chicago, its address on Chicago Avenue, and courted chic retail establishments, such as the Japonais Restaurant and an upscale David Barton Gym, to help make the building a hip destination, says Mr. Barket. Meanwhile, they also began filling the condo portion of the building. Developers were converting other nearby factories and offices into condos.

More than 20 office tenants now occupy 70% of the old Catalog House. As they enter the building each morning, nearly 2,000 workers navigate around eight-sided columns three feet thick, covered with steel sleeves meant to protect them from errant forklifts of the past. Exposed ceilings reveal copper and other metal pipes and large air vents that generate a low hum. Adding retro and modern touches, Centrum put a century-old electrical control panel from the warehouse on display next to the lobby elevators. Nearby, lighted plastic wall panels turn from blue to lime to magenta to orange.

"The types of workers that are there, they're making a lot of money, they're coming to work in jeans," says Mr. Barket. "They don't want a stuffy, corporate environment."

Several first-floor tenants—including a holistic fertility clinic called "Pulling Down the Moon" and a sports-medicine center—face onto the river walk. People from nearby condos walk their dogs outside the warehouse, and joggers in track suits pass by. The neighborhood also is home to subsidized apartments built to house displaced residents of the Cabrini-Green projects.

On the warehouse's third and fourth floors, Bankers Life & Casualty Co., a Chicago-based health insurer that focuses on the elderly, has occupied 220,000 square feet since 2004. It has 600 customer-service, billing and other back-office workers in the building and an option to take as much as 50,000 square feet more. "There was a sense that was an area in transition, but the question was, 'Is it going to make that transition?'" says Scott Perry, 43, the company's chief operating officer. "It's exceeded the expectations."

Japonais Restaurant co-owner Rick Wahlstedt, a friend of Mr. Barket's, says he moved in downstairs because he wanted the cachet of a "destination location" in an up-and-coming neighborhood. "Chicago to me is more of a recession-proof city than New York or Los Angeles," says Mr. Wahlstedt, who says he owns seven restaurants with partners in other cities. With sales at Japonais up 10% over a year ago, he says he plans to open a French *brasserie* across the street.

Bloomberg So Far

FRED SIEGEL AND HARRY SIEGEL

When Michael Bloomberg was elected mayor in 2001, New Yorkers had little idea what to expect from him. A liberal Democrat by disposition turned Republican by opportunity, the billionaire media baron had no previous political experience. He had used his fortune to conduct a stealth campaign, bombarding the public with direct mailings and television advertising and making virtually no unscripted appearances. Wrapped only in the halo of outgoing mayor Rudolph Giuliani's belated endorsement, and widely expected to lose, the would-be mayor was barely questioned, let alone tested, before he took office.

In the immediate wake of 9/11, Bloomberg's conciliatory and willfully apolitical style turned out to be well suited to the city's sense of trauma. The political neophyte seemed to promise Giuliani-like results without the ex-prosecutor's abrasive, stentorian style. Now, halfway through his tenure and with talk of the next mayoral election already in the air, Bloomberg has a record and an established public personality. He is far more of a known quantity, even if much of what can now be said about him is neither especially flattering nor encouraging for the future of New York.

To his credit, and despite his sometimes graceless efforts to escape his predecessor's shadow, Bloomberg has consolidated and even extended a number of Giuliani's most important achievements. Contrary to the expectations of many commentators, there has been no increase in crime in New York City, nor a renewed sense of urban dread and menace. In fact, since Bloomberg took office, the crime rate has dropped a further 10 percent, thanks in no small measure to the latitude that he has given to his police commissioner, Raymond Kelly. Moreover, as the mayor noted in his recent State of the City address, "We've done all this while protecting the nation's most important city against the constant threat of terror."

Bloomberg has also built upon the success of Compstat, the block-by-block breakdown of crime statistics that Giuliani instituted as a way to assign responsibility for public safety. Now the city has a similar system for quality-of-life problems, based on phoned-in complaints. By replicating the Compstat ethos of tracking data and quickly spotting undesirable trends, Bloomberg has made the city more responsive to the petty annoyances—potholes, noise violations, inadequate garbage pickups, cell-phone dead spots—that can make life in New York a daily trial.

Bloomberg's most significant accomplishment to date has been winning back mayoral control of the city's schools. For years, 110 Livingston Street, the Board of Education's downtown Brooklyn address, had been shorthand for Byzantine bureaucracy and wanton waste. Giuliani had paved the way for the takeover with his tough talk about the need to "blow up" the Board of Education; but the former mayor's enemies in Albany, where such decisions are made, refused to give him the victory. State lawmakers proved more receptive to Bloomberg's calm and conciliatory style.

From a purely administrative point of view, Bloomberg's reorganization of the schools has thus far been highly successful. Textbooks are delivered on time, and supplies are available. The powerful custodians' union, which has been ripping off the city for years, is being brought to heel through the partial privatization of janitorial services. More important, a mayor can no longer hide behind the Board when schools perform poorly while stepping forward to take credit for any and all signs of educational progress. Bloomberg has repeatedly said that if he fails to reform the education system, he should be voted out of office—a commendable pledge of accountability.

But there are other items than these on Bloomberg's ledger sheet, and too many of them fall decidedly into the debit column. Though there is no denying the importance of his having won mayoral control of the schools, his use of that control with respect to the curriculum has been irresponsible, even reckless. As a candidate, Bloomberg spoke of the need for a back-to-basics approach to education. But the instructional program imposed by the mayor and his schools chancellor, Joel Klein (formerly the Justice Department's lead counsel in the Microsoft case), is straight out of the left-wing fever swamps of Columbia Teachers College. Advised by Diana Lam, a well-known advocate of "progressive" education, Klein abandoned a variety of phonics programs that had shown some success in improving reading scores, replacing them with a one-size-fits-all "whole language" approach that has a long history of failure. Worse, the literacy effort has been micromanaged from Klein's office, which has told even experienced and successful teachers how to arrange every minute of their day and every inch of their classrooms. Blackboards, for example, are prohibited, as is arranging chairs in rows with the teacher in the front. (According to the slogan of progressive education, a teacher must act not as "a sage on the stage" but as a "guide on the side.") This attack on pedagogical authority has even extended to school discipline, emboldening unruly students and generating a surge in violence against teachers.

Education aside, Bloomberg has expended valuable political capital on various pet causes. The most notorious of these has been his anti-smoking campaign. He used much of the good will of his honeymoon in office to pass a draconian law that banned smoking in bars and other heretofore unregulated places and dramatically raised the cigarette tax—an issue he had not mentioned as a candidate. The predictable result has been a new and violent black market in out-of-state cigarettes and vastly increased noise levels outside bars, some of which have lost considerable business. Even voters sympathetic to his cause were offended when the mayor promoted it by warning the citizenry, with missionary zeal, that "more people [would] die from second-hand smoke than were killed in the World Trade Center."

A worthier effort, if one handled just as badly, was Bloomberg's campaign in 2003 to persuade voters to approve a ballot initiative establishing nonpartisan elections for mayor and City Council. The proposal was hardly revolutionary. Nonpartisan elections—already in place in eight of the country's ten largest cities—open up municipal government to a wider range of interests. In New York City, such a reform would help to break the powerful hold of the public-sector unions, whose highly organized members dominate the all important Democratic primary.

But it takes time to explain how nonpartisanship would make elections more competitive and politicians more accountable. Bloomberg insisted on rushing the matter, placing it on the ballot only a few months after it was officially proposed by a charter commission that he had appointed. Trying to replicate the stealth tactics that had helped him win the mayoralty, he blitzed voters with a last minute, $7.5-million direct-mail campaign. The results were predictable. Although nonpartisanship enjoyed a slight majority of support among the electorate as a whole, the 12 percent who bothered to vote in this off-year ballot—many of them drawn from the same pool of public-sector employees whose influence Bloomberg was trying to limit—defeated the proposal by a margin of more than 2 to 1. In what Dan Janison of *Newsday* called his "Evita moment," the mayor declared that what mattered was not the outcome but the effort: "I was a big winner yesterday."

Even a reform as intelligent as nonpartisan elections is no substitute for dealing more directly with the public-sector interests that have long been the fiscal albatross around New York City's neck. Like Giuliani before him, Bloomberg was given a poor economic hand. The city was in recession even before 9/11, and the new mayor was saddled with rising pension and Medicaid costs imposed during Giuliani's boom years. He arrived in office facing a budget deficit of $4 billion. But unlike Giuliani, Bloomberg played his poor hand poorly, especially in his dealings with his "friend," Governor George Pataki, on one side and with the public-sector unions on the other. In both cases his watchword was "partnership"—in contrast, presumably, with Giuliani's vaunted confrontationalism. Thus, lavishing praise on the Republican governor and donating $1 million of his personal money to the state GOP, Bloomberg went so far as to support an obviously unpopular fare hike imposed on the city's buses and subways by the Pataki-controlled transportation authority. What he got in exchange was worse than nothing. Pataki refused Bloomberg's reasonable request to help reinstate the city's small but symbolically important commuter tax, while permitting him to raise the city's sales and income taxes, already the highest in the region.

The story was similar with the public-sector unions. Perhaps the most dramatic incident occurred in December 2002, when Roger Toussaint, the radical president of the Transit Workers Union, threatened to strike rather than accept changes in work rules that would allow, among other things, subway cleaners to change light bulbs and do minor painting. Placed in a similar situation, Giuliani had made clear how much damage he could do to the union under the law; Bloomberg, instead, spoke plaintively of how much damage the union could do to the city. "A strike," he said, "would be more than inconvenient. It would endanger human life and devastate our economy." Toussaint largely got his way.

The pattern of behavior that Toussaint capitalized on had been set earlier. In what he declared to be a new "partnership" between the city and its public sector unions, Bloomberg had announced, before even sitting down to bargaining sessions, that he would do everything he could to avoid layoffs. Where Giuliani had restrained hiring through a vacancy-control board, Bloomberg quickly abolished the board. Where Giuliani had used the threat of privatization to win concessions from unions, Bloomberg promised to avoid such measures wherever possible. He also made no effort to renegotiate the unions' health, benefits, and pension plans, all of which are far more generous than similar plans in the private sector and in most other big cities.

In exchange for this new spirit of cooperation, Bloomberg expected good will from the other side. Naturally, it never materialized. But the mayor's naive expectation was costly, causing him to wait almost a year before imposing any kind of serious controls on hiring and spending. The results were devastating for the city's overall financial health. Where Giuliani reduced spending by 3 percent in his inaugural year, Bloomberg increased spending by almost as much—increments that amounted to much more than peanuts in New York City's massive budget. As the Manhattan Institute's E.J. McMahon has noted, if Bloomberg "had duplicated Rudy's spending restraint in his first two fiscal years, the city would now be spending about $2.5 billion less, and most of Bloomberg's tax and fee hikes wouldn't have been necessary."

"That Bloomberg has, in fact, closed the city's budget gap primarily through those "tax and hikes" has been especially galling to many who supported him. Bloomberg ran for office on a ringing pledge of no new taxes, confirming this in his first speech as mayor when he warned that higher taxes would only "drive people and business out of New York." But within a year, he had sharply raised cigarette, sales, and income taxes. Over the noisy protests of middle-class homeowners in every borough, he also pushed through a whopping 21-percent increase in the property tax. All of these hikes, insisted the mayor of a city that was already the most taxed in the nation, were unavoidable.

By the last quarter of 2003, Michael Bloomberg had achieved the unhappy distinction of possessing the lowest approval rating ever held by a modern mayor of New York. To explain his deep unpopularity, it is not enough, though, to catalogue his policy missteps. Bloomberg is disliked, even hated, not just because of what he has done but perhaps in equal measure because of how he has done it.

A self-made man who has accumulated a personal fortune of $4.5 billion, Bloomberg possesses an overweening self-confidence, acting at times as if it were demeaning to have to explain himself to others. Plainly, he is someone accustomed to having his word taken as law. But City Hall is a very different place from the boardroom, and rarely has a mayor shown himself, by temperament or forethought, to be less prepared to govern a major city.

Like Bloomberg, Giuliani had never held elected office prior to his victory in 1993. But Giuliani had spent years in the public sphere as a federal prosecutor. More important, he had already made one unsuccessful run for mayor, and after his defeat had gone to work studying every aspect of city policy. Once elected, Giuliani was single-minded in the performance of his job, immersing himself for eighteen hours a day in the details of government operations while at the same time keeping the big picture in sight.

What has stood out with Bloomberg, by contrast, is his aloofness, not just from the city (he often quietly escapes by private jet for weekends at his home in Bermuda) but from city government itself. Unlike his predecessor, he has neither taken a direct hand in running the city's maze of bureaucracies nor tried to give specific guidance to his appointees.

Moreover, for a hard-headed businessman who now presides over a budget larger than that of all but eight states, Bloomberg can seem appallingly naive. When he insisted (to guffaws) that "corruption, waste, and meaningless programs hardly exist in city government," he was declaring himself content with business as usual, and essentially denying that the city faced any sort of crisis.

For a great many New Yorkers whose wonted relationship to their mayor is visceral and intimate, this detachment has been too much to bear. Time and again, Bloomberg has proved that he simply does not understand average New Yorkers or empathize with their travails. As the possibility of a subway strike loomed, he dragged reporters along to watch him buy a $600 bicycle, and suggested that others should meet their transportation needs in the same way. At a time when middle-class New Yorkers were outraged by his tax hikes, he jauntily told an elite Manhattan business group that the city was "a high-end product, maybe even a luxury product." Further stoking the anger of his critics, he jibed that he, for one, was perfectly willing to pay higher taxes.

Has Bloomberg learned anything from the rocky first years of his tenure? Perhaps. In his State of the City address this January, he seemed intent on relaunching his mayoralty with an appeal to New York's outer boroughs. The highlight of the speech was a proposal to issue a $400 rebate against the huge property-tax increase he had imposed. Striking, too, was the tone of the address, with its stress on crime control and the city's quality of life—clear echoes of Giuliani's priorities. For the first time, the mayor seemed to be talking to—instead of at—voters.

What remains unclear is whether Bloomberg now understands the deeper issue for New York: the enduring and now-desperate need to shrink and reform the city's bloated public sector. If nothing else, he has certainly placed himself on a collision course with the unions, virtually all of whose major contracts are up for renegotiation this year. Working to close an estimated $2-billion deficit—and, thanks to his proposed rebate, with less money at hand—he has stipulated that any salary increase will have to be paid for by improvements in productivity. Needless to say, this position is fiercely opposed by the unions.

The grim reality facing New Yorkers concerned about the future of the city is that the billionaire incumbent, an accidental mayor who seems to have run for office primarily to test himself with a new challenge, may be their best hope among the available alternatives. Since the defeat of the initiative for non-partisan elections, Left-liberal rivals have been making ready their campaigns. They include Fernando (Freddy) Ferrer, an ally of Al Sharpton who almost won the Democratic mayoral nomination the last time around, and Gifford Miller, the speaker of the City Council and a young and willing accomplice of the city's spending interests. In short, Bloomberg could well be defeated in 2005 by a candidate backed by and ready to accommodate the same interests that are slowly strangling the city and driving away its middle class.

It is hard to exaggerate the danger of such a relapse. Bloomberg is fond of reassuring audiences that "smart people have to be here if they want to be successful." This, however, has become less true with each passing year, especially as New York's costs have risen in relation to those of its competitors. The last recession set a telling precedent. Usually the city and the region rise and fall together, but this time New Jersey and Connecticut, which have diversified their economies by attracting industries once based overwhelmingly in New York, recovered quickly—and left the city behind.

Behind the sparkle and dynamism of today's New York is the mundane fact that, with the exception of San Francisco, no other American city has lost residents at a higher rate over the past several years. Poor and ill-educated immigrants have continued to flow into the city, while highly skilled people with intellectual capital continue to decamp for places that offer them more and tax them less. For the city's Democratic politicians and the public employees they represent, this may be good news; the middle class has always been the chief political obstacle to their hold on power. For New York City as a whole—even for those precincts of it inhabited by the likes of Michael Bloomberg—such news is a portent of dark days ahead.

FRED SIEGEL is a professor at Cooper Union and was a member of the 2003 charter commission appointed by Mayor Bloomberg. HARRY SIEGEL, the editor-in-chief of *New Partisan*, is writing a book on gentrification in New York.

Mayors and Morality: Daley and Lindsay Then and Now

FRED SIEGEL

*Chicago's traditional tribalism looks remarkably similar
to the modern multiculturalism of the Democratic Party.*

—Paul McGrath, high-ranking advisor
to former Chicago mayor Jane Byrne

History seems to have come full circle for the Daleys of Chicago. In 1960 Mayor Richard J. Daley, who had been elected with black votes, temporarily made himself a hero to liberal Democrats when he played a key role in electing John Kennedy president. Forty years later his oldest son William Daley, working with Jesse Jackson, ran the campaign to put Al Gore into the White House. Over the past forty years of racial politics the Daleys have gone from darlings to demons and back again.

Political archetypes sometimes play tricks on us. Consider John Kennedy and Ronald Reagan. They were born just six years apart yet JFK is frozen in our memory as forever youthful, while few can imagine Reagan as anything but doddering. Mayors John Lindsay of New York and Richard J. Daley of Chicago are remembered as the antithetical embodiments of the 1960s urban crisis. Yet New York and Chicago are anything but typical. "New York," notes Saul Bellow, "is a European city though of no known nationality." While only a Bertolt Brecht could imagine that Chicago, a city of Slavs governed by Irishmen along the lines of European Christian Democracy, was typically American. Neither man's national reputation seemed to have survived the era's cauldron of racial politics. Both men reached their nadir in 1972: Lindsay in his brief but disastrous run for the presidency; Daley when his delegation was refused admittance to the Democratic convention only to be replaced by a group led by Jesse Jackson.

Nonetheless, the two mayors became ideograms frozen in the paratactic moments of urban rioting. The image of Lindsay that still endures is of a caring man walking the streets of Harlem, courageously keeping the city relatively calm as other cities went up in flames. The primary author of the Kerner Commission report on urban riots, Lindsay saw racism not only as a scourge but as virtually the sole explanation for African-American poverty. The jowly Daley by contrast was as rough-edged as Lindsay was smooth. His frustrated press secretary once blurted, "Print what he means not what he says." One of his most famous malapropisms was, "The policeman isn't there to create disorder; the policeman is there to preserve disorder." Daley's infamous "shoot to kill" arsonists order during the 1968 riots as well as the police riots that accompanied the Democratic Convention of that year are often the first things his name brings to mind.

Daley's and Lindsay's names were taken as the pole stars of city politics. Here's how *The Boston Globe* described the once-promising career of Mayor Kevin White when he left office: "Elected in 1967 as Boston's answer to John Lindsay, New York's young reform mayor, White left in 1984 as Boston's Richard Daley, the aging and resented Chicago machine boss." In the mid-1960s, Lindsay, his picture on the cover of all the newsweeklies, was seen as nothing less than the Second Coming of JFK. His youth, vigor, and moral commitment to racial equality gave him an extraordinary aura. There was even talk—talk that Lindsay encouraged—that he was likely to be president some day. But if Lindsay was once revered, this New York mayor who was supposed to represent the future of urban America has since been largely forgotten, while Daley, the man reviled as a dinosaur, is not only remembered but extolled as forerunner of today's successful new-wave mayors.

While Lindsay has been ranked as one of the worst big city mayors, the same poll of political scientists and historians selected Daley as the single best mayor of the late twentieth century and one of the ten best in American history. Today Daley's son, Richard M. Daley, reigns virtually unchallenged as his father's legatee. And at a time when mayors like to think of themselves as efficient managers rather than the social conscience of the country, the phrase "Boss Daley," popularized by Mike Royko, has, says Alan Ehrenhalt, "lost the evil connotation for most people that it seemed to have a quarter-century ago."

Why the reversal? In part, says political analyst Jim Chapin, it is a matter both of exoticism and of subtly shifting standards. In the sixties, jowly, aging, overweight machine politicians were old hat, a dime a dozen; the blow-dried dynamic Lindsay seemed different and promising. But today, in an era of smiling empty suits, Lindsay's style no longer looks promisingly authentic. Instead, a nostalgic haze glosses over the cigar chomping, backroom corruption, and police brutality of the Daley years. Today we can chuckle at the informal slogan of Fred Roti, a longtime First Ward alderman: "Vote for Fred Roti and no one gets hurt." The notorious mob-run First Ward also had Jackie "the Lackey" Cerone who, when described by the Associated Press as a "minor gangland figure," called to complain about the "minor."

At a time when liberals have largely given up on universalism, Daley's tribalism no longer seems so egregious. In retrospect, notes Paul McGrath, Daley was the least racist mayoral candidate of the 1950s and '60s in a city whose whites seethed with anti-black animus. Daley first won election in 1955 against the backdrop of a two-year-long, sometimes violent campaign by whites to keep blacks out of the far South Side of Chicago. The white incumbent Martin Kennelly openly courted backlash voters, while black voters backed Daley in order to bring down Kennelly. It was a measure of Daley's skill that he was endorsed by both *The Chicago Defender,* the city's leading black newspaper, and by white groups on the far South Side. Unable to adapt to the new climate of civil rights, Daley tried, with mixed success, to fit blacks into the machine politics mold. As he famously put it, "Why don't they act like the Poles, Jews, and the Irish?"

But if Daley was unable to see how the history of racism made the black condition distinctive, for Lindsay blacks were *sui generis.* Lindsay governed a liberal city that had already experienced something of a civil rights movement in the late 1940s and '50s. Yet by confronting the issue of race as simply a matter of white racism, Lindsay, the patrician paternalist, so empathized with black anger that he left his city far more polarized than he found it. While Daley couldn't see why the grandchildren of slaves and the children of semi-enslaved sharecroppers needed special help, Lindsay exempted African-Americans from any code of conduct. He explained away any and all behavior by those who claimed to speak for black anger.

Lindsay believed that government could save the cities and right innumerable wrongs. But three decades of HUD policy makes it hard to maintain that optimism. President Clinton's first HUD secretary, Henry Cisneros, testified to Congress in June 1993: "HUD has in many cases exacerbated the declining quality of life in America's cities." A dramatic case in point: the 1968 National Housing Act created the Section 235 program to provide subsidized loans to low-income families, with special assistance for welfare mothers, to buy houses. When the vast majority of the new owners defaulted on these loans there was widespread abandonment and devastation. Carl Levin, then Detroit City Council President, now a liberal Democratic senator, called the upshot "Hurricane HUD." *The Chicago Tribune* wrote that "no natural disaster on record has caused destruction on the scale of the government's housing programs. . . . " For a Gotham analog we have only to look to East New York in the 1960s, where urban renewal and HUD policy produced massive foreclosures in private properties bought with federal aid. More recently a real estate revival in Harlem has been stalled by a new HUD scandal in which the

Section 203(K) program created in 1978 to bring stability to low-income neighborhoods has been used, explains *The New York Times,* by "real estate speculators, mortgage lenders and nonprofit groups involved in a complex scheme in which they pocketed millions in rehabilitation money and profits from selling and reselling the buildings in quick succession."

As the passions of the sixties cooled and the costs of that era became apparent, Lindsay's moralism seems less alluring and his managerial failings seem more significant. New York's City Club (Lindsay himself was a member) complained that the mayoralty was "in the hands of people who know all about management—or its vocabulary—except how to get a job done." If Lindsay often viewed issues through a veil of abstraction aimed at impressing *The New York Times* editorial board, Daley emphasized the mundane housekeeping elements of the mayor's job which anticipated today's concern with quality of life issues. What Daley couldn't grasp was the liberal-moralist dimensions of racial politics. When Daley was confronted by Martin Luther King in 1968, he told the civil rights leader that "your goals are our goals" but offered very little in the way of either concrete changes or symbolic acknowledgment of white guilt. King was taken aback when Daley threw the ball back into his court, asking him, "What are your solutions, how do you eliminate slums and blight overnight?" When Jesse Jackson got his first audience with Daley, the mayor offered him a job as a toll-taker.

Daley had an immensely personal concern with the city, extending from everything: from individuals—it's said that he knew half of the city's forty thousand workers personally—to keeping the city clean and attractive. Today it is his son who has completed his vision of cleaning up the Chicago River for recreation.

Daley may have been dubbed a dinosaur in the 1960s, but Lindsay, the self-styled progressive, was on the wrong side of history when it came to the central issues of property and homeownership. While Daley was the champion of property-owning democracy, one of the few prominent Democrats in the sixties who empathized with the middle class, Lindsay was the product of New York political culture which mixed bohemianism, upper-class pretension, and leftist ideology into a coalition of contempt for the homeowning petty bourgeoisie. Lindsay had nothing but disdain for what his administration described, and I quote, as "the ticky-tacky" homes of Archie Bunker's Queens. The first-generation homeowners of the outer boroughs, fearful that their newly acquired middle class status might be stripped from them, returned the hostility. Lindsay seemed comfortable only with those too wealthy to need to work or those unable or unwilling to work. Daley, who had emerged from the ranks of the lower middle class, always understood the importance of homeownership for those newly arrived in positions of relative prosperity. He was the favorite of those white Chicagoans who owned modest homes in the "Bungalow Belt."

The hidden issue of homeownership produced an often unexamined clash between the two American ideals—the rights of private property and the right to equality of opportunity, both essential to the American creed. Lindsay honored the American ideal of equal opportunity by using city hiring to expand black employment opportunities. But his attempts to build housing for poor, racially oppressed black families with high rates of criminality in the midst of lower middle class white neighborhoods was a threat to American ideals of private property, particularly a home safe from government depredations. Lindsay was too arrogant, too sure that his was necessarily the path of righteousness, to be a hypocrite on these matters.

But Daley, like most effective politicians, was a practiced hypocrite. He protected the property rights of white homeowners at the cost of containing even black middle class families in the festering conditions of the inner city. Daley dragged his feet on expanding homeowning opportunities for African-Americans on political grounds. There was an intense and violent opposition when a black family moved into his own neighborhood of Bridgeport in 1955; the house was dismantled almost brick by brick. And the only time he was challenged politically came in 1963 from white critics who, shortly after the Robert Taylor homes had been constructed, said he had done too much for blacks. At the time, the Robert Taylor homes were seen as a big improvement, and they were built in black congressman William Dawson's district at his request and as his reward for service to the machine. Daley won re-election that year with overwhelming black support, while losing a majority of white voters.

A new book by photographer Wayne Miller chronicles the arrival of the people who moved into Robert Taylor. The modern viewer is struck by the still Southern character of the migrants as seen in photos of rabbits strung up across the sidewalk. Even more striking was the housing which looked like the rickety shacks that had been left behind in the Mississippi delta, except these were shacks piled up three and four stories high. These ramshackle homes were the site of innumerable fires, collapsed porches and buildings, garbage-strewn alleyways, rats rampant, an absence of indoor plumbing, disease.

Later, when they became vertical disasters, Daley's critics argued that he maliciously packed forty-thousand newly arrived African-Americans into the high-rise slum of the Robert Taylor homes. They note that "Robert Taylor construction was 'gold plated,' a gift to politically connected contractors. A licensed electrician belonging to a Daley-allied union had to be on site every time a refrigerator was plugged in." And federal money that might have gone into maintaining the vast complex was siphoned into the hands of Daley cronies who operated law firms and insurance companies. And if that wasn't bad enough, the Dan Ryan Expressway, like the Robert Taylor homes built with federal money "Daley was so good at getting," sealed the projects off from the rest of the city.

But Daley fought against high-rise buildings; "when I see my neighborhood I see all the neighborhoods of Chicago," he explained. In Washington he argued for walk-ups and row houses of the sort that other groups occupied as their first step on the housing ladder, but he was rebuffed by housing officials who insisted that only high-rises could meet federal cost

concerns. In other words, if we ask if the Taylor homes were a product of Daley's racism, the answer is both *yes* and *no*.

If liberals thought high-rises were reactionary in Chicago, they found them quite progressive when Lindsay proposed to build three twenty-four-story high-rise apartment buildings in the heart of a middle class Jewish neighborhood, Forest Hills, in Queens. Black and Italian middle class areas were vehemently opposed to the project, but Lindsay assumed the Jewish liberals who had voted for him in 1965 wouldn't object, and when they did he spoke of the project's "moral imperative" and denounced the opponents as "racists"—his favorite epithet. The residents of Forest Hills, it seems, were often people who had fled from Brownsville, Crown Heights, Hunts Point, and Far Rockaway into the safety of a pleasant neighborhood, and they didn't want to have to flee again.

Lindsay's narrow emphasis on race seems dated today. Consider the current controversy in Baltimore over an ACLU lawsuit designed to move welfare families into integrated working-to-middle-class neighborhoods in Northeast Baltimore with Section 8 vouchers. (Unsurprisingly, the ACLU lawyer who initiated the suit lives in a tony neighborhood entirely free of Section 8 tenants.)

City Council president Sheila Dixon and State Senator Joan Conway, both black representatives of Northeast Baltimore, are fighting the decision. Their city, they note, has a terrible track record in these matters. Keith Norris, a council member from the district who is also black, explains that he grew up in Park Heights and "witnessed firsthand its gradual decay . . . as a result of flawed public policy." He sees property ownership not only as an emblem of achievement but as a guarantee of social stability that is now threatened by government action.

"As a homeowner now," says Norris, "I don't want wilting property values to sap the spirit of residents . . . nor do I want to see the community used as a stage for a courtroom drama." If people are to be brought in "what must be different this time is the amount of support these families get...[such as] classes in home maintenance, landscaping, money management, and child care."

When I spoke to people in Northeast Baltimore, they snorted that "the government specializes in sending welfare populations into weak targets." "You won't see any welfare families sent to Roland Park," one black man snapped at me, referring to the Scarsdale-like neighborhood that resembles Rock Creek Park in the District of Columbia.

In other words, Daley's caution in these matters was more than a matter of racism, it was also—as a recent Chicago experiment with homeowners equity insurance suggests—a matter of helping lower middle class people protect their nest eggs. Derided as "black insurance" when the idea was proposed thirty years ago by the radical Saul Alinsky, homeowners equity insurance enables low-income homeowners to insure the current value of their property in order to prevent white flight. It was initially defeated by pressure from both real estate interests and black politicians, like Tim Evans, who were more concerned with maintaining black political majorities than better housing.

In the ten years since the program finally began under Daley Jr. in 1990, only ten homeowners on the Southwest Side have filed claims. Though the white population has shrunk to about 20 percent of the total (with the rest divided almost evenly between blacks and Hispanics), it is still far greater than in most surrounding areas. Perhaps most telling, property values have steadily climbed. The only catch is that participating residents are required to wait at least five years before a sale below the assessed value entitles them to file a claim. That catch has been crucial. Having committed to live with their new neighbors for at least a few years, many longtime white residents discovered that integration wasn't the horror they had expected.

Neighborhoods, notes *The Wall Street Journal's* Jonathan Eig, are class as well as race-sorting mechanisms:

> The home-equity program serves as a reminder that racial integration often is a matter of economic assimilation. Many of the black families that moved in a decade ago are now enrolling in the program because they fear that the new wave of Hispanic home buyers will damage property values, and Hispanic buyers are signing up because they're not so sure about the next generation of Hispanics.

Today the older Mayor Daley looks like a man ahead of his time on a variety of issues. He had doubts not only about high-rises but also about the social programs of the 1960s. He asked, "Is poor housing the cause of murder and arson?" Similarly, long before broken-windows policing became a great success, he understood that a city has to take care of the small things to maintain its quality of life.

The Lindsayites, however, seem stuck in the past. Recently I took part in a debate at the City University of New York Graduate Center on the question of whether John Lindsay was the worst New York mayor of the twentieth century. The event doubled as a Lindsay alumni reunion so the audience was packed with Lindsayites. And here I should note that the phrase "limousine liberal" is not merely a metaphor—after the debate, as I left the auditorium to go out onto Fifth Avenue, both sides of the street were lined with long black stretch limos.

During the course of the discussion the Lindsayites replied to every disaster, from the doubling of the welfare rolls in the midst of an economic boom to the bankruptcy Lindsay's policies visited on the city, with one of two responses. The first was that Lindsay was a "compassionate man": "Why, he even cried at the death of a black colleague's father." The other was to argue that no one who wasn't a part of the administration could understand or evaluate it. "You had to be there, you had to be inside the administration" to judge it, they insisted time and again. This argument, it so happens, was the favorite of the Lindsayites' archnemesis, Archie Bunker. When Bunker's son-in-law tried to explain to Archie why Vietnam was wrong, Archie replied that "Meathead" didn't know "nuttin'". If you wanted to judge a war, "you had to be there" just like Archie had been there in "the big one, World War II." The

Lindsayites' sanctimony had not only effectively sealed them off from learning from their failures, it had reduced them to the caricature they had once mocked.

Still, in putting Lindsay in his proper place we ought not elevate Daley beyond his. The Chicago mayor faced an impossible situation inadequately. But he wasn't nearly as bad as the critics of his time suggested, nor was he as good as nostalgists suggest. We can judge Daley senior in part by what his son has done differently in a Chicago largely shorn of both machine politics and patronage. Once the tough among cities, in the words of Lincoln Steffens, Chicago has turned soft, so to speak. Symbolically, the son has left the family's ancestral home in working-class Bridgeport, which is now slowly gentrifying, for the more cosmopolitan climes of downtown. And while Chicago still suffers from police and government corruption, both Daleys paid inordinate attention to detail. Like his father, Richard M. Daley is planting trees at every opportunity. But the son runs a far more inclusive regime.

Richard M. Daley has done far more than his father to Lindsay-like bring African-Americans into government while improving the services offered to the rapidly growing number of black homeowning neighborhoods. In 1960s terms he has co-opted the black opposition more effectively than his father ever did. Both father and son courted black ministers but Richard M. has done far more to include blacks in city pork, as when he cut African-American politicians in on the lucrative food franchises at the city-owned O'Hare Airport. And black contractors were given a sizable chunk of the action when Daley built the new police headquarters in the historically African-American neighborhood of Bronzeville. Young Daley has supported affirmative action, criticized police brutality, and subsidized church loans for social service corporations. He is now in the process of tearing down the high-rise projects his father built and then generally neglected in favor of dispersing the welfare population into low-rise walk-ups. In three terms as mayor, Daley has gone from 3 percent of the black vote in 1989 to 45 percent last year when he defeated Congressman and former Black Panther Bobby Rush in a landslide even greater than those won by his father. In short, the Daleys have adjusted to a powerful African-American political presence, and most of the black leadership has adjusted to Chicago's one-party political culture.

The "Boss's" mantra of emphasizing "loyalty, hard work, and playing by the rules" was revived for Democrats by the centrist Democratic Leadership Council. The council's chair, Bill Clinton, picked up Daley's themes in his successful 1992 run for president. "Daleyism," referring to the father, was recently defined by John Judis writing in *The New Republic,* as a "cross-racial, working-class and lower middle class voting majority with the financial support of business—which is what every Democrat wants to bottle and imbibe these days." That is one reason why older brother Bill Daley ran Al Gore's campaign.

If there's merit to Richard J. Daley's revival, it's oddly enough because the elder Daley was a man behind the times.

In the 1960s he was a fish out of water, a localist in an era that demanded a universalist racial ethic. But as cities have, for the most part, become more racially inclusive, they've generally been able to return to the time-honored approaches that have always worked. Daley's passion for both private homeownership and the details of city life point to the policies of today's most successful mayors. But it's only as race has receded as a defining issue that Daley's parochial perspective, which sees affirmative action as just another way of dividing the spoils, could once again define the Democrats. In Chicago, an inclusive tribalism looks remarkably similar to the multiculturalism of Jesse Jackson and the liberal wing of the Democratic Party.

FRED SIEGEL is the author of *The Future Once Happened Here* (1997).

From *Partisan Review*, Spring 2001, pp. 218–227. Copyright © 2001 by Fred Siegel. Reprinted by permission of Fred Siegel.

UNIT 6

Sprawl: Challenges to the Metropolitan Landscape

Unit Selections

Key Points to Consider

- Should the country build more highways to encourage growth beyond cities?

- Should cities and regional planning bodies develop extensive public transportation systems to ease the burden that uncontrolled sprawl has on the highway system? If this were to happen, how could it best be implemented?

- Why do city dwellers choose to move to suburbs and exurbs? Why do people move into cities from less dense areas?

- What effect does planning have on city life? Can cities cooperate with the regions they are part of, or must they compete with their suburbs for people and money?

Student Web Site
www.mhcls.com/online

Internet References
Further information regarding these Web sites may be found in this book's preface or online.

American Studies Web
  http://www.georgetown.edu/crossroads/asw
Sprawl Guide
  http://www.plannersweb.com/sprawl/home.html
Yahoo/Social Science/Urban Studies
  http://www.yahoo.com/Social_Science/Urban_Studies

It's impossible to think about cities without looking at sprawl, and the attraction of the suburbs and exurbs. As cities have thrived over the last decade, growth itself has at times become the problem. Decentralizing cities have spread into the countryside, replacing millions of acres of farmland and open space with new development. What to do about sprawl? What about the social, political, and economic implications? Is it possible to control the impact that sprawl has on highway systems? How much of sprawl is subsidized, and how much due to market forces? Can or should exurban development be slowed? Are there effective ways to balance development without upsetting the environment?

None of these questions has easy or universal answers. Only a few places in the country have tried to directly control sprawl;

in many communities zoning boards have been slow to react to the flood of extensive development. The economic enticement of new taxes that are generated by the new businesses that move into the suburban periphery often overcomes opposition to those developments.

With rapid growth, however, comes sharp increase in population and services that can quickly outstrip a community's capacity to effectively handle the new requirements. "Patio Man and the Sprawl People" and "Downtown Struggles While Neighbor Thrives" examine the centrifugal social and economic forces that are drawing people and businesses from cities into exurbs and suburbs. Two other articles in this section look at how cities and regions are planned, and the effect of these plans on the competition between city and suburb.

Patio Man and the Sprawl People

America's Newest Suburbs

DAVID BROOKS

I don't know if you've ever noticed the expression of a man who is about to buy a first-class barbecue grill. He walks into a Home Depot or Lowe's or one of the other mega hardware complexes and his eyes are glistening with a faraway visionary zeal, like one of those old prophets gazing into the promised land. His lips are parted and twitching slightly. Inside the megastore, the grills are just past the racks of affordable-house plan books, in the yard-machinery section. They are arrayed magnificently next to the vehicles that used to be known as rider mowers but are now known as lawn tractors, because to call them rider mowers doesn't really convey the steroid-enhanced M-1 tank power of the things.

The man approaches the barbecue grills and his face bears a trance-like expression, suggesting that he has cast aside all the pains and imperfections of this world and is approaching the gateway to a higher dimension. In front of him are a number of massive steel-coated reactors with names like Broilmaster P3, The Thermidor, and the Weber Genesis, because in America it seems perfectly normal to name a backyard barbecue grill after a book of the Bible.

The items in this cooking arsenal flaunt enough metal to suggest they have been hardened to survive a direct nuclear assault, and Patio Man goes from machine to machine comparing their features—the cast iron/porcelain coated cooking surfaces, the 328,000-Btu heat-generating capacities, the 1,600-degree-tolerance linings, the multiple warming racks, the lava rock containment dishes, the built-in electrical meat thermometers, and so on. Certain profound questions flow through his mind. Is a 542-square-inch grilling surface really enough, considering that he might someday get the urge to roast an uncut buffalo steak? Though the matte steel overcoat resists scratching, doesn't he want a polished steel surface on his grill so he can glance down and admire his reflection as he is performing the suburban manliness rituals, such as brushing tangy sauce on meat slabs with his right hand while clutching a beer can in an NFL foam insulator ring in his left?

Pretty soon a large salesman in an orange vest who looks like a human SUV comes up to him and says, "Howyadoin'," which is, "May I help you?" in Home Depot talk. Patio Man, who has so much lust in his heart it is all he can do to keep from climbing up on one of these machines and whooping rodeo-style with joy, manages to respond appropriately. He grunts inarticulately and nods toward the machines. Careful not to make eye contact at any point, the two manly suburban men have a brief exchange of pseudo-scientific grill argot that neither of them understands, and pretty soon Patio Man has come to the reasoned conclusion that it really does make sense to pay a little extra for a grill with V-shaped metal baffles, ceramic rods, and a side-mounted smoker box. Plus the grill he selects has four insulated drink holders. All major choices of consumer durables these days ultimately come down to which model has the most impressive cup holders.

Patio Man pays for the grill with his credit card, and is told that some minion will forklift his machine over to the loading dock around back. It is yet another triumph in a lifetime of conquest shopping, and as Patio Man heads toward the parking lot he is glad once again that he's driving that Yukon XL so that he can approach the loading dock guys as a co-equal in the manly fraternity of Those Who Haul Things.

He steps out into the parking lot and is momentarily blinded by sun bouncing off the hardtop. The parking lot is so massive that he can barely see the Wal-Mart, the Bed Bath & Beyond, or the area-code-sized Old Navy glistening through the heat there on the other side. This mall is in fact big enough to qualify for membership in the United Nations, and is so vast that shoppers have to drive from store to store, cutting diagonally through the infinity of empty parking spaces in between.

As Patio Man walks past the empty handicapped and expectant-mother parking spots toward his own vehicle, wonderful grill fantasies dance in his imagination: There he is atop the uppermost tier of his multi-level backyard patio/outdoor recreation area posed like an admiral on the deck of his destroyer. In his mind's eye he can see himself coolly flipping the garlic and pepper T-bones on the front acreage of his new grill while carefully testing the citrus-tarragon trout filets that sizzle fragrantly in the rear. On the lawn below he can see his kids, Haley and Cody, frolicking on the weedless community lawn that is mowed twice weekly by the people who run Monument Crowne Preserve, his town-home community.

Haley, 12, is a Travel Team Girl, who spends her weekends playing midfield against similarly pony-tailed, strongly calved soccer marvels. Cody, 10, is a Buzz Cut Boy, whose naturally blond hair has been cut to a lawn-like stubble and dyed an almost phosphorescent white. Cody's wardrobe is entirely derivative of fashions he has seen watching the X-Games.

In his vision, Patio Man can see the kids enjoying their child-safe lawn darts with a gaggle of their cul de sac friends, a happy gathering of Haleys and Codys and Corys and Britneys. It's a brightly colored scene: Abercrombie & Fitch pink spaghetti-strap tops on the girls and ankle length canvas shorts and laceless Nikes on the boys. Patio Man notes somewhat uncomfortably that in America today the average square yardage of boys' fashion grows and grows while the square inches in the girls' outfits shrink and shrink, so that while the boys look like tent-wearing skateboarders, the girls look like preppy prostitutes.

Nonetheless, Patio Man envisions his own adult softball team buddies lounging on his immaculate deck furniture watching him with a certain moist envy in their eyes as he mans the grill. They are fit, sockless men in dock siders, chinos, and Tommy Bahama muted Hawaiian shirts. Their wives, trim Jennifer Aniston women, wear capris and sleeveless tops that look great owing to their many hours of sweat and exercise at Spa Lady. These men and women may not be Greatest Generation heroes, or earthshaking inventors like Thomas Edison, but if Thomas Edison had had a Human Resources Department, and that Human Resources Department had organized annual enrichment and motivational conferences for mid-level management, then these people would have been the marketing executives for the back office outsourcing companies to the meeting-planning firms that hooked up the HR executives with the conference facilities.

They are wonderful people. And Patio Man can envision his own wife, Cindy, a Realtor Mom, circulating amongst them serving drinks, telling parent-teacher conference stories and generally spreading conviviality while he, Patio Man, masterfully runs the grill—again, to the silent admiration of all. The sun is shining. The people are friendly. The men are no more than 25 pounds overweight, which is the socially acceptable male paunch level in upwardly mobile America, and the children are well adjusted. It is a vision of the sort of domestic bliss that Patio Man has been shooting for all his life.

And it's plausible now because two years ago Patio Man made the big move. He pulled up stakes and he moved his family to a Sprinkler City.

Sprinkler Cities are the fast-growing suburbs mostly in the South and West that are the homes of the new style American Dream, the epicenters of Patio Man fantasies. Douglas County, Colorado, which is the fastest-growing county in America and is located between Denver and Colorado Springs, is a Sprinkler City. So is Henderson, Nevada, just outside of Las Vegas. So is Loudoun County, Virginia, near Dulles Airport. So are Scottsdale and Gilbert, Arizona, and Union County, North Carolina.

The growth in these places is astronomical, as Patio Men and their families—and Patio retirees, yuppie geezers who still like to grill, swim, and water ski—flock to them from all over. Douglas County grew 13.6 percent from April 2000 to July 2001, while Loudoun County grew 12.6 percent in that 16-month period. Henderson, Nevada, has tripled in size over the past 10 years and now has over 175,000 people. Over the past 50 years, Irving, Texas, grew by 7,211 percent, from about 2,600 people to 200,000 people.

The biggest of these boom suburbs are huge. With almost 400,000 people, Mesa, Arizona, has a larger population than Minneapolis, Cincinnati, or St. Louis. And this sort of growth is expected to continue. Goodyear, Arizona, on the western edge of the Phoenix area, now has about 20,000 people, but is projected to have 320,000 in 50 years' time. By then, Greater Phoenix could have a population of over 6 million and cover over 10,000 square miles.

Sprinkler Cities are also generally the most Republican areas of the country. In some of the Sprinkler City congressional districts, Republicans have a 2 or 3 or 4 to 1 registration advantage over Democrats. As cultural centers, they represent the beau ideal of Republican selfhood, and are becoming the new base— the brains, heart, guts, and soul of the emerging Republican party. Their values are not the same as those found in either old-line suburbs like Greenwich, Connecticut, where a certain sort of Republican used to dominate, or traditional conservative bastions, such as the old South. This isn't even the more modest conservatism found in the midwestern farm belt. In fact, the rising prominence of these places heralds a new style of suburb vs. suburb politics, with the explosively growing Republican outer suburbs vying with the slower-growing and increasingly Democratic inner suburbs for control of the center of American political gravity.

If you stand on a hilltop overlooking a Sprinkler City, you see, stretched across the landscape, little brown puffs here and there where bulldozers are kicking up dirt while building new townhomes, office parks, shopping malls, AmeriSuites guest hotels, and golf courses. Everything in a Sprinkler City is new. The highways are so clean and freshly paved you can eat off them. The elementary schools have spic and span playgrounds, unscuffed walls, and immaculate mini-observatories for just-forming science classes.

The lawns in these places are perfect. It doesn't matter how arid the local landscape used to be, the developers come in and lay miles of irrigation tubing, and the sprinklers pop up each evening, making life and civilization possible.

The roads are huge. The main ones, where the office parks are, have been given names like Innovation Boulevard and Entrepreneur Avenue, and they've been built for the population levels that will exist a decade from now, so that today you can cruise down these flawless six lane thoroughfares in traffic-less nirvana, and if you get a cell phone call you can just stop in the right lane and take the call because there's no one behind you. The smaller roads in the residential neighborhoods have pretentious names—in Loudoun County I drove down Trajan's Column Terrace—but they too are just as smooth and immaculate as a blacktop bowling alley. There's no use relying on a map to get around these places, because there's no way map publishers can keep up with the construction.

The town fathers try halfheartedly to control sprawl, and as you look over the landscape you can see the results of their ambivalent zoning regulations. The homes aren't spread out with quarter-acre yards, as in the older, close-in suburbs. Instead they are clustered into pseudo-urban pods. As you scan the horizon you'll see a densely packed pod of townhouses, then a stretch of a half mile of investor grass (fields that will someday contain 35,000-square-foot Fresh-Mex restaurants but for now are being kept fallow by investors until the prices rise), and then another pod of slightly more expensive detached homes just as densely packed.

The developments in the southeastern Sprinkler Cities tend to have Mini-McMansion Gable-gable houses. That is to say, these are 3,200-square-foot middle-class homes built to look like 7,000-square-foot starter palaces for the nouveau riche. And on the front at the top, each one has a big gable, and then right in front of it, for visual relief, a little gable jutting forward so that it looks like a baby gable leaning against a mommy gable.

These homes have all the same features as the authentic McMansions of the mid-'90s (as history flows on, McMansions come to seem authentic), but significantly smaller. There are the same vaulted atriums behind the front doors that never get used, and the same open kitchen/two-story great rooms with soaring palladian windows. But in the middle-class knockoffs, the rooms are so small, especially upstairs, that a bedroom or a master-bath suite would fit inside one of the walk-in closets of a real McMansion.

In the Southwest the homes tend to be tile and stucco jobs, with tiny mousepad lawns out front, blue backyard spas in the back, and so much white furniture inside that you have to wear sunglasses indoors. As you fly over the Sprinkler Cities you begin to see the rough pattern—a little pseudo-urbanist plop of development, a blank field, a plop, a field, a plop. You also notice that the developers build the roads and sewage lines first and then fill in the houses later, so from the sky you can see cul de sacs stretching off into the distance with no houses around them.

Then, cutting through the landscape are broad commercial thoroughfares with two-tier, big-box malls on either side. In the front tier is a line of highly themed chain restaurants that all fuse into the same Macaroni Grill Olive Outback Cantina Charlie Chiang's Dave & Buster's Cheesecake Factory mélange of peppy servers, superfluous ceiling fans, free bread with olive oil, and taco salad entrees. In the 21st-century migration of peoples, the food courts come first and the huddled masses follow.

Then in the back row are all the huge, exposed-air-duct architectural behemoths, which are the big-box stores.

Shopping experiences are now segregated by mood. If you are in the mood for some titillating browsing, you can head over to a Lifestyle Center, which is one of those instant urban streetscapes that developers put up in suburbia as entertainment/ retail/community complexes, complete with pedestrian zones, outdoor cafés, roller rinks, multiplexes, and high-attitude retail concepts such as CP Shades, a chain store that masquerades as a locally owned boutique.

If you are buying necessities, really shopping, there are Power Malls. These are the big-box expanses with Wal-marts, K-Marts,

Targets, price clubs, and all the various Depots (Home, Office, Furniture, etc.). In Sprinkler Cities there are archipelagoes of them—one massive parking lot after another surrounded by huge boxes that often have racing stripes around the middle to break the monotony of the windowless exterior walls.

If one superstore is in one mall, then its competitor is probably in the next one in the archipelago. There's a Petsmart just down from a Petco, a Borders nearby a Barnes & Noble, a Linens 'n' Things within sight of a Bed Bath & Beyond, a Best Buy cheek by jowl with a Circuit City. In Henderson, there's a Wal-Mart superstore that spreads over 220,000 square feet, with all those happy greeters in blue vests to make you feel small-town.

There are also smaller stores jammed in between the mega-outlets like little feeder fish swimming around the big boys. On one strip, there might be the ostentatiously unpretentious Total Wine & More, selling a galaxy of casual Merlots. Nearby there might be a Michaels discount women's clothing, a bobo bazaar such as World Market that sells raffia fiber from Madagascar, Rajasthani patchwork coverlets from India, and vermouth-flavored martini onions from Israel, and finally a string of store-front mortgage bankers and realtors serving all the new arrivals. In Sprinkler Cities, there are more realtors than people.

People move to Sprinkler Cities for the same reasons people came to America or headed out West. They want to leave behind the dirt and toxins of their former existence—the crowding and inconvenience, the precedents, and the oldness of what suddenly seems to them a settled and unpromising world. They want to move to some place that seems fresh and new and filled with possibility.

Sprinkler City immigrants are not leaving cities to head out to suburbia. They are leaving older suburbs—which have come to seem as crowded, expensive, and stratified as cities—and heading for newer suburbs, for the suburbia of suburbia.

One of the problems we have in thinking about the suburbs is that when it comes to suburbia the American imagination is motionless. Many people still have in their heads the stereotype of suburban life that the critics of suburbia established in the 1950s. They see suburbia as a sterile, dull, Ozzie and Harriet retreat from the creative dynamism of city life, and the people who live in the suburbs as either hopelessly shallow or quietly and neurotically desperate. (There is no group in America more conformist than the people who rail against suburbanites for being conformist—they always make the same critiques, decade after decade.)

The truth, of course, is that suburbia is not a retreat from gritty American life, it is American life. Already, suburbanites make up about half of the country's population (while city people make up 28 percent and rural folk make up the rest), and America gets more suburban every year.

According to the census data, the suburbs of America's 100 largest metro areas grew twice as fast as their central cities in the 1990s, and that was a decade in which many cities actually reversed their long population slides. Atlanta, for example, gained 23,000 people in the '90s, but its suburbs grew by 1.1 million people.

Moreover, newer suburbs no longer really feed off cities. In 1979, 74 percent of American office space was located in cities, according to the Brookings Institution's Robert Puentes. But now, after two decades in which the biggest job growth has been in suburban office parks, the suburbs' share of total office space has risen to 42 percent. In other words, we are fast approaching a time when the majority of all office space will be in the suburbs, and most Americans not only will not live in cities, they won't even commute to cities or have any regular contact with city life.

Encompassing such a broad swath of national existence, suburbs obviously cannot possibly be the white-bread places of myth and literature. In reality, as the most recent census shows, suburbs contain more non-family houses—young singles and elderly couples—than family households, married couples with children. Nor are they overwhelmingly white. The majority of Asian Americans, half of Hispanics, and 40 percent of American blacks live in suburbia.

And so now there are crucial fault lines not just between city and suburb but between one kind of suburb and another. Say you grew up in some southern California suburb in the 1970s. You graduated from the University of Oregon and now you are a systems analyst with a spouse and two young kids. You're making $65,000 a year, far more than you ever thought you would, but back in Orange County you find you can't afford to live anywhere near your Newport Beach company headquarters. So your commute is 55 minutes each way. Then there's your house itself. You paid $356,000 for a 1962 four-bedroom split level with a drab kitchen, low ceilings, and walls that are chipped and peeling. Your mortgage—that $1,800 a month—is like a tapeworm that devours the family budget.

And then you visit a Sprinkler City in Arizona or Nevada or Colorado—far from the coast and deep into exurbia—and what do you see? Bounteous roads! Free traffic lanes! If you lived here you'd be in commuter bliss—15 minutes from home on Trajan's Column Terrace to the office park on Innovation Boulevard! If you lived here you'd have an extra hour and a half each day for yourself.

And those real estate prices! In, say, Henderson, Nevada, you wouldn't have to spend over $400,000 for a home and carry that murderous mortgage. You could get a home that's brand new, twice the size of your old one, with an attached garage (no flimsy carport), and three times as beautiful for $299,000. The average price of a single-family home in Loudoun County, one of the pricier of the Sprinkler Cities, was $166,824 in 2001, which was an 11 percent increase over the year before. Imagine that! A mortgage under 200 grand! A great anvil would be lifted from your shoulders. More free money for you to spend on yourself. More free time to enjoy. More Freedom!

Plus, if you moved to a Sprinkler City there would be liberation of a subtler kind. The old suburbs have become socially urbanized. They've become stratified. Two sorts of people have begun to move in and ruin the middle-class equality of the development you grew up in: the rich and the poor.

There are, first, the poor immigrants, from Mexico, Vietnam, and the Philippines. They come in, a dozen to a house, and they introduce an element of unpredictability to what was a comforting milieu. They shout. They're less tidy. Their teenage boys seem to get involved with gangs and cars. Suddenly you feel you will lose control of your children. You begin to feel a new level of anxiety in the neighborhood. It is exactly the level of anxiety—sometimes intermingled with racism—your parents felt when they moved from their old neighborhood to the suburbs in the first place.

And then there are the rich. Suddenly many of the old ramblers are being knocked down by lawyers who proceed to erect 4,000-square-foot arts and crafts bungalows with two-car garages for their Volvos. Suddenly cars in the neighborhoods have window and bumper stickers that never used to be there in the past: "Yale," "The Friends School," "Million Mom March." The local stores are changing too. Gone are the hardware stores and barber shops. Now there are Afghan restaurants, Marin County bistros, and environmentally sensitive and extremely expensive bakeries.

And these new people, while successful and upstanding, are also. . . snobs. They're doctors and lawyers and journalists and media consultants. They went to fancy colleges and they consider themselves superior to you if you sell home-security systems or if you are a mechanical engineer, and in subtle yet patronizing ways they let you know it.

I recently interviewed a woman in Loudoun County who said she had grown up and lived most of her life in Bethesda, Maryland, which is an upscale suburb close to Washington. When I asked why she left Bethesda, she hissed "I hate it there now" with a fervor that took me by surprise. And as we spoke, it became clear that it was precisely the "improvements" she hated: the new movie theater that shows only foreign films, the explosion of French, Turkish, and new wave restaurants, the streets choked with German cars and Lexus SUVs, the doctors and lawyers and journalists with their educated-class one-upmanship.

These new people may live in the old suburbs but they hate suburbanites. They hate sprawl, big-box stores, automobile culture. The words they use about suburbanites are: synthetic, bland, sterile, self-absorbed, disengaged. They look down on people who like suburbs, their lawn statuary, their Hallmark greeting cards, their Ethan Allen furniture, their megachurches, the seasonal banners the old residents hang out in front of their houses, their untroubled attitude toward McDonald's and Dairy Queen, their Thomas Kinkade fantasy paintings. And all the original suburbanites who were peacefully enjoying their suburb until the anti-suburban suburbanites moved in notice the condescension, and they do what Americans have always done when faced with disapproval, anxiety, and potential conflict. They move away. The pincer movements get them: the rich and the poor, the commutes and the mortgages, the prices and the alienation. And pretty soon it's Henderson, Nevada, here we come.

George Santayana once observed that Americans don't solve problems, they just leave them behind. They take advantage of all that space and move. If there's an idea they don't like, they don't bother refuting it, they just go somewhere else, and if they can't go somewhere else, they just leave it in the past, where it dies from inattention.

And so Patio Man is not inclined to stay and defend himself against the condescending French-film goers and their Volvos. He's not going to mount a political campaign to fix the educational, economic, and social woes that beset him in his old neighborhood. He won't waste his time fighting a culture war. It's not worth the trouble. He just bolts. He heads for the exurbs and the desert. He goes to the new place where the future is still open and promising. He goes to fresh ground where his dreams might more plausibly come true.

The power of this urge to leave and create new places is really awesome to behold. Migration is not an easy thing, yet every year 43 million Americans get up and move. And it sets off a chain reaction. The migrants who move into one area push out another set of people, who then migrate to another and push out another set of people, and so on and so on in one vast cycle of creative destruction. Ten years ago these Sprinkler Cities didn't really exist. Fifteen years ago the institutions that dot them hadn't been invented. There weren't book superstores or sporting goods superstores or Petsmart or Petco, and Target was just something you shot arrows at. And yet suddenly metropolises with all these new stores and institutions have materialized out of emptiness. It's as if some Zeus-like figure had appeared out of the ether and slammed down a million-square-foot mall on the desert floor, then a second later he'd slammed down a 5,000-person townhome community, then a second later an ice rink and a rec center and soccer fields and schools and community colleges. How many times in human history have 200,000-person cities just materialized almost instantaneously out of nowhere?

The people who used to live in these empty places don't like it; they've had to move further out in search of valleys still pristine. But the sprawl people just love it. They talk to you like born-again evangelists, as if their life had undergone some magical transformation when they made the big move. They talk as if they'd thrown off some set of horrendous weights, banished some class of unpleasant experiences, and magically floated up into the realm of good climate, fine people, job opportunities, and transcendent convenience. In 2001, Loudoun County did a survey of its residents. Ninety-eight percent felt safe in their neighborhoods. Ninety-three percent rated their county's quality of life excellent or good. Only a third of the county's residents, by the way, have lived there for more than 10 years.

These people are so happy because they have achieved something that human beings are actually quite good at achieving. Through all the complex diversity of society, they have managed to find people who want pretty much the same things they want.

This is not to say they want white Ozzie and Harriet nirvana. The past 40 years happened. It never occurs to them to go back before rock, rap, women working, and massive immigration. They don't mind any of these things, so long as they complement the core Sprinkler City missions of orderly living, high achievement, and the bright seeking of a better future.

Recently three teams from the Seneca Ridge Middle School in Loudoun County competed in the National Social Studies Olympiad. The fifth grade team finished fifth out of 242 teams, while the eighth grade team finished twenty-third out of 210. Here are some of the names of the students competing for Loudoun: Amy Kuo, Arshad Ali, Samanth Chao, Katie Hempenius, Ronnel Espino, Obinna Onwuka, Earnst Ilang-Ilang, Ashley Shiraishi, and Alberto Pareja-Lecaros. At the local high school, 99 percent of seniors graduate and 87 percent go on to higher education.

When you get right down to it, Sprinkler Cities are united around five main goals:

- *The goal of the together life.* When you've got your life together, you have mastered the complexities of the modern world so thoroughly that you can glide through your days without unpleasant distractions or tawdry failures. Instead, your hours are filled with self-affirming reminders of the control you have achieved over the elements. Your lawn is immaculate. Your DVD library is organized, and so is your walk-in closet. Your car is clean and vacuumed, your frequently dialed numbers are programmed into your cell phone, your telephone plan is suited to your needs, and your various gizmos interface without conflict. Your wife is effortlessly slender, your kids are unnaturally bright, your job is rewarding, your promotions are inevitable, and you look great in casual slacks.

You can thus spend your days in perfect equanimity, the Sprinkler City ideal. You radiate confidence, like a professional golfer striding up the 18th fairway after a particularly masterful round. Compared with you, Dick Cheney looks like a disorganized hothead. George W. Bush looks like a self-lacerating neurotic. Professionally, socially, parentally, you have your life together. You may not be the most intellectual or philosophical person on the planet, but you are honest and straightforward. You may not be flamboyant, but you are friendly, good-hearted, and considerate. You have achieved the level of calm mastery of life that is the personality equivalent of the clean and fresh suburban landscape.

- *The goal of technological heroism.* They may not be stereotypical rebels, and nobody would call them avant-garde, but in one respect many Sprinkler City dwellers have the souls of revolutionaries. When Patio Man gets out of his Yukon, lowers his employee-badge necklace around his neck, and walks into his generic office building, he becomes a technological radical. He spends his long workdays striving to create some technological innovation, management solution, or organizing system breakthroughs that will alter the world. Maybe the company he works for has one of those indecipherable three-initial names, like DRG Technologies or SER Solutions, or maybe it's got one of those jammed together compound names that were all the rage in the 1990s until WorldCom and MicroStrategy went belly up.

Either way, Patio Man is working on, or longs to be working on, a project that is new and revolutionary. And all around him there are men and women who are actually achieving that goal, who are making that leap into the future. The biotech revolution is being conducted in bland suburban office parks by seemingly unremarkable polo-shirt-and-chino people at firms like Celera and Human Genome Sciences. Silicon Valley is just one long string of suburban office parks jutting out from San Jose. AOL is headquartered in Loudoun County. You walk down a path in a Sprinkler City corporate center and it leads you to a company frantically chasing some market-niche innovation in robotics, agricultural engineering, microtechnology, or hardware and software applications.

There are retail-concept revolutionaries, delivery-system radicals, market-research innovators, data-collection pioneers, computer-game Rembrandts, and weapons-systems analysts. They look like bland members of some interchangeable research team, but many of them are deeply engrossed in what they consider a visionary project, which if completed will help hurtle us all further into the Knowledge Revolution, the Information Millennium, the Age of MicroTechnology, the Biotech Century, or whatever transplendent future it is you want to imagine. They have broken the monopoly that cities used to have, and they have made themselves the new centers of creativity.

- *The goal of relaxed camaraderie.* The critics of suburbia believe that single-family homeowners with their trimmed yards and matching pansies are trying to keep up with the Joneses. But like most of what the critics assert, that's completely wrong. Sprinkler City people are competitive in the marketplace and on the sports field, but they detest social competition. That's part of why these people left inner-ring suburbs in the first place.

They are not emulating the rich; they are happy to blend in with each other. One of the comforts of these places is that almost nobody is far above you socially and almost nobody is far below. You're all just swimming in a pond of understated success.

So manners are almost aggressively relaxed. Everybody strives overtime to not put on airs or create friction. In style, demeanor, and mood, people reveal the language and values they have in common. They are good team members and demonstrate from the first meeting that they are team-able. You could go your entire life, from home to church to work to school, wearing nothing but Lands' End—comfortable, conservative, non-threatening activewear for people with a special fondness for navy blue. The dominant conversational tone is upbeat and friendly, like banter between Katie Couric and Matt Lauer on the "Today" show. The prevailing style of humor is ironic but not biting and owes a lot to ESPN's "SportsCenter."

- *The goal of the active-leisure lifestyle.* Your self-esteem is based on your success at work, but since half the time it's hard to explain to people what the hell it is you do, your public identity is defined by your leisure activities. You are the soccer family, engrossed by the politics and melodrama of your local league, or you are the T-ball coach and spend your barbecue conversations comparing

notes on new $200 titanium bat designs (there's a new bat called The Power Elite—even C. Wright Mills has been domesticated for the Little League set). You are Scuba Woman and you converse about various cruises you have taken. You are Mountain Bike Man and you make vague references to your high altitude injuries and spills. Or you are a golfer, in which case nobody even thinks of engaging you in conversation on any topic other than golf.

Religion is too hot a subject and politics is irrelevant, so if you are not discussing transportation issues—how to get from here to there, whether the new highway exit is good or bad—you are probably talking about sports. You're talking about your kids' ice hockey leagues, NBA salary levels, or the competition in your over-70 softball league—the one in which everybody wears a knee brace and it takes about six minutes for a good hitter to beat out a double. Sports sets the emotional climate of your life. Sports provides the language of easy camaraderie, self-deprecating humor, and (mostly) controlled competition.

- *The goal of the traditional, but competitive, childhood.* Most everything in Sprinkler Cities is new, but much of the newness is in the service of tradition. The families that move here are trying to give their children as clean and upright and traditional a childhood as they can imagine. They're trying to move away from parents who smoke and slap their kids, away from families where people watch daytime TV shows about transvestite betrayals and "My Daughter is a Slut" confessions, away from broken homes and, most of all, away from the company of children who are not being raised to achieve and succeed.

They are trying to move instead to a realm of clean neighborhoods, safe streets, competitive cheerleading, spirit squads, soccer tots academies, accelerated-reader programs, and adult-chaperoned drug-free/alcohol-free graduation celebrations.

For the fifth consecutive year, the Henderson, Nevada, high school Marine Corps Junior ROTC squad has won the National Male Armed Drill Team championship. The Female Unarmed Drill Team has come in first six out of the past eight years. In Loudoun County the local newspaper runs notices for various travel team tryouts. In one recent edition, I counted 55 teams announcing their tryouts, with names like The Loudoun Cyclones, the Herndon Surge, the Loudoun Volcanoes. (It's not socially acceptable to name your team after a group of people anymore, so most of the teams have nature names.) As you drive around a Sprinkler City you see SUVs everywhere with cheers scrawled in washable marker on the back windows: "Go Heat!" "#24 Kelly Jones!" "Regional Champs!"

The kids spend their days being chaperoned from one adult-supervised activity to another, and from one achievement activity to the next. They are well tested, well trophied, and well appreciated. They are not only carefully reared and nurtured, they are launched into a life of high expectations and presumed accomplishment.

The dominant ideology of Sprinkler Cities is a sort of utopian conservatism. On the one hand, the people who live here have made a startling leap into the unknown. They have, in great numbers and with great speed, moved from their old homes in California, Florida, Illinois, and elsewhere, to these brand new places that didn't really exist 10 years ago. These places have no pasts, no precedents, no settled institutions, very few longstanding groups you can join and settle into.

Their inhabitants have moved to towns where they have no family connections, no ethnic enclaves, and no friends. They are using their imaginations to draw pictures for themselves of what their lives will be like. They are imagining their golf club buddies even though the course they are moving near is only just being carved out of the desert. They are imagining their successful children's graduation from high school, even though the ground around the new school building is still rutted with the tracks of construction equipment. They are imagining outings with friends at restaurants that are now only investor grass, waiting to be built.

And when they do join groups, often the groups turn out to be still in the process of building themselves. The migrants join congregations that meet in school basements while raising the money to construct churches. They go to office parks at biotech companies that are still waiting to put a product on the market. They may vote, or episodically pay attention to national politics, but they don't get drawn into strong local party organizations because the local organizations haven't been built.

But the odd thing is that all this imaginative daring, these leaps into the future, are all in the service of an extremely conservative ideal. You get the impression that these people have fled their crowded and stratified old suburbs because they really want to live in Mayberry. They have this image of what home should be, a historical myth or memory, and they are going to build it, even if it means constructing an old fashioned place out of modern materials.

It's going to be morally upstanding. It's going to be relaxed and neighborly. It's going to be neat and orderly. Sprinkler City people seem to have almost a moral revulsion at disorder or anything that threatens to bring chaos, including out-of-control immigration and terrorist attacks. They don't think about the war on terror much, let alone some alleged invasion of Iraq, but if it could be shown that Saddam Hussein presented a threat to the good order of the American homeland, then these people would support his ouster with a fervor that would take your breath away. "They have strong emotions when dealing with security," says Tom Tancredo, a congressman from suburban Denver. "Border security, the security of their families, the security of their neighborhoods."

Of course, from the moment they move in, they begin soiling their own nest. They move in order to get away from crowding, but as they and the tens of thousands like them move in, they bring crowding with them. They move to get away from stratification, snobbery, and inequality, but as the new towns grow they get more stratified. In Henderson, the $200,000 ranch homes are now being supplemented by gated $500,000-a-home golf communities. People move for stability and old fashioned values, but they are unwilling to accept limits to opportunity. They are achievement oriented. They are inherently dynamic.

For a time they do a dance about preserving the places they are changing by their presence. As soon as people move into a Sprinkler City, they start lobbying to control further growth. As Tancredo says, they have absolutely no shame about it. They want more roads built, but fewer houses. They want to freeze the peaceful hominess of the town that was growing when they moved there five minutes before.

But soon, one senses, they will get the urge to move again. The Hendersons and the Douglas Counties will be tomorrow what the Newport Beaches and the Los Altoses and the White Plaines are today, places where Patio Man no longer feels quite at home. And the suburban middle-class folks in these places will again strike out as the avant-garde toward new places, with new sorts of stores and a new vision of the innocent hometown.

So the dynamism and volatility will continue—always moving aggressively toward a daring future that looks like an imagined picture of the wholesome past, striving and charging toward that dream of the peaceful patio, the happy kids, the slender friends, and, towering over it all, the massive barbecue grill.

DAVID BROOKS is a senior editor at *The Weekly Standard.*

Downtown Struggles While Neighbor Thrives

MICHAEL BRICK

Gary Barnett does not trade natural gas and electricity futures for a living, and there is no indication that he plans to do so. This is something of a disappointment for many people in Houston. Should Mr. Barnett ever take a shine to the idea of trading energy futures, he is the new owner of an ideal place to start, a place that many people here had hoped would be used for that purpose.

He is president of the **Intell Management and Investment Company,** which bought the building formerly known as Enron Center South through a bankruptcy court auction for $102 million, about a third of its construction cost. The sale closed on Dec. 30, and Intell has renamed the building 1500 Louisiana, a name that makes its address redundant.

The only tenant, the power trading operation that UBS Warburg bought from Enron, plans to move in May.

Henry J. Terech, a senior vice president at Intell who manages the 40-story tower and who previously oversaw its development as an Enron employee, said he was marketing space to a range of potential tenants.

"The conventional wisdom was this place was going to sell to a Dynegy or a Duke," Mr. Terech said, naming companies that are, in fact, in the business of trading energy futures. "When the energy market melted down, that wasn't the case."

The problems of the power trading companies have steepened the downward slope of a boom-and-bust real estate cycle in the central business district, an echo of previous patterns driven by traditional energy companies. But Houston has diversified its economic base, developing a medical complex about four miles south of downtown. That part of town is thriving, but the traditional downtown remains hostage to boom or bust.

Vacancy rates for top-class office space downtown have risen to 13.75 percent at the end of 2002, not including sublease space, from 4.94 percent a year earlier, and asking rents have fallen to an average of $24.01 a square foot, from $27.35, the real estate services firm Insignia/ESG said.

"The hope is that there's some large energy companies that can take that space," said Jerald King, a director of Insignia, citing as an example Exxon Mobil, which has offices here in a building that is more than 40 years old.

"I don't know that any of them will," Mr. King said. "At least for the Enron building, there's still a stigma to it that people can't get over."

Mr. Terech, the manager of 1500 Louisiana, said he planned to market the space at rates comparable to other buildings downtown, emphasizing its modern amenities.

Inside, there are four trading floors, each with a 53,000-square-foot floorplate raised 18 inches to accommodate a maze of 1.3 million feet of data network cable. The cables connect with 475 trading positions, desktops with file cabinets, dwarfed beneath 55 plasma screens.

From just outside an office once intended for Jeffrey K. Skilling, who was once the chief executive of Enron, a luna pearl granite staircase leads down to one trading floor. The building's exterior wall is reinforced to withstand hurricane-force winds; backup generators sit atop the garage; and boardrooms are wired with microphones and videoconferencing equipment.

A few miles away, Houston's other downtown is booming.

The Texas Medical Center, with 22 million square feet of space, is a city within a city, not quite half the 47 million square feet of office space in the central business district.

The medical center has about 6,000 hospital beds and 60,000 workers. Another 11 million square feet is under construction at a cost of about $1.8 billion, according to the nonprofit group that manages the area.

The group, the Texas Medical Center Corporation, owns 250 undeveloped acres, and the complex is bordered by a bayou, a park and university land. Inside its zone, the corporation leases buildings to medical institutions for 198 years at a dollar a year, so commercial developers and brokers are effectively frozen out.

"We have driven up the price of land by our success," said Richard E. Wainerdi, chief executive of the corporation, noting that it spent $15.7 million in 2000 to buy 22 acres including a 600,000-square-foot building from Nabisco.

Much of this real estate is research space and hospital facilities, along with hotels and restaurants. But the center has 3.6 million square feet of office space, and its market is among the tightest in the country. Insignia places the vacancy rate at zero for top-class buildings, and 10.42 percent for buildings described as Class C, a designation typically applied to older buildings nearing economic obsolescence.

"You've got fancy buildings downtown that can't get these kinds of rental rates," said Jeffrey P. Munger, a senior director of Holliday Fenoglio Fowler, a commercial mortgage banking firm, standing outside Medical Towers, an 18-story building that opened in 1954. Rental rates for older buildings in this part of the city range from $26 to $30 a square foot, Mr. Munger said.

Back downtown, brokers and building managers consistently cite its ever-increasing list of amenities as reason to think that tenants will return. A 7.5-mile, 16-station light rail system is being installed, and the city has promised that it will be complete, at least as far as the football stadium, in time for the Super Bowl in January.

A $100 million convention center expansion is under way, and there is a new $85 million performing arts center.

In addition, a developer, Tilman J. Fertitta, has built what might be described as a permanent carnival, the Downtown Aquarium. His $38 million complex on the edge of the central business district has 500,000 gallons of water and 200 species of marine life, as well as seafood restaurants and games and rides not unlike a sanitized Coney Island. His aquarium complex is packed with visitors, mostly children, even on school days.

In Houston, vacancy rates rise downtown, but a nearby medical complex booms.

Downtown brokers and landlords do not expect the aquarium to lure office tenants, and neither does Mr. Fertitta, but they consistently say that another attraction cannot hurt.

"The problem is the oil," Mr. Fertitta said. "Maybe Houston still needs to be a little bit more diversified."

While energy still looms large, its dominance has been diminishing. More than 51 percent of economic activity drawing money into Houston these days comes from sources other than energy, compared with 15.7 percent in 1981, according to the Institute for Regional Forecasting at the University of Houston.

Mr. Barnett, the owner of the former Enron Center South, is counting on that diversity. His building downtown is being marketed to companies in financial services, technology and traditional energy areas.

In addition to the former Enron building, Intell and its affiliates own or are developing 8 million square feet of commercial real estate around the country, including a 1.8-million-square-foot office building at 175 West Jackson Street in Chicago and the W Hotel in Times Square.

Mr. Barnett's hopes of developing an office tower near Times Square were frustrated last year when he and other property owners on the block lost a legal battle to prevent the state from condemning a site for a new headquarters for The New York Times Company.

Discussing his property in Houston, Mr. Barnett said, "We're seeing lots of interest in our building," adding that there are companies in the suburbs that want to move downtown and companies downtown that want to consolidate their space in more modern buildings.

"For years, there was no space in downtown Houston," he said. "You have the oil services business and the exploration and development, and those are doing really well now. The only ones that are hurting are the power traders."

Unscrambling the City

Archaic zoning laws lock cities into growth patterns that hardly anybody wants. Changing the rules can help set them free.

CHRISTOPHER SWOPE

Take a walk through Chicago's historic Lakeview neighborhood, and the new houses will jump right out at you. That's because they're jarringly incompatible with the old ones. On one quiet tree-lined street, you'll find a row of old two-story colonials with pitched roofs. Then you walk a little farther and it seems as though a giant rectangular box has fallen out of the sky. The new condominium building is twice as high as its older neighbors and literally casts shadows over their neat flower gardens and tiny front yards. Angry Lakeview residents have seen so many new buildings like this lately that they have come up with a sneering name for them. They call them "three-flats on steroids."

Listening to the complaints in Lakeview, you might wonder whether home builders are breaking the law and getting away with it, or at least bending the rules quite a bit. But that's not the case. If you take some time and study Chicago's zoning law, you'll find that these giant condos are technically by the book. It's not the new buildings that are the problem. The problem is Chicago's zoning ordinance. The code is nearly half a century old, and it is an outdated mishmash of vague and conflicting rules. Over the years, it has been amended repeatedly, to the point of nonsense. Above all, it's totally unpredictable. In Lakeview, zoning can yield anything from tasteful two-flats to garish McMansions, with no consideration at all for how they fit into the neighborhood.

Chicago's zoning problem lay dormant for decades while the city's economy sagged and population declined. Back in the 1970s and '80s, not much building was going on. But then the 1990s brought an economic boom and 112,000 new residents. While almost everyone is happy that the construction machine has been turned back on, so many Chicagoans are appalled by the way the new construction looks that Mayor Richard M. Daley decided it was time to rewrite the city's entire zoning code. Everything about Chicago land use is on the table: not just residential development but commercial and industrial as well. It is the largest overhaul of its kind in any U.S. city in 40 years.

But while few communities are going as far as Chicago, many are coming to a similar conclusion: The zoning laws on their books—most of them written in the 1950s and '60s—are all scrambled up. They are at once too vague and too complicated to produce the urban character most residents say they want.

The zoning problem afflicts both cities and suburbs and manifests itself in countless ways. It takes the form of oversized homes and farmland covered in cookie-cutter housing developments. It shows up as a sterile new strip mall opening up down the street from one that is dying. It becomes an obstacle when cities discover how hard it is to revive pedestrian life in their downtowns and neighborhood shopping districts. And it becomes a headache for city councils that spend half their time interpreting clumsy rules, issuing variances and haggling with developers.

What urban planners disagree about is whether the current system can be salvaged, or whether it should be scrapped altogether. Most cities are not ready to take the ultimate step. Chicago isn't going that far. Neither did Boston, Milwaukee, San Diego and San Jose. All of them retained the basic zoning conventions, even as they slogged through the process of streamlining the codes and rewriting them for the 21st century. According to researcher Stuart Meck, of the American Planning Association, there's a cyclical nature to all this. He points out that it's common for cities to update their laws after the sort of building boom many have enjoyed recently. "Cities are in growth mode again," Meck says, "but they're getting development based on standards that are 20, 30 or 40 years old."

Myriad Categories

For much of the past century, if you wanted to find out the latest thinking about zoning, Chicago was a good place to go. In 1923, it became one of the first cities, after New York, to adopt a zoning law. The motivation then was mostly health and safety. Smoke-spewing factories were encroaching on residential neighborhoods, and the city's first ordinance sought to keep them out. By the 1950s, when more people drove cars, Chicago

Picture-Book Zoning

While Chicago and a few other large cities struggle to update old zoning laws for the new century, some places are going in a new direction. They are experimenting with zoning concepts percolating out of the New Urbanist movement, writing codes that bear a closer resemblance to picture books than to laws. Conventional zoning, they have decided, is based on an abstract language that leaves too much to chance. They would rather start with a question—what does the community want to look like—and then work back from there. "It's not enough to change the zoning," says New Urbanist author Peter Katz. "Cities have to move to a new system. They should look at the streets they like and the public spaces they like and then write the rules to get more of what they like and less of what they don't. Conventional zoning doesn't do that. It just gives a use and a density and then you hope for the best."

One jurisdiction currently buying in to this new idea is Arlington, Virginia, a suburb of 190,000 people just across the river from Washington D.C. A few months ago, Arlington's county board adopted a "form-based" zoning code for a 3.5-mile corridor known as Columbia Pike, making it one of the largest experiments yet with this new idea.

Columbia Pike is a typical traffic-choked suburban drag, lined mostly with strip malls, drive-throughs and apartment complexes ringed by parking lots. Developers have ignored the area for years. County planners want to convert it into a place that more closely resembles a classic American Main Street. They want a walkable commercial thoroughfare, featuring ground-floor retail blended together with offices and apartments above. But the old zoning code made this nearly impossible.

Rather than starting with a clear vision of what Arlington wants Columbia Pike to look like, the old code starts with a letter and a number: "C-2." The "C" stands for commercial uses only, and the "2" means that development should be of a medium density. C-2 is so vague that it could yield any number of building types. But the code's ambiguities don't end there. Building size is regulated by "floor area ratio," a calculation that again says nothing about whether the building should be suitable for a Main Street or an interstate highway exit. Finally, the code doesn't say where on the lot the building should go—just that it shouldn't sit near the roadway. Mostly, developers have used this recipe to build strip malls. "The code is really absolute on things that don't matter to us at all," says Arlington board member Chris Zimmerman. "The tools are all wrong for the job we're trying to do."

The new code for Columbia Pike abandons these old tools. It begins with a picture: What does a Main Street look like? Rather than abstract language, the new code uses visuals to show the form that the buildings should take. Buildings are three to six stories tall. And they sit on the sidewalk, with ground-floor windows and front doors, not 50 feet back from the street.

Compared with traditional zoning, a form-based code doesn't focus on specific uses. It specifies physical patterns. Whether the buildings are occupied by coffee shops, law offices or upstairs renters makes little difference. "Traditionally," says Peter Katz, "zoning stipulates a density and a use and it's anyone's guess whether you'll get what the planners' renderings look like. Form-based codes give a way to achieve what you see in the picture with precision."

One of the most prominent New Urbanists, Miami architect Andres Duany, advocates taking the form-based idea even further. In Duany's view, it's not only buildings along a road like Columbia Pike that should be coded according to physical form rather than use: entire metropolitan regions should be thought of this way. Duany is pushing an alternative he calls "Smart Code."

The Smart Code is based on the concept of the "transect." The idea is that there is a range of forms that the built environment can take. At one end is downtown, the urban core. At the other end is wilderness. In between are villages, suburbs and more dense urban neighborhoods. As Duany sees it, conventional zoning has failed to maintain the important distinctions between these types of places. Instead, it has made each of them resemble suburbia. When suburban building forms encroach on wilderness, the result is sprawl. When they encroach on urban areas, the result is lifeless downtowns.

Nashville-Davidson County, Tennessee, is one of the first places to begin incorporating these concepts into its planning process. The transect isn't a substitute for a zoning code, says planning director Rick Bernhardt. But it helps planners think about how one part of the city fits into the region, and how to zone accordingly. "It's really understanding what the purpose is of the part of the community you're designing," Bernhardt says, "and then making sure that the streetscape, the intensity and the mix of land use are all consistent with that."

—*C.S.*

was a pioneer in rewriting the code to separate the places people live in from where they work and where they shop.

The 1957 zoning law was largely the creation of real estate developer Harry Chaddick, who proclaimed that the city was "being slowly strangled" by mixed uses of property. It classified every available parcel of land into myriad categories based on density. Residential neighborhoods, for example, were laid out in a range from "R1" (single family homes) to "R8" (high-rises).

Land use rules were so strict as to dictate where ice cream shops, coin stores and haberdasheries could go. Chaddick's code was hailed in its time as a national model.

But over the years, one patch after another in the 1957 law made it almost impossible to use. Some parts contradicted other parts. Two attorneys could read it and come away with completely opposite views of what the code allowed. Finally, in 2000, the mayor tapped Ed Kus, a longtime city zoning attorney, to take charge of a full-scale rewrite. Kus thinks the law in the works will be equally as historic as Chaddick's—and more durable. "I hope the ordinance we come up with will be good for the next 50 years," Kus says.

Besides its rigidity, the old code has been plagued by false assumptions about population growth. Back in the 1950s, Chicago was a city of 3.6 million people, and planners expected it to reach a population of 5 million. Of course, it didn't work out that way. Like every other major city, Chicago lost a huge proportion of its residents to the suburbs. By 1990, it was down to fewer than 2.8 million residents. But it was still zoned to accommodate 5 million.

That's essentially how Lakeview got its three-flats on steroids. Had the city's population grown as the code anticipated, it would have needed a supply of large new residential buildings to replace its traditional two-flats and bungalows. The law made it possible to build these in lots of neighborhoods, regardless of the existing architecture or character.

For decades, this made relatively little difference, because the declining population limited demand for new housing in most of the city. Once the '90s boom hit, however, developers took advantage. They bought up old homes and tore them down, replacing them with massive condo projects. They built tall, and sometimes they built wide and deep, eating up front yards and side yards and often paving over the back for parking. "Developers are building to the max," Kus says. "We have all these new housing types and the zoning ordinance doesn't govern them very well."

There are other glaring problems. Although many people think of the 1950s as the decade when America went suburban, most retail business in Chicago was still conducted in storefronts along trolley lines, both in the city and the older close-in suburbs. The code reflects that mid-century reality. Some 700 miles of Chicago's arterial streets are zoned for commercial use, much more than the current local retail market can bear. Worse, the old code is full of anachronistic restrictions on what kinds of transactions can be conducted where. A store that sells computers needs a zoning variance to set up shop next door to one that fixes them. "If you're in a 'B1' district"—a neighborhood business corridor—"you can hardly do any business," Kus says.

All of these archaic provisions are quietly being reconsidered and revised on the ninth floor of city hall, where Kus heads a small team that includes two planning department staffers and a consultant from the planning firm of Duncan Associates. Their work will go to the zoning reform commission, a panel whose 17 members were picked by the mayor to hold exhaustive public meetings and then vote on the plan. The commission includes aldermen, architects, planners, business representatives and a labor leader. Developers are conspicuously absent, which may come back to bite the whole project later. But for now, the rewrite is moving remarkably fast. The city council is expected to pass the new code this fall. That will set the stage

for an even more difficult task: drawing new maps to fit the changed rules.

In the past, Chicago's zoning reforms sought nothing less than to transform the face of the city. This time, however, there is more of a conservationist bent. What the reformers are trying to do is to lock in the qualities Chicagoans like about their oldest, most traditional neighborhoods. That's not to say they want to freeze the city in place. The building boom is quite popular. But it's also widely accepted that the character of Chicago's neighborhoods is the reason why the city is hot again, and that zoning should require new buildings to fit in. "Cities that will succeed in the future are the ones that maintain a unique character of place," says Alicia Mazur Berg, Chicago's planning commissioner. "People choose to live in many of our neighborhoods because they're attractive, they have front yards and buildings of the same scale."

Made for Walking

The new rules being drafted for residential areas are a good example of this thinking. Height limits will prevent new houses from towering over old ones. Neighborhoods such as Lakeview will likely be "downzoned" for less density. New homes will be required to have a green back yard, not a paved one, and builders will not be allowed to substitute a new creation known as a "patio pit" for a front yard. Garages will be expected to face an alley—not the street—and blank walls along the streetscape will be prohibited.

In the same spirit, the creators of the new zoning code are also proposing a new category, the Pedestrian Street, or "P-street." This is meant for a neighborhood shopping street that has survived in spite of the automobile and still thrives with pedestrian life. The new code aims to keep things that way. Zoning for P-streets will specifically outlaw strip malls, gas stations and drive-throughs, or any large curb cut that could interrupt the flow of pedestrians. It also will require new buildings to sit right on the sidewalk and have front doors and windows so that people walking by can see inside.

There are dozens of other ideas. The new code aims to liven up once-vibrant but now-dying neighborhood commercial streets by letting developers build housing there. For the first time ever, downtown Chicago will be treated as a distinct place, with its own special set of zoning rules. The code will largely ignore meaningless distinctions between businesses, such as whether they sell umbrellas or hats.

The new code also will recognize that the nature of manufacturing has changed. Light manufacturing will be allowed to mix with offices or nightclubs. But heavy industry will get zones of its own, not so much for the health reasons that were important in 1923 and 1957, but because the big manufacturers want it that way and Chicago doesn't want to lose them.

For all the changes, Chicago is still keeping most of the basic zoning conventions in place. It is also keeping much of the peculiar language of zoning—the designations such as "R2" and "C3" that sound more like droids from Star Wars than descriptions of places where people live, work and shop.

On the other hand, the new code will be different from the old code in one immediately identifiable way: It will be understandable. Pages of text are being slimmed down into charts and graphics, making the law easier to use for people without degrees in law or planning. An interactive version will go up on the city's Web site. "Predictability is important," says Ed Kus. "The average person should be able to pick up the zoning code and understand what can and can't be built in his neighborhood."

Is Regional Government the Answer?

FRED SIEGEL

Suburban sprawl, the spread of low-density housing over an ever-expanding landscape, has attracted a growing list of enemies. Environmentalists have long decried the effects of sprawl on the ecosystem; aesthetes have long derided what they saw as "the ugliness and banality of suburbia"; and liberals have intermittently insisted that suburban prosperity has been purchased at the price of inner-city decline and poverty. But only recently has sprawl become the next great issue in American public life. That's because suburbanites themselves are now calling for limits to seemingly inexorable and frenetic development.

Slow-growth movements are a response to both the cyclical swings of the economy and the secular trend of dispersal. Each of the great postwar booms have, at their cyclical peak, produced calls for restraint. These sentiments have gained a wider hearing as each new upturn of the economy has produced an ever widening wave of exurban growth. A record 96 months of peacetime economic expansion has produced the strongest slow-growth movement to date. In 1998, antisprawl environmentalists and "not-in-my-backyard" slow-growth suburbanites joined forces across the nation to pass ballot measures restricting exurban growth.

Undoubtedly, the loss of land and the environmental degradation produced by sprawl are serious problems that demand public attention. But sprawl also brings enormous benefits as well as considerable costs. It is, in part, an expression of the new high-tech economy whose campus-like office parks on the periphery of urban areas have driven the economic boom of the 1990s. And it's sprawl that has sustained the record rise in home ownership. Sprawl is not some malignancy to be summarily excised but, rather, part and parcel of prosperity. Dealing with its ill effects requires both an understanding of the new landscape of the American economy and a willingness to make subtle trade-offs. We must learn to curb its worst effects without reducing the wealth and freedom that permit sprawl to develop.

Rising incomes and employment, combined with declining interest rates, have allowed a record number of people, including minority and immigrant families, to purchase homes for the first time. Home ownership among blacks, which is increasingly suburban, has risen at more than three times the white rate; a record 45 percent of African Americans owned their own homes in 1998. Nationally, an unprecedented 67 percent of Americans are homeowners.

Sprawl is part of the price we're paying for something novel in human history—the creation of a mass upper middle class. Net household worth has been increasing at the unparalleled annual rate of 10 percent since 1994, so that while in 1970, only 3.2 percent of households had an annual income of $100,000 (in today's dollars), by 1996, 8.2 percent of American households could boast a six-figure annual income. The new prosperity is reflected in the size of new homes, many of whose owners no doubt decry the arrival of still more "McMansions" and new residents, clogging the roads and schools of the latest subdivisions. In the midst of the 1980's boom, homebuilders didn't have a category for mass-produced houses of more than 3,000 square feet: By 1996, one out of every seven new homes built was larger than 3,000 square feet.

Today's Tenement Trail

Sprawl also reflects upward mobility for the aspiring lower-middle class. Nearly a half-century ago, Samuel Lubell dedicated *The Future of American Politics* to the memory of his mother, "who pioneered on the urban frontier." Lubell described a process parallel to the settling of the West, in which families on "the Old Tenement Trail" were continually on the move in search of a better life. In the cities, they abandoned crowded tenements on New York's Lower East Side for better housing in the South Bronx, and from there, went to the "West Bronx, crossing that Great Social Divide—the Grand Concourse—beyond which rolled true middle-class country where janitors were called superintendents."

Today's "tenement trail" takes aspiring working- and lower-middle class Americans to quite different areas. Kendall, Florida, 20 miles southeast of Miami, is every environmentalist's nightmare image of sprawl, a giant grid carved out of the muck of swamp land that encroaches on the Everglades. Stripmalls and mega-stores abound for mile after mile, as do the area's signature giant auto lots. Yet Kendall also represents a late-twentieth-century version of the Old Tenement Trail. Kendall, notes the *New Republic*'s Charles Lane, is "the Queens of the late twentieth century," a place where immigrants are buying into America. Carved out of the palmetto wilderness, its population exploded from roughly 20,000 in 1970 to 300,000 today. Agricultural in the 1960s, and a hip place for young whites in the 1970s, Kendall grew increasingly Hispanic in the 1980s, as

Cubans, Nicaraguans, and others who arrived with very little worked their way up. Today, it's half Hispanic and a remarkable example of integration. In most of Kendall, notes University of Miami geographer Peter Muller, "You can't point to a white or Latino block because the populations are so intermixed."

Virginia Postrel, the editor of *Reason,* argues that the slow-growth movement is animated by left-wing planners' hostility to suburbia. Others mock slow-growthers as elitists, as in the following quip:

Q: What's the difference between an environmentalist and a developer?

A: The environmentalist already has his house in the mountains.

But, in the 1990s, slow-growth sentiment has been taking hold in middle- and working-class suburbs like Kendall, as development turns into overdevelopment and traffic congestion becomes a daily problem.

Regional Government

One oft-proposed answer to sprawl has been larger regional governments that will exercise a monopoly on land-use decisions. Underlying this solution is the theory—no doubt correct—that sprawl is produced when individuals and townships seek to maximize their own advantage without regard for the good of the whole community. Regionalism, however, is stronger in logic than in practice. For example, the people of Kendall, rather than embracing regionalism, are looking to slow down growth by *seceding* from their regional government. Upon examination, we begin to see some of the problems with regional government.

Kendall is part of Metro-Dade, the oldest major regional government, created in 1957. The largest of its 29 municipalities, Miami, the fourth poorest city in the United States, has 350,000 people; the total population of Metro-Dade is 2 million, 1.1 million of whom live in unincorporated areas. In Metro-Dade, antisprawl and antiregional government sentiments merge. Despite county-imposed growth boundaries, residents have complained bitterly of overdevelopment. The county commissioners—many of whom have been convicted of, or charged with, corruption—have been highly receptive to the developers who are among their largest campaign contributors. As one south Florida resident said of the developers, "It's a lot cheaper to be able to buy just one government." The south Florida secessionists want to return zoning to local control where developers' clout is less likely to overwhelm neighborhood interests.

When Jane Jacobs wrote, in *The Death and Life of Great American Cities,* that "the voters sensibly decline to federate into a system where bigness means local helplessness, ruthless oversimplified planning and administrative chaos," she could have been writing about south Florida. What's striking about Metro-Dade is that it has delivered neither efficiency nor equity nor effective planning while squelching local self-determination.

The fight over Metro-Dade echoes the conflicts of an earlier era. Historically, the fight over regional versus local government was an important, if intermittent, issue for many cities from 1910 to 1970. From about 1850 to 1910, according to urban historian Jon Teaford, suburbanites were eager to be absorbed by cities whose wealth enabled them to build the water, sewage, and road systems they couldn't construct on their own. "The central city," he explains, "provided superior service at a lower cost." But, in the 1920s, well before race became a central issue, suburbanites, who had increasingly sorted themselves out by ethnicity and class, began to use special-service districts and innovative financial methods to provide their own infrastructure and turned away from unification. Suburbanites also denounced consolidation as an invitation to big-city, and often Catholic, "boss rule" and as a threat to "self-government."

In the 1960s, as black politicians began to win influence over big-city governments, they also joined the anticonsolidation chorus. At the same time, county government, once a sleepy extension of rural rule, was modernized, and county executives essentially became the mayors of full-service governments administering what were, in effect, dispersed cities. But they were mayors with a difference. Their constituents often wanted a balance between commercial development, which constrained the rise of taxes, and the suburban ideal of family-friendly semirural living. When development seemed too intrusive, suburban voters in the 1980s, and again in the 1990s, have pushed a slow-growth agenda.

The New Regionalism

In the 1990s, regionalism has been revived as an effort to link the problem of sprawl with the problem of inner-city poverty. Assuming that "flight creates blight," regionalists propose to recapture the revenue of those who have fled the cities and force growth back into older areas by creating regional or metropolitan-area governments with control over land use and taxation.

The new regionalism owes a great deal to a group of circuit-riding reformers. Inspired by the arguments of scholars like Anthony Downs, one of the authors of the Kerner Commission report, and sociologist William Julius Wilson of Harvard, as well as the example of Portland, Oregon's metro-wide government, these itinerant preachers have traveled to hundreds of cities to spread the gospel of regional cooperation. The three most prominent new regionalists—columnist Neil Peirce, former Albuquerque mayor David Rusk, and Minnesota state representative Myron Orfield—have developed a series of distinct, but overlapping, arguments for why cities can't help themselves, and why regional solutions are necessary.

Peirce, in his book *Citistates,* plausibly insists that regions are the real units of competition in the global economy, so that there is a metro-wide imperative to revive the central city, lest the entire area be undermined. Less plausibly, Orfield in *Metropolitics* argues that what he calls "the favored quarter" of fast-growing suburbs on the periphery of the metro area have prospered at the expense of both the central city and the inner-ring suburbs. In order [for] both to revive the central city and save the inner suburbs from decline, Orfield proposes that these two areas join forces, redistributing money from the "favored quarter" to the older areas. Rusk argues, in *Baltimore Unbound,* that older cities, unable to annex the fast growing suburbs, are doomed to further decline. He insists that only "flexible cities"— that is, cities capable of expanding geographically and capturing the wealth of the suburbs—can truly deal with inner-city black poverty. Regionalism, writes Rusk, is "the new civil rights movement."

There are differences among them. Orfield and, to a lesser degree, Rusk operate on a zero-sum model in which gain for the suburbs comes directly at the expense of the central city. Peirce is less radical, proposing regional cooperation as the means to a win-win situation for both city and the surrounding region. But they all share a desire to disperse poverty across the region and, more importantly, recentralize economic growth in the already built-up areas. The latter goal is consistent with both the environmental thrust of the antisprawl movement and the push for regional government. In a speech to a Kansas City civic organization, Rusk laid out the central assumption of the new regionalism. "The greater the fragmentation of governments," he asserted, "the greater the fragmentation of society by race and economic class." Fewer governments, argue the new regionalists, will yield a number of benefits, including better opportunities for regional cooperation, more money for cash-strapped central cities, less racial inequality, less sprawl, and greater economic growth. However, all of these propositions are questionable.

Better Policies, Not Fewer Governments

Consider Baltimore and Philadelphia, cities that the regionalists have studied thoroughly. According to the 1998 *Greater Baltimore State of the Region* report, Philadelphia has 877 units of local government (including school boards)—or 17.8 per 100,000 people. Baltimore has only six government units of any consequence in Baltimore City and the five surrounding counties—or 2.8 per 100,000 people. Greater Baltimore has fewer government units than any other major metro area in the United States. As a political analyst told me: "Get six people in a room, and you have the government of 2,200 square miles, because the county execs have very strong powers." We might expect considerable regional cooperation in Baltimore, but not in Philadelphia. Regionalism has made no headway in either city, however. The failure has little to do with the number of governments and a great deal to do with failed policy choices in both cities.

Rusk does not mention the many failings of Baltimore's city government. He refers to the current mayor, Kurt Schmoke, just once and only to say that Baltimore has had "excellent political leadership." In Rusk's view, Baltimore is "programmed to fail" because of factors entirely beyond its control, namely, the inability to annex its successful suburbs. In the ahistorical world of the regionalist (and here, Peirce is a partial exception),

people are always pulled from the city by structural forces but never pushed from the city by bad policies.

Baltimore is not as well financed as the District of Columbia, which ruined itself despite a surfeit of money. But Baltimore, a favorite political son of both Annapolis and Washington, has been blessed with abundant financial support. Over the past decade, Schmoke has increased spending on education and health by over a half-billion dollars. He has also added 200 police officers and spent $60 million more for police over the last four years. "His greatest skill," notes the *Baltimore Sun,* "has been his ability to attract more federal and state aid while subsidies diminished elsewhere." But, notwithstanding these expenditures, middle-class families continue to flee the city at the rate of 1,000 per month, helping to produce the sprawl environmentalists decry.

Little in Baltimore works well. The schools have been taken over by the state, while the Housing Authority is mired in perpetual scandal and corruption. Baltimore is one of the few cities where crime hasn't gone down. That's because Schmoke has insisted, contrary to the experiences of New York and other cities, that drug-related crime could not be reduced until drug use was controlled through treatment. The upshot is that New York, with eight times more people than Baltimore, has only twice as many murders. Baltimore also leads the country in sexually transmitted diseases. These diseases have flourished among the city's drug users partly owing to Schmoke's de facto decriminalization of drugs. According to the Centers for Disease Control and Prevention (CDC), Baltimore has a syphilis rate 18 times the national average, 3 or 4 times as high as areas where the STD epidemic is most concentrated.

Flexible Cities

Rusk attributes extraordinary qualities to flexible cities. He says that they are able to both reduce inequality, curb sprawl, and maintain vital downtowns. Rusk was the mayor of Albuquerque, a flexible city that annexed a vast area, even as its downtown essentially died. The reduced inequality he speaks of is largely a statistical artifact. If New York were to annex Scarsdale, East New York's average income would rise without having any effect on the lives of the people who live there. As for sprawl, flexible cities like Phoenix and Houston are hardly models.

A recent article for *Urban Affairs Review,* by Subhrajit Guhathakurta and Michele Wichert, showed that within the elastic city of Phoenix, inner-city residents poorer than their outer-ring neighbors are subsidizing the building of new developments on the fringes of the metropolis. While sprawl is correlated with downtown decline in Albuquerque, in Phoenix it's connected with what *Fortune* described as "the remarkable rebound of downtown Phoenix, which has become a chic after-dark destination as well as a residential hot spot." There seems to be no automatic connection between regionalism and downtown revival.

Orfield's *Metropolitics* provides another version of an overdetermined structuralist argument. According to him, the favored quarter is sucking the inner city dry, and, as a result, central-city blight will inevitably engulf the older first-ring suburbs as well. He is right to see strong pressures on the inner-ring suburbs, stemming from an aging housing stock and population as well as an influx of inner-city poor. But it is how the inner-ring suburbs respond to these pressures that will affect their fate.

When Coleman Young was mayor of Detroit, large sections of the city returned to prairie. But the inner-ring suburbs have done fairly well precisely by not imitating Detroit's practice of providing poor services at premium prices. "Much like the new edge suburbs," explains the *Detroit News,* "older suburbs that follow the proven formula of promoting good schools, public safety and well-kept housing attract new investment." Suburban Mayor Michael Guido sees his city's well developed infrastructure as an asset, which has already been bought and paid for. "Now," says Mayor Guido, "it's a matter of maintenance . . . and we offer a sense of history and a sense of community. That's really important to people, to have a sense of belonging to a whole community rather than a subdivision."

Suburb Power

City-suburban relations are not fixed; they are various depending on the policies both follow. Some suburbs compete with the central city for business. In south Florida, Coral Gables more than holds its own with Miami as a site for business headquarters. Southfield, just outside Detroit, and Clayton, just outside St. Louis, blossomed in the wake of the 1960s' urban riots and now compete with their downtowns. Aurora, with a population of more than 160,000 and to the east of Denver, sees itself as a competitor, and it sees regional efforts at growth management as a means by which the downtown Denver elite can ward off competition.

Suburban growth can also help the central city. In the Philadelphia area, economic growth and new work come largely from the Route 202 high-tech corridor in Chester County, west of the city. While the city has lost 57,000 jobs, even in the midst of national economic prosperity, the fast growing Route 202 companies have been an important source of downtown legal and accounting jobs. At the same time, the suburbs are creating jobs for residents that the central city cannot produce, so that 20 percent of city residents commute to the suburbs while 15 percent of people who live in the suburbs commute to Philadelphia.

The "new regionalists" assume that the prosperity of the edge cities is a function of inner-city decline. But, in many cities, it is more nearly the case that suburban booms are part of what's keeping the central-city economy alive. It is the edge cities that have taken up the time-honored urban task of creating new work.

According to *INC* magazine, the 500 fastest growing small companies are all located in suburbs and exurbs. This is because local governments there are very responsive to the needs of start-up companies. These high-tech hotbeds, dubbed "nerdistans" by Joel Kotkin, are composed of networks of companies that are sometimes partners, sometimes competitors. They provide a pool of seasoned talent for start-ups, where engineers and techies who prefer the orderly, outdoor life of suburbia to the crowds and disorder of the city can move from project to project.

Henry Nicholas, CEO of Broadcom, a communications-chip and cable-modem maker, explained why he reluctantly moved to Irvine: "It's hard to relocate techies to LA. It's the congestion, the expensive housing—and there's a certain stigma to it."

Imagine what the United States would be like if the Bay Area had followed the New York model. In 1898, New York created the first regional government when it consolidated all the areas of the New York harbor—Manhattan, Brooklyn, Queens, the Bronx, and Staten Island—into the then-largest city in the world. The consolidation has worked splendidly for Manhattan, which thrives as a capital of high-end financial and legal services. But over time, the Manhattan-centric economy based on high taxes, heavy social spending, and extensive economic regulation destroyed Brooklyn's once vital shipping and manufacturing economy.

In 1912, San Francisco, the Manhattan of Northern California, proposed to create a unified regional government by incorporating Oakland in the East Bay and San Jose in the South. The plan for a Greater San Francisco was modeled on Greater New York and called for the creation of self-governing boroughs within an enlarged city and county of San Francisco. East Bay opposition defeated the San Francisco expansion in the legislature, and later attempts at consolidation in 1917, 1923, and 1928 also failed. But had San Francisco with its traditions of high taxation and heavy regulation succeeded, Silicon Valley might never have become one of the engines of the American economy. Similarly, it's no accident that the Massachusetts Route 128 high-tech corridor is located outside of the boundaries of Boston, even as it enriches the central city.

The Portland Model

The complex and often ironic history of existing regional governments has been obscured by the bright light of hope emanating from Portland. It seems that in every generation one city is said to have perfected the magic elixir for revival. In the 1950s, it was Philadelphia; today, it's Portland. In recent years, hundreds of city officials have traveled to Portland to study its metropolitan government, comprehensive environmental planning, and the urban-growth boundary that has been credited with Portland's revival and success.

While there are important lessons to be learned from Portland, very little of its success to date can be directly attributed to the growth boundary, which was introduced too recently and with boundaries so capacious as not yet to have had much effect. Thirty-five percent of the land within the boundary was vacant when it was imposed in 1979. And, at the same time, fast growing Clark County, just north of Portland but not part of the urban-growth boundary, has provided an escape valve for potential housing pressures. The upshot, notes demographer Wendell Cox, is that even with the growth boundary, Portland still remains a relatively low-density area with fewer people per square mile than San Diego, San Jose, or Sacramento.

Portland has also been run with honesty and efficiency, unlike Metro-Dade. Blessed with great natural resources, Portland—sometimes dubbed "Silicon forest," because chipmakers are drawn to its vast quantities of cheap clean water—has conserved its man-made as well as natural resources. A city with more cast-iron buildings than any place outside of Manhattan, it has been a leader in historic preservation. Time and again, Portland's leadership has made the right choices. It was one of the first cities to reconnect its downtown with the riverfront. Portland never built a circumferential freeway. And, in the 1970s, under the leadership of mayor Neil Goldschmidt, the city vetoed a number of proposed highway projects that would have threatened the downtown.

In 1978, Portland voters, in conjunction with the state government, created the first directly elected metropolitan government with the power to manage growth over three counties. Portland metro government has banned big-box retailers, like Walmart and Price Club, on the grounds that they demand too much space and encourage too much driving. This is certainly an interesting experiment well worth watching, but should other cities emulate Portland's land-management model? It's too soon to say.

Good government is always important. But aside from that, it's hard to draw any general lessons from the Portland experience. The growth boundaries may or may not work, and there's certainly no reason to think that playing with political boundaries will bring good government to Baltimore.

Living with Sprawl

What then is to be done? First, we can accept the consensus that has developed around preserving open space, despite some contradictory effects. The greenbelts around London, Portland, and Baltimore County pushed some development back toward the city and encouraged further sprawl as growth leapfrogged the open space. The push to preserve open space is only likely to grow stronger as continued growth generates both more congestion and more wealth, which can be used to buy up open land.

Secondly, we can create what Peter Salins, writing in *The Public Interest*,[1] described as a "level playing field" between the central cities and the suburbs. This can be done by ending exurban growth subsidies for both transportation as well as new water and sewer lines. These measures might further encourage the revival of interest in old fashioned Main Street living, which is already attracting a new niche of home buyers. State and local governments can also repeal the land-use and zoning regulations that discourage mixed-use development of the sort that produces a clustering of housing around Main Street and unsubsidized low-cost housing in the apartments above the streets' shops.

Because of our strong traditions of local self-government, regionalism has been described as an unnatural act among consenting jurisdictions. But regional cooperation needn't mean the heavy hand of all-encompassing regional government. There are some modest, but promising, experiments already under way in regional revenue sharing whose effects should be carefully evaluated. Allegheny County, which includes Pittsburgh, has created a Regional Asset District that uses a 1 percent sales tax increase to support cultural institutions and reduce other taxes. The Twin Cities have put money derived from the increase in assessed value of commercial and industrial properties into a pot to aid fiscally weaker municipalities. Kansas and Missouri created a cultural district that levies a small increase in the sales tax across the region. The money is being used to rehabilitate the area's most treasured architectural landmark, Kansas City's Union Station.

Cities and suburbs do have some shared interests, as in the growing practice of reverse commuting which links inner-city residents looking to get off welfare with fast growing suburban areas hampered by a shortage of labor. Regionalism can curb sprawl and integrate and sustain central-city populations if it reforms the misguided policies and politics that have sent the black and white middle class streaming out of cities like Baltimore, Washington, and Philadelphia. Regional co-operation between the sprawling high-tech suburbs and the central cities could modernize cities that are in danger of being left further behind by the digital economy. In that vein, the District of Columbia's Mayor Anthony Williams has seized on the importance of connecting his welfare population with the fast growing areas of Fairfax County in Northern Virginia. The aim of focused regional policies, argues former HUD Undersecretary Marc Weiss, should be economic, not political, integration.

Sprawl isn't some malignancy that can be surgically removed. It's been part and parcel of healthy growth, and curbing it involves difficult tradeoffs best worked out locally. Sprawl and the movement against sprawl are now a permanent part of the landscape. The future is summed up in a quip attributed to former Oregon Governor Tom McCall, who was instrumental in creating Portland's growth boundary. "Oregonians," he said, "are against two things, sprawl and density."

Note

1. "Cities, Suburbs, and the Urban Crisis," *The Public Interest*, No. 113 (Fall 1993).

Reprinted with permission from The Public Interest, Fall 1999, pp. 85–98.

Are Europe's Cities Better?

Pietro S. Nivola

Cities grow in three directions: *in* by crowding, *up* into multi-story buildings, or *out* toward the periphery. Although cities everywhere have developed in each of these ways at various times, nowhere in Europe do urban settlements sprawl as much as in the United States. Less than a quarter of the U.S. population lived in suburbia in 1950. Now well over half does. Why have most European cities remained compact compared to the hyperextended American metropolis?

At first glance, the answer seems elementary. The urban centers of Europe are older, and the populations of their countries did not increase as rapidly in the postwar period. In addition, stringent national land-use laws slowed exurban development, whereas the disjointed jurisdictions in U.S. metropolitan regions encouraged it.

But on closer inspection, this conventional wisdom does not suffice. It is true that the contours of most major urban areas in the United States were formed to a great extent by economic and demographic expansion after the Second World War. But the same was true in much of Europe, where entire cities were reduced to rubble by the war and had to be rebuilt from ground zero.

Consider Germany, whose cities were carpet bombed. Many German cities today are old in name only, and though the country's population as a whole grew less quickly than America's after 1950, West German cities experienced formidable economic growth and in-migrations. Yet the metropolitan population density of the United States is still about one-fourth that of Germany. New York, our densest city, has approximately one-third the number of inhabitants per square mile as Frankfurt.

Sprawl has continued apace even in places where the American population has grown little or not at all in recent decades. From 1970 to 1990, the Chicago area's population rose by only 4 percent, but the region's built-up land increased 46 percent. Metropolitan Cleveland's population actually declined by 8 percent, yet 33 percent more of the area's territory was developed.

The fragmented jurisdictional structure in U.S. metropolitan areas, wherein every suburban town or county has control over the use of land, does not adequately explain sprawl either. Since 1950, about half of America's central cities at least doubled their territory by annexing new suburbs. Houston covered 160 square miles in 1950. By 1980, exercising broad powers to annex its environs, it incorporated 556 square miles. In the same 30-year period, Jacksonville went from being a town of 30 square miles to a regional government enveloping 841 square miles—two-thirds the size of Rhode Island. True, the tri-state region of New York contains some 780 separate localities, some with zoning ordinances that permit only low-density subdivisions. But the urban region of Paris—Ile de France—comprises 1,300 municipalities, all of which have considerable discretion in the consignment of land for development.

To be sure, European central governments presumably oversee these local decisions through nationwide land-use statutes. But is this a telling distinction? The relationship of U.S. state governments to their local communities is roughly analogous to that of Europe's unitary regimes to their respective local entities. Not only are the governments of some of our states behemoths (New York State's annual expenditures, for example, approximate Sweden's entire national budget) but a significant number have enacted territorial planning legislation reminiscent of European guidelines. Indeed, from a legal standpoint, local governments in this country are mere "creatures" of the states, which can direct, modify, or even abolish their localities at will. Many European municipalities, with their ancient independent charters, are less subordinated.

The enforcement of land-use plans varies considerably in Europe. In Germany, as in America, some *Länder* (or states) are more restrictive than others. The Scandinavians, Dutch, and British take planning more seriously than, say, the Italians. The late Antonio Cederna, an astute journalist, wrote volumes about the egregious violations of building and development codes in and around Italy's historic centers. Critics who assume that land regulators in the United States are chronically permissive, whereas Europe's growth managers are always scrupulous and "smart," ought to contemplate, say, the unsightly new suburbs stretching across the northwestern plain of Florence toward Prato, and then visit Long Island's East End, where it is practically impossible to obtain a building permit along many miles of pristine coastline.

Big, Fast, and Violent

The more important contrasts in urban development between America and Europe lie elsewhere. With three and half million square miles of territory, the United States has had much more space over which to spread its settlements. And on this vast expanse, decentralizing technologies took root and spread decades earlier than in other industrial countries. In 1928, for example, 78 percent of all the motor vehicles in the world were located in the United States. With incomes rising rapidly, and the costs of producing vehicles declining, 56 percent of American families owned an automobile by that time. No European country reached a comparable level of automobile ownership until well after the Second World War. America's motorized multitudes were able to begin commuting between suburban residences and workplaces decades before such an arrangement was imaginable in any other advanced nation.

A more perverse but also distinctive cause of urban sprawl in the United States has been the country's comparatively high level of violent crime. Why a person is ten times more likely to be murdered in America than in Japan, seven times more likely to be raped than in France, or almost four times more likely to be robbed at gun point than in the United Kingdom, is a complex question. But three things are known.

First, although criminal violence has declined markedly here in the past few years, America's cities have remained dangerous by international standards. New York's murder rate dropped by two-thirds between 1991 and 1997, yet there were still 767 homicides committed that year. London, a mega-city of about the same size, had less than 130. Second, the rates of personal victimization, including murder, rape, assault, robbery, and personal theft, tend to be much higher within U.S. central cities than in their surroundings. In 1997, incidents of violent crime inside Washington, D.C., for instance, were six times more frequent than in the city's suburbs. Third, there is a strong correlation between city crime rates and the flight of households and businesses to safer jurisdictions. According to economists Julie Berry Cullen of the University of Michigan and Steven D. Levitt of the University of Chicago, between 1976 and 1993, a city typically lost one resident for every additional crime committed within it.

Opinion surveys regularly rank public safety as a leading consideration in the selection of residential locations. In 1992, when New Yorkers were asked to name "the most important reason" for moving out of town, the most common answer was "crime, lack of safety" (47.2 percent). All other reasons—including "high cost of living" (9.3 percent) and "not enough affordable housing" (5.3 percent)—lagged far behind. Two years ago, when the American Assembly weighed the main obstacles to business investments in the inner cities, it learned that businessmen identified lack of security as *the* principal impediment. In short, crime in America has further depopulated the cores of metropolitan areas, scattering their inhabitants and businesses.

The Not-So-Invisible Hand

In addition to these fundamental differences, the public agendas here and in major European countries have been miles apart. The important distinctions, moreover, have less to do with differing "urban" programs than with other national policies, the consequences of which are less understood.

For example, lavish agricultural subsidies in Europe have kept more farmers in business and dissuaded them from selling their land to developers. Per hectare of farmland, agricultural subventions are 12 times more generous in France than in the United States, a divergence that surely helps explain why small farms still surround Paris but not New York City.

Thanks to scant taxation of gasoline, the price of automotive fuel in the United States is almost a quarter of what it is in Italy. Is it any surprise that Italians would live closer to their urban centers, where they can more easily walk to work or rely on public transportation? On a per capita basis, residents of Milan make an average of 350 trips a year on public transportation; people in San Diego make an average of 17.

Gasoline is not the only form of energy that is much cheaper in the United States than in Europe. Rates for electric power and furnace fuels are too. The expense of heating the equivalent of an average detached U.S. suburban home, and of operating the gigantic home appliances (such as refrigerators and freezers) that substitute for neighborhood stores in many American residential communities, would be daunting to most households in large parts of Europe.

Systems of taxation make a profound difference. European tax structures penalize consumption. Why don't most of the Dutch and Danes vacate their compact towns and cities where many commuters ride bicycles, rather than drive sport-utility vehicles, to work? The sales tax on a new, medium-sized car in the Netherlands is approximately nine times higher than in the United States; in Denmark, 37 times higher. The U.S. tax code favors spending over saving (the latter is effectively taxed twice) and provides inducements to purchase particular goods—most notably houses, since the mortgage interest is deductible. The effect of such provisions is to lead most American families into the suburbs, where spacious dwellings are available and absorb much of the nation's personal savings pool.

Tax policy is not the only factor promoting home ownership in the United States. Federal Housing Administration and Veterans Administration mortgage guarantees financed more than a quarter of the suburban single-family homes built in the immediate postwar period. In Europe, the housing stocks of many countries were decimated by the war. Governments responded to the emergency by erecting apartment buildings and extending rental subsidies to large segments of the population. America also built a good deal of publicly subsidized rental housing in the postwar years, but chiefly to accommodate the most impoverished city-dwellers. Unlike the mixed-income housing complexes scattered around London or Paris, U.S. public housing projects further concentrated the urban poor in the inner cities, turning the likes of Chicago's South Side into breeding grounds of social degradation and violence. Middle-class city-dwellers fled from these places to less perilous locations in the metropolitan fringe.

Few decisions are more consequential for the shape of cities than a society's investments in transportation infrastructure. Government at all levels in the United States has committed hundreds of billions to the construction and maintenance of highways, passenger railroads, and transit systems. What counts, however, is not just the magnitude of the commitment but the *distribution* of the public expenditures among modes of transportation. In the United States, where the share claimed by roads has dwarfed that of alternatives by about six to one, an unrelenting increase in automobile travel and a steady decline in transit usage—however heavily subsidized—was inevitable.

Dense cities dissipate without relatively intensive use of mass transit. In 1945, transit accounted for approximately 35 percent of urban passenger miles traveled in the United States. By 1994, the figure had dwindled to less than 3 percent—or roughly one-fifth the average in Western Europe. If early on, American transportation planners had followed the British or French budgetary practice of allocating between 40 and 60 percent of their transport outlays to passenger railroads and mass transit systems, instead of nearly 85 percent for highways, there is little question that many U.S. cities would be more compressed today.

Dense cities also require a vibrant economy of neighborhood shops and services. (Why live in town if performing life's simplest everyday functions, like picking up fresh groceries for supper, requires driving to distant vendors?) But local shopkeepers cannot compete with the regional megastores that are proliferating in America's metropolitan shopping centers and strip malls. Multiple restrictions on the penetration and predatory pricing practices of large retailers in various European countries protect small urban businesses. The costs to consumers are high, but the convenience and intimacy of London's "high streets" or of the corner markets in virtually every Parisian *arrondissement* are preserved.

"Shift and Shaft" Federalism

Europe's cities retain their merchants and inhabitants for yet another reason: European municipalities typically do not face the same fiscal liabilities as U.S. cities. Local governments in Germany derive less than one-third of their income from local revenues; higher levels of government transfer the rest. For a wide range of basic functions—including educational institutions, hospitals, prisons, courts, utilities, and so on—the national treasury funds as much as 80 percent of the expense incurred by England's local councils. Localities in Italy and the Netherlands raise only about 10 percent of their budgets locally. In contrast, U.S. urban governments must largely support themselves: They collect two-thirds of their revenues from local sources.

In principle, self-sufficiency is a virtue; municipal taxpayers ought to pay directly for the essential services they use. But in practice, these taxpayers are also being asked to finance plenty of other costly projects, many of which are mandated, but underfunded, by the federal government. Affluent jurisdictions may be able to absorb this added burden, but communities strapped for revenues often cannot. To satisfy the federal government's paternalistic commands, many old cities have been forced to raise taxes and cut the services that local residents need or value most. In response, businesses and middle-class households flee to the suburbs.

America's public schools are perhaps the clearest example of a crucial local service that is tottering under the weight of unfunded federal directives. Few nations, if any, devote as large a share of their total public education expenditures to *nonteaching* personnel. There may be several excuses for this lopsided administrative overhead, but one explanation is almost certainly the growth of government regulation and the armies of academic administrators needed to handle the red tape.

Schools are required, among other things, to test drinking water, remove asbestos, perform recycling, insure "gender equity," and provide something called "special education." The latter program alone forces local authorities to set aside upwards of $30 billion a year to meet the needs of students with disabilities. Meanwhile, according to a 1996 report by the U.S. Advisory Commission on Intergovernmental Relations, the federal government reimburses a paltry 8 percent of the expense. Compliance costs for urban school districts, where the concentrations of learning-disabled pupils are high and the means to support them low, can be particularly onerous. Out of a total $850 million of local funds budgeted for 77,000 students in the District of Columbia, for instance, $170 million has been earmarked for approximately 8,000 students receiving "special education."

Wretched schools are among the reasons why most American families have fled the cities for greener pastures. It is hard enough for distressed school systems like the District's, which struggle to impart even rudimentary literacy, to compete with their wealthier suburban counterparts. The difficulty is compounded by federal laws that, without adequate recompense, divert scarce educational resources from serving the overwhelming majority of students.

Schools are but one of many municipal services straining to defray centrally dictated expenses. Consider the plight of urban mass transit in the United States. Its empty seats and colossal operating deficits are no secret. Less acknowledged are the significant financial obligations imposed by Section 504 of the Rehabilitation Act and subsequent legislation. To comply with the Department of Transportation's rules for retrofitting public buses and subways, New York City estimated in 1980 that it would need to spend more than $1 billion in capital improvements on top of $50 million in recurring annual operating costs. As the city's mayor, Edward I. Koch, said at the time, "It would be cheaper for us to provide every severely disabled person with taxi service than make 255 of our subway stations accessible."

Although the Reagan administration later lowered these costs, passage of the Americans with Disabilities Act in 1990 led to a new round of pricey special accommodations in New York and other cities with established transit systems. Never mind that the Washington Metro is the nation's most modern and well-designed subway system. It has been ordered to tear up 45 stations and install bumpy tiles along platform edges to accommodate the sight impaired, a multi-million dollar effort. At issue here, as in the Individuals with Disabilities Education Act, is not whether provisions for the handicapped are desirable and just. Rather, the puzzle is how Congress can sincerely claim to champion these causes if it scarcely appropriates the money to advance them.

Nearly two decades ago, Mayor Koch detailed in *The Public Interest* what he called the "millstone" of some 47 unfunded mandates.[1] The tally of national statutes encumbering U.S. local governments since then has surpassed at least one hundred. And this does not count the hundreds of federal court orders and agency rulings that micromanage, and often drain, local resources. By 1994, Los Angeles estimated that federally mandated programs were costing the city approximately $840 million a year. Erasing that debit from the city's revenue requirements, either by meeting it with federal and state aid or by substantial recisions, would be tantamount to reducing city taxes as much as 20 percent. A windfall that large could do more to reclaim the city's slums, and halt the hollowing out of core communities, than would all of the region's planned "empowerment zones," "smart growth" initiatives, and "livability" bond issues.

Follow Europe?

To conclude that greater fiscal burden sharing and a wide range of other public policies help sustain Europe's concentrated cities is not to say, of course, that all those policies have enhanced the welfare of Europeans—and hence, that the United States ought to emulate them. The central governments of Western Europe may assume more financial responsibilities instead of bucking them down to the local level, but these top-heavy regimes also levy much higher taxes. Fully funding all of Washington's many social mandates with national tax dollars would mean, as in much of Europe, a more centralized and bloated welfare state.

Most households are not better off when farmers are heavily subsidized, or when anticompetitive practices protect microbusinesses at the expense of larger, more efficient firms. Nor would most consumers gain greater satisfaction from housing strategies that encourage renter occupancy but not homeownership, or from gas taxes and transportation policies that force people out of their cars and onto buses, trains, or bicycles.

In fact, these sorts of public biases have exacted an economic toll in various Western European countries, and certainly in Japan, while the United States has prospered in part because its economy is less regulated, and its metropolitan areas have been allowed to decompress. So suffocating is the extreme concentration of people and functions in the Tokyo area that government planners now view decentralization as a top economic priority. Parts of the British economy, too, seem squeezed by development controls. A recent report by McKinsey and Company attributes lagging productivity in key sectors to Britain's land-use restrictions that hinder entry and expansion of the most productive firms.

The densely settled cities of Europe teem with small shops. But the magnetic small-business presence reflects, at least in part, a heavily regulated labor market that stifles entrepreneurs who wish to expand and thus employ more workers. As the *Economist* noted in a review of the Italian economy, "Italy's plethora of small firms is as much an indictment of its economy as a triumph: many seem to lack either the will or the capital to keep growing." The lack of will is not surprising; moving from small to midsize or large means taking on employees who are nearly impossible to lay off when times turn bad, and it means saddling a company with costly mandated payroll benefits. Italy may have succeeded in conserving clusters of small businesses

in its old cities and towns, but perhaps at the price of abetting double-digit unemployment in its economy as a whole.

Striking a Balance

America's strewn-out cities are not without their own inefficiencies. The sprawling conurbations demand, for one thing, virtually complete reliance on automotive travel, thereby raising per capita consumption of motor fuel to four times the average of cities in Europe. That extraordinary level of fossil-fuel combustion complicates U.S. efforts to lower this country's considerable contribution to the buildup of greenhouse gases. Our seemingly unbounded suburbanization has also blighted central cities that possess irreplaceable architectural and historic assets. A form of metropolitan growth that displaces only bleak and obsolescent urban relics, increasingly discarded by almost everyone, may actually be welfare-enhancing. A growth process that also blights and abandons a nation's important civic and cultural centers, however, is rightfully grounds for concern.

Still, proposals to reconfigure urban development in the United States need to shed several misconceptions. As research by Helen Ladd of Duke University has shown, the costs of delivering services in high-density settlements frequently increase, not decrease. Traffic congestion at central nodes also tends to worsen with density, and more people may be exposed to hazardous levels of soot and smog. (The inhabitants of Manhattan drive fewer vehicle miles per capita than persons who inhabit New York's low-density suburbs. Nevertheless, Manhattan's air is often less healthy because the borough's traffic is unremittingly thick and seldom free-flowing, and more people live amid the fumes.) Growth boundaries, such as those circumscribing Portland, Oregon, raise real estate values, so housing inside the boundaries becomes less, not more, "affordable." Even the preservation of farmland, a high priority of managed growth plans, should be placed in proper perspective. The United States is the world's most productive agricultural producer, with ample capacity to spare. Propping up marginal farms in urbanizing areas may not put this acreage to uses most valued by society.

In sum, the diffuse pattern of urban growth in the United States is partly a consequence of particular geographic conditions, cultural characteristics, and raw market forces, but also an accidental outcome of certain government policies. Several of these formative influences differ fundamentally from those that have shaped European cities. Critics of the low-density American cityscape may admire the European model, but they would do well to recognize the full breadth of hard policy choices, and tough tradeoffs, that would have to be made before the constraints on sprawl in this country could even faintly begin to resemble Europe's.

Note

1. Edward I. Koch, "The Mandate Millstone," *The Public Interest,* Number 61, Fall 1980.

UNIT 7

Urban Problems: Crime, Education, and Poverty

Unit Selections

Key Points to Consider

- Did the application of the Broken Windows theory—that is, the concept of order maintenance in crime prevention—lead to New York's dramatic decline in crime?

- What other examples of a change in thinking about crime can you describe, and what effect would these changes have on crime rates?

- What makes a successful public housing project? How can subsidized housing be constructed to create such results?

- What is the difference between bilingual education and English as a Second Language (ESL)? Which of the two approaches, in your opinion, helps urban schools better educate its children? How does the problem of segregation in the school system enter into your thinking?

- Can different classes, especially the rich and the poor, prosper at the same time in a city, or is success a zero-sum game?

Student Web Site
www.mhcls.com/online

Internet References
Further information regarding these Web sites may be found in this book's preface or online.

The Center for Innovation in Education, Inc.
http://www.center.edu
Justice Information Center
http://www.ncjrs.org
National Institute on the Education of At-Risk Students
http://www.ed.gov/offices/OERI/At-Risk
The Urban Institute
http://www.urban.org

occurred in some cities, but others like Washington, D.C., have yet to see improvement. New York has had steep declines both in crime and in police violence against civilians. Educational reform has been called the civil rights battleground for the twenty-first century, the institutional arena where equal opportunity will be expanded or curtailed. Urban schools have in general either stagnated or declined academically over the past quarter century, driving out middle class students, leaving behind the poor trapped in a system with no exit. Students in these schools suffer from slack standards and social promotion even when they do manage to graduate. A number of reform efforts have sprouted over the years to challenge or provide alternatives to large urban school systems. Currently, the most important ideas, from charter schools to vouchers, all provide low-income parents with a greater degree of school choice, something that middle class and more affluent parents take for granted.

School choice questions also entered the debate over the recent referendum in California that limited the number of years students can spend in bilingual classes. Parents of Spanish-surnamed children complained about having their kids forced into dead-end, bilingual programs that were largely monolingual in Spanish. School choice won a momentous legal victory in June 2002 when the Supreme Court upheld Cleveland's publicly funded voucher program.

Crime may be down in some cities, but it continues to undermine urban life in others. James Q. Wilson looks back on 20 years of Broken Windows to consider how the theory has worked, and how it could be improved. Harry Siegel looks at crimes outside of the Broken Windows frame, while several other essays look at the lessons learned over the past 10 years, and where space remains for improvement.

But even where crime rates are down, the question of those left behind by the gains of the past decade remains. Aaron Bernstein sees things differently in "An Inner-City Renaissance," arguing that the poor prospered during the boom of the 1990s, as crime went down, and employment and incomes in the inner city neighborhoods shot up.

The fact that cities have begun to solve some of their most egregious problems should not blind us to those that remain. Crime, in fact, falls into both categories. Steep declines have

How an Idea Drew People Back to Urban Life

Twenty Years After 'Broken Windows,' James Q. Wilson Assesses the Theory

JAMES Q. WILSON

Two decades ago, George Kelling and I published an article in the Atlantic Monthly entitled "Broken Windows: The Police and Neighborhood Safety." Maybe it was the catchy title, maybe it was the argument, but for some reason the phrase and maybe the idea spread throughout American policing, and now is being taken up by the police in many other countries. Today, I sometimes hear a police official explain to me that they have adopted the "broken windows" strategy as if I had never heard of it.

The idea was simple. Citizens want public order as much as they want crime reduced, and so the police ought to worry about public disorder as much as they worry about catching crooks. Disorder arises from minor offenses such as aggressive panhandling, graffiti sprayed on the outside of buildings, alcoholics wandering the streets, and hostile teenagers hanging around bus stops and delicatessens.

Even though chasing away or arresting people who did these things may not do much to reduce crime immediately and in any event would constitute at best a minor pinch that police officers rarely took seriously and that courts were likely to ignore, recreating public order would do two things: Convince decent citizens that they and not some hostile force were entitled to use the streets and (perhaps) reduce crime over time by inducing good people and discouraging bad ones from using the streets.

The idea arose from Mr. Kelling's study of the effects of foot patrol on crime and public attitudes in New Jersey. He worked for the Police Foundation as it carried out a rigorous evaluation of foot patrol in Newark when Hubert Williams was the police chief. The neighborhoods where the experiment took place were largely inhabited by blacks and the officers who did the patrolling were largely white. The theory was that foot patrol would make the streets safer.

By and large, police chiefs did not believe this; after all, an officer on foot could not do much to chase a burglar in a car, and besides thieves could easily avoid the streets where foot patrol officers were walking. Police officers did not much care for foot patrol either. Standing outside on a cold or rainy night in Newark was a lot less pleasant than sitting in a warm patrol car, and the arrests you were likely to make while on foot would probably be of small-time offenders that would not do much to advance your police career.

The research showed that the police chiefs were right: Foot patrol did not cut crime. But it showed something else as well: The citizens loved it.

Explaining this puzzle is why we wrote the article. Were the citizens just fooling themselves by liking foot patrol? Did the whole project mean that the cops got better public relations just by conning the voters? Or maybe the citizens were right. Maybe they valued public order as much as they valued less crime. Perhaps public order would later on reduce the chances of crime rates rising if enough good folk used the streets and fewer roughnecks did.

We think the citizens were right. Getting rid of graffiti, aggressive panhandling, and wandering drunks made the citizens happier and increased their support for the police. Moreover, the cops on foot actually liked the work because they got to meet a lot of decent people and learn how they thought instead of just getting out of a patrol car to arrest a crook. We went on to offer the speculation—and at the time it was only a guess—that more orderly neighborhoods would, over the long haul, become less dangerous ones.

Our idea survived the predictable onslaught. Many civil rights organizations began to protest against efforts to control panhandling. Such efforts, they argued, were directed at the poor, blacks and the homeless. The ACLU filed suits in some cities against aspects of broken-windows policing. They must have forgotten, or perhaps they never knew, that broken-windows policing was first tested in poor black neighborhoods that enthusiastically endorsed it.

Civil libertarians also complained that stopping begging in the New York subways denied people free speech, and even got a federal judge to agree with them. But the appeals court threw out the argument because begging was not speech designed to convey a message, it was simply solicitation for money.

Slowly our idea grew until now it is hard to find a police department that does not claim to practice community-oriented policing and follow a broken-windows strategy. Just what the police chief means by these terms is not always very clear; to some extent, these words have become buzz phrases, backed up by a federal government policy of giving money to cities if they practice community policing, somehow defined.

In 1996, Mr. Kelling and his wife, Catherine Coles, published a book, "Fixing Broken Windows," that reviewed what has been done by Robert Kiley, David Gunn, and William Bratton to restore decency and safety to the New York subways and Bratton's later efforts to cut crime citywide after he became commissioner of the New York Police Department. Similar efforts took place in Baltimore, San Francisco, and Seattle.

The New York Transit Authority experience was especially telling. Long before he became the NYPD commissioner, Mr. Bratton, working with Messrs. Kiley and Gunn, had cut crime dramatically in the city's subways by holding his subordinates accountable for reducing offenses and getting rid of the graffiti. The people and the editorial writers cheered and in time the number of cops on duty underground could be safely cut.

Everyone in New York will recall the key steps whereby the subway success became the whole city's achievement. Rudolph Giuliani got elected mayor after a tough anti-crime campaign. One of the first things the NYPD did after he took office was to emphasize a policy begun by former police commissioner Raymond Kelly (who is now commissioner again) to get tough on "squeegee-men," males who extort money from motorists by pretending to wash (and sometimes spitting on) their car windows. Traditionally, officers would at best give only tickets to squeegeers, who would usually ignore the tickets or at worst pay a small fine. But then the NYPD began issuing warrants for the arrest of squeegee-men who ignored their tickets. Getting the warrant for non-appearance meant jail time for the recipient, and suddenly squeegee harassment stopped.

It may have been a little thing, but every New York motorist noticed it. Almost overnight, the city seemed safer. No one can say it was safer from serious crime, but it appeared safer and the people loved it.

After Mr. Giuliani took office, the crime rate plummeted. Lots of criminologists think that this happened automatically or as a result of some demographic change. No doubt serious crime fell in a lot of cities, but it fell faster and more in New York than almost anywhere else.

I do not assume that broken-windows policing explains this greater drop. Indeed, my instinct is to think that Mr. Bratton's management style, and especially his effort to hold precinct commanders accountable by frequently reviewing their performance in rigorous CompStat hearings, was the chief factor.

But Mr. Kelling has gathered a lot of evidence that a broken-windows strategy also made a difference. He measured that strategy by counting the number of misdemeanor arrests in New York precincts and showing that an increase in such arrests was accompanied by a decrease in serious crime, even in areas where unemployment rates rose, drug use was common, and the number of young men in their crime-prone years had increased.

So maybe a broken-windows strategy really does cut crime. But we know that it draws people back into urban life. And that is no trivial gain.

Mr. Wilson is an emeritus professor at UCLA and a lecturer at Pepperdine University.

Windows Not Broken

HARRY SIEGEL

It's not that I take pleasure in seeing anyone get hurt, but I can't say I was upset when the natives violently crashed the pioneer party in Williamsburg. There were 25 or so hipsters, umbrellas, space pirates, or whatever you like to call them on the roof blazing copious quantities of high grade skunk, another six on the fire escape drinking loudly, and a brick holding the apartment's outside door open, Dr. Dre booming from a stereo system that well exceeded the monthly rent, plugged into a pricey new Apple loaded up with mp3s. I'd been there about an hour, with friends who had come to see friends of theirs, and still had no idea whose apartment I was in. It didn't seem to matter. Several people had apparently just ambled in, drawn by the noise, crowd, drugs, and women, uninvited and unchallenged.

Then come the Hispanics. Four, all men, one of them easily larger than anyone else at the party. Hip hop clothes, gold chains, one with a couple of knife scars on his cheek. Someone puts the music down and suddenly there's a lot more murmuring than yelling. As the noise goes does, the newcomers tense up. Quantum uncertainty in practice—the newcomers are trying discreetly to examine the party, the party is trying discreetly to examine them and everyone is stuck staring. One of the newcomers asks for a cigarette in a neutral voice—half the hipsters are smoking, no one offers a smoke. Within five minutes all the women in the room have retreated to the roof. Five minutes later, three fellows descend from it, trying to look serious and purposeful but coming off stoned and spooked. One of them steps up to the newcomers, and, to quote "Airplane," starts talking jive—"Yo fellas, I'm sayin, yo, no disrespect, knowh'Imean, but this is a private party, yo"—then puts his hand on the biggest guy's shoulder, as though to steer him to the door. Even after the young jive talker was smacked around, I still wasn't clear if he was the host of the party, but in any event no one stepped in to help him. The Hispanics left after that, unchallenged, and the party quickly petered out.

It's a testament to how much the city has changed since the Dinkins years that the hipsters at the party, many of them newcomers to the city, lacked the danger sense shared by most all New Yorkers. There is an almost unprecedented expectation of safety in Hipster Williamsburg (which shares little but a name with Hispanic Williamsburg and Hasidic Williamsburg), with its population of underemployed, oversexed recent college graduates and their ilk. There's a shared expectation that the L is a safe means of transportation at three in the morning, that there's nothing wrong with sitting in a park with a $2,000 laptop or leaving your apartment door open while throwing a party.

But this detachment is from the police as well as from hard men and low lives. The Giuliani revolution in controlling crime is barely noticed, taken as a given. Unlike those who live in poor or working class neighborhoods, the city's young hipsters feel neither compunction nor fear about smoking a joint while at home or at a party. While the poor and working class continue to face consequences for smoking pot, middle class pot use has been all but decriminalized—and this is, for the most part, a good thing.

Ask a hipster fresh off the boat or however it is they get here about juice bars, and odds are you'll hear about some spot on Houston Street that mixes a great blueberry smoothie. Ask about weed, and odds are you'll hear about a delivery service, some young entrepreneur from the neighborhood moving quarter-ounces.

But a decade ago, as the East Village, the Lower East Side, and Alphabet City were just beginning to gentrify, just about every juice bar in those areas—and there was a fair handful of them—sold nickel and dime bags. The quality was fairly low, ranging from dusted or otherwise laced up to pure schwag, but the quantities were generous. Most of the spots sold a particular brand of weed, or at least sold weed in little plastic bags branded with little logos, so that seeing the empty bags strewn on the sidewalk, anyone, smoker or otherwise, much plugged in knew where they came from—other than the police, evidently. The IRS could have conducted a half decent audit by collecting the bags in the neighborhood, which is where most all the weed was smoked—you left, went to a bodega for papers or a blunt, and then lit up outside.

The other classic setup was the bodega full of dusty cans and without any customers younger than 14 or older than 35. During the day, customers would buy a soda or a bag of plantain chips and the weed bag would be dropped in the paper bag. At night, all business was conducted from a bulletproof glass window facing the street. I've actually gone to such spots late night in search of household super basics, like garbage bags, only to be told, less politely, that "We don't do that now."

There were many variations. For a while there was an ice cream truck in on the action, taping bags to the bottom of ice cream cups—once or twice I saw parents buy their kids an ice cream while treating themselves.

Spots did get busted here and again, but new ones opened up, hydra-like. Those too impatient for word of mouth would drop in on a new deli that had that look, drop a ten spot, and see what ended up in their paper bag. If the ten was snickered at or disdainfully ignored, you knew you were in a coke or smack spot.

Nearly all these spots sold extremely low quantities that the police were evidently willing to overlook, or at least not go out of their way to find. But in consequence, most users were sparking up right after leaving the store, on the street. But of course these spots and street users added up to a classic broken windows scenario. Turning a blind eye to the spots (easily identified, among other ways, by the tremendously poor care they took of their stores and storefronts) told their customers it was alright to smoke in the streets, seeing people smoke in the streets gave the sign that it was alright to get rowdy, fight, and otherwise seriously disrupt the neighborhood's life, and so on. In short, the spots were central to a pervasive feeling of lawlessness and incivility.

Like many people about my age (25) who were born here, I have certain nostalgia for all that lawlessness and chaos and the weirdness and adventures that intermittently popped up around it.

But who in their right mind wants to live above a drug spot, with people getting high all around—yelling, fighting, pissing in the streets, and worse—or open a business adjacent to one? Some storeowners and neighborhood residents objected, but the response was most always some variation of "This is how it is" or "What do you expect living here?"

Rudy changed all that. Few people remember how controversial the whole idea of proactive, Broken Windows policing was in 1993. Today the idea that small crimes are signposts that larger crimes are acceptable, and that those who commit small crimes are likely to be involved in larger ones, seems conventional. But at the time, the idea of focusing on small crimes in a city overwhelmed by big ones was dismissed by Al Sharpton, the New York Times, and much of the city as absurd, if not outright villainous.

We now know that the idea was spot on. When Rudy's first police chief, Bill Bratton, started conducting massive arrest sweeps of turnstile jumpers, it turned out that one of every seven people arrested had an outstanding felony warrant. In little time, crime began to plummet, and as went the fare jumpers and squeegeemen, so went the drug fronts. By 1996, there was nary a spot left in Manhattan (Note to newcomers: Manhattan here is Bloomberg's luxury product, going only as far north as about 110th Street. Uptown is, of course, understood as a distinct sixth borough. I'm talking about the Manhattan you see on taxi maps.).

In their place came delivery services, stepping into the vacuum that the spots had left in Manhattan, Park Slope, Brooklyn Heights, Williamsburg, and the rest of the places the young, better off, and sometimes beautiful choose to live. Even low level delivery services tend to have a minimum sale of about an eighth of an ounce and to sell a higher grade of weed than did the five and dime spots.

The delivery quantities were too small, though, to be worth robbing, especially since most services had fairly small clienteles, gained through word of mouth and recommendations from trusted clients. This, combined with the price barrier to entry goes a fair ways toward filtering out the younger and wilder crowd. Often one or two man operations, with the delivery guy doubling as the CEO, they are for the most part discreet affairs that help to separate the drug economy from the criminal and quality of life concerns that accompany open air drug use and sales. Outside of their operations, these new dealers tend to be disconnected from the criminal economy, as do their clients, outside of their smoking. Neither tend to interact with any other sort of criminal element either during the sale or otherwise.

In short, all drug sales are not the same—spots have far more impact on the surrounding community than do delivery services. As George Kelling, co-author of the seminal 1982 Atlantic article "Broken Windows" that introduced the theory of the same name puts it, however distasteful it might be, "Suburban drug use ... doesn't compare with the violence associated with the fight for drug markets that has literally wiped out neighborhoods. The drug trade threatens the stability of poor neighborhoods—very few middle class neighborhoods are threatened by drug dealing or drug use."

I sat down in the big playground at Washington Square Park with Nancy—names have been changed to protect the guilty—an attractive (but married) red haired, chain smoking Hispanic woman in her late 20s, while her six year old son played on the swings. A lifelong Brooklynite and waitress at a popular Village restaurant, devoted martial artist, and former casual heroin user, she's been selling weed from a friend's place in the Village for the last six months, pocketing an extra $1,200 or so a month on about six ounces. "I'm thinking of expanding to low poundage," she told me. "If I was contactable, I could easily expand, but I've got no beeper and only answer my house phone when I recognize the number. No one can find me except physically. It's very Victorian."

Nancy entered into the pot business almost by accident, when her personal source vanished "and my new guy only sold in larger quantities than I could smoke, so I moved some along down the food chain, thus the better to help friends, make money, and live a happy life." After unsuccessfully staring down an eavesdropping mother staring daggers at us, Nancy expressed concern that the other mother might call the city's child services bureau and we moved the conversation out of the park, leaving her son to play with Nancy's sister.

When I then asked what concerns, moral or otherwise, she had about the business, Nancy, who has never had an encounter with the police while selling, said, "I don't think it's a problem or a vice anymore than cigarettes or chocolate. I'm not into the legalization people. It's not a moral issue . . . I don't think I'd sell to high school kids—it feels like mixing the crimes. I am conscious of the risks just because of the college student clients, who think oh no, I got a bright future. It's this chick who's, you know, not in college.' The clients are not very paranoid about the police, and neither am I, but I'm sometimes paranoid about the clients."

To her, the job means always having a bit of her own weed to smoke and "the difference between working full time to pay the bills and having money to spend. It's putting my child through private elementary school."

When I asked Kelling about delivery services, he surprised me by arguing that limited police resources necessitate a degree of tolerance for discrete delivery services. "I have never been an advocate of legalization but at the same time the ideas that we are going to have a drug free society or stop all drug dealing is a joke. The top priority of the police has to be with drug markets that threaten the stability of cities, and to come down very hard on such groups. It seems to me that if one is able to make substantial gains the threshold might change. At one moment in time the pattern of a group or gang might be minimally appropriate but once you've changed the threshold, you demand even more discrete drug dealing."

Given police success, the hope is to eventually define deviancy back up, but in the short haul, so long as the sellers are policing themselves and staying off the streets, the cops have other priorities. At this moment in the cycle, at least, the practical result is the essential decriminalization of low level middle class drug use. Suddenly, the window is all but unbroken, the war on drugs distinct from the war on crime on the local level. It is the extension of the free and open use of coke in high end bars otherwise free of disruptive or criminal dealings, and that handle what trouble does emerge in house. This is a whole new spin on the old adage, often invoked when the cops or other sorts of trouble approach, to "master your high." In short, to the extent that drug use in a neighborhood is distinct from other criminal or publicly disruptive activities, it becomes less and less of a police and prosecutorial priority.

Daniel is another example of a dealer below the present threshold. A nondescript white guy in his mid-20s, Brooklyn born and raised, he has been selling for half a decade, first at college and then in Park Slope, and has yet to encounter the police. He nets about $2,500 a month, labeling it "a decent bartender's salary, and I prefer my line of work."

He got his customers through socializing, a free mix of business and pleasure—"I have a pretty small client base of about 15 people ... I'm a local to my neighborhood. You know people—I play softball with some people, I play poker with other people, friends refer friends. Almost all my people are in the Slope and Prospect Heights."

Like Nancy, he has no moral qualms, and little fear of the police. "I don't really get worried when I carry. Maybe in the beginning, but at this stage in the game I'm pretty comfortable with everything. I don't meet people in the street—either in their homes or in a car. I don't have that guilty conscience. I really don't believe I'm doing anything wrong or that anyone has reason to think I am."

Julia Vitullo-Martin, the crime columnist for GothamGazette.com, makes a distinction similar to those of both Kelling and Daniel. "It comes back to the federal drug war and our motives for doing this. Do we have this war against drugs because like turn-of-the-century Protestants we think drugs, like alcohol, nicotine, gambling, and coffee are immoral? Is that what's driving this or is it because we object to drugs because with drugs come crime and it's really crime we don't want. I really don't care what anyone does at home if that person is not robbing, raping, or murdering. The war on drugs is premised on the idea that the addiction itself is what we should go after . . . I hesitate because I don't want to see anybody selling drugs on my street. I don't object to any low level dealer selling in his apartment but any selling on the street I object to because I think it always triggers bad stuff. I'd like to see the NYPD turn a blind eye to this low level stuff whenever it becomes private but as soon as it becomes public I object." The difficulty is in codifying common sense, and applying limited resources in a way that is both reasonable and fair, which are two very different, and sometimes contrary goals.

The upshot is that those with their own place, a fair amount of discretionary cash, and minimal prudence, most all of whom live within delivery zones such as Hipster Williamsburg, slide while nickel and dime bag buyers, like those in Hispanic Williamsburg, get no such free ride. I asked Vitullo-Martin, is this an unfair use of policing and prosecutorial discretion or an intelligent application of limited law enforcement resources?

Referring back to the crack epidemic of the 1980s, she replied that, "In cycles of public policy there is such a thing as shock treatment in which you're on some kind of downward spiral and you're just going to keep going down unless something shocking and practically brutal happens. Then the question becomes, how do you get out of that shock treatment, which is where we are right now. The shock treatment did work, but now what? . . . Some kind of basic equity requires that if you're going to bust the crack user with a small amount you've also got to slam the privileged kid drug user."

Daniel doesn't want to hear this. Now that he no longer sells to high school students—"These kids looks so suspicious, its ridiculous, and they have no sense of how things are supposed to flow"—he's had not even close shaves with cops or hardcore crooks. "I haven't been involved in any real shady shit. My partner who does his thing in the city had a gun put to his head and had 10 Gs taken in any attempted transaction. I only go out of my network if I get a referral. I carry no weapon. I'm not dealing with those kinds of clients and those kind of areas. I'm in a family biz and a family neighborhood."

On the subject of families, Nancy's husband "knows, but doesn't want to. As far as he's concerned, it's no moral issue, but breaking the law is liable to get you into trouble, and we have enough trouble anyway. It seems kind of sleazy. I think that's the main issue—it seems kind of low brow."

Or, as Vitullo-Martin has it, however much safer the city is these days, "this is not Greenwich, Connecticut."

Murder Mystery

In the 1990s, New York and Boston achieved dramatic decreases in homicide. One of them is still improving. The other is getting worse again. Why?

JOHN BUNTIN

Two dozen young African-American men, wearing orange, blue and tan jumpsuits, are sitting in a semicircle in a room at the Suffolk County House of Corrections in Boston. They are there because they are about to be released from prison, and because they are former gang members at high risk of returning to crime.

Sitting across from them is a whole battery of ministers, social workers, police and local and federal prosecutors. Each of them has something to offer the inmates. The ministers tell them about a mentoring program. The social workers say they can help arrange child support payments, get them IDs or driver's licenses, and find transitional living arrangements.

Then the prosecutors take over. Theirs is a different message: We're watching you, and if you return to your former lifestyle, we'll be there to make sure you regret it. "There are two messages," says Kurt Francois, who works for a program called the Safe Neighborhood Reentry Initiative: "It's time to change, and if you don't, you will bear the consequences."

There, in a nutshell, is Boston-style policing. It is based on an unusual collaboration between law enforcement agencies, social service organizations and local churches. It has given the city one of the nation's most admired police departments. Lately, however, local residents have been asking a blunt question: Does it really work?

Five years ago, the question would have seemed absurd. Between 1990 and 1999, as the Boston approach took hold, the city's homicide rate fell by 80 percent. Of course, other cities experienced big crime drops too, including some cities that did little in the way of innovative policing. But only two—Boston and New York—saw murder rates fall by double-digit figures year after year.

Both Boston and New York attributed the decline to new—and very different—approaches to policing. In New York, the police emphasized "quality of life" law enforcement, focusing on minor property and nuisance offenses as a key to serious crimes, and developed a high-tech mapping and accountability system to track police performance. Boston did some of that, but its emphasis was elsewhere: on the partnerships between police and parole officers, community leaders, "streetworkers," academics and ministers.

Because both systems produced impressive numbers, both departments became models for reform-minded policing across the country. But in the eyes of many, Boston had a clear edge: Whereas New York's reduced crime rate came at the cost of growing tension between police and minority activists, Boston accomplished the same result while police relations with the African-American community actually improved. U.S. Attorney General Janet Reno called it "the Boston Miracle."

Former New York chief William Bratton: Stopping crime is up to the police, not citizens.

It was almost too good to be true. And then the numbers started changing. Boston's homicide rate began creeping up again. It took a while for most of the country to notice, but New York noticed very quickly. Last December, in his nationally televised farewell address, Mayor Rudolph Giuliani made a pointed comparison. "In the last statistics put out by the FBI," the mayor said, "there has been a 67 percent increase in murder in Boston. During that same period of time, there was a 12 percent decrease in the city of New York. I don't know, which policing theory would you want to follow?" And then Giuliani answered his own question: "The reality is that the model that was adopted for dealing with crime in New York City is the very, very best way to assure that you can keep a city safe."

Officials in Boston wrote these remarks off as personal pettiness. "A shallow boast," sniffed the *Boston Globe* editorial board. "I can't tell you why he did it," said Boston Mayor Thomas Menino. "Maybe it was frustration because he wishes he could continue the job."

Whatever the motive, Giuliani's figures were accurate. In the past two years, Boston's homicide rate has increased by more than 100 percent. At the same time, the rate in New York City has continued to fall. Clearly, something must be going on. The question is what.

Does Boston's rising homicide rate reflect problems with the Boston model itself, as Giuliani charges, or is Boston suffering from new demographic trends that other cities can soon expect to see? It's a question whose answer has major implications for police departments around the nation. Looking at Boston and New York's divergent police styles isn't a bad way to begin studying this question.

Boston and New York began with a common problem. In the late 1980s and early '90s, both experienced a frightening epidemic of murder. In 1990, New York's homicide total hit the staggering number of 2,245—quadruple the figure in the 1960s. That same year, homicides in Boston reached 152—a number that sounds modest at first but in fact was almost identical to New York's on a per capita basis.

And the problem seemed certain only to get worse. "If there are two thousand murders this year," warned New York newspaper columnist Pete Hamill, "get ready for four thousand." A *Time* magazine survey found that 59 percent of New Yorkers would move out of town if they could. To many, it seemed the police had simply relinquished control of the streets to criminals.

The New York strategy was born in the waning days of Mayor David Dinkins' administration, when Commissioner Raymond Kelly publicly embraced the "broken windows" philosophy of policing, which held that "disorder and crime are usually inextricably linked." Kelly began with an aggressive crackdown on the notorious "squeegee men" who harassed the city's commuters.

Commissioner Paul Evans attributes the 'Boston Miracle' to a web of partnerships between police and the community.

The new approach wasn't enough to save Dinkins; he was unseated by Giuliani in November 1993. But Giuliani embraced "broken windows" and steadily built upon it. He replaced Kelly with William Bratton, the former Boston police commissioner, and Bratton added the critical innovation called Compstat.

The brainchild of Bratton's chief crime strategist, the late Jack Maple, Compstat married the idea of crime mapping with a new focus on precinct commander performance. Every week, precinct commanders from one of New York's eight patrol boroughs would come before the department's top brass to discuss the crime trends in their precincts. Commanders who failed to show sufficient familiarity with those trends, or who failed to come up with strategies for solving the problems, were quickly reassigned or demoted—two-thirds of the city's precinct commanders in all. The crime rate plummeted.

Criminologists continued to debate the effect of "broken windows" policing and Compstat, but the homicide rate continued to go down. It was 1,177 in 1995, 770 in 1997, 664 in 1999. Compstat quickly became one of the most admired innovations in American policing in decades.

But in the midst of the good news, some New Yorkers began to see a dark side to the aggressive style of policing that the New York system encouraged. Former Mayor Dinkins complained to the press that Bratton and Giuliani "seem more interested in 'kicking ass' than increasing peace." In 1999, when members of the elite Street Crimes Unit opened fire on Amadou Diallo, an unarmed African immigrant, much of New York's African-American leadership came out to protest against the NYPD.

Boston wasn't having those sorts of problems. And its murder rate was falling just as dramatically, from 152 in 1990 to 31 in 1999. Police officials there were quick to assert that the reason was their law enforcement philosophy, based on social service and neighborhood relations, not on the cold statistics and hard-nosed street tactics of the cops in New York. "It wasn't just tough enforcement," says Commissioner Paul Evans. "It was going out to the community, trying to prevent crime, trying to identify alternatives for young people, after-school programs, jobs." In short, he argues, it was the result of an extraordinary web of partnerships between local, state and federal law enforcement agencies, nonprofit organizations and social service agencies, and the city's African-American clergy.

The Boston strategy emerged, unlike New York's, not so much from numbers but from one horrifying event. In May 1992, a group of youths burst in on a funeral being held for a slain gang member at Morning Star Baptist Church in Mattapan. In the presence of 300 panicked witnesses, the youths repeatedly stabbed one of the mourners, whose presence they viewed as an insult to the deceased.

Boston responded to the Morning Star attack (and a string of youth homicides that followed) with a flurry of programs and partnerships, such as the 10 Point Coalition, a group of African-American ministers who decided to reach out to kids on the street and put aside their distrust of the police. The homicide rate started going down, but rather slowly. Between 1992 and late 1996, it declined to 70 deaths per year—a big improvement from 1990, but more than twice as many as the city's historical average.

Then in mid-1996, Boston's police added something new to its network of partnerships—the idea of "focused deterrence." It was the inspiration of an unlikely coalition: front-line police officers from the Youth Violence Strike Force; a neighborhood probation office; the Department of Youth Services; the Streetworkers, a youth outreach program; the FBI and Drug Enforcement Administration; the U.S. Attorney and county D.A.; and researchers from Harvard University's Kennedy School of Government. "Focused deterrence" began not with social work but with the recognition that a relatively small number of hard-core gang members were responsible for most of the carnage in Boston.

At first, this was a discouraging finding: These hard-core offenders scarcely seemed the type who would walk away from drug-dealing and gun-running for a temporary summer job. But officers in Boston decided to turn these kids' very criminality against them. Because these kids were so criminally active, they could potentially be deterred or punished in a number of ways. As the officers put it, there were "a lot of levers to pull." Kids who were on probation could be supervised more closely; kids who had been referred to the Department of Youth Services could be taken into protective custody and even transferred to rural western Massachusetts; kids who were repeat offenders could be subjected to federal prosecution and sent out of state.

The Youth Violence Strike Force had achieved good results using a limited trial of focused deterrence on a gun-happy Cape Verdean gang on Boston's crime-plagued Wendover Street: not only had there been an immediate drop in gun-related incidents, but many kids gave up their weapons voluntarily. Now the same approach was employed citywide, with police, probation officers and prosecutors all warning gang members that gun violence would bring down on them the full attention not only of local authorities but of the U.S. Attorney's Office, the DEA and the ATF.

This marked a major change from the way Boston police had dealt with homicide "hot spots" in the past. "Years ago," said Commissioner Evans, "we'd have shootings in neighborhoods and we'd do saturation patrols and warrant sweeps and we were going after anybody and everybody. Now . . . we know what's going on; we know who's involved in the shooting; we call them all in; they're all on probation; we use the levers. We tell them, 'Fellows, the violence stops . . . We're not going to let you kill each other.'"

In August 1996, Boston police and federal agents arrested 21 members of the Intervale Posse, one of Boston's most notorious gangs. Then, in a series of forums with other gangs in the city, the Ceasefire group quickly got the word out: If the shooting doesn't stop, this will happen to you, too. One notorious gangster found with a single bullet in his possession was sent to federal prison for 10 years. Soon the city's homicide rate was in a gratifying freefall.

Boston isn't the only city where this sort of intervention worked. Minneapolis, a city not normally associated with violent crime, experienced an explosion of gang-related violence in the mid-1990s. In 1997, it responded with a Ceasefire program. The same thing happened as in Boston—homicides fell dramatically. The city ended the year with 58 murders, down from 86 the previous year. In Stockton, California, gang-related killings fell from 20 to four with Boston-style tactics. Indianapolis and the city of Winston-Salem, North Carolina, reported similar results.

New York, meanwhile, was finding equal success with its different emphasis. Maple, the NYPD's chief strategist, stressed four guiding principles: "accurate and timely intelligence," "rapid deployment," "effective tactics and strategies" and "relentless follow-up and assessment." Partnerships and reeducation meetings were not at the top of his list of effective methods.

Nearly all the media coverage of New York's declining crime rate stressed Compstat and the constant use of computer data. But within the department, many believed that the key element in keeping crime down was the fourth one on Maple's list: follow-up.

"We're great at initiatives, but it's the follow-up that's crucial," notes Elizabeth Glazer, chief of staff of the New York City Department of Investigation. "What Compstat does is ensure that there's always follow-up."

And that may offer a partial clue to the puzzling discrepancy between Boston and New York crime rates in the past couple of years. Researchers who have studied Ceasefire-style interventions say they are weak when it comes to follow-up. They tend to produce dramatic initial results—and then fall apart. "They're hard to sustain," admits Harvard criminologist David Kennedy. "They take an awful lot of assembly. They're basically simple, but it takes a lot of moving parts to put it together. Some are so dramatically effective that there comes a time when there's really not much work to do. People gather around a table and ask each other, 'Has there been any violence?' People say, 'No,' and if that goes on long enough, the partnership weakens. Violence picks up and people move on, and the script has been forgotten."

As Boston's homicide rate was plunging in the late '90s, the Ceasefire group met less frequently. Key players were promoted or moved on to other tasks. The grant that had supported work on the program at the Kennedy School was phased out. While the Youth Violence Strike Force continued to hold an occasional Ceasefire forum, the gang members no longer received the sustained "focused deterrence" they once did. They didn't seem to need it.

In retrospect, it seems they may have needed it after all. By the spring of 2000, Boston's violent crime remission was over. After years of decreases, the number of gun incidents in the gang strongholds of Roxbury and Dorchester started to creep up again. The increased gunplay soon translated into a rising homicide rate. In 2000, Boston had 40 homicides. In 2001, the number jumped to 66.

There are plenty of explanations for that change that avoid the issue of police tactics altogether, and stress demographics. Many believe, for example, that the return of homicide is connected to convicts completing their prison terms and returning to their old neighborhood, settling old feuds and trying to regain control of the drug trade.

"You want my quick and dirty analysis for the jump in the numbers?" probation officer Billy Stewart told the *Boston Herald*. "Simple: They're b-a-a-ck! . . . and they're back smarter. They're back embittered. And that seasoned bitterness makes them extremely dangerous."

Some statistics do buttress this argument. A decade ago, the average age of the city's homicide perpetrators was between 20 and 25. Last year, the department says, it was 31. The average age of inmates released from the Suffolk County House of Correction in January 2001 was 32—considerably older than the prison population a decade ago. "When you look at the Boston Miracle or the Boston model," says Commissioner Evans, "it was really geared toward youth violence. Now what we've seen in the last year is a much older individual."

On the other hand, the release of prisoners back into the community is hardly a new phenomenon. The prisoner population at

Table 1 Body Count

Number of homicides

	Boston	N.Y.
1985	87	1,384
1986	105	1,582
1987	76	1,672
1988	93	1,896
1989	99	1,905
1990	143	2,245
1991	113	2,154
1992	73	1,995
1993	98	1,946
1994	85	1,561
1995	96	1,177
1996	59	983
1997	43	770
1998	34	633
1999	31	664
2000	40	671
2001	66	642

Note: Data up through 1999 are from BJS, 2000–2001 are from PDs.

Source: Bureau of Justice Statistics, Boston Police Department, New York Police Department

the Suffolk County House of Corrections peaked in 1999, when approximately 3,700 offenders were released. It's possible that these ex-cons are behind Boston's recent murder increase, but commanders in the field discount the notion. "I can look at some neighborhoods—Bowdoin, Geneva—a couple of guys got out of jail, and we saw things happen," says Captain Robert Dunford, "but in terms of citywide, no."

In contrast to the "ex-con" theory, some analysts say the explanation for increased homicide is exactly the opposite: a tough new batch of young kids. Back in the mid-1990s, criminologists such as James Alan Fox and John DiIulio were warning of a whole generation of "super predators"—teenage criminals more ruthless and more dangerous than any cohort that preceded them. "Although we would never use the term 'super predator,'" says the Reverend Eugene Rivers, co-chair of the National 10 Point Leadership Foundation, "this kid that we [have seen] emerging fits that description of that uncertain term. . . . A younger cohort of more violent young people [have been] surfacing."

There are problems with this explanation as well. Boston's youth population was growing steadily throughout the '90s, even as crime began to fall. In 1991, the percentage of homicide victims aged 24 and under (victim numbers generally track perpetrator numbers pretty well) was 48 percent. Last year, it was 41 percent. The story is much the same nationwide. According to a March report by the Urban Institute, a nonpartisan think tank in Washington, D.C., the youth population increased by 13 percent between 1990 and 2000. During that same period, the juvenile crime rate fell by a third, to its lowest level in two decades.

Given the inconsistencies in both of the demographic theories, it begins to seem more plausible to return to the issue of police strategy. And this is just what Boston is doing. However, rather than reinvigorating its efforts at "focused deterrence," the Boston police department seems to be redoubling its efforts at building partnerships, expanding social services and involving the community in the fight against crime.

This past January, the Boston police department laid out what it calls "Boston Strategy Part 2." It calls for redoubling the department's emphasis on "prevention, enforcement and intervention," for pushing more authority to the district commander level, and for creating a new law enforcement community coordinating group to direct the department's actions. "You can see with all of our strategies, we're not moving away from partnerships," says Superintendent Paul Joyce. "You can't put the responsibility of dealing with crime issues on the police or on the probation officer; it's really too much."

That's the kind of sentiment that Giuliani and his police commissioners scoffed at. "I'm from the school of thought that the average citizen doesn't want to be engaged in patrolling their own neighborhood," says Bratton, the police commissioner who first introduced community policing to Boston in the early '90s, before becoming Giuliani's first commissioner in 1993. "When I come home at night, I don't want to be looking over my shoulder or coming upstairs to get my flashlight, my armband, and go out and patrol the neighborhood. That's what the police are for." Indeed, the idea that the police couldn't reduce crime on their own was one of the ideas that Giuliani and Bratton set out to demolish. When Bratton was appointed police commissioner, he promised Giuliani that under his watch the NYPD would reduce crime by 30 percent in three years—and it did.

The NYPD doesn't exactly repudiate the partnership idea. "It's critical," says Deputy Commissioner Michael Farrell, "that there be productive relationships with communities, particularly with cities that have as much diversity in their makeup as we do." On the other hand, Farrell acknowledges, the department's emphasis continues to be placed on those strategies it believes are working: Compstat and quality of life.

Boston police are hopeful that their new efforts will work, too. They say they're encouraged by early indications that the homicide increases are leveling off in 2002. They're optimistic that initiatives such as the prisoner reentry program and the ongoing efforts to provide more resources to district commanders will further depress crime rates.

Still, Superintendent Joyce doubts that Boston will soon return to the homicide levels of a couple of years ago. "Most likely, we've seen our best days," he admits. "Crime will move up. It's how you monitor that and how you deal with that as crime trends start to move up again."

Meanwhile, in the first quarter of 2002, the homicide rate in New York City was down another 29 percent.

Police Line—Do Cross

Crack's not back—but the drug trade has resurged in the Bronx. To rein it in this time around, the NYPD and the community must learn to work as partners.

BOB ROBERTS

Standing in the half-light from the altar candle, Josefina Edwards, wearing a trim cloth coat, talks about her neighborhood while the members of her Charismatic prayer group file into their empty church. This Friday, as they have for the last five years, she and around a hundred of her fellow Our Lady of Refuge parishioners will make a procession around the church, at 196th Street and Briggs Avenue. At each street corner they will pause to sing hymns and offer a public witness to Jesus Christ over a hand-held loudspeaker. It's a social occasion as well as an act of worship—or was until recently. "Now we go right home," says Edwards. "There are so many people on the street you can't even walk down the sidewalk."

In the last two years the streets of the northwest Bronx neighborhood of Fordham Bedford have grown increasingly chaotic. At night, knots of drunken young men, many in their teens, lean against SUVs, stereos blaring at indescribable volume. Empty beer bottles explode against the sidewalk, and angry voices echo off brick walls, making sleep impossible.

During the day, junkies crowd the porch of a tumble-down house on Decatur Avenue, prepping their arms, while at a nearby Police Athletic League "play street" at P.S. 54, run by Fordham Bedford Children Services, kids and staff are bombarded by eggs, batteries and ice cubes hurled by mocking rooftop gangs. According to residents, dealers and their crews are creating what John Garcia, director of Fordham Bedford Children's Services, calls "an atmosphere of lawlessness." Citizens haven't seen such blatant trafficking since the bad old days of the 1980s. Elsewhere on Decatur, surly teenage crews camp out on doorsteps, glaring at passersby. Over on Creston, a beauty parlor is raided for chairs so dealers can conduct street-level business in style. "We made it through the crack epidemic okay," says Garcia, who grew up on the street where Edwards lives. "But now it's starting to look bad again."

The police from the 52nd Precinct are trying to maintain order. The latest citywide anticrime initiative, called Operation Impact, has flooded high-crime spots with cops and made foot patrols a visible presence on the street. Still, there's a perception among neighborhood residents that the police aren't taking action. "I see cops on the corner writing out tickets for seatbelt violations while there's dealing across the street!" scoffs

Edwards' son Remy, who runs Fordham Bedford's Heiskell Learning Center.

The truth is that these days, it's getting harder for police to handle the drug problem—to make arrests and put dealers out of business. The 52nd Precinct, covering Fordham Bedford, Bedford Park, Norwood and University Heights, has always been known as a "busy" area for the police, particularly notorious for burglary and armed robbery. In some respects, things have gotten better. Consistent with a decline in reported incidents throughout New York City and the nation, for the last 10 years crime in the 52nd Precinct is down—at least according to Compstat, the data-tracking system the NYPD uses to identify trouble spots.

Since its inception under the Giuliani administration, Compstat has provided a statistical profile of crime in New York City. But it measures some crimes and not others. Burglaries, robberies, assaults, rapes and, of course, murders are counted. The spectrum of offenses related to the drug trade—possession, sale, loitering and so on—is not. Since the department uses Compstat to determine where to assign its personnel, this has a direct effect on how police do their jobs on the street.

These decisions are now more important than ever. The NYPD has been losing cops at a steady rate since the end of the Giuliani administration, down to 37,000 from a high of 40,000. The 52nd Precinct itself is at a 10-year low. At the same time, Operation Atlas, New York City's anti-terror effort, is putting new demands on the department's manpower. Not only are thousands of uniformed police from precincts like the 52nd subject to immediate deployment during an alert—such as the May 22 bomb scare on the Brooklyn Bridge—but more than a thousand detectives have been shifted away from the Organized Crime Control Bureau (which oversees the citywide Narcotics Division) and ordinary precinct assignments to the NYPD's intelligence activities.

As the police shift their manpower to high-profile terror targets, neighborhoods like Fordham Bedford are losing many of the men and women who have kept the drug business at bay. "It's creeping back," admits Community Affairs Officer Mark Morisi, a 12-year veteran of the 52nd Precinct. "We're doing more with less. People don't want to believe it, but it's true."

Running roughly from 183rd to 198th Streets, from Fordham University to Jerome Avenue, the neighborhood of Fordham Bedford represents about one-fifth of the total area of the sprawling 52nd Precinct—and more than 40 percent of its crime.

There's been no shortage of recent efforts to try to turn that around. In 1999, the NYPD's Central Bronx Initiative flooded the 52 and two adjoining precincts with special anti-narcotics teams. That same year, on the crooked two-block-long stretch of Valentine Avenue from Kingsbridge Road to 196th Street, the NYPD set up road blocks and floodlights as part of its Model Block Initiative, which sought to purge dealers from the area, and organize residents to keep them out.

Both efforts yielded mixed results. Despite a temporary respite for residents, dealers simply moved off the block for awhile, then moved back. Community organizing under police auspices collapsed beneath constant intimidation from drug crews.

A sense of mistrust between the police and community residents, not uncommon in high-crime neighborhoods, complicates police efforts. "Cops here don't know where they are!" complained Garcia at a September Neighborhood Security meeting, which until recently has been held the first Tuesday of each month in the auditorium of Our Lady of Refuge Church. Residents are torn between a desire for a strong and accessible police presence and the predictable apprehension bred by 20 years of roadblocks, "stop-and-frisk" and no-knock warrants.

What they want is a cop they know and who knows them. "Beat cops would be ideal," agrees Officer Morisi, "They know the good guys on the block from the bad guys." But community policing died with the Dinkins administration.

If the neighborhood has a public face when it comes to its relations with the NYPD, it's that of Monsignor John Jenik, pastor of Our Lady of Refuge. Jenik has always been defiant of the drug business—and has often taken his parish into the streets in an effort to put public pressure on the police department, which he sees as indifferent to the neighborhood's concerns. In the 1980s, he held vigils and even said mass at drug-dealing hot spots. CNN broadcast one (and all the tires of its news truck got slashed). On another occasion, Jenik brought Cardinal O'Connor on a tour of the neighborhood, forcing panicked cops to line every rooftop. Through actions like these, Jenik got the city and the police department's attention during the critical years of the crack epidemic.

He's also the chair of the board of Fordham Bedford Housing Corporation (FBHC), the parent organization of John Garcia's group. More than two decades after a small group of activists started rehabbing a handful of abandoned buildings scattered throughout the neighborhood, the corporation has emerged as one of the city's more successful community development non-profits. It has fixed more than 70 buildings, started a loan fund for neighborhood residents and built a nursing home from scratch. When it opened a shelter for women and children in 1983, it was Jenik who secured funding from the Diocese to keep it afloat.

Jenik is caustic, often withering, in his assessment of police efforts in his neighborhood, and he rarely misses an opportunity to point out what he sees as the NYPD's shortcomings. Contemptuous of efforts like the Model Block, he calls police brass who tout complex solutions "modern-day Gnostics" who believe themselves possessed of arcane knowledge inaccessible to ordinary citizens. When he hears talk of making "big busts" to flush drugs from the neighborhood he replies sharply, "I've been hearing that since [former Police Commissioner] Ben Ward!"

Jenik cites the case of Wilson Ramos as a particularly egregious example of police incompetence. In May 2000, Ramos was standing on Briggs Avenue drinking a soda when he was struck in the head by a stray bullet during a shootout between officers and a man who had robbed a pot dealer's house, then hijacked a bus. "We had been vigiling in front of that house for months and it came up at every one of our monthly meetings!" insists Jenik. The shooting remains a black eye for cops and a sore point in the community. The priest has battled with three of the last four commanders of the 52, and he doesn't give a fig how the cops view him: "I've never been liked at the precinct and I don't care."

Despite this, Jenik and Fordham Bedford Housing Corporation have forced the police to listen to him anyway. For the last nine years, the precinct leadership has been coming to monthly Neighborhood Security meetings in the auditorium of Our Lady of Refuge to hear community concerns and figure out ways to respond. Within the NYPD, it's extraordinary for top precinct officials to meet regularly with an independent community group. It's all the more remarkable because when they show up to Our Lady of Refuge, the cops often get no mercy from their hosts, particularly Jenik, and spend the nights sitting under fluorescent lights listening to a litany of their sins.

Last September, when the 52's new precinct commander, Joseph Hoch, attended his first—and last—Neighborhood Security Meeting, harassment charges dominated the evening. As he attempted to deliver a set speech about his philosophy of policing, Hoch was quickly interrupted by angry citizens. Remy Edwards, visibly shaking with rage, described how a simple traffic violation turned into a confrontation as six officers, hands resting lightly on their holsters, surrounded him on the sidewalk. Jenik related how a volunteer at the church's thrift shop was stopped while walking with her child, called a crackhead, and made to uncuff her jeans by two uniformed officers. (As with many accounts of police malfeasance from Jenik, this one turned out to be exaggerated: The woman in question, Bernice Gonzalez, says she was not with her child when she was stopped on 198th Street and actually was accused of purchasing marijuana from a local dealer.)

Jenik then proceeded to make one of his key points: Cops listen to confidential informants but not to residents. Though the inspector had just taken command, the four-year-old Ramos case was brought up. As Hoch became visibly angry, the auditorium buzzed with tension. At one point an oldtimer in the front row questioned Hoch's "Bronxhood." (He was born here.)

But by the end of the night, the dynamic in the room was very different. Far from haranguing the precinct brass, residents were clustering around Hoch to talk with their new precinct commander about problems on their blocks.

It's this kind of communication between police and the community that Garcia, soft-spoken and diplomatic, has sought to cultivate in his year and a half of chairing Neighborhood Security Meetings. Since Fordham Bedford Children Services works with kids from three public schools, as well as Our Lady of Refuge's own parochial school, Garcia has a natural interest in seeing that schoolyards, playgrounds and student assembly areas are protected. While he shares many of Jenik's criticisms, he's still managed to maintain a close day-to-day working relationship, serving almost as a community liaison with the precinct. He makes a point of saying, "I always find the police helpful and professional when I talk to them." Officer Morisi has known Garcia for eight years and considers him "honest but fair."

Garcia knows that police harassment happens. He's experienced it himself. "The only time you deal with a police officer here is in a negative situation," observes Garcia. "Either you're getting stopped for a traffic violation or because you fit the identity of someone they're looking for." Three years ago, in an eerie echo of Diallo, he was stopped by officers with guns drawn as he was reaching under his shirt for his cell phone. "I took it in stride and said to myself, 'Man, that's the neighborhood.'"

The Our Lady of Refuge Neighborhood Security Meetings are currently in abeyance. Though Father Jenik doesn't want the issue to be "Jenik versus the precinct," there's little doubt that his antipathy toward the 52 is one of the main reasons that Inspector Hoch canceled regular police participation in the meetings. Says Hoch, "I never understood why one group gets a meeting all to themselves."

"Mistrust of the police is ingrained in the culture of the neighborhood," Remy Edwards maintains. But the police also sense that people in the community don't have cops' backs. On December 1, during the filming of a video for rap star Noriega on Decatur Avenue, a suspect who had been picked up on a possession warrant broke away from police. As they chased him down the block, cops were pelted with garbage from neighboring rooftops while the crowd cheered. Five shots were fired (no one was hurt, and the shooter was arrested the next day). When it comes to drugs, few residents are willing to come forward with the concrete details needed to make an arrest.

For people who live here, there's a sense of impotence. Most know who is selling what on which corner, and relations can become almost casual. "Every morning I see the local heroin dealer," relates Wanda Solomon, who lives on Valentine Avenue. "I say 'Hi' and 'Bye'—what else am I supposed to do? Once I saw him sweeping the sidewalk."

If you can look out your window on a Sunday morning and watch dealers in action, it's hard to figure out why the police aren't doing anything. Deputy Inspector Hoch, who took over the 52 last August after a stint leading the nearby 48th Precinct, hears complaints along those lines all the time. He says they are misguided. "I understand peoples' frustrations, but if you just call up and tell me that drugs are being sold on the corner, what can I do?" he asks. "My officers can't just walk up to [suspected dealers] and search them. Then they're breaking the law. At most, they can ask them to move on if they're somewhere they're not supposed to be. So the average person says, 'The cops did nothing.'"

What Deputy Inspector Hoch can do, if his precinct receives enough complaints, is deploy a Street Narcotics Enforcement Unit, or SNEU—a team of six officers and a sergeant—and begin the painstaking task of gathering enough information to make a legitimate arrest, using rooftop observation posts and criminal informants. Says Hoch, "It takes a little longer but it leads to better results."

Hoch happens to be an expert in this arena. Forty years old and rising rapidly through the ranks of the department, he served in the Bronx Narcotics Bureau before becoming a precinct commander. (He is also one of just a handful of orthodox Jews to hold high command in the NYPD.) The 52, in Hoch's estimation, merits two SNEU units. But since the precinct has lost close to a hundred officers in the last 10 years, he can only field one.

And that's not even the most critical shortfall Hoch is dealing with. Detectives from the Bronx Command of the NYPD's Narcotics Division provide critical support to precinct anti-drug efforts. Officers at the 52 won't talk about numbers, but David Palladino, vice-president of the Detective Endowment Association—who incidentally grew up in Fordham Bedford, attended Our Lady of Refuge's parochial school, and served in the 52 as a uniformed officer and a detective before retiring in 1991—explains the extent of the damage. According to his sources, more than 20 percent of Bronx Narcotics Division personnel have been shifted to counterterrorism work. Narcotics detectives confirm that the 52 has had its support teams cut from eight to three.

A shortage of undercover officers is also making a fundamental difference in how the precinct attacks drug trafficking, Palladino claims. Each undercover "module" consists of six officers, a sergeant, and two undercover cops. According to Palladino, there are now only two covering the entire 52 and the adjoining 47th Precinct. "The Bureau is starving for undercover cops," says Palladino, who maintains that even in the best of times it's tough to find volunteers for such a dangerous assignment. "They're the backbone of narcotics enforcement. Without them, cops have to rely on observation, and the dealers do surveillance too so they get 'made'"—recognized and promoted in the business. "The whole process becomes hit-and-miss."

What Hoch does have at his disposal are 50 rookie cops, compliments of Operation Impact, the program cited by Mayor Bloomberg and Commissioner Kelly as instrumental in making New York City "the safest big city in America." In the 52nd Precinct last year, all of those officers were concentrated within two "impact sectors" (there are currently 22 across the city)—one in the perennial neighborhood hot spot on Decatur Avenue between 193rd and 198th streets, the other covering the area just to the north of that, including the streets around Our Lady of Refuge. Hoch can claim that Fordham Bedford now boasts the largest concentration of foot patrols in its history.

The 52nd Precinct has reported a double-digit drop in Compstat crime in areas where the Operation Impact police officers have been deployed, and they're a welcome presence to residents. But they are not deterring "workers": professional drug dealers, masters of sleight of hand, who manipulate tiny glassine envelopes while surreptitiously pocketing cash.

The Impact cops, after all, are rookies, only months removed from a college classroom. They're naturally experiencing culture shock, in a multiethnic neighborhood with little to unite it socially or geographically. Nigerians work in the Arab chicken shop next door to the Mexican *carnecería*. The Cambodian grocery store does steady business. Men in dark suits stand in a long line outside an Albanian restaurant on a Friday night. And at its base, Fordham Bedford is still multiethnic Hispanic: Dominican, Puerto Rican, Mexican and Central American. It's overcrowded—doubling and tripling up among the increasing number of immigrants is common—and demographically it's one of the youngest neighborhoods in the Bronx. Despite Fordham Bedford Housing Corporation's remarkable expansion, the neighborhood simply lacks much organized community presence—a tenant group, a block association—that makes itself felt at street level.

As much as possible, Hoch is trying to keep the Impact cops on the same blocks so they can learn the social terrain. But the final say on their deployment is had downtown. At the beginning of each year, assignments are made according to the current Compstat figures. Confident at the beginning of his tour that he would retain his allotment of 50 cops, Hoch now has to cope with a cut to 30, and they will be moved across the Concourse to patrol St. James Park, deserting Decatur Avenue and the heart of the Fordham Bedford drug trade. The best Hoch can do now is deploy an eight-man "post-impact team" to pick up the slack.

Jenik and Garcia maintain that it's the threat of violence that inhibits community organizing against crime. Cops acknowledge that the concern is legitimate, but Inspector Raymond Rooney, who commanded the 52nd Precinct for three years before leaving to become head of the Operations for the Bronx Detective Bureau, also offers a critique of FBHC's institutional culture: "Fordham Bedford, the only thing missing is getting their hands dirty."

Unlike his predecessors and Inspector Hoch, Rooney enjoys a warm personal relationship with Jenik, whom he calls a "catalyst for the neighborhood," and he credits FBHC and "Chairman Monsignor" as the prime reason that the Fordham Bedford neighborhood has survived relatively intact. But, he asks, "When was the last time the good people in the neighborhood said, 'Let's have a block party, let's clean up this vacant lot. . .outside of a Fordham Bedford function, something that they just got a grant to do?'"

It's unlikely that the NYPD will have the resources anytime soon to stage another intensive anti-drug effort like the Valentine Avenue Model Block. Operation Impact may be an imaginative use of the department's limited resources, but—and both the cops and Father Jenik believe this—it's certainly no substitute for an adequately funded Narcotics Division.

Fordham Bedford can't do all the work the NYPD needs to help keep the community organized for order and safety, and the police still have a long way to go to connect with grassroots organizations that could also get involved. Mention of police strategies, Operation Impact, or the new commander draws blank looks at the Decatur Avenue offices of Part of the Solution (P.O.T.S.), a community service group founded in the early 1980s. P.O.T.S. enjoys a good reputation with its neighbors thanks to its legal clinic, run by the Urban Justice Center, and its soup kitchen on Webster Avenue, which feeds as many as 450 people a day. The group works with residents on Decatur Avenue below 198th Street—the heart of the area's drug zone. But even though police regularly visit the soup kitchen looking for open warrants, the organization reports no formal contact with the precinct. John Hoffman, project coordinator of P.O.T.S, has noticed, and welcomes, the increased presence of young officers on patrol in his neighborhood. He's also grateful for the free turkeys cops drop off around the holidays.

But Hoffman gets more excited about the prospects for street-level organizing. When asked about the possibility of starting a block association, his eyes light up: "Wow, that's a really interesting idea!" He's not talking about citizen patrols armed with walkie-talkies. P.O.T.S. founder Ned Kelly is thinking about getting his neighbors together to pick up dog shit.

Our Lady of Refuge and Fordham Bedford Housing Corporation have gotten the NYPD's attention, and their efforts have resulted in Fordham Bedford receiving as much attention from the precinct as it does. But they've also monopolized the dialogue. There's little chance, after years of conflict, that anything cops do now will satisfy Jenik. If there is a possibility for real cooperation between the precinct and citizens, it will probably consist of a handful of neighbors wearing plastic gloves collecting trash while a cop quietly stands on the corner, rather than the latest "cutting-edge" anti-drug initiative or "new model" of community organizing.

Few expect miracles. It's more than likely that 10 years from now, heroin will still be for sale on Decatur Avenue. But the police have no choice but to look on the bright side. "Ten years ago people were worried about getting killed," notes Morisi. "So there's been progress."

BOB ROBERTS is a Bronx-based freelance writer.

The Black Family—40 Years of Lies

Rejecting the Moynihan report caused untold, needless misery.

Kay S. Hymowitz

Read through the megazillion words on class, income mobility, and poverty in the recent *New York Times* series "Class Matters" and you still won't grasp two of the most basic truths on the subject: 1) entrenched, multigenerational poverty is largely black; and 2) it is intricately intertwined with the collapse of the nuclear family in the inner city.

By now, these facts shouldn't be hard to grasp. Almost 70 percent of black children are born to single mothers. Those mothers are far more likely than married mothers to be poor, even after a post-welfare-reform decline in child poverty. They are also more likely to pass that poverty on to their children. Sophisticates often try to dodge the implications of this bleak reality by shrugging that single motherhood is an inescapable fact of modern life, affecting everyone from the bobo Murphy Browns to the ghetto "baby mamas." Not so; it is a largely low-income—and disproportionately black—phenomenon. The vast majority of higher-income women wait to have their children until they are married. The truth is that we are now a two-family nation, separate and unequal—one thriving and intact, and the other struggling, broken, and far too often African-American.

So why does the *Times,* like so many who rail against inequality, fall silent on the relation between poverty and single-parent families? To answer that question—and to continue the confrontation with facts that Americans still prefer not to mention in polite company—you have to go back exactly 40 years. That was when a resounding cry of outrage echoed throughout Washington and the civil rights movement in reaction to Daniel Patrick Moynihan's Department of Labor report warning that the ghetto family was in disarray. Entitled "The Negro Family: The Case for National Action," the prophetic report prompted civil rights leaders, academics, politicians, and pundits to make a momentous—and, as time has shown, tragically wrong—decision about how to frame the national discussion about poverty.

To go back to the political and social moment before the battle broke out over the Moynihan report is to return to a time before the country's discussion of black poverty had hardened into fixed orthodoxies—before phrases like "blaming the victim," "self-esteem," "out-of-wedlock childbearing" (the term at the time was "illegitimacy"), and even "teen pregnancy" had become current. While solving the black poverty problem seemed an immense political challenge, as a conceptual matter it didn't seem like rocket science. Most analysts assumed that once the nation removed discriminatory legal barriers and expanded employment opportunities, blacks would advance, just as poor immigrants had.

Conditions for testing that proposition looked good. Between the 1954 *Brown* decision and the Civil Rights Act of 1964, legal racism had been dismantled. And the economy was humming along; in the first five years of the sixties, the economy generated 7 million jobs.

Yet those most familiar with what was called "the Negro problem" were getting nervous. About half of all blacks had moved into the middle class by the mid-sixties, but now progress seemed to be stalling. The rise in black income relative to that of whites, steady throughout the fifties, was sputtering to a halt. More blacks were out of work in 1964 than in 1954. Most alarming, after rioting in Harlem and Paterson, New Jersey, in 1964, the problems of the northern ghettos suddenly seemed more intractable than those of the George Wallace South.

Moynihan, then assistant secretary of labor and one of a new class of government social scientists, was among the worriers, as he puzzled over his charts. One in particular caught his eye. Instead of rates of black male unemployment and welfare enrollment running parallel as they always had, in 1962 they started to diverge in a way that would come to be called "Moynihan's scissors." In the past, policymakers had assumed that if the male heads of household had jobs, women and children would be provided for. This no longer seemed true. Even while more black men—though still "catastrophically" low numbers—were getting jobs, more black women were joining the welfare rolls. Moynihan and his aides decided that a serious analysis was in order.

Convinced that "the Negro revolution . . . , a movement for equality as well as for liberty," was now at risk, Moynihan wanted to make several arguments in his report. The first was empirical and would quickly become indisputable: single-parent families were on the rise in the ghetto. But other points were more speculative and sparked a partisan dispute that has lasted to this day. Moynihan argued that the rise in single-mother families was not due to a lack of jobs but rather to a destructive vein in ghetto culture that could be traced back to slavery and Jim Crow discrimination. Though black sociologist E. Franklin Frazier had already introduced the idea in the 1930s, Moynihan's argument defied conventional social-science wisdom. As he wrote later, "The work began in the most orthodox setting, the U.S. Department of Labor, to establish at some level of statistical conciseness what 'everyone knew': that economic conditions determine social conditions. Whereupon, it turned out that what everyone knew was evidently not so."

But Moynihan went much further than merely overthrowing familiar explanations about the cause of poverty. He also described, through pages of disquieting charts and graphs, the emergence of a "tangle of pathology," including delinquency, joblessness, school failure, crime, and fatherlessness that characterized ghetto—or what would come to be called underclass—behavior. Moynihan may have borrowed the term "pathology" from Kenneth Clark's *The Dark Ghetto,* also published that year. But as both a descendant and a scholar of what he called "the wild Irish slums"—he had written a chapter on the poor Irish in the classic *Beyond the Melting Pot*—the assistant secretary of labor was no stranger to ghetto self-destruction. He knew the dangers it posed to "the basic socializing unit" of the family. And he suspected that the risks were magnified in the case of blacks, since their "matriarchal" family had the effect of abandoning men, leaving them adrift and "alienated."

More than most social scientists, Moynihan, steeped in history and anthropology, understood what families do. They "shape their children's character and ability," he wrote. "By and large, adult conduct in society is learned as a child." What children learned in the "disorganized home[s]" of the ghetto, as he described through his forest of graphs, was that adults do not finish school, get jobs, or, in the case of men, take care of their children or obey the law. Marriage, on the other hand, provides a "stable home" for children to learn common virtues. Implicit in Moynihan's analysis was that marriage orients men and women toward the future, asking them not just to commit to each other but to plan, to earn, to save, and to devote themselves to advancing their children's prospects. Single mothers in the ghetto, on the other hand, tended to drift into pregnancy, often more than once and by more than one man, and to float through the chaos around them. Such mothers are unlikely to "shape their children's character and ability" in ways that lead to upward mobility. Separate and unequal families, in other words, meant that blacks would have their liberty, but that they would be strangers to equality. Hence Moynihan's conclusion: "a national effort towards the problems of Negro Americans must be directed towards the question of family structure."

Astonishingly, even for that surprising time, the Johnson administration agreed. Prompted by Moynihan's still-unpublished study, Johnson delivered a speech at the Howard University commencement that called for "the next and more profound stage of the battle for civil rights." The president began his speech with the era's conventional civil rights language, condemning inequality and calling for more funding of medical care, training, and education for Negroes. But he also broke into new territory, analyzing the family problem with what strikes the contemporary ear as shocking candor. He announced: "Negro poverty is not white poverty." He described "the breakdown of the Negro family structure," which he said was "the consequence of ancient brutality, past injustice and present prejudice." "When the family collapses, it is the children that are usually damaged," Johnson continued. "When it happens on a massive scale, the community itself is crippled."

Johnson was to call this his "greatest civil rights speech," but he was just about the only one to see it that way. By that summer, the Moynihan report that was its inspiration was under attack from all sides. Civil servants in the "permanent government" at Health, Education, and Welfare (HEW) and at the Children's Bureau muttered about the report's "subtle racism." Academics picked apart its statistics. Black leaders like Congress of Racial Equality (CORE) director Floyd McKissick scolded that, rather than the family, "[i]t's the damn system that needs changing."

In part, the hostility was an accident of timing. Just days after the report was leaked to *Newsweek* in early August, L.A.'s Watts ghetto exploded. The televised images of the South Central Los Angeles rioters burning down their own neighborhood collided in the public mind with the contents of the report. Some concluded that the "tangle of pathology" was the administration's explanation for urban riots, a view quite at odds with civil rights leaders' determination to portray the violence as an outpouring of black despair over white injustice. Moreover, given the fresh wounds of segregation, the persistent brutality against blacks, and the ugly tenaciousness of racism, the fear of white backsliding and the sense of injured pride that one can hear in so many of Moynihan's critics are entirely understandable.

Less forgivable was the refusal to grapple seriously—either at the time or in the months, years, even decades to come—with the basic cultural insight contained in the report: that ghetto families were at risk of raising generations of children unable to seize the opportunity that the civil rights movement had opened up for them. Instead, critics changed the subject, accusing Moynihan—wrongfully, as any honest reading of "The Negro Family" proves—of ignoring joblessness and discrimination. Family instability is a "peripheral issue," warned Whitney Young, executive director of the National Urban League. "The problem is discrimination." The protest generating the most buzz came from William Ryan, a CORE activist, in "Savage Discovery: The Moynihan Report," published in *The Nation* and later reprinted in the NAACP's official publication. Ryan, though a psychologist, did not hear Moynihan's point that as the family goes, so go the children. He heard code for the archaic charge of black licentiousness. He described the report as a "highly sophomoric treatment of illegitimacy" and insisted that whites' broader access to abortion, contraception, and adoption hid the fact that they were no less "promiscuous" than blacks. Most memorably, he accused Moynihan of "blaming the victim," a phrase that would become the title of his 1971 book and the fear-inducing censor of future plain speaking about the ghetto's decay.

That Ryan's phrase turned out to have more cultural staying power than anything in the Moynihan report is a tragic emblem of the course of the subsequent discussion about the ghetto family. For white liberals and the black establishment, poverty became a zero-sum game: either you believed, as they did, that there was a defect in the system, or you believed that there was a defect in the individual. It was as if critiquing the family meant that you supported inferior schools, even that you were a racist. Though "The Negro Family" had been a masterpiece of complex analysis that implied that individuals were intricately entwined in a variety of systems—familial, cultural, and economic—it gave birth to a hardened, either/or politics from which the country has barely recovered.

By autumn, when a White House conference on civil rights took place, the Moynihan report, initially planned as its centerpiece, had disappeared. Johnson himself, having just introduced large numbers of ground troops into Vietnam, went mum on the subject, steering clear of the word "family" in the next State of the Union message. This was a moment when the nation had the resources, the leadership (the president had been overwhelmingly elected, and he had the largest majorities in the House and Senate since the New Deal), and the will "to make a total … commitment to the cause of Negro equality," Moynihan lamented in a 1967 postmortem of his report in *Commentary*. Instead, he declared, the nation had disastrously decided to punt on Johnson's "next and more profound stage in the battle for civil rights." "The issue of the Negro family was dead."

W ell, not exactly. Over the next 15 years, the black family question actually became a growth industry inside academe, the foundations, and the government. But it wasn't the same family that had worried Moynihan and that in the real world continued to self-destruct at unprecedented rates. Scholars invented a fantasy family—strong and healthy, a poor man's Brady Bunch—whose function was not to reflect truth but to soothe injured black self-esteem and to bolster the emerging feminist critique of male privilege, bourgeois individualism, and the nuclear family. The literature of this period was so evasive, so implausible, so far removed from what was really unfolding in the ghetto, that if you didn't

know better, you might conclude that people actually *wanted* to keep the black family separate and unequal.

Consider one of the first books out of the gate, *Black Families in White America,* by Andrew Billingsley, published in 1968 and still referred to as "seminal." "Unlike Moynihan and others, we do not view the Negro as a causal nexus in a 'tangle of pathologies' which feeds on itself," he declared. "[The Negro family] is, in our view, an absorbing, adaptive, and amazingly resilient mechanism for the socialization of its children and the civilization of its society." Pay no attention to the 25 percent of poor ghetto families, Billingsley urged. Think instead about the 75 percent of black middle-class families—though Moynihan had made a special point of exempting them from his report.

Other black pride–inspired scholars looked at female-headed families and declared them authentically African and therefore a *good* thing. In a related vein, Carol Stack published *All Our Kin,* a 1974 HEW-funded study of families in a midwestern ghetto with many multigenerational female households. In an implicit criticism of American individualism, Stack depicted "The Flats," as she dubbed her setting, as a vibrant and cooperative urban village, where mutual aid—including from sons, brothers, and uncles, who provided financial support and strong role models for children—created "a tenacious, active, lifelong network."

In fact, some scholars continued, maybe the nuclear family was really just a toxic white hang-up, anyway. No one asked what nuclear families did, or how they prepared children for a modern economy. The important point was simply that they were not black. "One must question the validity of the white middle-class lifestyle from its very foundation because it has already proven itself to be decadent and unworthy of emulation," wrote Joyce Ladner (who later became the first female president of Howard University) in her 1972 book *Tomorrow's Tomorrow*. Robert Hill of the Urban League, who published *The Strengths of Black Families* that same year, claimed to have uncovered science that proved Ladner's point: "Research studies have revealed that many one-parent families are more intact or cohesive than many two-parent families: data on child abuse, battered wives and runaway children indicate higher rates among two-parent families in suburban areas than one-parent families in inner city communities." That science, needless to say, was as reliable as a deadbeat dad.

Feminists, similarly fixated on overturning the "oppressive ideal of the nuclear family," also welcomed this dubious scholarship. Convinced that marriage was the main arena of male privilege, feminists projected onto the struggling single mother an image of the "strong black woman" who had always had to work and who was "superior in terms of [her] ability to function healthily in the world," as Toni Morrison put it. The lucky black single mother could also enjoy more equal relationships with men than her miserably married white sisters.

If black pride made it hard to grapple with the increasingly separate and unequal family, feminism made it impossible. Fretting about single-parent families was now not only racist but also sexist, an effort to deny women their independence, their sexuality, or both. As for the poverty of single mothers, that was simply more proof of patriarchal oppression. In 1978, University of Wisconsin researcher Diana Pearce introduced the useful term "feminization of poverty." But for her and her many allies, the problem was not the crumbling of the nuclear family; it was the lack of government support for single women and the failure of business to pay women their due.

With the benefit of embarrassed hindsight, academics today sometimes try to wave away these notions as the justifiably angry, but ultimately harmless, speculations of political and academic activists. "The depth and influence of the radicalism of the late 1960s and early 1970s are often exaggerated," historian Stephanie Coontz writes in her new book, *Marriage, a History: From Obedience to Intimacy, or How Love Conquered Marriage.* This is pure revisionism. The radical delegitimation of the family was so pervasive that even people at the center of power joined in. It made no difference that so many of these cheerleaders for single mothers had themselves spent their lives in traditional families and probably would rather have cut off an arm than seen their own unmarried daughters pushing strollers.

Take, for instance, Supreme Court Justice William Brennan, who wrote a concurring assent in the 1977 *Moore* v. *City of East Cleveland* decision. The case concerned a woman and her grandson evicted from a housing project following a city ordinance that defined "family" as parents—or parent—and their own children. Brennan did not simply agree that the court should rule in favor of the grandmother—a perfectly reasonable position. He also assured the court that "the extended family has many strengths not shared by the nuclear family." Relying on Robert Hill's "science," he declared that delinquency, addiction, crime, "neurotic disabilities," and mental illness were more prevalent in societies where "autonomous nuclear families prevail," a conclusion that would have bewildered the writers of the Constitution that Brennan was supposedly interpreting.

In its bumbling way and with far-reaching political consequences, the executive branch also offered warm greetings to the single-parent family. Alert to growing apprehension about the state of the American family during his 1976 presidential campaign, Jimmy Carter had promised a conference on the subject. Clearly less concerned with conditions in the ghetto than with satisfying feminist advocates, the administration named a black single (divorced) mother to lead the event, occasioning an outcry from conservatives. By 1980, when it finally convened after numerous postponements, the White House Conference on the Family had morphed into the White House Conference on Families, to signal that all family forms were equal.

Instead of the political victory for moderate Democrats that Carter had expected, the conference galvanized religious conservatives.

Later, conservative heavyweight Paul Weyrich observed that the Carter conference marked the moment when religious activists moved in force into Republican politics. Doubtless they were also more energized by their own issues of feminism and gay rights than by what was happening in the ghetto. But their new rallying cry of "family values" nonetheless became a political dividing line, with unhappy fallout for liberals for years to come.

Meanwhile, the partisans of single motherhood got a perfect chance to test their theories, since the urban ghettos were fast turning into nuclear-family-free zones. Indeed, by 1980, 15 years after "The Negro Family," the out-of-wedlock birthrate among blacks had more than doubled, to 56 percent. In the ghetto, that number was considerably higher, as high as 66 percent in New York City. Many experts comforted themselves by pointing out that white mothers were also beginning to forgo marriage, but the truth was that only 9 percent of white births occurred out of wedlock.

And how was the black single-parent family doing? It would be fair to say that it had not been exhibiting the strengths of kinship networks. According to numbers crunched by Moynihan and economist Paul Offner, of the black children born between 1967 and 1969, 72 percent received Aid to Families with Dependent Children before the age of 18. School dropout rates, delinquency, and crime, among the other dysfunctions that Moynihan had warned about, were rising in the cities. In short, the 15 years since the report was written had witnessed both the birth of millions of fatherless babies and the entrenchment of an underclass.

Liberal advocates had two main ways of dodging the subject of family collapse while still addressing its increasingly alarming fallout. The first, largely the creation of Marian Wright Edelman, who in 1973 founded the Children's Defense Fund, was to talk about children not as the offspring of individual mothers and fathers responsible for rearing them, but as an oppressed class living in generic, nebulous, and never-to-be-analyzed "families." Framing the problem of ghetto children in this way, CDF was able to mount a powerful case for a host of services, from prenatal care to day care to housing subsidies, in the name of children's developmental needs, which did not seem to include either a stable domestic life or, for that matter, fathers. Advocates like Edelman might not have viewed the collapsing ghetto family as a welcome occurrence, but they treated it as a kind of natural event, like drought, beyond human control and judgment. As recently as a year ago, marking the 40th anniversary of the Civil Rights Act, CDF announced on its website: "In 2004 it is morally and economically indefensible that a black preschool child is three times as likely to depend solely on a mother's earnings." This may strike many as a pretty good argument for addressing the prevalence of black single-mother families, but in CDF-speak it is a case for federal natural-disaster relief.

The Children's Defense Fund was only the best-known child-advocacy group to impose a gag rule on the role of fatherless families in the plight of its putative constituents. The Carnegie Corporation followed suit. In 1977, it published a highly influential report by Kenneth Keniston called *All Our Children: The American Family Under Pressure.* It makes an obligatory nod toward the family's role in raising children, before calling for a cut in unemployment, a federal job guarantee, national health insurance, affirmative action, and a host of other children's programs. In a review in *Commentary,* Nathan Glazer noted ruefully that *All Our Children* was part of a "recent spate of books and articles on the subject of the family [that] have had little if anything to say about the black family in particular and the matter seems to have been permanently shelved." For that silence, children's advocates deserve much of the credit—or blame.

The second way not to talk about what was happening to the ghetto family was to talk instead about teen pregnancy. In 1976 the Alan Guttmacher Institute, Planned Parenthood's research arm, published "Eleven Million Teenagers: What Can Be Done About the Epidemic of Adolescent Pregnancy in the United States?" It was a report that launched a thousand programs. In response to its alarms, HEW chief Joseph Califano helped push through the 1978 Adolescent Health Services and Pregnancy Prevention and Care Act, which funded groups providing services to pregnant adolescents and teen moms. Nonprofits, including the Center for Population Options (now called Advocates for Youth), climbed on the bandwagon. The Ford and Robert Wood Johnson Foundations showered dollars on organizations that ran school-based health clinics, the Charles Stewart Mott Foundation set up the Too Early Childbearing Network, the Annie E. Casey Foundation sponsored "A Community Strategy for Reaching Sexually Active Adolescents," and the Carnegie, Ford, and William T. Grant Foundations all started demonstration programs.

There was just one small problem: *there was no epidemic of teen pregnancy.* There was an *out-of-wedlock* teen-pregnancy epidemic. Teenagers had gotten pregnant at even higher rates in the past. The numbers had reached their zenith in the 1950s, and the "Eleven Million Teenagers" cited in the Guttmacher report actually represented a decline in the rate of pregnant teens. Back in the day, however, when they found out they were pregnant, girls had either gotten married or given their babies up for adoption. Not this generation. They were used to seeing children growing up without fathers, and they felt no shame about arriving at the maternity ward with no rings on their fingers, even at 15.

In the middle-class mind, however, no sane girl would want to have a baby at 15—not that experts mouthing rhetoric about the oppressive patriarchal family would admit that there was anything wrong with that. That middle-class outlook, combined with post-Moynihan mendacity about the growing disconnect between ghetto childbearing and marriage, led the policy elites to frame what was really the broad cultural problem of separate and unequal families as a simple lack-of-reproductive-services problem. Ergo, girls "at risk" must need sex education and contraceptive services.

But the truth was that underclass girls often *wanted* to have babies; they didn't see it as a problem that they were young and unmarried. They did not follow the middle-class life script that read: protracted adolescence, college, first job, marriage—and only then children. They did not share the belief that children needed mature, educated mothers who would make their youngsters' development the center of their lives. Access to birth control couldn't change any of that.

At any rate, failing to define the problem accurately, advocates were in no position to find the solution. Teen pregnancy not only failed to go down, despite all the public attention, the tens of millions of dollars, and the birth control pills that were thrown its way. *It went up*—peaking in 1990 at 117 pregnancies per 1,000 teenage girls, up from 105 per 1,000 in 1978, when the Guttmacher report was published. About 80 percent of those young girls who became mothers were single, and the vast majority would be poor.

Throughout the 1980s, the inner city—and the black family—continued to unravel. Child poverty stayed close to 20 percent, hitting a high of 22.7 percent in 1993. Welfare dependency continued to rise, soaring from 2 million families in 1970 to 5 million by 1995. By 1990, 65 percent of all black children were being born to unmarried women.

In ghetto communities like Central Harlem, the number was closer to 80 percent. By this point, no one doubted that most of these children were destined to grow up poor and to pass down the legacy of single parenting to their own children.

The only good news was that the bad news was so unrelentingly bad that the usual bromides and evasions could no longer hold. Something had to shake up what amounted to an ideological paralysis, and that something came from conservatives. Three thinkers in particular—Charles Murray, Lawrence Mead, and Thomas Sowell—though they did not always write directly about the black family, effectively changed the conversation about it. First, they did not flinch from blunt language in describing the wreckage of the inner city, unafraid of the accusations of racism and victim blaming that came their way. Second, they pointed at the welfare policies of the 1960s, not racism or a lack of jobs or the legacy of slavery, as the cause of inner-city dysfunction, and in so doing they made the welfare mother the public symbol of the ghetto's ills. (Murray in particular argued that welfare money provided a disincentive for marriage, and, while his theory may have overstated the role of economics, it's worth noting that he was probably the first to grasp that the country was turning into a nation of separate and unequal families.) And third, they believed that the poor would have to change their behavior instead of waiting for Washington to end poverty, as liberals seemed to be saying.

By the early 1980s the media also had woken up to the ruins of the ghetto family and brought about the return of the repressed Moynihan report. Declaring Moynihan "prophetic," Ken Auletta, in his 1982 *The Underclass,* proclaimed that "one cannot talk about poverty in America, or about the underclass, without talking about the weakening family structure of the poor." Both the *Baltimore Sun* and the *New York Times* ran series on the black family in 1983, followed by a 1985 *Newsweek* article called "Moynihan: I Told You So" and a 1986 CBS documentary, *The Vanishing Black Family,* produced by Bill Moyers, a onetime aide to Lyndon Johnson, who had supported the Moynihan report. The most symbolic moment came when Moynihan himself gave Harvard's prestigious Godkin lectures in 1985 in commemoration of the 20th anniversary of "The Negro Family."

For the most part, liberals were having none of it. They piled on Murray's 1984 *Losing Ground,* ignored Mead and Sowell, and excoriated the word "underclass," which they painted as a recycled and pseudoscientific version of the "tangle of pathology." But there were two important exceptions to the long list of deniers. The first was William Julius Wilson. In his 1987 *The Truly Disadvantaged,* Wilson chastised liberals for being "confused and defensive" and failing to engage "the social pathologies of the ghetto." "The average poor black child today appears to be in the midst of a poverty spell which will last for almost two decades," he warned. Liberals have "to propose thoughtful explanations for the rise in inner city dislocations." Ironically, though, Wilson's own "mismatch theory" for family breakdown—which hypothesized that the movement of low-skill jobs out of the cities had sharply reduced the number of marriageable black men—had the effect of extending liberal defensiveness about the damaged ghetto family. After all, poor single mothers were only adapting to economic conditions. How could they do otherwise?

The research of another social scientist, Sara McLanahan, was not so easily rationalized, however. A divorced mother herself, McLanahan found Auletta's depiction of her single-parent counterparts in the inner city disturbing, especially because, like other sociologists of the time, she had been taught that the Moynihan report was the work of a racist—or, at least, a seriously deluded man. But when she surveyed the science available on the subject, she realized that the research was so sparse that no one knew for sure how the children of single mothers were faring. Over the next decade, McLanahan analyzed whatever numbers she could find, and discovered—lo and behold—that children in single-parent homes were not doing as well as children from two-parent homes on a wide variety of measures, from income to school performance to teen pregnancy.

Throughout the late eighties and early nineties, McLanahan presented her emerging findings, over protests from feminists and the Children's Defense Fund. Finally, in 1994 she published, with Gary Sandefur, *Growing Up with a Single Parent.* McLanahan's research shocked social scientists into re-examining the problem they had presumed was not a problem. It was a turning point. One by one, the top family researchers gradually came around, concluding that McLanahan—and perhaps even Moynihan—was right.

In fact, by the early 1990s, when the ghetto was at its nadir, public opinion had clearly turned. No one was more attuned to this shift than triangulator Bill Clinton, who made the family a centerpiece of his domestic policy.

In his 1994 State of the Union Address, he announced: "We cannot renew our country when, within a decade, more than half of our children will be born into families where there is no marriage." And in 1996, despite howls of indignation, including from members of his own administration (and mystifyingly, from Moynihan himself), he signed a welfare-reform bill that he had twice vetoed—and that included among its goals increasing the number of children living with their two married parents.

So, have we reached the end of the Moynihan report saga? That would be vastly overstating matters. Remember: *70 percent of black children are still born to unmarried mother*s. After all that ghetto dwellers have been through, why are so many people still unwilling to call this the calamity it is? Both NOW and the National Association of Social Workers continue to see marriage as a potential source of female oppression. The Children's Defense Fund still won't touch the subject. Hip-hop culture glamorizes ghetto life: " 'cause nowadays it's like a badge of honor/to be a baby mama" go the words to the current hit "Baby Mama," which young ghetto mothers view as their anthem. Seriously complicating the issue is the push for gay marriage, which dismissed the formula "children growing up with their own married parents" as a form of discrimination. And then there is the American penchant for to-each-his-own libertarianism. In opinion polls, a substantial majority of young people say that having a child outside of marriage is okay—though, judging from their behavior, they seem to mean that it's okay, not for them, but for other people. Middle- and upper-middle-class Americans act as if they know that marriage provides a structure that protects children's development. If only they were willing to admit it to their fellow citizens.

All told, the nation is at a cultural inflection point that portends change. Though they always caution that "marriage is not a panacea," social scientists almost uniformly accept the research that confirms the benefits for children growing up with their own married parents. Welfare reform and tougher child-support regulations have reinforced the message of personal responsibility for one's children. The Bush administration unabashedly uses the word "marriage" in its welfare policies. There are even raw numbers to support the case for optimism: teen pregnancy, which finally started to decline in the mid-nineties in response to a crisper, teen-pregnancy-is-a-bad-idea cultural message, is now at its lowest rate ever.

And finally, in the ghetto itself there is a growing feeling that mother-only families don't work. That's why people are lining up to see an aging comedian as he voices some not-very-funny opinions about their own parenting. That's why

so many young men are vowing to be the fathers they never had. That's why there has been an uptick, albeit small, in the number of black children living with their married parents.

If change really is in the air, it's taken 40 years to get here—40 years of inner-city misery for the country to reach a point at which it fully signed on to the lesson of Moynihan's report. Yes, better late than never; but you could forgive lost generations of ghetto men, women, and children if they found it cold comfort.

Big Cities Balk Over Illegal Migrants

JUDY KEEN

Despite a federal effort to enlist help from local police to catch illegal immigrants, some of the USA's biggest cities are declining to enforce immigration laws.

Police chiefs, mayors and city councils are ordering local cops not to get involved as federal agents crack down on people in the country illegally.

"Vulnerable people have always needed to see the police as being there to protect and serve, and that can't happen when the first words out of a cop's mouth are, 'I need to see your papers,'" Minneapolis Mayor R.T. Rybak said.

U.S. Immigration and Customs Enforcement has been visiting police conventions in an effort to have departments join a voluntary program. ICE has trained officers in seven jurisdictions to identify, process and detain illegal immigrants, said Robert Hines, who heads the program started in 1996. Participants include state police in Alabama and Florida, the Arizona corrections department and sheriff's departments in San Bernardino, Los Angeles and Riverside counties in California and Mecklenburg County, N.C.

Several jurisdictions have refused to help. Chicago police and city workers are prohibited from asking immigrants about their legal status. Rybak asked ICE agents last month to stop identifying themselves as "police." New York City's public hospitals promised last month that they would keep secret an immigrant's legal status.

In the broadest signal of opposition, a national group representing 57 big-city police chiefs warned this month that local enforcement of federal immigration laws would "undermine trust and cooperation" among immigrants.

The Major Cities Chiefs Association said in recommendations to President Bush and Congress that police have long worked with federal agents to pursue illegal immigrants suspected of crimes. The group said helping identify those suspected only of being in the USA illegally could backfire.

"We have spent many years . . . getting special communities to talk to us, to report crime, to be witnesses," said Houston Police Chief Harold Hurtt. "If we stop individuals (to ask about immigration status), we would lose all of that."

The association—including police chiefs from Los Angeles, Detroit, Seattle and Miami—said most departments can't afford to spend time quizzing immigrants. Members fear that "the call for local enforcement of immigration laws signals the beginning of a trend towards local police agencies being asked to enter other areas of federal regulation or enforcement."

Hines said, "The cooperation we get for the most part is outstanding." Illegal immigration "is all of our problem, because these people are here in violation of law."

Segregation in New York under a Different Name

Exposes the separate and unequal status of bilingual education

J. P. AVLON

Segregation exists in New York City public schools under the name of bilingual education. What began as a well-intentioned program to aid non-English speaking newcomers has become an entitlement program that promotes separate classrooms and unequal results along ethnic lines. Having gained control over the school system, Mayor Bloomberg is suddenly in a position to mend—and possibly end—bilingual education as we know it.

Last February the Board of Education unanimously passed the first and only fundamental reform of bilingual education in the program's 26-year history. Among other things, the plan sought to give parents a new high-speed English immersion alternative to traditional bilingual education programs and began aiming in earnest to have students transition out of bilingual education within three years. This hard-won reform was trumpeted as one of the key victories of Harold Levy's tenure as Chancellor. He had succeeded where virtually every leader of the Board of Education had failed since the early 1980s. But after the fanfare died down, bilingual education reform died the lonely death of most reforms entrusted to the Board of Education—it was never implemented due to a fight over funding.

The losers were the roughly 160,000 "English Language Learners" in the public schools, who speak more than 145 different languages and dialects.

These students are split between traditional bilingual education classes, which are taught primarily in the student's native language, and English as a Second Language classes, which are taught primarily in English. In bilingual classes, 90% of the students are Spanish speaking. ESL courses tend to be offered to a linguistically and ethnically diverse array of students.

The stated purpose of bilingual education is to make students fluent in their native language before teaching them English—a process that bilingual advocates say can take between five and seven years. Bilingual education is also not limited to immigrant students—increasingly, native-born Americans who speak Spanish at home are placed in these programs. Many bilingual

education teachers are not bilingual—they can't speak English themselves, and 27% are not certified.

Of the students who entered bilingual programs in the first grade, 22% were still enrolled in the program nine years later. 54% of students who began bilingual programs in the sixth grade in 1991 had not transitioned into a mainstream classroom by 1999; and 85% of the students who entered bilingual programs in ninth grade in 1991 did not transition out within four years—the traditional end of high school.

Bilingual education programs also have a negative effect on school scores. In 1999 only 6.9% of the middle school English Language Learner population who took the Citywide Reading Test could read at grade level. In the Citywide Math Test, which is given in the student's native language, only 15% of middle school English Language Learners scored at or above grade level, and more than 55% of them fell below the 25th percentile.

And despite the fact that bilingual education classes were created in part to address high drop out rates, students who stay in bilingual programs beyond six years are nearly 50% more likely to drop out than students in the general population.

At every level, students in ESL classes performed better on tests and transferred into mainstream English-speaking classes more rapidly than their counterparts in bilingual. The 18-month study conducted by Mayor Giuliani's Bilingual Education Reform Task Force (on which I served as a staff member) confirmed the findings of the 1994 report commissioned by Chancellor Raymond Cortines, which stated that "Students in ESL-only programs consistently tested out of entitlement faster than students served in bilingual programs, even when baseline differences in English were taken into effect."

Mr. Bloomberg seems to understand the limitations of bilingual education, and the need for such programs to rededicate themselves to English acquisition. Beginning with next year's sophomore high school class, all students will be required to pass five Regents examinations, including English, in order to receive a diploma at the end of high school. Effective reforms must be enacted to avoid a debacle in 2005, which is incidentally an election year here in New York City.

California has successfully taken the bold step of ending bilingual education entitlement programs, replacing them with intensive English immersion programs. Critics and activists claimed that this an abandonment of non-English speaking students and predicted a steep decline in test scores. In fact, the opposite has happened—in the four years since the elimination of California's bilingual programs, test scores have gone up consistently in every category. California's success has spurred other states, including Arizona and Colorado, to dump bilingual education. Will New York be next?

Mr. Bloomberg could presumably implement the Board of Education's already approved reforms single-handedly now that he has control of the school system. But if he wants to end bilingual education in New York, he'll have to take his fight to court.

The Mayor will find that his ability to institute bilingual education reforms is severely restricted by the Aspira Consent Decree, which began bilingual programs for Spanish-speaking students here in the city of New York in 1974. The decree was originally intended to allow Spanish speaking students "full and equal educational opportunity" in the learning process while ensuring that students "avoid isolation and segregation from their peers."

But Aspira now undermines its original purpose. A 1975 Board of Education pamphlet defining Board policy at the outset of bilingual education stated that parents "are to be notified of their child's entitlement and of the nature of the program to be provided. Every effort is to be made to inform parents of the educational value of the [bilingual] program and no attempt is to be made to invite parents to withdraw from the program." This institutional bias in favor of bilingual education has had disastrous effects for several generations. It has created segregated educational programs rather than ending them. The results are separate and unequal.

The sad fact is that bilingual education has become an entitlement program. It is defended by those with an interest the status quo, despite the fact that the system is clearly broken beyond repair. Professional bilingual advocates are strikingly out of touch with the constituents they claim to represent. A Zogby poll measured support for "all public school instruction to be conducted in English, and for students not fluent in English to be placed in an intensive one-year English immersion program." Seventy-nine percent of all New York voters surveyed supported this proposal—72% of Democrats, 87% of Republicans, and 62% of Latino voters. This is consistent with a poll conducted by the non-partisan, non-profit group Public Agenda which showed that two out of three immigrant parents believe that "it is more important for public schools to teach English as quickly as possible, even if they fall behind in other subjects."

In 1644, a Jesuit missionary named Father Isaac Jogues visited our city and counted 18 different languages being spoken. Our city has always been a melting pot, and immigration has always been the secret to our success. For the most diverse city in the history of the world to thrive, it must have a common currency of communication. We have an important opportunity to emphasize in theory as well as practice that bilingual education exists to help the children of all immigrants as quickly as possible so that they might participate fully in the pursuit of the American dream.

MR. AVLON'S column appears weekly. His e-mail address is jpavlon@nysun.com.

An Inner-City Renaissance

The nation's ghettos are making surprising strides. Will the gains last?

AARON BERNSTEIN

Take a stroll around Harlem these days, and you'll find plenty of the broken windows and rundown buildings that typify America's ghettos. But you'll also see a neighborhood blooming with signs of economic vitality. New restaurants have opened on the main drag, 125th Street, not far from a huge Pathmark supermarket, one of the first chains to offer an alternative to overpriced bodegas when it moved in four years ago. There's a Starbucks—and nearby, Harlem U.S.A., a swank complex that opened in 2001 with a nine-screen Magic Johnson Theatres, plus Disney and Old Navy stores and other retail outlets. Despite the aftermath of September 11 and a sluggish economy, condos are still going up and brownstones are being renovated as the middle classes—mostly minorities but also whites—snap up houses that are cheap by Manhattan standards.

It's not just Harlem, either. Across the U.S., an astonishing economic trend got under way in the 1990s. After half a century of relentless decline, many of America's blighted inner cities have begun to improve. On a wide range of economic measures, ghettos and their surrounding neighborhoods actually outpaced the U.S. as a whole, according to a new study of the 100 largest inner cities by Boston's Initiative for a Competitive Inner City, a group founded in 1994 by Harvard University management professor Michael E. Porter.

Consider this: Median inner-city household incomes grew by 20% between 1990 and 2000, to a surprising $35,000 a year, the ICIC found, while the national median gained only 14%, to about $57,000. Inner-city poverty fell faster than poverty did in the U.S. as a whole, housing units and homeownership grew more quickly, and even the share of the population with high school degrees increased more. Employment growth didn't outdo the national average, with jobs climbing 1% a year between 1995 and 2001, vs. 2% nationally. Still, the fact that inner cities, which are 82% minority, created any jobs at all after decades of steady shrinkage is something of a miracle.

Scent of Opportunity

Nor are the gains just the byproduct of the superheated economy of the late 1990s. Rather, they represent a fundamental shift in the economics of the inner city as falling crime rates and crowded suburbs lure the middle-class back to America's downtowns. After decades of flight out of inner cities, companies as diverse as Bank of America, Merrill Lynch, and Home Depot have begun to see them as juicy investment opportunities. National chains are opening stores, auto dealerships, and banks to tap into the unfulfilled demand of inner cities.

Wall Street, too, is jumping in, making loans and putting up equity for local entrepreneurs. "Smart businesspeople gravitate toward good opportunities, and it has become clear that inner cities are just that," says David W. Tralka, chairman of Merrill Lynch & Co.'s Business Financial Services group. In 2002, his group, which caters to small business, began formally targeting inner cities. It now offers financing and commercial mortgages for hundreds of inner-city entrepreneurs around the country.

Is it possible that America at last has started to solve one of its most intractable social ills? True, the progress so far is minuscule compared with the problems created by decades of capital flight, abysmal schools, and drug abuse. And some inner cities, like Detroit's, have made little sustained progress. Ghettos also have been hit by the joblessness of this latest recovery. The national poverty rate has jumped by nearly a percentage point since 2000, to 12.1% last year, so it almost certainly did likewise in inner cities, which the ICIC defined as census tracts with poverty rates of 20% or more.

But as the economy recovers, a confluence of long-term trends is likely to continue to lift inner cities for years. The falling crime rate across the country has been a key factor, easing fears that you take your life in your hands by setting foot in an inner city. At the same time, larger demographic shifts—aging boomers turned empty nesters, more gays and nontraditional households without children, homeowners fed up with long commutes—have propelled Americans back into cities. When they arrive, slums suddenly look like choice real estate at bargain prices.

Beyond Philanthropy

Political and civic leaders helped lay the groundwork, too. After floundering for decades following the exodus of factories to the suburbs in the 1950s, many cities finally found new economic missions in the 1990s, such as tourism, entertainment, finance,

Inner Cities and Their Residents . . .

The Boston-based Initiative for a Competitive Inner City has completed the first-ever analysis of the 100-largest inner cities in the U.S. and finds the once-dismal picture brightening

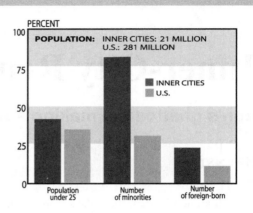

PERCENT

POPULATION: INNER CITIES: 21 MILLION
U.S.: 281 MILLION

■ INNER CITIES
▨ U.S.

Population under 25 · Number of minorities · Number of foreign-born

. . . Did Better Than the Nation As a Whole in the 90s . . .

Change between 1990 and 2000 Census data

	INNER CITIES	U.S
Population	24%	13%
Household income	20%	14%
Housing unit growth	20%	13%
High school graduates*	55 to 61%	75 to 80%
College graduates*	10 to 13%	20 to 24%
Home ownership	29 to 32%	64 to 66%
Poverty rate	34 to 30%	13 to 12%

*Of those 25 and over

. . . Although There's Still a Long Way to Go

2000 Census data

	INNER CITIES	U.S
High school graduates*	61%	80%
College graduates*	13%	24%
Poverty rate	31%	11.3%
Unemployment rate	12.8%	5.8%
Home ownership rate	32%	66%
Average household income	$34,755	$56,600
Aggregate household income	$250 billion	$6 trillion

Data: Initiative for a Competitive Inner City

and services. This has helped boost the geographic desirability of inner-city areas. New state and federal policies brought private capital back, too, by putting teeth into anti-redlining laws and by switching housing subsidies from public projects to tax breaks for builders. As a result, neighborhoods like the predominantly African-American Leimert Park in South Central Los Angeles are becoming thriving enclaves.

The outcome has been a burst of corporate and entrepreneurial activity that already has done more to transform inner cities than have decades of philanthropy and government programs. "What we couldn't get people to do on a social basis they're willing to do on an economic basis," says Albert B. Ratner, co-chairman of Forest City Enterprises Inc., a $5 billion real estate investment company that has invested in dozens of inner-city projects across the country.

Emerging Markets

The new view of ghettos began to take hold in the mid-1990s, when people such as Bill Clinton and Jesse Jackson started likening them to emerging markets overseas. Porter set up the ICIC in 1994 as an advocacy group to promote inner cities as

overlooked investment opportunities. Since then, it has worked with a range of companies, including BofA, Merrill Lynch, Boston Consulting Group, and PricewaterhouseCoopers to analyze just how much spending power exists in inner cities.

The new study, due to be released on Oct. 16, uses detailed census tract data to paint the first comprehensive economic and demographic portrait of the 21 million people who live in the 100 largest inner cities. The goal, says Porter, "is to get market forces to bring inner cities up to surrounding levels."

Taken together, the data show an extraordinary renaissance under way in places long ago written off as lost causes. America's ghettos first began to form early in the last century, as blacks left Southern farms for factory jobs in Northern cities. By World War II, most major cities had areas that were up to 80% black, according to the 1993 book *American Apartheid,* co-authored by University of Pennsylvania sociology professor Douglas S. Massey and Nancy A. Denton, a sociology professor at the State University of New York at Albany. Ghettos grew faster after World War II as most blacks and Hispanics who could follow manufacturing jobs to the suburbs did so, leaving behind the poorest and most un-employable. Immigrants poured in, too, although most tended to leave as they assimilated.

Figure 1   Benchmarks of Progress.

In this context, the solid gains the ICIC found in the 1990s represent an extraordinary shift in fortunes. One of the biggest changes has come in housing. As cities have become desirable places to live again, the number of inner-city housing units jumped by 20% in the 1990s, vs. 13% average for the U.S. as a whole.

A number of companies were quick to see the change. BofA, for example, has developed a thriving inner-city business since it first began to see ghettos as a growth market six years ago. In 1999 it pulled together a new unit called Community Development Banking, which focuses primarily on affordable housing for urban, mostly inner-city, markets, says CDB President Douglas B. Woodruff. His group's 300 associates are on track this year to make $1.5 billion in housing loans in 38 cities, from Baltimore to St. Louis. They will do an additional $550 million in equity investments, mostly real estate.

Shelled Out

Pension funds and other large investors are putting in cash, too. The Los Angeles County Employee Retirement Assn. has sunk $210 million into urban real estate since 2000, including $87 million in August for a bankrupt, 2,496-room apartment complex in Brooklyn, N.Y. The plan is to do things like fix the broken elevators, hire security guards, and kick out nonpaying tenants. "We believe there are opportunities that weren't there before or that we weren't aware of," says board member Bruce Perelman.

One question is whether the ICIC's findings represent not so much progress by the poor as their displacement by middle-class newcomers. In other words, inner-city incomes could be rising simply because affluent new home buyers jack up the average. But experts think gentrification explains only a small part of what's going on. "It's certainly a local phenomenon, but if you aggregate 100 inner cities, gentrification is a small trend," says ICIC research director Alvaro Lima, who spearheaded the study.

In Chicago, for instance, a $65 million redevelopment of the notorious Cabrini-Green housing project has replaced three slummy high-rises with mixed-income units. The area has a new library, new schools, and a new retail center featuring a major grocery store, Starbucks, and Blockbuster (BBI)—all staffed by scores of local residents. "The goal is not gentrification, it's to integrate the classes," says Phyllis L. Martin, the head of a local committee that's trying to lure more than $50 million in private capital to help the city replace 3,245 public housing units in another blighted area, Bronzeville.

"We're just beginning to undo all the damage."

Despite the brightening picture, the decay of most inner cities is so advanced that half a dozen years of progress makes only a dent. The degree of poverty—a measure of how many poor people there are in a census tract—fell 11% in 60 large cities in the 1990s, according to an analysis by U Penn's Massey that parallels ICIC's approach. While that's a significant decline, it only begins to offset the doubling of poverty concentrations in prior decades, he found. "The gains are the first positive news since at least the 1950s, but we're just beginning to undo all the damage," says Massey.

Badge of Shame

What's more, too many inner cities remain untouched. More than a third of the ICIC's 100 cities lost jobs between 1995 and 2001. Detroit's ghetto has seen little new development and shed one-fifth of its jobs over this period. Residents did gain from the booming auto industry, which hired many locals and pushed up their median incomes at a 3.2% annual pace in the 1990s—the third highest increase of the ICIC 100. But with auto makers now shedding jobs again, those gains are likely to be short-lived. More broadly, improving inner cities won't come close to wiping out poverty in the U.S. While the inner-city poverty rate of 31% is nearly three times the national average, the 6.5

million poor people who live there represent less than a fifth of the country's 34.6 million poor.

Still, America's ghettos have been a national badge of shame for so long that any real gain is news. The change in perspective also seems to be an enduring one, not just a 1990s blip. For evidence, consider Potamkin Auto Group, which owns 70 dealerships around the country and will break ground in Harlem in late October on a $50 million development that will include Cadillac, Chevrolet, Hummer, and Saturn dealers.

Potamkin also has a project in another inner city and is mulling a national expansion. "We see opportunities there," says Robert Potamkin, president of the family-owned company. This view, that inner cities can be a good place to do business, may be the most hopeful news about the country's urban blight in decades.

Aaron Bernstein in Washington, with **Christopher Palmeri** in Los Angeles and **Roger O. Crockett** in Chicago

The Rise, Fall, and Rise Again of Public Housing

HARRY SIEGEL

They tend to be isolated outposts: segregated from surrounding neighborhoods, folded in upon themselves, cut off from the street grid, avoided by outsiders other than troublemakers. More than their utilitarian ugliness, it is the red brick that gives them away, and how they huddle in masses so that each removes any doubt as to its neighbor's identity. Though of the city, public housing and its residents are too often set apart from its sprawling, mixed-use life.

Urban public housing came into vogue in the 1930s, when cities began to move beyond ward politics, and planners and politicians attempted to conceive of the city as a single unit or system, and to plan (and zone) housing accordingly. Modern in its ideas, architectural and otherwise, it was envisioned as a superior way of housing the poor replacing the run-down tenements. It continued in the years during and following World War II as a way to compensate for the sudden cessation in housing growth as resources were diverted into the war effort, and to prepare for the surge in population as veterans returned home and began having families.

The projects were also initially a source of valuable political capital, both in spreading construction monies and in housing the connected. Today they come to attention only during social or fiscal crises. And yet the great urban conflicts of the past half century—group versus individual rights, big government versus limited government, and of course race—have often been fought in these laboratories of social policy.

Professor Lawrence J. Vale, the head of MIT's department of urban studies and planning, has taken on the question of what makes a successful project in his new book. He focuses his attention on three Boston housing projects—Franklin Field, Commonwealth, and West Broadway—to see why the first is now considered a failure, the second a success, and the third a bit of each. What emerges is a picture of what successful public housing might look like, and the obstacles to creating such a system.

Public housing, Mr. Vale shows, is racked by competing interests. Should it strive to maintain a stable core of residents with a sense of ownership or to move residents up and on as quickly as possible? Should it be aimed at the poorest, who are often the most troubled, or at those with less need but more responsibility? Should residents of a neighborhood have priority for public housing? Mr. Vale uses the three projects to demonstrate the consequences of the varying implementation of public housing.

The three Boston projects he takes on are in different neighborhoods and serve very different tenant-constituents. All three opened in the decade following World War II and were intended primarily for white veterans and their families. In the time-honored manner of city politics, local and city leaders used the projects to spread wealth during construction and then to reward the politically loyal and connected with subsidized housing—evidenced by the large number of chauffeurs in residence.

Most of the city's projects originally excluded blacks through income and family structure criteria. This was brought to a halt by court orders in the 1960s, but because "standards" had served as a way to Jim Crow blacks, standards were done away with almost entirely. The Boston Housing Authority (BHA) began actively catering to the poorest and least capable applicants, including the mentally ill. This had deleterious effects on the quality of life of working-class residents, a situation exacerbated by the collapse of the BHA, which went into receivership in 1975, and the consequent erosion of the housing stock. Revitalization attempts began in the 1980s and have met with mixed success.

Though overwhelmingly white, West Broadway was always disliked in its predominantly Irish Lower End neighborhood. Initially more prosperous than the neighboring blocks, the project declined when the original residents took advantage of the low mortgage rates and loan opportunities of the postwar era, and left the neighborhood. Their replacements were poorer, and the project began a long downward spiral. (This pattern was typical of all the city's projects.) The few minority residents who dared to move in were met with pervasive hostility and violence that the police and the BHA for the most part ignored.

By contrast, Franklin Field—originally intended for Jewish war veterans and their families—was built in a Jewish neighborhood that was rapidly becoming black. As the Jewish residents migrated to the suburbs, a disastrous program encouraged black home ownership by providing mortgages for housing-in-disrepair with minimal down payments.

This was a con game dressed as social policy; more than 70% of these mortgages failed, and the neighborhood fell into severe disrepair.

The project and the neighborhood became a destination of last resort—a poorly maintained, crime-ridden slum with no shopping or bus service, adjacent to a dangerous and unkept park. The situation was compounded by the 1980s crack explosion. Residents felt completely powerless to get standard maintenance done, let alone effect change, and they lacked any political voice.

In the 1980s, the BHA set out to revive both projects. The money that went into West Broadway brought a renewed interest in its integration, although the violent hostility of neighborhood whites continued to be such that few minorities wanted to live there. A more radical renovation in the 1990s was largely successful in creating a greater sense of ownership on the part of the tenants, who except for a committed few had previously seen themselves as wards of the BHA. This improved the perceived quality of life, but has yet to translate into actual upward mobility.

Franklin Field has not fared nearly as well. An attempted renovation of the project in the late 1980s indulged in as much graft and shoddy workmanship as possible before declaring bankruptcy. It actually worsened conditions in the eyes of most residents.

The BHA had determined that Franklin Field was one of the places where a renovation was the least likely to succeed, and it received funding only as a black beard to allow predominantly white West Broadway to be renovated. Once the money was allocated, no one in power seemed to care how it was spent, and residents who felt powerless over their lives and environments to begin with felt even further removed from self-sufficiency and responsibility.

Commonwealth is the success story of the three, and the reasons why are obvious. It was set on prime property in an affluent neighborhood, and its neighbors invested in its success. Though the property rapidly deteriorated from 1975–80, tenants remained well-organized and active. The BHA allowed them to sign a deal with a private management company, which has worked exceedingly well.

But the success of Commonwealth has been more about improving the residents' frame of mind and quality of life than in creating or even encouraging an upwardly mobile lower class. The illegitimacy rate in the Boston housing projects is well over 50%, and employment is under 25%. The question is what should be done with the projects, particularly those deemed by reasonable factors to be beyond repair.

For this reason and others, public housing remains a difficult problem. Part of the answer lies in involvement by the residents themselves. The people who live in public housing must be held to a standard of conduct and be able to demand a standard of service.

If citizens and housing authorities are willing to do this, it may not be too late to return to the original vision of a lower class on the rise.

MR. SIEGEL is a writer living in New York City.

UNIT 8

Cities and Disasters: Viewing 9/11 and Katrina, and Preparing for What's Next

Unit Selections

Key Points to Consider

- How did the events of September 11, 2001, affect the way Southerners see New York? How will 21st Century cities resemble 20th Century cities? How will they be different? What steps can cities take to plan for terrorist attacks or natural disasters?

- Will new terror attacks affect how Americans feel about cities? How willing how they continue to be to live in cities?

- How did Hurricane Katrina affect how Americans see New Orleans? How will the rebuilt city resemble the old one?

- What went wrong with planning and response to Katrina? What can be improved in responding to future catastrophes?

Student Web Site
www.mhcls.com/online

Internet References
Further information regarding these Web sites may be found in this book's preface or online.

Department of State International Information Programs
  http://usinfo.state.gov
Metropolis Archives: Sustainability
  http://www.metropolismag.com/html/content_1001/sup/index_b.html
SocioSite: University of Amsterdam
  http://www.pscw.uva.nl/sociosite/TOPICS
United Nations
  http://www.unsystem.org
Urban Education Web
  http://iume.tc.columbia.edu

American cities faced new challenges in 2004, even as they continued to build on major reforms introduced by a wave of innovative new mayors in the 1990s. The terrorist attack on September 11, 2001, exposed the vulnerabilities of cities, those dense concentrations of diverse people and modern sensibilities that create targets for massive destruction.

Tough, brave, working class New York cops and firemen stand tall amidst the rubble and massive destruction that the terrorists inflicted, overshadowing and displacing, at least temporarily, those difficult New Yorkers whom the rest of the country loves to hate, in John Shelton Reed's "A View From the South." The internal contradictions within New York, America's most urban city, stood out during the heroic responses to September 11.

Yet there is still room, even after September 11 and the economic downturn that the attacks exacerbated, for cautious optimism: the revitalizing effects of some of the new immigrants, the growing awareness of economic opportunities in our cities, the successes of new wave mayors who've stopped looking to the federal government for their salvation, the surprising economic vitality of sophisticated new businesses, and the remarkable drops in crime and welfare in some of our most hard-hit, industrial cities.

City downtowns can offer the liveliness and energy lacking in even the most grandiose of suburban malls. A variety of older cities from Kansas City and Chicago to Cincinnati and Philadelphia are bringing people back into the downtown after working hours. Their aim is to make their downtowns into residential and recreational areas that attract a 24-hour population.

A View from the South

How New York City looks from way, way outside Manhattan

JOHN SHELTON REED

In the days after September 11, when Americans were watching a lot of television, many of us heard a Texas man-in-the-street tell a network interviewer something like, "Being a Texan or New Yorker just isn't very important right now. We're all Americans." Soon after that, we heard about some South Carolina middle-school students who raised the money to buy a truck for some Brooklyn firefighters who lost theirs (along with seven comrades) at the World Trade Center.

What's going on here? Texans and South Carolinians playing kissy-face with *New York City?* Isn't New York the heart of Yankeedom? Isn't it the city Southerners love to *hate?*

Well, like other Americans in that great red Republican interior on the 2000 Presidential election map, many Southerners do think at least occasionally of New York City as the Great Wen, the cesspool of iniquity, home of everything alien and vile. It has been suggested, not entirely in jest, that the city's evolution vindicates the Confederacy. The bill of particulars has several components.

First of all, there's a lot for *everybody* to dislike about New York: the welfare culture, deranged street people, dysfunctional public schools, periodic brushes with bankruptcy, wack-job politicians—even many New Yorkers complain about this stuff (often while taking a perverse sort of pride in being able to cope with it).

But Southerners have had some special reasons to dislike New York, starting with the fact that it is simply the most *urban* corner of America. A good many Southerners have seen city life as bad for both morals and manners. When Thomas Jefferson celebrated individual ownership of land and the farming life as the only sound bases for culture and society, he was writing in what was already an old Souther tradition. The most eloquent statement of the Southern case against big cities probably came in 1930, with a manifesto by twelve Southern men of letters called *I'll Take My Stand: The South and the Agrarian Tradition.* More recently, Hank Williams Jr. has often put the sentiment to music: In "Dixie on My Mind," for example, he complains, "These people never smile or say a word/They're all too busy trying to make an extra dime."

In addition, although this may be changing, many Southerners have also taken a dim view of New York for serving as the great reception center and repository for foreign immigration. Our Chambers of Commerce, after all, used to brag about our "native-born" labor force, and Atlanta Brave John Rocker of Macon, Georgia is not the only Southern boy who thinks Americans ought to speak English.

The attacks have highlighted a different, less obnoxious kind of New Yorker, one many Southerners and other Americans find more sympathetic.

In general, ever since New York displaced Boston as the home of the ultra-Yankee, Southerners have tended to see whatever we dislike about Northerners as concentrated there. When we describe ourselves to pollsters as friendly, polite, hospitable, leisurely, traditional, conservative—well, it goes without saying who is *not* that way.

And what many of us *really* dislike about Northerners, and thus loathe in spades about New Yorkers, is their view of Southerners as yokels—if not as *Deliverance*-style Neanderthals. Wherever Northerners got their ideas of the South (and of course a Southerner wrote *Deliverance*), some of them have indeed been inclined to view us as a lesser breed. Consider Kirkpatrick Sale's scare-mongering 1975 book, *Power Shift: The Rise of the Southern Rim and Its Challenge to the Eastern Establishment,* which extrapolated from economic and demographic trends to project the sort of nightmare future in which Sales' Northeastern readers would have to choose between, say, a governor of Texas and a former senator from Tennessee for President. (One of the few pleasures of the 1992 Democratic convention for this Southerner was watching the expression on Mario Cuomo's face every time he said the word "Arkansas.")

I could go on, but the point is that there has been no love lost, in either direction, between New York City and the South. And in this, the South has merely been a 100-proof stand-in for places like Omaha, Idaho, Ohio, and many other parts of what some New Yorkers call "flyover country." We all know this, don't we?

But, of course, it hasn't been quite that simple. Southerners, like other American heartlanders, have always been of two minds about the city. Some have looked on New York and New Yorkers with admiration, occasionally envy. Most of us can find at least something to admire about the place and its people.

For decades, of course, New York looked pretty good to *black* Southerners. In the first half of the twentieth century, hundreds of thousands, especially from Georgia and the Carolinas, packed their worldly goods and box lunches and rode the Chickenbone Special out of the Jim Crow South, following the drinking gourd to seek a better life in Harlem and Bedford Stuyvesant.

Many whites joined this exodus, especially a certain type of young Southern intellectual for whom The City has always been where it's happening (whatever "it" may be). North Carolina's Thomas Wolfe set the pattern in the 1920s, and 40 years later Mississippi's Willie Morris epitomized it. Morris's wince-making memoir *New York Days* is awash in isn't-it-wonderful-that-I'm-a-part-of-you-New-York-New-York gush. Even as confident and self-aware an expat as Tom Wolfe the younger (the Virginian who pretty well peeled, cored, and sliced the Big Apple in *Bonfire of the Vanities*) once confessed, "I still find New York exciting, to tell the truth. It's not the easiest way to live in the world, but I still get a terrific kick out of riding down Park Avenue in a cab at 2:30 in the morning and seeing the glass buildings all around. I have a real cornball attitude towards it, I suppose, which I think only somebody born far away from there would still have."

Southern writers and artists have historically *had* to look north to New York, because that's pretty much where the literacy and artistic action was. Yet arty folk aren't the only ones who have feared, deep down, that nothing signifies unless it is noticed on that thin sliver of asphalt stretching between the Hudson and the East River; plenty of hardheaded business-people feel the same. Atlanta, in particular, is full of the kind of strivers Tom Wolfe nailed in *A Man in Full,* for whom "the one thing they can't stand is the idea that somebody in New York might be calling them Southern hicks." (Houstonians, for some reason, don't have as bad a case of what the Australians call "cultural cringe": On the rare occasions when they think of New Yorkers at all, they're likely to feel sorry for them because they're not Texans.)

No matter where we grew up, few of us have entirely escaped the romance of The City. We know about the mean streets, sure, but we can't shake the image of Gene Kelly dancing in them.

One might have thought that the South's astonishing economic development, the rise of Southern cities, and the end of *de jure* segregation—all of which have made the South more like New York—would make New York City less alluring to some, and less repugnant to others. Increasingly, Southerners don't have to leave home to find urban, cosmopolitan, polyglot settings. Now that we have our own street crime, pollution, and traffic problems, there should be less reason to feel superior. Now that we have our own operas and publishing houses and big-league sports, there would seem less reason to feel inferior. But we still think of New York as different, and, in some ways, special.

No matter where we grew up, few of us have entirely escaped the romance of The City. We know about the mean streets, sure, but we can't shake the image of Gene Kelly dancing in them. Thanks to *Mad* magazine and the *New Yorker,* to Irving Berlin and Hollywood, I knew about Wall Street and Madison Avenue and Broadway and Coney Island and Harlem long before I ever set foot in New York. I recognized that socialites lived on Park Avenue, bums in the Bowery, bohemians in Greenwich Village. I understood who worked on Wall Street, and Madison Avenue, and Broadway, and Tin Pan Alley.

New York City is part of the mental furniture of all Americans, and—this is important—many of us think of the good things about New York as in some sense *ours*. We have proprietary feelings about the Metropolitan Opera, the Rockettes, the Statue of Liberty, and, yes, the World Trade Center. We feel attached to them whether we've seen them or not (and we may actually be more likely than the natives to have visited them). To say that those who destroyed the Twin Towers attacked New York City is like calling an assault on Mount Rushmore an attack on South Dakota.

But [they reminded] us that the New Yorkers we most often hear from are not the only people who live there. When Southerners and other outsiders dislike (or fawn on) "New Yorkers," the people they usually have in mind are the media and show business figures, politicians, business titans, and intellectuals we encounter on television—in short, "the people who run things": sophisticated, worldly, cosmopolitan (if you admire them); supercilious, smug, arrogant (if you don't).

These people are still there, of course, and they sure can grate. Shortly after September 11, I heard Fran Leibowitz making snide comments on NPR about President Bush's reference to the "folks" responsible for the attacks. She apparently had that word associated with hayrides. But many of these obnoxious figures have been uncharacteristically subdued since last fall, and the attacks have highlighted a different kind of New Yorker, one many Southerners and other Americans find more sympathetic.

There has always been more to New York City than the "people who run things." Ever since the heyday of Jacksonian Democracy, an on-again off-again alliance has existed between ordinary Southerners (that is, most of us) and New York's working people. After the Civil War and Reconstruction, this coalition was famously described as one of "rum, Romanism, and rebellion." Later, it elected Franklin Roosevelt to four terms. Later still, it reassembled to elect Richard Nixon and Ronald Reagan.

Most Southerners who know New York (I lived there for five years) know that there's a kind of outer borough New

York guy (it's almost always a guy) we get along with just fine. He is working-class and usually Irish, Jewish, or Italian, but these days sometimes black or Latino. He is what historian Paul Fussell called a "high prole," largely defined by his skills and "pride and a conviction of independence." When Fussell identifies disdain for social climbing, fondness for hunting and gambling and sports, and unromantic attitudes toward women as his other traits, Southerners should recognize the Northern variety of what we used to call a "good old boy" (before the label escaped captivity and lost all precision). "A solid, reliable, unpretentious, stand-up, companionable, appropriately loose, joke-sharing feller," in the description of Roy Blount Jr.

> **To say that those who destroyed the Twin Towers attacked New York City is like calling an assault on Mount Rushmore an attack against South Dakota.**

The bond between Southerners and this kind of Northerner often does have to do with sports. Recall that "Broadway Joe" Namath of the New York Jets, the Pennsylvanian who became an archetypal New Yorker, launched his public persona as "Joe Willie" Namath of the Alabama Crimson Tide. (Namath even played a Confederate soldier in a seriously bad movie called *The Last Rebel*.)

Or consider Coach Frank McGuire, from St. Xavier High School and St. John's University in Queens, who steered the North Carolina Tar Heels to an undefeated season and a national championship, and later coached at South Carolina. The New York players McGuire recruited used to bemuse the locals with their habit of crossing themselves before foul shots. And then there's Coach Jimmy Valvano of North Carolina State University, another New Yorker who led a Southern team to a national championship and endeared himself even to fans of rival teams with his good-old-boy humor. (After his team blew a lead to lose to the arch-rival Tar Heels, Valvano claimed a fan wrote him "If you ever do that again, I'll come over and shoot your dog." Valvano said he wrote back saying he didn't have a dog and the man replied: "I'm sending you a dog. But don't get too attached to him.")

These are the kinds of New Yorkers we saw on television after September 11: policemen, firemen, rescue workers—ordinary folks. Their accents may have sounded funny to Southern ears, but they're our kind of Yankee: unpretentious, hard working when they have to be, offhandedly courageous. Mayor Giuliani may or may not be one of them by nature, but in that context he sure looked it, and most of us found him wholly admirable.

The post-9/11 fortitude and determination of New York's plain folk has led many of us to conclude that Tom Wolfe was wrong when, in one of his most famous essays, he described the stockcar racer Junior Johnson, from Ingle Hollow, Wilkes County, North Carolina, as "the last American hero." We have learned that there are some guys from places like Red Hook, Brooklyn, New York, who qualify as well.

JOHN SHELTON REED, a professor at the University of North Carolina, is author of *Whistling Dixie* and other books on the South.

Debunking the Myths of Katrina

The Lessons of Katrina

Camas Davis, Nicole Davis, Christian DeBenedetti, Brad Reagan, Kristin Roth

No One Should Have Been Surprised

Not the federal agencies tasked with preparing for catastrophes. Not the local officials responsible for aging levees and vulnerable populations. Least of all the residents themselves, who had been warned for decades that they lived on vulnerable terrain. But when Hurricane Katrina struck the Gulf Coast on Aug. 29, 2005, it seemed as though the whole country was caught unawares. Accusations began to fly even before floodwaters receded. But facts take longer to surface. In the months since the storm, many of the first impressions conveyed by the media have turned out to be mistaken. And many of the most important lessons of Katrina have yet to be absorbed. But one thing is certain: More hurricanes will come. To cope with them we need to understand what really happened during modern America's worst natural disaster. *Popular Mechanics* editors and reporters spent more than four months interviewing officials, scientists, first responders and victims. Here is our report.—*The editors*

Government Responded Rapidly

Myth: *"The aftermath of Katrina will go down as one of the worst abandonments of Americans on American soil ever in U.S. history."*—Aaron Broussard, president, Jefferson Parish, La., Meet the Press, NBC, Sept. 4, 2005

Reality: Bumbling by top disaster-management officials fueled a perception of general inaction, one that was compounded by impassioned news anchors. In fact, the response to Hurricane Katrina was by far the largest—and fastest-rescue effort in U.S. history, with nearly 100,000 emergency personnel arriving on the scene within three days of the storm's landfall.

Dozens of National Guard and Coast Guard helicopters flew rescue operations that first day—some just 2 hours after Katrina hit the coast. Hoistless Army helicopters improvised rescues, carefully hovering on rooftops to pick up survivors. On the ground, "guardsmen had to chop their way through, moving trees and recreating roadways," says Jack Harrison of the National Guard. By the end of the week, 50,000 National Guard troops in the Gulf Coast region had saved 17,000 people; 4000 Coast Guard personnel saved more than 33,000.

These units had help from local, state and national responders, including five helicopters from the Navy ship Bataan and choppers from the Air Force and police. The Louisiana Department of Wildlife and Fisheries dispatched 250 agents in boats. The Federal Emergency Management Agency (FEMA), state police and sheriffs' departments launched rescue flotillas. By Wednesday morning, volunteers and national teams joined the effort, including eight units from California's Swift Water Rescue. By Sept. 8, the waterborne operation had rescued 20,000.

While the press focused on FEMA's shortcomings, this broad array of local, state and national responders pulled off an extraordinary success—especially given the huge area devastated by the storm. Computer simulations of a Katrina-strength hurricane had estimated a worst-case-scenario death toll of more than 60,000 people in Louisiana. The actual number was 1077 in that state.

Next Time: Any fatalities are too many. Improvements hinge on building more robust communications networks and stepping up predisaster planning to better coordinate local and national resources.

PM Prescription

Improving Response

One of the biggest reminders from Katrina is that FEMA is not a first responder. It was local and state agencies that got there first and saved lives. Where the feds can contribute is in planning and helping to pay for a coordinated response. Here are a few concrete steps.

Think Locally: "Every disaster starts and ends as a local event," says Ed Jacoby, who managed New York state's emergency response to 9/11. All municipalities must assess their own risk of disasters—both natural and man-made.

Include Business Help: "Companies realize that if a city shuts down, they shut down," says Barry Scanlon, former FEMA director of corporate affairs. During Katrina, many companies coordinated their own mini relief efforts. That organizational power can augment public disaster management. "If 10 Fortune 100 members made a commitment to the Department of Homeland Security," says Scanlon, "the country would take a huge leap forward."

Prearrange Contracts: Recovery costs skyrocket with high demand during a crisis. Contracts with local firms must be signed before disaster strikes. "You know beforehand that everyone is ready to move," says Kate Hale, emergency management director of Florida's Miami-Dade County during Hurricane Andrew in 1992. "The government blows the whistle and the contractors go to work."

Better First-Responder Gear

In disasters, the right tools are everything. PM chose three Katrina-tested technologies that should be part of every emergency manager's arsenal.

Mobile Command When Katrina knocked out communications, confusion followed. Some emergency experts recommend mobile field headquarters such as this $500,000 LDV communication and command truck, which enables incident commanders to coordinate response when infrastructure goes down. Up to six communication officers can work at a dispatch center with landline phones and satellite, cellular and radio links that operate over multiple frequencies to link incompatible systems.

Fresh Water Portable reverse-osmosis water filtration (such as the USFilter system) uses high-pressure membranes to clean brackish water at an output of 288,000 gal. of potable water per day. The cost: about $4 per 1000 gal.—a fraction of the cost of trucking in bottled water.

Homing Signals The Thales 25, from Thales Communications, is among the smallest, fully interoperable digital radios available to first responders, bridging the communications gap between multiple agencies. The handheld device can also transmit GPS data to locate team members and victims.

Katrina wasn't a Superstorm

Myth: *"This is a once-in-a-lifetime event."*—New Orleans Mayor C. Ray Nagin, press conference, Aug. 28, 2005

Reality: Though many accounts portray Katrina as a storm of unprecedented magnitude, it was in fact a large, but otherwise typical, hurricane. On the 1-to-5 Saffir-Simpson scale, Katrina was a midlevel Category 3 hurricane at landfall. Its barometric pressure was 902 millibars (mb), the sixth lowest ever recorded, but higher than Wilma (882mb) and Rita (897mb), the storms that followed it. Katrina's peak sustained wind speed at landfall 55 miles south of New Orleans was 125 mph; winds in the city barely reached hurricane strength.

By contrast, when Hurricane Andrew struck the Florida coast in 1992, its sustained winds were measured at 142 mph. And meteorologists estimate that 1969's Category 5 Hurricane Camille, which followed a path close to Katrina's, packed winds as high as 200 mph. Two factors made Katrina so devastating. Its radius (the distance from the center of the storm to the point of its maximum winds, usually at the inner eye wall) was 30 miles—three times wider than Camille's. In addition, Katrina approached over the Gulf of Mexico's shallow northern shelf, generating a more powerful storm surge—the water pushed ashore by hurricanes—than systems that move across deeper waters. In Plaquemines Parish, south of New Orleans, the surge topped out at 30 ft.; in New Orleans the surge was 25 ft.—enough to overtop some of the city's floodwalls.

Next Time: According to the National Hurricane Center in Miami, the Atlantic is in a cycle of heightened hurricane activity due to higher sea-surface temperatures and other factors. The cycle could last 40 years, during which time the United States can expect to be hit by dozens of Katrina-size storms. Policymakers—and coastal residents—need to start seeing hurricanes as routine weather events, not once-in-a-lifetime anomalies.

Floodwalls Were Built Properly

Myth: *"Perhaps not just human error was involved [in floodwall failures]. There may have been some malfeasance."*—Raymond Seed, civil engineering professor, UC, Berkeley, testifying before a Senate committee, Nov. 2, 2005

Reality: Most of the New Orleans floodwall failures occurred when water up to 25 ft. high overtopped the barriers, washing out their foundations. But three breached floodwalls—one in the 17th Street Canal and two in the London Avenue Canal—showed no signs of overtopping. Accusations of malfeasance were born after the Army Corps of Engineers released seismic data suggesting that the sheet-pile foundations supporting those floodwalls were 7 ft. shorter than called for in the design—a possible cause for collapse. In December 2005, PM watched Corps engineers pull four key sections of the 17th Street Canal foundation out of the New Orleans mud. The sections were more than 23 ft. long—as per design specifications. "I had heard talk about improper building before the sheet-pile pull," the Corps' Wayne Stroupe says. "But not much since."

Next Time: The Corps is restoring levees at a cost of more than $1 billion in time for the 2006 hurricane season (June 1), driving foundations 50 ft. deep—almost three times the depth of the existing foundations.

Floodwall Failures

Overtopping

Most New Orleans flood barriers are simple earthen embankments, or levees, supporting a wall of steel sheet piles, some of which are capped with reinforced concrete I-walls. Breaches occurred when storm surges poured over the walls, washing away, or scouring, interior soil foundations. This weakened their lateral stability. Pressure from the floodwaters then caused collapse.

Foundation Failure

The cause of breaches on the 17th Street and London Avenue canals remains a mystery. Over-dredging in the 17th Street Canal may have removed lining sediments near the floodwall's sheet-pile wall, allowing water to percolate through deep levee soils. Swimming pools and other structures built too close to the barrier may have compromised its integrity by compressing its foundation.

PM Prescription

Keeping New Orleans Dry

In 1965, the same year Hurricane Betsy swamped large sections of New Orleans (including the Lower Ninth Ward), the Army Corps of Engineers presented Congress with an audacious blueprint for protecting the city from a fast-moving Category 3 storm. The $85 million Barrier Plan proposed sealing off Lake Pontchartrain from the gulf with massive, retractable flood barriers. The goal: Stop storm surges 25 miles east of the levees that encircle New Orleans. After Betsy, the plan was expanded to include gates on two of the four drainage canals that slice into the city from Pontchartrain (two of which breached their floodwalls after Katrina). But, environmental groups objected to the impact that the Pontchartrain floodgates might have on wildlife and wetlands. The Sewer and Water Board of New Orleans vetoed gates on the canals. So the Corps instead built higher levees and floodwalls.

Now, 40 years later, the Corps is again studying how to design gates for Pontchartrain and the New Orleans canals that will have minimal impact on the environment and navigation, but will still be able to block Katrina-strength storm surges. The report's due date: January 2008. Meanwhile, engineers are also studying how to strengthen the existing levees. One idea is to replace fragile I-wall barriers with more robust T-walls, which use three rows of foundation pilings that can withstand pressure generated by hurricane-force floodwaters. A wide concrete slab, or "skirt," on the protected side deflects overflowing water that could otherwise wash away supporting soil. T-walls held throughout Katrina without a leak.

Anarchy Didn't Take Over

Myth: *"They have people . . . been in that frickin' Superdome for five days watching dead bodies, watching hooligans killing*

people, raping people."—New Orleans Mayor C. Ray Nagin, The Oprah Winfrey Show, Sept. 6, 2005

Reality: Both public officials and the press passed along lurid tales of post-Katrina mayhem: shootouts in the Superdome, bodies stacked in a convention center freezer, snipers firing on rescue helicopters. And those accounts appear to have affected rescue efforts as first responders shifted resources from saving lives to protecting rescuers. In reality, although looting and other property crimes were widespread after the flooding on Monday, Aug. 29, almost none of the stories about violent crime turned out to be true. Col. Thomas Beron, the National Guard commander of Task Force Orleans, arrived at the Superdome on Aug. 29 and took command of 400 soldiers. He told PM that when the Dome's main power failed around 5 am, "it became a hot, humid, miserable place. There was some pushing, people were irritable. There was one attempted rape that the New Orleans police stopped."

The only confirmed account of a weapon discharge occurred when Louisiana Guardsman Chris Watt was jumped by an assailant and, during the chaotic arrest, accidently shot himself in the leg with his own M-16.

When the Superdome was finally cleared, six bodies were found—not the 200 speculated. Four people had died of natural causes; one was ruled a suicide, and another a drug overdose. Of the four bodies recovered at the convention center, three had died of natural causes; the fourth had sustained stab wounds.

Anarchy in the streets? "The vast majority of people [looting] were taking food and water to live," says Capt. Marlon Defillo, the New Orleans Police Department's commander of public affairs. "There were no killings, not one murder." As for sniper fire: No bullet holes were found in the fuselage of any rescue helicopter.

Next Time: "Rumors are fueled by a shortage of truth," says Ted Steinberg, author of *Acts of God: The Unnatural History of Natural Disasters in America.* And truth was the first casualty of the information breakdown that followed the storm. Hardening communications lines will benefit not just first responders, but also the media. Government officials have a vital role in informing the public. Ensuring the flow of accurate information should be part of disaster planning at local, state and federal levels.

EVAC Plans Worked

Myth: *"The failure to evacuate was the tipping point for all the other things that . . . went wrong."*—Michael Brown, former FEMA director, Sept. 27, 2005

Reality: When Nagin issued his voluntary evacuation order, a contraflow plan that turned inbound interstate lanes into outbound lanes enabled 1.2 million people to leave New Orleans out of a metro population of 1.5 million. "The Corps estimated we would need 72 hours [to evacuate that many people]," says Brian Wolshon, an LSU civil engineer. "Instead, it took 38 hours." Later investigations indicated that many who stayed did so by choice. "Most people had transportation," says

Col. Joe Spraggins, director of emergency management in Harrison County, Ala. "Many didn't want to leave." Tragic exceptions: hospital patients and nursing home residents.

Next Time: All states should adopt a Florida-style registry, which enables people who will need evacuation assistance to notify their city or state officials.

Repetitive Property Loss Breakdown

A repetitive-loss property is one with multiple insured losses due to floods within a 10-year period. The five Gulf Coast states account for more than half the claims filed—a clear indication of the vulnerability of property in Hurricane Alley.

Government Subsidies Encourage Bad Planning

Myth: *"We will rebuild [the Gulf Coast] bigger and better than ever."*—Haley Barbour, Miss. Gov., The Associated Press, Sept. 3, 2005

Reality: In the past 25 years, the tiny community of Dauphin Island, Ala., has been hit by at least six hurricanes. Residents there carry insurance backed by the federal government, and they've collected more than $21 million in taxpayer money over the years to repair their damaged homes. Not bad, considering their premiums rarely go up and they are seldom denied coverage—even after Katrina almost completely demolished the barrier island at the entrance to Mobile Bay.

"It's like a guy getting inebriated and wrecking his Ferrari four or five times," says David Conrad of the National Wildlife Federation (NWF). "Eventually, a private insurer would say no. It doesn't work that way with the federal flood insurance program."

The National Flood Insurance Program (NFIP), administered by FEMA, was started in 1968 for homeowners who live in flood-prone areas considered too great a risk by private insurers. And for more than 30 years, the program was self-supporting. But studies by Conrad's NWF team revealed a disturbing fact: Just 1 to 2 percent of claims were from "repetitive-loss properties"—those suffering damage at least twice in a 10-year period. Yet, those 112,000 properties generated a remarkable 40 percent of the losses—$5.6 billion. One homeowner in Houston filed 16 claims in 18 years, receiving payments totaling $806,000 for a building valued at $114,000.

Just as significantly, the five Gulf Coast states accounted for half the total of repetitive-loss costs nationwide. Taxpayers across the country are paying for a minute number of people to rebuild time and time again in the path of hurricanes.

That is proving to be an expensive habit. Following Katrina, Rita and Wilma in 2005, claims could exceed $22 billion—more than the total amount paid in premiums in the program's 38-year history. In mid-November, the NFIP ran out of money; to pay claims, Congress will have to authorize FEMA to borrow more money.

Next Time: Folks in Tornado Alley and along the San Andreas fault don't get federally backed insurance, so why should taxpayers subsidize coastal homes, many of them vacation properties? Before we start rebuilding "bigger and better," Congress should reform the flood insurance program. A good start: Structure premiums so the program is actuarially sound and clamps down on repetitive claims.

Another option is for the government to buy out homeowners in vulnerable communities, just as it did along the Mississippi River following the floods of 1993. "The only problem is that it is going to cost more to buy out properties along the shore than it is to do it in North Dakota," says Andrew Coburn of Duke University's Program for the Study of Developed Shorelines. "The concept is still solid. It's just going to take more dollars."

PM Prescription

Rethinking the Coast

Katrina was the sixth storm in 20 years to flood Pete Melich's house on Dauphin Island, Ala., yet the rain had barely stopped when he made plans for a $500,000 home on the lot next door. This one will not be built on a slab, but on 13-ft. pilings, with walls engineered to withstand 175-mph winds. "There will never be another flood claim on my house," Melich says proudly.

The impulse is to rebuild quickly, only bigger and more expensively than before. Yes, the federal flood insurance program described on the previous page helps fuel that drive. Yet, some people, like Melich, would still live in vulnerable areas, even without federal insurance. "The price I pay for living on the gulf is hurricanes," Melich says. "I'm willing to deal with them."

Coastal development critics argue that a total retreat from the beach makes economic and environmental sense. Realistically, that's not going to happen. But Duke University's Coburn says that there are feasible steps that can make coastal communities more storm resistant. Coburn's first step is to restore natural buffers between the beach and developed areas. He recommends wider setbacks from the beach (the equivalent of at least two rows of housing); the creation of additional dune fields; curvilinear roads that reduce the velocity and scouring of floodwaters; and redesigned beach access points so they can't act as conduits for storm surge and ebb. A second step: If people must build on the beach, they should follow Melich's lead on tougher construction.

The Energy Infrastructure Survived

Myth: *"You have a major energy network that is down . . . We could run out of gasoline or diesel or jet fuel in the next two weeks here."*—Roger Diwan, managing director, Oil Markets Group, PFC Energy, *Business Week,* Sept. 1, 2005

Reality: Initially, the pictures from the gulf looked bleak: oil rigs washed up along the coast, production platforms wrecked. In truth, Katrina inflicted minimal damage to the offshore energy infrastructure. Only 86 of the gulf's 4000 drilling rigs and platforms were damaged or destroyed, and most of those were older, fixed platforms atop unproductive wells.

Then, a month later, Rita—a Category 5 storm when it tore through the gulf—knocked out 125 more. Although no offshore wells or underground pipelines ruptured, and no lives were lost, Katrina and Rita each shut down nearly all the gulf's offshore output (which represents 29 percent of domestic oil production and 19 percent of domestic natural gas production) for more than a week. A third Cat 5 hurricane, Wilma, also slowed the recovery. It took two months to get 60 percent of those wells back on line.

Refineries were hit harder. Katrina shut down nine of the gulf's 36 facilities; a month later, Rita disabled 15. Combined, the stoppages affected 30 percent of the country's refining capacity. But recovery came more quickly than many experts predicted. By the end of the year, overall production was down just 8 percent, and only three refineries were still off line. "This is by far the worst we've ever seen," says Ed Murphy, who is a refinery expert at the American Petroleum Institute. "That we've recovered so quickly is really quite extraordinary."

Despite fears that the energy infrastructure would break down, the system proved surprisingly robust. Consumers did experience a spike in gas prices. But, it was temporary and only partly attributable to the storms; a surge in worldwide demand had already driven up prices. (Two weeks before Katrina, a *Newsday* headline read: "Gas, Oil Prices Again Reach New Records.") Although high prices were aggravating, they helped hold down demand, encouraged new supply sources and ensured that gas stations and fuel depots did not run dry.

Next Time: Three major policy changes could help make our energy system more resilient in the face of disasters. 1) Loosen restrictions on refinery construction to encourage new refineries in more diverse locations. 2) Expand port facilities for Liquefied Natural Gas to help supplement domestic supply. 3) Relax the current ban on offshore natural gas drilling along the Atlantic and Pacific coasts. Clearly, all three options require overcoming NIMBY resistance and striking a careful balance between environmental and energy concerns.

Prescription

Re-Engineering the Mississippi

For nearly 300 years the interests of landowners, farmers, fishermen, oil companies, businessmen and politicians have all conspired against the natural will of the third largest drainage basin in the world. The Mississippi River was once a meandering, interconnected system of large streams. It flooded often, changed its course every 1500 years or so, and built up coastal deltas and wetlands by depositing 400 million tons of clay, sand and silt on southern Louisiana's coastline each year.

With a federal mandate to improve navigation and flood control, the Army Corps of Engineers began building levees in the late 1800s, and by the 1940s had largely tamed the river. In the past few decades, however, scientists realized that the Corps' control structures, dams and levees were either trapping sediment upstream or spitting it out past the continental shelf, which meant that new coastal wetlands could no longer form and existing ones were diminishing. This, combined with rising sea levels, has meant that in the past century Louisiana has lost 1.2 million acres of coastal marshes, swamps and barrier islands.

Engineers and scientists refer to the Mississippi basin as a "wicked problem," a term used to describe inherently intractable challenges with solutions that only lead to more complex problems. The Corps' wicked problem is this: How do we re-engineer the lower Mississippi to restore coastal wetlands while maintaining the flood controls and navigation structures that led to their destruction? In 1998 Louisiana answered with the $14 billion Coast 2050, a 60-project program that rivaled the Everglades restoration in scope. Too long-range and expensive, said the White House Office of Management and Budget. The Corps responded with the $2 billion Louisiana Coastal Area plan, with five projects, which are still under review. Other scientists and engineers also have proposed solutions, both sweeping and modest. Post-Katrina, it is time to bring a national commitment to applying the best of these ideas.

Redirecting Silt: To maintain navigability, the Corps regularly dredges the river, but Robert Twilley, professor of oceanography and coastal science at Louisiana State University, claims the Corps "wastes millions of cubic feet per year of sediment that's tossed into the ocean. Instead we should transport those dredged materials by pipeline, and spew silt from the river over the coastal floodplain to nourish the landscape." Since 1990, the Corps has initiated dozens of such projects, although their scope and impact remain small when compared with the natural processes of the river. Kerry St. Pé, director of the Barataria-Terrebonne National Estuary Program, advocates 36-in. pipelines to carry 70 million cubic yards of dredged silt annually from the Mississippi west to vanishing wetlands.

Build Bigger Diversions: To boost natural productivity, the Corps mimics the effects of historical annual flooding by diverting fresh water into receding, increasingly saline coastal estuaries. Two diversion structures—at Caernarvon and Davis Pond—feature drainage holes called box culverts that are cut into the levees to introduce controlled flows of 8000 to 10,000 cubic feet per second (cfs) of fresh water into overly saline estuaries.

Baton Rouge engineer Sherwood Gagliano proposes a grander diversion project called the Third Delta. (Two areas of natural delta building are at the mouths of the Mississippi and Atchafalaya rivers.) Its centerpiece: a 60-ft.-deep channel from the Mississippi, near Donaldsonville, that will deliver 360,000 cfs of water and sediment to the Barataria and Terrebonne basins flanking stagnant Bayou Lafourche.

Dismantle Obsolete Structures: Southeastern Louisiana is crosshatched with unused canals, many of them dredged by mineral companies, that channel fresh water and sediment to the gulf instead of into wetlands. "We need to break down [obsolete] levees," Twilley says, "and backfill canals so that water and sediment flow west."

The Gathering Storm

One year after Hurricane Katrina, what if it's not just once in a lifetime? Making sense of our disaster-prone future.

ELAINE KAMARCK

The lingering anger in New Orleans over the poor federal response to Hurricane Katrina is such that you can buy a T-shirt that reads "FEMA: Federal Employees Missing in Action." By now, one year after Hurricanes Katrina and Rita hit New Orleans and the Gulf Coast, most people are familiar with the catalogue of missteps by the Federal Emergency Management Agency (FEMA) in the days after the storm first hit. They read like recollections from a bureaucratic nightmare. FEMA denied local officials' requests for rubber rafts needed to rescue victims because it was afraid the polluted waters would ruin them. It issued a press release telling first responders in neighboring states not to respond to the hurricane without being requested and lawfully dispatched by state and local authorities. It turned away trucks filled with water and refused to accept much-needed generators. It wouldn't allow food to be delivered to New Orleans by the Red Cross. It ignored Amtrak's offer of trains to evacuate victims. It tied up valuable offers of foreign aid in the form of water-purification systems and rescue ships. And it left 20,000 trailers, desperately needed for temporary housing, sitting in Atlanta.

Why was the response to Katrina so inadequate, and can FEMA be fixed? On the surface, the outlines of the problem are clear enough: By placing FEMA, formerly an independent agency, into a new Department of Homeland Security (DHS), the Bush Administration severely weakened FEMA, causing problems that can only be fixed by restoring its independence. But, beyond this reshuffling of boxes on the federal government's organization chart, FEMA's response points to a deeper and more serious problem. Hurricane Katrina may not be the once-in-a-century storm it was thought to be. Rather, in all likelihood it is a harbinger for what is likely to come in an era of global warming. Just as the attacks of September 11 served as a wake-up call for what could be decades of catastrophic terrorism, Katrina must be seen as a wake-up call for an era of potentially new and explosively expensive natural disasters.

Taken together, we can expect a future where today's "emergencies," both natural and man-made, are more common—and more deadly. Yet our federal government—the only institution that can coordinate and pay for disaster response—is woefully unprepared to respond to, and pay for, these emergencies. Three

major problems loom: The local-state-federal arrangements that have governed emergency response may no longer work in an era where disasters are so large that they overwhelm first responders; our system of emergency supplemental budgeting risks creating a fiscal emergency in which successive disasters push the nation into deeper and deeper fiscal trouble; and our seriousness about preventing disasters in the first place involves a level of political commitment previously unheard of in the United States. In other words, reforming FEMA is just a first step. Ultimately, the federal government must rethink its entire approach to disaster prevention and response.

FEMA's Failed Past

Created in 1979, FEMA was, throughout the 1980s, the dumping ground for political appointees; one report in the early '90s showed that it had 10 times the number of appointees as other agencies. The low point for the agency prior to Katrina came in 1992, with its failure to respond effectively to Hurricane Andrew, which left 250,000 homeless. FEMA's response to Andrew was similar to that during Katrina, perhaps because the director at the time was a man who—like Michael Brown, the director during Katrina—had no prior disaster experience. Instead of preparing his agency to handle disasters, Director Wallace Stickney's major claim to fame had been forcing an openly gay employee of FEMA to reveal the identities of other gay employees.

This began to change in 1993, when President Bill Clinton appointed James Lee Witt, who had been his head of emergency response in Arkansas, to run FEMA. At the time, there were calls in Congress to abolish the agency because of its poor performance during Andrew. Witt, however, performed the government equivalent of a corporate turnaround, slashing tiers of bureaucracy and draining the patronage swamp. Witt reorganized FEMA around an "all-hazards response" approach and improved the agency's performance so much that during the 1994 Northridge earthquake in California, FEMA was applauded for its timely payments and assistance to victims. FEMA's re-organization and subsequent performance was so good that it became the poster child for Vice President Al Gore's reinventing government initiative. FEMA continued to perform well in the first year of the Bush Administration, particularly after September 11. In those days, many of Witt's reforms were still in place, and the agency was headed by Joe Allbaugh, a man who, like Witt, was a close confidante of the sitting president.

The re-deterioration of FEMA began in the third year of the Bush Administration, when it was placed in the Department of Homeland Security. Including FEMA in DHS blurred its mission and focus, a not-unusual occurrence when an independent agency is folded into an enormous new department. Prior to Katrina, warnings were issued by the Government Accountability Office (GAO), as well as a host of state and local emergency preparedness planners, that FEMA's preparedness mission was getting lost in layers of bureaucracy; it was likewise unclear how terrorism fit into the all-hazards paradigm. When FEMA's state-grant-making process got rolled into an overall departmental grant-making process, states found that they could get grants to buy protective gear against a biochemical attack, but they could not get grants for more traditional and probable threats like flooding. And, predictably, as FEMA's mission was blurred and its autonomy stripped away, it began to lose its longtime executives. The first to go was Allbaugh, whose departure meant the loss of direct access to the president, a feature of emergency response that is nearly as important as prior experience.

By the time Katrina made landfall, then, FEMA had spent slightly more than two years suffocating within DHS. Its vision was blurred, its morale sapped, its talent gone, and its leadership practically nonexistent. Those who remained were uncertain of their own authority and their relationship to the rest of the government. It is no surprise that so many mistakes were made and so much confusion reigned. This history, and the agency's performance during Katrina, has led many to accuse the Administration of setting up the agency to fail in the face of a major emergency. The solution has been just as clear: In the immediate aftermath of Katrina, Senator Hillary Clinton introduced legislation to restore FEMA's independence. And by the spring of 2006, two House committees had approved legislation that would pull FEMA out of DHS.

Such a correction, to make FEMA a freestanding agency once again, is important for a variety of reasons. First, making the agency report directly to the president would make it possible to recruit top talent to lead FEMA. Second, a freestanding FEMA is the only way to allow it broad authority for action across the federal government, a vital step in the face of disasters that could easily overwhelm first responders and require broad federal action. Third, it would clarify some of the thorny issues of federalism that have arisen through the thicket of the DHS grant-making process. As the disaster simulation known as "Dark Winter" proved, for example, a smallpox attack on the United States could cause massive confusion and death across the country, a scenario that only can be handled with clear lines of authority and communication between the state governments and Washington. Such lines do not exist now, nor did they during Dark Winter. In fact, during the exercise, jurisdictional conflict quickly broke out, leading former Senator Sam Nunn, who played the President of the United States, to say, "We're going to have absolute chaos if we start having war between the federal government and the state government."

Hurricane Katrina: The Canary in the Coalmine

An independent and empowered FEMA would go a long way toward better preparing the United States for disaster response. But such a move alone would prepare the federal government to respond merely to the threat landscape of the past, not the unsettling and turbulent one of the future: global warming and international terrorism.

Former Vice President Gore's recent book *An Inconvenient Truth* makes the case, known to scientists for some time, that global warming has contributed to an increase in both the number and intensity of extreme weather events. A growing raft of studies indicates that warmer ocean waters fuel more powerful hurricanes, containing more moisture and more wind. In 2004, Florida experienced four unusually powerful hurricanes; Japan set an all-time record for the number of typhoons; and in the United States the record for tornadoes was broken. In 2005, so many hurricanes hit the United States that we ran out of letters of the alphabet and had to start using Greek letters as hurricane designations, a step never before reached. In addition, as Gore points out, "The science textbooks had to be rewritten in 2004. They used to say, 'It's impossible to have hurricanes in the South Atlantic.' But that year, for the first time ever, a hurricane hit Brazil."

Hurricanes are not the only cataclysm on the rise. The number of major floods in the United States increased from less than 25 in the 1950s to just under 200 in the 1990s, a rate of change that was mirrored in Asia and in Europe. As Gore goes on to point out, one of the ironies of more flooding, and more precipitation in general, is that the phenomenon is uneven across the globe—producing more drought and desertification at the same time. The number of square miles of desert created in the 1990s is more than double what it was in the 1970s. And the number of major wildfires in the Americas went from less than 10 in the 1950s to close to 50 in the 1990s. Thus, Hurricane Katrina may well have been the canary in the coalmine, alerting us to the fact that "once-in-a-century storms" will occur much more frequently than that. The emerging scientific consensus is that global warming equals extreme weather, and national wealth and power are no protection against Mother Nature. That images from the aftermath of Katrina looked eerily similar to the pictures from the Asian tsunami a year earlier was no accident. We in the United States are as vulnerable to extreme weather events as anyone else in the world.

A similar situation exists regarding large-scale terrorism. As the terrorism expert Brian Jenkins points out, the nature of terrorism changed in the late twentieth century, from terrorism directed at precise political objectives to terrorism driven by fanatical religious objectives directed at societies in general.

Even before September 11, we were seeing an increase in the number of lives taken in terrorist attacks. And, as nuclear proliferation expert Graham Allison has written so persuasively, the decreasing cost of scientific and computing information has meant that it is not only inconceivable, but, in fact, quite possible, that sometime in the next decade a major city will be attacked with a small-scale nuclear device. All the trappings of modern life—bridges, tunnels, airplanes, computer networks, electricity grids, and power plants—have been, and will continue to be, targets of terrorists intent upon inflicting maximum damage to civilian populations.

Redesigning Emergency Response

Global warming and terrorist attacks have drastically different implications when it comes to prevention, but for purposes of emergency response the two issues are nearly identical (the only real difference is that, in addition to emergency response, the scene of a terrorist attack is also treated like a crime scene). The levees in New Orleans could have been blown up by terrorists instead of being destroyed by Hurricane Katrina. An explosion and meltdown in a nuclear power plant can come about as the result of carelessness on the part of an employee as easily as it can come about from intentional terrorist activity. Whatever the cause of the disaster, people need to be rescued and treated, fires and other second-stage disasters need to be fought, and property needs to be rebuilt.

Moving forward, therefore, the federal government must establish a set of guiding principles for responding to large-scale disasters, be they natural or man-made. The first is that a determination must be made, as early as possible, whether first responders have been overwhelmed and have become, in fact, victims themselves. This goes against established doctrine, embodied by the Stafford Act, which dictates that response efforts should start with local and state resources. It is the Stafford Act that sets up the process whereby a governor formally asks the federal government for assistance in the case of a catastrophe. But, as we saw with Katrina, it is possible to experience disasters of such a scale that they decimate even the local government's ability to communicate merely the extent of the damage, let alone initiate a response. New Orleans Mayor Ray Nagin had to operate out of the Hyatt Hotel for several days, unable to establish communications with anyone; many state and local public safety agencies suffered water and wind damage to their equipment (evacuation buses, for one, were underwater); and the breakdown of communications led to an inability to coordinate state and local responses. In other words, in Katrina, from the Mayor of New Orleans on down, the first responders were victims.

Katrina must be seen as a wake-up call for an era of potentially new and explosively expensive natural disasters.

Interestingly enough, the Bush Administration, in its National Response Plan, had, in fact, anticipated that there would be events in which first responders were incapacitated and immediate federal intervention would be necessary. A presidential directive issued eight months before Katrina allowed the secretary of homeland security to declare a disaster to be an Incident of National Significance, essentially a federal takeover of the response effort, drawing resources from across the federal government. But this step wasn't taken by Secretary Michael Chertoff until days after the hurricane hit, thus delaying to a dangerous degree the mobilization of federal, especially military, resources. The sad truth is that, had New Orleans' leadership been incapacitated by a dirty bomb, the federal response would have been more quickly forthcoming. Such a disparity between the federal response to natural and terrorist-made disasters must be reconciled. In the future, the federal government will need to make an immediate determination about the fitness of first responders and direct a federal, often military, response within hours—not days.

Another requirement for disaster strategy is the need for a standing emergency-response budget. Over time, America's natural disasters have become steadily less deadly—but also steadily more expensive. The hurricane that hit Galveston, Texas, in 1900 resulted in 8,000 dead, but the property damage (under $10 billion) was minimal by today's standards. In contrast, Hurricane Katrina, the deadliest disaster in recent American history, killed 1,330, but the property damage cost the government nearly $100 billion, by far the most expensive natural disaster in American history. Similarly, the September 11 attacks on New York and Washington cost the nation $64 billion, above and beyond what had been budgeted for homeland defense as of the summer of 2002 (this number reflects only the emergency spending; it does not take into account the increases in regular spending that have come as a result of those attacks). In the context of a federal budget that is expected to total $2.7 trillion in 2006, these emergency expenditures are small. But if major disasters are increasingly a way of life in this country, then such numbers take on an added significance. They are, in effect, less and less contingent costs; increasingly, they are fixed, mandatory costs—in other words, entitlements. Thus, one way to understand how to budget for disasters is to look at the history of the federal government's budgets for entitlements.

With each decade of the twentieth century, as entitlements grew, the "rest" of the government made up a smaller and smaller portion of the whole. This was not supposed to be. But the sympathies elicited by the beneficiaries—aged people on Medicare and Social Security—made it impossible to cap expenditures; so as people lived longer lives and began to rely more on federal benefits, the size of federal entitlements rose accordingly. In 1937, when Social Security was passed, no one thought that it would turn out to be the enormous expenditure that it has become. In that year, there were 53,236 beneficiaries, and their benefits cost the federal government just over $1 million. In 1941, Social Security outlays were less than 1 percent of the federal budget; today the old age program alone accounts for 22 percent (all entitlements combined for 55 percent). The universal nature of the program and the pure political fact that

Congress can't say no to old people has created a program that overwhelms all other spending.

A similar situation is likely to play out regarding emergency expenditures. Like Social Security, spending on emergency relief is directed toward people who are in extreme need and who command the sympathy and support of Americans and their political leaders. Just as all Americans realize that they, too, will be old someday, every American realizes that he or she could wind up in the middle of some natural or man-made disaster. So, as with Social Security, there is a political imperative to spend whatever is needed in the wake of disasters. As Witt told a Senate subcommittee a decade ago, "Disasters are very political events." But, unlike entitlement spending, which can be predicted with a fair degree of accuracy using demographic data, emergency spending is assumed to be unpredictable. This is why we have gotten into the habit of appropriating emergency-response money in what are called "supplemental appropriations"—spending bills that come up outside the regular budget process. Outside of supplementals for military action, almost all such appropriations are for emergency response.

Indeed, the amount of money spent on disaster supplementals has been rising. In the 1990s, non-defense supplemental spending came to $22 billion and covered a variety of natural disasters, such as Hurricanes Hugo, Andrew, and Iniki; the Loma Prieta and Northridge earthquakes; and the Chicago floods; as well as two man-made emergencies, the Oklahoma City bombing and the Los Angeles riots. Such spending was a significant increase over the 1980s, but it pales in comparison to what has been spent in the first half of the first decade of the twenty-first century. Driven mostly by one man-made disaster (September 11) and one natural disaster (Hurricane Katrina), supplemental authority for non-defense spending from 2000 to 2005 is already more than $167 billion, or more than seven times as high as it was for the entire previous decade. The emergency supplementals for the September 11 disaster roughly equaled all spending by the Department of Education for 2004, and emergency supplementals for Hurricane Katrina were slightly higher than all spending by the Department of Agriculture in 2006. At this rate of growth, emergency-response spending will quickly devour what remains of the discretionary budget and dwarf appropriations for health, education, criminal justice, and a host of other programs.

When the bill for natural disasters exacts a pound of flesh from the federal budget, the pound of cure promised by prevention looks ever more appealing.

Attempts by conscientious members of Congress to actually put aside money for disasters have failed time and time again. And, for obvious good human reasons, the political will to place limits on aid to victims of disasters or to mitigate further disasters simply doesn't exist. The simple solution to this budgeting crisis is to appropriate, each and every year, money that would go into a kind of rainy day fund, protected from government spending and allowed to grow in years when there are no major emergencies. But the failure of calls for a similar protected fund—the once-maligned, now-pined-for Social Security "lock box"—does not offer much hope that this could actually be accomplished in the present political climate.

When the bill for natural disasters exacts a pound of flesh from the federal budget, the pound of cure promised by prevention looks ever more appealing. The most obvious solutions to the impending fiscal crisis are to take sensible, less costly steps to prevent disasters in the first place. Of course, such steps are often impossible in the absence of political courage and will. For instance, in the case of hurricanes, wetlands act as natural sponges, absorbing some of the shock of the ocean before it hits dry land. The New Orleans levees were built on the assumption that they would have 40 or 50 miles of protective swamp between the city and the Gulf of Mexico. But successive administrations at all levels of government have allowed for development on wetlands. Today, the Gulf of Mexico is 20 miles closer to land than it was in 1965, which makes hurricanes consequently more destructive. Thus one step in trying to reduce the destructiveness of natural disasters would be to protect wetlands, in contrast to the Bush Administration's policy of allowing development in these previously protected ecosystems.

The lack of political will to take such common-sense steps of mitigation will come back to haunt the federal taxpayer. The private insurance industry is not nearly as skeptical about global warming as is the Bush Administration. "The big European insurers and re-insurers—Lloyd's, Munich Re, Swiss Re and Allianz, for example—are vocal in calling for the industry to take the climate change threat seriously," says an article in *Reactions*, the magazine of the re-insurance industry. Since the private market is not subject to political pressures, it will not insure much of what used to be New Orleans. So it is left up to the National Flood Insurance Program, which, instead of living up to its promise to reduce flood damage, is knowingly using old maps that significantly underestimate the danger from flooding. The cost of this short-sighted political gamesmanship will be endured by all taxpayers.

Just as steps should be taken to "harden" potential targets of terrorist assault, we need policies that will invest government dollars and political capital in making environmentally sensitive areas less susceptible to natural disasters. Wetlands policies should be strengthened. Federal aid should be provided to move people out of flood plains, and the people who run the federal flood insurance program should be forced to take a much tougher look at the risk levels they are underwriting. And, of course, the most important thing we can do is to get serious about global warming. Since the United States contributes more to global warming than any other country, our leadership alone can make a significant difference in terms of the effect we can have and the example we can set.

It is tempting, of course, to look at the first five years of this decade as an aberration, to simply write off September 11 and Hurricane Katrina as extraordinary events—literally. In fact, Katrina and September 11 are only the beginning of what is likely to be a decade or more of enormous spending on disasters and disaster relief. It is easy to see emergency-response spending topping $200 billion in this decade and steadily increasing—eating what is left of the discretionary portion of the federal budget. By refusing to pay attention to the environment on the one hand and by waging a wasteful and ineffective war against terrorism on the other, we have all but guaranteed that emergency-response capabilities will become an ever larger and more important federal function.

Turning this around means mustering the political will to engage in serious prevention. This will not be an easy thing to do. It means telling Americans that they can no longer live in the places where they've lived before and giving them resources to relocate. It means getting serious about reducing global warming. And it means understanding that nothing will undermine our government and our way of life more than lurching from one catastrophe to another. In so many ways, the costs of Katrina are still being tallied. But if the cost of successive natural disasters is that of a government that is unable to act and innovate, it will be a price too large to bear.

ELAINE KAMARCK teaches at the John F. Kennedy School of Government at Harvard University. Prior to that she was Senior Policy Advisor to Vice President Al Gore, where she created and managed the Clinton Administration's reinventing government initiative.

Test Your Knowledge Form

We encourage you to photocopy and use this page as a tool to assess how the articles in *Annual Editions* expand on the information in your textbook. By reflecting on the articles you will gain enhanced text information. You can also access this useful form on a product's book support Web site at *http://www.mhcls.com/online/*.

NAME: _____   DATE: _____

TITLE AND NUMBER OF ARTICLE: _____

BRIEFLY STATE THE MAIN IDEA OF THIS ARTICLE:

_____

LIST THREE IMPORTANT FACTS THAT THE AUTHOR USES TO SUPPORT THE MAIN IDEA:

_____

WHAT INFORMATION OR IDEAS DISCUSSED IN THIS ARTICLE ARE ALSO DISCUSSED IN YOUR TEXTBOOK OR OTHER READINGS THAT YOU HAVE DONE? LIST THE TEXTBOOK CHAPTERS AND PAGE NUMBERS:

_____

LIST ANY EXAMPLES OF BIAS OR FAULTY REASONING THAT YOU FOUND IN THE ARTICLE:

_____

LIST ANY NEW TERMS/CONCEPTS THAT WERE DISCUSSED IN THE ARTICLE, AND WRITE A SHORT DEFINITION:

We Want Your Advice

ANNUAL EDITIONS revisions depend on two major opinion sources: one is our Advisory Board, listed in the front of this volume, which works with us in scanning the thousands of articles published in the public press each year; the other is you—the person actually using the book. Please help us and the users of the next edition by completing the prepaid article rating form on this page and returning it to us. Thank you for your help!

ANNUAL EDITIONS: Urban Society 13/e

ARTICLE RATING FORM

Here is an opportunity for you to have direct input into the next revision of this volume.
We would like you to rate each of the articles listed below, using the following scale:

1. **Excellent: should definitely be retained**
2. **Above average: should probably be retained**
3. **Below average: should probably be deleted**
4. **Poor: should definitely be deleted**

Your ratings will play a vital part in the next revision.
Please mail this prepaid form to us as soon as possible.
Thanks for your help!

RATING	ARTICLE	RATING	ARTICLE
	1. Fear of the City, 1783 to 1983		24. Rocking-Chair Revival
	2. The Death and Life of America's Cities		25. In New York City, Fewer Find They Can Make It
	3. Interview with Jane Jacobs		26. Winds of Change—Tale of a Warehouse Shows How Chicago Weathers a Decline
	4. Broken Windows		
	5. Back to the Fortress of Brooklyn and the Millions of Destroyed Men Who Are My Brothers		27. Bloomberg So Far
			28. Mayors and Morality: Daley and Lindsay Then and Now
	6. My L.A.		
	7. Chicago, City of Champions		29. Patio Man and the Sprawl People
	8. A Play at Contrition		30. Downtown Struggles While Neighbor Thrives
	9. The Rise of the Creative Class		31. Unscrambling the City
	10. Too Much Froth		32. Is Regional Government the Answer?
	11. Packaging Cities		33. Are Europe's Cities Better?
	12. Urban Warfare		34. How an Idea Drew People Back to Urban Life
	13. The Geography of Cool		35. Windows Not Broken
	14. The Best of Mates		36. Murder Mystery
	15. Return to Center		37. Police Line—Do Cross
	16. The Fall and Rise of Bryant Park		38. The Black Family—40 Years of Lies
	17. Ground Zero in Urban Decline		39. Big Cities Balk Over Illegal Migrants
	18. Saving Buffalo from Extinction		40. Segregation in New York Under a Different Name
	19. Movers and Shakers		41. An Inner-City Renaissance
	20. The Gentry, Misjudged As Neighbors		42. The Rise, Fall, and Rise Again of Public Housing
	21. Red Hook—Wounded by Good Intentions		43. A View from the South
	22. The Essence of Uptown		44. Debunking the Myths of Katrina
	23. In Parts of U.S. Northwest, a Changing Face		45. The Gathering Storm

URBAN SOCIETY, 13/e

ABOUT YOU

Name

Date

Are you a teacher? ☐ A student? ☐
Your school's name

Department

Address   City   State   Zip

School telephone #

YOUR COMMENTS ARE IMPORTANT TO US!

Please fill in the following information:
For which course did you use this book?

Did you use a text with this ANNUAL EDITION? ☐ yes ☐ no
What was the title of the text?

What are your general reactions to the Annual Editions concept?

Have you read any pertinent articles recently that you think should be included in the next edition? Explain.

Are there any articles that you feel should be replaced in the next edition? Why?

Are there any World Wide Web sites that you feel should be included in the next edition? Please annotate.

May we contact you for editorial input? ☐ yes ☐ no
May we quote your comments? ☐ yes ☐ no

GUN CONTROL
RESTRICTING RIGHTS OR PROTECTING PEOPLE?

DATE DUE

ISSN 1534-1909

GUN CONTROL
RESTRICTING RIGHTS OR PROTECTING PEOPLE?

Laurie DiMauro

INFORMATION PLUS® REFERENCE SERIES
Formerly Published by Information Plus, Wylie, Texas

GALE
CENGAGE Learning·

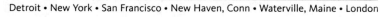

Detroit • New York • San Francisco • New Haven, Conn • Waterville, Maine • London

GALE
CENGAGE Learning®

Gun Control: Restricting Rights or Protecting
People?

Laurie DiMauro

Kepos Media, Inc.: Paula Kepos and Janice
Jorgensen, Series Editors

Project Editors: Kathleen J. Edgar, Elizabeth
    Manar, Kimberley McGrath

Rights Acquisition and Management: Margaret
    Chamberlain-Gaston

Composition: Evi Abou-El-Seoud, Mary Beth
    Trimper

Manufacturing: Rita Wimberley

For product information and technology assistance, contact us at
Gale Customer Support, 1-800-877-4253.
For permission to use material from this text or product,
submit all requests online at **www.cengage.com/permissions.**
Further permissions questions can be e-mailed to
permissionrequest@cengage.com

Cover photograph: © April Turner/Shutterstock.com.

Gale
27500 Drake Rd.
Farmington Hills, MI 48331-3535

ISBN-13: 978-0-7876-5103-9 (set)   ISBN-10: 0-7876-5103-6 (set)
ISBN-13: 978-1-4144-8143-2   ISBN-10: 1-4144-8143-8

ISSN 1534-1909

This title is also available as an e-book.
ISBN-13: 978-1-5730-2285-9 (set)
ISBN-10: 1-5730-2285-3 (set)
Contact your Gale sales representative for ordering information.

Printed in the United States of America
2 3 4 5 6   17 16 15 14 13

TABLE OF CONTENTS

PREFACE

Gun Control: Restricting Rights or Protecting People? is part of the *Information Plus Reference Series*. The purpose of each volume of the series is to present the latest facts on a topic of pressing concern in modern American life. These topics include the most controversial and studied social issues of the 21st century: abortion, capital punishment, care for the elderly, child abuse, crime, energy, the environment, health care, immigration, minorities, national security, social welfare, women, youth, and many more. Even though this series is written especially for high school and undergraduate students, it is an excellent resource for anyone in need of factual information on current affairs.

By presenting the facts, it is the intention of Gale, Cengage Learning to provide its readers with everything they need to reach an informed opinion on current issues. To that end, there is a particular emphasis in this series on the presentation of scientific studies, surveys, and statistics. These data are generally presented in the form of tables, charts, and other graphics placed within the text of each book. Every graphic is directly referred to and carefully explained in the text. The source of each graphic is presented within the graphic itself. The data used in these graphics are drawn from the most reputable and reliable sources, such as from the various branches of the U.S. government and from private organizations and associations. Every effort has been made to secure the most recent information available. Readers should bear in mind that many major studies take years to conduct and that additional years often pass before the data from these studies are made available to the public. Therefore, in many cases the most recent information available in 2013 is dated from 2010 or 2011. Older statistics are sometimes presented as well, if they are landmark studies or of particular interest and no more-recent information exists.

Although statistics are a major focus of the *Information Plus Reference Series*, they are by no means its only content. Each book also presents the widely held positions and important ideas that shape how the book's subject is discussed in the United States. These positions are explained in detail and, where possible, in the words of their proponents. Some of the other material to be found in these books includes historical background, descriptions of major events related to the subject, relevant laws and court cases, and examples of how these issues play out in American life. Some books also feature primary documents or have pro and con debate sections that provide the words and opinions of prominent Americans on both sides of a controversial topic. All material is presented in an evenhanded and unbiased manner; readers will never be encouraged to accept one view of an issue over another.

HOW TO USE THIS BOOK

Gun control is a topic that elicits passionate emotions. On one side are those who believe that guns should be banned or restricted because they are too often used to commit crimes and many innocent lives are lost because of their misuse. This side contends that there is no longer a compelling need for "people to keep and bear arms" as there was at the birth of this nation. On the other side are arrayed those who believe that gun ownership is an individual right guaranteed by the Second Amendment and not to be infringed, as well as that guns are vital for self-protection.

Gun Control: Restricting Rights or Protecting People? consists of 10 chapters and four appendixes. Each chapter is devoted to a particular aspect of gun control in the United States. For a summary of the information covered in each chapter, please see the synopses provided in the Table of Contents. Chapters generally begin with an overview of the basic facts and background information on the chapter's topic, then proceed to examine subtopics of particular interest. For example, Chapter 5: Firearms and Crime begins with an overview of statistics on the frequency and ways in which guns are used to commit crimes. The chapter then presents data on firearm homicides, including sections on murder weapons, circumstances, and the age, race, and gender of both homicide victims and offenders. The chapter then discusses how the nature of firearms allows perpetrators to keep physically and mentally distant from victims, a feature that makes guns a suitable weapon for those intent on multiple-homicides or mass murders such as the shooting at the Century Aurora theater in Aurora, Colorado, in July 2012 that killed 12 and wounded 58 others. Chapter 5 also provides information on the use of firearms in other violent crimes, such as robbery or aggravated assault, and on shootings in the workplace or at school. (Chapter 7 includes additional information on school shootings, including coverage of major events of this type from 1998 through 2012.) Statistics in Chapter 5 address the demographics of firearm victimization and an examination of what is known about where criminals get their guns, including a subsection on Operation Fast and Furious, the controversial federal program that allowed an estimated 2,200 firearms to be trafficked illegally from the United States into Mexico between 2009 and 2011. Other sections in Chapter 5 bring together information on firearm deaths and injuries to law enforcement officers, justifiable homicides involving firearms, and police initiatives to reduce the number of illegal guns on the streets. Readers can find their way through a chapter by looking for the section and subsection headings, which are clearly set off from the text. They can also refer to the book's extensive Index if they already know what they are looking for.

Statistical Information

The tables and figures featured throughout *Gun Control: Restricting Rights or Protecting People?* will be of particular use to readers in learning about this issue. These tables and figures represent an extensive collection of the most recent and important statistics on gun ownership, gun violence, and gun control legislation, as well as the trends—for example, graphics outline the percentage of Americans who own various types of firearms, the number and result of criminal background checks under the Brady gun control laws, and a demographic breakdown of firearm-related deaths from 1970 to 2009. Gale, Cengage Learning believes that making this information available to readers is the most important way to fulfill the goal of this book: to help readers understand the issues and controversies surrounding gun control in the United States and reach their own conclusions.

Each table or figure has a unique identifier appearing above it, for ease of identification and reference. Titles for the tables and figures explain their purpose. At the end of each table or figure, the original source of the data is provided.

To help readers understand these often complicated statistics, all tables and figures are explained in the text. References in the text direct readers to the relevant statistics. Furthermore, the contents of all tables and figures are fully indexed. Please see the opening section of the Index at the back of this volume for a description of how to find tables and figures within it.

Appendixes

Besides the main body text and images, *Gun Control: Restricting Rights or Protecting People?* has four appendixes. The first appendix lists the 50 states and cites the specific articles of the 44 states that have constitutional provisions regarding weapons. The second appendix is the Important Names and Addresses directory. Here, readers will find contact information for a number of government and private organizations that can provide further information on aspects of gun control. The third appendix is the Resources section, which can also assist readers in conducting their own research. In this section, the author and editors of *Gun Control: Restricting Rights or Protecting People?* describe some of the sources that were most useful during the compilation of this book. The final appendix is the Index. It has been greatly expanded from previous editions and should make it even easier to find specific topics in this book.

ADVISORY BOARD CONTRIBUTIONS

The staff of Information Plus would like to extend its heartfelt appreciation to the Information Plus Advisory Board. This dedicated group of media professionals provides feedback on the series on an ongoing basis. Their comments allow the editorial staff who work on the project to continually make the series better and more user-friendly. The staff's top priority is to produce the highest-quality and most useful books possible, and the Information Plus Advisory Board's contributions to this process are invaluable.

The members of the Information Plus Advisory Board are:

- Kathleen R. Bonn, Librarian, Newbury Park High School, Newbury Park, California
- Madelyn Garner, Librarian, San Jacinto College, North Campus, Houston, Texas
- Anne Oxenrider, Media Specialist, Dundee High School, Dundee, Michigan
- Charles R. Rodgers, Director of Libraries, Pasco-Hernando Community College, Dade City, Florida
- James N. Zitzelsberger, Library Media Department Chairman, Oshkosh West High School, Oshkosh, Wisconsin

COMMENTS AND SUGGESTIONS

The editors of the *Information Plus Reference Series* welcome your feedback on *Gun Control: Restricting Rights or Protecting People?* Please direct all correspondence to:

Editors
Information Plus Reference Series
27500 Drake Rd.
Farmington Hills, MI 48331-3535

CHAPTER 1
THE HISTORY OF THE RIGHT TO BEAR ARMS

The right to bear arms has long been an American tradition. From the time colonists settled on North American soil, Americans have held weapons to protect themselves. Armed citizen-soldiers won America's freedom from English rule more than two centuries ago. Partly because of this long-standing tradition, attempts to restrict a citizen's right to own a gun evoke strong emotions.

The modern debate over gun control erupted after a series of high-profile assassinations during the 1960s, including the assassinations of President John F. Kennedy (1917–1963), the civil rights leader Martin Luther King Jr. (1929–1968), and Senator Robert F. Kennedy (1925–1968). In the decades that followed, the debate gained new urgency as gun-related violence continued to increase. The Bureau of Justice Statistics indicates in "Homicide Trends in the United States" (June 17, 2010, http://bjs.ojp.usdoj.gov/content/homicide/weapons.cfm) that gun-related homicides rose sharply in the late 1970s and peaked in 1980, and that the number of homicides rose again beginning in the late 1980s and peaked in the mid-1990s. Even though gun-related homicides dropped after the mid-1990s' peak, shootings such as the 1999 massacre at Columbine High School in Colorado, the 2007 gun rampage at Virginia Polytechnic Institute and State University, the shooting spree at Fort Hood, Texas, in 2009, and three 2012 attacks (at a movie theater in Aurora, Colorado; a shopping mall near Portland, Oregon; and an elementary school in Newtown, Connecticut) keep the issue of gun control in the forefront of the collective American consciousness.

At the heart of the gun control debate is the interpretation of the Second Amendment to the U.S. Constitution. One side claims that gun ownership is an individual right guaranteed by the Second Amendment and that guns are vital for self-protection. The other side believes guns should be banned or restricted because many innocent lives are lost due to their misuse. Gun control advocates say there is no longer a compelling need for people to "keep and bear arms" as there was when the Constitution was ratified in 1788. They sometimes add the argument that the constitutionally guaranteed right was never meant to apply to individuals. Regardless, Table 1.1 shows that the majority (74%) of Americans in 2010 understood the Second Amendment as supporting an individual's right to bear arms, either independent of (43%) or in conjunction with a state's right to form a militia (31%).

The right of the individual to keep and use weapons has a long tradition in Western civilization. The Greek philosopher Aristotle (384–322 BC) wrote in *Politics* that ownership of weapons was necessary for true citizenship and participation in the political system. By contrast, another Greek philosopher, Plato (428–348 BC), wrote in the *Republic* that he believed in a monarchy with few liberties and saw the disarming of the populace as essential to the maintenance of an orderly and autocratic system. The Roman politician Marcus Tullius Cicero (106–43 BC) wrote in *De Officiis* of his support of bearing arms for self-defense of the individual and for public defense against tyranny. The Italian political philosopher Niccolò Machiavelli (1469–1527) advocated in *Discourse* an armed populace of citizen-soldiers to keep headstrong rulers in line.

AN EARLY PRECEDENT: MILITIAS AND THE OWNERSHIP OF WEAPONS

One of the first documents to link the bearing of arms with a militia (an army composed of citizens called to action in time of emergency) was the English *Assize of Arms* of 1181, which directed every free man to have access to weaponry. Henry II of England (1133–1189) signed this law to enable the rapid creation of a militia when needed, but the law also permitted carrying arms in self-defense and forbade the use of arms only when the intention was to "terrify the King's subjects." In 1328,

TABLE 1.1

Poll respondents' views on the meaning of the Second Amendment, 2008 and 2010

"THE SECOND AMENDMENT OF THE U.S. CONSTITUTION READS: "A WELL REGULATED MILITIA BEING NECESSARY TO THE SECURITY OF A FREE STATE, THE RIGHT OF THE PEOPLE TO KEEP AND BEAR ARMS SHALL NOT BE INFRINGED." WHICH OF THE FOLLOWING DO YOU BELIEVE THE SECOND AMENDMENT SUPPORTS?"

| | 2008 | 2010 | Political party | | | Own guns | |
			Rep.	Dem.	Ind.	Yes	No
	%	%	%	%	%	%	%
An individual's right to bear arms	41	43	53	38	44	51	37
A State's right to form a militia	17	13	6	19	13	7	17
Neither	5	5	2	9	4	2	8
Both	29	31	34	24	33	35	29
Not sure	7	8	4	10	5	4	10

Note: Percentages may not add to 100% because of rounding.

SOURCE: David Krane, "Table 4. Meaning of Second Amendment," in *Americans Should Be Allowed to Have Guns, Say Large Majorities*, The Harris Poll, June 16, 2010, http://www.harrisinteractive.com/vault/HI-Harris-Poll-Gun-Control-2010-06-16.pdf (accessed August 27, 2012)

under the reign of King Edward III (1312–1377), Parliament enacted the Statute of Northampton, which prohibited the carrying of arms in public places but did not overrule the right to carry arms in self-defense.

EARLY GUN CONTROL LAWS

The 17th century was a period of great turmoil in England as Parliament and the monarchy struggled for control of the government. When a series of civil wars erupted in 1642, a critical issue was whether the king or Parliament had the right to control the militia. When the wars ended in early 1660, England fell briefly under the control of a military government, which authorized its officers to search for and seize all arms owned by Catholics or any other person deemed dangerous. In late 1660 the English monarchy was restored with the coronation of Charles II (1630–1685), but the battle between Parliament and the monarchy continued.

The Game Act of 1671, an early example of a gun control law, was enacted to keep the ownership of hunting lands and weaponry in the hands of the wealthy and to restrict hunting and gun ownership among the peasants. People without an annual income of at least 40 to 100 pounds could no longer keep weapons, even for self-defense. In 1689 Queen Mary II (1662–1694) and King William III (1650–1702) were installed as corulers of England. When the pair took their oaths of office, they were presented with a new Bill of Rights (2008, http://avalon.law.yale.edu/17th_century/england.asp), which outlined the relationship of Parliament and the monarchy to the people. This Bill of Rights included a specific right of "Protestants [to] arms for their defence suitable to their conditions and as allowed by law." It also condemned abuses committed by standing armies (armies maintained by the government on a long-term basis, even while at peace) and declared "that the raising or keeping a standing army within the kingdom in time of peace, unless it be with consent of Parliament, is against law." Furthermore, the

Bill of Rights removed the word *guns* from the list of items the poor were forbidden to own by the Game Act of 1671. From this time on, the right to keep and bear arms belonged to all Englishmen, whether rich or poor.

THE AMERICAN MILITIA AND THE RIGHT TO BEAR ARMS

Much of U.S. law is rooted in the system of laws developed in England (called common law) because most American colonists came from England, bringing with them English values, traditions, and legal concepts. Many of the English were familiar with the famous judge Sir William Blackstone (1723–1780), who listed in his *Commentaries* (2000, http://press-pubs.uchicago.edu/founders/documents/v1ch16s5.html) the "right of having and using arms for self-preservation and defense." This right, brought to North America by the English, was exercised by the colonists against the English during the Revolutionary War and was later incorporated into the U.S. Constitution.

During the mid-18th century an increasing British military presence in the colonies alerted colonists to the danger of a standing army. When British soldiers shot and killed five men on the streets of Boston in 1770, an event that became known as the Boston Massacre, colonists grew further concerned. The Boston Massacre became a milestone on the road to the Revolutionary War. In 1775 the British army encountered the Massachusetts militia at Lexington—famously recalled in "Concord Hymn" by the poet Ralph Waldo Emerson (1803–1882) as "the shot heard round the world"—and the ensuing seizure of colonial arms and munitions convinced other colonies that a militia was necessary to achieve the "security of a free state."

Because the individual colonies did not have enough money to purchase weapons, each man was required to maintain a firearm so he could report immediately for duty and form a militia. It was taken for granted by the colonists that the right to individually possess and bear arms was inseparable from the right to form a militia—without these privileges, the right to organize a militia would have little meaning. Thomas Jefferson (1743–1826) stated, "No freeman shall be debarred the use of arms (within his own lands or tenements)," and Richard Henry Lee (1732–1794) of Virginia observed that "to preserve liberty, it is essential that the whole body of the people always possess arms."

In *The Federalist, No. 29* ([January 9, 1788] November 11, 2011, http://www.constitution.org/fed/fedea29.htm), one of a series of papers written after the Revolutionary War to convince the colonists to ratify the Constitution, Alexander Hamilton (1755?–1804) spoke of the right to bear arms in the sense of an unorganized militia, which consisted of the "people at large." He suggested that this militia could mobilize against a standing army if the army usurped the government's authority or if it supported a tyrannical government. Such a standing army, declared Hamilton, could "never be formidable to the liberties of the people while there is a large body of citizens, little, if at all, inferior to them in discipline and the use of arms, who stand ready to defend their own rights and those of their fellow-citizens."

James Madison (1751–1836) attributed the colonial victory to armed citizens. In *The Federalist, No. 46* ([January 29, 1788] November 11, 2011, http://www.constitution.org/fed/federa46.htm), he wrote, "Besides the advantage of being armed, which the Americans possess over the people of almost every other nation, the existence of subordinate governments, to which the people are attached, and by which the militia officers are appointed, forms a barrier against the enterprises of ambition, more insurmountable than any which a simple government of any form can admit of. Notwithstanding the military establishments in the several kingdoms of Europe, which are carried as far as the public resources will bear, the governments are afraid to trust the people with arms."

THE U.S. CONSTITUTION, THE RIGHT TO BEAR ARMS, AND THE MILITIA

The Revolutionary War ended in 1783. In 1787, 39 men gathered in Philadelphia, Pennsylvania, to sign the newly written Constitution. Three refused to sign because the document did not include a Bill of Rights. One reluctant signer protested that, without a Bill of Rights, Congress "at their pleasure may arm or disarm all or any part of the freemen of the United States."

By 1791 James Madison had written the 10 amendments to the Constitution that became known as the Bill of Rights. He was influenced by state bills of rights and many amendment suggestions from the state conventions that ratified the Constitution. Overall, four basic beliefs were assimilated into the Second Amendment: the right of the individual to possess arms, the fear of a professional army, the dependence on militias regulated by the individual states, and the control of the military by civilians.

According to the Constitution Society in *Documents on the First Congress Debate on Arms and Militia* (February 25, 2005, http://www.constitution.org/mil/militia_debate_1789.htm), the ratifying state conventions offered similar suggestions about the militia and the right to bear arms. Even though New Hampshire did not mention the militia, it did state that "no standing Army shall be Kept up in time of Peace unless with the consent of three-fourths of the Members of each branch of Congress, nor shall Soldiers in Time of Peace be Quartered upon private Houses without the consent of the Owners."

Another New Hampshire amendment read, "Congress shall never disarm any Citizen unless such as are or have been in Actual Rebellion." Maryland proposed five separate amendments, which Virginia consolidated by stating: "That the people have a right to keep and bear arms; that a well regulated Militia composed of the body of the people trained to arms is the proper, natural and safe defence of a free State. That standing armies in time of peace are dangerous to liberty, and therefore ought to be avoided, as far as the circumstances and protection of the Community will admit; and that in all cases the military should be under strict subordination to and governed by the Civil power."

The New York convention offered more than 50 amendments, including the following: "That the People have a right to keep and bear Arms; that a well regulated Militia, including the body of the People capable of bearing Arms, is the proper, natural and safe defence of a free State."

As early as 1776 Congress had advised the colonies to form new governments "such as shall best conduce to the happiness and safety of their constituents." Within a year after the Declaration of Independence was signed, nearly every state had drawn up a new constitution. The constitutions of several states guaranteed the rights of individuals to bear arms but forbade the maintenance of a standing army. In *State Constitutional Right to Keep and Bear Arms Provisions, by Date* (April 18, 2008, http://www.law.ucla.edu/volokh/beararms/statedat.htm), Eugene Volokh of the University of California, Los Angeles, notes that Pennsylvania's constitution ensured "that the people have a right to bear arms, for the defence of the State; and, as standing armies, in time of peace, are dangerous to liberty, they ought not to be kept up; and that the military should be kept under strict subordination to, and governed by, the civil power."

Because of their fear of tyranny and repression by a standing army, the colonists preferred state militias to provide protection and order. Such militias could also act as counterbalances against any national standing army. Some people believe that the individual right to bear arms was guaranteed by state laws providing for a militia made up of people trained to use arms.

The Bill of Rights was adopted in 1791. The Second Amendment states: "A well regulated Militia, being necessary to the security of a free State, the right of the people to keep and bear Arms, shall not be infringed."

THE MODERN DEBATE

Efforts to control gun ownership are usually a response to gun-related violence. An effort to decrease crime in the early 1930s led to an unsuccessful attempt by President Franklin D. Roosevelt (1882–1945) to pass legislation requiring the registration of handguns. Nonetheless, the National Firearms Act was passed in 1934, which imposed a tax on the manufacture and sale of "Title II weapons" and mandated the registration of those weapons. Title II weapons include machine guns, short-barreled rifles, short-barreled shotguns, destructive devices (such as grenades), and a catchall category that includes novelty devices such as pen guns and cane guns. It did not, however, include handguns. Table 1.2 lists the types of firearms used in crime and defines many of the types of weapons mentioned here.

The next major piece of gun control legislation—the Gun Control Act of 1968—was passed after the assassinations of King and Senator Kennedy. As of October 2012, the Gun Control Act of 1968 comprised the Title I portion of the U.S. federal firearms laws, and the National Firearms Act comprised the Title II portion. Title I has provisions that include requiring serial numbers on all guns, setting standards for gun dealers, prohibiting mail-order and interstate sales of firearms, prohibiting the importation of guns not used for sporting purposes, and setting penalties for carrying and using firearms in crimes of violence or drug trafficking. It also prohibits certain categories of people, such as convicted felons, drug addicts, illegal aliens, and minors, from buying or possessing firearms. However, there was no efficient national system for carrying out background checks until the Brady Handgun Violence Prevention Act was passed in 1993.

The Brady Handgun Violence Prevention Act (the Brady law) was named for James S. Brady (1940–), an official in the administration of President Ronald Reagan (1911–2004). Brady was shot during a 1981 assassination attempt on the president. The Brady law imposed a five-day waiting period on handgun purchases and a background check on buyers to determine whether they were illegal aliens or had a history of criminal behavior, mental illness, or drug use. It required state and local law enforcement agencies to carry out the background checks until a national system could be established. These early background checks were never carried out to any great

TABLE 1.2

Types of firearms used in crime

Types	
Handgun	A weapon designed to fire a small projectile from one or more barrels when held in one hand with a short stock designed to be gripped by one hand.
Revolver	A handgun that contains its ammunition in a revolving cylinder that typically holds five to nine cartridges, each within a separate chamber. Before a revolver fires, the cylinder rotates, and the next chamber is aligned with the barrel.
Pistol	Any handgun that does not contain its ammunition in a revolving cylinder. Pistols can be manually operated or semiautomatic. A semiautomatic pistol generally contains cartridges in a magazine located in the grip of the gun. When the semiautomatic pistol is fired, the spent cartridge that contained the bullet and propellant is ejected, the firing mechanism is cocked, and a new cartridge is chambered.
Derringer	A small single- or multiple-shot handgun other than a revolver or semiautomatic pistol.
Rifle	A weapon intended to be fired from the shoulder that uses the energy of the explosive in a fixed metallic cartridge to fire only a single projectile through a rifled bore for each single pull of the trigger.
Shotgun	A weapon intended to be fired from the shoulder that uses the energy of the explosive in a fixed shotgun shell to fire through a smooth bore either a number of ball shot or a single projectile for each single pull of the trigger.
Firing action	
Fully automatic	Capability to fire a succession of cartridges so long as the trigger is depressed or until the ammunition supply is exhausted. Automatic weapons are considered machine guns subject to the provisions of the National Firearms Act.
Semiautomatic	An autoloading action that will fire only a single shot for each single function of a trigger.
Machine gun	Any weapon that shoots, is designed to shoot, or can be readily restored to shoot automatically more than one shot without manual reloading by a single function of the trigger.
Submachine gun	A simple fully automatic weapon that fires a pistol cartridge that is also referred to as a machine pistol.
Ammunition	
Caliber	The size of the ammunition that a weapon is designed to shoot, as measured by the bullet's approximate diameter in inches in the United States and in millimeters in other countries. In some instances, ammunition is described with additional terms, such as the year of its introduction (.30/06) or the name of the designer (.30 Newton). In some countries, ammunition is also described in terms of the length of the cartridge case (7.62×63 mm).
Gauge	For shotguns, the number of spherical balls of pure lead, each exactly fitting the bore, that equals one pound.

SOURCE: Marianne W. Zawitz, "What Are the Different Types of Firearms?" in *Guns Used in Crime*, U.S. Department of Justice, Office of Justice Programs, Bureau of Justice Statistics, July 1995, http://bjs.ojp.usdoj.gov/content/pub/pdf/GUIC.PDF (accessed August 17, 2012)

extent because Congress did not provide the funds, and in 1997 the requirement was found unconstitutional by the U.S. Supreme Court under the 10th Amendment (states' rights). The court stated in *Printz v. United States* (521 U.S. 898) that the federal government had no right to order state and local law enforcement agencies to carry out federal programs.

The five-day waiting period and the background check requirement were eventually replaced by a national database for background checks, which became effective on November 30, 1998, and was still effective as of October 2012. Known as the National Instant Criminal

Background Check System (NICS), this computerized system is managed by the Federal Bureau of Investigation (FBI). It is used to perform background checks on people seeking to buy handguns or long guns from federal firearms licensees. (Commonly referred to as an FFL, a federal firearms license is usually required for anyone selling a firearm.) In *National Instant Criminal Background Check System (NICS): Operations 2010* (August 9, 2012, www.fbi.gov/about-us/cjis/nics/reports/2010-operations-report/2010-operations-report-pdf), the FBI reports that by December 31, 2010, the system had completed a total of 124.4 million background checks; in 91.3% of cases the results of background checks were available within seconds to minutes of the data entry.

"Collective Rights" versus "Individual Rights"

The modern debate over gun control is described by Robert J. Spitzer in *The Politics of Gun Control* (2008) as a split between a "collective rights" interpretation and an "individual rights" interpretation of the Second Amendment. Spitzer, a professor of political science at the State University of New York at Cortland, calls the Second Amendment a "touchstone of the gun debate."

Proponents of the collective rights argument favor stricter control of guns. They point to the opening words of the Second Amendment—"A well regulated militia, being necessary to the security of a free state"—as an indication that the amendment was intended to guarantee the right of states to maintain militias. They argue that since colonial times the concept of a citizens' militia has fallen from use, having been replaced by the National Guard. By this view, the general population does not need unfettered access to guns, as they are no longer expected to form a militia during times of need.

In contrast, proponents of the individual rights argument hold that individuals have a right to keep and bear arms. Opponents of extensive gun control add that the phrase "right of the people" is used in the Second Amendment, as well as in other amendments in the Bill of Rights, and in each case it refers to a right of individuals. Courts have ruled in favor of both interpretations.

In November 2001 the U.S. Court of Appeals for the Fifth Circuit held in *United States v. Emerson* (No. 99-10331) that the Second Amendment protects the right of individuals to "privately possess and bear their own firearms." Conversely, in December 2002 the U.S. Court of Appeals for the Ninth Circuit ruled in *Silveira v. Lockyer* (No. 01-15098) that the Second Amendment does not grant Americans a personal right to carry firearms. The court's ruling said that the purpose of the Second Amendment was to maintain effective state militias. In December 2003 the U.S. Supreme Court declined to hear a challenge of this ruling, leaving the question of gun ownership rights in limbo. Then in

November 2007 the High Court announced that it would hear an appeal involving the constitutionality of a District of Columbia law banning the use or possession of all handguns. *District of Columbia v. Heller* (554 U.S. ___ [2008]) was argued in March 2008. In June 2008 the U.S. Supreme Court ruled in a 5–4 decision that the Second Amendment guarantees individuals the right to bear arms. This ruling affected federal jurisdictions only, but in June 2010, with the ruling in *McDonald v. Chicago* (561 U.S. ___ [2010]), the High Court extended the same interpretation of the Second Amendment to include state and local jurisdictions.

Is Handgun Control Unconstitutional?

With the guarantee of the right to bear arms, however, came a provision for gun control legislation. The majority opinion in *Heller*, written by Justice Antonin Scalia (1936–), noted that "it is not a right to keep and carry any weapon whatsoever in any manner whatsoever and for whatever purpose." For example, the District of Columbia requires that firearms be registered and bans the carrying of guns in public, both openly and concealed. Keeping a loaded gun in one's home is legal. The provision for gun control legislation applies to state and local jurisdictions in the *McDonald v. Chicago* ruling as it does to federal jurisdictions in *Heller*.

Nonetheless, gun control legislation is surrounded by disagreement. Handguns are a particular point of contention in the gun control debate because they are seen as the weapon of choice for criminals. Advocates of gun rights point out, however, that upstanding citizens use handguns for self-defense and argue that any attempt to control handgun use is unconstitutional. Those opposing this argument reply that no gun control legislation—including legislation affecting handguns—has ever been declared unconstitutional by the Supreme Court under the Second Amendment.

Arguments for and against Gun Control

One of the key issues in the debate over gun control is whether placing greater restrictions on gun ownership will make society safer. Many opponents of extensive gun control think that access to guns makes it possible for law-abiding Americans to protect themselves and deter crime. By contrast, proponents of extensive gun control hold that Americans infrequently use guns for this purpose.

Estimates vary widely as to the number of times handguns are used in self-defense annually. In their study *Tough Targets: When Criminals Face Armed Resistance* (2012, http://www.cato.org/publications/white-paper/tough-targets-when-criminals-face-armed-resistance-citizens), coauthors Clayton E. Cramer of the College of Western Idaho and David Burnett of the organization Students for Concealed Carry note that "estimates of defensive gun use range between the tens of thousands to as high as two million each year." Estimating self-defense uses is complicated, they argue, because many cases are never reported. Cramer and Burnett explain that "when a gun is simply brandished, criminals often flee the scene and are not apprehended. With no shot fired, no injuries, and no suspect in custody, news organizations sometimes report nothing at all."

In one of the most cited studies of the topic, *Armed: New Perspectives on Gun Control* (2001), Gary Kleck and Don Kates provide a scholarly and wide-ranging review and analysis of the studies on the use of guns and self-defense. They conclude that "the best survey on defensive gun use frequency indicates 2.55 million defensive gun uses a year in the United States…and this estimate has been repeatedly confirmed by all surveys of comparable technical merit. Until a methodologically better national survey yields a substantially different estimate, honest scholars will have to continue to accept, however tentatively, that millions of Americans use guns for self-protection each year." As a result, Kleck and Kates reject the "rare-defensive gun use theory" of gun control proponents. They support moderate gun control measures, such as background checks for those purchasing guns, but oppose the prohibition of gun ownership.

The statistics appear to indicate that millions of Americans use guns to defend themselves annually, and gun rights advocates suggest that more violent crimes are stopped by guns than are committed by guns. Advocates of extensive gun control or gun prohibition argue that the defensive use of handguns does not offset the offensive use of handguns by criminals, which accounts for thousands of deaths and hundreds of thousands of injuries annually. Spitzer, a gun control advocate, notes that "on an individual level, a gun in the hand of a victim can thwart or stop a crime. On an aggregate level, however, more guns mean more gun problems, even though many citizens believe that guns make them safer."

Gun control advocates point out that guns are often used to commit suicide or are involved in accidental shootings, especially involving children. Gun rights advocates often counter that even if guns were not available, suicides and accidental deaths would still happen. People who use guns to commit suicide may also commit this act in other ways, such as with poison or by hanging. Children who are accidentally shot and killed can also die in car accidents or by drinking toxic chemicals in the home, yet no background check or waiting period is required for the purchase of cars or toxic household chemicals. The right to keep and bear these items is not constitutionally protected, they argue, and society might be safer without them as well. Spitzer counters by noting that "the suicide rate among the adult population would probably undergo a measurable reduction without guns because some would not seek other methods, and guns

are more lethal than other suicide methods." However, he admits that reducing the availability of guns would have only a modest effect on gun accidents.

Spitzer also contends that gun proliferation among law-abiding citizens will start an arms race with criminals, who will upgrade their weapons and be more willing to use them to kill. This, Spitzer believes, will inevitably result in an increase in gun-related crimes and accidents. Indeed, some law enforcement officers claim they are already outgunned by criminals with more powerful weapons.

The Second Amendment Foundation, a nonprofit group that promotes the right to bear arms, counters that just because the quality of handguns, like most consumer products, has improved is no reason to override the Second Amendment. Furthermore, it does not believe that stricter gun control measures will actually keep weapons out of the hands of criminals. The foundation argues that law-abiding citizens would be perilously exposed to lawbreakers if the government interpreted the Second Amendment to control or restrict gun use. Their access to guns through legal channels would become limited, whereas criminals would continue to acquire weapons through illegal means.

Spitzer argues that in the interest of national security a compromise must be reached between those who favor gun control and those who favor gun rights. He suggests that citizens should not have access to assault weapons, that access to handguns should be limited, and that ownership of hunting and sporting weapons should be protected.

Approaching Gun Violence as a Public Health Issue

In *Private Guns, Public Health* (2006), David Hemenway suggests approaching the issue of gun control as a public health concern. He contends, "Considering that each year tens of thousands of Americans die from gunshot wounds, the reduction of firearm injuries—and the reduction of the accompanying dread and fear of firearm violence—is clearly within the purview of public health."

Hemenway compares gun violence to major public health issues of the 20th century, such as tuberculosis, tobacco use, and motor vehicle safety. In all these instances the government at the national, state, and local levels mobilized in varying degrees to rally political and social support to effectively address the problems. Hemenway outlines several goals of a public health approach to gun violence, including:

• Add new analytic tools, new research sources, and professionals from public health and medical communities to gather scientific knowledge about gun violence and to create programs to combat it.

- Mobilize national, state, and local governmental and non-governmental agencies to work to reduce gun violence.

- Create a new government agency that is empowered to regulate firearms as a consumer product and to maintain a national death-data system that will track gun fatalities of all types.

- Strengthen the systematic effort to stop the supply of guns to criminals through gun tracing and other methods, instead of focusing only on locking up criminals after a crime is committed.

- License and register all gun owners, thus allowing officials to track all legal firearm transfers.

- Change the belief that gun violence is a part of the national culture and cannot be altered.

To reduce the problem of gun violence, Hemenway proposes a public health approach that uses multiple strategies and many partners. He concludes that the public health approach is ideally suited to deal with gun violence: "Public health emphasizes prevention rather than fault-finding, blame, or revenge. It uses science rather than belief as its basis and relies on accurate data collection and scientific analysis. It promotes a wide variety of interventions—environmental as well as individual—and integrates the activities of a wide variety of disciplines and institutions. Most important, public health brings a pragmatic [practical] attitude to problems—finding innovative solutions and eliminating the fatalistic and complacent beliefs that little can be done to reduce the problem."

CHAPTER 2
HOW MANY GUNS ARE THERE, AND WHO OWNS THEM?

OWNERSHIP BY PRIVATE CITIZENS

There Can Only Be Estimates

"How many guns are there?" is a question that cannot be answered with exact figures for the United States due to differences among the states. Each has its own system of counting and classifying guns. Some states do not require registration of guns, and unregistered guns cannot be included in an official count. In addition, some types of gun data are restricted from public access. The result is that there can only be estimates of the total number of guns that U.S. residents possess.

The ATF Estimates

The Bureau of Alcohol, Tobacco, Firearms, and Explosives (ATF) is a law enforcement organization in charge of reducing violent crime, among other tasks. One of its duties is to keep firearms out of the hands of criminals. The ATF is also responsible for estimating the total number of firearms in the United States. It does this by adding domestic firearms production and imports since 1899, then subtracting firearms exports during the same period. The ATF does not take into account guns that are destroyed or that no longer work. The ATF statistics also do not account for guns that are smuggled into or out of the United States or guns that are manufactured illegally.

According to the ATF, in *Firearms Commerce in the United States—2001/2002* (2002), from 1899 to 1999 an estimated 248 million guns became available for sale in the United States (not including those produced for the military). This number included more than 87 million rifles, 86 million handguns, and 72 million shotguns. The ATF estimates that there were 1.5 million guns produced in the United States in 1950, 3.7 million in 1970, 5.6 million in 1980, 3.8 million in 1990, and 4 million in 1999. The ATF data suggest that the number of imported rifles, shotguns, and handguns combined averaged 1 million per year during the 1990s, with handguns

accounting for roughly half of that figure. Exports averaged fewer than 400,000 per year. Putting all estimates together, by the end of 1999 the total number of guns privately owned or available for sale in the United States came to approximately 260 million.

No further published reports from the ATF on the number of guns in the United States were available as of October 2012. However, Table 2.1, Table 2.2, and Table 2.3 provide statistics from the ATF on the number of firearms manufactured (42.8 million from 2000 to 2010), firearms imported (23.8 million from 2000 to 2010), and firearms exported (2.2 million from 2000 to 2010). Using these data and using 260 million guns as a baseline for 1999, there were about 324.4 million guns privately owned or available for sale in the United States by the end of 2010. Table 2.2 shows an additional year of data for firearm imports, bringing the total number of guns in the United States to at least 327.7 million in 2011.

THE TIAHRT AMENDMENT: RESTRICTING PUBLIC ACCESS TO GUN INFORMATION. Even though the ATF expected to report annually on firearms commerce (the buying and selling of guns), *Firearms Commerce in the United States—2001/2002* was the last such document published. Beginning in 2003 the ATF was legally prohibited from publishing certain statistics concerning the production and imports of firearms under an amendment sponsored by Representative Todd Tiahrt (1951–; R-KS). The amendment, which was approved as part of legislation that provided funding for the Departments of Commerce, Justice, and State, also made it illegal for the agency to report on sales of multiple handguns and firearms tracing statistics (gun trace statistics).

The concept of gun trace statistics is explained by the ATF in the fact sheet "ATF's National Tracing Center" (March 2010, http://www.atf.gov/publications/factsheets/factsheet-national-tracing-center.html): "Firearms tracing is the systematic tracking of the movement of a recovered

TABLE 2.1

Firearms manufactured, 1986–2010

Calendar year	Pistols	Revolvers	Rifles	Shotguns	Misc. firearms*	Total firearms
1986	662,973	761,414	970,507	641,482	4,558	3,040,934
1987	964,561	722,512	1,007,661	857,949	6,980	3,559,663
1988	1,101,011	754,744	1,144,707	928,070	35,345	3,963,877
1989	1,404,753	628,573	1,407,400	935,541	42,126	4,418,393
1990	1,371,427	470,495	1,211,664	848,948	57,434	3,959,968
1991	1,378,252	456,966	883,482	828,426	15,980	3,563,106
1992	1,669,537	469,413	1,001,833	1,018,204	16,849	4,175,836
1993	2,093,362	562,292	1,173,694	1,144,940	81,349	5,055,637
1994	2,004,298	586,450	1,316,607	1,254,926	10,936	5,173,217
1995	1,195,284	527,664	1,411,120	1,173,645	8,629	4,316,342
1996	987,528	498,944	1,424,315	925,732	17,920	3,854,439
1997	1,036,077	370,428	1,251,341	915,978	19,680	3,593,504
1998	960,365	324,390	1,535,690	868,639	24,506	3,713,590
1999	995,446	335,784	1,569,685	1,106,995	39,837	4,047,747
2000	962,901	318,960	1,583,042	898,442	30,196	3,793,541
2001	626,836	320,143	1,284,554	679,813	21,309	2,932,655
2002	741,514	347,070	1,515,286	741,325	21,700	3,366,895
2003	811,660	309,364	1,430,324	726,078	30,978	3,308,404
2004	728,511	294,099	1,325,138	731,769	19,508	3,099,025
2005	803,425	274,205	1,431,372	709,313	23,179	3,241,494
2006	1,021,260	385,069	1,496,505	714,618	35,872	3,653,324
2007	1,219,664	391,334	1,610,923	645,231	55,461	3,922,613
2008	1,609,381	431,753	1,734,536	630,710	92,564	4,498,944
2009	1,868,258	547,195	2,248,851	752,699	138,815	5,555,818
2010	2,258,450	558,927	1,830,556	743,378	67,929	5,459,240

*Miscellaneous firearms are any firearms not specifically categorized in any of the firearms categories defined on the ATF Form 5300.11 Annual Firearms Manufacturing and Exportation Report (AFMER). (Examples of miscellaneous firearms would include pistol grip firearms, starter guns, and firearm frames and receivers.)
Notes: The AFMER report excludes production for the U.S. military but includes firearms purchased by domestic law enforcement agencies. The report also includes firearms manufactured for export.
AFMER data is not published until one year after the close of the calendar year reporting period because the proprietary data furnished by filers is protected from immediate disclosure by the Trade Secrets Act. For example, calendar year 2009 data was due to ATF (Bureau of Alcohol, Tobacco, Firearms and Explosives) by April 1, 2010, but not published until January 2011.

SOURCE: "Exhibit 1. Firearms Manufactured (1986–2010)," in *Firearms Commerce in the United States: Annual Statistical Update, 2012*, U.S. Department of Justice, Bureau of Alcohol, Tobacco, Firearms and Explosives, May 4, 2012, http://www.atf.gov/publications/firearms/050412-firearms-commerce-in-the-us-annual-statistical-update-2012.pdf (accessed August 17, 2012)

firearm from its manufacturer or introduction into U.S. commerce by the importer through the distribution chain (wholesaler/retailer) to the first retail purchase. A firearms trace is typically conducted when a law enforcement agency discovers a firearm at a crime scene and wishes to know the origin of that firearm in order to develop investigative leads." Firearms tracing is used in criminal investigations to link particular firearms to criminals, to identify gun traffickers, and to detect patterns in the sources and types of guns used in crime.

Between 2003 and 2006 the Tiahrt Amendment became more restrictive. In 2007, however, the amendment allowed the ATF to release gun trace statistics to federal, state, and local agencies for use in criminal investigations. In addition, the ATF was allowed to release state-by-state crime gun trace data to the public (http://www.atf.gov/statistics/).

In March 2008 the Firearms Information Use Act was introduced in the U.S. Senate to repeal the Tiahrt Amendment. Those in favor of retaining the amendment argued that all guns are not crime guns and that data on all guns should be restricted to protect noncriminals and the gun industry. In addition, the advocates said that public access to crime gun data permits anyone to know the names of investigators,

targeted gun dealers, and other information related to criminal investigations, which jeopardizes not only those investigations but also individuals involved in those investigations. Those against the amendment (in favor of repealing the amendment) argued that the amendment was too restrictive and that it impeded efforts by officials to investigate national patterns of gun trafficking and identify gun dealers who are most involved in illegal gun sales. Furthermore, opponents said that the amendment's restrictions did not allow the public to have information about guns and crime. In spite of these arguments, the movement to repeal the amendment failed and the bill did not become law.

Also in 2008 presidential candidate Barack Obama (1961–) vowed to repeal the Tiahrt Amendment if elected. After Obama took office in 2009, however, he removed only the restriction that police and prosecutors need an investigative reason to obtain gun trace data. He added restrictions that gun trace data cannot be released if criminal cases or undercover officers can be jeopardized by those data and made it illegal to release trace data to the public under any circumstances. The Tiahrt Amendment became permanent law in the 2010 budget, meaning that annual appropriations amendments would no longer be needed.

TABLE 2.2

Firearm imports, 1986–2011

Calendar year	Shotguns	Rifles	Handguns	Total
1986	201,000	269,000	231,000	701,000
1987	307,620	413,780	342,113	1,063,513
1988	372,008	282,640	621,620	1,276,268
1989	274,497	293,152	440,132	1,007,781
1990	191,787	203,505	448,517	843,809
1991	116,141	311,285	293,231	720,657
1992	441,933	1,423,189	981,588	2,846,710
1993	246,114	1,592,522	1,204,685	3,043,321
1994	117,866	847,868	915,168	1,880,902
1995	136,126	261,185	706,093	1,103,404
1996	128,456	262,568	490,554	881,578
1997	106,296	358,937	474,182	939,415
1998	219,387	248,742	531,681	999,810
1999	385,556	198,191	308,052	891,799
2000	331,985	298,894	465,903	1,096,782
2001	428,330	227,608	710,958	1,366,896
2002	379,755	507,637	741,845	1,629,237
2003	407,402	428,837	630,263	1,466,502
2004	507,050	564,953	838,856	1,910,859
2005	546,403	682,100	878,172	2,106,675
2006	606,820	659,393	1,166,309	2,432,522
2007	725,752	631,781	1,386,460	2,743,993
2008	535,960	602,364	1,468,062	2,606,386
2009	558,679	864,010	2,184,417	3,607,106
2010	509,913	547,449	1,782,585	2,839,947
2011	529,056	998,072	1,725,276	3,252,404

Note: Statistics prior to 1992 are for fiscal years; 1992 is a transition year with five quarters.

SOURCE: "Exhibit 3. Firearms Imports (1986–2011)," in *Firearms Commerce in the United States: Annual Statistical Update, 2012*, U.S. Department of Justice, Bureau of Alcohol, Tobacco, Firearms and Explosives, May 4, 2012, http://www.atf.gov/publications/firearms/050412-firearms-commerce-in-the-us-annual-statistical-update-2012.pdf (accessed August 17, 2012)

U.S. FIREARMS MANUFACTURING

Table 2.1 shows the number of firearms manufactured in the United States from 1986 to 2010, except for machine guns and all other National Firearms Act (NFA) weapons. NFA weapons include machine guns, short-barreled rifles, short-barreled shotguns, silencers, and destructive devices. (See Chapter 1 for a description of the National Firearms Act of 1934. In addition, Table 1.2 in Chapter 1 lists and describes several types of firearms.) In 1986 Congress banned the manufacture of machine guns for private sale, but they can be manufactured for export, for the military, and for law enforcement personnel. The annual manufacture of machine guns increased from 1998 to 2001. Likewise, the annual manufacture of other NFA weapons increased from 1998 to 2000. After 2001 machine gun and other NFA weapons data were no longer available to the public. Nearly 3.2 million NFA weapons were registered in the United States in 2012, including 488,065 machine guns. (See Table 2.4.) California (268,479), and Texas (258,204) had the most NFA weapons registered in 2012.

Table 2.1 also shows the numbers of pistols, revolvers, rifles, and shotguns manufactured in the United States between 1986 and 2010. Pistol manufacture rose from 662,973 weapons in 1986 to 2,093,362 in 1993, an increase of 216%, and then dropped to a low of 626,836 in 2001.

After that year, pistol production began a period of increase, rising eventually to an all-time high of 2,258,450 in 2010, which represented a 21% increase over the previous year's total of 1,868,258 pistols.

Rifle manufacture as shown in Table 2.1 ranged between roughly 1 million and 1.5 million annually throughout much of the period from 1986 to 2006, before increasing to a high of 2,248,851 in 2009. However, the year 2010, with manufacture of 1,830,556 rifles, saw a 19% decrease from the previous year. The manufacture of shotguns rose from 641,482 in 1986 to a high of 1,254,926 in 1994, but then fell to a low of 630,710 in 2008. Shotgun manufacturing rebounded somewhat in 2009 (752,699 weapons) and 2010 (743,378). (See Table 2.1.)

As shown in Table 2.1, the manufacture of revolvers declined 40% from 761,414 in 1986 to 456,966 in 1991 and then recovered somewhat before leveling off in the 300,000 to 400,000 range for much of the period 1997 to 2007. The 547,195 revolvers manufactured in 2009 represented the first time the figure was above the half-million mark since 1995. The upward trend continued in 2010 with a 2% increase over the previous year with the manufacture of 558,927 revolvers.

FIREARMS IMPORTS

The United States imports a sizeable number of guns each year. According to the Gun Control Act of 1968, imported firearms must be "generally recognized as particularly suitable for or readily adaptable to sporting purposes, excluding surplus military firearms." Gun import statistics from the U.S. International Trade Commission show that firearm imports for the U.S. civilian market more than quadrupled from 1986 to 1993, from about 701,000 in 1986 to more than 3 million in 1993. Firearms imports, however, declined by more than a million units the following year and remained below 1.5 million annually through 2001. The first decade of the 21st century saw an increase in the number of firearms imported into the United States, surpassing 2 million units in 2005 and reaching an all-time high of 3,607,106 firearms imported in 2009. Although slightly below the 2009 figure, firearm imports in 2011 (3,252,404) again exceeded 3 million units. (See Table 2.2.)

Table 2.5 shows the countries from which firearms were imported in 2011, with the top three countries—Brazil (846,619 total firearms), Austria (522,638), and Germany (313,528)—supplying more than half (52%) of all firearms imported into the United States. More handguns (53%) were imported in 2011 than rifles (31%) and shotguns (16%) combined. (See Figure 2.1.)

The top three countries from which the United States imported handguns in 2011 were Austria (515,396), Brazil (359,846), and Germany (265,092). (See Table 2.5.) As shown in the same table, the top three countries from

TABLE 2.3

Firearms exported, 1986–2010

Calendar year	Pistols	Revolvers	Rifles	Shotguns	Misc. firearms	Total firearms
1986	16,511	104,571	37,224	58,943	199	217,448
1987	24,941	134,611	42,161	76,337	9,995	288,045
1988	32,570	99,289	53,896	68,699	2,728	257,182
1989	41,970	76,494	73,247	67,559	2,012	261,282
1990	73,398	106,820	71,834	104,250	5,323	361,625
1991	79,275	110,058	91,067	117,801	2,964	401,165
1992	76,824	113,178	90,015	119,127	4,647	403,791
1993	59,234	91,460	94,272	171,475	14,763	431,204
1994	93,959	78,935	81,835	146,524	3,220	404,473
1995	97,969	131,634	90,834	101,301	2,483	424,221
1996	64,126	90,068	74,557	97,191	6,055	331,997
1997	44,182	63,656	76,626	86,263	4,354	275,081
1998	29,537	15,788	65,807	89,699	2,513	203,344
1999	34,663	48,616	65,669	67,342	4,028	220,318
2000	28,636	48,130	49,642	35,087	11,132	172,627
2001	32,151	32,662	50,685	46,174	10,939	172,611
2002	22,555	34,187	60,644	31,897	1,473	150,756
2003	16,340	26,524	62,522	29,537	6,989	141,912
2004	14,959	24,122	62,403	31,025	7,411	139,920
2005	19,196	29,271	92,098	46,129	7,988	194,682
2006	144,779	28,120	102,829	57,771	34,022	367,521
2007	45,053	34,662	80,594	26,949	17,524	204,782
2008	54,030	28,205	104,544	41,186	523	228,488
2009	56,402	32,377	61,072	36,455	8,438	194,744
2010	80,041	25,286	76,518	43,361	16,771	241,977

*Miscellaneous firearms are any firearms not specifically categorized in any of the firearms categories defined on the Bureau of Alcohol, Tobacco and Firearms (ATF) Form 5300.11 Annual Firearms Manufacturaing and Exportation Report (AFMER). (Examples of miscellaneous firearms would include pistol grip firearms, starter guns, and firearm frames and receivers.)

Note: The ARMER report excludes production for the U.S. military but includes firearms purchased by domestic law enforcement agencies. The report also includes firearms manufactured for export.

source: "Exhibit 2. Firearms Manufacturers' Exports (1986–2010)," in *Firearms Commerce in the United States: Annual Statistical Update, 2012*, U.S. Department of Justice, Bureau of Alcohol, Tobacco, Firearms and Explosives, May 4, 2012, http://www.atf.gov/publications/firearms/050412-firearms-commerce-in-the-us-annual-statistical-update-2012.pdf (accessed August 17, 2012)

which the United States imported rifles in 2011 were Brazil (381,097), Canada (194,995), and Russia (148,556); the top three countries from which the United States imported shotguns were Italy (137,768), Turkey (122,682), and Brazil (105,676).

FIREARMS EXPORTS

Table 2.3 shows the number of firearms exported by U.S. manufacturers from 1986 to 2010. Between 1986 and 1993 the export of firearms nearly doubled from 217,448 to 431,204. From that peak, however, firearm exports began a period of decline, reaching a low of 139,920 in 2004. After 2004 firearms exports increased dramatically in 2005 (194,682) and 2006 (367,521) but did not sustain that level, declining to 204,782 in 2007. The year 2010 again saw an increase, with U.S. firearm exports counted at 241,977.

AUTOMATIC AND SEMIAUTOMATIC FIREARMS

The Firearms Owners' Protection Act, which amended the Gun Control Act of 1968, was signed into law in May 1986 and banned private ownership of any machine gun not already lawfully owned. Machine guns are fully automatic weapons, which means they can fire a steady stream of bullets. (See Table 1.2 in Chapter 1.)

Then in 1989 the ATF issued an order banning the importation of 43 models of semiautomatic assault-type guns following a schoolyard shooting in Stockton, California, that killed 5 people and wounded 29 others. Assault-type guns, or assault weapons, generally refer to military-style semiautomatic firearms. Military-style simply means the weapons look like guns used in the military; however, they are not military weapons. Semiautomatic means the weapons fire only a single shot for each pull of the trigger, but that bullets are automatically loaded into the chamber. Regardless, the phrase "assault weapons" is often used by the media and the public to refer to machine guns, which are military weapons. Thus, the meaning of the phrase "assault weapons" is not always clearly understood or defined.

The Violent Crime Control Act of 1994 banned the sale and possession of 19 assault-type firearms and copycat models, including the Uzi, the TEC-9, and the Street Sweeper. The act also limited the capacity of newly manufactured magazines to 10 bullets. A magazine is a cartridge holder that feeds the gun chamber automatically. (Chapter 3 describes this law in more detail.)

Those in favor of gun control argued that semiautomatic firearms are lethal and effective killing tools that should be banned because they are suitable only for criminal purposes. The National Rifle Association of America

TABLE 2.4

National Firearms Act registered weapons by state, March 2012

State	Any other weapon[a]	Destructive device[b]	Machinegun[c]	Silencer[d]	Short barreled rifle[e]	Short barreled shotgun[f]	Total
Alabama	1,133	47,421	15,653	8,550	1,327	2,075	76,159
Alaska	311	3,317	1,617	2,085	508	1,101	8,939
Arkansas	591	41,962	4,827	7,218	1,091	1,017	56,706
Arizona	1,080	67,185	16,879	15,860	5,492	1,851	108,347
California	3,698	212,800	28,774	7,303	3,738	12,166	268,479
Colorado	910	37,444	6,040	6,475	2,217	1,389	54,475
Connecticut	643	9,886	22,023	5,170	1,068	960	39,750
District of Columbia	69	34,841	4,278	160	440	1,048	40,836
Delaware	32	2,183	569	302	94	507	3,687
Florida	3,113	101,418	29,128	28,312	7,432	6,125	175,528
Georgia	1,759	48,026	22,081	29,259	3,563	9,422	114,110
Hawaii	34	5,503	429	105	55	59	6,185
Iowa	876	11,737	3,262	301	343	936	17,455
Idaho	588	14,049	4,342	9,839	1,103	398	30,319
Illinois	958	83,363	24,651	1,071	1,214	1,674	112,931
Indiana	1,430	34,628	17,019	16,735	2,343	8,581	80,736
Kansas	674	19,379	3,289	2,266	1,095	850	27,553
Kentucky	1,019	22,239	10,703	12,046	1,379	1,638	49,024
Louisiana	517	44,821	6,182	4,359	1,577	1,508	58,964
Massachusetts	837	12,878	6,555	3,679	1,315	887	26,151
Maryland	933	45,037	23,709	7,024	1,713	3,771	82,187
Maine	570	2,517	4,664	1,290	1,420	410	10,871
Michigan	1,061	21,221	9,090	2,887	700	1,121	36,080
Minnesota	2,633	36,066	6,828	619	1,183	1,011	48,340
Missouri	1,330	24,986	8,230	4,913	1,864	2,266	43,589
Mississippi	410	6,776	3,886	3,368	572	712	15,724
Montana	404	2,852	1,892	2,303	497	345	8,293
North Carolina	820	69,005	11,234	8,609	2,850	2,542	95,060
North Dakota	199	1,605	1,480	1,826	260	211	5,581
Nebraska	717	5,068	2,049	2,273	895	768	11,770
New Hampshire	430	3,459	9,863	2,782	1,457	385	18,376
New Jersey	425	37,700	6,895	965	688	2,316	48,989
New Mexico	277	60,764	3,709	2,920	1,094	607	69,371
Nevada	679	30,778	6,843	6,671	2,621	767	48,359
New York	2,012	35,707	7,521	1,153	1,370	7,342	55,105
Ohio	1,776	71,814	18,013	10,407	2,842	3,822	108,574
Oklahoma	1,110	13,004	7,972	11,964	1,787	1,470	37,307
Oregon	1,487	17,492	6,442	9,841	2,346	1,309	38,917
Pennsylvania	2,043	148,700	17,384	12,914	3,853	12,323	197,217
Rhode Island	42	2,710	595	27	106	112	3,592
South Carolina	670	26,358	6,010	7,457	1,380	3,655	45,530
South Dakota	344	3,352	1,495	2,022	264	175	7,652
Tennessee	1,502	32,848	13,442	9,571	2,623	5,538	65,524
Texas	6,169	159,805	28,690	47,712	9,271	6,557	258,204
Utah	403	13,960	6,076	5,857	1,927	1,160	29,383
Virginia	2,514	161,841	30,220	15,736	6,720	6,272	223,303
Vermont	221	2,216	1,070	68	134	94	3,803
Washington	1,726	34,693	3,805	8,400	1,174	752	50,550
Wisconsin	747	25,316	6,385	4,416	1,419	1,106	39,389
West Virginia	431	8,318	2,438	2,325	682	548	14,742
Wyoming	286	102,723	1,659	1,103	369	373	106,513
Other US territories	6	320	175	16	11	47	575
Total	**54,649**	**2,064,091**	**488,065**	**360,534**	**93,486**	**124,079**	**3,184,804**

(NRA) defended the use of semiautomatic firearms for hunting, informal target shooting, and competitive target shooting. The NRA also claimed that many other guns offer criminals the same capacity to kill and that the only way to stop their use is to control the criminals, not the weapons. The assault weapons ban expired in September 2004. Bills were introduced in the U.S. House of Representatives in 2007 and 2008 to reinstate and extend the assault weapons ban, but neither bill became law.

During his 2008 presidential campaign, Barack Obama supported the reinstatement of the assault weapons ban. However, only a few months into Obama's presidency,

Sam Youngman and Bob Cusack reported in "Some Obama Promises Get Punted" (April 2, 2009, http://thehill.com/hom enews/news/19065-some-obama-promises-get-punted) that the president was taking a "hands off" approach to the issue. By October 2012, almost four years after Obama took office, the assault weapons ban had not been reinstated. However, President Obama reaffirmed his support of such a ban during his re-election campaign in a presidential debate with his opponent, Mitt Romney (1947–), at Hofstra University in Hempstead, New York, on October 16, 2012. In response to a question about what President Obama's administration had done or plans to do "to limit the availability of assault weapons," the president suggested he might reintroduce an

aThe term "any other weapon" means any weapon or device capable of being concealed on the person from which a shot can be discharged through the energy of an explosive, a pistol or revolver having a barrel with a smooth bore designed or redesigned to fire a fixed shotgun shell, weapons with combination shotgun and rifle barrels 12 inches or more, less than 18 inches in length, from which only a single discharge can be made from either barrel without manual reloading, and shall include any such weapon which may be readily restored to fire. Such term shall not include a pistol or a revolver having a rifled bore, or rifled bores, or weapons designed, made, or intended to be fired from the shoulder and not capable of firing fixed ammunition.
bDestructive device generally is defined as (a) Any explosive, incendiary, or poison gas (1) bomb, (2) grenade, (3) rocket having a propellant charge of more than 4 ounces, (4) missile having an explosive or incendiary charge of more than one-quarter ounce, (5) mine, or (6) device similar to any of the devices described in the preceding paragraphs of this definition; (b) any type of weapon (other than a shotgun or a shotgun shell which the Director finds is generally recognized as particularly suitable for sporting purposes) by whatever name known which will, or which may be readily converted to, expel a projectile by the action of an explosive or other propellant, and which has any barrel with a bore of more than one-half inch in diameter; and (c) any combination of parts either designed or intended for use in converting any device into any destructive device described in paragraph (a) or (b) of this section and from which a destructive device may be readily assembled. The term shall not include any device which is neither designed nor redesigned for use as a weapon; any device, although originally designed for use as a weapon, which is redesigned for use as a signaling, pyrotechnic, line throwing, safety, or similar device; surplus ordnance sold, loaned, or given by the Secretary of the Army pursuant to the provisions of section 4684(2), 4685, or 4686 of title 10, United States Code; or any other device which the Director finds is not likely to be used as a weapon, is an antique, or is a rifle which the owner intends to use solely for sporting, recreational, or cultural purposes.
cMachinegun is defined as any weapon which shoots, is designed to shoot, or can be readily restored to shoot, automatically more than one shot, without manual reloading, by a single function of the trigger. The term shall also include the frame or receiver of any such weapon, any part designed and intended solely and exclusively, or combination of parts designed and intended, for use in converting a weapon into a machine gun, and any combination of parts from which a machine gun can be assembled if such parts are in the possession or under the control of a person.
dSilencer is defined as any device for silencing, muffling, or diminishing the report of a portable firearm, including any combination of parts, designed or redesigned, and intended for the use in assembling or fabricating a firearm silencer or firearm muffler, and any part intended only for use in such assembly or fabrication.
eShort-barreled rifle is defined as a rifle having one or more barrels less than 16 inches in length, and any weapon made from a rifle, whether by alteration, modification, or otherwise, if such weapon, as modified, has an overall length of less than 26 inches.
fShort-barreled shotgun is defined as a shotgun having one or more barrels less than 18 inches in length, and any weapon made from a shotgun, whether by alteration, modification, or otherwise, if such weapon as modified has an overall length of less than 26 inches.

SOURCE: "Exhibit 8. National Firearms Act Registered Weapons by State (March 2012)," in *Firearms Commerce in the United States: Annual Statistical Update, 2012*, U.S. Department of Justice, Bureau of Alcohol, Tobacco, Firearms and Explosives, May 4, 2012, http://www.atf.gov/publications/firearms/050412-firearms-commerce-in-the-us-annual-statistical-update-2012.pdf (accessed August 17, 2012)

---

assault weapons ban as part of a larger strategy to reduce gun violence. He said, "I...share your belief that weapons that were designed for soldiers in war theaters don't belong on our streets. And so what I'm trying to do is to get a broader conversation about how do we reduce the violence generally. Part of it is seeing if we can get an assault weapons ban reintroduced, but part of it is also looking at other sources of the violence." Romney, speaking to the same question, said that he did not support reinstating the ban even though he had signed an assault weapons ban in 2004 while serving as governor of Massachusetts. He explained, "In my state, the pro-gun folks and the anti-gun folks came together and put together a piece of legislation, and it's referred to as an assault weapons ban, but it had at the signing of the bill both the pro-gun and the anti-gun people...because it provided opportunities for both that both wanted."

GUNS IN THE HOME

Percentages of Adults Having Guns in the Home

Trends in the percentages of adults having guns in their homes are presented in Figure 2.2 and Table 2.6. Figure 2.2 shows the results of Gallup polls from 1960 to 2011 that asked adult Americans: "Do you have a gun in your home?" During the 1960s about half of all respondents answered "yes" to this question. In general, the proportion of people answering "yes" dropped in the decades that followed, with ups and downs along the way. By 2011 the percentage of those having a gun in the home had risen again to 45%, not much different from 49% in 1960.

Table 2.6 shows the results from the General Social Surveys conducted from 1973 to 2008 by the National Opinion Research Center at the University of Chicago. Survey results show that 47.3% of adults had a gun in the home in 1973, compared with 32.5% of adults in 2000. After 2000, however, the percentage of people with guns in the home remained relatively stable for several years, with 34.4% of respondents saying they had a gun in the home in 2008. In 2010, 40.9% of respondents reported having a gun at home, the highest level of gun ownership in the survey since the mid-1990s. (See Table 2.6.)

Table 2.6 also shows that having long guns in the home (shotguns and rifles) is more popular with American gun owners than having handguns in the home (pistols or revolvers). In 2010, 21.7% of those with guns in the home reported having pistols or revolvers, whereas 49.4% had shotguns (24.9%) or rifles (24.5%).

Research on Guns in the Home and Safety

Guns in the home can be used to protect those in the home from intruders, but are they associated with a risk of increased injury and death to those residing in the home? The Bureau of Justice Statistics reports in *Criminal Victimization in the United States, 2008* (May 2011, http://bjs.ojp.usdoj.gov/content/pub/pdf/cvus0804.pdf) that 18.4% of the violent crimes committed in the United States in 2007 occurred at or in the victim's home. (See Table 2.7.) Even though not all in-home violent crimes are perpetrated with a gun, studies have been conducted to explore the relationship between guns and crime in the home.

TABLE 2.5

Firearms imported, by country, 2011

	Handguns	Rifles	Shotguns	Total firearms
Brazil	359,846	381,097	105,676	846,619
Austria	515,396	7,191	51	522,638
Germany	265,092	46,288	2,148	313,528
Italy	104,911	12,222	137,768	254,901
Russia	16,900	148,556	50,837	216,293
Croatia	211,001	0	0	211,001
Canada	2	194,995	13	195,010
Turkey	22,899	1,153	122,682	146,734
China[a]	0	1,450	90,952	92,402
Argentina	71,838	0	0	71,838
Japan	0	59,471	1,834	61,305
Philippines	54,247	1,430	950	56,627
Romania	13,775	38,048	1	51,824
Czech Republic	20,003	20,236	6	40,245
Belgium	9,769	16,317	114	26,200
Finland	0	23,417	6	23,423
Poland	20,895	1,081	11	21,987
Ukraine	0	20,600	0	20,600
Costa Rica	19,500	0	0	19,500
United Kingdom	4,376	4,046	8,254	16,676
Spain	322	10,015	1,328	11,665
Israel	9,995	157	0	10,152
Serbia	720	7,562	0	8,282
Mexico	0	0	4,284	4,284
Other[b]	1,348	2,246	16	3,610
Portugal	0	0	2,115	2,115
Switzerland	991	494	10	1,495
Bulgaria	1,450	0	0	1,450
Totals	**1,725,276**	**998,072**	**529,056**	**3,252,404**

[a]On May 26, 1994, the United States instituted a firearms imports embargo against China. Shotguns, however, are exempt from the embargo.
[b]Imports of fewer than 1,000 per country.

SOURCE: "Exhibit 5. Firearms Imported into the United States by Country 2011," in *Firearms Commerce in the United States: Annual Statistical Update, 2012*, U.S. Department of Justice, Bureau of Alcohol, Tobacco, Firearms and Explosives, May 4, 2012, http://www.atf.gov/publications/firearms/050412-firearms-commerce-in-the-us-annual-statistical-update-2012.pdf (accessed August 17, 2012)

FIGURE 2.1

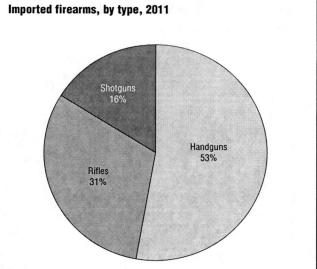

Imported firearms, by type, 2011

SOURCE: "Exhibit 5a. Imported Firearms by Type 2011," in *Firearms Commerce in the United States: Annual Statistical Update, 2012*, U.S. Department of Justice, Bureau of Alcohol, Tobacco, Firearms and Explosives, May 4, 2012, http://www.atf.gov/publications/firearms/050412-firearms-commerce-in-the-us-annual-statistical-update-2012.pdf (accessed August 17, 2012)

In "Do Guns Provide Safety? At What Cost?" (*Southern Medical Journal*, vol. 103, no. 2, February 2010), Puneet Narang et al. provide a review that focuses on whether guns provide safety for their owners and families. The researchers state that guns in U.S. homes have been associated "with high rates of suicide, accidental injury, homicide, and domestic violence." Narang et al. also mention that the "presence of a firearm in the home reportedly results in death or injury to household members or visitors over 12 times more often than to an intruder."

Gary Kleck and Don Kates study defensive gun use and published a review of their findings in *Armed: New Perspectives on Gun Control* (2001), the most recent, large-scale study on this topic as of 2012. The authors conclude that estimates of defensive gun use are usually low due to errors in research methodology and that guns are used for defense more than 2.5 million times per year in the United States. Kleck and Kates posit that this estimate has been confirmed many times "by all surveys of comparable technical merit." They also contend that the study of guns and violence in general, and the study of guns and self-defense in particular,

are plagued with "advocacy scholarship" and "junk science." Their work puts into question the data presented in reviews such as Narang's and other studies on the comparison of defensive and nondefensive gun use in the home.

CHARACTERISTICS OF PRIVATELY OWNED FIREARMS AND THEIR OWNERS

Lisa Hepburn et al. conducted a national telephone survey in 2004 "to explore the characteristics of privately owned firearms in the US" and published their findings in "The U.S. Gun Stock: Results from the 2004 National Firearms Survey" (*Injury Prevention*, vol. 13, no. 1, 2007), the most recent study on this topic as of 2012. The researchers determine that in 2004, 33% of the firearms owned in the United States were rifles, 21% were shotguns, 6% were other long guns, 20% were revolvers, 14% were semiautomatic pistols, 5% were other handguns, and 1% were other guns.

Hepburn et al. also determine the demographic characteristics of the owners of these firearms. In 2004 gun ownership varied with many factors including gender, geographic location, military service, age, and race. Men (42%) were far more likely to own guns than were women (11%). More respondents in the South (32%) said they owned a firearm, compared with 27% of those in the Midwest, 24% of those in the West, and 17% of those in the Northeast. Veterans of military service (53%) were much more likely to own a firearm than those currently in the military (31%) or people with no military service (22%). People aged 45 to 64 years were the most likely to own a firearm (30%), compared with those over the age of 65 (27%) or those aged 25 to 44 years (26%). People younger

FIGURE 2.2

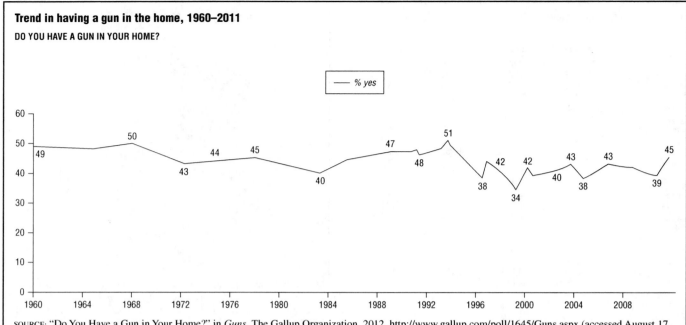

Trend in having a gun in the home, 1960–2011

DO YOU HAVE A GUN IN YOUR HOME?

— % yes

TABLE 2.6

Trends in having a gun in the home, by type of firearm and ownership, selected years 1973–2010

	% of adults with gun in home	Of adults with gun in home, % with pistol or revolver in home	Of adults with gun in home, % with shotgun in home	Of adults with gun in home, % with rifle in home	Of adults with gun in home, % who own the gun
1973	47.3	19.9	27.6	29.2	—
1976	46.7	21.6	28.1	28.2	—
1980	47.7	23.2	29.6	29.2	61.8
1984	45.2	21.4	27.7	27.3	56.1
1988	40.1	22.6	23.9	24.2	59.9
1990	42.7	23.5	25.9	25.4	66.2
1994	40.7	24.5	24.3	24.5	68.3
1996	40.2	22.3	24.7	23.3	66.2
1998	34.9	19.6	20.8	20.8	65.2
2000	32.5	19.7	18.6	19.7	66.5
2002	33.5	19.5	21.1	19.8	74.9
2004	35.7	20.7	18.9	19.7	70.3
2006	33.2	20.0	19.3	19.1	64.8
2008	34.4	24.3	23.8	23.7	68.3
2010	40.9	21.7	24.9	24.5	64.8

Note: The percentages of types of guns do not equal 100% for each year shown, because some persons refused to answer and some had types of guns not listed here.

than 25 years were the least likely to own a firearm (16%). Whites were twice as likely to own a gun (30%) as non-whites (15%).

GUN-CARRYING REASONS, BEHAVIORS, AND DEMOGRAPHICS

The National Opinion Research Center (NORC) at the University of Chicago has been conducting social science research on a variety of topics since its establishment in 1941. The General Social Survey (GSS), which began in 1972 and monitors social change in the United States, is one of the NORC's major survey projects. The National Gun Policy Survey is included in the GSS, but not all questions are asked with each survey, and reports are produced only occasionally. Tom W. Smith of the NORC indicates in *1997–98 National Gun Policy Survey of the National Opinion Research Center: Research Findings* (September 1998) that participants in the survey who did not personally own a gun were asked to give reasons for not owning a firearm.

TABLE 2.7

Place of occurrence of violent crimes, 2008

Type of crime	Number of incidents	Total	At or in respondent's home	Near home	On the street near home	At, in, or near a friend's, relative's or neighbor's home	Inside a restaurant, bar, or nightclub	Other commercial building	Parking lot or garage	Inside school building/on school property	In apartment yard, park, field, or playground	On street other than near own home	On public transportation or inside station	Other
Crimes of violence	**4,581,260**	**100%**	**18.4**	**10.9**	**5.9**	**9.1**	**3.2**	**8.9**	**7.0**	**13.3**	**1.9**	**13.6**	**0.7**	**7.1**
Completed violence	1,291,780	100%	27.7	4.8	6.9	12.3	2.9*	3.7	8.8	11.4	1.9*	14.7	1.6*	3.4
Attempted/threatened violence	3,289,490	100%	14.7	13.2	5.5	7.9	3.3	10.9	6.3	14.1	2.0	13.1	0.4*	8.6
Rape/sexual assault[a]	200,520	100%	35.0	4.2*	3.4*	18.3*	0.0*	6.0*	0.0*	12.1*	7.2*	10.9*	0.0*	2.9*
Robbery	504,110	100%	16.0	6.6*	10.2	8.5	0.8*	4.2*	17.0	5.9*	0.0*	25.6	0.4*	4.9*
Completed/property taken	346,240	100%	19.5	7.0*	12.5	8.2*	1.1*	0.0*	15.5	7.1*	0.0*	23.7	0.5*	4.8*
With injury	127,290	100%	19.6*	8.6*	16.0*	6.5*	3.1*	0.0*	17.7*	5.4*	0.0*	16.5*	1.4*	5.2*
Without injury	218,950	100%	19.5	6.1*	10.4*	9.2*	0.0*	0.0*	14.2*	8.0*	0.0*	27.9	0.0*	4.6*
Attempted to take property	157,870	100%	8.3*	5.7*	5.2*	8.9*	0.0*	13.5*	20.2*	3.3*	0.0*	29.6	0.0*	5.2*
With injury	56,800	100%	14.4*	0.0*	5.3*	5.7*	0.0*	13.3*	15.5*	3.5*	0.0*	42.3*	0.0*	0.0*
Without injury	101,070	100%	4.9*	8.9*	5.2*	10.8*	0.0*	13.6*	22.9*	3.2*	0.0*	22.5*	0.0*	8.0*
Assault	3,876,640	100%	17.8	11.8	5.5	8.7	3.7	9.6	6.1	14.3	1.9	12.2	0.8*	7.6
Aggravated	768,770	100%	16.4	13.0	6.2	11.0	2.9*	7.2	10.0	7.3	3.1*	15.9	0.9*	6.1
Simple	3,107,870	100%	18.2	11.5	5.3	8.2	3.9	10.2	5.1	16.1	1.6	11.3	0.8*	8.0
Purse snatching/pocket picking	136,710	100%	8.7*	0.0*	5.9*	2.4*	17.8*	13.0*	10.0*	4.8*	0.0*	24.4*	8.9*	4.0*
Property crimes														
Motor vehicle theft	795,160	100%	4.5*	41.8	16.9	1.8*	—	2.3*	21.1	0.9*	0.0*	8.3	—	2.5*
Completed	593,360	100%	5.3*	41.4	14.4	2.4*	—	3.0*	21.6	1.1*	0.0*	7.8	—	2.8*
Attempted	201,800	100%	1.9*	43.0	24.1	0.0*	—	0.0*	19.5	0.0*	0.0*	9.8*	—	1.6*
Theft	12,335,400	100%	11.0	42.1	6.9	3.8	1.5	4.5	11.9	7.3	0.8	3.7	0.8	5.7

Note: Detail may not add to total shown because of rounding.

*Estimate is based on 10 or fewer sample cases.

—Not applicable

[a]Includes verbal threats of rape and threats of sexual assault.

SOURCE: Michael R. Rand and Jayne E. Robinson, "Table 61. Selected Personal and Property Crimes, 2008: Percent Distribution of Incidents, by Type of Crime and Place of Occurrence," in *Criminal Victimization in the United States, 2008—Statistical Tables*, U.S. Department of Justice, Office of Justice Programs, Bureau of Justice Statistics, May 2011, http://bjs.ojp.usdoj.gov/content/pub/pdf/cvus0804.pdf (accessed August 27, 2012)

The major reason, given by 35.2%, was a lack of interest in having a gun. Other reasons included opposition to guns on ethical grounds (11.6%), having children in the house (11%), and feeling that guns were more a threat than a source of protection (8.4%).

In *2001 National Gun Policy Survey of the National Opinion Research Center: Research Findings* (December 2001, http://www.norc.org/PDFs/publications/SmithT_Nat _Gun_Policy_2001.pdf), the most recent study on this topic as of 2012, Smith examines the gun-carrying behaviors of gun owners and the prevalence of such behaviors. He indicates that in 2001 Americans carried guns for a number of reasons: target practice (70.1%), hunting (46.7%), protection (41.6%), and work purposes (10.7%). Smith also measures how often owners carried their guns, where they took their guns, how they carried their weapons, and whether they had a permit to carry a weapon (33.3% did, whereas 62.2% did not).

Smith discusses how gun ownership made the owner feel. For a significant majority of the people interviewed in 2001, carrying a gun resulted in feelings of safety and protection (59.4%). Yet 9.8% of the respondents indicated that carrying a gun made them feel less safe. For 26.5% of the respondents, they felt the same whether they carried a gun or not.

Smith presents a further breakdown of gun ownership behavior by sociodemographics, based on data found in the 2001 NORC National Gun Policy Survey. Regarding gender, more men than women carried a gun for work (13.2% versus 4.8%), carried a gun for protection (42.7% versus 39%), usually carried their gun unloaded (43.5% versus 31.5%), and carried their gun in their car (53% versus 48.2%). However, more women (61.5%) than men (54.2%) carried their gun concealed. Regarding race, more African-Americans than whites carried a gun for work (16.3% versus 9.8%), carried a gun for protection (57% versus 40.2%), usually carried their gun unloaded (46.5% versus 39.7%), and carried their gun concealed (60.3% versus 54.6%). However, more whites (53%) than African-Americans (49.4%) carried their gun in their car.

STATES ALLOWING GUN CARRYING

According to the NRA's Institute for Legislative Action (http://www.nraila.org/gun-laws/articles/2012/right-to-carry-2012.aspx), as of February 2012 there were 41 right-to-carry (RTC) states, which means that those states allowed individuals to carry firearms for protection. Of the 41 RTC states, 38 had "shall-issue" laws. (See Figure 2.3.) These laws required local officials to issue a concealed handgun carry permit to anyone who applied, unless the applicant was prohibited by law from carrying a weapon. Of the shall-issue states, Alaska, Arizona, and Wyoming did not require a permit yet had a shall-issue system. Two of the RTC states (Alabama and Connecticut) that did not have shall-issue laws had

discretionary-issue laws, in which individuals were generally granted permits unless the state determined that it had cause to deny the permit. Vermont did not have shall-issue laws and did not require a permit for any adult who was legally allowed to possess a firearm. In July 2010 Arizona joined Alaska and Vermont in not requiring a permit to carry a concealed weapon.

The remaining nine states were non-RTC states: California, Delaware, Hawaii, Illinois, Maryland, Massachusetts, New York, New Jersey, and Rhode Island. Eight of the non-RTC states generally did not allow handguns to be carried in public areas, but they had very limited and restrictive issue laws that allowed concealed handgun carry permits to be granted in certain circumstances. Illinois (and the District of Columbia) prohibited individuals from carrying guns.

The phrase "open carry" means that a person is allowed to carry a firearm in plain view while in public. States that expressly prohibited open carry as of 2012 included Arkansas, California, Florida, Illinois, New York, South Carolina, and Texas. The Brady Center to Prevent Gun Violence conducted a survey in April 2010 with Lake Research Partners on attitudes toward open carry gun laws. Figure 2.4 shows the opinions of respondents when asked if they would feel more or less safe if people could carry guns openly in public. Half (50%) of respondents said they would feel less safe, with 31% responding that they would feel much less safe. Conversely, 38% said they would feel more safe, with 24% responding that they would feel much more safe. When shown by gender, however, the divide between men and women is striking. Nearly half (49%) of men said they would feel safer if people could carry guns openly, whereas 63% of women said they would feel less safe.

WOMEN AND GUNS

The number of females who own firearms can only be estimated, and these estimates vary. In "Changes in Firearm Ownership among Women, 1980–1994" (*Journal of Criminal Law and Criminology*, vol. 86, no. 1, Autumn 1995), Tom W. Smith and Robert J. Smith show that female gun ownership increased slightly between 1980 and 1994—from an estimated 10.5% of women in 1980 to 12.7% in 1994. The researchers conclude that even though gun manufacturers had begun targeting the female market beginning in the early 1980s, women were little more likely to buy guns in 1994 than they had been in 1980. The percent of women gun owners seemed to remain steady through the end of the century. Smith notes in *1997–98 National Gun Policy Survey of the National Opinion Research Center* that by 1997–98 only 11.4% of the U.S. female population owned a gun.

This figure was the same in 2004 as reported by Hepburn et al. Beginning about this time, however, an

FIGURE 2.3

Right-to-carry-weapons laws, 2012

Right to carry—shall issue

State law that provides that, upon completion of specified requirements, a law-abiding person shall be granted a permit to carry concealed firearms.

Right to carry—discretionary/reasonable issue

State law that provides the government with some discretion over the issuance of a carry permit, but which generally grants permits to all law-abiding persons.

Right to carry—no permit required

State law that allows individuals to carry concealed firearms for lawful purposes without a permit.

Right to carry—rights restricted—very limited issue

State law that gives the government complete discretion over the issuance of carry permits, and where the discretion is normally used to deny the issuance of permits.

Right to carry—rights infringed/non-issue

State law that completely prohibits carrying firearms for personal protection outside the home or place of business.

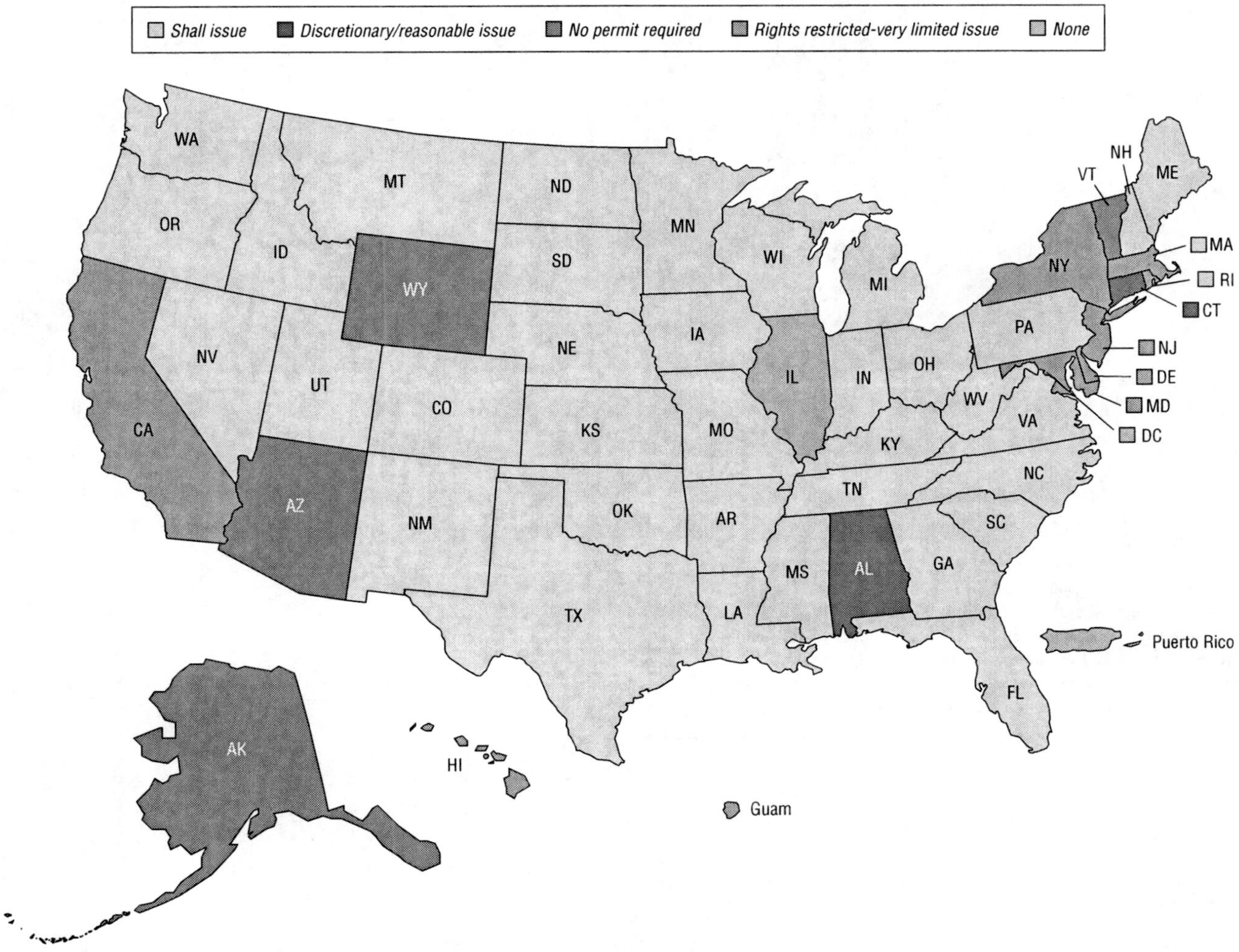

☐ *Shall issue* ■ *Discretionary/reasonable issue* ▦ *No permit required* ▨ *Rights restricted-very limited issue* ☐ *None*

SOURCE: "State Laws at a Glance: Right to Carry Laws," in *Gun Laws*, National Rifle Association, Institute for Legislative Action, 2012, http://www.nraila.org/gun-laws.aspx (accessed September 28, 2012)

upturn seems to have begun that continued through 2011. Joseph Carroll of the Gallup Organization reports in *Gun Ownership and Use in America* (November 22, 2005, http://www.gallup.com/poll/20098/gun-ownership-use-america.aspx) that in 2005, 13% of women owned guns. In *Self-Reported Gun Ownership in U.S. Is Highest since 1993*, Lydia Saad reports (October 26, 2011, http://www.gallup.com/poll/150353/Self-Reported-Gun-Owner ship-Highest-1993.aspx) that 23% of women respondents said they owned a gun in October 2011.

Why do women buy guns? In "More Women May Be Turning to Firearms" (*Washington Times*, March 30, 2010), Kristin Volk and Joseph Weber cite a 2009 study that was conducted by the National Shooting Sports Foundation in conjunction with Southwick Associates that revealed that

FIGURE 2.4

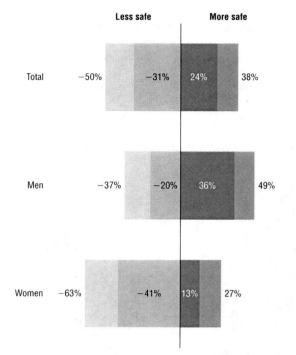

Public opinion on personal safety if people carry guns openly in public, April 2010

Note: The darker colors represent a stronger response and lighter colors a less strong response.

SOURCE: Celinda Lake, Joshua Ulibarri, and Christopher Panetta, "There is a clear gender divide when it comes to personal safety. Men are likely to tilt toward feeling safe with allowing people to carry openly in public, by 13 points. Women overwhelmingly feel less safe by 36 points. That gender gap of 49 points is one of the largest divides seen on current issues," in *Findings from a National Survey of 600 Registered Voters April 26–28, 2010*, Brady Center to Prevent Gun Violence and Lake Research Partners, 2010, http://www .bradycampaign.org/xshare/bcam/legislation/open_carry/polling-overview-slides.ppt (accessed August 27, 2012)

80% of women who bought guns did so for self-defense, 35% for target practice, and 24% for hunting. (The percentages do not add to 100% because respondents were able to cite multiple reasons for their gun purchases.) The study also noted that gun shop owners said more women were purchasing guns in 2009 than in past years.

CHAPTER 3
FIREARM LAWS, REGULATIONS, AND ORDINANCES

FEDERAL GOVERNMENT REGULATION OF GUNS

Americans have long debated the issue of federal regulation of firearms. Those in favor of regulation argue that only federal firearm laws can limit access by criminals, juveniles, and other high-risk people, thereby reducing violent crime. Supporters of regulation also contend that without federal laws, states with few firearms restrictions will supply guns illegally to states with stiffer restrictions. Opponents of federal involvement advance Second Amendment arguments against any kind of gun control. They also argue that federal gun laws only cause extra burdens for law-abiding citizens who seek to buy and sell firearms.

Until the 1920s the states made their own decisions about whether and how to regulate firearms. The federal government stepped in following ratification of the 18th Amendment (1919), which made it illegal to manufacture, transport, and sell "intoxicating liquors" in the United States. Known as Prohibition, the ban sparked a national crime wave as gangsters built empires on the illegal manufacture and sale of alcohol. For the first time, crime was seen as a national problem, and people debated solutions at the federal level.

The first federal law regulating firearms was passed in 1927 (18 USC 1715). The law outlawed mailing any firearm other than a shotgun or rifle through the U.S. Postal Service, except for firearms shipped for official law enforcement purposes. This law, which was still in effect as of 2012, was intended to curb the mail-order business in handguns, and it inspired many states to pass their own regulations regarding the sale and use of handguns. Supporters of the federal law tried to get a law passed forbidding the shipment of handguns across state lines by all commercial carriers, but they failed. Instead, commercial carriers other than the U.S. Postal Service were allowed to carry handguns across state lines.

The next federal regulation was the National Firearms Act of 1934, which was designed to make it more difficult to acquire especially dangerous "gangster-type" weapons such as machine guns, sawed-off shotguns, and silencers. The legislation placed heavy taxes on all aspects of the manufacture and distribution of these firearms and required registration of each firearm through the entire production, distribution, and sales process. This law was still in force, with amendments, as of 2012.

Ordinary firearms were the subject of the Federal Firearms Act of 1938. The act required any manufacturer or dealer who sent or received firearms across state lines to have a federal firearms license and to keep a record of the names and addresses of people purchasing firearms. Firearms could not be sent to anyone who was a fugitive from justice or had been convicted of a felony. It became illegal to transport stolen guns from which the manufacturer's mark had been rubbed out or changed. This act was replaced with the passage of the Gun Control Act of 1968.

THE GUN CONTROL ACT OF 1968

The Gun Control Act of 1968 was passed in the wake of the assassinations of President John F. Kennedy (1917–1963), the civil rights leader Martin Luther King Jr. (1929–1968), and Senator Robert F. Kennedy (1925–1968). It repealed the Federal Firearms Act of 1938 and amended the National Firearms Act of 1934 by adding bombs and other destructive devices to machine guns and sawed-off shotguns as items strictly controlled by the government. Its purpose was to assist federal, state, and local law enforcement agencies in reducing crime and violence.

The Gun Control Act of 1968 had two major sections. Title I required anyone dealing in firearms or ammunition—whether locally or across state lines—to be federally licensed under tough new standards and to keep records of all commercial gun sales. Title I also prohibited the interstate mail-order sale of all firearms and ammunition, the interstate sale of handguns generally, and the interstate sale of long guns (rifles and shotguns), except under certain conditions. It forbade sales to minors and those with criminal records, outlawed the importation of nonsporting firearms, and established special penalties for the use or carrying of a firearm while committing a crime of violence or drug trafficking. However, Title I did not forbid the importation of unassembled weapons parts, and some individuals and companies were suspected of importing separate firearms parts and then reassembling them into a complete weapon as a means of getting around the law.

Title II, the National Firearms Act, reenacted the 1934 National Firearms Act and extended the Gun Control Act to cover private ownership of destructive devices such as submachine guns, bombs, and grenades. Enforcement of the federal laws became the responsibility of the U.S. Department of the Treasury, which in 1972 created the Bureau of Alcohol, Tobacco, and Firearms (ATF). The ATF has since come under the control of the U.S. Department of Justice and has been renamed the Bureau of Alcohol, Tobacco, Firearms, and Explosives.

Efforts to Amend the Gun Control Act of 1968

After the passage of the Gun Control Act of 1968, Congress found itself under siege from both pro- and anti-gun groups. Firearms owners and dealers complained about ATF enforcement efforts, which seemed to target law-abiding citizens while neglecting criminals with firearms and people selling firearms illegally. Others voiced concern that the act penalized sportsmen. By contrast, those urging tighter control on guns believed the act did not go far enough in keeping firearms out of the hands of criminals. Every Congress from 1968 to 1986 introduced dozens of pieces of legislation to strengthen, repeal, or diminish the requirements of the 1968 act. In 1986 the gun control advocates were successful.

THE FIREARMS OWNERS' PROTECTION ACT OF 1986

In 1986, nearly 20 years after the passage of the Gun Control Act of 1968, Congress passed major legislation amending the 1968 law. The Firearms Owners' Protection Act of 1986, commonly referred to as the Gun Control Act of 1986, was still in effect as of 2012. The battle over this piece of legislation was fierce. David T. Hardy describes in "The Firearm Owners' Protection Act of 1986: A Historical and Legal Perspective" (*Cumberland Law Review*, vol. 17, 1986) the reactions of those in favor and those opposed to its passage. Those in favor of the act called its passage "necessary to restore fundamental fairness and clarity to our nation's firearms laws." Those opposed called it an "almost monstrous idea" and a "national disgrace." The following sections compare the 1968 act with the current standards under the 1986 act.

Changes Implemented with the Gun Control Act of 1986 and Further Amendments

PROHIBITED PEOPLE. The 1968 legislation identified the categories of people to whom firearms could not be sold by a federally licensed firearms dealer, also called a federal firearms licensee (FFL). These included convicted felons, drug abusers, and the mentally ill. The 1986 legislation clarified some inconsistencies in the 1968 act and made it unlawful for anyone, whether licensed or not, to sell a gun to a high-risk individual. The definition of the term *high risk* has been refined over the years and includes groups such as felons, fugitives, illegal aliens, and those subject to a restraining order.

The 1996 enactment of the Domestic Violence Offender Gun Ban (generally known as the Lautenberg Amendment after its sponsor Senator Frank R. Lautenberg [1924–; D-NJ]) to the Gun Control Act of 1968 expanded the group of people prohibited from legally obtaining a gun. The Lautenberg Amendment made it a felony for anyone convicted of a misdemeanor crime of domestic violence (e.g., assault or attempted assault on a family member) to ship, transport, possess, or receive firearms or ammunition. There was no exception for military personnel or law enforcement officers engaged in official duties unless their record has been expunged (erased). The amendment also made it a felony for anyone to sell or issue a firearm or ammunition to a person with such a conviction. The Lautenberg Amendment was ruled unconstitutional in 1999, but that ruling was reversed two years later. It was challenged and upheld again in 2009 in *United States v. Hayes* (555 U.S. 415), and, as of 2012, the Lautenberg Amendment was still in force.

The Omnibus Consolidated and Emergency Supplemental Appropriations Act of 1999 also amended the Gun Control Act of 1968 by prohibiting aliens admitted under a nonimmigrant visa from obtaining firearms. This included people traveling temporarily in the United States, those studying in the United States who maintained a residence abroad, and some foreign workers. Exceptions included people entering the United States for lawful hunting or sporting purposes, official representatives of a foreign government, and foreign law enforcement officers from friendly foreign governments who entered the United States on official business. In addition, the U.S. attorney general had the authority to waive the prohibition on submission of a petition by an alien.

INTERSTATE SALES. Under the 1968 act it was unlawful to sell or deliver a firearm to anyone from another state, except for long guns, which could be sold to residents of contiguous (bordering) states with laws allowing such sales. Interstate over-the-counter sales of long guns by those licensed to sell them became legal as long as the laws of both states permitted them.

Following the implementation of the National Instant Criminal Background Check System (NICS) in 1998, in the first years of the 21st century, advocates sought to ease restrictions and procedures for interstate firearm sales. In May 2006 Representative Phil Gingrey (1942–; R-GA) introduced the Firearms Commerce Modernization Act, which would allow individuals to buy handguns and long guns from licensed dealers in another state, subject to a background check requirement. However, this bill never became law. (See Representative Gingrey's testimony in Chapter 10.) In February 2009 Representative Steve Scalise (1965–; R-LA) introduced the Firearms Interstate Commerce Reform Act in the U.S. House of Representatives, and in March 2009 Senator David Vitter (1961–; R-LA) introduced the Firearms Transfer Improvement Act in the U.S. Senate. Both bills were similar to the Gingrey bill, and neither bill passed. Similar legislation was proposed in 2011 by Senator Mark Begich (1962–; D-AK) in the Senate and by Scalise in the House of Representatives. Neither bill had been reported out of committee by October 2012.

PURCHASING FIREARMS AND AMMUNITION. The Gun Control Act of 1968 stated that firearms and ammunition could be purchased only on the premises of an FFL and that FFLs were required to record all firearms and ammunition transactions. The 1986 law made the purchase of ammunition and gun components by mail legal. Under the new law firearms dealers were required to keep records only of armor-piercing ammunition sales. Establishments selling only ammunition (no firearms) would not have to be licensed, thus allowing stores that previously may not have carried ammunition because of licensing requirements to do so.

The Treasury and General Government Appropriations Act of 2000 amended the Gun Control Act to require that firearms owners who pawn their weapons must undergo a background check when they seek to redeem the weapons.

CARRYING A GUN BETWEEN JURISDICTIONS. The 1968 act did not address the effects of state and local regulations concerning the intrastate (within a state) transportation of weapons. The 1986 act made it legal to transport any legally owned gun through a jurisdiction where it would otherwise be illegal, provided the possession and transporting of the weapon were legal at the point of origin and the point of destination. In addition, the gun needed to be unloaded and placed in a locked container or in the trunk of a vehicle during transport.

FEDERAL CRIMES. The 1968 legislation prohibited the carrying or use of a firearm during or in relation to a federal crime of violence. In addition, anyone convicted of such a crime would be subject to a minimum penalty over and above any sentence received for the primary offense. The 1986 act added serious drug offenses to the category of prohibited crimes, and it doubled the existing penalty for use of a machine gun or a gun equipped with a silencer.

FORFEITURE OF FIREARMS AND AMMUNITION. Before 1986 any firearm or ammunition involved in, used in, or intended to be used in violation of the Gun Control Act or other federal criminal law could be taken away from the gun owner. However, under the Gun Control Act of 1986, forfeiture is no longer automatic. For some offenses, a willful element must be demonstrated; for others, knowledge of an offense is enough. In the case of a firearm being "intended for use" in a violation, "clear and convincing evidence" of the intent must be shown. In addition, only specified crimes now justify forfeiture, including crimes of violence, drug-related offenses, and certain violations of the Gun Control Act. In all cases forfeiture proceedings must begin within 120 days of seizure, and the court will award attorney fees to the owner if the owner wins the case.

CRIMINAL PENALTIES. The 1968 law stated that a demonstration of willfulness was not needed as an element of proof of violation of any provision of the act, whereas the Gun Control Act of 1986 required proof of willful violations and/or knowing violations to prosecute. The 1986 act also reduced licensee record-keeping violations from felonies to misdemeanors.

LEGAL DISABILITIES. Under the 1968 law, any person who had been convicted of a crime and sentenced to prison for more than one year was restricted from shipping, transporting, or receiving a firearm and could not be granted an FFL. State pardons could not erase the conviction for federal purposes. However, a convicted felon could make a special request to the U.S. secretary of the treasury to be allowed to possess a firearm. The secretary of the treasury had to certify that the possession of a firearm by the convicted felon was not contrary to public interest and safety and that the applicant did not commit a crime involving a firearm or violate federal gun control laws.

Under the 1986 act, however, state pardons can erase convictions for federal purposes, unless the person is specifically denied the right to possess or receive firearms. The act allows those who violated the law to appeal—even those whose crime involved the use of a firearm or the violation of federal gun control laws.

MACHINE GUN FREEZE. The National Firearms Act of 1934 imposed production and transfer taxes and registration requirements on firearms typically associated with criminal activity. These restrictions applied specifically to machine guns; destructive devices such as bombs, missiles, and grenades; and firearm silencers. The definition of a machine gun included "any combination of parts designed and intended for use in converting a weapon to a machine gun."

The Firearms Owners' Protection Act of 1986 made it "unlawful for any person to transfer or possess a machine gun" unless it was manufactured and legally owned before May 19, 1986. In addition, the definition was revised to include any combination of parts "designed and intended solely and exclusively for use in conversion." By refusing to review a lower court's decision in *Farmer v. Higgins* (907 F.2d 1041 [11th Cir. 1990]), the U.S. Supreme Court upheld the ban on machine-gun ownership.

THE LAW ENFORCEMENT OFFICERS' PROTECTION ACT OF 1986

The Law Enforcement Officers' Protection Act of 1986 also amended the 1968 Gun Control Act. This act banned the manufacture or importation of certain varieties of armor-piercing ammunition. Called "cop-killers," these bullets are capable of penetrating police officers' bullet-proof vests. The law defined the banned ammunition as handgun bullets made of specific hard metals: tungsten alloys, steel, brass, bronze, iron, beryllium copper, or depleted uranium. (Standard ammunition is made from lead.) It also decreed that the licenses of dealers who knowingly sold such ammunition should be revoked.

In 1994 the Violent Crime Control and Law Enforcement Act broadened the ban to include other metal-alloy ammunition. Both laws limit the sale of such bullets to the U.S. military or to the police.

The legislation banning armor-piercing ammunition was politically significant because it polarized two traditionally allied groups: the National Rifle Association of America (NRA) and the police. The NRA had long assisted in training police officers in marksmanship. The police saw the ammunition ban as a personal issue, because the cop-killer bullets were intended to harm them. A police lobby, the Law Enforcement Steering Committee (LESC), was formed to get this and other legislation passed. The NRA opposed the legislation as originally written because, it said, the legislation would have also banned most of the types of ammunition used for hunting and target shooting. The final version of the legislation exempted bullets made for rifles and sporting purposes.

THE UNDETECTABLE FIREARMS ACT OF 1988

Highly publicized aircraft hijackings during the 1980s prompted Congress to begin hearings in 1986 to determine if plastic firearms represented a danger to airline passengers if used by terrorists. The passage of the Undetectable Firearms Act of 1988 followed. It banned the manufacture, import, sale, transfer, or possession of a plastic firearm. The act also stated: "If the major parts of the firearms do not permit an accurate X-ray picture of the gun's shape, the firearm is [also defined as] a plastic

firearm, even if the firearm contains more than 3.7 ounces of electromagnetically detectable metal."

The NRA called the proposed legislation unnecessary and the first step toward a total ban on handguns. The lobbying efforts of police officers on the LESC convinced the U.S. attorney general Edwin Meese (1931–) that plastic weapons posed an unacceptable hazard to public safety and that this bill was a necessary piece of legislation. The ban was renewed and made permanent in December 2003.

THE "TOY GUN LAW," 1988

A law requiring that a "toy, look-alike, or imitation firearm shall have as an integral part, permanently affixed, a blaze orange plug inserted in the barrel of such toy, look-alike, or imitation firearm" was passed as section four of the Federal Energy Management Improvement Act of 1988. The law provided for alternative markings if the orange plug could not be used. However, the plug could be removed and the markings painted over.

Ending Sales of Look-Alike Toy Guns

By November 1994 three major toy retailers announced that they would stop selling toy guns designed to look like real guns, because the look-alikes had led to tragic consequences. On September 27, 1994, 13-year-old Nicholas Heyward Jr. was shot and killed by a police officer in Brooklyn, New York, when the officer confronted the boy in a dimly lit stairwell. The appearance of the gun and clicking sounds that occurred led the officer to believe that he was about to be shot. He fired and killed the boy. Later that evening in Brooklyn, 16-year-old Jamiel Johnson was seriously wounded by a plainclothes police officer when the boy pointed his look-alike toy pistol at the officer. Kay-Bee Toy Stores, Toys "R" Us, and Bradlees decided to stop selling these guns, even though the sale of them had generated almost $250 million in 1993. A report by the New York Police Department showed that realistic-looking toy guns had been used in 534 felonies up until October 1994.

Despite pledges by toy retailers to halt their sales of realistic-looking toy guns, the sales did not stop. In 2004, after a New York City council investigation found that 20% of all toy and discount stores in the city were still selling the realistic-looking toy guns, Mayor Michael Bloomberg (1942–) announced a renewed effort to eliminate the guns from local stores' shelves. In 2005 the retail stores CVS and Kmart were levied large fines for selling realistic-looking toy guns. In April 2008 the chain store Party City was accused by the New York City Department of Consumer Affairs of having hundreds of realistic-looking toy guns on its store shelves. In October 2008 the chain store reached a $500,000 settlement with the department for violating the city law.

In "New York City Takes Aim at Illegal Sales of Realistic-Looking Toy Guns" (*New York Daily News*, December 9, 2009), Frank Lombardi reports on a New York City advertising campaign that was conducted between December 2009 and January 2010. The ads were the continuation of New York City's attack on the illegal sales of realistic-looking toy guns and also the result of criminals painting real guns the luminous, bright colors required of toy guns. In the ad the real gun was luminous red and the realistic-looking toy gun was black. The ad was designed to show how difficult it was to determine which gun was the real, deadly weapon. The city also passed legislation to raise its fines for illegal sales of realistic-looking toy guns.

THE GUN-FREE SCHOOL ZONES ACT OF 1990

Congressional passage of the Gun-Free School Zones Act, which was part of the Crime Control Act of 1990, stipulated that it was unlawful for anyone to knowingly possess firearms in school zones. Considered quite strict, the law made it illegal to carry even unloaded firearms in an unlocked case or bag while on public sidewalks in designated school zones. This applied to the sidewalk in front of the firearm owner's residence as well, if that portion of the walkway was within 1,000 feet (305 m) of the grounds of any public or private school—whether or not school was in session. Gun control advocates thought the legislation was needed to send a message to teachers and law enforcement personnel that the federal government was behind them in the effort to get guns out of schools.

Gun rights advocates condemned this attempt to restrict their rights. The act was challenged as unconstitutional and was struck down by the Supreme Court in *United States v. Lopez* (514 U.S. 549 [1995]). The court upheld state and local authority in the regulation of schools and ruled that Congress had exceeded its power in passing the original act. In response to the court's ruling, Congress approved a slightly revised version of the Gun-Free School Zones Act in 1996. The focus of the act was changed from possessing a firearm in a school zone to possessing a firearm "that has moved in or that otherwise affects interstate or foreign commerce" in a school zone.

THE BRADY HANDGUN VIOLENCE PREVENTION ACT OF 1993

In 1981 a mentally disturbed young man named John W. Hinckley Jr. (1955–)—armed with a handgun—shot and seriously wounded the presidential press secretary James S. Brady (1940–) during an assassination attempt on President Ronald Reagan (1911–2004). After the attempt, Hinckley was quickly apprehended, placed in custody, tried, and found not guilty by reason of insanity. His violent act was the impetus behind the Brady Handgun Violence Prevention Act, which was passed by Congress in November 1993 after years of debate.

After the court decision, Hinckley was treated and confined at St. Elizabeth's Hospital in Washington, D.C. As his mental state improved, he was allowed visits to his mother's home in Virginia and some other time away from the hospital. According to the article "Court Gives Would-Be Assassin More Freedom" (CNN.com, June 17, 2009), in June 2009 Hinckley was granted longer visits to his mother's home, a driver's license, and increased time away from the hospital. Prosecutors had objected to the increased freedom, stating that Hinckley continued "to maintain inappropriate thoughts of violence." In late 2011 and early 2012, U.S. District Court Judge Paul Friedman (1944–) presided over hearings to determine whether Hinckley could be granted increased time away from the hospital. Carol Cratty reports in "Virginia Health Facility Bows Out of Proposed Treatment Plan for John Hinckley Jr." (August 17, 2012, http://www.cnn.com/2012/08/17/us/virginia-hinckley-treatment/index.html) that doctors at St. Elizabeth's Hospital proposed allowing him to extend visits home from 10 days per month to 17 days and then to 24 days per month to determine whether or not he could be ultimately granted "convalescent leave." In August 2012 the facility in Virginia that had been proposed as the site of Hinckley's future group therapy sessions dropped out of the plan, and as of October 2012 no ruling had been granted in the case.

"Interim Brady": The Five-Day Waiting Period

The Brady Handgun Violence Prevention Act (commonly referred to as the Brady law), which went into effect on February 28, 1994, established a national five-day waiting period for a person to purchase a handgun. This waiting period allowed time for local law enforcement officers to conduct background checks on handgun purchasers for mental instability or criminal records. The waiting time also provided a cooling-off period to reduce gun-related crimes of passion. Provisions for a waiting period and for background checks by local law enforcement officials were interim measures of the Brady law that could be dropped after a computerized national instant criminal identification system was developed. Such a system became operational in the United States in 1998.

Before 1998, within the first day of the waiting period, licensed firearms dealers were required to send a copy of the purchaser's sworn statement to the chief law enforcement officer where the purchaser resided. The purchaser was asked many questions, including whether he or she was a fugitive from justice, addicted to drugs, illegally in the United States, or convicted of a crime. The dealer could complete the sale after five business days unless the police notified the dealer that the sale would violate the law. It also required the police to respond within 20 business days to any request for a written explanation of a request denial. If the sale was not denied, local law enforcement officials were required to destroy the sworn statement and any other record of the transaction within 20 business days.

In 1997 the Brady law's interim provision requiring law enforcement officers to conduct background checks was ruled unconstitutional by the Supreme Court. Consequently, gun purchasers were no longer required to fill out the Brady Handgun Purchase Form. However, the five-day waiting period remained in place until November 30, 1998, when it expired. It was replaced by a mandatory computerized criminal background check through the National Instant Check System (NICS) before any firearm purchase from a federally licensed firearms dealer.

People Who May Not Purchase Firearms under the Brady Law

The Brady law prohibits firearms sales to any person who:

- Is charged with a crime punishable by imprisonment for more than one year or has been convicted of such a crime
- Is a fugitive from justice
- Is an unlawful user of a controlled substance
- Has been judged mentally ill or has been committed to a mental institution
- Has renounced U.S. citizenship
- Is subject to a court order restraining him or her from harassing, stalking, or threatening an intimate partner or a child
- Has been convicted of domestic violence
- Is an illegal alien
- Has been dishonorably discharged from the military

"PERMANENT BRADY": THE NICS

On November 30, 1998, the five-day waiting period for handgun purchasers was replaced by the NICS, which was designed to quickly screen purchasers of both handguns and long guns. As a result, all FFLs must verify the identity of a customer and receive authorization for the sale from the NICS, which usually takes less than a minute. This is a permanent provision of the Brady law.

How the NICS Works

Under the NICS, FFLs call a toll-free telephone number and provide information on prospective firearms buyers. The Federal Bureau of Investigation (FBI) checks the NICS, which consists of three databases containing more than 40 million criminal history records and other prohibiting records (e.g., a history of drug addiction). In 2011 the system conducted about 16.5 million background checks, the largest number since the system was

instituted. (See Table 3.1.) By July 31, 2012, the NICS had processed more than 151 million background checks.

From 1999 to 2005 the number of background checks conducted each year remained relatively constant, ranging from 8.5 million to 9 million. (See Table 3.1.) After 2005 the number of NICS background checks increased steadily from 10 million in 2006 to 16.5 million in 2011. In general, the summer months generate the lowest number of checks until August, and then the number of checks increases steadily during the fall through December, the hunting and holiday seasons. During October 2001—after the September 11, 2001, terrorist attacks on the United States—NICS transactions were substantially higher than in previous and subsequent Octobers until 2008.

In many states some or all inquiries are directed to the state's designated point of contact (POC), which will then conduct a background check through the NICS. In states without a designated POC, gun dealers contact the FBI directly, and the FBI runs the check through the NICS. Figure 3.1 shows the components of the national firearm check system and how the NICS fits into the system. (The firearm transferee is the person buying the gun. The federal firearm licensee is the person licensed to sell the gun.) The FFL must initiate a background check on the person wanting to buy a gun. Depending on the state, the FFL does this by contacting either the NICS directly or a state-designated POC. In the POC states, the states act as intermediaries between the FFLs and the NICS.

As of September 2011, 29 states, five territories, and the District of Columbia were non-POC entities, which means the FBI conducted all the NICS checks. (See Figure 3.2.) Thirteen states were full POC states, which means that they maintained their own Brady NICS Program and conducted their own background checks by electronically accessing the NICS. The rest of the states were partial POC states, in that they conducted NICS checks on handgun transfers and had the FBI conduct checks on long gun transfers.

Table 3.2 lists the checking agencies (FBI or state POC checking agency) for each state on December 31, 2009, for handguns, long guns, and pawn redemptions. The "purchase check or permit" column refers to the agencies conducting NICS background checks for a gun purchase. The dashes in this column mean that the FBI conducts the purchase checks. Some states have their own background checking systems and permit statutes. States with purchase permit systems require a buyer to obtain a government-issued permit, license, or identification card that must be presented to a seller to receive a firearm. Even though NICS checks usually occur immediately, checks under purchase permit systems may take up to 30 days. The "exempt carry permit" column refers to agencies conducting background checks for state carry permits that provide the holder with an exemption from

TABLE 3.1

Total National Instant Criminal Background Check System (NICS) checks, November 30, 1998–July 31, 2012

Year	Jan	Feb	Mar	Apr	May	Jun	Jul	Aug	Sep	Oct	Nov	Dec	Totals
1998	—	—	—	—	—	—	—	—	—	—	21,196	871,644	892,840
1999	591,355	696,323	753,083	646,712	576,272	569,493	589,476	703,394	808,627	945,701	1,004,333	1,253,354	9,138,123
2000	639,972	707,070	736,543	617,689	538,648	550,561	542,520	682,501	782,087	845,886	898,598	1,000,962	8,543,037
2001	640,528	675,156	729,532	594,723	543,501	540,491	539,498	707,288	864,038	1,029,691	983,186	1,062,559	8,910,191
2002	665,803	694,668	714,665	627,745	569,247	518,351	535,594	693,139	724,123	849,281	887,647	974,059	8,454,322
2003	653,751	708,281	736,864	622,832	567,436	529,334	533,289	683,517	738,371	856,863	842,932	1,008,118	8,481,588
2004	695,000	723,654	738,298	642,589	542,456	546,847	561,773	666,598	740,260	865,741	890,754	1,073,701	8,687,671
2005	685,811	743,070	768,290	658,954	557,058	555,560	561,358	687,012	791,353	852,478	927,419	1,164,582	8,952,945
2006	775,518	820,679	845,219	700,373	626,270	616,097	631,156	833,070	919,487	970,030	1,045,194	1,253,840	10,036,933
2007	894,608	914,954	975,806	840,271	803,051	792,943	757,884	917,358	944,889	1,025,123	1,079,923	1,230,525	11,177,335
2008	942,556	1,021,130	1,040,863	940,961	886,183	819,891	891,224	956,872	973,003	1,183,279	1,529,635	1,523,426	12,709,023
2009	1,213,885	1,259,078	1,345,096	1,225,980	1,023,102	968,145	966,162	1,074,757	1,093,230	1,233,982	1,223,252	1,407,155	14,033,824
2010	1,119,229	1,243,211	1,300,100	1,233,761	1,016,876	1,005,876	1,069,792	1,089,374	1,145,798	1,368,184	1,296,223	1,521,192	14,409,616
2011	1,323,336	1,473,513	1,449,724	1,351,255	1,230,953	1,168,322	1,157,041	1,310,041	1,253,752	1,340,273	1,534,414	1,862,327	16,454,951
2012	1,377,301	1,749,903	1,727,881	1,427,343	1,316,226	1,302,660	1,300,704	—	—	—	—	—	10,202,018
Total													**151,084,417**

Note: These statistics represent the number of firearm background checks initiated through the NICS. They do not represent the number of firearms sold. Based on varying state laws and purchase scenarios, a one-to-one correlation cannot be made between a firearm background check and a firearm sale.

SOURCE: "Total NICS Background Checks November 30, 1998–July 31, 2012," Federal Bureau of Investigation, August 1, 2012, http://www.fbi.gov/about-us/cjis/nics/reports/080112_1998_2012_Monthly_Yearly_Totals .pdf (accessed August 17, 2012)

FIGURE 3.1

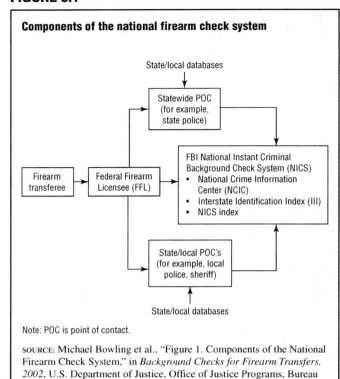

Components of the national firearm check system

State/local databases

Statewide POC
(for example,
state police)

Firearm
transferee

Federal Firearm
Licensee (FFL)

FBI National Instant Criminal
Background Check System (NICS)
• National Crime Information
  Center (NCIC)
• Interstate Identification Index (III)
• NICS index

State/local POC's
(for example, local
police, sheriff)

State/local databases

Note: POC is point of contact.

SOURCE: Michael Bowling et al., "Figure 1. Components of the National Firearm Check System," in *Background Checks for Firearm Transfers, 2002*, U.S. Department of Justice, Office of Justice Programs, Bureau of Justice Statistics, September 2003, http://bjs.ojp.usdoj.gov/content/pub/pdf/bcft02.pdf (accessed August 28, 2012)

an NICS check. The dashes in this column mean that the jurisdiction does not issue exempt carry permits. Exempt carry permits usually expire after a certain length of time.

When the NICS check is initiated, one or more of the following things can happen:

• No disqualifying information is found (the search takes 30 seconds or less) and the transaction can *proceed* immediately.

• The transaction is briefly *delayed* because it is necessary for the FBI to look outside the NICS for data.

• The FBI contacts state or local law enforcement for information because it is not possible to conduct an NICS check electronically. The FBI has three business days to complete its background check. If the check cannot be completed in three days, the transaction may still occur, even though potentially disqualifying information might exist in the NICS. This is called a *default proceed* transaction. The dealer does not, however, have to complete the sale, and the FBI will continue to review the case for two more weeks. If disqualifying information is discovered after three business days, the FBI then contacts the dealer to find out whether the gun was transferred (sold) under the default proceed rule. Default proceed transactions are a matter of particular concern because potentially disqualifying information on a gun buyer may well exist. This sometimes occurs when

information about a person's recent arrest or conviction has not been entered into the national database.

• The dealer transfers a gun to a prohibited person in a default proceed transaction. If this occurs, the FBI may later notify local law enforcement agencies and the ATF in an attempt to retrieve the gun and take appropriate action, if any, against the buyer.

• The NICS check returns disqualifying information on the buyer and the transfer is *denied*.

Table 3.3 shows the reasons the NICS denies gun transfers. The most common reason, which accounted for 60% of denials from November 30, 1998, to December 31, 2011, was because the applicant had been convicted of a felony—a serious crime punishable by a minimum term of one year in a state penitentiary. The FBI also includes misdemeanors in this group, which are less serious crimes punishable by fines or imprisonment in a local jail, but the misdemeanors included in Table 3.3 are only those with jail sentences of two years or more. Other reasons for rejection due to criminal record include substance abuse and crimes of domestic violence. Among the noncriminal reasons for rejection of a firearm purchase application are status as an illegal alien, a dishonorable discharge from the U.S. armed forces, and an individual's renunciation of U.S. citizenship.

Table 3.4 shows the categories of denial data for 2009 and 1999–2009. As in Table 3.3, the most common reason for denial was a felony indictment or conviction. Table 3.4 also shows denials by the checking agency. The data represent attempted purchases from FFLs only; they do not indicate whether rejected purchasers later obtained a gun through other legal or illegal means, or how many applications were rejected because of inaccurate information in the background checkers' files.

Comparing Permit Denials under Interim and Permanent Brady Periods

Table 3.5 presents permit rejection data from 1994 to 2009. The table divides the information into the rejection rates during the "interim period" (1994–98; which had an average denial rate of 2.4%) and the "permanent Brady" period (1998–2009; which had an average denial rejection rate of 1.7%). The interim period in Table 3.5 includes the years of the five-day waiting period, and the permanent Brady period includes the years from the inception of the NICS to 2008. During the permanent Brady years, the denial rate was initially close to that of the Brady interim period at 2.2% in 1998 and 2.4% in 1999, but the rate fell steadily through 2003, remained at 1.6% from 2003 to 2007, and then fell to 1.5% in 2008 and 1.4% in 2009.

Permit Denials under Permanent Brady

Table 3.6 shows the number of applications and denials under permanent Brady by type of agency and

FIGURE 3.2

The National Instant Criminal Background Check System (NICS) participation map, September 2011

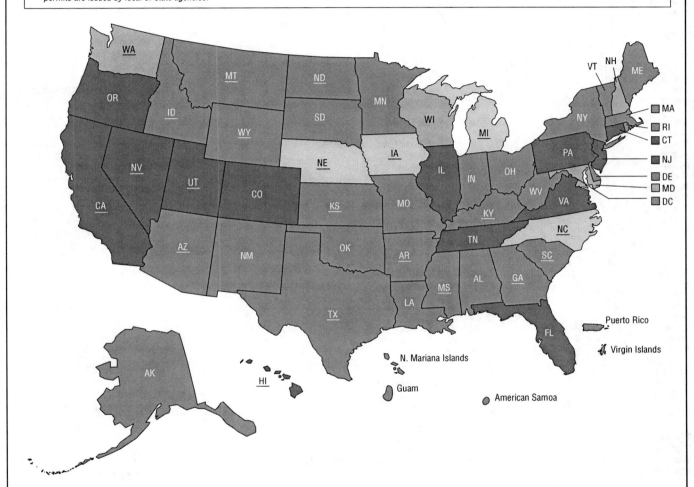

■ 13 (CA, CO, CT, FL, HI, IL,NJ, NV, OR, PA, TN, UT, VA) Full POC: Contact state/territory for all firearms background checks including permits

■ 4 (MD, NH, WA, WI) Partial, POC: Contact state for handgun and FBI for long gun background checks

□ 4 (IA, MI, NC, NE) Partial, POC: Contact state for handgun permit and FBI for long gun background checks

■ 35 (AK, ID, MT, WY, AZ, NM, ND, SD, KS, OK, TX, MN, MO, AR, LA, IN, OH, KY, MS, AL, GA, SC, WV, NY, VT, ME, MA, RI, DE, DC, Puerto Rico, Virgin Islands, American Samoa, N. Mariana Islands, Guam) Non-POC: Contact FBI for all firearms background checks

— 21 (AR, AZ, CA, GA, HI, IA, ID, KS, KY, MI, MS, MT, NC, ND, NE, NV, SC, TX, UT, WA, WY) Denotes that the state has at least one ATF-Qualified Alternate Permit. The permits are issued by local or state agencies.

POC = Point of Contact; ATF = Alcohol, Tobacco, Firearms and Explosives

SOURCE: "NICS Participation Map," in *The National Instant Criminal Background Check System (NICS)*, U.S. Department of Justice, Federal Bureau of Investigation, Criminal Justice Information Services Division, September 2011, http://www.fbi.gov/about-us/cjis/nics/general-information/participation-map (accessed August 17, 2012)

type of check from December 1999 to 2009 and for 2009 alone. From 1999 to 2009, 95.1 million checks were processed—40.9 million through state and local agencies and 54.2 million directly through the FBI's NICS section. Federal (1.4%) and state (1.6%) denial rates were lower in 2009 than the average denial rates from December 1999 to 2009 (1.7% and 2.1%, respectively) overall. However, local agencies denied applications at a slightly higher rate (1.9%) in 2009 compared with the 10-year

average of 1.8% overall. Purchase permits issued by state agencies were also denied at a slightly higher rate (2.5%) in 2009 than the 10-year average (2.4%), as were empty carry permits issued by local agencies (1.8% in 2009, compared with the 10-year average of 1.6%).

Impact of the Brady Law on Gun Violence

Philip J. Cook and Jens Ludwig examine in "The Effects of the Brady Act on Gun Violence" (Bernard E. Harcourt, ed.,

TABLE 3.2

Agencies conducting firearm background checks, by state, December 31, 2009

Jurisdiction	Names or description of checking agencies	
	Purchase check or permit	Exempt carry permit[a]
United States	Federal Bureau of Investigation	—
Alabama	—	—
Alaska	—	—
Arizona	—	Department of Public Safety
Arkansas	—	State Police
California	Department of Justice Firearms Division	—
Colorado	Bureau of Investigation Insta-Check Unit	—
Connecticut	State Police Special Licensing & Firearms	—
Delaware	State Police Bureau of Identification	Three county superior courts
Florida	Department of Law Enforcement	—
Georgia	—	159 county probate courts
Hawaii	Four police departments	—
Idaho	—	44 county sheriffs
Illinois	State Police FOID and FTIP units	—
Indiana	—	—
Iowa	Dept. of Public Safety/99 county sheriffs	Dept. of Public Safety/99 county sheriffs
Kansas	—	—
Kentucky	—	State Police
Louisiana	—	—
Maine	—	—
Maryland	State Police Firearms Enforcement Division	—
Massachusetts	351 police departments	351 police departments
Michigan	595 sheriffs and police departments	County licensing boards
Minnesota	568 sheriffs and police departments	87 county sheriffs
Mississippi	—	Department of Public Safety
Missouri	—	—
Montana	—	56 county sheriffs
Nebraska	95 sheriffs and police departments	—
Nevada	Department of Public Safety	—
New Hampshire	Department of Safety	—
New Jersey	State Police/505 local police departments	—
New Mexico	—	—
New York[b]	58 county sheriffs; some police departments	—
North Carolina	100 county sheriffs	100 county sheriffs
North Dakota	—	Bureau of Criminal Investigation
Ohio	—	—
Oklahoma	—	—
Oregon	State Police Firearms Unit	—
Pennsylvania	State Police Firearms Division	—
Rhode Island	39 police departments	—
South Carolina	—	Law Enforcement Division
South Dakota	—	—
Tennessee	Bureau of Investigation Instant Check	—
Texas	—	Department of Public Safety
Utah	Bureau of Criminal Identification	Bureau of Criminal Identification
Vermont	—	—
Virginia	State Police Firearm Transaction Program	—
Washington	291 sheriffs and police departments	—
West Virginia	—	—
Wisconsin	Department of Justice Handgun Hotline	—
Wyoming	—	Wyoming Attorney General

FOID = Firearm Owner's Identification Card.
FTIP = Firearm Transfer Inquiry Program.
—FBI conducts purchase checks or jurisdiction has no exempt permits.
[a]Agencies listed issue carry permits that may be used to waive a purchase check.
[b]License required for purchase may also allow carrying.

SOURCE: Michael Bowling et al., "Appendix Table 1. Agencies Conducting Firearm Background Checks, December 31, 2009," in *Background Checks for Firearms Transfers, 2009—Statistical Tables*, U.S. Department of Justice, Office of Justice Programs, Bureau of Justice Statistics, October 2010, http://bjs.ojp.usdoj.gov/content/pub/html/bcft/2009/bcft09st.pdf (accessed August 17, 2012)

Guns, Crime, and Punishment in America, 2003) the impact of the Brady law on gun violence. They conclude:

> We do not find evidence that the background-check requirement of the Brady Act has reduced lethal violence or affected the choice of weapons by killers. The Brady Act may have reduced firearm suicides among older Americans, the population at highest risk for suicide, although this decline is at least partially offset by some

increase in non-gun suicides.... Our analysis of the Brady Act highlights the difficulty of reducing gun violence in America through regulation of the primary market [transactions taking place through FFLs] without some change in policy toward secondary-market transfers [transactions between individuals or between non-FFL dealers and individuals at flea markets and gun shows, which can take place within states that do not regulate such sales].

TABLE 3.3

Reasons for federal firearm transfer denials by the National Instant Criminal Background Check System (NICS), November 30, 1998–December 31, 2011

Rank	Prohibited category description	Total	Percent of total
1	Convicted of a crime punishable by more than one year or a misdemeanor punishable by more than two years	540,210	60.08%
2	Misdemeanor crime of domestic violence conviction	95,820	10.66%
3	Fugitive from justice	77,916	8.67%
4	Unlawful user/addicted to a controlled substance	72,189	8.03%
5	Protection/restraining order for domestic violence	39,186	4.36%
6	State prohibitor	34,754	3.86%
7	Under indictment/information	14,231	1.58%
8	Illegal/unlawful alien	10,950	1.22%
9	Adjudicated mental health	7,879	0.87%
10	Federally denied persons file	5,296	0.59%
11	Dishonorable discharge	618	0.07%
12	Renounced U.S. citizenship	50	0.01%
Total federal denials		**899,099**	**100.00%**

Note: Federal in this case = FBI

SOURCE: "Federal Denials: Reasons Why the NICS Section Denies, November 30, 1998–December 31, 2011," in *National Instant Criminal Background Check System (NICS)*, Federal Bureau of Investigation, January 3, 2012, http://www.fbi.gov/about-us/cjis/nics/reports/010312denials-1.pdf (accessed August 17, 2012)

TABLE 3.4

Reasons for denial of firearm transfer applications, by checking agency, 1999–2009

Reason for denial	2009			1999–2009		
	FBI[a]	State	Local	FBI[a]	State	Local
Total	**100%**	**100%**	**100%**	**100%**	**100%**	**100%**
Felony indictment/conviction	48.5	39.4	21.7	64.5	52.8	26.4
State law prohibition	11.2	10.7	6.3	2.6	7.7	12.4
Domestic violence	11.5	13.5	15.8	16.0	13.6	13.5
Misdemeanor conviction	7.2	10.2	13.9	11.6	10.1	11.6
Restraining order	4.3	3.3	1.9	4.4	3.5	1.9
Fugitive	16.8	7.1	1.0	6.6	6.8	1.3
Illegal alien	1.0	0.3	0.7	1.3	0.4	0.5
Mental illness or disability	1.4	6.2	5.3	0.6	2.5	4.4
Drug user/addict	9.3	1.6	15.2	7.7	1.1	8.9
Local law prohibition	—	—	1.5	—	—	5.1
Other prohibitions[b]	0.3	21.2	32.5	0.7	15.1	27.5

Note: Reasons for denials are based on 18 U.S.C. 922 and state laws.
FBI = Federal Bureau of Investigation.
—Not available or Not applicable
[a]During 2008 the FBI began a new classification system and reclassified all denials from 1999 to 2008. Thus, cumulative totals are not comparable with those in prior years.
[b]Includes juveniles, persons dishonorably discharged from the armed services, persons who have renounced U.S. citizenship, and other unspecified persons.

SOURCE: Devon B. Adams and Allina D. Boutilier, "Table 4. Reasons for Denial of Firearm Transfer Applications, by Type of Checking Agency, 1999–2009," in *Background Checks for Firearm Transfers, 2009—Statistical Tables*, U.S. Department of Justice, Office of Justice Programs, Bureau of Justice Statistics, October 19, 2010, http://bjs.ojp.usdoj.gov/content/pub/html/bcft/2009/tables/bcft09st04.pdf (accessed August 17, 2012)

Steven A. Sumner, Peter M. Layde, and Clare E. Guse of the Medical College of Wisconsin contend in "Firearm Death Rates and Association with Level of Firearm Purchase Background Check" (*American Journal of Preventive Medicine*, vol. 35, no. 1, July 2008) that the agencies conducting background checks under the Brady law often lack the necessary data to conduct a complete search. The researchers suggest that this situation is likely due to multiple factors, including incomplete digitalization of state records, laws that prevent sharing of local data, or budgetary constraints. They determine that states conducting local checks at the time of a firearm purchase showed a lower rate of both homicide and suicide across all age groups. Sumner, Layde, and Guse conclude that "methods to increase local-level agency

background checks, such as authorizing local police or sheriff's departments to conduct them, or developing the capability to share local-level records with federal databases, should be evaluated as a means of reducing firearm deaths."

Controversies over Brady Provisions

Major ongoing Brady law controversies center on four issues:

1. The elimination of the five-day waiting period, beginning on November 30, 1998

2. The length of time the FBI can retain records of gun transactions

TABLE 3.5

Number of applications and estimates of denials for firearm transfers, 1994–2009

	Number of applications		
	Received	Denied	Percent denied
Total	107,845,000	1,925,000	1.8%
Brady interim period[a]			
1994–1998	12,740,000	312,000	2.4%
Permanent Brady[b]	95,105,000	1,613,000	1.7%
1998[c]	893,000	20,000	2.2
1999	8,621,000	204,000	2.4
2000	7,699,000	153,000	2.0
2001	7,958,000	151,000	1.9
2002	7,806,000	136,000	1.7
2003	7,831,000	126,000	1.6
2004	8,084,000	126,000	1.6
2005	8,278,000	132,000	1.6
2006	8,612,000	135,000	1.6
2007	8,658,000	136,000	1.6
2008	9,900,000	147,000	1.5
2009	10,764,000	150,000	1.4

Note: Counts are rounded to the nearest 1,000; therefore, annual numbers may not sum to cumulative totals in other tables.
[a]From March 1, 1994, to November 29, 1998, background checks on applicants were conducted by state and local agencies, mainly on handgun transfers.
[b]The National Instant Criminal Background Check System (NICS) began operations. Checks on handgun and long gun transfers are conducted by the Federal Bureau of Investigation (FBI), and by state and local agencies. Totals combine Firearm Inquiry Statistics (FIST) estimates for state and local agencies with transactions and denials reported by the FBI.
[c]November 30 to December 31, 1998. Counts are from the NICS operations report for the period and may include multiple transactions for the same application.

SOURCE: Devon B. Adams and Allina D. Boutilier, "Table 1. Number of Applications and Estimates of Denials for Firearm Transfers or Permits since the Inception of the Brady Act, 1994–2009," in *Background Checks for Firearm Transfers, 2009—Statistical Tables*, U.S. Department of Justice, Office of Justice Programs, Bureau of Justice Statistics, October 19, 2010, http://bjs.ojp.usdoj.gov/content/pub/html/bcft/2009/tables/bcft09st01.pdf (accessed August 17, 2012)

3. The provision of the law that exempts certain people from background checks

4. The regulation of sales at gun shows (the gun-show loophole)

ELIMINATION OF THE WAITING PERIOD. The elimination of the waiting period is probably the thorniest issue connected to the Brady law. Gun control advocates support legislation to establish a minimum three-day waiting period. Gun rights advocates claim that 24 hours is adequate. Gun control advocates maintain that a longer waiting period allows local police to search records that might not be in the NICS and that a waiting requirement of at least three days allows a "cooling-off" period, thereby preventing many crimes of passion. They worry that the speed of the background checks may help some of the targets to evade the Brady law. This could happen if state and local records have not made it into the national database. For example, the NICS may miss individuals who have only recently been convicted of crimes. However, some states have mandatory waiting periods that must be respected before a person can purchase a firearm.

RETENTION OF RECORDS. Soon after the NICS started operations in 1998, the NRA filed a lawsuit arguing, among other things, that records relating to a background check should be immediately destroyed to prevent the formation of a central registry of gun buyers—a registry the NRA considers an invasion of privacy. The Department of Justice noted that the records would be kept, generally, for 90 days but for no more than six months to conduct audits to make sure gun dealers were following the law and to check for identity fraud and other abuses of the system. In July 2000 the federal court of appeals in the District of Columbia upheld in *NRA v. Reno* (No. 99-5270) the legality of the regulation, allowing the FBI to conduct periodic security audits of NICS records. In June 2001 the Supreme Court declined to hear the NRA's appeal of that decision, thereby allowing the lower court's decision to stand.

Only days later the U.S. attorney general John D. Ashcroft (1942–), a gun rights advocate and the head of the Department of Justice, proposed destroying the critical NICS records within one business day. Congress asked the U.S. General Accounting Office (GAO; now the U.S. Government Accountability Office) to investigate the implications of such a quick destruction of records. In July 2002 the GAO published *Gun Control: Potential Effects of Next-Day Destruction of NICS Background Check Records* (http://www.gao.gov/new.items/d02653.pdf). The GAO stated that 97% of the guns retrieved from illegal purchasers who had been incorrectly approved to buy guns between July 2001 and January 2002 would not have been detected under the attorney general's one-day destruction plan.

Two years later, under an amendment sponsored by Representative Todd Tiahrt (1951–; R-KS), the FBI was mandated to destroy the NICS records of a gun sale within 24 hours of allowing the sale to proceed. The amendment was approved as part of legislation that provided funding for the Departments of Commerce, Justice, and State and made it illegal for the agency to report on sales of multiple handguns and gun trace statistics.

In April 2008 Senator Lautenberg introduced the Preserving Records of Terrorist and Criminal Transactions Act to the Senate. This bill would require the FBI to retain records of approved firearm transactions for at least 180 days. If a background check revealed someone suspected of terrorist activity, the FBI would be required to retain the record for at least 10 years. The bill died in committee when the 110th Congress ended, but Senator Lautenberg reintroduced the bill in December 2009 to the 111th Congress. This bill also lapsed.

EXEMPTION FROM BACKGROUND CHECKS. The Brady law exempts gun buyers from NICS background checks if they have a state permit that meets certain criteria established by the ATF, including holding a right-to-carry permit. However, states that issue permits are expected to incorporate an NICS check into their permit process. Buyers who do not have a permit must have an NICS check, and

TABLE 3.6

Number of applications and denials for firearm transfers, by type of agency and type of check, 1999–2009

Type of checks conducted	2009			1999–2009[a]		
	Applications	Denials	Percent denied	Applications	Denials	Percent denied
National total (FIST and FBI)	10,764,237	150,013	1.4%	95,104,599	1,613,953	1.7%
FBI total	6,083,428	67,324	1.1	54,242,433	748,229	1.4
State and local total (FIST)[b]	4,680,809	82,689	1.8	40,862,166	865,724	2.1
State agencies						
Total	**4,067,155**	**65,662**	**1.6%**	**35,042,085**	**733,884**	**2.1%**
Instant checks[c]	2,610,548	43,053	1.6	24,131,328	547,867	2.3
Purchase permits[d]	439,023	11,025	2.5	3,641,934	86,961	2.4
Exempt carry permits[e]	479,370	5,712	1.2	2,578,132	49,138	1.9
Other approvals[f]	538,214	5,872	1.1	4,690,691	49,918	1.1
Local agencies[g]						
Total	**920,304**	**17,027**	**1.9%**	**7,128,269**	**131,840**	**1.8%**
Purchase permits[d]	508,060	10,313	2.0	4,332,109	91,749	2.1
Exempt carry permits[e]	344,615	6,296	1.8	2,210,132	35,433	1.6
Other approvals[f]	67,629	418	0.6	586,028	4,658	0.8

FIST = Firearm Inquiry Statistics.
FBI = Federal Bureau of Investigation.
[a]Totals for the 10-year period include December 1998.
[b]Agencies that conduct exempt carry permit checks in Arizona, Arkansas, Kentucky, Mississippi, North Dakota, South Carolina, Texas, and Wyoming request an FBI background check, but the state agency makes the decision to approve or deny an applicant. Applications in these states are included in FBI checks but denials are included in state and local checks, causing a reduction of FIST total applications by 306,650 in 2009 and by 1,308,188 for 1999 to 2009.
[c]Instant check requires a seller to transmit a buyer's application to a checking agency by telephone or computer; the agency is required to respond immediately or as soon as possible.
[d]Purchase permit systems require a buyer to obtain, after a background check, a government-issued document such as a permit, license, or identification card that must be presented to a seller in order to receive a firearm.
[e]Exempt carry permit is a state concealed weapons permit, issued after a background check, that exempts the holder from a new check at the time of purchase under an ATF ruling or state law.
[f]Other approval systems require a seller to transmit an application to a checking agency, with transfers delayed until a waiting period expires or the agency completes a check.
[g]Totals were estimated.

SOURCE: Devon B. Adams and Allina D. Boutilier, "Table 2. Number of Applications and Denials, by Type of Agency and Type of Check, 1999–2009," in *Background Checks for Firearm Transfers, 2009—Statistical Tables*, U.S. Department of Justice, Office of Justice Programs, Bureau of Justice Statistics, October 19, 2010, http://bjs.ojp.usdoj.gov/content/pub/html/bcft/2009/tables/bcft09st02.pdf (accessed August 17, 2012)

people renewing their permit must undergo an NICS check at that time. In "Compendium of State Laws Governing Firearms 2010" (June 2010, http://www.nraila.org/media/PDFs/Compendium.pdf), the NRA's Institute for Legislative Action lists state firearms laws and whether they allow NICS exemptions.

GUN SHOW REGULATION. The background-check requirement on potential gun buyers applies to federally licensed gun dealers, manufacturers and importers, and pawnshop brokers. People who are not gun dealers and cannot be described as "engaged in the business" of selling firearms do not have to be licensed by the federal government to sell guns, nor do they need to perform background checks on their buyers. This means that someone who is not a gun dealer but who offers a gun or guns for sale at gun shows or flea markets, through classified ads, or through personal sale is not subject to the Brady law. (Both Craigslist and eBay prohibit sales of firearms and related items.)

Legislation was introduced in Congress in 2001, 2003, 2004, 2005, 2007, and 2008 seeking to close the gun-show loophole, but the legislation did not advance. Such legislation was reintroduced in April 2009 (Gun Show Background Check Act) by Senator Lautenberg and in May 2009 (Gun Show Loophole Closing Act) by Representative Michael N. Castle (1939–; R-DE). When the 112th Congress convened,

Senator Lautenberg in the Senate and Representative Carolyn McCarthy (1944–; D-NY) in the House of Representatives introduced versions of legislation designed to close the gun-show loophole. Referred to committee in January 2011 in the Senate and February 2011 in the House of Representatives, the bills remained in committee with no further action as of October 2012.

Rather than waiting for federal legislation, some states closed the gun-show loophole through their own authority and required background checks for gun purchases at gun shows. As reported by the Coalition to Stop Gun Violence (2012, http://www.csgv.org/issues-and-campaigns/gun-show-loophole), California, Colorado, Connecticut, Florida, Hawaii, Iowa, Illinois, Maryland, Massachusetts, Michigan, Nebraska, New Jersey, New York, North Carolina, Oregon, Pennsylvania, and Rhode Island had state laws in place that required background checks for gun show sales.

THE VIOLENT CRIME CONTROL AND LAW ENFORCEMENT ACT OF 1994
Banning Assault Weapons

Federal laws have banned the possession of automatic-fire guns (machine guns) since 1934 and their importation and manufacture for private use since 1986. A machine gun shoots a stream of bullets when the trigger is pulled, instead of a single shot.

In 1989 a semiautomatic firearm was used by Patrick Purdy (1964–1989) to kill five children at an elementary school in Stockton, California. This type of firearm shoots only one bullet each time the trigger is pulled, but the shooter does not have to do anything to "ready" the next shot; therefore, the shooter can fire as fast as he or she can pull the trigger. Some semiautomatic guns can be converted to automatic firearms.

In response to Purdy's crime, several states passed laws banning the sale and possession of semiautomatic weapons. It also led to the passage of the Violent Crime Control and Law Enforcement Act of 1994, which included a subsection commonly known as the Semiautomatic Assault Weapons Ban. This act banned the manufacture, transfer, and possession of semiautomatic firearms but did not outlaw such firearms lawfully possessed before its enactment.

According to the act, banned weapons were defined as guns with a detachable magazine (ammunition holder) and two or more of the following: a bayonet lug (a metal mount for a thrusting knife), a flash suppressor, a protruding pistol grip, a folding stock (which allows the gun to be stored in a smaller space), or a threaded muzzle (used to attach other devices). The act also banned the making or sale of large-capacity ammunition magazines capable of holding more than 10 rounds (bullets). The federal law listed 19 types of banned semiautomatic firearms, including the Uzi, the TEC-9, the Street Sweeper, and their copycats, all of which are often referred to as "assault weapons." The definition of this term is not clear-cut, but an assault weapon is most frequently defined as a semiautomatic rifle, shotgun, or pistol with a combination of any or all the characteristics and accessories banned by the Violent Crime Control and Law Enforcement Act.

The act exempted at least 650 different sporting rifles. Furthermore, it was legal under this law to buy the accessories to convert these semiautomatic guns to automatic firearms, but the conversion itself was against federal law.

Even though the act had several different provisions pertaining to guns, the focus of the debate over its passage was a proposed ban on semiautomatic military-style weapons. Pro-gun supporters repeatedly stressed that the use of the term *assault weapons* to describe the weapons banned under the law was misleading. They complained that the legislation was intended to ban military-style weapons but actually encompassed some ordinary rifles used in hunting and target shooting—weapons that are seldom used to commit crimes. The Semiautomatic Assault Weapons Ban Subsection of the Violent Crime Control and Law Enforcement Act expired on September 13, 2004, despite broad support for its renewal; as of 2012 it had not been renewed. Chapter 9 offers congressional testimony about renewing the semiautomatic assault weapons ban.

Banning Juveniles from Possessing Handguns or Ammunition

The 1994 Violent Crime Control and Law Enforcement Act also prohibited the possession of a handgun or ammunition by a juvenile under 18 years of age. In addition, it prohibited the sale or private transfer of a handgun or ammunition to juveniles. Exemptions included cases in which the juvenile temporarily used the handgun for employment, with the permission of the owner, such as in ranching or farming where predatory animals often kill livestock. Other exemptions included using a handgun for target practice, hunting, or a course of instruction on the safe and lawful use of a handgun.

Implementing New Regulations for Obtaining FFLs

Table 3.7 shows the number of active firearms licensees from 1975 through 2011. Even before the changes that came when the 1994 Violent Crime Control and Law Enforcement Act was implemented, the ATF realized that it needed to strengthen the procedures for obtaining an FFL. Between late 1992 and early 1993 news stories, such as Josh Sugarmann's "Gun Market Is Wide Open in America" (*Christian Science Monitor*, April 23, 1993), revealed just how easy it was to get an FFL. The charge for a three-year license was a mere $10, and the only check was a short computer criminal history query. As a result of the publicity, the number of FFL applications and FFLs issued per year rose dramatically, surpassing 280,000 active FFLS in 1992 and 1993. (See Table 3.7.)

The ATF took steps to curtail the number of active FFLs. The Brady law raised the fee to $200 for a three-year license and $90 for a three-year renewal. In March 1994 the ATF sent out new application forms requiring each applicant to submit fingerprint cards and a photograph. These new regulations, as well as an extra step to ensure that the person applying for an FFL complied with state and local laws, was included as part of the Violent Crime Control and Law Enforcement Act. The act also required each licensee to report the theft or loss of a firearm within 48 hours.

There are 11 types of FFLs, including the Type 3 license—collector of curio and relic firearms. Many of the types of FFLs are specific to importers and manufacturers of firearms, their components, and their ammunition. The Type 1 FFL is for a dealer or gunsmith, and the Type 2 FFL is for a pawnbroker who deals in guns.

In *Federal Firearms Licensees: Various Factors Have Contributed to the Decline in the Number of Dealers* (March 1996, http://www.gao.gov/archive/1996/gg96078.pdf), the GAO states that beginning in 1994, due to the revisions in the law, the number of FFLs and the number of FFL applications started to drop sharply. According to the ATF, in *Firearms Commerce in the United States—2001/2002*, this decline is reflected in the number of active FFLs in 1993 (283,193), compared with 1996 (124,286). However,

TABLE 3.7

Federal firearms licensees, 1975–2011

| Fiscal year | Dealer | Pawn-broker | Collector | Manufacturer of | | Importer | Destructive device | | | Total |
				Ammunition	Firearms		Dealer	Manufacturer	Importer	
1975	146,429	2,813	5,211	6,668	364	403	9	23	7	161,927
1976	150,767	2,882	4,036	7,181	397	403	4	19	8	165,697
1977	157,463	2,943	4,446	7,761	408	419	6	28	10	173,484
1978	152,681	3,113	4,629	7,735	422	417	6	35	14	169,052
1979	153,861	3,388	4,975	8,055	459	426	7	33	12	171,216
1980	155,690	3,608	5,481	8,856	496	430	7	40	11	174,619
1981	168,301	4,308	6,490	10,067	540	519	7	44	20	190,296
1982	184,840	5,002	8,602	12,033	675	676	12	54	24	211,918
1983	200,342	5,388	9,859	13,318	788	795	16	71	36	230,613
1984	195,847	5,140	8,643	11,270	710	704	15	74	40	222,443
1985	219,366	6,207	9,599	11,818	778	881	15	85	45	248,794
1986	235,393	6,998	10,639	12,095	843	1,035	16	95	52	267,166
1987	230,888	7,316	11,094	10,613	852	1,084	16	101	58	262,022
1988	239,637	8,261	12,638	10,169	926	1,123	18	112	69	272,953
1989	231,442	8,626	13,536	8,345	922	989	21	110	72	264,063
1990	235,684	9,029	14,287	7,945	978	946	20	117	73	269,079
1991	241,706	9,625	15,143	7,470	1,059	901	17	120	75	276,116
1992	248,155	10,452	15,820	7,412	1,165	894	15	127	77	284,117
1993	246,984	10,958	16,635	6,947	1,256	924	15	128	78	283,925
1994	213,734	10,872	17,690	6,068	1,302	963	12	122	70	250,833
1995	158,240	10,155	16,354	4,459	1,242	842	14	118	71	191,495
1996	105,398	9,974	14,966	3,144	1,327	786	12	117	70	135,794
1997	79,285	9,956	13,512	2,451	1,414	733	13	118	72	107,554
1998	75,619	10,176	14,875	2,374	1,546	741	12	125	68	105,536
1999	71,290	10,035	17,763	2,247	1,639	755	11	127	75	103,942
2000	67,479	9,737	21,100	2,112	1,773	748	12	125	71	103,157
2001	63,845	9,199	25,145	1,950	1,841	730	14	117	72	102,913
2002	59,829	8,770	30,157	1,763	1,941	735	16	126	74	103,411
2003	57,492	8,521	33,406	1,693	2,046	719	16	130	82	104,105
2004	56,103	8,180	37,206	1,625	2,144	720	16	136	84	106,214
2005	53,833	7,809	40,073	1,502	2,272	696	15	145	87	106,432
2006	51,462	7,386	43,650	1,431	2,411	690	17	170	99	107,316
2007	49,221	6,966	47,690	1,399	2,668	686	23	174	106	108,933
2008	48,261	6,687	52,597	1,420	2,959	688	29	189	113	112,943
2009	47,509	6,675	55,046	1,511	3,543	735	34	215	127	115,395
2010	47,664	6,895	56,680	1,759	4,293	768	40	243	145	118,487
2011	48,676	7,075	59,227	1,895	5,441	811	42	259	161	123,587

SOURCE: "Exhibit 10. Federal Firearms Licensees Total (1975–2011)," in *Firearms Commerce in the United States: Annual Statistical Update, 2012*, U.S. Department of Justice, Bureau of Alcohol, Tobacco, Firearms and Explosives, May 4, 2012, http://www.atf.gov/publications/firearms/050412-firearms-commerce-in-the-us-annual-statistical-update-2012.pdf (accessed August 17, 2012)

beginning in 1997 the decline appeared to level off, with the overall number of licenses stabilizing between 1997 (106,710) and 2001 (104,840); after that year the number of licenses began to increase.

Figure 3.3 shows the number of active FFLs for selected years from 2002 to 2012. The total number of active FFLs slowly increased during this period. In 2012 there were 128,849 active FFLs, compared with 103,411 active FFLs in 2002, an increase of nearly 25%. Interestingly, the number of active Type 3 FFLs (collector's licenses) roughly doubled from 30,157 in 2002 to 61,416 in 2012, whereas the number of active commercial FFLs decreased from 73,254 in 2002 to 67,433 in 2012.

Other Provisions of the Violent Crime Control and Law Enforcement Act

The Violent Crime Control and Law Enforcement Act imposed stiffer penalties for using a gun during a violent crime or drug felony. Amendments to the act and policies enacted by the ATF prohibited the possession of firearms by people guilty of domestic abuse. It also tightened rules and regulations for firearms dealers.

GUN LAWS PASSED IN RESPONSE TO SEPTEMBER 11, 2001

Some new gun laws were passed in the wake of the September 11, 2001, terrorist attacks on the United States. In November 2002 Congress passed the Arming Pilots against Terrorism Act, which allows airline pilots to carry handguns in the cockpit. The Law Enforcement Officers Safety Act, signed into law in 2004, allows off-duty or retired police officers with firearms training to travel the country with a concealed weapon.

GUN LAWS PASSED IN RESPONSE TO THE VIRGINIA TECH MASSACRE

The NICS Improvement Amendments Act of 2007 was signed into law by President George W. Bush (1946–) in January 2008. This legislation mandates that information that would prohibit individuals from possessing or purchasing

FIGURE 3.3

Number of active federal firearms licenses (FFLs), selected years 2002–12

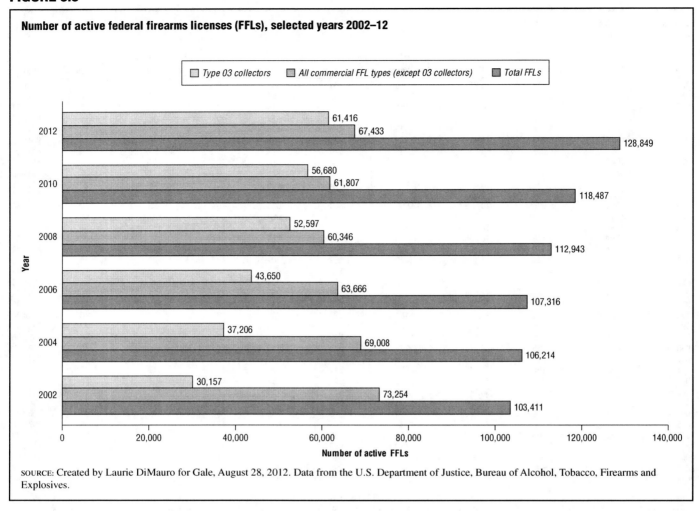

SOURCE: Created by Laurie DiMauro for Gale, August 28, 2012. Data from the U.S. Department of Justice, Bureau of Alcohol, Tobacco, Firearms and Explosives.

firearms be transmitted from state and local governments and federal agencies to the NICS. States are provided financial assistance to do this work and receive penalties if they fail to comply.

The law was enacted in response to Seung-Hui Cho's (1984–2007) shooting rampage on April 16, 2007, at Virginia Polytechnic Institute and State University (Virginia Tech) in Blacksburg, Virginia. Cho had been ordered by a judge to receive mental health treatment, but that information was never entered into the NICS database. It would have disqualified Cho from purchasing the 9mm semiautomatic handgun and .22-caliber pistol he used to kill 32 students and teachers, and then himself. Even though this law had been proposed in Congress since 2002, it languished until the Virginia Tech tragedy brought the issue to wide public attention.

STATE FIREARMS CONTROL LAWS

The Brady Campaign to Prevent Gun Violence annually publishes state "report cards" that rank states according to the strength or weakness of their gun laws. The state scorecard rankings for 2011 are shown in Table 3.8. Each

state can earn up to 100 points, the highest and best number. States earn points based on their gun control laws. States with many and strong comprehensive gun control laws earn the most points. States with few effective gun control laws earn low scores.

According to the Brady Campaign, the states that had the most effective gun control laws in 2011—those scoring at least 50 points—were (from highest to lowest) California, New Jersey, Massachusetts, New York, Connecticut, and Hawaii. (See Table 3.8.) The lowest-ranked states—those scoring only two points or below—were (from lowest to highest) Utah, Arizona, Alaska, Oklahoma, North Dakota, Montana, Louisiana, Kentucky, and Idaho. Thirty-nine states (78%) scored 16 points or less. (See Table 3.8.)

Laws and constitutional provisions relating to the purchase, ownership, and use of firearms differ dramatically from state to state and just as sharply from county to county and town to town. In most states the right to gun ownership was protected in the state constitution. (See Table 3.9.) As of 2012, only six states—California, Iowa, Maryland, Minnesota, New Jersey and New York—did not have such a provision. Some states, including Connecticut, Illinois,

TABLE 3.8

Brady Campaign state scorecard rankings, 2011

Rank	State	2011 points	Stars
1	California	81	4 Stars
2	New Jersey	72	3 Stars
3	Massachusetts	65	3 Stars
4	New York	62	3 Stars
5	Connecticut	58	3 Stars
6	Hawaii	50	3 Stars
7	Maryland	45	2 Stars
8	Rhode Island	44	2 Stars
9	Illinois	35	2 Stars
10	Pennsylvania	26	2 Stars
11	Michigan	25	2 Stars
12	North Carolina	16	1 Star
T-15	Colorado	15	1 Star
T-15	Oregon	15	1 Star
T-15	Washington	15	1 Star
T-17	Alabama	14	1 Star
T-17	Minnesota	14	1 Star
18	Delaware	13	1 Star
19	Virginia	12	1 Star
T-22	Georgia	8	
T-22	South Carolina	8	
T-22	Tennessee	8	
T-25	Iowa	7	
T-25	Maine	7	
T-25	Ohio	7	
T-27	New Hampshire	6	
T-27	Vermont	6	
T-29	Nebraska	5	
T-29	Nevada	5	
T-39	Arkansas	4	
T-39	Indiana	4	
T-39	Kansas	4	
T-39	Mississippi	4	
T-39	Missouri	4	
T-39	New Mexico	4	
T-39	South Dakota	4	
T-39	Texas	4	
T-39	West Virginia	4	
T-39	Wyoming	4	
T-41	Florida	3	
T-41	Wisconsin	3	
T-47	Idaho	2	
T-47	Kentucky	2	
T-47	Louisiana	2	
T-47	Montana	2	
T-47	North Dakota	2	
T-47	Oklahoma	2	
T-50	Alaska	0	
T-50	Arizona	0	
T-50	Utah	0	

SOURCE: "2011 Brady Campaign State Scorecard," Brady Campaign to Prevent Gun Violence, 2012, http://www.bradycampaign.org/xshare/stateleg/scorecard/2011/2011_Brady_Campaign_State_Scorecard_Rankings.pdf (accessed August 17, 2012)

Massachusetts, New Jersey, New York, and Virginia, and the District of Columbia, had laws prohibiting or tightly restricting ownership of certain weapons, primarily machine guns and assault weapons.

Even though gun laws vary among states, all states had a waiting period for handgun purchases in the first five years after passage of the 1993 interim Brady law—they either complied with the federal waiting period of five business days or had alternative requirements. As of 2012, all states had instant background checks, but some had waiting periods as well. (See Table 3.9.) Furthermore, 14 states plus the

District of Columbia required permits or licenses to purchase handguns and four states and the District of Columbia required permits for long guns.

Registration, which is not required by federal law, is a record of the transfer or ownership of a specific firearm. As of September 2012, five states and the District of Columbia required registration of handguns, with several others requiring registration of long guns, assault weapons, or maintaining levels of documentation of transfers or permits that comprise a type of de facto registry (existing in reality whether with lawful authority or not). (See Table 3.9.)

Concealed Weapons

All states and the District of Columbia have some type of concealed-carry laws. As of 2012, 38 states had a shall-issue permit system, which made it easy for almost anyone to carry a hidden gun. Table 3.10 shows state policies regarding concealed weapons permits relative to the Brady background check as of 2011. In Alaska, for example, concealed weapons permits marked "NICS-Exempt" qualify as alternatives to the background check requirements of the Brady law. A concealed weapons permit must be valid under state law to qualify as an alternative to a Brady background check. Regardless of any dates shown on the chart, concealed weapons permits qualify as alternatives to the background check for no more than five years from the date of issuance.

Carrying Firearms Openly

Even though few people exercise the option to openly carry firearms, 25 states and the District of Columbia had laws prohibiting this action as of September 2012. For the 25 states that did allow open carry, some placed restrictions on its practice. For example, in Ohio a person with a concealed handgun license could transport a loaded handgun in a vehicle if it was in a holster. In Alabama, Michigan, and Pennsylvania a gun owner needed a license to carry a handgun openly in a vehicle. In Minnesota a Carrying Concealed Weapons permit was needed to carry a firearm openly. In Arkansas carrying a firearm "with a purpose to employ it as a weapon against a person" was banned; in Tennessee carrying "with the intent to go armed" was forbidden; and in Vermont carrying a firearm "with the intent or purpose of injuring another" was outlawed. In California, North Dakota, and Utah the carrying of a loaded firearm was prohibited. In Colorado municipalities could prohibit open carrying in government buildings if a sign was posted to that effect. In Washington local municipalities could override state law and provide legislation that allowed openly carrying a firearm.

Many states and municipalities allow carrying firearms openly, but some businesses in those jurisdictions have banned this action in their establishments. As a result, some of the businesses that have not followed suit have been

TABLE 3.9

Firearm purchase laws, by state, 2012

State	Constitutional provision	Permit required to purchase		Waiting period		Registration	
		Long guns	Handguns	Long guns	Handguns	Long guns	Handguns
Alabama	Article 1, Section 26	No	No	None	None	No	No[a]
Alaska	Article 1, Section 19	No	No	None	None	No	No
Arizona	Article 2, Section 26	No	No	None	None	No	No
Arkansas	Article 2, Section 5	No	No	None	None	No	No
California	None	No	Yes[b]	10 days	10 days	No[c]	Yes
Colorado	Article 2, Section 13	No	No	None	None	No	No
Connecticut	Article 1, Section 15	No	Yes	14 days	None	Yes[f]	No[a]
Delaware	Article 1, Section 20	No	No	None	None	No	No
Florida	Article 1, Section 8	No	No	None	3–5 days[d]	No	No
Georgia	Article 1, Section 1	No	No	None	None	No	No
Hawaii	Article 1, Section 17	Yes	Yes	14–20 days	14–20 days	Yes	Yes
Idaho	Article 1, Section 11	No	No	None	None	No	No
Illinois	Article 1, Section 22	Yes	Yes	24 hours	7 days	No	No
Indiana	Article 1, Section 32	No	No	None	None	No	No
Iowa	None	No	Yes	None	3 days	No	No
Kansas	Bill of Rights, Section 4	No	No	None	None	No	No
Kentucky	Article 1, Section 1	No	No	None	None	No	No
Louisiana	Article 1, Section 11	No	No	None	None	No[e]	No
Maine	Article 1, Section 16	No	No	None	None	No	No
Maryland	None	No	No	7 days[f]	7 days	No[f]	Yes
Massachusetts	Part 1, Article 17	Yes	Yes	None	None	No[a]	No[a]
Michigan	Article 1, Section 6	No	Yes	None	None	No	No[a]
Minnesota	None	No	Yes[f]	7 days[f]	7 days	No	No
Mississippi	Article 3, Section 12	No	No	None	None	No	No
Missouri	Article 1, Section 23	No	No	None	None	No	No
Montana	Article 2, Section 12	No	No	None	None	No	No
Nebraska	Article 1, Section 1	No	Yes	None	None	No	No
Nevada	Article 1, Section 11	No	No	None	None	No	No
New Hampshire	Part 1, Article 2-a	No	No	None	None	No	No
New Jersey	None	Yes	Yes	None	7 days	No	Yes
New Mexico	Article 2, Section 6	No	No	None	None	No	No
New York	None	No[g]	Yes	None	None	No[g]	Yes
North Carolina	Article 1, Section 30	No	Yes	None	None	No	No[a]
North Dakota	Article 1, Section 1	No	No	None	None	No	No
Ohio	Article 1, Section 4	No	No	None	None	No	No
Oklahoma	Article 2, Section 26	No	No	None	None	No	No
Oregon	Article 1, Section 27	No	No	None	None	No	No[a]
Pennsylvania	Article 1, Section 21	No	No	None	None	No	No[a]
Rhode Island	Article 1, Section 22	No	Yes[b]	7 days	7 days	No	No
South Carolina	Article 1, Section 20	No	No	None	None	No	No
South Dakota	Article 6, Section 24	No	No	None	None	No	No
Tennessee	Article 1, Section 26	No	No	None	None	No	No
Texas	Article 1, Section 23	No	No	None	None	No	No
Utah	Article 1, Section 6	No	No	None	None	No	No
Vermont	Chapter 1, Article 16	No	No	None	None	No	No
Virginia	Article 1, Section 13	No	No	None	None	No	No
Washington	Article 1, Section 24	No	Yes	None	5 days	No	No[a]
West Virginia	Article 3, Section 22	No	No	None	None	No	No
Wisconsin	Article 1, Section 25	No	No	None	48 hours	No	No
Wyoming	Article 1, Section 24	No	No	None	None	No	No
District of Columbia	N/A	Yes	Yes	10 days	10 days	Yes	Yes

Notes
[a]Though not a complete registry of ownership, varying levels of documentation of transfers or permits are maintained in these states.
[b]Completion of a safety course is required.
[c]Registration law takes effect on January 1, 2014.
[d]The statewide 3-day waiting period may be extended by local jurisdictions.
[e]Pertains to shotguns and rifles less than 26 inches long.
[f]For assault weapons; in Minnesota for "a pistol or semiautomatic military-style assault weapon."
[g]Stricter gun control laws have been enacted in New York City, including requiring a permit to purchase a rifle or shotgun and restricting permission to carry firearms, even during transport to or from a target range.

SOURCE: Compiled by Laurie DiMauro for Gale, 2012.

criticized, in particular Starbucks. In the press release "Starbucks Position on Open Carry Gun Laws" (March 3, 2010, http://news.starbucks.com/article_display.cfm?article_id=3 32), the company responds to this criticism by explaining that it complies with the laws and statutes in the communities it serves by allowing open carry in jurisdictions where it is legal and not allowing it where it is legally banned. The company believes that advocacy groups on both sides of the issue "have chosen to use Starbucks as a way to draw attention to their positions." Those in favor of open carry

TABLE 3.10

Permanent Brady permit chart, 2011

[Last updated: August 26, 2011]

State/territory	Qualifying permits
Alabama	None
Alaska	Concealed weapons permits marked NICS-Exempt
American Samoa	None
Arizona	Concealed weapons permits qualify.
Arkansas	Concealed weapons permits issued on or after April 1, 1999 qualify.*
California	Entertainment Firearms Permit only
Colorado	None
Connecticut	None
Delaware	None*
District of Columbia	None*
Florida	None*
Georgia	Georgia firearms licenses qualify.
Guam	None*
Hawaii	Permits to acquire and licenses to carry qualify.
Idaho	Concealed weapons permits qualify.
Illinois	None
Indiana	None
Iowa	Permits to acquire and permits to carry concealed weapons qualify.
Kansas	Kansas licenses to carry a concealed handgun qualify.
Kentucky	Concealed weapons permits issued on or after July 12, 2006 qualify.
Louisiana	None*
Maine	None*
Maryland	None*
Massachusetts	None*
Michigan	Licenses to purchase a pistol qualify. Concealed Pistol Licenses (CPLs) issued on or after November 22, 2005, qualify as an alternative to a National Instant Criminal Background Check System (NICS) check. CPLs issued prior to November 22, 2005 and Temporary Concealed Pistol Licenses do not qualify as NICS alternative.
Minnesota	None*
Mississippi	License to carry concealed pistol or revolver issued to individuals under Miss. Stat. Ann. § 45-9-101 qualify. (NOTE: security guard permits issued under Miss. Stat. Ann. § 97-37-7 do not qualify).
Missouri	None*
Montana	Concealed weapons permits qualify.
Nebraska	Concealed handgun permit qualifies as an alternative. Handgun purchase certificates qualify.
Nevada	Concealed carry permits issued on or after July 1, 2011, qualify.
New Hampshire	None
New Jersey	None
New Mexico	None
New York	None
North Carolina	Permits to purchase a handgun and concealed handgun permits qualify.
North Dakota	Concealed weapons permits issued on or after December 1, 1999 qualify.*
Northern Mariana Islands	None
Ohio	None
Oklahoma	None*
Oregon	None*
Pennsylvania	None
Puerto Rico	None
Rhode Island	None
South Carolina	Concealed weapons permits qualify.
South Dakota	None*
Tennessee	None
Texas	Concealed weapons permits qualify.
U.S. Virgin Islands	None
Utah	Concealed weapons permits qualify.
Vermont	None
Virginia	None

TABLE 3.10

Permanent Brady permit chart, 2011 [CONTINUED]

[Last updated: August 26, 2011]

State/territory	Qualifying permits
Washington	Concealed pistol licenses issued on or after July 22, 2011 qualify.
West Virginia	None
Wisconsin	None
Wyoming	Concealed weapons permits qualify.

*While certain permits issued in these states prior to November 30, 1998 were "grandfathered" as Brady alternatives, none of these grandfathered permits would still be valid under State law as of November 30, 2003.

Note: Notwithstanding the dates set forth below, permits qualify as alternatives to the background check requirements of the Brady law for no more than 5 years from the date of issuance. The permit must be valid under State law in order to qualify as a Brady alternative.

SOURCE: "Permanent Brady Permit Chart," in *Brady Law*, U.S. Department of Justice, Bureau of Alcohol, Tobacco, Firearms, and Explosives, Enforcement Programs and Services, August 26, 2011, http://www.atf.gov/firearms/brady-law/permit-chart.html (accessed August 17, 2012)

hold that they are able to protect themselves and unarmed individuals from criminals and that their gun-carrying is a visible symbol of their right to bear arms and of a free society. Those opposed to open carry believe the practice is provocative and dangerous. Starbucks notes that it will not ask law-abiding customers to leave its coffeehouses and that "the political, policy and legal debates around these issues belong in the legislatures and courts, not in our stores."

Allowing the open carry of firearms outside of events at which President Barack Obama (1961–) will speak has also been criticized. In jurisdictions that allow open carry, this behavior is lawful. However, those carrying weapons, whether openly carried or concealed, are not allowed to enter the venue.

Minors

During the 1990s Americans became concerned with what the U.S. surgeon general called an epidemic of youth violence. In *Youth Violence: A Report of the Surgeon General* (January 2001, http://www.surgeongeneral.gov/library/youthviolence/default.htm), the surgeon general describes the sharply rising arrest rates of young people for violent crimes between 1983 and 1993–94. The surgeon general also notes that juvenile homicides increased 65% between 1987 and 1993. The number of older juveniles killed with firearms accounted for nearly all the growth.

Even though arrest rates later declined, the surgeon general explains that some states passed tougher laws prohibiting juveniles from possessing firearms and/or punishing those who supplied them with guns. These state laws are in addition to the federal law that prohibits FFLs from selling or delivering handguns to people under the age of 21 (18 U.S.C. 922[b][l]) and the federal law that prohibits people under the age of 18 from possessing handguns (18 U.S.C. Sect. 922[x]). Federal law allows the sale of handguns to people between the ages of 18 and 21 at gun shows, unless specifically prohibited by state law.

LOCAL ORDINANCES

Many laws regulating guns are local ordinances passed by town, city, and county governments. Most of these statutes regulate the sale of weapons, restricting who can buy firearms and imposing waiting periods on firearms purchases. Among the most notable of these are statutes in effect in New York City, which are more restrictive than the laws in place throughout the rest of the state. For example, the city does not recognize firearm permits from any other jurisdiction, including permits issued by the state of New York. Other restrictions include prohibiting possession of a gun by anyone under 21 years of age, requiring a license to purchase a firearm, requiring handguns being transported in vehicles in New York City to be unloaded and in a locked container, with ammunition in a separate locked container.

CHAPTER 4

COURT RULINGS ON FIREARMS

The U.S. Constitution and most state constitutions guarantee the right to bear arms, but the courts have ruled that this right may be strictly controlled. Many laws and regulations have been enacted at the local, state, and federal levels to regulate firearms. When these laws have been challenged, state and federal courts have consistently upheld the right of governments to require the registration of firearms, to determine how these weapons may be carried, and even to forbid the sale or use of some weapons under certain circumstances. Courts have also been asked to decide if manufacturers, dealers, or sometimes even relatives of the gun carrier should be held responsible when guns are used to commit crimes.

Table 4.1 presents a list of reasons an individual may be denied the right to bear arms in the United States in 2012. It is generally accepted that gun ownership will be denied to convicted felons, individuals who are not of sound mind, and individuals regarded as incapable due to a mental condition. Restrictions such as these, however, have also been challenged in court. The following selection of court cases includes landmark decisions and more recent rulings on gun rights and regulations at the federal, state, and local levels.

SECOND AMENDMENT INTERPRETATIONS
The Bill of Rights: Federal versus State Protections

The "right of the people to keep and bear arms" is the essence of the Second Amendment, which is part of the Bill of Rights (ratified 1791) to the U.S. Constitution. For many years, when deciding cases based on any guarantee granted by the Bill of Rights, including the Second Amendment, the courts relied on the 1833 U.S. Supreme Court decision in *Barron v. City of Baltimore* (32 U.S. 243). In that case the court ruled that the Bill of Rights does not apply to or restrict the states. This meant that the Bill of Rights was a limitation to the federal government only; its protections applied to federal laws.

Under this interpretation, a state did not have to allow people "to keep and bear arms" unless the state's constitution guaranteed that right. If the state constitution did not ensure that right, then state or local authorities could arrest a person who possessed a firearm; nevertheless, federal law enforcement officials could not because of the Bill of Rights. Thus, state constitutions—rather than the Second Amendment of the U.S. Constitution—decided most gun cases. This situation, however, changed during the years of Chief Justice Earl Warren (1891–1974). Warren was the chief justice from 1953 to 1969, when most of the guarantees of the Bill of Rights were held to apply to the states through the 14th Amendment, which states, "No state shall make or enforce any law which shall abridge the privileges or immunities of citizens."

The Individual Rights Interpretation versus the Collective Rights Interpretation

Gun rights advocates interpret the Second Amendment as a guarantee to individuals of the right to keep and bear arms without governmental interference. Favoring stricter control of guns, proponents of the collective rights argument disagree and point to the opening words of the Second Amendment—"A well regulated militia, being necessary to the security of a free state"—as an intention to guarantee the right of states to maintain militias. The modern militia of the United States is the National Guard. Thus, collective rights advocates argue that the general population does not need unfettered access to guns, because they are no longer expected to form a militia during times of need.

A middle ground was struck in the landmark decision *District of Columbia v. Heller* (554 U.S. ___ [2008]), in which the U.S. Supreme Court made it clear that the government can "interfere" with the right to keep and bear arms, while interpreting the Second Amendment as upholding an individual's right to own and use firearms for lawful purposes. In this case, the court ruled that the District of Columbia's ban on handguns was unconstitutional, but it stressed that handgun regulation was lawful.

TABLE 4.1

Individuals prohibited from shipping, transporting, receiving, or possessing firearms, 2012

These categories include any person:

- Under indictment or information in any court for a crime punishable by imprisonment for a term exceeding one year;
- Convicted of a crime punishable by imprisonment for a term exceeding one year;
- Who is a fugitive from justice;
- Who is an unlawful user of or addicted to any controlled substance;
- Who has been adjudicated as a mental defective or has been committed to any mental institution;
- Who is an illegal alien;
- Who has been discharged from the military under dishonorable conditions;
- Who has renounced his or her United States citizenship;
- Who is subject to a court order restraining the person from harassing, stalking, or threatening an intimate partner or child of the intimate partner; or
- Who has been convicted of a misdemeanor crime of domestic violence.

SOURCE: "Identify Prohibited Persons," U.S. Department of Justice, Bureau of Alcohol, Tobacco, Firearms, and Explosives, 2012, http://www.atf.gov/firearms/how-to/identify-prohibited-persons.html (accessed August 28, 2012)

FEDERAL COURT CASES

United States v. Cruikshank: Right to Bear Arms?

The first major federal case dealing with the Second Amendment was *United States v. Cruikshank* (92 U.S. 542 [1875]). The defendants were members of the Ku Klux Klan, a white supremacist group, and were convicted of conspiracy to deprive two African-American men of their right of assembly and free speech and their right to keep and bear arms as guaranteed by the U.S. Constitution. The Supreme Court ruled, "'Bearing arms for a lawful purpose.' This is not a right granted by the Constitution. Neither is it in any manner dependent upon that instrument for its existence. The second amendment declares that it shall not be infringed; but this... means no more than that it shall not be infringed by Congress. This is one of the amendments that has no other effect than to restrict the powers of the national government."

In this ruling, the Supreme Court agreed with a lower court ruling that the right to keep and bear arms is a birthright. It is not a right created or conferred by the Constitution. The Constitution, however, guarantees that this right shall not be impaired by the state or federal government. In addition, it is the duty of the state to protect and enforce this right.

United States v. Miller: Possession of Gangster-Type Weapons

The Supreme Court first tackled the Second Amendment in the late 1930s, in a case involving a violation of the National Firearms Act of 1934, a federal law designed to make it more difficult to acquire especially dangerous "gangster-type" weapons. Jack Miller and Frank Layton were arrested by federal agents in 1938 and charged with traveling with an unregistered, gangster-type, sawed-off shotgun. A federal district court judge dismissed the case on the grounds that the National Firearms Act violated the Second Amendment. The U.S. government appealed to the Supreme Court in *United States v. Miller* (307 U.S. 174 [1939]).

The federal government argued that if the Second Amendment protected an individual's right to keep and bear arms, the only arms protected were those suitable to military purposes, not weapons such as sawed-off shotguns that "constitute the arsenal of the 'public enemy' and the 'gangster'"—weapons that the National Firearms Act was intended to regulate.

The Supreme Court reversed the lower court's ruling and upheld the federal law. Because Miller had fled and was not present to plead his case, the court heard only the government's side of the issue and did not hear a strong argument for permitting a citizen to maintain such a weapon. In the end, the Supreme Court denied Miller the right to carry a sawed-off shotgun, noting that no evidence had been presented as to the usefulness "at this time" of a sawed-off shotgun for military purposes. The court stated, "In the absence of any evidence tending to show that possession or use of a 'shotgun having a barrel of less than eighteen inches in length' at this time has some reasonable relationship to the preservation or efficiency of a well regulated militia, we cannot say that the Second Amendment guarantees the right to keep and bear such an instrument. Certainly it is not within judicial notice that this weapon is any part of the ordinary military equipment or that its use could contribute to the common defense."

Referring back to the debates of the Constitutional Convention and the discussion of the militia, the court observed that such deliberations showed "plainly enough that the Militia comprised all males physically capable of acting in concert for the common defense, 'A body of citizens enrolled for military discipline.' And further, that ordinarily when called for service these men were expected to appear bearing arms supplied by themselves and of the kind in common use at the time."

For the next seven decades *Miller* was the major Supreme Court ruling and precedent concerning gun control until the *District of Columbia v. Heller* ruling in 2008 (discussed later in this chapter). Regardless, what did the court mean in *Miller*? The ruling has been used to support both sides of the gun rights debate. Was the court protecting an individual's right to bear arms or not? Do those arms have to have some military usefulness? The sawed-off shotgun was used in Vietnam as an effective military weapon. Does this mean that it can be shown to contribute to the common defense in modern times? What of the machine gun, which as of 2012 was forbidden under federal law but has also been used in war? Could that weapon, too, be considered as potentially helpful to the common defense? Should Americans be allowed to bear machine guns? Gun control advocates say the court's decision in *Miller* allows the reasonable regulation of firearms and that the Second Amendment right applies only to people on active duty in official state militias.

USING *MILLER* AS A PRECEDENT. The case of *United States v. Tot* (131 F.2d 261 [1942]) originated in the arrest of Frank Tot for stealing cigarettes from an interstate shipment. Tot had previously been convicted of a crime of violence. At the time of his arrest, a .32-caliber Colt automatic pistol was seized during a search of his home. The Third Circuit Court of Appeals did not accept Tot's argument that the Second Amendment prohibited the state of New Jersey from denying him the right to own a gun even if he was a convicted felon. Citing *Miller* as a precedent, the circuit court reasoned that "one could hardly argue seriously that a limitation upon the privilege of possessing weapons was unconstitutional when applied to a mental patient of the maniac type. The same would be true if the possessor were a child of immature years.... Congress has prohibited the receipt of weapons from interstate transactions by persons who have previously, by due process of law, been shown to be aggressors against society. Such a classification is entirely reasonable and does not infringe upon the preservation of the well regulated militia protected by the Second Amendment."

The circuit court noted that the Second Amendment, "unlike those providing for protection of free speech and freedom of religion, was not adopted with individual rights in mind, but as a protection for the States in the maintenance of their militia organizations against possible encroachments by the federal power."

In 1942 the First Circuit Court of Appeals cited *Miller* in *Cases v. United States* (131 F.2d 916) in an attempt to uphold the Federal Firearms Act of 1938. Jose Cases Velazquez had been convicted of a violent crime and, under the federal law, could not own a gun. The circuit court observed, "The Federal Firearms Act undoubtedly curtails to some extent the right of individuals to keep and bear arms.... [This] is not a right conferred upon the people by the federal constitution."

These rulings (*Tot* and *Cases*) and others were consistent with the thinking in *Miller*. Furthermore, they expanded on *Miller* by disagreeing with the argument of gun rights advocates that the Second Amendment extends firearms rights to individuals independent of the need to ensure a well-regulated militia.

Miller was also cited by the Fifth Circuit Court of Appeals in *U.S. v. Emerson* (270 F.3d 203 [2001]). In this case Timothy Joe Emerson was charged with violating the Lautenberg Amendment to the 1994 Gun Act, which prohibits possession of a firearm by people under a domestic violence restraining order. Emerson's estranged wife had obtained such an order from a judge in 1998, after Emerson had acknowledged his mental instability. He was subsequently indicted for illegally possessing two 9mm pistols,

a semiautomatic SKS assault rifle with bayonet, a semiautomatic M-14 assault rifle, and an M1 carbine. At his trial in district court, his lawyers argued that the case should be dismissed on the grounds that the federal ban on gun possession by those under a protective order for domestic violence violated the Second Amendment. The district court sided with Emerson and dismissed the charges, reasoning that the provision of the 1994 law violates the Second Amendment because it allows a state court divorce proceeding to deprive a citizen of his or her right to keep and bear arms, even when that citizen has not been found guilty of anything.

In its ruling, the district court noted that it interpreted the Second Amendment as conferring individual rights on U.S. citizens. Nevertheless, U.S. Department of Justice (DOJ) prosecutors appealed the court's decision, stating that it directly conflicted with the long-established legal precedent (the collective rights interpretation) laid down by the Supreme Court in *Miller*.

When the Fifth Circuit Court of Appeals reversed the lower court decision and upheld the domestic violence gun ban against Emerson, gun control advocates viewed the decision as a victory for domestic violence victims and a safeguard for women across the country. Gun rights advocates also found something to praise in the decision, because it seemed to provide support for the argument that individuals are guaranteed the right under the U.S. Constitution to bear arms independent of the provision of a well-regulated militia. The decision of the court stated, "We conclude that *Miller* does not support the government's collective rights or sophisticated collective rights approach to the Second Amendment. Indeed, to the extent that *Miller* sheds light on the matter it cuts against the government's position."

The *Emerson* case sparked conflicting views of the Second Amendment within the DOJ. In arguing the government's case in *Emerson*, the DOJ contended that it is "well settled" that the Second Amendment creates a right held by the states and does not protect an individual's right to bear arms. When Emerson filed his brief on appeal, he attached a copy of a letter from the U.S. attorney general John D. Ashcroft (1942–) to the National Rifle Association of America dated May 17, 2001. The letter stated in part, "Let me state unequivocally my view that the text and the original intent of the Second Amendment clearly protects the right of individuals to keep and bear firearms."

Emerson was quickly seized on by gun rights advocates. In 2000 the attorney Gary Gorski filed a lawsuit in the Eastern District Court in California. The case, *Silveira v. Lockyer* (312 F.3d 1052 [2002]), sought to overturn California's ban on semiautomatic rifles on the basis of the individual right of a person to keep and bear arms under the Second Amendment. The *Silveira* lawsuit lost in the Eastern District Court and was appealed to the Ninth Circuit Court in 2002, which upheld the lower court's decision. The Ninth Circuit Court's written decision strongly rejected the reasoning behind the *Emerson* decision, stating "the debates of the founding era demonstrate that the second of the first ten amendments to the Constitution was included in order to preserve the efficacy of the state militias for the people's defense—not to ensure an individual right to possess weapons."

Silveira has been viewed by some observers as a significant setback for gun rights advocates.

United States v. Synnes: Gun Possession by a Convicted Felon

In *United States v. Synnes* (438 F.2d 764 [1971]), another case involving the possession of a firearm by a convicted felon, the Eighth Circuit Court of Appeals said this about the Second Amendment, "We see no conflict between [a law prohibiting the possession of guns by convicted criminals] and the Second Amendment since there is no showing that prohibiting possession of firearms by felons obstructs the maintenance of a 'well-regulated militia.'"

Most supporters of handgun possession have accepted the right of federal and state governments to deny weapons to former felons, drug abusers, and mentally disabled individuals.

United States v. Warin: Possession of a Machine Gun

In *United States v. Warin* (530 F.2d 103 [1976]), the defendant Francis J. Warin appealed his conviction for possessing an unlicensed submachine gun. Warin tried to convince the Sixth Circuit Court of Appeals that a federal law prohibiting the possession of the gun violated his Second Amendment rights. The court upheld Warin's conviction, stating that it is an "erroneous supposition that the Second Amendment is concerned with the rights of individuals rather than those of the States."

Smith v. United States: Enhanced Penalties for "Use" of Firearms in a Drug Crime

The Supreme Court ruled in *Smith v. United States* (508 U.S. 223 [1993]) that the federal law authorizing stiffer penalties if the defendant "during and in relation to . . . [a] drug trafficking crime uses . . . a firearm" applies not only to the use of firearms as weapons but also to firearms used as commerce, such as in a bartering or trading transaction. John Angus Smith and a companion went from Tennessee to Florida to buy cocaine, which they planned to resell for profit. During a drug transaction, an undercover agent posing as a pawnshop dealer examined Smith's MAC-10, a compact and lightweight firearm that can be equipped with a silencer and is popular among criminals. Smith told the agent he could have the gun in

exchange for 2 ounces (56.7 grams) of cocaine. The officer said he would try to get the drugs and return in an hour. In the meantime Smith became suspicious and fled, and after a high-speed chase officers apprehended him.

A grand jury was convened to decide whether there was enough evidence to justify formal charges and a trial. Smith was charged with drug trafficking crimes and with knowingly using the MAC-10 in connection with a drug trafficking crime, among other offenses. Under 18 U.S.C. Section 924(c)(1)(B)(ii), a defendant who uses a firearm in such a way must be sentenced to five years' imprisonment, and if the firearm "is a machine gun or a destructive device, or is equipped with a firearm silencer or firearm muffler," as it was in this case, the sentence is 30 years. Smith was convicted on all counts.

On appeal Smith argued that the law applied only if the firearm was used as a weapon. The 11th Circuit Court disagreed, ruling that the federal legislation did not require that the firearm be used as a weapon—"any use of 'the weapon to facilitate in any manner the commission of the offense' suffices." In a similar case, *United States v. Harris* (959 F.2d 246 [1992]), the Court of Appeals for the District of Columbia Circuit had arrived at the same conclusion. By contrast, the Court of Appeals for the Ninth Circuit held in *United States v. Phelps* (877 F.2d 28 [1989]) that trading a gun during a drug-related transaction was not "using" it within the meaning of the statute. To resolve the conflict among the different circuit courts, the Supreme Court heard Smith's appeal.

In a 6–3 decision, the court ruled in *Smith v. United States* that the "exchange of a gun for narcotics constitutes 'use' of a firearm 'during and in relation to . . . [a] drug trafficking crime' within the meaning" of the federal statute. Delivering the opinion of the majority, Justice Sandra Day O'Connor (1930–) wrote that "when a word is not defined by statute, we normally construe it in accord with its ordinary or natural meaning." Definitions for the word *use* from various dictionaries and *Black's Law Dictionary* show the word to mean "convert to one's service; to employ; to carry out a purpose or action by means of." In trying to exchange his MAC-10 for drugs, the defendant "used" or employed the gun as an item of trade to obtain drugs. The phrase "as a weapon" does not appear in the statute. O'Connor reasoned that if Congress had meant the narrow interpretation of "use" (as a weapon only), it would have worded the statute differently.

Justice Antonin Scalia (1936–) dissented from the majority's definition of "use." Defining the normal usage of a gun as discharging, brandishing, or using as a weapon, he observed:

> The Court does not appear to grasp the distinction between how a word can be used and how it ordinarily is used. It would, indeed, be "both reasonable and normal to say that petitioner 'used' his MAC-10 in his

drug trafficking offense by trading it for cocaine." ...It would also be reasonable and normal to say that he "used" it to scratch his head. When one wishes to describe the action of employing the instrument of a firearm for such unusual purposes, "use" is assuredly a verb one could select. But that says nothing about whether the ordinary meaning of the phrase "uses a firearm" embraces such extraordinary employments. It is unquestionably not reasonable and normal, I think, to say simply "do not use firearms" when one means to prohibit selling or scratching with them.

Bailey v. United States: New Interpretations of "Use"

In 1995 the Supreme Court narrowed the definition of the word *use* that had been established in *Smith*. In *Bailey v. United States* (516 U.S. 137), the court considered the separate criminal misdeeds of Roland J. Bailey and Candisha Robinson.

In 1988 Bailey had been stopped in his car by Washington, D.C., police officers because he was missing a front license plate and an inspection sticker. When Bailey could not produce a driver's license, an officer searched Bailey's car and found ammunition and just over 1 ounce (30 grams) of cocaine. Another officer found a loaded pistol and more than $3,200 in small bills in the trunk. At his trial, Bailey was convicted of possession of cocaine with intent to deliver and using or carrying a firearm in connection with a drug offense. He appealed to the Court of Appeals for the District of Columbia Circuit.

In June 1991 an undercover police officer approached Candisha Robinson to buy crack cocaine with a marked $20 bill. The officer noticed that she obtained the drugs from her one-bedroom apartment. Later, while executing a search warrant on Robinson's apartment, officers found a .22-caliber derringer, two rocks of crack cocaine, and the marked bill. Robinson was found guilty of cocaine distribution and, among other things, the use or carrying of a firearm during and in relation to a drug trafficking offense. She appealed to the Court of Appeals for the District of Columbia Circuit.

In Bailey's appeal, *United States v. Bailey* (995 F. 2d 1113 [CADC 1993]), the defense argued there was no evidence that he had used the gun in connection with a drug offense. Robinson argued in her appeal, *United States v. Robinson* (997 F. 2d 884 [CADC 1993]), that during the drug sale to the officer, the gun was unloaded and in a locked trunk and was not used in the commission of or in relation to a drug trafficking offense.

The court of appeals rejected Bailey's claim of insufficient evidence and held that he could be convicted for "using" a firearm if the jury could reasonably infer that the gun had assisted in the commission of a drug offense. In Robinson's case the court reversed her conviction for "using or carrying," because the presence of an unloaded gun in a locked trunk in a bedroom closet was not evidence

of actual use. Because the decisions were contradictory, the court of appeals consolidated the two cases and reheard them. A majority of the judges then found that there was sufficient evidence to establish that each defendant had used a firearm in relation to a drug trafficking offense. Bailey and Robinson then jointly appealed to the Supreme Court, which granted their petition to clarify the meaning of "use."

In 1995 the Supreme Court unanimously held that to establish "use," the government must show that the defendant actively employed a firearm so as to make it an "operative factor in relation to the predicate offense." This definition includes hiding a gun in a shirt or pants, threatening to use a gun, or actually using the gun during the commission of a drug crime. The court also found that Bailey's and Robinson's "use" convictions could not be supported because the evidence did not indicate that either defendant actively employed firearms during drug crimes.

In 1998 the Supreme Court put a much broader interpretation on the federal law, which mandates a five-year prison term for a person who "uses or carries" a gun "during and in relation to" a drug-trafficking crime. The three defendants in this case carried guns in the trunks of their cars. The court ruled in *Muscarello v. United States* (524 U.S. 125 [1998]) that having a gun in a car from which a person is dealing drugs fits the meaning of "carries" for purposes of the sentencing statutes.

United States v. Lopez: Possession of a Firearm near a School

The Gun-Free School Zones Act of 1990 made it unlawful for any individual to knowingly possess a firearm in a school zone, defined as within 1,000 feet (305 m) of school grounds, regardless of whether school was in session. Two federal appeals courts came to different conclusions about the constitutionality of the act.

FIFTH CIRCUIT COURT OF APPEALS: THE GUN-FREE SCHOOL ZONES ACT IS UNCONSTITUTIONAL. In March 1992 high school senior Alfonso Lopez Jr. carried a concealed revolver and five cartridges into Edison High School in San Antonio, Texas. School officials caught him, and the student was subsequently charged with violating the Gun-Free School Zones Act. Lopez's attorneys moved to dismiss the changes because, they contended, the law was unconstitutional. The trial court did not accept their argument and convicted Lopez. The case then went to the U.S. Court of Appeals for the Fifth Circuit, which disagreed with the trial court, ruling in *United States v. Lopez* (2 F.3d 1342 [1993]) that Congress had exceeded the power granted to it under the commerce clause of the U.S. Constitution when it enacted the Gun-Free School Zones Act. The commerce clause gives Congress the power to regulate conduct that crosses state borders. According to the court, with few specific exceptions, "federal laws proscribing firearm possession require the government to prove a connection to commerce."

Congress had made no attempt to link the Gun-Free School Zones Act to commerce in the debates before the law was enacted and in the law itself. The appeals court asserted:

> Both the management of education, and the general control of simple firearms possession by ordinary citizens, have traditionally been a state responsibility.... We are unwilling to ourselves simply assume that the concededly intrastate conduct of mere possession by any person of any firearm substantially affects interstate commerce, or the regulation thereof, whenever it occurs, or even most of the time that it occurs, within 1,000 feet of the grounds of any school, whether or not then in session. If Congress can thus bar firearms possession because of such a nexus [connection] to the grounds of any public or private school, and can do so without supportive findings or legislative history, on the theory that education affects commerce, then it could also similarly ban lead pencils, "sneakers," Game Boys, or slide rules.

Following this reasoning, the appeals court found the Gun-Free School Zones Act unconstitutional.

NINTH CIRCUIT COURT OF APPEALS: THE GUN-FREE SCHOOL ZONES ACT IS CONSTITUTIONAL. By contrast, the U.S. Court of Appeals for the Ninth Circuit ruled in *United States v. Edwards III* (13 F.3d 291 [1993]) that the commerce clause of the U.S. Constitution did, indeed, give Congress the power to pass a law such as the Gun-Free School Zones Act. In 1991 Sacramento, California, police officers and school officials approached Ray Harold Edwards III and four other males at Grant Union High School. The officers discovered a .22-caliber rifle and a sawed-off rifle in the trunk of Edwards's car. One of the charges against Edwards was violation of the Gun-Free School Zones Act.

Edwards appealed, claiming the law violated the 10th Amendment because Congress did not have the authority under the commerce clause or any other delegated power to enact the Gun-Free School Zones Act. The 10th Amendment states that "the powers not delegated to the United States by the Constitution, nor prohibited by it to the States, are reserved to the States respectively, or to the people."

Disagreeing with *United States v. Lopez*, the court of appeals ruled that the Gun-Free School Zones Act "does not expressly require the Government to establish a nexus between the possession of a firearm in a school zone and interstate commerce.... It is unnecessary for Congress to make express findings that a particular activity or class of activities affects interstate commerce in order to exercise its legislative authority pursuant to the commerce clause."

The court of appeals used *United States v. Evans* (928 F.2d 858 [1991]) as a precedent, which upheld legislation that made it illegal to possess an unregistered machine gun. In *Evans* the court ruled that "violence created through the possession of firearms adversely affects the national economy, and consequently, it was reasonable for Congress to regulate the possession of firearms pursuant to the commerce clause."

THE U.S. SUPREME COURT: THE GUN-FREE SCHOOL ZONES ACT IS UNCONSTITUTIONAL. In 1995 the Supreme Court struck down the Gun-Free School Zones Act in *United States v. Lopez* (514 U.S. 549) on the grounds that Congress had overstepped its bounds because it had based the law on the commerce clause of the U.S. Constitution. The commerce clause empowers Congress to regulate interstate commerce, but Congress had failed to connect gun-free school zones with commerce. Chief Justice William H. Rehnquist (1924–2005) wrote that Congress had used the commerce clause as a general police power in a way that is generally retained by states. He also warned that the Gun-Free School Zones Act "is a criminal statute that by its terms has nothing to do with 'commerce' or any sort of economic enterprise, however broadly one might define those terms.... If we were to accept the Government's arguments, we are hard-pressed to posit any activity by an individual that Congress is without power to regulate."

Congress responded in 1996 by approving a slightly revised version of the Gun-Free School Zones Act in the form of amendments to the Department of Defense Appropriations Act of 1997. The amendments required prosecutors to prove an impact on interstate commerce as an element of the offense.

Printz v. United States: The Constitutionality of the Brady Law

Opponents of the Brady Handgun Violence Prevention Act of 1993 challenged its constitutionality soon after it passed. Under the Brady law, Congress had ordered local chief law enforcement officials nationwide to conduct background checks on prospective handgun purchasers who bought their guns through federally licensed dealers. Two sheriffs, Jay Printz of Ravalli County, Montana, and Richard Mack of Graham County, Arizona, charged that Congress exceeded its powers under the 10th Amendment of the U.S. Constitution, which defines the separation of powers—the relationship between the federal government and the sovereign powers of the individual states. They argued that the federal government had placed federal burdens on local police agencies with no federal compensation. Representing the federal government, the U.S. acting solicitor general Walter Dellinger (1941–) argued that the government had the right to require local agencies to carry out federal orders as long as those agencies were not forced to make policy.

In *Printz v. United States* (521 U.S. 898 [1997]), the Supreme Court struck down the Brady law provisions that required local chief law enforcement officials to conduct background checks on prospective handgun buyers and to accept the form on which that background check is based. The court declared that these provisions violated the 10th Amendment to the U.S. Constitution. Justice Scalia wrote, "The Federal Government may neither issue directives requiring the States to address particular problems, nor command the States' officers, or those of their political subdivisions, to administer or enforce a federal regulatory program."

The court unanimously upheld the Brady law's five-day waiting period for handgun purchases because the waiting period was directed at gun store owners and was not a federal mandate to state officials. Most chief law enforcement officers continued to conduct background checks voluntarily until the National Instant Check System, which was instituted by the Brady law, became effective in November 1998.

Bryan v. United States: Selling Guns without a License

The Firearms Owners' Protection Act of 1986 prohibits any person other than a licensed dealer from dealing in firearms. Anyone who "willfully violates" this law is subject to a fine and can be sentenced up to five years in prison. Sillasse Bryan bought several pistols in Ohio by using straw purchasers (legally qualified buyers who purchase for someone who is not legally qualified). After filing the serial numbers off the guns, he resold the weapons in New York City, in areas known for drug dealing. At his trial the defense argued that Bryan could be convicted only if he knew of the specific federal licensing requirement of the law. His argument failed, and Bryan was convicted. In *Bryan v. United States* (524 U.S. 184 [1998]), the Supreme Court interpreted "willfully violates" to mean that the defendant only needs to know that he was selling guns illegally. Bryan's conviction was upheld.

United States v. Bean: Federal Guns-for-Felons Program

According to the Supreme Court ruling in *United States v. Bean* (537 U.S. 71 [2002]), courts cannot restore firearm privileges to anyone convicted of a felony. In this case Thomas Lamar Bean, a registered gun dealer in Texas, drove to Mexico for dinner with his associates one night after a gun show in 1998. Even though he had asked one of his associates to remove the firearms and ammunition from his car, the Mexican police found one box of ammunition remaining inside. Bean was convicted of importing ammunition to Mexico, which is a felony. As a result of his conviction, he was subsequently barred from "possessing, receiving, or distributing firearms or ammunition" in the United States. Under Title 18, Section 925(c), however, Bean was allowed to petition the Bureau of Alcohol, Tobacco, Firearms and Explosives (ATF) for reinstatement of his gun privileges, known as the guns-for-felons program. The ATF turned him down, stating that it had no money to process his application

after the 1992 Appropriations Act passed by Congress had barred the ATF from spending money on such activities. Bean filed suit in the U.S. District Court in Texas, which decided to lift his prohibition. The Fifth Circuit Court of Appeals affirmed that decision.

In 2002 the Supreme Court rejected Bean's contention that the ATF's failure to act amounted to a de facto (existing in reality whether with lawful authority or not) denial of his application. In the decision, Justice Clarence Thomas (1948–) stated that "mere inaction by ATF does not invest a district court with independent jurisdiction to act on an application." The court also ruled unanimously that the federal "relief from disabilities" guns-for-felons program could not be revived by federal judges. Under the "relief from disabilities" program, convicted felons were given the right to apply for "relief" from the "disability" of not being able to buy or possess a gun. The Supreme Court did not comment on Bean's claim that he had a Second Amendment right to get his guns back.

United States v. Stewart: Possession of Homemade Machine Guns

Robert Wilson Stewart Jr. was a convicted felon who sold parts kits to make Maadi-Griffin .50-caliber rifles. He advertised the kits on the Internet and in magazines. The ATF began investigating Stewart when it realized that he had a prior conviction for the possession and transfer of a machine gun. During the investigation an ATF agent purchased parts kits from Stewart and determined that they could be used to make an unlawful firearm. After obtaining a warrant, the ATF searched Stewart's residence and discovered 31 firearms, including five machine guns that Stewart had machined and assembled. Stewart was convicted of being a felon in possession of a firearm, of unlawful possession of a machine gun, and of possessing several unregistered, homemade machine guns.

The case against Stewart had been based, in part, on an interpretation of the commerce clause of the U.S. Constitution that prohibits anyone except a licensed importer, manufacturer, or dealer of firearms to import, manufacture, or deal in firearms. In his appeal, Stewart claimed that Congress had exceeded its commerce clause power and violated the Second Amendment.

In *United States v. Stewart* (348 F.3d 1132 [2003]), the Ninth Circuit Court of Appeals overturned the lower court's ruling on violating the commerce clause, saying that Stewart did not have a substantial effect on interstate commerce. The court, however, affirmed his conviction for being a felon in possession of a firearm.

In 2005 the DOJ appealed the case to the Supreme Court. The High Court would not hear the case but instructed the Ninth Circuit Court of Appeals to further consider the case in light of its recent ruling in *Gonzales v. Raich* (545 U.S. 1 [2005]). That case allowed Congress to use the commerce clause to ban the cultivation and possession of homegrown marijuana for personal medical use because, the court said, the marijuana could affect the supply and demand of the drug, thereby affecting interstate commerce. In June 2006 the Ninth Circuit Court of Appeals ruled that Congress has the power to regulate the sales of homemade machine guns because they can enter the interstate market and affect supply and demand. Thus, Congress had not exceeded its commerce clause power and had not violated the Second Amendment.

District of Columbia v. Heller: The Constitutionality of the District of Columbia's Handgun Ban

In 2008 the Supreme Court was once again confronted with making a decision that hinged on the Second Amendment and would issue its first decision interpreting the Second Amendment since the 1939 *Miller* decision. This time the interpretation was in the context of the District of Columbia's ban on the possession of handguns. The High Court was expected to make a landmark ruling on the centuries-old question of whether the Constitution's Second Amendment refers to an individual's right to gun ownership or strictly to militia service.

In 1976 the District of Columbia passed a law that banned the private possession of handguns and that required rifles and shotguns in the home to be outfitted with a trigger lock or kept unloaded and disassembled. Dick Anthony Heller was the named party in the suit, but the attorney Robert A. Levy (1941–) personally financed the lawsuit and worked on bringing it to the Supreme Court with the purpose of addressing the Second Amendment question. Attorneys for the District of Columbia contended the Second Amendment does not give individuals the right to bear arms, whereas Levy and the other attorneys for Heller contended it does.

In 2007 a three-judge panel of the U.S. Court of Appeals for the District of Columbia struck down the gun control ordinance on Second Amendment grounds. Senior Judge Laurence H. Silberman (1935–) wrote for the two-to-one majority that the amendment provides an individual right just as other provisions of the Bill of Rights do. Handguns fall under the definition of "arms"; thus, the District of Columbia may not ban them.

The District of Columbia appealed the case to the Supreme Court. In March 2008 the High Court heard arguments, and in June 2008 the court rendered its decision in *District of Columbia v. Heller*. The 5–4 landmark ruling interpreted the Second Amendment as protecting the individual's right to own a gun, thus supporting the 2007 decision of the U.S. Court of Appeals for the District of Columbia. The majority opinion, written by Justice Scalia, provided for gun control legislation by noting that "like most rights, the Second Amendment right is not unlimited. It is not a right to keep and carry any weapon whatsoever in any manner whatsoever and for whatever purpose." Justice

John Paul Stevens (1920–), writing for the minority (dissenting) opinion, noted, "The Court's announcement of a new constitutional right to own and use firearms for private purposes upsets that settled understanding, but leaves for future cases the formidable task of defining the scope of permissible regulations."

McDonald v. Chicago: Must States Follow the Same Second Amendment Rules as the Federal Government?

The District of Columbia is under federal jurisdiction. As a result, the *Heller* ruling does not necessarily apply to state and local jurisdictions. One day after *Heller* was decided, Otis McDonald and three other Chicago residents filed suit in the U.S. District Court for the Northern District of Illinois in an attempt to determine whether states must follow the same Second Amendment rules as federal jurisdictions and to overturn a decades-long ban on handguns in the city of Chicago. In *McDonald v. Chicago* (No. 08 C 3645 [2008]), the district court ruled in favor of the city. The petitioners appealed the case to the Seventh Circuit Court of Appeals. In *McDonald v. Chicago* (567 F 3d 856 [7th Cir. 2009]), the appeals court upheld the decision of the district court, noting that the city's handgun ban did not violate the Constitution because the Supreme Court had not yet declared whether its decision in the *Heller* case established a fundamental right to guns applicable throughout the United States. The Supreme Court agreed to hear the case, *McDonald v. Chicago* (561 U.S. ___ [2010]), which was argued in March 2010. In June 2010 the High Court returned its ruling. In a 5–4 decision, the court stated that the "Second Amendment right is fully applicable to the States."

STATE LAWS

Most state constitutions guarantee the right to bear arms, and this right has either been enacted or strengthened in more than a dozen states since 1970 (see the Appendix). Some states clearly tie this right to the militia, whereas other state constitutions and courts have ruled from the perspective of personal defense or self-protection. States that have enacted laws to protect the right to use of weapons, including deadly force, in self-defense are shown in Figure 4.1. Two classic examples of cases involving self-defense are *Schubert v. DeBard* (398 NE.2d 1339 [1980]) and *State v. Kessler* (614 P.2d 94 [1980]).

Schubert v. DeBard: The Right to Possess a Handgun for Self-Defense Protected in Indiana

Joseph L. Schubert Jr. wanted a handgun to protect himself from his brother, who he believed was mailing him anonymous threats. Indiana law required that "a person desiring a license to carry a handgun shall apply to the chief of police or corresponding police officer"—in this case Robert L. DeBard, the superintendent of the Indiana State Police. The resulting investigation by DeBard's office found what it considered to be evidence that Schubert was mentally unstable and denied his request. When his application was denied, Schubert filed a petition for review.

Schubert's defense attorney accepted the conclusion of the police investigation that Schubert had some psychological problems, but he argued that they were irrelevant to the matter at hand. Article 1, Section 32, of the Indiana constitution guarantees that "the people shall have a right to bear arms, for the defense of themselves and the State." Therefore, the attorney argued, when self-defense was properly indicated as the reason for desiring a firearms license, and the applicant was otherwise qualified, the license could not be withheld because an administrative official had subjectively determined that the applicant's need to defend himself was not justified. (At that point, Schubert had not been found to be mentally incompetent, which is an accepted reason to deny permission to carry a gun.)

The Third District Court of Appeals of the State of Indiana agreed with Schubert. After studying the debates surrounding the creation of the Indiana constitution in 1850, most of the appeals court judges concluded, "We think it clear that our constitution provides our citizenry the right to bear arms for their self-defense." If it were left to a police official to determine a "proper reason" for a person to claim self-defense, "it would supplant a right with a mere administrative privilege." Based on this conclusion, the court sent the case back to the lower court, asking it to determine if Schubert was mentally incompetent, which was an accepted basis for denying him the right to purchase a weapon.

Doe v. Portland Housing Authority: Maine State Law Preempts the Portland Public Housing Authority Provision against Gun Possession

Most state constitutions guarantee the right to bear arms, but state laws regulate their possession. The case of *Doe v. Portland Housing Authority* (656 A.2d 1200 [1995])

FIGURE 4.1

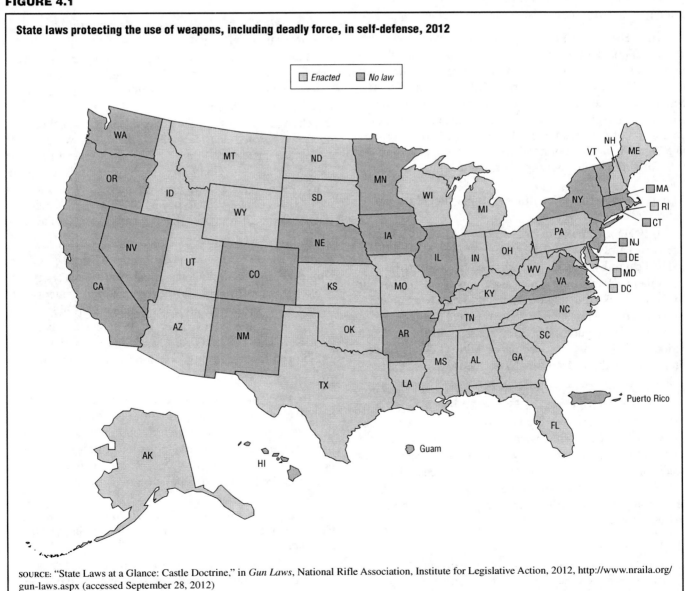

State laws protecting the use of weapons, including deadly force, in self-defense, 2012

SOURCE: "State Laws at a Glance: Castle Doctrine," in *Gun Laws*, National Rifle Association, Institute for Legislative Action, 2012, http://www.nraila.org/gun-laws.aspx (accessed September 28, 2012)

is an example of such regulation and its preemption (taking precedence) of a public housing authority provision.

A Maine couple identified as John and Jane Doe, who had lived in public housing since 1981, were threatened with eviction after the Portland Housing Authority (PHA) in Maine discovered guns in their apartment. John Doe was a veteran of the U.S. Marine Corps, a former firearms dealer, and a licensed hunter. Jane Doe, a target shooter, reported that she kept a handgun for self-protection when her husband worked late. The Does filed a petition to prevent the PHA from enforcing a provision in their lease that banned the possession of firearms.

The Does argued that a state law that regulates the possession of firearms preempted the lease. The Maine preemption statute declares, "The State intends to occupy and preempt the entire field of legislation concerning the regulation of firearms.... No political subdivision of the State, including, *but not limited to*, municipalities, counties, townships and village corporations, may adopt any ... [law] concerning ... firearms, components, ammunition or supplies."

The PHA claimed that the state law could not preempt its resolutions because the PHA is not a political subdivision listed in the statute. In 1995 the Maine Supreme Court ruled in *Doe v. Portland Housing Authority* that the PHA was indeed a political subdivision. The court also found that the state legislature intended to regulate uniformly the possession of firearms by all Maine residents whether they live in public housing or not. The case was appealed to the U.S. Supreme Court, but the court declined to hear it.

State v. Owenby: Mental Illness Limits the Right to Bear Firearms in Oregon

In 1991 the Circuit Court of Multnomah County, Oregon, ruled that Patrick Owenby, who suffered from mental illness and had carefully planned a murder, was a danger to himself and others. Because Owenby was unwilling, unable, or unlikely to seek voluntary treatment, the court had him committed to a psychiatric facility. It then ordered that Owenby be prohibited from purchasing or possessing firearms for a period of five years, in accordance with Oregon statutes. Unhappy with this order, Owenby decided to appeal the case.

The Oregon Court of Appeals ruled in *State v. Owenby* (111 Or. App. 270, 826 P.2d 51 [1992]) that the statute in question was a narrowly drawn and reasonable restriction on the right to bear arms; was not in violation of the state constitution; was supported by clear and convincing evidence; and did not violate the federal due process clause as expressed in the 14th Amendment: "Nor shall any State deprive any person of life, liberty, or property, without due process of law."

The court stated:

> The right to bear arms is not absolute. In the exercise of its police power, the legislature may enact reasonable regulations limiting the right and has done so.

> Given the nature of firearms ... the danger that the statute seeks to avert is a serious one. The restriction on the right of mentally ill people to bear arms, on the other hand, is a relatively minor one. The statute is narrowly drawn and may be invoked only when it is shown that the prohibition is *necessary* "as a result of the mentally ill person's mental or psychological state," as demonstrated by past behavior that involves unlawful violence.

Benjamin v. Bailey: Ban on Semiautomatic Firearms in Connecticut Upheld

In 1995 the Connecticut Supreme Court upheld in *Benjamin v. Bailey* (234 Conn. 455, 662 A.2d 1226) a 1993 state law banning the sale, possession, or transfer of 67 types of automatic and semiautomatic or burst-fire firearms, ruling that the ban did not violate the state constitutional right to bear arms. The decision made Connecticut one of the first states to have an assault-weapons ban pass legal challenge even though the right of self-defense was specified in its constitution.

State v. Wilchinski: Child Access Prevention in Connecticut Challenged

Florida was the first state to pass a child access prevention law (1989). Often referred to as the safe-storage law, it requires adults to either keep loaded guns in a place reasonably inaccessible to children or use a device to lock the gun. If a child (defined as anyone under the age of 16) obtains an improperly stored and loaded gun, the adult owner is held criminally liable. According to the Law Center to Prevent Gun Violence in "Child Access Prevention Policy Summary" (May 21, 2012, http://smartgunlaws.org/child-access-prevention-policy-summary/), as of 2012, 26 additional states and the District of Columbia had passed similar laws.

Among these states is Connecticut, whose law was challenged by Joseph Wilchinski, a police officer employed by Central Connecticut State University. He was charged with criminal negligence and sentenced to three years' probation after his teenage son and another boy found a loaded revolver in Wilchinski's bedroom in 1993. The boy was shot and died two days later. Wilchinski appealed his conviction, claiming the law was unconstitutionally vague.

In 1997 the Connecticut Supreme Court upheld the law, declaring in *State v. Wilchinski* (242 Conn. 211) that the requirement to store firearms in a "securely locked box or other container or in a location which a reasonable person would believe to be secure" was sufficiently clear to inform Wilchinski of safe-storage practices.

American Shooting Sports Council, Inc. v. Attorney General: A Challenge to Gun Safety Regulations in Massachusetts

Regulations applying consumer product safety guidelines to all handguns made or sold within the state of Massachusetts were set forth in October 1997 by Scott

Harshbarger (1941–), the state attorney general. They rank among the nation's strongest gun-safety regulations. The day before the rules took effect, the American Shooting Sports Council and a group of Massachusetts gun manufacturers sued to block them, arguing that the attorney general had exceeded his authority. The case ultimately made its way to the Supreme Judicial Court of Massachusetts, which reversed the trial court's ruling in favor of the gun manufacturers. The matter was then sent back to the trial court, where a final ruling in favor of the attorney general was entered in *American Shooting Sports Council, Inc. v. Attorney General* (429 Mass. 871, 711 N.E.2d 899 [1999]). On April 3, 2000, Harshbarger announced that the regulations were in effect immediately.

Coalition of New Jersey Sportsmen v. Whitman: New Jersey's Assault Weapons Ban Challenged

A group of gun clubs and arms manufacturers sought to overturn New Jersey's 1999 ban on assault weapons on the grounds of vagueness, free speech, and equal protection. The U.S. District Court for the District of New Jersey rejected their challenge in March 1999. The court held in *Coalition of New Jersey Sportsmen v. Whitman* (44 F. Supp. 2d 666) that the statute banning assault weapons was not vague because it "addresses an understandable core of banned guns and adequately puts gun owners on notice that their weapon could be prohibited." In the ruling, the court further held that the statute's ban on specifically named weapons "does not violate anyone's free speech," nor does the statute infringe on equal protection rights "because the rationality of the link between public safety and proscribing assault weapons is obvious." The federal court's decision was affirmed in March 2001 by the U.S. Court of Appeals for the Third Circuit (No. 99-5296).

Oklahoma: Guns on Corporate Property Challenged

On November 1, 2004, amendments to the Oklahoma Firearms Act and the Oklahoma Self-Defense Act took effect, allowing guns in locked vehicles on corporate property in Oklahoma. The amendments were passed after 12 workers at an Oklahoma Weyerhaeuser paper mill were fired for violating a company ban on firearms in the company parking lot. Whirlpool Corporation, Williams Companies Inc., and ConocoPhillips filed a lawsuit against the state in federal court, arguing that the amendments were unconstitutional and prevented them from banning firearms in their parking lots to help ensure safe workplaces. A U.S. district court judge issued a temporary restraining order to prevent the amendments from going into effect until the courts made a final ruling.

In March 2005 the Oklahoma Court of Criminal Appeals ruled that the amendments were criminal in nature, rather than civil. This ruling was necessary to guide the U.S. district court judge in his determination. In October 2007 Terence C. Kern (1944–), the U.S. district judge, placed a permanent injunction against the Oklahoma amendments, ruling that they were in conflict with federal safety laws meant to protect employees at their jobs, primarily denoted in the Occupational Safety and Health Act of 1970 (OSH Act or OSHA). However, the issue remained in dispute, and in February 2009, the U.S. Court of Appeals for the 10th Circuit lifted the injunction in *Ramsey Winch Inc. v. Henry* (555 F.3d 1199). In its ruling, the court found:

> the district court held that gun-related workplace violence was a "recognized hazard" under the general duty clause, and, therefore, an employer that allows firearms in the company parking lot may violate the OSH Act. We disagree. OSHA has not indicated in any way that employers should prohibit firearms from company parking lots. OSHA's website, guidelines, and citation history do not speak at all to any such prohibition. In fact, OSHA declined a request to promulgate a standard banning firearms from the workplace.... In declining this request, OSHA stressed reliance on its voluntary guidelines and deference "to other federal, state, and local law-enforcement agencies to regulate workplace homicides."

By 2012, in addition to Oklahoma, states that had enacted laws that forbade employers from banning weapons on their property (in other words, laws that allowed employees to keep guns in locked vehicles on corporate property) included Alaska, Arizona, Florida, Georgia, Idaho, Indiana, Kansas, Kentucky, Louisiana, Maine, Minnesota, Mississippi, North Dakota, Texas, and Utah. (See Figure 4.2.)

Paula Fiscal et al. v. City and County of San Francisco et al.: California State Law Preempts San Francisco Ordinance that Bans Handguns in the City

The 2008 California Supreme Court ruling in *Paula Fiscal et al. v. City and County of San Francisco et al.* (70 Cal.Rptr.3d 324) is an example of state law preempting a local ordinance. California state law regulates firearms within California, including their manufacture, distribution, sale, possession, and transfer. In November 2005 San Francisco voters passed Proposition H, a citywide ordinance that would ban the manufacture, distribution, sale, and transfer of firearms and ammunition within San Francisco, as well as prohibit San Francisco residents from possessing handguns within the city.

A few days after Proposition H was passed by city voters, the National Rifle Association of America and the Second Amendment Foundation, a nonprofit group that promotes the right to bear arms, filed suit to block the ordinance. In June 2006 Judge James Warren of the San Francisco Superior Court struck down the ordinance, stating that its key aspects were preempted by state law.

FIGURE 4.2

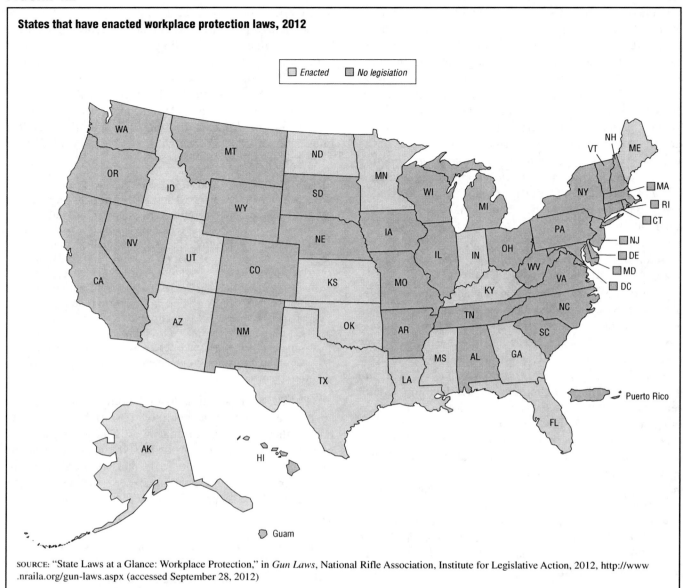

States that have enacted workplace protection laws, 2012

☐ Enacted ☐ No legislation

SOURCE: "State Laws at a Glance: Workplace Protection," in *Gun Laws*, National Rifle Association, Institute for Legislative Action, 2012, http://www
.nraila.org/gun-laws.aspx (accessed September 28, 2012)

He held that under California law local officials cannot ban the possession of firearms from law-abiding citizens.

The city appealed the superior court decision, and in January 2008 a three-judge panel of the California State Court of Appeals unanimously ruled to uphold the lower court's decision. The city then appealed the decision to the California Supreme Court, which upheld the previous two decisions. The April 2008 decision by California's high court exhausted the city's possibilities to appeal the case further.

LOCAL RULINGS
Portland, Oregon: Possession of Guns Regulated

The city of Portland, Oregon, passed an ordinance prohibiting "any person on a public street or in a public place to carry a firearm upon his person, or in a vehicle under his control or in which he is an occupant, unless all ammunition has been removed from the chamber and from the cylinder, clip, or magazine" (Portland Ordinance, PCC 14.138210). In 1982 Michael Boyce was convicted of violating this statute. He appealed, contending that the law violated Article 1, Section 27, of the Oregon constitution, which states, "The people shall have the right to bear arms for the defence of themselves, and the State, but the Military shall be kept in strict subordination to the civil power."

Boyce based his case on *State v. Kessler* (289 Or. 359 [1980]), in which the Oregon Supreme Court upheld the right to possess a billy club or any other type of small weapon for self-defense, and *State v. Blocker* (291 Or. 255, 630 P.2d 824 [1981]), in which the Oregon Supreme Court declared unconstitutional an Oregon law banning a number of weapons, including switchblades, billy clubs, and blackjacks. The court of appeals, however, did not see the similarities and upheld in *State v. Boyce* (658 P.2d 577 [1983]) the lower court's conviction. The court of appeals observed that the statute in *Kessler* and *Blocker* forbids the "mere possession" of certain weapons and that was the characteristic that made it unconstitutional. The statute in this case regulates only the manner of possession, something both *Kessler* and *Blocker* recognized as permissible when the regulation was reasonable. As such, the city of Portland could regulate the use of weapons within its borders.

In fulfilling its obligation to protect the health, safety, and welfare of its citizens, a government body must sometimes pass legislation that touches on a right guaranteed by the state or federal constitution. Such an encroachment is permissible when the unrestricted exercise of the right poses a clear threat to the interests and welfare of the public in general, and the means chosen by the government body do not unreasonably interfere with the right.

The court of appeals agreed that individuals had a right to protect their property and themselves:

> When a threat to person or property arises in the victim's defense capacity. It is true, on the other hand, that, when the threat arises in a public place, the fact that a person must have any ammunition separated from his firearm will hinder him to the extent that he is put to the trouble of loading the weapon.
>
> However, given the magnitude of the city's felt need to protect the public from an epidemic of random shootings, we think that the hindrance is permissible.

Renton, Washington: Guns Not Permitted Where Alcohol Is Served

The city of Renton, Washington, enacted Municipal Ordinance 3477-59, which states, "It is unlawful for anyone on or in any premise in the City of Renton where alcoholic beverages are dispensed by the drink to . . . carry any rifle, shotgun, or pistol, whether said person has a license or permit to carry said firearm or not, and whether said firearm is concealed or not."

Four residents, with the support of the Second Amendment Foundation, went to court seeking an injunction on the ordinance, claiming it violated state law and was unconstitutional. The Superior Court of King County upheld the city ordinance, so the Second Amendment Foundation took the case to the Court of Appeals of Washington.

Article 1, Section 24, of the Washington constitution states, "The right of the individual citizen to bear arms in defense of himself, or the state, shall not be impaired, but nothing in this section shall be construed as authorizing individuals or corporations to organize, maintain or employ an armed body of men."

The court indicated in *Second Amendment Foundation v. City of Renton* (668 F.2d 596 [1983]) that "it has long been recognized that the constitutional right to keep and bear arms is subject to reasonable regulation by the State under its police power." It also stated that simply because a right is guaranteed by either the state or federal constitution does not mean that it cannot be regulated. According to the court:

> The scope of permissible regulation must depend upon a balancing of the public benefit to be derived from the regulation against the degree to which it frustrates the purposes of the constitutional provision. The right to own and bear arms is only minimally reduced by limiting their possession in bars. The benefit to public safety by reducing the possibility of armed conflict while under the influence of alcohol outweighs the general right to bear arms in defense of self and state.
>
> . . . On balance, the public's right to a limited and reasonable exercise of police power must prevail against the individual's right to bear arms in public places where liquor is served.

Furthermore, the court stated that the statutes "do not expressly state an unqualified right to be in possession of a firearm at any time or place." Had the city of Renton instituted "an absolute and unqualified local prohibition against possession of a pistol by the holder of a state permit," it would have conflicted with state law and Washington's constitution. This it did not do. Rather, the city had instituted a law "which is a limited prohibition reasonably related to particular places and necessary to protect the public safety, health, morals, and general welfare."

Finally, the Court of Appeals of Washington noted that "while 36 states have constitutional provisions concerning the right to bear arms, in none is the right deemed absolute." Furthermore, "those states with constitutional provisions similar to ours (Alabama, Michigan, Wyoming, Oregon, Indiana) have uniformly held the right subject to reasonable exercise of the police power." The city of Renton was within its rights when it passed the ordinance barring firearms from bars, and the court upheld the decision of the lower court.

Morton Grove, Illinois: Handguns Are Banned

As soon as Morton Grove, Illinois, a Chicago suburb, passed an ordinance banning handguns in 1981, handgun owners challenged the city in court. Article 1, Section 22, of the Illinois constitution provides that "subject only to the police power, the right of the individual citizen to keep and bear arms shall not be infringed." Handgun owners argued that the right to bear arms was protected by state and federal constitutions and further contended that if Morton Grove were allowed to pass such laws in contradiction to other towns and cities, a "patchwork quilt" situation would result, in that handgun owners would never know if they were violating a law when traveling from town to town.

Morton Grove defended itself, claiming it was within its power to limit or ban the possession of handguns if city officials believed handgun possession was a threat to peace and stability. The city further claimed that its ordinance did not violate Section 22 of the Illinois constitution because it guaranteed the right to keep "some guns." The Morton Grove law did not ban all guns, only handguns.

LEGAL PROCEEDINGS. The cases of Victor Quilici, Robert Stengl, George Reichert, and Robert Metler were combined and brought to the Federal District Court of Northern Illinois in *Quilici v. Village of Morton Grove* (532 F.Supp. 1169 [1981]), in which the court upheld the town's right to ban handguns. The U.S. Court of Appeals, Seventh District, also upheld in *Quilici v. Village of Morton Grove* (695 F.2d 261 [7th Cir. 1982]) the findings of the district court, saying "the right to keep and bear handguns is not guaranteed by the Second Amendment." The case was appealed to the U.S. Supreme Court. The High Court refused to hear the case, so the ruling of the lower court of appeals stood.

A NEW ROUTE. The Morton Grove handgun owners then went to the Circuit Court of Cook County for an injunction to prevent Morton Grove from instituting the ordinance that banned handguns. The county circuit court upheld the validity of the ordinance. The handgun owners next appealed to the Appellate Court of Illinois, First District, Third Division. In *Kalodimos v. Village of Morton Grove* (447 NE.2d 849 [1983]), the court upheld the decisions of the lower courts. Even though the court agreed with the handgun owners that "gun control legislation could vary from municipality to municipality, we find that the framers [of the Illinois constitution] envisioned this kind of local control."

The case was again appealed, and in October 1984 the Illinois Supreme Court upheld in *Kalodimos v. Village of Morton Grove* (53 LW 2233) the lower courts' decisions. Agreeing with earlier observations, the state's highest court noted that "while the right to possess firearms for the purposes of self-defense may be necessary to protect important personal liberties from encroachment by others, it does not lie at the heart of the relationship between individuals and their government." Thus, Morton Grove needed only to have had a "rational basis" for instituting its ban on handguns. The Illinois Supreme Court concluded, "Because of the comparative ease with which handguns can be concealed and handled, a ban on handguns could rationally have been viewed as a way of reducing the frequency of premeditated violent attacks as well as unplanned criminal shootings in the heat of passion or an overreaction to fears of assault, accidental shootings by children or by adults who are unaware that a handgun is loaded, or suicides. The ordinance is a proper exercise of the police power."

Chicago: Limits on Handgun Possession

On March 19, 1982, the Chicago City Council passed an ordinance prohibiting the registration of any handgun after April 10, 1982, the effective date of the ordinance,

unless it was "validly registered to a current owner in the City of Chicago" before April 10, 1982 (*Municipal Code of the City of Chicago*, Chapter 8-20-050[c][1]). Jerome Sklar lived in neighboring Skokie, Illinois, when the law was passed. He owned a handgun and held a valid Illinois Firearms Identification Card. On April 15, 1982, after the ordinance had gone into effect, he moved to Chicago. He could not register the weapon and, therefore, was unable to bring it into the city.

Sklar went to court, claiming that the city of Chicago had violated the equal protection clause of the U.S. Constitution because he was unable to register the gun that he owned, whereas owners of firearms who resided in Chicago before the effective date of the ordinance had an opportunity to take advantage of the law's registration requirements. By this time, *Quilici v. Village of Morton Grove* had been decided in the Seventh Circuit Court of Appeals, a decision that applied to this judicial region. Therefore, the U.S. District Court for the Northern District of Illinois indicated in *Sklar v. Byrne* (727 F.2nd 633 [1983]) that because of the *Quilici* ruling it "concluded that the Chicago firearms ordinance does not infringe any federal constitutional right." The court indicated that the city of Chicago had legitimately and rationally used its police power to promote the health and safety of its citizens. Sklar's argument that Chicago could have chosen better ways to protect its citizens from the negative effects of firearms was irrelevant.

The court concluded that the ordinance did not violate the equal protection clause of the U.S. Constitution by limiting new registrations instead of banning handguns altogether. The city was under no legal requirement to take an all or nothing approach to limiting handguns.

Sklar appealed the district court's decision to the U.S. Court of Appeals, Seventh Circuit, the same court that had ruled on *Quilici v. Village of Morton Grove*. In his appeal, Sklar claimed that his constitutionally guaranteed right to travel had been violated, because he could not move into Chicago without giving up his gun. In *Sklar v. Byrne* (727 F.2d 633 [1984]), the court upheld the lower court's decision, citing the precedent established in *Quilici*. The court did not believe that a fundamental constitutional issue was involved. Therefore, the city of Chicago had a right to institute local regulations as long as it did not go overboard. The court stated:

> The Chicago handgun ordinance as a whole promotes legitimate government goals. The city council set forth its purposes in the preamble to the ordinance. The council found that handguns and other firearms play a major role in crimes and accidental deaths and injuries, and that the "convenient availability" of firearms and ammunition contributed to deaths and injuries in Chicago. The council therefore enacted the ordinance to restrict the availability of firearms and thereby to prevent some deaths and injuries among Chicago citizens. The city's primary goals

are thus classic examples of the city's police power to protect the health and safety of its citizens.

Sklar argued that it was irrational and "inconsistent with the overall purposes of the ordinance" to allow some people to have handguns and others not to, and not to classify gun owners on the basis of their ability to handle handguns safely. In dismissing his claim, the court stated, "that argument essentially asks this court to second-guess the judgment of the city council. The Constitution does not require the city council to act with a single purpose or to be entirely consistent. Indeed, the council is a political body for the accommodation of many conflicting interests.... The Constitution does not require the city council to enact the perfect law. The council may proceed step by step, 'adopting regulations that only partially ameliorate a perceived evil and deferring complete elimination of the evil to future regulations.'"

In both *Quilici* and *Sklar*, the courts were not saying that handgun control is or is not a good decision for any local authority to make. They did not see the possession of a handgun as a fundamental right protected by either the federal or the state constitution. The courts stated that a town or city, under the police powers granted it by American tradition and the Illinois constitution, has the right to decide and implement such an ordinance for its own people. A local ordinance does not have to be consistent, as long as the city council can prove that it thought out its decision rationally.

As noted above in this chapter, the U.S. Supreme Court held in *McDonald v. Chicago* that the Second Amendment right of individuals to keep and bear arms for self-defense may not be preempted by state or local laws. The High Court found that the restrictions on gun ownership in Chicago and neighboring Oak Park, Illinois, were too restrictive because they denied citizens the right to legally possess a gun in their own home for self-defense. The Court left open the possibility, however, that some state and local gun-control measures could withstand constitutional scrutiny applied in the case. Writing for the majority, Justice Samuel Alito (1950–) noted that "incorporation does not imperil every law regulating firearms," and Chicago and other municipalities throughout the country immediately began revising their gun-control policies.

West Hollywood, California: Saturday Night Specials Banned

In 1998 the California Supreme Court let stand a ruling by the California Court of Appeals on inexpensive handguns known as Saturday Night Specials. The court of appeals had upheld a municipal ban by the city of West Hollywood on the sale of this type of weapon. In its opinion, the court rejected the gun lobby's claim that California state law preempted the ordinance; furthermore, the court found that the ban did not violate the principles of equal protection or due process. Gun rights advocates maintained that singling out inexpensive weapons denies poor people an affordable means of self-defense.

Denver, Colorado: State Law Does Not Override Denver's Right to Ban Certain Guns

In 2003 the Colorado state legislature passed gun legislation that preempted many of Denver's local firearms laws. The city of Denver filed a lawsuit against the state of Colorado and Governor Bill Owens (1950–) to retain its city ordinances. Judges Joseph E. Meyer III and Lawrence Manzanares (1956–2007) of the Denver District Court ruled that the state legislation did and could override some of Denver's minor ordinances, but that the city still had the right to ban certain guns such as assault weapons and some handguns.

Seattle, Washington: State Law Overrides City Gun Ban

In October 2009 the Second Amendment Foundation and several other gun rights groups sued the city of Seattle, claiming that the city had no right to ban guns in certain places, such as parks and community centers. Judge Catherine Shaffer of the King County Superior Court ruled in February 2010 that Washington State law did not allow Seattle to regulate the possession of firearms. The city of Seattle appealed the ruling to the U.S. District Court on Second Amendment grounds, citing *Heller*. In March 2010 Judge Marsha J. Pechman (1951–) of the U.S. District Court for the Western District of Washington upheld the lower court ruling and stated that the *Heller* ruling applied only to federal jurisdictions. However, the U.S. Supreme Court ruling in *McDonald v. Chicago* in June 2010 clarified that Second Amendment rights also apply to the states. The article "Justices Extend Gun Owner Rights Nationwide; McKenna Statement Inside" (June 30, 2010, http://www .khq.com/Global/story.asp?S=12721580) quotes Rob McKenna (1962–), the attorney general of Washington State, as saying that he was "gratified that the U.S. Supreme Court has affirmed that the Second Amendment may not be infringed by state and local governments" and that "the right to bear arms shouldn't be infringed just because a person crosses state or city lines."

RESPONSIBILITY FOR HANDGUN DEATHS

The cases presented thus far on the federal, state, and local levels focus primarily on the right to bear arms. The following cases probe the responsibilities and liabilities associated with the use of those arms. Some victims of the use of certain weapons have tried to place that responsibility and liability on the manufacturers of the weapons, whereas others fault the people who made the weapons available to criminals. Each of the decisions presented here was based on state laws that differ greatly.

California: Gun Dealers Can Be Held Liable for Gun Violations of Others

Nineteen-year-old Jeff Randa had mentioned to a gun dealer many times that he wanted to buy a handgun and ammunition. The dealer told the youth that he could not buy a gun until he was 21 years old. Randa asked if his grandmother could purchase the weapon. The dealer replied that if she were a qualified buyer she could, but that the dealer could not sell her the weapon "just so she could give the gun to her grandson."

Subsequently, Randa's grandmother came into the store with him and purchased the handgun the youth wanted. Twelve days later, Randa went to a party with the gun. Bryan Hoosier, who was also at the party, told Randa to point the gun and shoot. Randa did so, killing Hoosier, and was later convicted of voluntary manslaughter.

Hoosier's father sued the gun dealer for negligence, accusing the dealer of knowing that the gun would be given to a minor after being sold to an adult. The dealer argued that it could not be liable and that the state laws imposed criminal penalties only on violators.

The California Court of Appeals ruled in *Hoosier v. Randa* (17 Cal. Rptr. 2d 518, 521 [Cal. Ct. App. 1993]) that the dealer was indeed liable for injuries. The state gun control laws were passed not only to establish criminal penalties but also to protect the public. If a dealer violated the law, he also violated his responsibility of care owed to the public. Consequently, any person harmed by such a violation may sue the violator.

Ohio: Gun Show Promoters Must Provide Adequate Security against Juvenile Gun Theft

During a 1992 gun show that was promoted by Niles Gun Show Inc., four youths under the age of 18 stole several handguns. The corporation from which the vendors rented space had no policy that required the vendors to protect their wares from being stolen, although it had an unenforced policy barring minors from entering the show.

After leaving the show, the youths also stole a car. While driving around in the car, the juveniles confronted two men, Greg L. Pavlides and Thomas E. Snedeker. One of the boys, Edward A. Tilley III, shot Pavlides in the chest and Snedeker in the head with one of the stolen guns. Tilley was arrested, charged, and convicted of two counts of attempted murder and one count of unauthorized use of a motor vehicle.

Pavlides and Snedeker survived their injuries and sued Niles Gun Show for negligence for not protecting them and the rest of the public from criminal acts by third parties who stole weapons that had not been properly secured. The trial court dismissed the case, stating that the promoters had no such responsibility, but the Ohio Court of Appeals reversed the lower court's decision, sending the case back to be tried.

The court ruled that the promoters of gun shows have a duty to provide adequate security to protect the public from criminal acts that might occur if the guns were stolen. The court explained that gun show operators should require vendors to secure their firearms and make a reasonable effort to bar minors from stealing or purchasing weapons and ammunition. The court further stated that it is "common knowledge" that minors possessing guns can create dangerous situations, and consequently gun show promoters should have been aware that minors stealing guns might use them in criminal activity.

Texas: Gun Seller Not Liable for Purchaser's Suicide

In December 1980 James J. Robertson purchased a handgun. Eighteen months later he used that gun to kill himself. Robertson's family brought a wrongful-death suit against the seller of the handgun before the 298th Judicial District Court, Dallas County, Texas. In *Robertson v. Grogan Investment Company* (710 SW.2d 678 [1986]), the district court found in favor of the defendant, Grogan Investments, because "the sale of handguns . . . to the general public is an abnormally dangerous and ultrahazardous activity . . . . Texas courts, when confronted with the opportunity to apply strict liability for ultrahazardous activities, have declined to do so and have consistently required some other showing, such as negligence or trespass, for recovery."

Florida: Store Responsible in Criminal Act for Selling Ammunition to Juveniles

In 1991 a Florida Wal-Mart store employee sold ammunition to two teenagers without asking about age or requesting identification, which is a violation of federal law. Several hours later the teenagers used the ammunition in a robbery of an auto parts store, during which they shot and killed Billy Wayne Coker. Coker's wife filed suit against Wal-Mart.

Even though Wal-Mart acknowledged that the sale was illegal, it argued that the perpetrators' intervening act of murder was not foreseeable and, therefore, the illegal sale was not the legal cause of Coker's death. The court agreed with this argument and dismissed the case. The Florida Court of Appeals, however, ruled that an ammunition vendor's illegal sale could be the legal cause of an injury or death caused by the buyer's intentional or criminal act. In July 1998 the Florida Supreme Court upheld in *Wal-Mart Stores, Inc. v. Coker* (1998 Fla. Lexis 861) the $2.6 million verdict against Wal-Mart for negligence in selling handgun ammunition to underaged buyers.

GUN INDUSTRY AND LIABILITY FOR GUNSHOT INJURIES
Maryland: *Kelley v. R.G. Industries Inc.*

In 1981 Olen J. Kelley was injured when he was shot in the chest during an armed robbery of the grocery store where he worked. The gun used was a Rohm revolver handgun model RG-38S that was designed and marketed by Rohm Gesellschaft, a German corporation. The handgun was assembled and initially sold by R.G. Industries Inc., a Miami-based subsidiary of the German corporation. Kelley and his wife filed suits against Rohm Gesellschaft and R.G. Industries in the Circuit Court of Montgomery County, Maryland.

Two counts charged that the handgun was "abnormally dangerous" and "defective in its marketing, promotion, distribution, and design." A third count charged negligence. The case revolved around whether or not the gun in question was a Saturday Night Special, which was banned from import by the ATF. The Federal District Court of Baltimore, where the case was first brought, asked the state court for a ruling on whether the manufacturer could be held liable under Maryland law.

The Maryland Court of Appeals ruled in *Kelley v. R.G. Industries Inc.* (497 A.2d 1143 [1985]) that the manufacturer and marketers could not be held strictly liable because handguns are "abnormally dangerous products" and their manufacturing and marketing are "abnormally dangerous activit[ies]." In its decision, the court noted, "Contrary to Kelley's argument, a handgun is not defective merely because it is capable of being used during criminal activity to inflict harm. A consumer would expect a handgun to be dangerous, by its very nature, and to have the capacity to fire a bullet with deadly force."

The court of appeals also stated that Kelley confused a product's normal function, which may be dangerous by its very nature, with a defect in its design and function. Kelley had cited as an example that a car is dangerous if it is used to run down pedestrians. The injury that results is from the nature of the product—the ability to be propelled to great speeds at great force. Nevertheless, if the gas tank of the car leaked in such a way as to cause an explosion in the event of a rear-end collision, then the design of the product would be defective, and the manufacturer would be liable. The court concluded that to impose "strict liability upon the manufacturers or marketers of handguns for gunshot injuries resulting from the misuse of handguns by others, would be contrary to Maryland public policy."

The Maryland court's opinion differed on Saturday Night Specials, which it defined as guns "characterized by short barrels, light weight, easy concealability, low cost, use of cheap quality materials, poor manufacture, inaccuracy and unreliability." The court considered these guns "largely unfit for any of the recognized legitimate uses sanctioned by the Maryland gun control legislation. They are too inaccurate, unreliable and poorly made for use by law enforcement personnel, sportsmen, homeowners or businessmen . . . . The chief 'value' a Saturday Night Special handgun has is in criminal activity, because of its easy concealability and low price."

The court determined that manufacturers and marketers are liable because they should know that this type of gun is made primarily for criminal activity. Judge John C. Eldridge (1933–) quoted an R.G. Industries salesperson as telling a prospective handgun marketer, "If your store is anywhere near a ghetto area, these ought to sell real well. This is most assuredly a ghetto gun." The salesperson allegedly went on to say that even though the gun sold well, it was virtually useless, and that he would be afraid to fire it.

The court of appeals did not rule on whether the gun in question fell within the category of Saturday Night Specials but referred that decision to the U.S. District Court. The court of appeals, however, did indicate that strong evidence had been presented that the gun fit many of the qualifications; if it were found to be a Saturday Night Special, liability against both the manufacturer and marketer could be imposed. This decision applied only in Maryland, and the Maryland legislature soon passed a law overriding it. Few courts have accepted this interpretation.

New Mexico: *Armijo v. Ex Cam Inc.*

Dolores Armijo's brother, Steven Armijo, shot and killed James Salusberry, Dolores's husband, in front of Dolores and her daughter. He then tried to shoot them, but the gun jammed. Dolores, claiming the gun used was a Saturday Night Special, sued Ex Cam Inc., the importer and distributor of the weapon.

The suit was based on four theories: strict product liability (the product was defective and unreasonably dangerous; therefore, the manufacturer was responsible for the actions of the product), "ultra-hazardous activity" liability (a gun is a dangerous product and the manufacturer is accountable for the results of its use), negligence liability (the manufacturer did not show reasonable care while marketing a product that carried some degree of risk that it might be used to commit a crime), and a narrow form of strict product liability for Saturday Night Specials put forth in *Kelley v. R.G. Industries Inc.*

The U.S. District Court in New Mexico did not believe that any court in New Mexico would ever recognize any of these theories as the basis of a court case under New Mexico law. In *Armijo v. Ex Cam Inc.* (656 F.Supp. 771 [1987]), the court said:

> It would be evident to any potential consumer that a gun could be used as a murder weapon. So could a knife, an axe, a bow and arrows, a length of chain. The mere fact that a product is capable of being misused to criminal ends does not render the product defective.

> [Based on New Mexico law, such a case] would not result in liability for a manufacturer of guns, as guns are commonly distributed and the dangers . . . are so obvious as to not require any manufacturers' warnings.

The court showed little respect for *Kelley v. R.G. Industries Inc.*, indicating that it went against common law in the state of New Mexico; therefore, it would not be considered. Furthermore, the court concluded that "all firearms are capable of being used for criminal activity. Merely to impose liability upon the manufacturers of the cheapest types of handguns will not avoid that basic fact. Instead, claims against gun manufacturers will have the anomalous [unusual] result that only persons shot with cheap guns will be able to recover, while those shot with expensive guns, admitted by the *Kelley* court to be more accurate and therefore deadlier, would take nothing."

Washington, D.C.: *Delahanty v. Hinckley*

In 1981 John W. Hinckley Jr. (1955–) tried to assassinate President Ronald Reagan (1911–2004). An individual injured during the assassination attempt sued to hold the gun manufacturer liable based on negligence, strict product liability, and a "social utility" claim founded on strict liability for unusually dangerous products.

In *Delahanty v. Hinckley* (DC, No. 88-488 [1989]), the Washington, D.C., court rejected the plaintiff's claims. There was no issue that the gun did not work properly. Furthermore, a manufacturer had no duty to warn a buyer "when the danger, or potentiality of danger, is generally known and recognized."

The court did not believe the marketing of a handgun was in and of itself dangerous; rather, the danger resulted from the action of a third party. The plaintiff had shown no connection between the gun manufacturer and Hinckley, nor had the plaintiff shown a reasonable way in which the gun manufacturer could have prevented Hinckley from using the weapon to try to assassinate President Reagan. The court also dismissed the *Kelley* argument because it could not accept a ruling that categorizes one type of product as liable for negligence simply because it is inexpensive and/or poorly made.

Washington, D.C.: The Federal Government Settles the Manufacturer Liability Issue

In 1998, after the tobacco industry was found to be responsible for lung cancer deaths caused by smoking cigarettes, many cities and counties across the United States began filing lawsuits against gun manufacturers and dealers. At issue was the gun distribution system, which was thought to allow guns to pass too easily to criminals and youth. Regardless, Fox Butterfield reports in "Gun Industry Is Gaining Immunity from Suits" (*New York Times*, September 1, 2002) that by 2002, 30 states had passed laws granting immunity to the gun industry from these civil lawsuits. In a countermeasure, California passed a bill repealing such an immunity law in its state.

In 2005 Congress settled this issue with the passage of the Protection of Lawful Commerce in Arms Act. President George W. Bush (1946–) signed the bill into law in October 2005. This act prohibits liability actions (charging legal responsibility) against firearms and ammunition manufacturers and sellers for unlawful misuse of their products. An exception to the act allows petitioners to sue firearms manufacturers and dealers if they knowingly violate state or federal statutes. The act also prohibits the sale of a handgun unless the purchaser is provided with a secure gun storage or safety device, and it provides for particular sentences when armor-piercing ammunition is used in certain crimes.

According to David Stout, in "Justices Decline New York Gun Suit" (*New York Times*, March 9, 2009), since the passage of the Protection of Lawful Commerce in Arms Act, many city and state officials have sued gun manufacturers without success, but some litigants have won suits against gun dealers.

Williams v. Beemiller: Gun Industry May Be Liable When Engaged in Illegal Trafficking

In *Williams v. Beemiller, Inc.* ([Appeal No. 1] ___ AD3d ___ [2012]) the New York Court of Appeals, Fourth Judicial Department, reversed a lower court's dismissal of a case in which a shooting victim brought suit against the gun manufacturer, distributor, and dealer who supplied the weapon used to injure him. *Williams v. Beemiller* stemmed from a drive-by shooting that occurred in Buffalo, New York, in 2003. In a case of mistaken identity, teenager Daniel Williams was shot by gang member Cornell Caldwell with a 9mm Hi-Point handgun that had been acquired by James Nigel Bostic in a "straw purchase," with his girlfriend as the buyer of record. Bostic had purchased about 250 guns in Ohio that he sold illegally in Buffalo; 140 of the guns were purchased from one dealer, Charles Brown, and 87 guns were exchanged in the transaction that included the one that was used to shoot Williams. Caldwell was apprehended, tried, found guilty, and was sent to prison for the crime.

Williams, who survived the shooting, filed a suit against the manufacturer of the gun, the distributor, and Brown, who he claimed should have recognized that Bostic was involved in criminal activity from the number and type of weapons that he purchased. Brown claimed that Bostic told him he was planning to open a gun shop. In 2011 the defendants had sought and received a dismissal of the case based on the Protection of Lawful Commerce in Arms Act; however, the New York State Court of Appeals overturned that dismissal in October 2012. Justice Erin Peradotto of the Appellate Division, Fourth Department, stated in the ruling, "Although the complaint does not specify the statutes allegedly violated (by the defendants), it sufficiently alleges facts supporting a finding that defendants knowingly violated federal gun laws." The ruling allowed Williams's case to move forward, therefore, holding open the possibility that the gun industry may be criminally liable when engaged in illegal sales.

CHAPTER 5
FIREARMS AND CRIME

Many of the statistics on the frequency and ways in which guns are used to commit crimes come from the Federal Bureau of Investigation (FBI) of the U.S. Department of Justice (DOJ), which collects crime statistics through its Uniform Crime Reports program. Its annual publication *Crime in the United States* is a primary source for statistical information on crime. The FBI's crime statistics are based solely on police investigation reports and arrests; crimes that are not reported to the police are not included. The most recent report from the Uniform Crime Reports program is *Crime in the United States, 2010* (September 2011, http://www.fbi.gov/about-us/cjis/ucr/crime-in-the-u.s/2010/crime-in-the-u.s.-2010).

The FBI reports in *Crime in the United States, 2010* that 1,181,579 violent crimes (murder and nonnegligent manslaughter, forcible rape, robbery, and aggravated assault) were reported to law enforcement agencies in 2010, a decrease of 5.8% from the previous year. (See Table 5.1.) Moreover, the violent crime rate as reported by the FBI decreased from 666.9 per 100,000 inhabitants in 1989 to 466.9 per 100,000 inhabitants in 2007 and then to 403.6 violent crimes per 100,000 inhabitants in 2010.

Table 5.1 shows that offenses in all of the four violent crime categories decreased from 2009 to 2010: murder and nonnegligent manslaughter decreased 4%, forcible rape decreased 3.8%, robbery decreased 9.7%, and aggravated assault decreased 4%. Cities with populations of 250,000 to 499,999 (medium-sized cities such as St. Louis, Missouri) had the largest decrease for violent crimes from 2009 to 2010, at 6.7%. Small cities (such as Nome, Alaska) with populations under 10,000 had the smallest decrease for violent crimes, at 4.7%.

In *Uniform Crime Reporting Handbook* (2004, http://www.fbi.gov/ucr/handbook/ucrhandbook04.pdf), the most recent revision as of October 2012, the FBI defines the following terms with respect to the four types of violent crimes shown in Table 5.1. Murder and nonnegligent

manslaughter are one type of criminal homicide and are defined as "the willful (nonnegligent) killing of one human being by another," such as deaths caused by injuries received in a fight or assault. (The other type of criminal homicide is manslaughter by negligence, which is defined as "the killing of another person through gross negligence," such as deaths caused by one person shooting and killing another by accident when target shooting.) Thus, murder and nonnegligent manslaughter mean the same thing, and both are a type of criminal homicide. Forcible rape is defined as "the carnal knowledge of a female forcibly and against her will," such as when a man forces or attempts to force intercourse on a woman. Sexual attacks on men are counted as aggravated assaults or sex offenses. Statutory rape, "nonforcible sexual intercourse with a person who is under the statutory age of consent," is counted as a sex offense. Robbery is defined as "the taking or attempting to take anything of value from the care, custody, or control of a person or persons by force or threat of force or violence and/or by putting the victim in fear." Aggravated assault is defined as "an unlawful attack by one person upon another for the purpose of inflicting severe or aggravated bodily injury. This type of assault usually is accompanied by the use of a weapon or by means likely to produce death or great bodily harm."

HOMICIDE AND MURDER
Murders, Weapons, and Circumstances

The Bureau of Justice Statistics (BJS) shows in *Homicide Trends in the United States: Long Term Trends and Patterns* (June 25, 2010, http://bjs.ojp.usdoj.gov/content/homicide/hmrt.cfm#) that the homicide victimization rate (the number of people killed by another per 100,000 population) was relatively low during the 1950s and the early 1960s, under five homicides per 100,000 people in most years. By the mid-1960s, however, the rate rose dramatically and continued to rise through the mid-1970s, reaching nearly 10 homicides per 100,000 people. Following a slight dip, it peaked in 1980 at 10.2 homicides per 100,000 people.

TABLE 5.1

Crime trends by population group, 2009–10

Population group	Year	Violent crime	Murder and nonnegligent manslaughter	Forcible rape	Robbery	Aggravated assault	Property crime	Burglary	Larceny-theft	Motor vehicle theft	Arson	Number of agencies	2010 estimated population
Total all agencies:	2009	1,253,786	14,668	79,306	394,107	765,705	8,783,560	2,068,376	5,950,908	764,276	56,477	14,706	291,385,855
	2010	1,181,579	14,077	76,322	355,795	735,385	8,543,699	2,034,268	5,801,900	707,531	52,191		
	Percent change	−5.8	−4.0	−3.8	−9.7	−4.0	−2.7	−1.6	−2.5	−7.4	−7.6		
Total cities	2009	998,731	11,318	58,265	343,360	585,788	6,875,514	1,515,174	4,754,923	605,417	41,914	10,611	197,239,780
	2010	943,322	10,861	56,651	310,450	565,360	6,666,087	1,489,019	4,615,865	561,203	39,169		
	Percent change	−5.5	−4.0	−2.8	−9.6	−3.5	−3.0	−1.7	−2.9	−7.3	−6.5		
Group I (250,000 and over)	2009	453,671	5,808	18,889	184,802	244,172	2,240,358	521,170	1,440,506	278,682	15,164	75	57,354,512
	2010	428,565	5,731	18,673	167,555	236,606	2,164,781	509,242	1,392,700	262,839	14,006		
	Percent change	−5.5	−1.3	−1.1	−9.3	−3.1	−3.4	−2.3	−3.3	−5.7	−7.6		
1,000,000 and over (Group I subset)	2009	193,010	2,369	6,105	85,436	99,100	842,014	178,035	555,477	108,502	4,587	10	25,823,829
	2010	183,262	2,316	6,062	78,293	96,591	810,287	172,991	535,650	101,646	3,890		
	Percent change	−5.1	−2.2	−0.7	−8.4	−2.5	−3.8	−2.8	−3.6	−6.3	−15.2		
500,000 to 999,999 (Group I subset)	2009	146,001	1,903	6,501	55,448	82,149	798,436	192,180	509,521	96,735	5,405	25	17,415,371
	2010	138,348	1,813	6,658	49,429	80,448	767,672	185,280	491,214	91,178	5,291		
	Percent change	−5.2	−4.7	+2.4	−10.9	−2.1	−3.9	−3.6	−3.6	−5.7	−2.1		
250,000 to 499,999 (Group I subset)	2009	114,660	1,536	6,283	43,918	62,923	599,908	150,955	375,508	73,445	5,172	40	14,115,312
	2010	106,955	1,602	5,953	39,833	59,567	586,822	150,971	365,836	70,015	4,825		
	Percent change	−6.7	+4.3	−5.3	−9.3	−5.3	−2.2	*	−2.6	−4.7	−6.7		
Group II (100,000 to 249,999)	2009	165,046	1,875	10,022	56,341	96,808	1,198,242	275,636	808,869	113,737	6,686	203	30,280,703
	2010	156,707	1,744	9,481	51,275	94,207	1,155,269	273,363	778,735	103,171	6,426		
	Percent change	−5.1	−7.0	−5.4	−9.0	−2.7	−3.6	−0.8	−3.7	−9.3	−3.9		
Group III (50,000 to 99,999)	2009	131,509	1,272	8,769	42,113	79,355	1,040,159	228,051	728,515	83,593	6,346	458	31,381,299
	2010	123,175	1,248	8,492	37,895	75,540	1,006,803	223,639	706,049	77,115	5,886		
	Percent change	−6.3	−1.9	−3.2	−10.0	−4.8	−3.2	−1.9	−3.1	−7.7	−7.2		
Group IV (25,000 to 49,999)	2009	95,293	934	7,198	28,129	59,032	861,663	177,532	630,329	53,802	4,881	808	27,927,972
	2010	89,599	914	7,107	25,031	56,547	839,961	178,140	612,266	49,555	4,427		
	Percent change	−6.0	−2.1	−1.3	−11.0	−4.2	−2.5	+0.3	−2.9	−7.9	−9.3		
Group V (10,000 to 24,999)	2009	82,409	748	6,906	20,435	54,320	819,189	170,827	604,783	43,579	3,985	1,743	27,712,113
	2010	77,803	700	6,481	18,285	52,337	796,254	166,235	590,495	39,524	3,754		
	Percent change	−5.6	−6.4	−6.2	−10.5	−3.7	−2.8	−2.7	−2.4	−9.3	−5.8		
Group VI (under 10,000)	2009	70,803	681	6,481	11,540	52,101	715,903	141,958	541,921	32,024	4,852	7,324	22,583,181
	2010	67,473	524	6,417	10,409	50,123	703,019	138,400	535,620	28,999	4,670		
	Percent change	−4.7	−23.1	−1.0	−9.8	−3.8	−1.8	−2.5	−1.2	−9.4	−3.8		
Metropolitan counties	2009	200,546	2,407	14,784	46,206	137,149	1,489,728	405,436	953,993	130,299	10,893	1,710	67,489,063
	2010	186,939	2,369	13,844	41,111	129,615	1,450,064	396,185	934,912	118,967	9,608		
	Percent change	−6.8	−1.6	−6.4	−11.0	−5.5	−2.7	−2.3	−2.0	−8.7	−11.8		
Nonmetropolitan counties[a]	2009	54,509	943	6,257	4,541	42,768	418,318	147,766	241,992	28,560	3,670	2,385	26,657,012
	2010	51,318	847	5,827	4,234	40,410	427,548	149,064	251,123	27,361	3,414		
	Percent change	−5.9	−10.2	−6.9	−6.8	−5.5	+2.2	+0.9	+3.8	−4.2	−7.0		

TABLE 5.1

Crime trends by population group, 2009–10 [CONTINUED]

Population group	Violent crime	Murder and nonnegligent manslaughter	Forcible rape	Robbery	Aggravated assault	Property crime	Burglary	Larceny-theft	Motor vehicle theft	Arson	Number of agencies	2010 estimate dpopulation
Suburban areas[b]												
2009	348,688	3,684	25,803	86,425	232,776	3,018,216	702,080	2,093,365	222,771	18,895		
2010	326,791	3,606	24,748	77,080	221,357	2,940,843	688,618	2,049,413	202,812	16,860	7,765	123,142,328
Percent change	−6.3	−2.1	−4.1	−10.8	−4.9	−2.6	−1.9	−2.1	−9.0	−10.8		

[a]Includes state police agencies that report aggregately for the entire state.
[b]Suburban areas include law enforcement agencies in cities with less than 50,000 inhabitants and county law enforcement agencies that are within a Metropolitan Statistical Area. Suburban areas exclude all metropolitan agencies associated with a principal city. The agencies associated with suburban areas also appear in other groups within this table.
*Less than one-tenth of 1 percent.

SOURCE: "Table 12. Crime Trends, by Population Group, 2009–2010," in *Crime in the United States, 2010*, U.S. Department of Justice, Federal Bureau of Investigation, September 2011, http://www.fbi.gov/about-us/cjis/ucr/crime-in-the-u.s./2010/crime-in-the-u.s.-2010/tables/10tbl12.xls (accessed August 17, 2012)

After a decline to 7.9 homicides per 100,000 people in 1984, the homicide rate rose again in the late 1980s and early 1990s to 9.8 homicides per 100,000 people in 1991. The homicide rate fell throughout the 1990s. In 2000 it reached the lowest national homicide rate since 1966, at 5.5 homicides per 100,000 people, and remained stabilized through 2008.

DEMOGRAPHICS OF HOMICIDE. The vast majority of murderers and murder victims are men. In *Homicide Trends in the United States, 1980–2008* (November 2011, http://bjs.ojp.usdoj.gov/content/pub/pdf/htus8008.pdf), Alexia Cooper and Erica L. Smith of the Bureau of Justice Statistics note that males are almost nine times more likely than females to be homicide offenders and three times more likely to be homicide victims. Overall during the period 1980 through 2008, more than three-quarters of homicide victims (76.8%) and nine out of 10 homicide offenders (89.5%) were men. (See Table 5.2.) African-Americans, who made up just 12.6% of the population during the period 1980 to 2008, were disproportionately represented as both homicide victims (47.4%) and offenders (52.5%). Similarly, young people aged 18 to 24 made up only 10.6% of the population between 1980 and 2008 but accounted for 24.4% of homicide victims and 37.5% of offenders.

Figure 5.1 shows homicide victimization rate trends by age for the period 1980 through 2008. At the beginning of the period reflected in the figure, the homicide rate was highest among those in the 25 to 34 age group (18.6

TABLE 5.2

Homicide victims and offenders, by demographic group, 1980–2008

	Percent of—			Rate per 100,000	
	Victims	Offenders	Population	Victims	Offenders
Total	**100%**	**100%**	**100%**	**7.4**	**8.3**
Age					
Under 14	4.8%	0.5%	20.0%	1.8	0.2
14–17	5.2	10.6	5.8	6.6	15.0
18–24	24.4	37.5	10.6	17.1	29.3
25–34	28.7	28.0	15.6	13.7	14.9
35–49	22.8	17.1	21.1	8.0	6.7
50–64	8.9	4.9	14.7	4.5	2.7
65 or older	5.1	1.6	12.3	3.1	1.1
Sex					
Male	76.8%	89.5%	48.9%	11.6	15.1
Female	23.2	10.5	51.1	3.4	1.7
Race					
White	50.3%	45.3%	82.9%	4.5	4.5
Black	47.4	52.5	12.6	27.8	34.4
Other*	2.3	2.2	4.4	3.8	4.1

*Other race includes American Indians, Native Alaskans, Asians, Native Hawaiians, and other Pacific Islanders.

SOURCE: Alexia Cooper and Erica L. Smith, "Table 1. Victims and Offenders, by Demographic Group, 1980–2008," in *Homicide Trends in the United States, 1980–2008*, U.S. Department of Justice, Office of Justice Programs, Bureau of Justice Statistics, November 2011, http://bjs.ojp.usdoj.gov/content/pub/pdf/htus8008.pdf (accessed August 28, 2012)

FIGURE 5.1

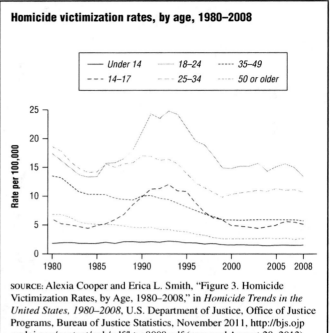

Homicide victimization rates, by age, 1980–2008

SOURCE: Alexia Cooper and Erica L. Smith, "Figure 3. Homicide Victimization Rates, by Age, 1980–2008," in *Homicide Trends in the United States, 1980–2008*, U.S. Department of Justice, Office of Justice Programs, Bureau of Justice Statistics, November 2011, http://bjs.ojp.usdoj.gov/content/pub/pdf/htus8008.pdf (accessed August 28, 2012)

homicides per 100,000 population); in 2008, the highest rate was registered among 18- to 24-year-olds (13.4 homicides per 100,000). The figure shows a sharp rise for teenagers and young adults during the late 1980s and early 1990s, peaking in 1993 at 12 homicides per 100,000 for those aged 14 to 17 and at 24.8 homicides per 100,000 for those aged 18 to 24. The homicide victimization rate for those under the age of 14 remained relatively flat throughout the period 1980 to 2008, peaking in 1993 at a rate of 2.2 homicide victims per 100,000. The rate of 1.5 in 2008 was only slightly higher than the lowest rate recorded for those under age 14 during the period, 1.4 homicides per 100,000 population in 2004.

There are a number of hypotheses as to why the homicide rate fell so dramatically during the 1990s, including the strong economy of the 1990s, changing demographics, better policing strategies, tougher gun control laws, laws allowing the carrying of concealed weapons, increased use of capital punishment, increases in the number of police, the rising prison population, the receding crack epidemic, and the legalization of abortion two decades earlier.

In "Understanding Why Crime Fell in the 1990s: Four Factors That Explain the Decline and Six That Do Not" (*Journal of Economic Perspectives*, vol. 18, no. 1, Winter 2004), Steven D. Levitt of the University of Chicago analyzes these hypotheses. He concludes that the first six factors do not explain the decline but that the last four factors do. His research shows that "police are the first line of defense against crime." During the 1990s the number of police officers in the United States increased about 14%. In addition, imprisonment of criminals increased during the decade, removing offenders from the streets and deterring others from committing crimes. He also suggests that as the crack epidemic receded, it had the effect of lowering the violent crime rate. Levitt also notes that a growing body of evidence shows that "unwanted" children are at a greater risk for crime than "wanted" children. As a result, the legalization of abortion with the *Roe v. Wade* (410 U.S. 113 [1973]) decision about two decades before the mid-1990s led to a reduction in the number of unwanted births and, therefore, to a reduction in the number of children who would have been at a greater risk for crime. During the first decade of the 21st century the effects of the factors resulting in this decline had been realized and the homicide victimization rate leveled out.

WEAPONS USED IN HOMICIDES. What types of weapons are used in homicides? From 1980 to 2008 handguns were the weapons most often used. (See Figure 5.2.) Following a peak of homicides by handguns in 1980 and a subsequent decline, incidents involving handguns increased beginning in the mid-1980s. By 1993 handgun use began a dramatic decline as did the homicide rate. The number of homicide victims killed by handguns from 2002 to 2007 increased slightly from the low point in 1999 to 2001, but in 2008 it declined again.

CIRCUMSTANCES SURROUNDING HOMICIDES. In *Homicide Trends in the United States, 1980–2008*, Cooper and Smith address the circumstances surrounding incidents of homicide between 1980 and 2008, finding that arguments were the most frequently cited circumstance of homicides

with known circumstances. Cooper and Smith report that a gun was used as the murder weapon in about 60% of homicides that stemmed from an argument in 2008, a proportion that had shown a slight decline since 1980. (See Figure 5.3.) Gang-related homicides, which comprised about 1% of homicides in 1980 and 6% of homicides in 2008, were the most likely to involve a gun throughout the period 1980 to 2008; in 1980 nearly three-quarters of gang homicides involved guns, whereas in 2008 the proportion had increased to more than nine out of 10 (92%).

Table 5.3 shows murder circumstances by weapon for 2010. In that year, handguns were the weapon most frequently used, accounting for 6,009 out of 12,996 murders (46.2%), shotguns were used in 373 murders (2.9%), and rifles were used in 358 murders (2.8%). Including "other" guns, over two-thirds (67.5%) of all murders in the United States in 2010 were committed using a firearm. A knife or other cutting instrument was used in 13.1% of murders (1,704 out of 12,996); personal weapons such as fists, hands, or feet in 742 murders (5.7%); blunt objects in 540 (4.2%); and other weapons, such as poisons, fire, and explosives, in the remainder.

Table 5.4 shows murder by state and type weapon for 2010. The states with the fewest murders in 2010 were Vermont (7), Wyoming (8), and North Dakota (9). Firearms were involved in two of the murders in Vermont, five of the murders in Wyoming, and four of the murders in North Dakota. California was the state that had the highest number of murders in 2010: 1,811. More than two-thirds of these

FIGURE 5.2

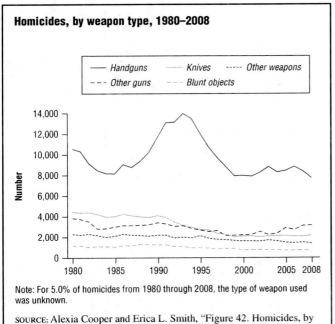

Homicides, by weapon type, 1980–2008

Note: For 5.0% of homicides from 1980 through 2008, the type of weapon used was unknown.

SOURCE: Alexia Cooper and Erica L. Smith, "Figure 42. Homicides, by Weapon Type, 1980–2008," in *Homicide Trends in the United States, 1980–2008*, U.S. Department of Justice, Office of Justice Programs, Bureau of Justice Statistics, November 2011, http://bjs.ojp.usdoj.gov/content/pub/pdf/htus8008.pdf (accessed August 28, 2012)

FIGURE 5.3

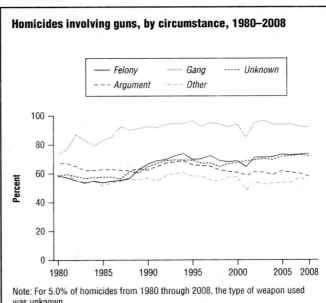

Homicides involving guns, by circumstance, 1980–2008

Note: For 5.0% of homicides from 1980 through 2008, the type of weapon used was unknown.

SOURCE: Alexia Cooper and Erica L. Smith, "Figure 41. Homicides Involving Guns, by Circumstance, 1980–2008," in *Homicide Trends in the United States, 1980–2008*, U.S. Department of Justice, Office of Justice Programs, Bureau of Justice Statistics, November 2011, http://bjs.ojp.usdoj.gov/content/pub/pdf/htus8008.pdf (accessed August 28, 2012)

TABLE 5.3

Murder circumstances, by weapon, 2010

Circumstances	Total murder victims	Total firearms	Handguns	Rifles	Shotguns	Other guns or type not stated	Knives or cutting instruments	Blunt objects (clubs, hammers, etc.)	Personal weapons (hands, fists, feet, etc.)	Poison	Pushed or thrown out window	Explosives	Fire	Narcotics	Drowning	Strangulation	Asphyxiation	Other
Total	12,996	8,775	6,009	358	373	2,035	1,704	540	742	11	3	4	74	39	10	122	98	874
Felony type total:	1,923	1,391	976	53	60	302	190	84	61	0	0	0	31	12	1	31	17	105
Rape	41	0	0	0	0	0	7	7	7	0	0	0	0	0	0	10	5	5
Robbery	780	603	463	16	19	105	69	44	27	0	0	0	1	0	0	7	3	26
Burglary	80	49	29	3	3	14	14	4	5	0	0	0	2	0	0	2	0	4
Larceny-theft	20	11	7	0	1	3	2	1	3	0	0	0	0	0	0	0	2	1
Motor vehicle theft	37	15	9	0	0	6	7	5	1	0	0	0	0	0	0	0	2	7
Arson	35	7	3	0	0	4	4	0	0	0	0	0	22	0	0	0	0	2
Prostitution and commercialized vice	5	1	0	0	0	1	1	0	1	0	0	0	0	0	0	1	0	1
Other sex offenses	14	3	3	0	0	0	3	1	3	0	0	0	0	0	0	2	0	2
Narcotic drug laws	463	391	264	7	12	108	37	8	3	0	0	0	1	10	1	3	0	9
Gambling	7	6	5	0	1	0	1	0	0	0	0	0	0	0	0	0	0	0
Other, not specified	441	305	193	27	24	61	45	14	11	0	0	0	5	2	0	6	5	48
Suspected felony type	66	44	31	2	2	9	10	1	3	0	0	0	0	0	0	4	0	4
Other than felony type total:	6,351	3,960	2,842	187	204	727	1,032	275	530	9	2	3	28	20	6	56	56	374
Romantic triangle	90	59	43	4	4	8	19	6	3	0	0	0	0	0	0	2	0	1
Child killed by babysitter	36	1	1	0	0	0	0	2	23	1	0	0	0	0	0	0	0	9
Brawl due to influence of alcohol	121	55	38	4	8	5	37	9	9	0	0	0	1	0	0	0	1	9
Brawl due to influence of narcotics	58	29	24	1	1	3	6	6	2	0	0	0	0	9	0	2	1	5
Argument over money or property	181	112	79	11	10	12	34	10	17	0	1	0	0	0	0	2	1	3
Other arguments	3,215	1,937	1,346	91	120	380	686	152	228	2	1	0	10	3	1	26	20	149
Gangland killings	176	160	102	4	3	51	11	1	0	0	0	0	0	0	0	0	0	4
Juvenile gang killings	673	624	529	10	7	78	31	4	5	0	0	0	0	0	0	0	0	9
Institutional killings	17	0	0	0	0	0	0	2	5	0	0	0	0	0	0	1	3	3
Sniper attack	3	3	0	3	0	0	0	0	0	0	0	0	0	0	0	0	0	0
Other, not specified	1,781	980	680	59	51	190	205	83	238	6	0	3	16	8	5	25	30	182
Unknown	4,656	3,380	2,160	116	107	997	472	180	148	2	1	1	15	7	3	31	25	391

SOURCE: "Expanded Homicide Data Table 11. Murder Circumstances by Weapon, 2010," in *Crime in the United States, 2010*, U.S. Department of Justice, Federal Bureau of Investigation, September 2011, http://www.fbi.gov/about-us/cjis/ucr/crime-in-the-u.s/2010/crime-in-the-u.s.-2010/tables/10shrtbl11.xls (accessed August 20, 2012)

TABLE 5.4

Murder, by state and type of weapon, 2010

State	Total murders[a]	Total firearms	Handguns	Rifles	Shotguns	Firearms (type unknown)	Knives or cutting instruments	Other weapons	Hands, fists, feet, etc.[b]
Alabama	199	135	112	0	23	0	23	24	17
Alaska	31	19	3	5	1	10	4	4	4
Arizona	352	232	152	14	10	56	51	62	7
Arkansas	130	93	49	7	4	33	12	21	4
California	1,811	1,257	953	59	44	201	250	201	103
Colorado	117	65	34	0	4	27	20	21	11
Connecticut	131	97	72	0	1	24	20	8	6
Delaware	48	38	25	0	2	11	8	0	2
District of Columbia	131	99	32	0	0	67	20	7	5
Georgia	527	376	315	19	21	21	64	85	2
Hawaii	24	7	6	0	0	1	6	5	6
Idaho	21	12	12	0	0	0	4	2	3
Illinois[c]	453	364	355	3	1	5	30	43	16
Indiana	198	142	83	11	7	41	19	25	12
Iowa	38	21	9	1	4	7	4	9	4
Kansas	100	63	30	4	1	28	13	18	6
Kentucky	180	116	76	6	16	18	19	25	20
Louisiana	437	351	263	19	11	58	42	31	13
Maine	24	11	4	2	1	4	6	1	6
Maryland	424	293	272	3	12	6	59	53	19
Massachusetts	209	118	52	0	1	65	50	31	10
Michigan	558	413	239	25	14	135	43	71	31
Minnesota	91	53	43	2	8	0	14	16	8
Mississippi	165	120	98	3	12	7	21	19	5
Missouri	419	321	189	26	4	102	35	49	14
Montana	21	12	6	2	4	0	3	5	1
Nebraska	51	32	29	1	2	0	8	5	6
Nevada	158	84	57	5	6	16	22	34	18
New Hampshire	13	5	2	0	2	1	5	3	0
New Jersey	363	246	216	7	2	21	50	39	28
New Mexico	118	67	36	6	2	23	29	15	7
New York	860	517	135	6	12	364	173	148	22
North Carolina	445	286	188	21	25	52	56	72	31
North Dakota	9	4	3	0	1	0	0	4	1
Ohio	460	310	176	7	2	125	40	93	17
Oklahoma	188	111	86	8	7	10	24	32	21
Oregon	78	36	20	1	2	13	16	17	9
Pennsylvania	646	457	367	8	11	71	67	94	28
Rhode Island	29	16	2	1	1	12	5	6	2
South Carolina	280	207	136	8	7	56	22	34	17
South Dakota	14	8	3	0	1	4	2	4	0
Tennessee	356	219	146	12	11	50	35	83	19
Texas	1,246	805	581	34	48	142	202	130	109
Utah	52	22	16	0	1	5	7	12	11
Vermont	7	2	1	1	0	0	1	2	2
Virginia	369	250	137	9	12	92	47	50	22
Washington	151	93	73	4	2	14	24	22	12
West Virginia	55	27	16	0	4	7	11	9	8
Wisconsin	151	97	63	5	6	23	13	22	19
Wyoming	8	5	0	2	0	3	1	1	1
Virgin Islands	50	41	36	1	0	4	4	5	0

[a]Total number of murders for which supplemental homicide data were received.
[b]Pushed is included in hands, fists, feet, etc.
[c]Limited supplemental homicide data were received.

SOURCE: "Table 20. Murder, by State, Types of Weapons, 2010," in *Crime in the United States, 2010*, U.S. Department of Justice, Federal Bureau of Investigation, September 2011, http://www.fbi.gov/about-us/cjis/ucr/crime-in-the-u.s/2010/crime-in-the-u.s.-2010/tables/10tbl20.xls (accessed August 20, 2012)

murders (1,257 murders, or 69.4%) were committed with a firearm. In Texas, the state with the second-highest number of murders in 2010, 64.6% of the murders (805 out of 1,246) were committed with firearms.

Murder is often the work of acquaintances or family: in 2010, 43.6% (5,657) of the murder victims knew their killers, with 13.9% (1,802) of murder victims related to their killers and 29.7% (3855) having other relationships, such as acquaintance, friend, neighbor, or girlfriend. (See Figure 5.4.) When the FBI published these 2010 crime statistics, the relationship of the offender to the victim was not known in 44% (5,724) of the murders. Strangers were the known perpetrators in 12.4% (1,615) of cases.

In *When Men Murder Women: An Analysis of 2010 Homicide Data* (September 2012, http://www.vpc.org/studies/wmmw2012.pdf), the Violence Policy Center (VPC), a national nonprofit educational foundation that conducts research on violence in the United States, links male-female and acquaintance murder data and determines that "for homicides in which the victim to offender relationship could be identified, 94 percent of female victims (1,571 out of 1,669) were murdered by a male they knew." In addition, nearly two-thirds (65%, or 1,017) of female homicide victims were murdered by their husband or an intimate acquaintance, such as a common-law husband, ex-husband, or boyfriend. In addition, the VPC finds that in 2010 more women were killed with firearms (52%) than with any other type of weapon. Of the homicides committed with firearms, almost three-quarters (70%) involved handguns.

In another study, *American Roulette: Murder-Suicide in the United States* (May 2012, http://www.vpc.org/studies/amroul2012.pdf), the VPC found that 280 of the 313 murder-suicides that occurred during the first half of 2011 were committed with a firearm (89.5%). For all murder-suicides during that time span, 17.9% involved a handgun as the only weapon, 4.5% involved only a shotgun, 3.8% involved solely

FIGURE 5.4

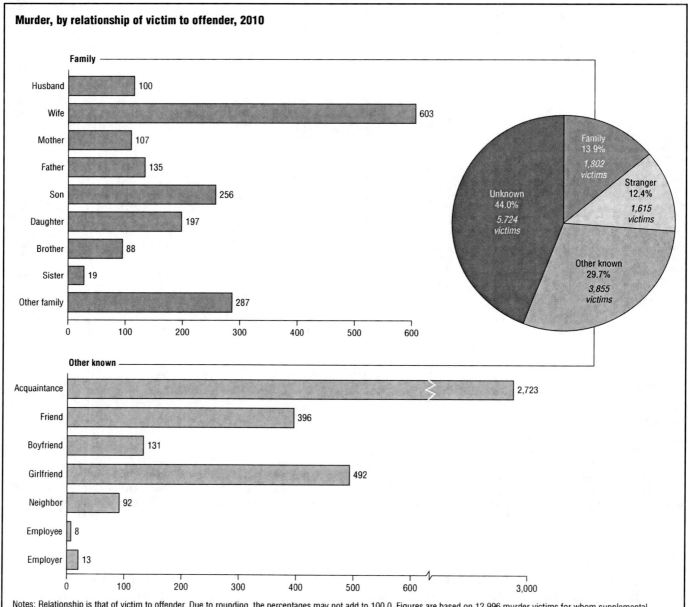

Murder, by relationship of victim to offender, 2010

Notes: Relationship is that of victim to offender. Due to rounding, the percentages may not add to 100.0. Figures are based on 12,996 murder victims for whom supplemental homicide data were received, and includes the 5,724 victims for which the relationship was unknown.

SOURCE: "Expanded Homicide Data Figure. Murder by Relationship, Percent Distribution, Volume by Relationship, 2010," in *Crime in the United States, 2010*, U.S. Department of Justice, Federal Bureau of Investigation, September 2011, http://www.fbi.gov/about-us/cjis/ucr/crime-in-the-u.s/2010/crime-in-the-u.s.-2010/offenses-known-to-law-enforcement/expanded/expanded-homicide-data-figure (accessed August 20, 2012)

a rifle, and 60.1% involved an unspecified type of firearm or multiple firearms. Multiple weapons (of which at least one was a firearm) were used in 3.2% of murder-suicides, and other weapons or means were involved in 9.3%.

The Criminal Advantages of Guns

A gun offers a criminal several advantages over other weapons. A gun offender can keep a greater physical distance from the victim to ensure his or her own safety and increase the chances of escaping. Moreover, a gun allows the offender to maintain a psychological distance as well, keeping the confrontation more impersonal and minimizing the emotional involvement. Control over potential victims can be easier to maintain with a gun; victims are less likely to run from a gun-carrying offender than from those brandishing other types of weapons, such as knives, for fear of being shot from a distance. For reasons such as these, between 1980 and 2008 multiple-victim homicides were more likely to involve the use of guns than single homicides. (See Figure 5.5.) In 2008 more than three-quarters of multiple-victim homicides (77.5%) involved the use of firearms, compared with about two-thirds (65.7%) of single-victim homicides.

Mass murders are usually carried out with a firearm because they make it possible to kill the greatest number of people in a limited amount of time. An example of this type of crime is the mass shooting at the Century Aurora movie theater in Aurora, Colorado, in July 2012 that killed 12 and wounded 58 others. With the theater darkened during a midnight screening of the film *The Dark Knight Rises*, a gunman in protective gear ignited tear gas canisters in the

FIGURE 5.5

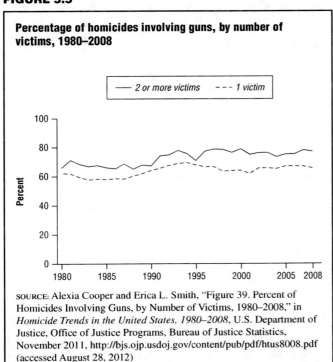

Percentage of homicides involving guns, by number of victims, 1980–2008

SOURCE: Alexia Cooper and Erica L. Smith, "Figure 39. Percent of Homicides Involving Guns, by Number of Victims, 1980–2008," in *Homicide Trends in the United States, 1980–2008*, U.S. Department of Justice, Office of Justice Programs, Bureau of Justice Statistics, November 2011, http://bjs.ojp.usdoj.gov/content/pub/pdf/htus8008.pdf (accessed August 28, 2012)

theater auditorium and then opened fire on the disoriented audience members. The theater audience was particularly vulnerable because of the relaxed atmosphere of the entertainment venue, the darkness inside the theater, the fact that theater patrons were seated in a confined area and had no easy avenue of escape, and the surprising nature of the attack, but because guns can kill from a great distance, they are also the most effective weapon against well-guarded targets. Perhaps the best example of this phenomenon is the use of firearms in political assassinations or assassination attempts. Also, it is unlikely that a felon would try to rob a well-guarded institution with many customers and multiple exits, such as a bank, while wielding a club or knife.

Shootings in the Workplace and at School

Table 5.5 is a time line that shows some notable incidents of multiple shootings since 1997. The workplace and schools are sometimes targets for these atrocities. The time line, it should be noted, focuses exclusively on multiple killings in the United States, but such attacks are not limited to one country. One of the most notorious of such cases occurred in Norway on July 22, 2011. Anders Behring Breivik (1979–) detonated a car bomb near government buildings in Oslo, and then later, impersonating a police officer conducting a security check in response to the earlier bombing, traveled to an island summer camp where a political youth conference was being held and began shooting at the participants. Eight people were killed and more than 200 injured in the car bomb incident; 69 people were killed and more than 100 were injured on the island, where Breivik spent more than an hour shooting his victims with a Ruger Mini semiautomatic carbine and a Glock 34 pistol. He had obtained his firearms legally in Norway, where licensing regulations require permits to purchase. In August 2012 Breivik was sentenced to a form of open-ended detention with a minimum sentence of 10 years, a maximum of 21 years, and the possibility of extension if he remains a danger to society.

AT THE WORKPLACE. Dana Loomis of the ASIS Foundation, an organization of security professionals, states in *Preventing Gun Violence in the Workplace* (2008, http://www.asisonline.org/foundation/guns.pdf) that:

> Workplace violence affects more than two million workers in the United States every year and accounts for about 20% of all violent crime. Although most workplace violence is not fatal, an average of 500 homicides occur in U.S. workplaces each year, which costs society approximately $800,000 for each death.

> More than three-quarters of workplace homicides are committed with guns. About two-thirds of workplace homicides are related to robbery; the remainder result from conflicts between workers and clients, coworkers, acquaintances, or family members.

In the fact sheet "Workplace Shootings" (July 14, 2010, http://www.bls.gov/iif/oshwc/cfoi/osar0014.htm), the Bureau of Labor Statistics reports that between 2004 and 2008 an average of 564 workplace homicides

TABLE 5.5

Notable multiple shootings, 1997–2012

2012

Adam Lanza, 20, killed 20 children and six adults at Sandy Hook Elementary School in Newtown, Connecticut. Lanza, who had shot and killed his mother at their home earlier that day, ended the rampage by killing himself.

2012

Wade Michael Page, 40, killed six people and wounded four at a Sikh temple in Oak Creek, WI. Page, who took his own life at the scene after being wounded by police gunfire, used a 9mm semiautomatic handgun in the spree.

2012

Shortly after the beginning of a midnight screening of the film *The Dark Knight Rises*, a gunman in protective gear ignited tear gas canisters in a theater auditorium in Aurora, CO, and then opened fire on the disoriented audience members, killing 12 and wounding 58 others. The alleged shooter, James Holmes, 24, was arrested outside the theater moments later with a .223-caliber assault rifle, a 12-gauge shotgun, and a .40-caliber handgun.

2011

U.S. Representative Gabrielle Giffords (D-AZ) was among the injured victims when Jared Loughner, 22, opened fire with a 9mm semiautomatic handgun at a political event near Tucson, AZ. Six people were killed and 13 were wounded in the incident, with an additional victim sustaining injuries in the ensuing chaos.

2010

Christopher Bryan Speight, a 39-year-old security guard, shot and killed his sister and brother-in-law, two other adults, three teenagers and a four-year old in an Appomattox, VA, house and surrounding yard.

2009

At the American Civic Association in Binghampton, NY, Jiverly Antares Wong, 41, entered the building and opened fire without saying a word, killing 13 and wounding four others. Many of the victims were immigrants participating in an English class at the center.

2009

In a spree that lasted less than an hour, 28-year old gunman Michael Kenneth McLendon killed 11 people and four dogs in two communities in Geneva County, AL, before killing himself. Among those fatally shot were his mother, grandmother, and several other family members; five additional victims survived their wounds.

2009

Major Nidal Malik Hasan, a 39-year-old practicing psychiatrist at the Darnall Army Medical Center at Fort Hood, TX, opened fire at the base's processing center. Using two handguns, Hasan killed 12 and wounded 31.

2008

On the campus of Northern Illinois University in DeKalb, Illinois, former graduate student Steven Phillip Kazmierczak, 27, entered an auditorium lecture hall and began shooting at the teacher and students assembled for the class. Armed with several weapons, including a 12-gauge shotgun and a 9mm Glock semiautomatic pistol, he killed five students and wounded 21 others before killing himself.

2008

At the Kirkwood, MO, city hall, Charles Lee "Cookie" Thornton, 52, stormed a city council meeting, shooting and killing the public works director, two city council members, and two police officers. He seriously injured the city's mayor and wounded a newspaper reporter. Police at the scene shot and killed Thornton, who was said to have a long-standing feud with the city.

2007

In the deadliest shooting rampage by a single gunman in U.S. history, Seung-Hui Cho, a 23-year-old college student, killed 32 students and faculty members at Virginia Polytechnic Institute and State University (Virginia Tech). In the shooting spree, 15 people were also wounded. Cho then shot and killed himself.

2003

Wielding a semiautomatic pistol, Jonathan Russell, 25, killed three of his co-workers and injured five others before killing himself outside of Modine Manufacturing Co., Jefferson City, MO.

2002

John Allen Muhammad, 41, who qualified as an expert marksman with the M-16 in the U.S. Army, and his stepson, 17-year-old John Lee Malvo, killed 10 people and wounded three others in Washington, DC, and vicinity, in a three-week killing spree with a .232-caliber Bushmaster XM15 semi-automatic rifle.

2000

In Queens, NY, two young gunmen bound, gagged, and shot seven employees in a Wendy's restaurant with a .380-caliber gun. Five of the workers were killed.

1999

In Los Angeles, five were wounded and a postal worker was fatally shot by Buford O. Furrow Jr., 37, at the North Valley Jewish Community Center.

1999

In Atlanta, GA, Mark Barton, 44, killed 9 people and wounded 13 at two brokerage firms before killing himself.

1999

Benjamin Nathaniel Smith, 21, killed two people and injured nine in a three-day rampage through Indiana and Illinois, before shooting himself.

1999

At Columbine High School in Littleton, CO, Dylan Klebold, 17, and Eric Harris, 18, killed 12 fellow-students and a teacher, and wounded 23 others, before shooting and killing themselves.

1998

In Springfield, OR, 15-year-old Kip Kinkel fired more than 50 rounds from a .22-caliber semiautomatic rifle into a high-school cafeteria. Two male students died and 23 other students were injured. The boy also shot and killed his parents.

occurred each year in the United States, with 526 workplace homicides in 2008. Of these, 421 were fatal workplace shootings, about one-quarter of which (24%) took place in retail establishments, 17% occurred in the leisure and hospitality sector, 14% were in government, and 11% were in the transportation and warehousing industry. In 2008, 30 of the workplace homicide incidents included multiple firearm fatalities. An average of two

TABLE 5.5

Notable multiple shootings, 1997–2012 [CONTINUED]

1998

Four middle-school students and a teacher were killed and 10 other students were injured in Jonesboro, AR, when a 13-year-old and an 11-year-old shot at the school from a nearby wooded area.

1997

Using a gun, Ali Hassan Abu Kamal, 69, killed one person and injured six others before taking his own life on the observation deck of the Empire State Building in Manhattan.

SOURCE: Created by Sandra Alters and updated by Laurie DiMauro for Gale, 2012.

people were killed in each firearm incident that had multiple fatalities, including a total of 67 victims, seven of them suicides. In 2008, 12% of the assailants in workplace shootings were coworkers or former coworkers of the victims, and 40% were robbers. The remaining fatal workplace shootings were committed by relatives, acquaintances of the victims, or other assailants.

Workplace murders and firearm homicides in 2010 were slightly lower than in 2008, with 518 workplace homicides that year (405 fatal shootings), as indicated by the BLS in "Occupational Homicides by Selected Characteristics, 1997–2010" (April 23, 2012, http://www.bls.gov/iif/oshwc/cfoi/work_hom.pdf). Of the 405 firearm workplace homicides in 2010, robbers and other assailants accounted for 273 (67%) of the murders (robbers specifically were responsible for 152 deaths [38%]), coworkers and former coworkers for 50 (12%), and customers and clients of the victims for 43 firearm deaths (11%). (See Table 5.6.)

AT SCHOOL. As the number of students enrolling in postsecondary institutions rose over the decades, so did the number of directed assaults, although the increase from the number of directed assaults that occurred in the 1980s to the number that occurred in the 1990s was the sharpest. In *Campus Attacks: Targeted Violence Affecting Institutions of Higher Education* (April 2010, http://www2.ed.gov/admins/lead/safety/campus-attacks.pdf), Diana A. Drysdale, William Modzeleski, and Andre B. Simons note that some of the increase in directed assaults against postsecondary students during the past two decades may be explained by increased enrollments, more media coverage, and digital reporting of such events.

Drysdale, Modzeleski, and Simons analyzed in depth 272 incidents of directed assaults against postsecondary students on or off campus that occurred between January 1, 1900, and December 31, 2008. The researchers define the phrase "directed assaults" in detail, but in general the phrase means that a postsecondary student or institution was targeted by a perpetrator who was able to inflict deadly force. Drysdale, Modzeleski, and Simons explain that "for incidents that took place off-campus and involved two persons in a romantic, spousal, or cohabitant/roommate relationship, both the subject and the target must have been affiliated with the affected IHE [institution of higher education], with at least one of their affiliations current."

The researchers find that firearms were used in 54% of the directed assaults against postsecondary students. Knives and bladed weapons were used in 21% of the assaults, and a combination of weapons or methods were used in 10% of the assaults. Strangulation and stabbing was the most frequent combination. The 272 directed assaults analyzed in the study resulted in 281 deaths and 247 injuries.

The time line in Table 5.5 includes reference to some school and campus shootings, including the 1999 incident in which Dylan Klebold and Eric Harris killed 13 people and wounded 23 others at Columbine High School in Littleton, Colorado, before shooting and killing themselves. Klebold and Harris used a TEC-DC9 handgun, a sawed-off double-barreled shotgun, a pump-action shotgun, and a 9mm semiautomatic rifle. The time line also includes the 2007 massacre at Virginia Polytechnic Institute and State University, in which a mentally ill student used two handguns to kill 32 students and faculty members and injure 15 others before fatally shooting himself. Another episode of gun violence included in Table 5.5 is that which occurred on the campus of Northern Illinois University on February 14, 2008. In that incident a former student of the university gunned down students attending an oceanography lecture, killing five people, wounding 21 others, and fatally shooting himself. Chapter 7 includes more information on school shootings.

POLICE DEATHS AND INJURIES

According to the National Law Enforcement Officers Memorial Fund Bulletin, in "Law Enforcement Officer Deaths: Preliminary 2011 Report" (February 22, 2012, http://www.nleomf.org/assets/pdfs/reports/2011-EOY-Report.pdf), 4,162 federal, state, and local law enforcement officers have been killed in firearms-related incidents during the past 50 years. From a high of 156 fatalities in 1973, the number of officers killed annually declined over the ensuing decades, reaching a low of 40 in 2008. However, the number of law officers killed by firearms increased after 2008, rising 70% from that year to 2011, when 68 officers died in firearm incidents.

The FBI indicates in *Law Enforcement Officers Killed and Assaulted, 2010* (October 2011, http://www.fbi.gov/about-us/cjis/ucr/leoka/leoka-2010) that 56 law enforcement officers were killed in the line of duty in 2010, with nearly

TABLE 5.6

Workplace firearm homicides by assailant-victim relationship, 1997–2010

| Years | Total occupational homicides from all causes (e.g. hitting, kicking, beating, shooting, stabbing, other) | Total occupational homicides resulting from shooting | Assailant | | | | | | | | | | |
| | | | Robbers and other assailants | | Work associates | | | Relatives | | | Other personal acquaintance | | |
			Total	Robber	Total	Co-worker, former co-worker	Customer, client	Total	Spouse	Other relative	Total	Boyfriend, ex-boyfriend, girlfriend, ex-girlfriend	Other acquaintance
1997	860	708	609	285	59	45	14	23	18	5	17	11	6
1998	714	574	463	243	70	52	18	15	9	6	26	10	16
1999	651	509	396	205	74	45	29	23	20	*	16	9	7
2000	677	533	426	249	74	51	23	25	20	5	8	5	—
2001	643	509	411	206	57	43	14	18	14	—	23	12	11
2002	609	469	375	202	65	49	16	20	12	8	9	7	—
2003	632	487	386	208	71	53	18	12	9	—	18	7	11
2004	559	421	334	191	56	35	21	12	9	—	19	7	12
2005	567	441	343	177	59	29	30	19	13	6	20	14	6
2006	540	436	312	177	85	48	37	16	11	5	23	10	13
2007	628	503	372	205	94	34	60	20	16	—	17	5	12
2008	526	421	298	168	84	49	35	14	11	—	25	10	15
2009	542	434	308	182	87	56	31	18	15	—	21	7	14
2010	518	405	273	152	93	50	43	15	9	6	24	10	14
Totals	**8,666**	**6,850**	**5,306**	**2,850**	**1,028**	**639**	**389**	**250**	**186**	**64**	**266**	**124**	**142**

*Dashes indicate no data reported or data that do not meet publication criteria. Census of Fatal Occupational Injury fatality counts exclude illness-related deaths unless precipitated by an injury event.

Note: Totals for 2001 exclude fatal injuries resulting from the September 11 terrorist attacks.

SOURCE: Adapted from "Occupational Homicides by Selected Characteristics, 1997–2010," U.S. Department of Labor, Bureau of Labor Statistics, April 24, 2012, http://www.bls.gov/iif/oshwc/cfoi/work_hom.pdf (accessed August 29, 2012)

all (55) of those deaths from firearms. (See Table 5.7.) Handguns (38 fatalities, or 69% of the total) were the most frequently used firearm in incidents that killed law enforcement officers in 2010. All fatal incidents in the Northeast, Midwest, and West resulted from firearms. Only in the South, where more law enforcement officers were killed than in any other region of the country, was an officer killed by an instrument other than a gun; in that case, the officer was purposely struck by a vehicle.

Table 5.8 details the circumstances under which federal, state, and local police officers were killed feloniously (criminally) from 2001 to 2010. Note that the 72 deaths of law enforcement officers resulting from the terrorist attacks of September 11, 2001, are not included in the following figures. Of the 541 officers in this group, the greatest number of killings took place in arrest situations (123, or 23%) and the second-greatest in ambush situations (120, or 22%). Traffic pursuits/stops were third (95, or 18%).

Law enforcement officers are also killed in accidents while on duty. Of the 72 officers who were accidentally killed while on duty in 2010, the FBI reports in *Law Enforcement Officers Killed and Assaulted, 2010* that three were shot accidentally during crossfire or as a result of a firearm mishap. The highest number of law enforcement officers killed accidentally in 2010 died as a result of an automobile accident (45); 11 others were struck by vehicles, and 7 officers died in motorcycle accidents. Table 5.9 shows the numbers of law enforcement officers accidentally killed by region and state from 2001 to 2010. Nearly half (48.6%; 349 out of 718) were accidentally killed in the South.

Officers Assaulted

Table 5.10 shows the number of assaults on federal officers from 2006 to 2010. During this period there were 7,963 assaults on federal law enforcement officers. Firearms were not the most frequent weapons used in assaults; they were used in 426 incidents, which comprised only 5.3% of the total. Most often used were personal weapons (e.g., fists), which were used 28.7% (2,288) of the time. In 2010 there were 1,886 assaults against federal officers, including one

fatality. That fatality was U.S. Border Patrol Agent Brian Terry (1970–2010), who was killed by gunfire from an AK-47 assault rife in December 2010 while attempting to apprehend suspected thieves near Rio Rico, Arizona. (The weapon used to kill Terry was connected with the controversial ATF program known as Operation Fast and Furious, which is discussed later in this chapter.)

In 2010, 53,469 state and local law enforcement officers were assaulted. (See Table 5.11.) A large majority (43,764, or 81.8% of victim officers) were attacked with personal weapons such as fists and feet. A lesser number, 6,990 (13.1%), were attacked with weapons other than guns or knives, with firearms (1,831, or 3.4%), or with knives (884, or 1.7%). Nearly one out of three (32.2%, 590 out of 1,831) of the incidents in which officers were assaulted with firearms involved disturbance calls. In 14% (257 out of 1,831) of firearm assaults on officers in 2010, the victim officer was investigating a suspicious person or circumstance. A smaller percentage (11.8%, 216 out of 1,831) involved an attempted arrest other than in a robbery, burglary, or disturbance situation.

VIOLENT CRIMES INVOLVING FIREARMS

In *Key Facts at a Glance: Crime Type* (April 23, 2010, http://bjs.ojp.usdoj.gov/content/glance/guncrime.cfm), the BJS indicates that the number of firearm crimes reported to the police (taken from the FBI's Uniform Crime Reports) rose from 361,141 in 1973 to a high of 581,697 crimes in 1993. Firearm crimes then fell dramatically to 1999, when the number was 338,535, and from 1999 through 2004 firearm crime reports ranged from approximately 339,000 to 358,000 per year. Rising to 368,178 in 2005, firearm crime continued an upward trend in 2006, when the number of crimes reported to police was 388,897. The BJS indicates a slight decrease to 385,178 in 2007.

In *Key Facts at a Glance: Crime Type*, the BJS further reports that during the period 1973 to 2007 the percentage of violent crimes involving firearms declined from 44.1% in 1973 to 29.2% in 2007. The percent of murders in which

TABLE 5.7

Law enforcement officers killed, by type of weapon and region, 2010

Region	Total	Total firearms	Handgun	Rifle	Shotgun	Knife or other cutting instrument	Bomb	Blunt instrument	Personal weapons	Vehicle	Other
Number of victim officers	**56**	**55**	**38**	**15**	**2**	**0**	**0**	**0**	**0**	**1**	**0**
Northeast	3	3	2	1	0	0	0	0	0	0	0
Midwest	10	10	10	0	0	0	0	0	0	0	0
South	22	21	17	4	0	0	0	0	0	1	0
West	18	18	6	10	2	0	0	0	0	0	0
Puerto Rico and other outlying areas	3	3	3	0	0	0	0	0	0	0	0

SOURCE: "Table 29. Law Enforcement Officers Feloniously Killed, Region by Type of Weapon, 2010," in *Law Enforcement Officers Killed and Assaulted, 2010*, U.S. Department of Justice, Federal Bureau of Investigation, Criminal Justice Information Services Division, October 2011, http://www.fbi.gov/about-us/cjis/ucr/leoka/leoka-2010/tables/table29-leok-feloniously-region-by-type-weapon-10.xls (accessed August 23, 2012)

TABLE 5.8

Law enforcement officers killed, by circumstance at scene of incident, 2001–10

Circumstance	Total	2001[a]	2002	2003	2004	2005	2006	2007	2008	2009	2010
Number of victim officers											
Total	541	70	56	52	57	55	48	58	41	48	56
Disturbance call											
Total	75	13	9	10	10	7	8	5	1	6	6
Disturbance (bar fight, person with firearm, etc.)	33	5	4	5	1	2	6	3	1	4	2
Domestic disturbance (family quarrel, etc.)	42	8	5	5	9	5	2	2	0	2	4
Arrest situation											
Total	123	24	10	8	13	8	12	17	9	8	14
Burglary in progress/pursuing burglary suspect	14	3	0	1	2	1	0	1	2	1	3
Robbery in progress/pursuing robbery suspect	43	4	4	1	7	4	6	7	1	3	6
Drug-related matter	17	8	3	1	0	0	2	1	1	0	1
Attempting other arrest	49	9	3	5	4	3	4	8	5	4	4
Civil disorder (mass disobedience, riot, etc.)											
Total	0	0	0	0	0	0	0	0	0	0	0
Handling, transporting, custody of prisoner											
Total	12	2	0	2	1	1	1	1	1	2	1
Investigating suspicious person/circumstance											
Total	61	8	6	4	7	7	6	4	7	4	8
Ambush situation											
Total	120	9	17	9	15	8	10	16	6	15	15
Entrapment/premeditation	42	3	4	6	6	4	1	9	1	6	2
Unprovoked attack	78	6	13	3	9	4	9	7	5	9	13
Investigative activity (surveillance, search, interview, etc.)											
Total	11	0	0	2	0	4	0	1	2	0	2
Handling person with mental illness											
Total	12	3	4	0	2	2	1	0	0	0	0
Traffic pursuit/stop											
Total	95	8	10	14	6	15	8	11	8	8	7
Felony vehicle stop	35	5	6	4	0	5	0	5	5	2	3
Traffic violation stop	60	3	4	10	6	10	8	6	3	6	4
Tactical situation (barricaded offender, hostage taking, high-risk entry, etc.)											
Total	32	3	0	3	3	3	2	3	7	5	3

[a]The deaths of the 72 law enforcement officers that resulted from the events of September 11, 2001, are not included in this table.

SOURCE: "Table 19. Law Enforcement Officers Feloniously Killed, Circumstance at Scene of Incident, 2001–2010," in *Law Enforcement Officers Killed and Assaulted, 2010,* U.S. Department of Justice, Federal Bureau of Investigation, Criminal Justice Information Services Division, October 2011, http://www.fbi.gov/about-us/cjis/ucr/leoka/leoka-2010/tables/table19-leok-feloniously-circumstance-01-10.xls (accessed August 23, 2012)

firearms were used was 67% in 1973 and 68% percent in 2007, but in the intervening years the figure had fallen to as low as 58.3% in 1983 before climbing to a high of 70% in 1994. The percentage of robberies involving a firearm also fell during the period, from 63% in 1973 to 42.8% in 2007; however, the percentage for 1973 was the highest recorded throughout the period, with all other years ranging between 33% and 44%. The percentage of aggravated assaults in which a firearm was used was 25.7% in 1973 and generally remained in the 20% to 25% range through the period, dipping to a low of 18% in 1999; the percentage of aggravated assaults involving a firearm in 2007 was 21.4%.

From 1993 to 2009 the number of both the victims and the incidents of nonfatal firearm-related violent crime fell. (See Table 5.12.) In 1993 and 1994 nonfatal firearm-related violent incidents numbered slightly more than 1 million.

By 2004 such incidents numbered only about 281,000—a dramatic decrease. Likewise, in 1994 there were nearly 1.3 million victims of nonfatal firearm-related violent crime. By 2004 the victims numbered about one-fourth of that figure—331,630. In 2005, however, the number of nonfatal firearm-related violent incidents rose to 417,000, and the number of nonfatal firearm-related victims increased to 474,000. No data are shown for 2006, but in 2007 a decline was apparent that continued in 2008, nearly returning the numbers of both victims of nonfatal firearm-related violent crime and nonfatal firearm-related violent incidents to their 2004 levels. Both the number of nonfatal firearm incidents and victims increased again in 2009, to 326,090 incidents and 352,810 victims. Figure 5.6 presents a visual representation of the decline in nonfatal firearm-related violent incidents and victimizations between 1993 and 2009.

TABLE 5.9

Law enforcement officers accidentally killed, by region, geographic division, and state, 2001–10

Area	Total	2001	2002	2003	2004	2005	2006	2007	2008	2009	2010
Number of victim officers	718	76	75	81	82	67	66	83	68	48	72
Northeast	73	5	5	10	10	7	5	6	11	6	8
New England	16	2	0	3	0	2	1	2	1	2	3
Connecticut	5	0	0	1	0	0	1	0	1	0	2
Maine	0	0	0	0	0	0	0	0	0	0	0
Massachusetts	8	1	0	0	0	2	0	2	0	2	1
New Hampshire	0	0	0	0	0	0	0	0	0	0	0
Rhode Island	1	1	0	0	0	0	0	0	0	0	0
Vermont	2	0	0	2	0	0	0	0	0	0	0
Middle Atlantic	57	3	5	7	10	5	4	4	10	4	5
New Jersey	18	1	1	3	1	3	1	2	2	0	4
New York	22	0	3	2	5	1	2	2	3	3	1
Pennsylvania	17	2	1	2	4	1	1	0	5	1	0
Midwest	115	12	10	12	15	13	14	11	5	9	14
East North Central	76	7	4	7	12	9	14	5	5	6	7
Illinois	23	0	2	3	5	3	6	1	0	0	3
Indiana	19	3	1	0	2	3	2	2	2	2	2
Michigan	13	1	0	2	3	3	2	0	0	2	0
Ohio	15	3	1	1	1	0	3	2	2	1	1
Wisconsin	6	0	0	1	1	0	1	0	1	1	1
West North Central	39	5	6	5	3	4	0	6	0	3	7
Iowa	2	0	0	1	0	0	0	1	0	0	0
Kansas	4	0	0	1	0	0	0	1	0	0	2
Minnesota	4	0	2	0	1	0	0	1	0	0	0
Missouri	26	5	4	2	2	4	0	3	0	2	4
Nebraska	1	0	0	0	0	0	0	0	0	1	0
North Dakota	0	0	0	0	0	0	0	0	0	0	0
South Dakota	2	0	0	1	0	0	0	0	0	0	1
South	349	39	39	38	39	30	26	46	32	21	39
South Atlantic	158	16	21	18	16	12	11	22	14	12	16
Delaware	2	1	0	0	1	0	0	0	0	0	0
District of Columbia	3	0	1	0	0	0	0	1	0	0	1
Florida	43	7	2	4	8	3	2	8	4	1	4
Georgia	27	0	2	5	3	3	3	3	3	2	3
Maryland	15	0	3	2	2	0	0	2	3	0	3
North Carolina	28	6	6	4	2	1	0	4	2	3	0
South Carolina	17	0	5	2	0	3	1	1	1	2	2
Virginia	20	1	2	1	0	2	5	2	1	3	3
West Virginia	3	1	0	0	0	0	0	1	0	1	0
East South Central	61	8	6	8	9	4	6	6	4	4	6
Alabama	17	1	2	1	4	2	1	3	2	1	0
Kentucky	6	0	1	1	0	0	2	1	0	0	1
Mississippi	14	2	1	2	1	0	1	2	1	2	2
Tennessee	24	5	2	4	4	2	2	0	1	1	3
West South Central	130	15	12	12	14	14	9	18	14	5	17
Arkansas	10	1	1	2	0	2	1	0	2	1	0
Louisiana	19	1	1	4	1	2	2	4	0	1	3
Oklahoma	11	1	1	0	0	3	1	0	3	1	1
Texas	90	12	9	6	13	7	5	14	9	2	13
West	164	19	19	18	15	14	20	19	17	12	11
Mountain	67	9	9	4	5	3	9	10	6	8	4
Arizona	20	1	3	1	3	2	4	2	2	1	1
Colorado	7	2	1	0	1	1	0	2	0	0	0
Idaho	3	0	0	1	0	0	0	0	0	2	0
Montana	7	0	1	1	0	0	2	1	1	1	0
Nevada	7	1	1	0	1	0	0	1	1	2	0
New Mexico	15	4	2	0	0	0	1	4	1	2	1
Utah	7	1	1	1	0	0	1	0	1	0	2
Wyoming	1	0	0	0	0	0	1	0	0	0	0

Table 5.12 also indicates that the rate of nonfatal firearm victims per 1,000 population fell dramatically beginning in the mid-1990s, reaching its lowest level in 2004 at 1.4 victims per 1,000 residents. That rate rose in 2005, to 1.9 victims per 1,000 residents. By 2008 the victimization rate of nonfatal firearm-related crimes returned to the 2004 rate, where it remained in 2009. Figure 5.7 presents a visual representation of the declining victimization rate in nonfatal firearm-related crimes between 1993 and 2009.

As mentioned earlier, the FBI's Uniform Crime Reports collect data only on crimes reported to law enforcement agencies. To give a better picture of actual crime occurrence in the United States—including unreported crime—the DOJ has conducted the National Crime Victimization Survey (NCVS) since 1973. The statistics appear in the annual report *Criminal Victimization in the United States* and accompanying statistical tables. The NCVS crime rate is sometimes spoken of as the "actual" or "estimated" crime

TABLE 5.9

Law enforcement officers accidentally killed, by region, geographic division, and state, 2001–10 [CONTINUED]

Area	Total	2001	2002	2003	2004	2005	2006	2007	2008	2009	2010
Pacific	97	10	10	14	10	11	11	9	11	4	7
Alaska	2	1	1	0	0	0	0	0	0	0	0
California	74	5	6	10	7	10	9	7	11	3	6
Hawaii	5	1	0	1	2	0	1	0	0	0	0
Oregon	6	2	2	1	0	0	0	1	0	0	0
Washington	10	1	1	2	1	1	1	1	0	1	1
Puerto Rico and other outlying areas	17	1	2	3	3	3	1	1	3	0	0
American Samoa	0	0	0	0	0	0	0	0	0	0	0
Guam	1	0	0	0	0	0	0	1	0	0	0
Mariana Islands	0	0	0	0	0	0	0	0	0	0	0
Puerto Rico	15	1	2	3	3	3	1	0	2	0	0
U.S. Virgin Islands	1	0	0	0	0	0	0	0	1	0	0

SOURCE: "Table 48. Law Enforcement Officers Accidentally Killed, Region, Geographic Division, and State, 2001–2010," in *Law Enforcement Officers Killed and Assaulted, 2010*, U.S. Department of Justice, Federal Bureau of Investigation, Criminal Justice Information Services Division, October 2011, http://www.fbi.gov/about-us/cjis/ucr/leoka/leoka-2010/tables/table48-leok-accidentally-region-division-state-01-10.xls (accessed August 23, 2012)

TABLE 5.10

Assaults on federal officers, by extent of injury and type of weapon, 2006–10

Year	Extent of injury	Total	Firearm	Knife or other cutting instrument	Bomb	Blunt instrument	Personal weapons	Vehicle	Other
Number of victim officers	Total	7,963	426	65	0	79	2,288	497	4,608
2006[a]	Total	1,273	109	4	0	17	484	96	563
	Killed	0	0	0	0	0	0	0	0
	Injured	212	7	2	0	6	130	26	41
	Not injured	1,061	102	2	0	11	354	70	522
2007	Total	1,650	71	17	0	14	553	131	864
	Killed	0	0	0	0	0	0	0	0
	Injured	257	3	5	0	3	191	21	34
	Not injured	1,393	68	12	0	11	362	110	830
2008	Total	1,347	71	11	0	11	400	85	769
	Killed	2	1	0	0	0	0	1	0
	Injured	188	2	2	0	6	125	19	34
	Not injured	1,157	68	9	0	5	275	65	735
2009	Total	1,807	89	16	0	21	464	109	1,108
	Killed	1	1	0	0	0	0	0	0
	Injured	181	6	3	0	8	83	18	63
	Not injured	1,625	82	13	0	13	381	91	1,045
2010[b]	Total	1,886	86	17	0	16	387	76	1,304
	Killed	1	1	0	0	0	0	0	0
	Injured	351	12	0	0	3	117	18	201
	Not injured	1,534	73	17	0	13	270	58	1,103

[a]Data for 2006 were not collected from the Bureau of Land Management.
[b]Prior to 2010, data were not collected from the U.S. Customs and Border Protection, Office of Air and Marine.

SOURCE: "Table 77. Federal Law Enforcement Officers Killed and Assaulted, Extent of Injury of Victim Officer by Type of Weapon, 2006–2010," in *Law Enforcement Officers Killed and Assaulted, 2010*, U.S. Department of Justice, Federal Bureau of Investigation, Criminal Justice Information Services Division, October 2011, http://www.fbi.gov/about-us/cjis/ucr/leoka/leoka-2010/tables/table77-federal-leoka-extent-of-injury-by-type-weapon-06-10.xls (accessed August 23, 2012)

rate. (Because of changes in the methodology of the survey in 2006, results for that year cannot be compared with results from previous years.)

The NCVS is divided into violent and property crime categories. Violent crime includes rape, robbery, aggravated assault, and simple assault (no weapon is involved). When publishing its data, the NCVS includes the murder rate, which is taken from the FBI's reports.

NCVS estimates reveal that nearly 4.6 million personal crimes of violence were committed in 2008, including rape, robbery, and assault. (See Table 5.13.) Overall, no weapon was involved in 73.7% of the crimes of violence in 2008. In 19.8% of the incidents a weapon was used, with firearms used in 6.6% of the cases. Most often the firearm was a handgun, which was used in 5.8% of personal crimes of violence overall in 2008. Nonetheless, in certain crimes of

TABLE 5.11

Law enforcement officers assaulted, by circumstance at scene of incident and type of weapon, 2010

Circumstance	Total	Percent distribution	Firearm Total	Firearm Percent distribution	Knife or other cutting instrument Total	Knife or other cutting instrument Percent distribution	Other dangerous weapon Total	Other dangerous weapon Percent distribution	Personal weapons Total	Personal weapons Percent distribution
Number of victim officers	**53,469**	**100.0**	**1,831**	**3.4**	**884**	**1.7**	**6,990**	**13.1**	**43,764**	**81.8**
Disturbance call	**17,646**	100.0	590	3.3	411	2.3	1,606	9.1	15,039	85.2
Burglary in progress/pursuing burglary suspect	**899**	100.0	65	7.2	20	2.2	197	21.9	617	68.6
Robbery in progress/pursuing robbery suspect	**450**	100.0	101	22.4	13	2.9	95	21.1	241	53.6
Attempting other arrest	**7,881**	100.0	216	2.7	82	1.0	819	10.4	6,764	85.8
Civil disorder (mass disobedience, riot, etc.)	**765**	100.0	12	1.6	7	0.9	83	10.8	663	86.7
Handling, transporting, custody of prisoner	**6,910**	100.0	23	0.3	40	0.6	528	7.6	6,319	91.4
Investigating suspicious person/circumstance	**5,074**	100.0	257	5.1	95	1.9	710	14.0	4,012	79.1
Ambush situation	**248**	100.0	53	21.4	10	4.0	58	23.4	127	51.2
Handling person with mental illness	**1,043**	100.0	26	2.5	76	7.3	159	15.2	782	75.0
Traffic pursuit/stop	**4,752**	100.0	208	4.4	35	0.7	1,592	33.5	2,917	61.4
All other	**7,801**	100.0	280	4.0	95	1.0	1,143	14.7	6,283	80.5

Note: Because of rounding, the percentages may not add to 100.0.

SOURCE: "Table 73. Law Enforcement Officers Assaulted, Circumstance at Scene of Incident by Type of Weapon and Percent Distribution, 2010," in *Law Enforcement Officers Killed and Assaulted, 2010*, U.S. Department of Justice, Federal Bureau of Investigation, Criminal Justice Information Services Division, October 2011, http://www.fbi.gov/about-us/cjis/ucr/leoka/leoka-2010/tables/table73-leo-assaulted-circumstance-by-type-weapon-percent-10.xls (accessed August 23, 2012)

TABLE 5.12

Nonfatal firearm-related violent crimes, 1993–2009

Year	Firearm incidents	Firearm victims	Firearm crime rate (victims per 1,000 residents)	Firearm crimes as a percent of all violent incidents
1993	1,054,820	1,248,250	5.9	11%
1994	1,060,800	1,286,860	6	11
1995	902,680	1,050,900	4.9	10
1996	845,220	989,930	4.6	10
1997	680,900	795,560	3.6	9
1998	557,200	670,480	3	8
1999	457,150	562,870	2.5	7
2000	428,670	533,470	2.4	7
2001	467,880	524,030	2.3	9
2002	353,880	430,930	1.9	7
2003	366,840	449,150	1.9	7
2004	280,890	331,630	1.4	6
2005	416,940	474,110	1.9	9
2006*				
2007	348,910	394,580	1.6	7
2008	303,880	343,550	1.4	7
2009	326,090	352,810	1.4	8

*Victimization rate trends excludes National Crime Victimization Survey (NCVS) estimates for 2006 because of methodogical inconsistencies between the data for that year and the data for other years.

SOURCE: "Nonfatal Firearm-Related Violent Crimes, 1993–2009," in *Key Facts at a Glance*, U.S. Department of Justice, Office of Justice Programs, Bureau of Justice Statistics, August 26, 2012, http://bjs.ojp.usdoj.gov/content/glance/tables/firearmnonfataltab.cfm (accessed August 26, 2012)

violence guns were used more frequently. For example, firearms were used in 23.7% of all robberies in 2008.

Additional information on victimizations involving firearms is available online using the National Criminal Victimization Study (NCVS) Victimization Analysis Tool (2012, http://bjs.ojp.usdoj.gov/index.cfm?ty=nvat), an interactive data site maintained by the BJS. As of the launch it included 18 years of data drawn from the NCVS. Table 5.14, a table generated using the site, reports violent victimizations by weapon use and by weapon type for the years 1994 through 2010. It shows that firearm crimes as a percent of total violent victimization were highest in 1994, when 1,568,176 of 17,059,005 victimizations (9.2%) involved a firearm. The lowest percentage was reached in 2008, when firearms were used in 371,289 out of 6,393,471 violent victimizations (5.8%). In 2010 firearms were involved in 415,003 out of 4,935,983 violent victimizations (8.4%).

As shown in Table 5.15, in violent crimes cases in which the weapon was known in 2012, firearms were the most prevalent weapon used overall, and the most likely to have been used in rape/sexual assaults and robberies.

Armed Robbery

As in the case of murder, armed robberies are recorded from police investigations. Thus, they do not include incidents that were never reported, but they do include incidents in which the accused robbers were never convicted in court.

FIGURE 5.6

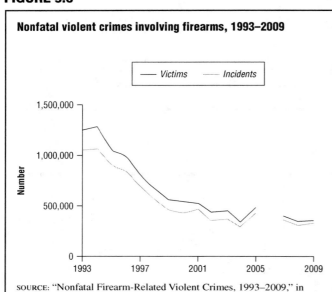

Nonfatal violent crimes involving firearms, 1993–2009

SOURCE: "Nonfatal Firearm-Related Violent Crimes, 1993–2009," in *Gun Violence*, U.S. Department of Justice, Office of Justice Programs, National Institute of Justice, October 26, 2010, http://www.nij.gov/topics/crime/gun-violence/ (accessed August 26, 2012)

The impact of robbery on its victims cannot be measured only in terms of monetary loss. The goal of robbing someone is usually to obtain money or property, but the crime always involves force, and many victims suffer serious personal injury. Moreover, the psychological trauma can be severe and can affect the victim for the rest of his or her life. Jennifer L. Truman of the BJS indicates in *Criminal Victimization, 2010* (September 2011, http://bjs.ojp.usdoj.gov/content/pub/pdf/cv10.pdf) that in 2010 there were 480,750 robberies.

Of the robberies committed in 2010 and reported to the police, 41.4% involved firearms. (See Table 5.16.) The use of strong-arm tactics (bullying) occurred in 42% of the robberies overall, knives or cutting instruments were involved in 7.9%, and other weapons were used in the remaining 8.8% of robberies. Guns were used most frequently in robberies that took place in the South (49.5%) and least frequently in the West (31.8%).

Aggravated Assault

The FBI reports in *Crime in the United States, 2010* that in 2010 there were 778,901 aggravated assaults reported to police, which was a 4.1% decrease over the previous year's figure of 812,514. The rate of victimization declined as well, from 264.7 aggravated assaults per 100,000 inhabitants in 2009 to 252.3 per 100,000 in 2010.

In 2010 firearms were used in 20.6% of aggravated assaults, and knives or other cutting instruments were used in 19% of aggravated assaults. (See Table 5.17.) In the remaining weapons categories, personal weapons such as hands or feet were used in 27.4% of the aggravated assaults, and other weapons, such as clubs, were used in the remainder (33.1%). Table 5.17 categorizes the weapons used for aggravated assaults by region. These data

FIGURE 5.7

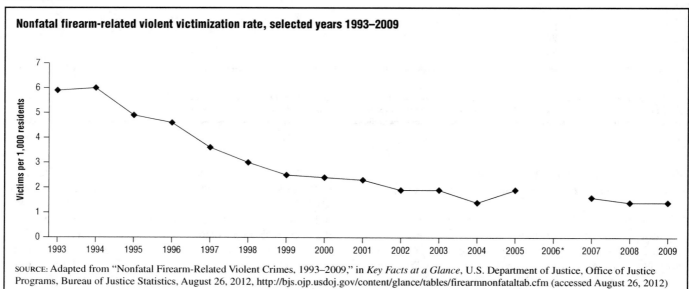

Nonfatal firearm-related violent victimization rate, selected years 1993–2009

SOURCE: Adapted from "Nonfatal Firearm-Related Violent Crimes, 1993–2009," in *Key Facts at a Glance*, U.S. Department of Justice, Office of Justice Programs, Bureau of Justice Statistics, August 26, 2012, http://bjs.ojp.usdoj.gov/content/glance/tables/firearmnonfataltab.cfm (accessed August 26, 2012)

TABLE 5.13

Use of weapons in personal crimes of violence, by type of crime and victim-offender relationship, 2008

All incidents	Total incidents Number	Percent	No weapon used	Weapon used Total	Total firearm	Hand gun	Other gun	Gun type unknown	Knife	Sharp object	Blunt object	Other weapon	Type unknown	Don't know if weapon present
Crimes of violence	**4,581,260**	**100%**	**73.7**	**19.8**	**6.6**	**5.8**	**0.8***	**0.1***	**4.9**	**1.2**	**3.9**	**1.8**	**1.5**	**6.6**
Completed violence	1,291,780	100%	69.5	25.3	9.8	8.2	1.4*	0.2*	5.4	0.8*	4.6	2.7*	2.1*	5.3
Attempted/threatened violence	3,289,490	100%	75.3	17.6	5.4	4.8	0.6*	0.0*	4.7	1.3	3.6	1.4	1.2	7.1
Rape/sexual assault[a]	200,520	100%	79.6	1.4*	0.0*	0.0*	0.0*	0.0*	1.4*	0.0*	0.0*	0.0*	0.0*	19.0
Robbery	504,110	100%	49.3	39.9	23.7	21.4	2.3*	0.0*	9.3	1.5*	2.8*	1.2*	1.4*	10.9
Completed/property taken	346,240	100%	46.2	44.7	28.8	25.4	3.4*	0.0*	9.9*	1.2*	2.5*	1.2*	1.2*	9.2*
With injury	127,290	100%	58.4	33.9	25.3*	21.0*	4.2*	0.0*	5.5*	3.2*	0.0*	0.0*	0.0*	7.7*
Without injury	218,950	100%	39.1	50.9	30.8	28.0	2.8*	0.0*	12.5*	0.0*	3.9*	1.8*	1.9*	10.0*
Attempted to take property	157,870	100%	56.1	29.3	12.7*	12.7*	0.0*	0.0*	7.9*	2.1*	3.3*	1.2*	2.0*	14.6*
With injury	56,800	100%	74.9	11.1*	0.0*	0.0*	0.0*	0.0*	5.3*	5.9*	0.0*	0.0*	0.0*	13.9*
Without injury	101,070	100%	45.6	39.5	19.8*	19.8*	0.0*	0.1*	9.4*	0.0*	5.2*	1.9*	3.1*	15.0*
Assault	3,876,640	100%	76.5	18.1	4.8	4.0	0.7*	0.1*	4.5	1.2	4.2	1.9	1.5	5.4
Aggravated	768,770	100%	8.0	91.2	24.0	20.3	3.3*	0.4*	22.6	5.9	21.3	9.7	7.7	0.8*
With injury	236,600	100%	25.9	71.5	11.4*	7.4*	2.7*	1.2*	13.6*	2.8*	21.2	13.0*	9.6*	2.5*
Threatened with weapon	532,170	100%	0.0*	100.0	29.6	26.0	3.6*	0.0*	26.6	7.3	21.4	8.3	6.9*	0.0*
Simple[b]	3,107,870	100%	93.5	—	—	—	—	—	—	—	—	—	—	6.5
With minor injury	589,360	100%	97.7	—	—	—	—	—	—	—	—	—	—	2.3*
Without injury	2,518,500	100%	92.5	—	—	—	—	—	—	—	—	—	—	7.5
Involving strangers														
Crimes of violence	2,285,170	100%	67.2	23.4	10.6	9.5	1.2*	0.0*	4.9	1.3*	3.8	1.3*	1.4*	9.4
Rape/sexual assault[a]	70,630	100%	68.0	0.0*	0.0*	0.0*	0.0*	0.0*	0.0*	0.0*	0.0*	0.0*	0.0*	32.0*
Robbery	340,480	100%	38.3	49.1	33.2	29.8	3.4*	0.0*	10.3*	2.2*	1.5*	0.6*	1.2*	12.7
Aggravated assault	399,380	100%	6.6*	91.9	32.6	28.9	3.7*	0.0*	19.5	5.5*	20.5	6.9*	6.9*	1.5*
Simple assault[b]	1,474,680	100%	90.3	—	—	—	—	—	—	—	—	—	—	9.7
Involving nonstrangers														
Crimes of violence	2,296,090	100%	80.1	16.2	2.6	2.0	0.5*	0.1*	4.8	1.0*	3.9	2.2	1.5*	3.8
Rape/sexual assault[a]	129,880	100%	85.9	2.1*	0.0*	0.0*	0.0*	0.0*	2.1*	0.0*	0.0*	0.0*	0.0*	12.0*
Robbery	163,630	100%	72.2	20.7*	4.0*	4.0*	0.0*	0.0*	7.0*	0.0*	5.3*	2.5*	1.9*	7.1*
Aggravated assault	369,400	100%	9.5*	90.5	14.6	11.0	2.9*	0.8*	26.1	6.3*	22.2	12.7	8.6*	0.0*
Simple assault[b]	1,633,190	100%	96.4	—	—	—	—	—	—	—	—	—	—	3.6

Note: Responses for weapons use are tallied once, based on a hierarchy. In previous editions, multiple responses for weapons were tallied.
*Estimate is based on 10 or fewer sample cases.
—Not applicable.
[a]Includes verbal threats of rape and threats of sexual assault.
[b]Simple assault, by definition, does not involve the use of a weapon.

SOURCE: Michael R. Rand and Jayne E. Robinson, "Table 66. Personal Crimes of Violence, 2008: Percent of Incidents, by Type of Crime, Victim-Offender Relationship, and Weapons Use," in *Criminal Victimization in the United States, 2008—Statistical Tables*, U.S. Department of Justice, Office of Justice Programs, Bureau of Justice Statistics, May 2011, http://bjs.ojp.usdoj.gov/content/pub/pdf/cvus/current/cv0866.pdf (accessed August 23, 2012)

TABLE 5.14

Violent victimization by use of weapon and weapon type, selected years 1994–2010

Crime type	1994	1996	1998	2000	2002	2004	2006	2008	2010
Violent victimization	17,059,005	14,059,520	12,010,551	8,502,602	742,450	6,726,060	8,430,430	6,393,471	4,935,983
No, offender did not have weapon	11,481,149	9,492,811	8,444,644	5,940,913	5,265,494	4,486,700	5,891,230	4,756,419	3,547,152
Yes, offender had weapon									
Firearm	1,568,176	1,100,809	835,423	610,219	539,973	456,512	614,406	371,289	415,003
Knife	1,005,281	806,846	616,358	537,262	514,780	501,148	593,866	335,740	262,957
Other type weapon	1,311,245	1,317,474	874,401	704,755	448,424	618,224	698,305	376,297	312,252
Type of weapon unknown	260,124	147,552	238,496	86,509	100,261	74,543	119,287	73,310	77,321
Do not know if offender had weapon	1,433,030	1,194,028	1,001,229	622,944	555,618	588,933	513,336	480,416	321,299

Notes:
Special tabulations from the National Crime Victimization Survey (NCVS) Victimization Analysis Tool (NVAT).
Detail may not sum to total due to rounding and/or missing data.

SOURCE: Adapted from "Number of Violent Victimizations by Weapon Use and Weapon Category, 1993–2010," in *National Criminal Victimization Study (NCVS) Victimization Analysis Tool*, Bureau of Justice Statistics, http://bjs.ojp.usdoj.gov/index.cfm?ty=nvat (accessed July 17, 2012)

TABLE 5.15

Violent victimizations involving a weapon, by type of crime and type of weapon, 2010

Presence of offender's weapon	Violent crime		Rape/sexual assault		Robbery		Simple and aggravated assault	
	Number	Percent	Number	Percent	Number	Percent	Number	Percent
Total	3,817,380	100%	188,380	100%	480,760	100%	3,148,250	100%
No weapon	2,643,420	69%	149,740	79%	196,850	41%	2,296,820	73%
Weapon	852,660	22%	22,600	12%	212,390	44%	617,670	20%
Firearm	337,960	9	12,630	7	140,640	29	184,700	6
Knife	192,230	5	4,540	2	48,260	10	139,440	4
Other	266,620	7	—	—	10,200	2	256,420	8
Unknown	55,850	1	5,440	3	13,290	3	37,120	1
Don't know	321,300	8%	16,040	9%	71,510	15%	233,750	7%

Note: Detail may not sum to total due to rounding. If the offender was armed with more than one weapon, the crime was classified based on the most serious weapon present.
—Less than 0.5%.

SOURCE: Jennifer L. Truman, "Table 4. Violent Victimizations Involving a Weapon, by Type of Crime and Type of Weapon, 2010," in *Criminal Victimization, 2010*, U.S. Department of Justice, Office of Justice Programs, Bureau of Justice Statistics, September 2011, http://www.bjs.gov/content/pub/pdf/cv10.pdf (accessed August 23, 2012)

TABLE 5.16

Robbery, by type of weapon used and region, 2010

Region	Total all weapons*	Armed			
		Firearms	Knives or cutting instruments	Other weapons	Strong-arm
Total	100.0	41.4	7.9	8.8	42.0
Northeast	100.0	33.4	10.2	8.6	47.7
Midwest	100.0	45.0	5.4	9.2	40.3
South	100.0	49.5	7.0	8.2	35.3
West	100.0	31.8	9.1	9.4	49.7

*Because of rounding, the percentages may not add to 100.0.

SOURCE: "Robbery Table 3. Robbery, Types of Weapons Used, Percent Distribution by Region, 2010," in *Crime in the United States, 2010*, U.S. Department of Justice, Federal Bureau of Investigation, September 2011, http://www.fbi.gov/about-us/cjis/ucr/crime-in-the-u.s/2010/crime-in-the-u.s.-2010/tables/10robtbl3.xls (accessed August 26, 2012)

TABLE 5.17

Types of weapons used in aggravated assaults, by region, 2010

Region	Total all weapons*	Firearms	Knives or cutting instruments	Other weapons (clubs, blunt objects, etc.)	Personal weapons (hands, fists, feet, etc.)
Total	**100.0**	**20.6**	**19.0**	**33.1**	**27.4**
Northeast	100.0	14.9	22.4	34.2	28.4
Midwest	100.0	23.6	17.1	29.5	29.8
South	100.0	22.8	19.6	33.4	24.2
West	100.0	17.5	17.4	34.0	31.1

*Because of rounding, the percentages may not add to 100.0.

SOURCE: "Aggravated Assault Table. Aggravated Assault, Types of Weapons Used, Percent Distribution by Region, 2010," in *Crime in the United States, 2010,* U.S. Department of Justice, Federal Bureau of Investigation, September 2011, http://www.fbi.gov/about-us/cjis/ucr/crime-in-the-u.s/2010/crime-in-the-u.s.-2010/tables/10aggvtbl.xls (accessed August 26, 2012)

show that states in the Midwest had the highest rate of firearms use in the commission of aggravated assaults (23.6 %), followed closely by southern states (22.8%).

Justifiable Homicide

The FBI also compiles data on the category of justifiable homicide, which it defines in *Crime in the United States, 2010* as "the killing of a felon by a peace officer in the line of duty" or as "the killing of a felon, during the commission of a felony, by a private citizen."

Table 5.18 shows the data for justifiable homicides committed by law enforcement officers from 2006 to 2010. The vast majority of incidents involved firearms. A firearm was used in all 386 cases in which a felon was killed by a law officer in the line of duty in 2006. In 2010, all but two cases out of 387 involved the use of the officer's firearm. For each of the years shown in Table 5.18 handguns were the most frequently used weapon in cases of justifiable homicide by a law enforcement officer. In 2010, out of 385 cases in which a firearm was used, 315 (81.8%) involved a handgun.

Table 5.19 shows the data for justifiable homicides committed by private citizens from 2006 to 2010. There was an upward trend in justifiable homicides during the period shown, from 238 incidents in 2006 to 278 in 2010, an increase of 16.8%. There was also an increase in the percentage of cases of justifiable homicide involving guns. Firearms were used in 192 out of 238 cases (80.1%) of justifiable homicide by private citizens in 2006 and in 232 out of 278 cases (83.5%) in 2010. Handguns were used most frequently in cases of private citizen justifiable homicide in 2010 (170 cases out of 232 cases involving a firearm, or 73.3% of cases in which a firearm was used).

DEMOGRAPHICS OF VICTIMIZATION

Table 5.20 shows the percentages of violent crime and personal theft reported to the police out of all the violent crime and personal theft that occurred as measured by surveys in 2010 by race and gender of the victim. Violent crimes against Hispanics were more likely to be reported to the police (53.4% of all violent crimes against Hispanic

male victims and 62.5% of all violent crimes against Hispanic female victims) than were violent crimes against whites (50% of male victims and 52.4% of female victims) or African-Americans (48% of all African-American male victims and 55.4% of female victims).

Table 5.21 shows the victimization rates of violent crime in 2010 by race, gender, and age of the victim. Native Americans or Alaskan Natives (42.2 per 1,000 people age 12 or older) were more likely than African-Americans (20.8 per 1,000 people), Hispanics (15.6 per 1,000), or whites (13.6 per 1,000) to be victims of violent crimes. Those identified as being of two or more races were even more likely to be victims of violent crimes (52.6 per 1,000 people). Those identified as Asian or Pacific Islander had the lowest violent crime victimization rate in 2010, at 6.3 per 1,000 people.

In 2010 those aged 12 to 24 years were far more likely to be victims of violent crime than people aged 25 years and older. (See Table 5.21.) Of the younger age groups, 18- to 20-year-olds had the highest rate of violent victimization (33.9 per 1,000 people), followed by 12- to 14-year-olds (27.5 per 1,000 people), and 21- to 24-year-olds (26.9 per 1,000 people); among 12- to 24-year-olds, those aged 15 to 17 had the lowest rate (23 per 1,000 people). The age group with the lowest violent victimization rate included those aged 65 years and older, at 2.4 per 1,000 people. Moreover, after age 20 the rate of violent victimization declined with age in 2010.

The rates of violent crime and personal theft are broken down into additional demographic categories in Table 5.22. The table shows that individuals with annual household incomes of less than $15,000 had higher victimization rates for crimes of violence in 2008 than those living in households with greater annual incomes. Individuals residing in households that earned more than $75,000 annually had the lowest victimization rates for violent crime in 2008.

WHERE DO CRIMINALS GET FIREARMS?

How do criminals acquire guns? Even with background checks and other regulations in place, many criminals obtain their guns legally. For example, James Holmes (1987–),

TABLE 5.18

Weapons used by law enforcement officers in justifiable homicides, 2006–10

Year	Total	Total firearms	Handguns	Rifles	Shotguns	Firearms, type not stated	Knives or cutting instruments	Other dangerous weapons	Personal weapons
2006	386	386	330	25	11	20	0	0	0
2007	398	395	351	19	8	17	1	1	1
2008	378	373	305	30	13	25	1	2	2
2009	414	411	326	29	6	50	0	3	0
2010	387	385	315	26	6	38	1	1	0

Note: The killing of a felon by a law enforcement officer in the line of duty.

source: "Expanded Homicide Data Table 14. Justifiable Homicide, by Weapon, Law Enforcement, 2006–2010," in *Crime in the United States, 2010*, U.S. Department of Justice, Federal Bureau of Investigation, September 2011, http://www.fbi.gov/about-us/cjis/ucr/crime-in-the-u.s/2010/crime-in-the-u.s.-2010/tables/10shrtbl14.xls (accessed August 26, 2012)

TABLE 5.19

Weapons used by private citizens in justifiable homicides, 2006–10

Year	Total	Total firearms	Handguns	Rifles	Shotguns	Firearms, type not stated	Knives or cutting instruments	Other dangerous weapons	Personal weapons
2006	238	192	154	12	15	11	31	12	3
2007	257	202	161	8	21	12	37	8	10
2008	265	219	171	13	13	22	35	9	2
2009	266	218	167	9	19	23	30	10	8
2010	278	232	170	8	26	28	30	11	5

Note: The killing of a felon, during the commission of a felony, by a private citizen.

source: "Expanded Homicide Data Table 15. Justifiable Homicide, by Weapon, Private Citizen, 2006–2010," in *Crime in the United States, 2010*, U.S. Department of Justice, Federal Bureau of Investigation, September 2011, http://www.fbi.gov/about-us/cjis/ucr/crime-in-the-u.s/2010/crime-in-the-u.s.-2010/tables/10shrtbl15.xls (accessed August 26, 2012)

TABLE 5.20

Violent and property victimizations, by gender and race of victim, 2010

Demographic characteristic of victim	Violent victimization	Property victimization
Total	51.0%	39.3%
Male	48.8%	41.1%
White*	50.0	41.1
Black*	48.0	42.5
Hispanic	53.4	36.1
Other*	19.1	46.7
American Indian or Alaskan Native*	16.4	64.9
Asian or Pacific Islander*	22.4	41.7
Two or more races*	37.5	50.3
Female	53.3%	37.6%
White*	52.4	38.4
Black*	55.4	39.6
Hispanic	62.5	33.1
Other*	74.4	32.0
American Indian or Alaskan Native*	44.5	38.7
Asian or Pacific Islander*	86.1	28.9
Two or more races*	17.5	34.1

Note: For violent victimizations, the characteristics apply to the victim. For property victimizations, the characteristics apply to the head of household.
*Excludes persons of Hispanic origin.

source: Jennifer L. Truman, "Table 8. Victimizations Reported to the Police, by Sex, Race, and Hispanic Origin of Victim, 2010," in *Criminal Victimization, 2010*, U.S. Department of Justice, Office of Justice Programs, Bureau of Justice Statistics, September 2011, http://www.bjs.gov/content/pub/pdf/cv10.pdf (accessed August 23, 2012)

accused of killing 12 people and wounding 58 others in the Aurora, Colorado, movie theater shooting in July 2012, was armed with an AR-15 assault rifle, a Remington 12-gauge shotgun, and two Glock handguns at the time of the incident. His four weapons had been purchased at shops in the Denver area, and he bought a supply of ammunition online. In Colorado no permit or waiting period is required for gun purchases. However, firearms dealers are required by law to maintain records on all sales, including personal information about the purchaser, the serial number and identifying information about the gun, and the date and terms of the sale. Speaking at a press conference reported by ABC News on July 20, 2012 (http://abcnews.go.com/US/colorado-movie-theater-shooting-suspect-bought-guns-6000/story?id=16817842#.UHbBQa4fjd4), the Aurora chief of police, Dan Oates, said of Holmes, "All the ammunition he possessed, he possessed legally, all the weapons he possessed, he possessed legally, all the clips he possessed, he possessed legally."

Perpetrators of crime who cannot or who do not want to obtain the guns they want legally, can obtain them illegally in a variety of ways, primarily by stealing them or by illegally buying or trading them on the black market. Beginning in 2003 the Bureau of Alcohol, Tobacco, Firearms, and Explosives (ATF) was legally prohibited from

TABLE 5.21

Violent victimizations, by type of crime, sex, race, Hispanic origin, and age of victim, 2010

Demographic characteristic of victim	Population	Percent of total population	Violent victimizations per 1,000 persons age 12 or older					
			Total	Rape/sexual assault	Robbery	Total assault	Aggravated assault	Simple assault
Total	255,961,940	100%	14.9	0.7	1.9	12.3	2.8	9.5
Sex								
Male	124,987,510	48.8%	15.7	0.1	2.4	13.1	3.4	9.7
Female	130,974,430	51.2	14.2	1.3	1.4	11.5	2.3	9.2
Race/Hispanic origin								
White*	173,740,280	67.9%	13.6	0.7	1.4	11.6	2.6	9.0
Black*	30,371,120	11.9	20.8	1.1	3.6	16.1	4.7	11.4
Hispanic	35,836,220	14.0	15.6	0.8	2.7	12.0	2.3	9.8
American Indian or Alaskan Native*	1,373,440	0.5	42.2	—	4.3	37.9	19.5	18.3
Asian or Pacific Islander*	12,135,210	4.7	6.3	0.6	1.1	4.5	0.5	4.0
Two or more races*	2,505,670	1.0	52.6	1.2	8.0	43.5	8.5	34.9
Age								
12–14	12,102,730	4.7%	27.5	2.7	0.7	24.1	5.8	18.3
15–17	12,332,800	4.8	23.0	1.7	2.7	18.6	3.9	14.7
18–20	13,109,120	5.1	33.9	1.1	5.9	26.9	6.9	20.0
21–24	16,757,880	6.5	26.9	1.5	3.7	21.7	8.0	13.7
25–34	41,712,030	16.3	18.8	1.3	2.5	15.0	3.3	11.7
35–49	63,157,240	24.7	12.6	0.6	1.5	10.4	1.9	8.6
50–64	58,096,490	22.7	10.9	—	1.3	9.7	2.1	7.6
65 or older	38,693,630	15.1	2.4	0.1	0.6	1.7	0.2	1.5

*Excludes persons of Hispanic origin.
—Less than 0.05.

SOURCE: Jennifer L. Truman, "Table 9. Violent Victimizations, by Type of Crime, Sex, Race, Hispanic Origin, and Age of Victim, 2010," in *Criminal Victimization, 2010*, U.S. Department of Justice, Office of Justice Programs, Bureau of Justice Statistics, September 2011, http://www.bjs.gov/content/pub/pdf/cv10.pdf (accessed August 23, 2012)

publishing certain statistics on the sales of multiple handguns and on firearms tracing statistics (gun trace statistics). Thus, it is difficult to get up-to-date information on where criminals get their guns. (See Chapter 2 for a more detailed discussion on this topic.)

The largest study conducted by the government on where criminals get their guns was released in 2001 and was based on interviews with 18,000 state prison inmates. In *Firearm Use by Offenders* (November 2001, http://bjs.ojp.usdoj.gov/content/pub/pdf/fuo.pdf), Caroline Wolf Harlow of the BJS presents results that show that 13.9% of those who carried a firearm during the offense for which they were serving time in 1997 bought their gun from a retail store, pawn shop, flea market, or gun show. This figure was down from 20.8% in 1991, when the previous survey was conducted. Another 39.6% acquired their firearms from family or friends, up from 33.8% in 1991. The remaining 39.2% acquired their firearms "on the street" from an illegal source, down from 40.8% in 1991.

The coalition Mayors against Illegal Guns (MAIG), a group headed by the mayors of New York City and Boston, hired an investigative services firm to determine where criminals get their guns. The results of this investigation were published in *Inside Straw Purchasing: How Criminals Get Guns Illegally* (April 2008, http://www.mayorsagainstillegalguns.org/downloads/pdf/inside-straw-purchases.pdf).

The coalition presents findings on straw purchasing, a situation in which a person who would be denied a gun purchase, such as a convicted felon or an underaged buyer, has another person (the straw purchaser) fill out the paperwork and obtain the gun for him or her. Sometimes a straw purchaser is used when a person simply does not want a gun purchase listed in his or her name.

The coalition explains that straw purchasing occurred frequently in so-called easy stores. Straw purchasers often paid for their purchases with both money and drugs and bought many guns at one time. Gun dealers appear to be the key in this illegal activity: some encourage straw purchases and actually coach straw purchasers, whereas others discourage the practice by asking many probing questions until the straw purchaser leaves the store. These dealers also train their employees how to spot straw purchasers and thwart them.

Many criminals get their guns from the black market (a market where products are bought and sold illegally). Sometimes, these guns are legally purchased in states with less restrictive gun laws and are then transported to states with strong gun laws, a phenomenon known as gunrunning or gun trafficking (buying, moving, and selling guns illegally). In *Trace the Guns: The Link between Gun Laws and Interstate Gun Trafficking* (September 2010, http://mayorsagainstillegalguns.org/downloads/pdf/trace_the_guns_report.pdf), the

TABLE 5.22

Rates of personal violent crimes, by type of crime and annual family income of victims, 2008

	Rate per 1,000 persons age 12 or older						
Type of crime	Less than $7,500	$7,500– $14,999	$15,000– $24,999	$25,000– $34,999	$35,000– $49,999	$50,000– $74,999	$75,000 or more
All personal crimes	44.0	41.3	26.5	25.7	23.1	16.5	12.9
Crimes of violence	43.5	40.4	26.0	25.4	22.4	15.9	12.6
Completed violence	17.9	10.2	7.0	9.4	5.5	2.4	3.3
Attempted/threatened violence	25.6	30.2	19.0	16.1	16.9	13.5	9.3
Rape/sexual assault	4.4*	2.1*	1.0*	0.6*	1.0*	0.0*	0.5*
Rape/attempted rape	3.2*	1.5*	0.4*	0.3*	1.0*	0.0*	0.3*
Rape	2.4*	0.3*	0.2*	0.0*	0.5*	0.0*	0.1*
Attempted rapeª	0.8*	1.2*	0.2*	0.3*	0.4*	0.0*	0.2*
Sexual assaultᵇ	1.2*	0.6*	0.5*	0.3*	0.0*	0.0*	0.2*
Robbery	5.9	4.8	3.0	3.7	2.0	1.3	1.4
Completed/property taken	4.1*	3.6*	1.7*	2.4	1.2*	0.7*	0.8
With injury	1.8*	1.7*	0.7*	0.6*	0.4*	0.5*	0.3*
Without injury	2.3*	2.0*	1.0*	1.8*	0.8*	0.2*	0.5*
Attempted to take property	1.8*	1.1*	1.3*	1.2*	0.8*	0.7*	0.6*
With injury	0.0*	0.4*	0.5*	0.3*	0.6*	0.5*	0.2*
Without injury	1.8*	0.8*	0.8*	0.9*	0.2*	0.1*	0.4*
Assault	33.1	33.5	22.0	21.2	19.3	14.6	10.7
Aggravated	9.3	8.6	5.3	3.4	3.8	3.0	1.9
With injury	4.7*	1.9*	1.3*	1.0*	1.3*	0.7*	0.4*
Threatened with weapon	4.6*	6.7	4.0	2.4	2.5	2.3	1.4
Simple	23.8	24.9	16.8	17.8	15.5	11.6	8.8
With minor injury	6.2	3.7	3.4	5.9	2.4	1.1*	1.7
Without injury	17.6	21.2	13.4	11.9	13.1	10.5	7.1
Purse snatching/pocket picking	0.5*	0.9*	0.6*	0.2*	0.7*	0.6*	0.3*
Population age 12 or older	6,760,710	10,261,320	17,538,250	19,522,830	28,963,880	33,797,170	59,992,830

Note: Detail may not add to total shown because of rounding. Excludes data on persons whose family income level was not ascertained.
*Estimate is based on 10 or fewer sample cases.
ªIncludes verbal threats of rape.
ᵇIncludes threats.

SOURCE: Michael R. Rand and Jayne E. Robinson, "Table 14. Personal Crimes, 2008: Victimization Rates for Persons Age 12 or Older, by Type of Crime and Annual Family Income of Victims," in *Criminal Victimization in the United States, 2008—Statistical Tables*, U.S. Department of Justice, Office of Justice Programs, Bureau of Justice Statistics, May 2011, http://bjs.ojp.usdoj.gov/content/pub/pdf/cvus/current/cv0814.pdf (accessed August 23, 2012)

MAIG analyzes data related to guns recovered from crime scenes in 2009 and gun laws in the states in which the guns were purchased, finding that states with weak gun laws were more likely to serve as a source state in supplying guns to criminals. The coalition reports that the ATF was able to identify the source state of 145,321 out of 238,107 guns (61%) that were recovered at U.S. crime scenes in 2009. Of this number, 70% of the guns (102,067) were used in crimes in the same state in which they were purchased, and 30% of the traced guns (43,254) were recovered in a different state. Nearly half (20,996 firearms, or 48.5%) of the traced guns that were used in crimes in other states in 2009 originated in just 10 states: Georgia (2,781), Florida (2,640), Virginia (2,557), Texas (2,240), Indiana (2,011), Ohio (1,806), Pennsylvania (1,777), North Carolina (1,775), California (1,772), and Arizona (1,637). In 2009 the states that had the highest rates of guns recovered at crime scenes in other states (that is, the number of guns that were used in crimes in other states per 100,000 inhabitants) were: Mississippi (50.3), West Virginia (46.8), Kentucky (34.9), Alaska (33.4), Alabama (33.2), South Carolina (33), Virginia (32.4), Indiana (31.3), Nevada (30.6), and Georgia (28.3). All of these states had rates that were more than twice the national average of 14.1 per 100,000 inhabitants.

In *Trace the Guns*, the MAIG also analyzes "Time-to-Crime" (TTC) data (the time between the initial sale of a gun and the time it is recovered at a crime scene) to determine the likelihood that the gun was acquired illegally before being used in a crime. Firearms that have a TTC of less than two years are considered most likely to have been trafficked illegally. The national average TTC in 2009 was 10.8 years. The MAIG reports that the 10 states with the highest gun export rates also had a higher proportion of guns recovered in other states in less than two years from the initial retail sale.

In addition, the report finds that states that had enacted strong gun laws were less likely to serve as a source for interstate trafficking of firearms in 2009. When used together, state regulations that require the prosecution of straw purchasers or those who falsify purchase information, stipulate background checks for handgun sales at gun shows, require purchase permits, authorize local officials to approve or deny concealed carry permits, deny guns to people convicted of violent misdemeanors, require owners to report missing guns to law enforcement, support local firearms regulations, and require state oversight of gun dealers, seemed to offer some effectiveness in limiting illegal trafficking. The MAIG finds that the states that had not

TABLE 5.23

Arrest trends, by offense, 2001–10

[8,726 agencies; 2010 estimated population 194,771,628; 2001 estimated population 180,336,272]

	Number of persons arrested								
	Total all ages			Under 18 years of age			18 years of age and over		
Offense charged	2001	2010	Percent change	2001	2010	Percent change	2001	2010	Percent change
Total[a]	8,468,019	8,221,468	−2.9	1,360,895	1,040,453	−23.5	7,107,124	7,181,015	+1.0
Murder and nonnegligent manslaughter	8,071	7,027	−12.9	822	627	−23.7	7,249	6,400	−11.7
Forcible rape	16,745	12,588	−24.8	2,788	1,821	−34.7	13,957	10,767	−22.9
Robbery	68,293	71,393	+4.5	15,946	16,841	+5.6	52,347	54,552	+4.2
Aggravated assault	304,692	268,512	−11.9	41,002	28,161	−31.3	263,690	240,351	−8.9
Burglary	184,076	190,440	+3.5	57,329	42,478	−25.9	126,747	147,962	+16.7
Larceny-theft	741,163	813,493	+9.8	227,017	184,154	−18.9	514,146	629,339	+22.4
Motor vehicle theft	85,303	44,125	−48.3	27,707	9,406	−66.1	57,596	34,719	−39.7
Arson	11,059	7,514	−32.1	5,902	3,132	−46.9	5,157	4,382	−15.0
Violent crime[b]	397,801	359,520	−9.6	60,558	47,450	−21.6	337,243	312,070	−7.5
Property crime[b]	1,021,601	1,055,572	+3.3	317,955	239,170	−24.8	703,646	816,402	+16.0
Other assaults	819,796	829,525	+1.2	150,182	134,420	−10.5	669,614	695,105	+3.8
Forgery and counterfeiting	73,248	47,845	−34.7	3,849	1,046	−72.8	69,399	46,799	−32.6
Fraud	216,503	120,764	−44.2	5,578	3,634	−34.9	210,925	117,130	−44.5
Embezzlement	13,690	11,301	−17.5	1,308	310	−76.3	12,382	10,991	−11.2
Stolen property; buying, receiving, possessing	75,552	62,274	−17.6	16,494	9,850	−40.3	59,058	52,424	−11.2
Vandalism	172,579	161,668	−6.3	68,771	50,326	−26.8	103,808	111,342	+7.3
Weapons; carrying, possessing, etc.	99,723	98,067	−1.7	23,108	19,715	−14.7	76,615	78,352	+2.3
Prostitution and commercialized vice	47,256	36,805	−22.1	882	654	−25.9	46,374	36,151	−22.0
Sex offenses (except forcible rape and prostitution)	57,263	46,089	−19.5	11,885	8,056	−32.2	45,378	38,033	−16.2
Drug abuse violations	961,056	1,014,383	+5.5	123,686	107,164	−13.4	837,370	907,219	+8.3
Gambling	4,913	3,046	−38.0	402	244	−39.3	4,511	2,802	−37.9
Offenses against the family and children	88,528	69,571	−21.4	6,097	2,275	−62.7	82,431	67,296	−18.4
Driving under the influence	860,398	836,018	−2.8	12,509	7,238	−42.1	847,889	828,780	−2.3
Liquor laws	403,068	321,255	−20.3	90,293	61,561	−31.8	312,775	259,694	−17.0
Drunkenness	399,835	373,886	−6.5	13,160	8,859	−32.7	386,675	365,027	−5.6
Disorderly conduct	380,646	350,773	−7.8	105,894	89,340	−15.6	274,752	261,433	−4.8
Vagrancy	16,788	21,252	+26.6	1,674	1,490	−11.0	15,114	19,762	+30.8
All other offenses (except traffic)	2,261,825	2,339,901	+3.5	250,660	185,698	−25.9	2,011,165	2,154,203	+7.1
Suspicion	2,300	537	−76.7	620	86	−86.1	1,680	451	−73.2
Curfew and loitering law violations	95,950	61,953	−35.4	95,950	61,953	−35.4	—	—	—

[a]Does not include suspicion.
[b]Violent crimes are offenses of murder and nonnegligent manslaughter, forcible rape, robbery, and aggravated assault. Property crimes are offenses of burglary, larceny-theft, motor vehicle theft, and arson.

SOURCE: "Table 32. Ten-Year Arrest Trends, Totals, 2001–2010," in *Crime in the United States, 2010*, U.S. Department of Justice, Federal Bureau of Investigation, September 2011, http://www.fbi.gov/about-us/cjis/ucr/crime-in-the.u.s/2010/crime-in-the-u.s.-2010/tables/10tbl32.xls (accessed August 26, 2012)

enacted these laws were twice as likely to serve as a source state for guns used in crimes in other states and for guns with a short TTC.

Operation Fast and Furious

In a case that drew attention to the role of the U.S. government in supplying guns to criminals, ATF agents allowed an estimated 2,200 firearms to be trafficked illegally from U.S. border states into the arsenals of Mexican narcotics cartels. Beginning in October 2009, agents in what was known as Operation Fast and Furious were instructed by their superiors not to arrest those on the lowest end of the crime organization, the so-called "straw purchasers," who falsified information required to purchase guns, but rather to allow the guns to be traded on the black market in the hope that U.S. agents could infiltrate the notoriously violent Mexican crime groups at a higher level of leadership. Sari Horwitz of the *Washington Post* (July 25, 2011,

http://www.washingtonpost.com/investigations/us-anti-gun-running-effort-turns-fatally-wrong/2011/07/14/gIQAH5d6YI_story.html) explains, "In drug-trafficking cases, investigating agents, by law, cannot let drugs 'walk' onto the street. Since gun sales are legal, agents on surveillance are not required to step in and stop weapons from hitting the streets." However, a group of agents in Phoenix, Arizona, became increasingly alarmed about the potential negative effects of the operation, and when U.S. Border Patrol Agent Brian Terry was killed in a firefight in December 2010 with a gang using an AK-47 assault rife that had been trafficked to Mexico through Fast and Furious connections, they made the operation public and a Congressional investigation ensued. As reported by Horwitz, of the 2,200 firearms known to have been trafficked in the case, 227 had been recovered in connection with crimes in Mexico, 390 had been recovered in U.S. crime cases, and 1,430 remained "on the streets" as of July 2011.

TABLE 5.24

Arrests, by race and age group, 2010

[12,221 agencies; 2010 estimated population 240,100,189]

Offense charged	Total arrests					Percent distribution[a]				
	Total	White	Black	American Indian or Alaskan Native	Asian or Pacific Islander	Total	White	Black	American Indian or Alaskan Native	Asian or Pacific Islander
Total	10,177,907	7,066,154	2,846,862	145,612	119,279	100.0	69.4	28.0	1.4	1.2
Murder and nonnegligent manslaughter	8,641	4,261	4,209	91	80	100.0	49.3	48.7	1.1	0.9
Forcible rape	15,503	10,178	4,925	214	186	100.0	65.7	31.8	1.4	1.2
Robbery	87,587	37,906	48,154	617	910	100.0	43.3	55.0	0.7	1.0
Aggravated assault	317,435	202,275	106,382	4,854	3,924	100.0	63.7	33.5	1.5	1.2
Burglary	225,775	152,210	69,541	1,961	2,063	100.0	67.4	30.8	0.9	0.9
Larceny-theft	998,476	687,609	282,246	14,323	14,298	100.0	68.9	28.3	1.4	1.4
Motor vehicle theft	55,278	35,009	18,797	696	776	100.0	63.3	34.0	1.3	1.4
Arson	8,766	6,592	1,978	100	96	100.0	75.2	22.6	1.1	1.1
Violent crime[b]	429,166	254,620	163,670	5,776	5,100	100.0	59.3	38.1	1.3	1.2
Property crime[b]	1,288,295	881,420	372,562	17,080	17,233	100.0	68.4	28.9	1.3	1.3
Other assaults	1,004,273	659,171	318,117	14,848	12,137	100.0	65.6	31.7	1.5	1.2
Forgery and counterfeiting	60,538	40,167	19,350	342	679	100.0	66.4	32.0	0.6	1.1
Fraud	144,214	95,126	46,493	1,253	1,342	100.0	66.0	32.2	0.9	0.9
Embezzlement	12,930	8,568	4,037	88	237	100.0	66.3	31.2	0.7	1.8
Stolen property; buying, receiving, possessing	74,122	48,303	24,494	598	727	100.0	65.2	33.0	0.8	1.0
Vandalism	197,015	145,284	46,306	3,279	2,146	100.0	73.7	23.5	1.7	1.1
Weapons; carrying, possessing, etc.	123,278	71,772	49,443	874	1,189	100.0	58.2	40.1	0.7	1.0
Prostitution and commercialized vice	48,154	26,156	20,405	342	1,251	100.0	54.3	42.4	0.7	2.6
Sex offenses (except forcible rape and prostitution)	56,125	41,406	13,182	744	793	100.0	73.8	23.5	1.3	1.4
Drug abuse violations	1,270,443	846,736	404,609	8,766	10,332	100.0	66.6	31.8	0.7	0.8
Gambling	7,512	2,160	5,071	32	249	100.0	28.8	67.5	0.4	3.3
Offenses against the family and children	84,812	56,233	26,470	1,533	576	100.0	66.3	31.2	1.8	0.7
Driving under the influence	1,082,301	927,516	124,467	13,980	16,338	100.0	85.7	11.5	1.3	1.5
Liquor laws	396,942	329,895	47,529	14,129	5,389	100.0	83.1	12.0	3.6	1.4
Drunkenness	440,688	362,396	66,837	8,583	2,872	100.0	82.2	15.2	1.9	0.7
Disorderly conduct	480,080	305,154	162,521	8,415	3,990	100.0	63.6	33.9	1.8	0.8
Vagrancy	24,759	14,092	9,935	567	165	100.0	56.9	40.1	2.3	0.7
All other offenses (except traffic)	2,877,687	1,905,436	893,018	43,634	35,599	100.0	66.2	31.0	1.5	1.2
Suspicion	903	582	310	5	6	100.0	64.5	34.3	0.6	0.7
Curfew and loitering law violations	73,670	43,961	28,036	744	929	100.0	59.7	38.1	1.0	1.3

Offense charged	Arrests under 18					Percent distribution[a]				
	Total	White	Black	American Indian or Alaskan Native	Asian or Pacific Islander	Total	White	Black	American Indian or Alaskan Native	Asian or Pacific Islander
Total	1,281,738	849,251	399,249	15,760	17,478	100.0	66.3	31.1	1.2	1.4
Murder and nonnegligent manslaughter	781	332	439	4	6	100.0	42.5	56.2	0.5	0.8
Forcible rape	2,181	1,369	787	15	10	100.0	62.8	36.1	0.7	0.5
Robbery	21,062	6,670	14,046	101	245	100.0	31.7	66.7	0.5	1.2
Aggravated assault	34,879	19,612	14,482	418	367	100.0	56.2	41.5	1.2	1.1
Burglary	51,135	31,539	18,657	400	539	100.0	61.7	36.5	0.8	1.1
Larceny-theft	221,901	143,791	70,833	2,912	4,365	100.0	64.8	31.9	1.3	2.0
Motor vehicle theft	12,223	6,721	5,166	172	164	100.0	55.0	42.3	1.4	1.3
Arson	3,552	2,677	784	39	52	100.0	75.4	22.1	1.1	1.5
Violent crime[b]	58,903	27,983	29,754	538	628	100.0	47.5	50.5	0.9	1.1
Property crime[b]	288,811	184,728	95,440	3,523	5,120	100.0	64.0	33.0	1.2	1.8
Other assaults	162,389	96,994	61,847	1,694	1,854	100.0	59.7	38.1	1.0	1.1
Forgery and counterfeiting	1,306	873	404	8	21	100.0	66.8	30.9	0.6	1.6
Fraud	4,557	2,700	1,753	52	52	100.0	59.2	38.5	1.1	1.1
Embezzlement	341	212	119	3	7	100.0	62.2	34.9	0.9	2.1
Stolen property; buying, receiving, possessing	11,564	6,486	4,865	80	133	100.0	56.1	42.1	0.7	1.2
Vandalism	60,265	46,992	11,858	747	668	100.0	78.0	19.7	1.2	1.1
Weapons; carrying, possessing, etc.	24,355	15,112	8,771	178	294	100.0	62.0	36.0	0.7	1.2
Prostitution and commercialized vice	804	306	476	9	13	100.0	38.1	59.2	1.1	1.6
Sex offenses (except forcible rape and prostitution)	10,082	7,228	2,640	71	143	100.0	71.7	26.2	0.7	1.4

TABLE 5.24

Arrests, by race and age group, 2010 [CONTINUED]

[12,221 agencies; 2010 estimated population 240,100,189]

Offense charged	Arrests under 18					Percent distribution[a]				
	Total	White	Black	American Indian or Alaskan Native	Asian or Pacific Islander	Total	White	Black	American Indian or Alaskan Native	Asian or Pacific Islander
Drug abuse violations	132,481	98,039	31,575	1,425	1,442	100.0	74.0	23.8	1.1	1.1
Gambling	1,039	86	942	3	8	100.0	8.3	90.7	0.3	0.8
Offenses against the family and children	2,948	2,114	746	72	16	100.0	71.7	25.3	2.4	0.5
Driving under the influence	9,290	8,468	532	156	134	100.0	91.2	5.7	1.7	1.4
Liquor laws	75,397	66,720	5,288	2,360	1,029	100.0	88.5	7.0	3.1	1.4
Drunkenness	10,003	8,862	850	221	70	100.0	88.6	8.5	2.2	0.7
Disorderly conduct	120,514	69,470	48,808	1,283	953	100.0	57.6	40.5	1.1	0.8
Vagrancy	1,690	1,282	391	5	12	100.0	75.9	23.1	0.3	0.7
All other offenses (except traffic)	231,223	160,564	64,120	2,588	3,951	100.0	69.4	27.7	1.1	1.7
Suspicion	106	71	34	0	1	100.0	67.0	32.1	0.0	0.9
Curfew and loitering law violations	73,670	43,961	28,036	744	929	100.0	59.7	38.1	1.0	1.3

Offense charged	Arrests under 18 and over					Percent distribution[a]				
	Total	White	Black	American Indian or Alaskan Native	Asian or Pacific Islander	Total	White	Black	American Indian or Alaskan Native	Asian or Pacific Islander
Total	**8,896,169**	**6,216,903**	**2,447,613**	**129,852**	**101,801**	**100.0**	**69.9**	**27.5**	**1.5**	**1.1**
Murder and nonnegligent manslaughter	7,860	3,929	3,770	87	74	100.0	50.0	48.0	1.1	0.9
Forcible rape	13,322	8,809	4,138	199	176	100.0	66.1	31.1	1.5	1.3
Robbery	66,525	31,236	34,108	516	665	100.0	47.0	51.3	0.8	1.0
Aggravated assault	282,556	182,663	91,900	4,436	3,557	100.0	64.6	32.5	1.6	1.3
Burglary	174,640	120,671	50,884	1,561	1,524	100.0	69.1	29.1	0.9	0.9
Larceny-theft	776,575	543,818	211,413	11,411	9,933	100.0	70.0	27.2	1.5	1.3
Motor vehicle theft	43,055	28,288	13,631	524	612	100.0	65.7	31.7	1.2	1.4
Arson	5,214	3,915	1,194	61	44	100.0	75.1	22.9	1.2	0.8
Violent crime[b]	370,263	226,637	133,916	5,238	4,472	100.0	61.2	36.2	1.4	1.2
Property crime[c]	999,484	696,692	277,122	13,557	12,113	100.0	69.7	27.7	1.4	1.2
Other assaults	841,884	562,177	256,270	13,154	10,283	100.0	66.8	30.4	1.6	1.2
Forgery and counterfeiting	59,232	39,294	18,946	334	658	100.0	66.3	32.0	0.6	1.1
Fraud	139,657	92,426	44,740	1,201	1,290	100.0	66.2	32.0	0.9	0.9
Embezzlement	12,589	8,356	3,918	85	230	100.0	66.4	31.1	0.7	1.8
Stolen property; buying, receiving, possessing	62,558	41,817	19,629	518	594	100.0	66.8	31.4	0.8	0.9
Vandalism	136,750	98,292	34,448	2,532	1,478	100.0	71.9	25.2	1.9	1.1
Weapons; carrying, possessing, etc.	98,923	56,660	40,672	696	895	100.0	57.3	41.1	0.7	0.9
Prostitution and commercialized vice	47,350	25,850	19,929	333	1,238	100.0	54.6	42.1	0.7	2.6
Sex offenses (except forcible rape and prostitution)	46,043	34,178	10,542	673	650	100.0	74.2	22.9	1.5	1.4
Drug abuse violations	1,137,962	748,697	373,034	7,341	8,890	100.0	65.8	32.8	0.6	0.8
Gambling	6,473	2,074	4,129	29	241	100.0	32.0	63.8	0.4	3.7
Offenses against the family and children	81,864	54,119	25,724	1,461	560	100.0	66.1	31.4	1.8	0.7
Driving under the influence	1,073,011	919,048	123,935	13,824	16,204	100.0	85.7	11.6	1.3	1.5
Liquor laws	321,545	263,175	42,241	11,769	4,360	100.0	81.8	13.1	3.7	1.4
Drunkenness	430,685	353,534	65,987	8,362	2,802	100.0	82.1	15.3	1.9	0.7
Disorderly conduct	359,566	235,684	113,713	7,132	3,037	100.0	65.5	31.6	2.0	0.8
Vagrancy	23,069	12,810	9,544	562	153	100.0	55.5	41.4	2.4	0.7
All other offenses (except traffic)	2,646,464	1,744,872	828,898	41,046	31,648	100.0	65.9	31.3	1.6	1.2
Suspicion	797	511	276	5	5	100.0	64.1	34.6	0.6	0.6
Curfew and loitering law violations	—	—	—	—	—	—	—	—	—	—

[a]Because of rounding, the percentages may not add to 100.0.
[b]Violent crimes are offenses of murder and nonnegligent manslaughter, forcible rape, robbery, and aggravated assault. Property crimes are offenses of burglary, larceny-theft, motor vehicle theft, and arson.

SOURCE: "Table 43. Arrests, by Race, 2010," in *Crime in the United States, 2010*, U.S. Department of Justice, Federal Bureau of Investigation, September 2011, http://www.fbi.gov/about-us/cjis/ucr/crime-in-the-u.s/2010/crime-in-the-u.s.-2010/tables/table-43 (accessed August 26, 2012)

In September 2012 Michael E. Horowitz, the U.S. inspector general, released the report *A Review of ATF's Operation Fast and Furious and Related Matters* (September 19, 2012, http://www.justice.gov/oig/reports/2012/s1209.pdf), the result of a review of more than 100,000 documents and interviews with more than 100 individuals connected with the case. In the report, Horowitz finds "a series of misguided strategies, tactics, errors in judgment, and management failures that permeated ATF Headquarters and the Phoenix Field Division, as well as the

U.S. Attorney's Office for the District of Arizona." Although disciplinary action was recommended for some personnel in the operation, no recommendations for criminal prosecution were made. Further, the report states that the U.S. Attorney General Eric Holder (1951–), who had been a key target of Republican critics of the case, had not been fully advised of the operation and was thus cleared of responsibility.

GUNS AND THE LOCAL POLICE
Police Shootings

Firearms are a valuable aid to law enforcement officers. As mentioned previously, justifiable homicide is defined as the killing of a felon by a law enforcement officer in the line of duty or by another person while the felon is committing a crime. As noted above, Table 5.18 shows the number of justifiable homicides by law enforcement officers from 2006 to 2010. Of the 387 justifiable homicides in 2010, almost all (385) were committed with firearms: 315 with handguns, 26 with rifles, 6 with shotguns, and 38 with unspecified firearms. Police justifiably kill over 350 felons each year. Most often, the felon is shot.

A Tool to Detect Gunfire

Some law enforcement officers, especially those who work in cities plagued by gangs and random shootings, have spoken of the frustration they feel when responding to reports of gunfire. Because it is difficult for the human ear to determine the direction from which a gunshot originates, callers cannot locate the source accurately, and police officers are sometimes unable to respond appropriately. This increases the chance of serious injury or death to victims. Furthermore, once police finally arrive on the scene, the person with the gun may be already gone.

To help locate the source of gunfire to within 20 feet (6.1 m), acoustic sensors (devices similar to those used to detect earthquake epicenters) can be used. In June 1996 Redwood City, California, became one of the first communities in the nation to employ them. Mounted on buildings and telephone poles throughout the city, the sensors transmit the time of the gunshots to a central computer that displays the location. This allows police to respond to gunfire before police dispatchers begin to receive phone calls reporting the shots. According to field tests conducted by the Redwood City Police Department, the sensors identified gunfire locations within seconds.

Mapping and communications systems work with the sensors to identify "hot spots" and to call homes and businesses in the area when shots are detected. Those called respond to automated questions by pressing buttons on their phones. This process helps law enforcement officers determine who needs help and who would be useful to interview for additional information. According to SST, Inc., a manufacturer of acoustic surveillance systems, more than 70 U.S. cities had installed its

systems at the time gunshot location technology was implemented in Kansas City, Missouri, in September 2012 (September 27, 2012, http://www.shotspotter.com/news-and-events/press-releases/kansas-city-mo-police-department-implements-sst-incs-shotspotter-flex).

Targeted Patrols Reduce Gun Crime

Faced with rising rates of violent crime in the early 1990s, Kansas City, Missouri, was the first city in the United States to experiment with the use of targeted patrols to reduce violent crime. The experiment was conducted by the Kansas City Police Department and evaluated by Lawrence W. Sherman, James W. Shaw, and Dennis P. Rogan in "The Kansas City Gun Experiment" (*Research in Brief*, January 1995) and by Sherman and Rogan in "The Effects of Gun Seizures on Gun Violence: 'Hot Spots' Patrol in Kansas City" (*Justice Quarterly*, vol. 12, no. 4, December 1995). Kansas City police officers were trained to search for illegal guns and then were assigned to a police beat with high levels of violent crime. Their job was to stop and search individuals for illegal guns when they were stopped for other offenses. The Kansas City Police Department's efforts led to a 65% increase in seizures of illegal firearms. This in turn was associated with a 50% decrease in gun-related crime in the targeted area.

By 2012 police departments in many cities (such as Albuquerque, New Mexico; Pittsburgh, Pennsylvania; and Tulsa, Oklahoma) were conducting targeted patrols to reduce a variety of crimes, including the possession of illegal guns. In "Newark Police Ramp Up Gun Seizures, See Violence Go Down" (July 31, 2012, http://www.nj.com/news/index.ssf/2012/07/newark_police_ramp_up_gun_seiz.html), James Queally reports that targeted firearms investigations by the police department and the FBI in Newark, New Jersey, in 2011 led to the seizure of 696 firearms that year, a 60% increase in gun seizures over 2010 (438 weapons). Queally indicates that "as the gun seizures have gone up, violence has slowly gone down. There were 43 homicides in the city as of July 11, down from 52 at the same time in 2011. Shootings and aggravated assaults have also dropped during that time, records show."

WEAPONS OFFENSES

Weapons offenses are violations of statutes or regulations that control deadly weapons, which include firearms and their ammunition, silencers, explosives, and certain knives. All 50 states, many cities and towns, and the federal government have laws concerning deadly weapons, including restrictions on their possession, carrying, use, sales, manufacturing, importing, and exporting.

Table 5.23 shows arrest trends for crimes committed in 2001 and in 2010, based on reports from 8,726 law enforcement agencies. Total arrests across all age groups decreased 2.9% during this 10-year period, and arrests for weapons offenses across all age groups decreased 1.7%.

Characteristics of Weapons Offenders

According to Table 5.23, the number of arrests of people under the age of 18 for weapons offenses was 23,108 in 2001 and 19,715 in 2010, a decline of 14.7%. Arrests for weapons offenses within this age group accounted for 23.2% of all arrests for weapons offenses in 2001 (23,108 arrests out of 99,723) and 20.1% in 2010 (19,715 arrests out of 98,067).

Arrests by race and age for crimes committed in 2010 are shown in Table 5.24; the data in this table differ slightly from the data in Table 5.23 because more law enforcement agencies (12,221) reported arrest figures used in Table 5.24 than in Table 5.23 (8,726). According to the U.S. Census Bureau in *Overview of Race and Hispanic Origin: 2010*

(March 2011, http://www.census.gov/prod/cen2010/briefs/ c2010br-02.pdf), white people made up 72.4% of the population in 2010, but Table 5.24 shows they accounted for only 58.2% of the arrests for weapons offenses across all age groups. African-Americans, who made up 12.6 % of the population in 2010, accounted for 40.1% of the arrests for weapons offenses across all age groups.

Comparing the percentage of arrests of people under the age of 18 to people aged 18 years and older for weapons offenses indicates that underaged whites accounted for a higher percentage of weapons arrests in their age group (62%) than did adult whites in their age group (57.3%). The converse is true for African-Americans. For weapons offenses, underaged African-Americans accounted for a lower percentage of weapons arrests in their age group (36%) than did adult African-Americans (41.1%).

CHAPTER 6
GUN-RELATED INJURIES AND FATALITIES

The public health community, which is represented at the national level by the Centers for Disease Control and Prevention (CDC), believes that collecting comprehensive data on firearm injuries and deaths—such as who was shot, under what circumstances, and with what kind of weapon—is the first step in reducing these injuries and deaths. The next step, it believes, may be a campaign similar to those that eradicated polio and reduced traffic fatalities. For example, according to the National Highway Traffic Safety Administration's Fatality Analysis Reporting System (2012, http://www-fars.nhtsa.dot.gov/Main/index.aspx), the rate of traffic fatalities decreased from 23.2 fatalities per 100,000 licensed drivers in 1994 to 15.7 fatalities per 100,000 licensed drivers in 2010.

The CDC's National Center for Injury Prevention and Control administers a system that tracks the numbers of firearm-related injuries. The data are available through the Web-Based Injury Statistics Query and Reporting System (WISQARS; http://www.cdc.gov/injury/wisqars/index.html). This interactive, user-friendly database provides reports of injury-related data of all types, including firearm injuries, both fatal and nonfatal.

The CDC also has a state-based system, the National Violent Death Reporting System (NVDRS; http://www.cdc.gov/ViolencePrevention/NVDRS/index.html), that collects information about violent deaths, including firearm deaths, from a variety of sources in some states. These sources include law enforcement, medical examiners and coroners, crime laboratories, and death certificates. These data help detail the circumstances that might have contributed to the firearm death. Furthermore, they help each participating state design and implement prevention and intervention efforts tailored to that state's needs.

In "National Violent Death Reporting System State Profiles" (July 13, 20122, http://www.cdc.gov/ViolencePrevention/NVDRS/stateprofiles.html), the CDC notes that as of July 2011 it funded the NVDRS in 18 states:

Alaska, Colorado, Georgia, Kentucky, Maryland, Massachusetts, Michigan, New Jersey, New Mexico, North Carolina, Ohio, Oklahoma, Oregon, Rhode Island, South Carolina, Utah, Virginia, and Wisconsin. The CDC's goal is to have all 50 states, all U.S. territories, and the District of Columbia be part of the system.

NONFATAL GUNSHOT INJURIES

Table 6.1 shows WISQARS data for the numbers of nonfatal gunshot injuries and the rates per 100,000 population from 2001 to 2010. The number and rate of nonfatal gunshot injuries rose and fell during this period, but overall there was a noticeable increase for both. Regardless, the number and rate of nonfatal gunshot injuries across all races, ages, and sexes was so low that this type of nonfatal injury was not one of the 10 leading causes of nonfatal injury listed by WISQARS from 2001 to 2010. As reported by the CDC in WISQARS (2012, http://www.cdc.gov/Injury/wisqars/), the leading causes of nonfatal unintentional injuries across all age groups from 2001 to 2010 were (from most to least common) falls, being struck by or against an object, overexertion, traffic accidents, being cut, and being assaulted; the leading causes for 2010 were the same as those that constituted the overall trend.

Nagesh N. Borse et al. of the CDC report in *CDC Childhood Injury Report: Patterns of Unintentional Injuries among 0–19 Year Olds in the United States, 2000–2006* (December 2008, http://www.cdc.gov/safechild/images/CDC-ChildhoodInjury.pdf) that nonfatal gunshot injuries are not a frequent source of injury for children. Table 6.2 lists nonfatal unintentional injury rates among children from birth to age 19 from 2001 to 2006. The rates of being shot unintentionally by a pellet gun or another type of firearm were among the least likely ways that children were unintentionally hurt. As a comparison, the rate of unintentional childhood injury from falls during this

TABLE 6.1

Nonfatal gunshot injuries and rates per 100,000 population, 2001–10

Year	Injuries	Population	Age-adjusted rate
2001	63,012	284,968,955	21.68
2002	58,841	287,625,193	20.16
2003	65,834	290,107,933	22.34
2004	64,389	292,805,298	21.79
2005	69,825	295,516,599	23.43
2006	71,417	298,379,912	23.61
2007	69,863	301,231,207	23.04
2008	78,622	304,093,966	25.77
2009	66,769	306,771,529	21.68
2010	73,505	308,745,538	23.97

Note: Standard population is 2,000, all races, both sexes.
Age adjusting: Some injuries occur more often among certain age groups than others. For instance, falls are more common among the elderly than among any other age group. Age adjustment enables you to compare injury rates without concern that differences are because of differences in the age distributions between different populations or for the same population over time.

SOURCE: "Overall Firearm Gunshot Nonfatal Injuries and Rates per 100,000, 2001–2010, United States, All Races, Both Sexes, All Ages, Disposition: All Cases," in *Web-Based Injury Statistics Query and Reporting System (WISQARS)*, U.S. Department of Health and Human Services, Centers for Disease Control and Prevention, National Center for Injury Prevention and Control, Office of Statistics and Programming, 2011, http://webappa.cdc .gov/sasweb/ncipc/nfirates2001.html (accessed August 26, 2012)

period was 3,420 per 100,000 population from birth to age 19, whereas the rate for being nonfatally shot by a pellet gun was 16 per 100,000 population and by another type of firearm was 5 per 100,000 population.

Table 6.3 shows that nonfatal firearm injuries—both those from pellet guns and from other types of firearms—rose with age in children in 2010. The highest rate was for nonfatal firearm injuries for males aged 15 to 19 years, at 110.7 injuries per 100,000 males of this age group; this age group also registered the highest rate for females, at 12.7 nonfatal firearm injuries per 100,000 population.

FIREARM FATALITIES

Table 6.4 shows the trend from 1970 to 2009 of deaths attributable to firearms by age, race, Hispanic origin, and gender of the victims as reported by the CDC in *Health, United States, 2011. With Special Feature on Socioeconomic Status and Health* (May 2012, http://www.cdc.gov/nchs/ hus.htm). The overall age-adjusted death rate from firearm-related injuries remained somewhat stable from 1970 to 1990 at about 14 deaths per 100,000 population. The rate then dropped to 13.4 deaths per 100,000 population in 1995, and it continued to drop to 10.2 deaths per 100,000 population in 2000. Thereafter, it stabilized at about 10 deaths per 100,000 population from 2000 to 2009.

The WISQARS data in Table 6.5 also show this stabilization in the rate of firearm deaths from 1999 to 2009, even though the numbers of deaths increased. The number of fatal gunshot injuries increased from 28,874 in 1999 to 31,347 in 2009. This apparent anomaly between

a stabilization in the rate of firearm deaths and an increase in the number of firearm deaths is easy to explain: the population rose during these years so that the modest rise in fatal gunshot injuries did not keep pace with the increasing population, by which the rate is calculated. In 1999 the rate of fatal gunshot injuries was 10.3 deaths per 100,000 population, and the rate fell slightly to 10.1 deaths per 100,000 population in 2009.

Deaths from firearm injuries do not result only from intentional use of a firearm to cause injury or death in another but also from unintentional use. Results from the NVDRS from 16 states show the number and percentage of deaths resulting from the unintentional use of firearms and the circumstances of those deaths in from 2005 through 2009. (See Table 6.6.) During the period shown in the table, the total number of unintentional firearm deaths dropped 33% from 99 in 2005 to 66 in 2009. The highest number of deaths for all the years shown occurred while someone was playing with a gun (20 deaths, or 30.3% in 2009). In 2009, the second-highest number of deaths occurred while hunting (18 deaths, or 27.3%). Concerning the circumstances of the injury in 2009, 13 deaths (19.7%) occurred when a gun was discharged that was thought to be unloaded. In "Surveillance for Violent Deaths—National Violent Death Reporting System, 16 States, 2009" (*Morbidity and Mortality Weekly Report*, vol. 61, no. SS-6, September 14, 2012), Debra L. Karch et al. of the CDC explain that unintentional firearm deaths accounted for 0.5% of the violent deaths that occurred in the NVDRS states in 2009 and occurred at a rate of 0.1 deaths per 100,000 population.

The CDC Injury Prevention and Control Center (March 9, 2012, http://www.cdc.gov/Injury/wisqars/pdf/ Leading_Causes_injury_Deaths_Age_GRoup_Highlighting _Unintentional_Injury%20Deaths_US_2009-a.pdf) notes that 18,735 suicide firearm injuries occurred in 2009, making it the fourth-leading cause of injury deaths in the United States that year. Motor vehicle accident injuries (34,485) were the first-leading cause of injury deaths in 2009, followed by unintentional poisonings (31,758) and unintentional falls (24,792).

According to Karch et al., among suicide deaths alone in 2009, firearms were used most often (51.8%), followed by hanging/strangulation/suffocation (24.7%), and intentional poisoning (17.2%). By gender, males most often committed suicide with firearms (56.7%), whereas females most often used poison (36.9%), followed closely by firearms (33.8%). Among homicide deaths alone in 2009, firearms were used most often overall (66.5%), and in homicides of males (72.1%) and females (48.8%). Sharp instruments were the second-most used method of homicide overall (12.9%), followed by blunt objects (7%).

TABLE 6.2

Nonfatal unintentional injury rates among children aged 0 to 19, by sex and cause, 2001–06

Cause	Overall		Males rate per 100,000 population*	Females rate per 100,000 population*
	Weighted estimate	Rate per 100,000 population*		
Fall	16,708,081	3,420	3,871	2,946
Struck by/against	12,034,546	2,463	3,163	1,728
Overexertion	4,976,839	1,019	1,102	931
MV-occupant	4,050,659	829	741	922
Cut/pierce	3,646,945	746	944	539
Other bite/sting	2,288,653	468	495	441
Pedal cyclist	1,924,756	394	559	221
Unknown/unspecified	1,920,436	393	530	250
Foreign body	1,483,355	304	313	294
Other transport	1,285,877	263	277	249
Fire/burn	942,978	191	206	174
Other specified	930,531	193	206	179
Dog bite	924,203	189	212	166
Poisoning	819,725	168	173	163
Motorcyclist	358,069	73	124	20
Pedestrian	351,764	72	83	61
Suffocation	143,709	22	23	21
Machinery	108,729	29	46	12
BB/pellet gunshot	77,491	16	27	4
Natural/environment	50,265	10	15	5
Nonfatal drowning	23,826	5	6	4
Firearm gunshot	23,421	5	8	1
Total	**55,074,860**	**11,272**	**13,122**	**9,331**

*Population 2001–2006: Overall 488,582,677; Males 250,264,225; Females 238,318,452.

SOURCE: Nagesh N. Borse et al., "Appendix 5A: Nonfatal Unintentional Injury Rates among Children 0 to 19 Years, by Sex and Cause, United States, 2001–2006," in *CDC Childhood Injury Report: Patterns of Unintentional Injuries among 0–19 Year Olds in the United States, 2000–2006*, U.S. Department of Health and Human Services, Centers for Disease Control and Prevention, National Center for Injury Prevention and Control, Division of Unintentional Injury Prevention, December 2008, http://www.cdc.gov/safechild/images/CDC-ChildhoodInjury.pdf (accessed August 30, 2012)

TABLE 6.3

Numbers and rates per 100,000 of nonfatal BB/pellet gun and firearm injuries for persons aged 0–19 by sex, 2010

Age group	Sex	Population	Overall BB/pellet injuries	Rate	Firearm injuries	Rate
0–4 yrs	Both	20,201,362	200*	0.99	200*	0.99
	Male	10,319,427	176*	1.71	75*	0.73
	Female	9,881,935	23*	0.24	125*	1.26
5–9 yrs	Both	20,348,657	987*	4.85	240*	1.18
	Male	10,389,638	856*	8.24	209*	2.01
	Female	9,959,019	131*	1.31	31*	0.31
10–14 yrs	Both	20,677,194	3,388	16.38	1,265*	6.12
	Male	10,579,862	2,991	28.27	957*	9.05
	Female	10,097,332	397*	3.93	308*	3.05
15–19 yrs	Both	22,040,343	4,678	21.23	13,870	62.93
	Male	11,303,666	4,036	35.71	12,507	110.65
	Female	10,736,677	642*	5.98	1,363*	12.70

*Injury estimate is unstable because of small sample size. Use with caution.

SOURCE: Adapted from "Overall BB/Pellet Gunshot Nonfatal Injuries and Rates per 100,000, 2010, United States, All Races, Both Sexes, Ages 0 to 19" and "Overall Firearm Gunshot Nonfatal Injuries and Rates per 100,000, 2010, United States, All Races, Both Sexes, Ages 0 to 19," in *Web-Based Injury Statistics Query and Reporting System (WISQARS)*, U.S. Department of Health and Human Services, Centers for Disease Control and Prevention, National Center for Injury Prevention and Control, Office of Statistics and Programming, 2012, http://webappa.cdc.gov/sasweb/ncipc/nfirates2001.html (accessed August 27, 2012)

In "Variation in Pediatric and Adolescent Firearm Mortality Rates in Rural and Urban US Counties" (*Pediatrics*, vol. 125, no. 6, June 2010), Michael L. Nance et al. examine whether children and youth died from firearms at varying rates depending on whether they lived in rural, suburban, or urban settings. The researchers report that their analysis of death data files from the National Center for Health Statistics National Vital Statistics System from 1999 to 2006 reveal that children and youth aged 0 to 19 years in the most rural counties had firearm mortality rates that were equivalent to those for children and youth of the same age range in the most urban counties. The

TABLE 6.4

Death rates for firearm-related injuries, by sex, race, Hispanic origin, and age, selected years 1970–2009

[Data are based on death certificates]

Sex, race, Hispanic origin, and age	1970[a]	1980[a]	1990[a]	1995[a]	2000[b]	2005[b]	2008[b]	2009[b]
All persons								
All ages, age-adjusted[c]	14.3	14.8	14.6	13.4	10.2	10.2	10.3	10.1
All ages, crude	13.1	14.9	14.9	13.5	10.2	10.4	10.4	10.2
Under 1 year	*	*	*	*	*	*	*	*
1–14 years	1.6	1.4	1.5	1.6	0.7	0.7	0.6	0.6
1–4 years	1.0	0.7	0.6	0.6	0.3	0.4	0.5	0.4
5–14 years	1.7	1.6	1.9	1.9	0.9	0.8	0.7	0.7
15–24 years	15.5	20.6	25.8	26.7	16.8	16.2	15.7	14.6
15–19 years	11.4	14.7	23.3	24.1	12.9	12.5	12.0	11.4
20–24 years	20.3	26.4	28.1	29.2	20.9	20.0	19.4	17.8
25–44 years	20.9	22.5	19.3	16.9	13.1	13.6	13.4	13.0
25–34 years	22.2	24.3	21.8	19.6	14.5	15.7	15.2	14.2
35–44 years	19.6	20.0	16.3	14.3	11.9	11.6	11.7	11.8
45–64 years	17.6	15.2	13.6	11.7	10.0	10.6	11.3	11.5
45–54 years	18.1	16.4	13.9	12.0	10.5	11.2	11.6	11.9
55–64 years	17.0	13.9	13.3	11.3	9.4	9.8	10.9	11.0
65 years and over	13.8	13.5	16.0	14.1	12.2	11.8	11.7	11.9
65–74 years	14.5	13.8	14.4	12.8	10.6	10.3	10.9	11.2
75–84 years	13.4	13.4	19.4	16.3	13.9	13.7	13.3	13.2
85 years and over	10.2	11.6	14.7	14.4	14.2	12.0	11.3	11.9
Male								
All ages, age-adjusted[c]	24.8	25.9	26.1	23.8	18.1	18.3	18.2	17.7
All ages, crude	22.2	25.7	26.2	23.6	17.8	18.3	18.2	17.8
Under 1 year	*	*	*	*	*	*	*	*
1–14 years	2.3	2.0	2.2	2.3	1.1	1.0	0.9	0.8
1–4 years	1.2	0.9	0.7	0.8	0.4	0.5	0.6	0.5
5–14 years	2.7	2.5	2.9	2.9	1.4	1.2	1.0	1.0
15–24 years	26.4	34.8	44.7	46.5	29.4	28.7	27.5	25.5
15–19 years	19.2	24.5	40.1	41.6	22.4	22.0	21.1	19.9
20–24 years	35.1	45.2	49.1	51.5	37.0	35.3	34.0	31.1
25–44 years	34.1	38.1	32.6	28.4	22.0	23.1	22.7	21.9
25–34 years	36.5	41.4	37.0	33.2	24.9	27.2	26.2	24.1
35–44 years	31.6	33.2	27.4	23.6	19.4	19.2	19.3	19.7
45–64 years	31.0	25.9	23.4	20.0	17.1	18.3	19.3	19.5
45–54 years	30.7	27.3	23.2	20.1	17.6	18.9	19.4	19.6
55–64 years	31.3	24.5	23.7	19.8	16.3	17.4	19.3	19.4
65 years and over	29.7	29.7	35.3	30.7	26.4	25.1	24.9	25.1
65–74 years	29.5	27.8	28.2	25.1	20.3	19.7	20.8	21.1
75–84 years	31.0	33.0	46.9	37.8	32.2	30.8	29.5	28.7
85 years and over	26.2	34.9	49.3	47.1	44.7	35.4	31.7	34.8
Female								
All ages, age-adjusted[c]	4.8	4.7	4.2	3.8	2.8	2.7	2.7	2.8
All ages, crude	4.4	4.7	4.3	3.8	2.8	2.7	2.8	2.8
Under 1 year	*	*	*	*	*	*	*	*
1–14 years	0.8	0.7	0.8	0.8	0.3	0.4	0.4	0.3
1–4 years	0.9	0.5	0.5	0.5	*	0.3	0.3	0.3
5–14 years	0.8	0.7	1.0	0.9	0.4	0.4	0.4	0.3
15–24 years	4.8	6.1	6.0	5.9	3.5	3.0	3.2	3.1
15–19 years	3.5	4.6	5.7	5.6	2.9	2.4	2.5	2.5
20–24 years	6.4	7.7	6.3	6.1	4.2	3.6	4.0	3.7
25–44 years	8.3	7.4	6.1	5.5	4.2	3.9	3.8	3.9
25–34 years	8.4	7.5	6.7	5.8	4.0	3.8	3.6	3.9
35–44 years	8.2	7.2	5.4	5.2	4.4	4.0	4.0	3.9
45–64 years	5.4	5.4	4.5	3.9	3.4	3.3	3.6	3.8
45–54 years	6.4	6.2	4.9	4.2	3.6	3.7	4.0	4.3
55–64 years	4.2	4.6	4.0	3.5	3.0	2.8	3.1	3.2
65 years and over	2.4	2.5	3.1	2.8	2.2	2.1	2.1	2.2
65–74 years	2.8	3.1	3.6	3.0	2.5	2.5	2.4	2.6
75–84 years	1.7	1.7	2.9	2.8	2.0	2.1	2.0	2.2
85 years and over	*	1.3	1.3	1.8	1.7	1.3	1.5	1.3

type of death varied, however. In urban counties youth firearm deaths were more frequently related to homicide, whereas in rural counties youth firearm deaths were more frequently related to suicide and unintentional gunshot wounds.

Age

Table 6.4 provides the firearm death rates for all age groups. In 1970 those aged 25 to 34 years had the highest death rate from firearm-related injuries, at 22.2 deaths per 100,000 population. Those aged 20 to 24 years

TABLE 6.4

Death rates for firearm-related injuries, by sex, race, Hispanic origin, and age, selected years 1970–2009 [CONTINUED]

[Data are based on death certificates]

Sex, race, Hispanic origin, and age	1970[a]	1980[a]	1990[a]	1995[a]	2000[b]	2005[b]	2008[b]	2009[b]
White male[d]								
All ages, age-adjusted[c]	19.7	22.1	22.0	20.1	15.9	15.7	15.9	15.8
All ages, crude	17.6	21.8	21.8	19.9	15.6	15.8	16.2	16.0
1–14 years	1.8	1.9	1.9	1.9	1.0	0.8	0.7	0.7
15–24 years	16.9	28.4	29.5	30.8	19.6	18.2	17.7	16.8
25–44 years	24.2	29.5	25.7	23.2	18.0	17.9	18.0	17.5
25–34 years	24.3	31.1	27.8	25.2	18.1	18.6	18.2	17.2
35–44 years	24.1	27.1	23.3	21.2	17.9	17.2	17.8	17.8
45–64 years	27.4	23.3	22.8	19.5	17.4	19.0	20.4	20.5
65 years and over	29.9	30.1	36.8	32.2	28.2	27.1	26.8	27.2
Black or African American male[d]								
All ages, age-adjusted[c]	70.8	60.1	56.3	49.2	34.2	36.4	34.4	32.1
All ages, crude	60.8	57.7	61.9	52.9	36.1	38.7	36.7	34.2
1–14 years	5.3	3.0	4.4	4.4	1.8	2.1	2.1	1.6
15–24 years	97.3	77.9	138.0	138.7	89.3	86.8	81.3	73.6
25–44 years	126.2	114.1	90.3	70.2	54.1	63.6	59.9	56.0
25–34 years	145.6	128.4	108.6	92.3	74.8	88.4	81.4	71.6
35–44 years	104.2	92.3	66.1	46.3	34.3	38.7	36.8	38.5
45–64 years	71.1	55.6	34.5	28.3	18.4	17.8	17.7	18.1
65 years and over	30.6	29.7	23.9	21.8	13.8	13.6	13.4	12.4
American Indian or Alaska Native male[d]								
All ages, age-adjusted[c]	—	24.0	19.4	19.4	13.1	15.7	13.3	13.5
All ages, crude	—	27.5	20.5	20.9	13.2	16.7	13.6	13.8
15–24 years	—	55.3	49.1	40.9	26.9	32.7	27.4	27.6
25–44 years	—	43.9	25.4	31.2	16.6	23.2	20.3	19.6
45–64 years	—	*	*	14.2	12.2	13.0	8.0	12.6
65 years and over	—	*	*	*	*	*	*	*
Asian or Pacific Islander male[d]								
All ages, age-adjusted[c]	—	7.8	8.8	9.2	6.0	5.3	4.5	4.7
All ages, crude	—	8.2	9.4	10.0	6.2	5.5	4.6	4.7
15–24 years	—	10.8	21.0	24.3	9.3	12.1	9.0	6.5
25–44 years	—	12.8	10.9	10.6	8.1	6.4	5.4	6.4
45–64 years	—	10.4	8.1	8.2	7.4	5.7	4.8	5.5
65 years and over	—	*	*	*	*	*	4.4	4.7
Hispanic or Latino male[d, e]								
All ages, age-adjusted[c]	—	—	27.6	23.8	13.6	13.3	11.8	11.5
All ages, crude	—	—	29.9	26.2	14.2	14.2	12.0	11.4
1–14 years	—	—	2.6	2.8	1.0	0.7	0.5	0.7
15–24 years	—	—	55.5	61.7	30.8	33.0	28.2	25.6
25–44 years	—	—	42.7	31.4	17.3	18.8	15.9	15.0
25–34 years	—	—	47.3	36.4	20.3	22.9	18.5	17.5
35–44 years	—	—	35.4	24.2	13.2	13.4	12.7	12.0
45–64 years	—	—	21.4	17.2	12.0	9.1	8.9	9.5
65 years and over	—	—	19.1	16.5	12.2	9.8	9.7	10.3
White, not Hispanic or Latino male[e]								
All ages, age-adjusted[c]	—	—	20.6	18.6	15.5	15.3	16.1	16.0
All ages, crude	—	—	20.4	18.5	15.7	15.9	17.0	16.9
1–14 years	—	—	1.6	1.6	1.0	0.8	0.7	0.7
15–24 years	—	—	24.1	23.5	16.2	13.9	14.5	13.8
25–44 years	—	—	23.3	21.4	17.9	17.4	18.5	18.0
25–34 years	—	—	24.7	22.5	17.2	16.9	17.9	16.7
35–44 years	—	—	21.6	20.4	18.4	17.8	19.0	19.2
45–64 years	—	—	22.7	19.5	17.8	20.0	21.8	21.9
65 years and over	—	—	37.4	32.5	29.0	28.2	28.1	28.4
White female[d]								
All ages, age-adjusted[c]	4.0	4.2	3.8	3.5	2.7	2.6	2.7	2.8
All ages, crude	3.7	4.1	3.8	3.5	2.7	2.6	2.7	2.8
15–24 years	3.4	5.1	4.8	4.5	2.8	2.3	2.3	2.4
25–44 years	6.9	6.2	5.3	4.9	3.9	3.7	3.7	3.8
45–64 years	5.0	5.1	4.5	4.0	3.5	3.6	4.0	4.2
65 years and over	2.2	2.5	3.1	2.8	2.4	2.3	2.2	2.5

had the second-highest rate of 20.3 deaths per 100,000 population. By 1980, however, these age groups had changed places, with 20- to 24-year-olds experiencing 26.4 deaths per 100,000 population because of firearm-related injuries. Those aged 25 to 34 years were in second place, with 24.3 deaths per 100,000 population. The death

TABLE 6.4

Death rates for firearm-related injuries, by sex, race, Hispanic origin, and age, selected years 1970–2009 [CONTINUED]

[Data are based on death certificates]

Sex, race, Hispanic origin, and age	1970[a]	1980[a]	1990[a]	1995[a]	2000[b]	2005[b]	2008[b]	2009[b]
Black or African American female[d]								
All ages, age-adjusted[c]	11.1	8.7	7.3	6.2	3.9	3.6	3.5	3.4
All ages, crude	10.0	8.8	7.8	6.5	4.0	3.7	3.6	3.5
15–24 years	15.2	12.3	13.3	13.2	7.6	6.7	8.2	6.9
25–44 years	19.4	16.1	12.4	9.8	6.5	6.0	5.4	5.8
45–64 years	10.2	8.2	4.8	4.1	3.1	2.7	2.1	2.4
65 years and over	4.3	3.1	3.1	2.6	1.3	1.3	1.3	*
American Indian or Alaska Native female[d]								
All ages, age-adjusted[c]	—	5.8	3.3	3.8	2.9	2.4	2.7	2.9
All ages, crude	—	5.8	3.4	4.1	2.9	2.6	2.7	2.9
15–24 years	—	*	*	*	*	*	*	*
25–44 years	—	10.2	*	7.0	5.5	*	4.2	4.4
45–64 years	—	*	*	*	*	*	*	*
65 years and over	—	*	*	*	*	*	*	*
Asian or Pacific Islander female[d]								
All ages, age-adjusted[c]	—	2.0	1.9	2.0	1.1	0.9	0.8	1.0
All ages, crude	—	2.1	2.1	2.1	1.2	0.9	0.9	1.0
15–24 years	—	*	*	3.9	*	2.3	*	*
25–44 years	—	3.2	2.7	2.7	1.5	1.0	1.2	1.2
45–64 years	—	*	*	*	*	*	*	1.3
65 years and over	—	*	*	*	*	*	*	*
Hispanic or Latina female[d, e]								
All ages, age-adjusted[c]	—	—	3.3	3.1	1.8	1.6	1.5	1.5
All ages, crude	—	—	3.6	3.3	1.8	1.6	1.5	1.4
15–24 years	—	—	6.9	6.1	2.9	2.6	2.9	2.8
25–44 years	—	—	5.1	4.7	2.5	2.7	2.0	2.0
45–64 years	—	—	2.4	2.4	2.2	1.2	1.7	1.5
65 years and over	—	—	*	*	*	*	*	*
White, not Hispanic or Latina female[e]								
All ages, age-adjusted[c]	—	—	3.7	3.4	2.8	2.7	2.9	3.0
All ages, crude	—	—	3.7	3.5	2.9	2.8	3.0	3.1
15–24 years	—	—	4.3	4.1	2.7	2.2	2.2	2.2
25–44 years	—	—	5.1	4.8	4.2	4.0	4.1	4.2
45–64 years	—	—	4.6	4.1	3.6	3.8	4.2	4.5
65 years and over	—	—	3.2	2.8	2.4	2.4	2.4	2.6

*Rates based on fewer than 20 deaths are considered unreliable and are not shown.
—Data not available.
[a]Underlying cause of death was coded according to the 8th Revision of the *International Classification of Diseases* (ICD) in 1970 and 9th Revision in 1980–1998.
[b]Starting with 1999 data, cause of death is coded according to ICD-10.
[c]Age-adjusted rates are calculated using the year 2000 standard population. Prior to 2003, age-adjusted rates were calculated using standard million proportions based on rounded population numbers. Starting with 2003 data, unrounded population numbers are used to calculate age-adjusted rates.
[d]The race groups, white, black, Asian or Pacific Islander, and American Indian or Alaska Native, include persons of Hispanic and non-Hispanic origin. Persons of Hispanic origin may be of any race. Death rates for the American Indian or Alaska Native, Asian or Pacific Islander, and Hispanic populations are known to be underestimated.
[e]Prior to 1997, excludes data from states lacking an Hispanic-origin item on the death certificate.
Notes: Starting with *Health, United States, 2003*, rates for 1991–1999 were revised using intercensal population estimates based on the 2000 census. Rates for 2000 were revised based on 2000 census counts. Rates for 2001 and later years were computed using 2000-based postcensal estimates. Age groups were selected to minimize the presentation of unstable age-specific death rates based on small numbers of deaths and for consistency among comparison groups.
Starting with 2003 data, some states allowed the reporting of more than one race on the death certificate.
The multiple-race data for these states were bridged to the single-race categories of the 1977 Office of Management and Budget standards, for comparability with other states.
Data for additional years are available.

SOURCE: "Table 40. Death Rates for Firearm-Related Injuries, by Sex, Race, Hispanic Origin, and Age: United States, Selected Years 1970–2009," in *Health, United States, 2011. With Special Feature on Socioeconomic Status and Health*, U.S. Department of Health and Human Services, Centers for Disease Control and Prevention, National Center for Health Statistics, 2012, http://www.cdc.gov/nchs/data/hus/2011/040.pdf (accessed August 26, 2012)

rates continued to rise for the 20- to 24-year-old group through 1995 when the rate reach 29.2 per 100,000, whereas the rates fell to 19.6 per 100,000 for the 25- to 34-year-old group during the same period, widening the gap between them. However, death rates fell dramatically for both groups in 2000 and stabilized through 2005 and then began to fall again. In 2009 the firearm injury rate for

20- to 24-year-olds was 17.8 per 100,000 population, and for the 25- to 34-year-old group it was 14.2.

Race

Table 6.4 also provides the firearm death rates for race. African-American males were the racial group with the highest rate of firearm deaths from 1970 to 2006.

TABLE 6.5

Fatal gunshot injuries and rates per 100,000, 1999–2009

Year	Deaths	Population	Age-adjusted rate
1999	28,874	279,040,181	10.30
2000	28,663	281,421,906	10.14
2001	29,573	285,081,556	10.31
2002	30,242	287,803,914	10.43
2003	30,136	290,326,418	10.28
2004	29,569	293,045,739	9.98
2005	30,694	295,753,151	10.26
2006	30,896	298,593,212	10.22
2007	31,224	301,579,895	10.23
2008	31,593	304,374,846	10.23
2009	31,347	307,006,550	10.05
Total	**332,811**		

Note: Standard population is 2,000, all races, both sexes.
Age adjusting: Some injuries occur more often among certain age groups than others. For instance, falls are more common among the elderly than among any other age group. Age adjustment enables you to compare injury rates without concern that differences are because of differences in the age distributions between different populations or for the same population over time.

SOURCE: "1999–2009, United States Firearm Deaths and Rates per 100,000, All Races, Both Sexes, All Ages," in *Web-Based Injury Statistics Query and Reporting System (WISQARS)*, U.S. Department of Health and Human Services, Centers for Disease Control and Prevention, National Center for Injury Prevention and Control, Office of Statistics and Programming, 2012, http://webappa.cdc.gov/sasweb/ncipc/mortrate10_us.html (accessed August 26, 2012)

African-American men aged 25 to 34 years experienced a death rate of 145.6 deaths per 100,000 population in 1970, which declined to 74.8 per 100,000 by 2000. This age group had the highest number of deaths from firearm-related injuries in 1970 and 1980. In 1990, however, a sharp rise in firearm-related deaths in the 15- to 24-year-old age group, to 138 per 100,000, surpassed the death rate of 108.6 per 100,000 for the 25- to 34-year-old age group. The death rates for both groups fell in 2000, and continued to fall in 2005 for those aged 15 to 24 years. For 25- to 34-year-olds, however, the rate of firearm deaths rose after 2000 to 88.4 per 100,000 in 2005, which was slightly higher than the rate for 15- to 24-year-olds at 86.8 per 100,000. In 2008 the rates for both age groups were nearly even at 81.3 per 100,000 for the younger group and 81.4 per 100,000 for the older. In 2009 the death rates for firearm-related injuries were 71.6 per 100,000 population for African-American males aged 25 to 34 years and 73.6 per 100,000 population for those aged 15 to 24 years.

Hispanic men in general experienced a dramatic decrease in firearm-related deaths from 1990 to 2000, with the rate then dropping slightly through 2009. (See Table 6.4.) Most dramatically, those aged 15 to 24 years had a death rate from firearm-related injuries of 55.5 per 100,000 population in 1990. This number rose to 61.7 per 100,000 in 1995 but dropped to 30.8 per 100,000 in 2000. By 2009 the rate dropped again, to 25.6 per 100,000. Equally dramatic was the decline in firearm-related deaths in the 25- to 34-year-old age group. In 1990 the

firearm-related death rate for this group was 47.3 per 100,000 population. In 2000 the rate declined to 20.3 per 100,000 population, rising slightly to 22.9 per 100,000 population in 2005, but then falling to 17.5 per 100,000 population in 2009.

Gender

Men are not only more likely than women to be the victims of gun homicides but also they are more likely to be the perpetrators of homicides committed with a gun. Figure 6.1 graphs cumulative data from 1980 to 2008. During this period 82.6% of U.S. gun homicide victims were male, whereas only 17.4% were female. Approximately 92.1% of U.S. gun homicide offenders were male, whereas only 7.9% were female.

Because there exists a gender difference in favor of males being the victims of gun homicides, firearm-related death rates are also higher for men than for women. Nevertheless, firearm-related death rates for both sexes have decreased over the past few decades. Table 6.4 shows that the age-adjusted death rate among males from firearm-related injuries fell from 24.8 per 100,000 population in 1970 to 18.1 per 100,000 population in 2000. In 2009 the rate was 17.7 deaths per 100,000 population. For women, the rate dropped from 4.8 deaths per 100,000 population in 1970 to 2.8 deaths per 100,000 population in 2000 and remained stable to 2009. In that year African-American females, as compared with other female race or ethnicity groups, had the highest death rate from firearm-related injuries (3.4 per 100,000 population). Asian or Pacific Islander females had the lowest rate at 1 death per 100,000 population.

THE COST OF FIREARM INJURIES

In "Medical Costs and Productivity Losses Due to Interpersonal and Self-Directed Violence in the United States" (*American Journal of Preventive Medicine*, vol. 32, no. 6, 2007), Phaedra S. Corso et al. state that the estimated total lifetime cost of firearm injuries due to assaults occurring in 2000 was about $17.4 billion—$822 million for medical treatment and $16.6 billion for lost work and household productivity. Costs were much higher for males than for females, with males accounting for 90% of the total costs. The estimated total lifetime cost of firearm injuries due to assaults occurring in 2000 for males was $15.7 billion—$734 million for medical treatment and $14.9 billion for lost productivity—and for females was $1.8 billion—$88 million for medical treatment and $1.7 billion for lost productivity.

Corso et al. also indicate that the estimated total lifetime cost of self-inflicted (suicide) firearm injuries occurring in 2000 was only about $1 billion less, at $16.4 billion—$124 million for medical treatment and $16.3 billion for lost productivity. Once again, costs were

TABLE 6.6

Unintentional firearm death counts and percentages by circumstances, 16 states, 2005–09

Circumstance	2005		2006		2007		2008		2009	
	Death counts	%	Death counts	%	Death counts	%	Death counts	%	Death counts	%
All persons with known circumstances	99	100	84	100	75	100	64	100	66	100
Hunting	21	21.2	11	13.1	19	25.3	8	12.5	18	27.3
Target shooting	*	*	*	*	*	*	*	*	*	*
Justifiable self-defense/law enforcement	0	0	0	0	0	0	0	0	0	0
Celebratory firing	*	*	0	0	0	0	*	*	0	0
Gun fired during loading/unloading	7	7.1	11	13.1	8	10.7	8	12.5	8	12.1
Cleaning gun	*	*	8	9.5	*	*	*	*	6	9.1
Showing gun to others	17	17.2	13	15.9	11	14.7	13	20.3	8	12.1
Playing with gun	33	33.3	29	34.5	23	30.7	25	39.1	20	30.3
Other context of injury	25	25.3	23	27.4	16	21.3	17	26.6	17	25.8
Thought safety was engaged	6	6.1	0	0	*	*	*	*	*	*
Thought unloaded magazine disengaged	*	*	9	10.7	10	13.3	7	10.9	*	*
Thought gun was unloaded-other	11	11.1	21	25	10	13.3	9	14.1	13	19.7
Unintentionally pulled trigger	20	20.2	16	19.1	16	21.3	16	25	8	12.1
Bullet ricochet	0	0	*	*	*	*	0	0	*	*
Gun defect or malfunction	*	*	*	*	*	*	*	*	*	*
Fired while holstering/unholstering	*	*	*	*	0	0	*	*	*	*
Dropped gun	12	12.1	9	10.7	*	*	*	*	*	*
Fired while operating safety/lock	0	0	*	*	0	0	0	0	*	*
Gun mistaken for toy	*	*	*	*	*	*	*	*	*	*
Other mechanism of injury	23	23.2	24	28.6	20	26.7	18	28.1	25	37.9

Note: Victims can have one or more circumstances; therefore, subcategories may not sum to all known circumstances.
*The number of deaths are 5 or fewer; the number has been suppressed to retain confidentiality.

SOURCE: Adapted from "2005–2009, 16 NVDRS States: AK, CO, GA, KY, MD, MA, NJ, NM, NC, OK, OR, RI, SC, UT, VA, WI Death Counts by Circumstances of Death, Abstracter Assigned Mode Unintentional Firearm Circumstances, Mechanism: Firearm All Races, Both Sexes, All Ages," in *Web-Based Injury Statistics Query and Reporting System (WISQARS)*, U.S. Department of Health and Human Services, Centers for Disease Control and Prevention, National Center for Injury Prevention and Control, Office of Statistics and Programming, 2012, http://www.cdc.gov/injury/wisqars/nvdrs.html (accessed August 27, 2012)

much higher for males than for females, with males accounting for 90% of the total costs. The estimated total lifetime cost of self-inflicted firearm injuries occurring in 2000 for males was $14.9 billion—$101 million for medical treatment and $14.8 billion for lost productivity— and for females was $1.6 billion—$23 million for medical treatment and $1.6 billion for lost productivity.

Notice that the proportion of the costs for medical treatment versus lost productivity was lower for the self-inflicted injuries than for the assault injuries. This difference is because the death rate for self-inflicted firearm injuries is higher than the death rate for firearm injuries due to assaults. Medical treatment costs are low with a high proportion of deaths, but costs due to lost productivity are very high. Corso et al. reveal that in 2000 the overall fatal rate for firearm injuries because of assault was 4 per 100,000 population, whereas the overall fatal rate for self-inflicted firearm injuries was 6 per 100,000 population. For men, the rates were 7 per 100,000 population when firearm injuries were inflicted during assaults and 11 per 100,000 population when self-inflicted. For women, the rates were 1 per 100,000 population and 2 per 100,000 population, respectively.

Concerning the cost in terms of years of life expectancy lost because of gunshot injuries to the brain and spinal cord, Therese S. Richmond and Jean Lemaire

determine in "Years of Life Lost Because of Gunshot Injury to the Brain and Spinal Cord" (*American Journal of Physical Medicine and Rehabilitation*, vol. 87, no. 8, August 2008) that the overall "life expectancy in the United States is reduced by 3.1 days because of the shorter lifespan for individuals who survive an initial gunshot wound to the brain or spinal cord." The researchers added these data to a previous study that Lemaire conducted on the loss of days of life expectancy because of the shorter lifespan for individuals who died immediately from gunshot wounds. Calculations revealed that the U.S. life expectancy is reduced by 106.7 days due to gunshot wounds. In addition, the researchers find that African-American males lost over three times as many days of life expectancy (371 days) than did the general population (106.7 days).

In 2012 the CDC released cost of injury reports for firearm-related deaths and injuries in 2005 in its Web-Based Injury Statistics Query and Reporting System ([WISQARS] May 2012, http://wisqars.cdc.gov:8080/ costT/). The estimates, expressed in 2005 dollars, were produced with data from the National Center for Health Statistics and the U.S. Consumer Product Safety Commission, and with cost estimates from the Pacific Institute for Research and Evaluation. The CDC estimates that for the 30,179 nonfatal firearm injuries for which the victim was treated in a hospital emergency room and released in

FIGURE 6.1

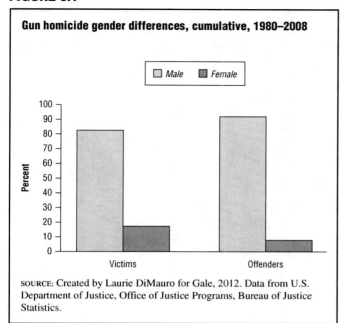

Gun homicide gender differences, cumulative, 1980–2008

SOURCE: Created by Laurie DiMauro for Gale, 2012. Data from U.S. Department of Justice, Office of Justice Programs, Bureau of Justice Statistics.

2005, the total costs were about $111.9 million, with the average medical bill estimated at $931 and lost work time averaging a loss of $2,775 per victim. For the 38,844 gunshot injuries in 2005 that resulted in a hospital stay for the victim, the average medical cost rose to $14,716 and lost work time amounted to an average $79,615; the CDC estimates the total cost of firearm injuries that resulted in the hospitalization of the victim in 2005 to be $3.7 billion. For the 30,694 firearm-related fatal injuries in 2005, the CDC estimates the medical costs averaged $3,676 per victim and totaled more than $112.8 million overall. When costs associated with $1.2 million in average lifetime lost work for each victim were added, the overall cost for firearm fatalities surpassed $37 billion in 2005.

GUNS AND SELF-DEFENSE

It is impossible to determine accurately how many times each year guns are used for self-defense, but there are estimates. As of 2012, the following four studies were the most up to date. Studies on guns and self-defense are relatively rare in the literature, possibly because such incidents are difficult to document and rely on self-reported data during a stressful time. Such data are often considered unreliable. Gary Kleck and Don Kates address these and other research design methodology issues in detail in one of the most cited examinations of this topic, *Armed: New Perspectives on Gun Control* (2001).

Kleck and Kates use data from their National Self-Defense Survey (NSDS), the first survey conducted solely on armed self-defense. The researchers suggest that this survey yielded highly reliable data because of its careful design and wide scope, which involved nearly 5,000 completed interviews spanning all states in the continental United States. Kleck and Kates contend that surveys conducted previous to the NSDS yielded less reliable data because of design flaws and a much smaller scope. The researchers calculate that guns in general are used in self-defense about 2.2 million to 2.5 million times per year and that between 1.5 million and 1.9 million of those self-defense cases involve handguns.

Deborah Azael and David Hemenway surveyed 1,906 adults across the United States to determine whether individuals had been threatened or intimidated with a gun at home or had used a gun in self-defense at home. They indicate in "'In the Safety of Your Own Home': Results from a National Survey on Gun Use at Home" (*Social Science and Medicine*, vol. 50, no. 2, January 2000) that 5% of the respondents reported having a gun displayed against them in the home within five years before the survey. Less than 1% reported using a gun in self-defense in the home during that same period. After analyzing the complete data, Azael and Hemenway conclude that "in the home, hostile gun displays against family members may be more common than gun use in self-defense, and that hostile gun displays are often acts of domestic violence directed against women."

Craig Perkins of the Bureau of Justice Statistics reports in "Weapon Use and Violent Crime" (September 2003, http://bjs.ojp.usdoj.gov/content/pub/pdf/wuvc01.pdf) that in 2003 well over half (60.5%) of victims of violent crime reported taking self-defensive measures during an assault. Most victims used non-aggressive means, such as getting help or trying to escape. Thirteen percent of victims tried to threaten or attack their offender—0.7% of these victims used a gun to ward off their attacker.

David Hemenway and Matthew Miller surveyed approximately 5,800 California adolescents aged 12 to 17 years to determine the prevalence of gun threats versus the use of guns for self-defense among them. In "Gun Threats against and Self-Defense Gun Use by California Adolescents" (*Archives of Pediatric Adolescent Medicine*, vol. 158, no. 4, April 2004), they state that about 4% of those surveyed reported ever being threatened with a gun. Only 0.3% reported ever using a gun in self-defense. Hemenway and Miller conclude that self-defense gun use in adolescents is rare.

SAFE STORAGE OF GUNS IN THE HOME

If a gun is to be used for self-defense, does it make sense to keep it unloaded and locked up? This is a question asked by people who oppose safe-storage laws and laws that hold gun owners criminally liable for any injury caused by a child gaining unsupervised access to a gun. The Law Center to Prevent Gun Violence notes in *Child Access Prevention*

Policy Summary (May 21, 2012, http://smartgunlaws.org/child-access-prevention-policy-summary/) that most states and the District of Columbia had child access prevention (CAP) laws. The Law Center to Prevent Gun Violence reports that as of 2012 the following states did not specifically regulate minors' access to guns: Alabama, Alaska, Kansas, Louisiana, New Mexico, New York, Ohio, Oregon, Pennsylvania, South Carolina, Vermont, Washington, and Wyoming. Gun control advocates are pressing for such legislation at the federal level.

Lisa Hepburn et al. conclude in "The Effect of Child Access Prevention Laws on Unintentional Child Firearm Fatalities, 1979–2000" (*Journal of Trauma Injury, Infection, and Critical Care*, vol. 61, no. 2, August 2006) that CAP laws may have influenced the continued reduction in unintentional firearm death rates that occurred from 1979 to 2000 nationally among children. The researchers determine that "the decrease in rates of unintentional firearm deaths for children aged 0 to 14 in CAP law states exceeded the average for states without CAP laws in 9 of the 14 states for which data were available." According to Hepburn et al., statistical analyses of the data "showed a significant association between CAP laws and rates of unintentional firearm deaths for children 0 to 14 years old."

Some argue that if society chooses to hold people accountable for negligent actions or child endangerment, it should do so with all such actions and not single out firearms. The category "Accidents (unintentional injuries)" (primarily from motor vehicle accidents, drowning, fires and burns, firearms, suffocation, falls, and traffic accidents) was the leading cause of death among 15- to 24-year-olds from 1999 to 2009. (See Table 6.7.) According to Kenneth D. Kochanek, et al. of the CDC, in "Deaths: Final Data for 2010" (*National Vital Statistics Reports*, vol. 60, no. 3, December 29, 2011), unintentional injuries were also the leading cause of death for children under the age of 15 during this same period.

CAP laws are intended not only to protect children from unintentional injury from firearms but also from gaining access to firearms to commit suicide. Table 6.7 shows that intentional self-harm (suicide) was the third-leading cause of death from 1999 to 2009 for those aged 15 to 24 years. Suicide was the fourth-leading cause of death for children aged 5 to 14 years, after accidents, cancer, and homicide, respectively. Jeffrey A. Bridge et al. report in "Changes in Suicide Rates by Hanging and/or Suffocation and Firearms among Young Persons Aged 10–24 Years in the United States: 1992–2006" (*Journal of Adolescent Health*, vol. 46, no. 5, May 2010) that from 1992 to 2006 youth suicides committed with firearms decreased; the researchers, however, do not know if the decrease was due to CAP laws. They note that suicide by poisoning and other methods declined as well in this age

TABLE 6.7

Leading causes of death for 15-to-24-year-olds, 1999–2009

[Rates on an annual basis per 100,000 population in specified group; age-adjusted rates are per 100,000 U.S. standard population. Rates are based on populations enumerated as of April 1 for 2000 and estimated as of July 1 for all other years.]

Cause of death and year	Age 15–24 years
Accidents (unintentional injuries)	
2009	28.9
2008	33.1
2007	37.4
2006	38.2
2005	37.4
2004	37.0
2003	37.1
2002	38.0
2001	36.1
2000	36.0
1999	25.3
Assault (homicide)	
2009	11.3
2008	12.4
2007	13.1
2006	13.5
2005	13.0
2004	12.2
2003	13.0
2002	12.9
2001*	13.3
2000	12.6
1999	12.9
Intentional self-harm (suicide)	
2009	10.1
2008	10.1
2007	9.7
2006	9.9
2005	10.0
2004	10.3
2003	9.7
2002	9.9
2001	9.9
2000	10.2
1999	10.1
Malignant neoplasms	
2009	3.8
2008	3.9
2007	3.9
2006	3.9
2005	4.1
2004	4.1
2003	4.0
2002	4.3
2001	4.3
2000	4.4
1999	4.5
Disease of heart	
2009	2.4
2008	2.5
2007	2.6
2006	2.5
2005	2.7
2004	2.5
2003	2.7
2002	2.5
2001	2.5
2000	2.6
1999	2.8

group and that suicide by hanging and suffocation increased concurrently. These data suggest to Bridge et al. a selection of suffocation and hanging rather than a thwarting of other methods. The researchers indicate

*Figures include September 11, 2001 related deaths for which death certificates were filed as of October 24, 2002.

SOURCE: Adapted from Kenneth D. Kochanek et al., "Table 9. Death Rates by Age and Age-Adjusted Death Rates for the 15 Leading Causes of Death in 2009: United States, 1999–2009," in "Deaths: Final Data for 2009," *National Vital Statistics Reports*, vol. 60, no. 3, December 29, 2011, http://www.cdc.gov/nchs/data/nvsr60/nvsr60_03.pdf (accessed August 27, 2012)

that hanging and suffocation were the leading methods of suicide among youth in many countries, such as England, Australia, and New Zealand, and recommend that future research investigate the reasons for this preference so that public health programs might be developed to curb this method of suicide.

Safety Programs to Protect Young Children

In 1988 the National Rifle Association of America (NRA) created the Eddie Eagle GunSafe Program (http://www.nrahq.org/safety/eddie/) for gun safety. Eddie Eagle is a school-based program that teaches gun safety to young children (preschool to third grade). With the help of the cartoon character Eddie the Eagle, kids are taught that when they find a gun they should not touch it, but instead leave the area and tell an adult. The Violence Policy Center contends in "Joe Camel with Feathers: How the NRA with Gun and Tobacco Industry Dollars Uses Its Eddie Eagle Program to Market Guns to Kids" (November 1997, http://www.vpc.org/studies/eddiecon.htm) that the program is a marketing tool for the NRA: "The Eddie Eagle program employs strategies similar to those utilized by America's tobacco industry—from youth 'educational' programs that are in fact marketing tools to the use of appealing cartoon characters that aim to put a friendly face on a hazardous product. The hoped-for result is new customers for the industry and new members for the NRA." The Violence Policy Center's study was conducted with the Global Survival network and was the most detailed study on the program as of 2012.

According to Brian J. Gatheridge et al., in "Comparison of Two Programs to Teach Firearm Injury Prevention Skills to 6- and 7-Year-Old Children" (*Pediatrics*, vol. 114, no. 3, September 2004), the Eddie Eagle GunSafe Program is effective in teaching young children to verbalize the safety skills message. The researchers, however, conclude that children who received behavior skills training (programs that incorporate active learning approaches such as modeling, rehearsal, and feedback) are more likely to exhibit the desired safety skills around guns.

In "Peer Tutoring to Prevent Firearm Play: Acquisition, Generalization, and Long-Term Maintenance of Safety Skills" (*Journal of Applied Behavior Analysis*,

vol. 41, no. 1, 2008), Candace M. Jostad et al. of North Dakota State University support the behavioral skills training approach and show that six- and seven-year-old children acquire and maintain firearm safety skills when behavioral skills training is used and is taught by other children trained in the techniques.

NATIONAL GOALS: *HEALTHY PEOPLE 2020*

Released in December 2010, *Healthy People 2020* (http://www.healthypeople.gov/) is a set of national health objectives developed under the leadership of a variety of U.S. governmental agencies, such as the CDC, the Health Resources and Services Administration, the President's Council on Sports, Fitness, and Nutrition, and the U.S. Food and Drug Administration. This national health initiative builds on previous programs that began with *Healthy People: The Surgeon General's Report on Health Promotion and Disease Prevention* (1979, http://profiles.nlm.nih.gov/NN/B/B/G/K/) and have been updated and reassessed in each decade since. *Healthy People 2020* replaces the previous initiative, *Healthy People 2010* (January 2000, http://www.cdc.gov/nchs/healthy_people/hp2000.htm).

The *Healthy People 2020* objectives with regard to firearms are included in the section outlining Injury and Violence Prevention (IVP) goals:

• IVP-30: To reduce the rate of firearm-related deaths 10%, from 10.2 firearm-related deaths per 100,000 population in 2007 to 9.2 deaths per 100,000 population in 2020

• IVP-31: To reduce the rate of nonfatal firearm-related injuries by 10%, from 20.7 nonfatal firearm-related injuries per 100,000 population in 2007 to 18.6 injuries per 100,000 population in 2020

The CDC provides monitoring data on each of the *Healthy People 2020* goals on the website Health Indicators Warehouse (http://healthindicators.gov/). As of October 2012, the data for IVP-30 showed progress toward the goal, with firearm-related deaths declining from 10.2 per 100,000 population in 2007 to 10.1 in 2009. The data for IVP-31 had not been updated from the 2007 rates that served as a starting point for the initiative, but some progress toward lowering the firearm injury rate could be seen by comparing the 2020 objective with a similar goal in the previous program. The beginning point for nonfatal firearm-related injuries (20.7 per 100,000 population in 2007) in *Healthy People 2020* IVP-31 was lower than the baseline rate of 24 injuries per 100,000 population in 1997 used in *Healthy People 2010*.

Although setting forth national objectives, the *Healthy People 2020* program depends on state and local entities for implementation, offering tools for the development of plans to foster improvement. Each objective area on the Healthy People website includes a link to community interventions and program models. In response to the goals outlined in *Healthy People 2010*, for example, the state of Washington developed its own strategies to address specific areas of concern related to firearm deaths and injuries in that state. In *Firearm-Related Injury* (June 2008, http://www.doh.wa.gov/por tals/1/Documents/2900/DOH530090Firear.pdf), the state Department of Health advised developing a multifaceted approach to preventing firearm deaths and injuries by implementing a combination of public awareness campaigns and community-based coalitions to reduce access to firearms, improve firearm safety, and augment data collection related to firearm injuries.

CHAPTER 7

GUNS AND YOUTH

During the 1980s and 1990s young people in the United States began to resolve disputes more and more often with guns. Youth gangs and school shootings dominated news headlines. During the first decade of the 21st century school security became a major issue in American culture as weapons in schools were viewed as commonplace, and parents wondered if any school was safe.

DEADLY ASSAULTS

In *Homicide Trends in the United States, 1980–2008* (November 2011, http://bjs.ojp.usdoj.gov/content/pub/pdf/htus8008.pdf), Alexia Cooper and Erica L. Smith of the Bureau of Justice Statistics (BJS) attribute the increase in homicides during the late 1980s and early 1990s and the subsequent decline to gun violence among teenagers and young adults; homicide victimization rates for teens (aged 14 to 17) peaked in 1993 at 12 homicides per 100,000 and declined after that time to 5.1 homicides per 100,000 in 2008. Similarly, homicide offending reached a high of 30.7 teen offenders per 100,000 in that age group in 1993; since 2000 the rate of homicide offenders among teenagers has remained relatively stable at a level similar to that which occurred in 1985 (9.5 per 100,000).

Figure 7.1 shows homicide trends over the period 1980 to 2008 by victim/offender relationship and weapon use. The rise in gun-related homicides from 1984 to 1994 is evident in homicides by friends and acquaintances and is even more pronounced in homicides by strangers. Gun violence among family members and those in intimate relationships showed a gradual decline during the 1980s and 1990s; among family members, other weapons (a category that includes knives, sharp instruments, and blunt objects as well as personal weapons such as hands and feet) overtook guns as the most likely type of weapon to be used in a homicide.

Table 7.1 presents the number and rate of firearm deaths for those aged 19 and under in 2009. The highest victimization rate occurred among male teenagers aged 15 to 19 years at 19.85 firearm deaths per 100,000 population; females in this same age group (2.50 per 100,000) registered the highest rate among girls. The lowest rates of firearm deaths among both males and females was experienced in 2009 by those aged 5 to 9 years, with boys having a victimization rate of 0.39 per 100,000 and girls even lower (0.25 per 100,000).

Youthful Offenders

Figure 7.2 shows trends in homicide offenders by age group from 1980 to 2008. Some main themes emerge from the three graphs: homicides involving weapons other than guns declined slightly for all age groups during this period, with few significant increases or decreases from year to year; the same general pattern held true for gun homicides committed by offenders age 25 or older. Gun homicides committed by teens and adults aged 14 to 24, however, increased dramatically during the late 1980s, peaked in the early 1990s, and then declined.

The U.S. courts define a juvenile as a person under the age of 18, unless he or she is to be tried as an adult. Figure 7.3 shows the number of juveniles who committed homicide with and without guns from 1980 to 2010. The graph shows a dramatic rise in the number of juveniles who committed homicide with a gun beginning in 1984 and peaking in 1994. In *Juvenile Offenders and Victims: 2006 National Report* (March 2006, http://ojjdp.ncjrs.org/ojstatbb/nr2006/downloads/NR2006.pdf), Howard N. Snyder and Melissa Sickmund of the National Center for Juvenile Justice provide an explanation for the 1984 to 1994 rise. According to the researchers, 90% of the overall increase occurred with males killing nonfamily members with guns, usually handguns. Snyder and Sickmund state, "This type of murder increased 400% between 1984 and 1994. A closer look at these crimes reveals that the increase was somewhat greater for murders of acquaintances than strangers and somewhat greater for juveniles acting with other

FIGURE 7.1

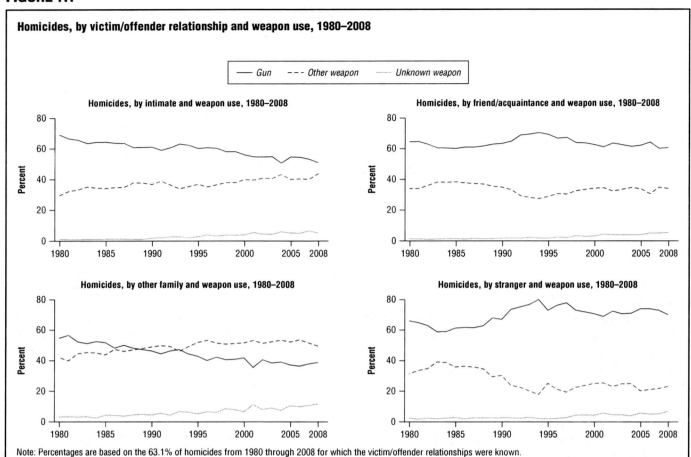

Homicides, by victim/offender relationship and weapon use, 1980–2008

— Gun   – – – Other weapon   ······· Unknown weapon

Homicides, by intimate and weapon use, 1980–2008

Homicides, by friend/acquaintance and weapon use, 1980–2008

Homicides, by other family and weapon use, 1980–2008

Homicides, by stranger and weapon use, 1980–2008

Note: Percentages are based on the 63.1% of homicides from 1980 through 2008 for which the victim/offender relationships were known.

SOURCE: Adapted from Alexia Cooper and Erica L. Smith, "Figure 25a. Homicides, by Intimate and Weapon Use, 1980–2008," "Figure 25b. Homicides, by Other Family and Weapon Use, 1980–2008," "Figure 25c. Homicides, by Friend/Acquaintance and Weapon Use, 1980–2008," and " Figure 25d. Homicides, by Stranger and Weapon Use, 1980–2008," in *Homicide Trends in the United States, 1980–2008*, U.S. Department of Justice, Office of Justice Programs, Bureau of Justice Statistics, November 2011, http://bjs.ojp.usdoj.gov/content/pub/pdf/htus8008.pdf (accessed August 28, 2012)

TABLE 7.1

Numbers and rates per 100,000 of firearm deaths for persons aged 0–19 by sex, 2009

Age group	Sex	Number of deaths	Population	Rate
0–4 yrs	Both	86	21,299,656	0.40
	Males	50	10,887,008	0.46
	Females	36	10,412,648	0.35
5–9 yrs	Both	66	20,609,634	0.32
	Males	41	10,535,900	0.39
	Females	25	10,073,734	0.25
10–14 yrs	Both	203	19,973,564	1.02
	Males	166	10,222,522	1.62
	Females	37	9,751,042	0.38
15–19 yrs	Both	2,456	21,537,837	11.40
	Males	2,194	11,051,289	19.85
	Females	262	10,486,548	2.50

SOURCE: Adapted from "2009, United States Firearm Deaths and Rates per 100,000, All Races, Both Sexes, Ages 0 to 19," in *Web-Based Injury Statistics Query and Reporting System (WISQARS)*, U.S. Department of Health and Human Services, Centers for Disease Control and Prevention, National Center for Injury Prevention and Control, Office of Statistics and Programming, 2012, http://webappa.cdc.gov/sasweb/ncipc/mortrate10_us .html (accessed August 27, 2012)

offenders than for a juvenile offender acting alone. Nearly three-quarters of the increase was the result of crimes committed by black and other minority males—and in two-thirds of these murders, the victims were minority males." Interestingly, the number of juveniles who committed murder with a gun declined from 1994 to 2002 as dramatically as it had risen between 1984 and 1994.

Why did gun-related homicides rise from 1984 to 1994? The Virginia Youth Violence Project at the University of Virginia's Curry School of Education suggests in "Juvenile Homicide" (2010) that violent juvenile crime during that time was linked to many factors, including the introduction of crack cocaine, the availability of cheap handguns, inadequate after-school supervision, and the prevalence of violence in the media. Reasons for the subsequent fall include increases in the number of police, the receding crack epidemic, and the legalization of abortion two decades earlier, which resulted in fewer children at risk for violence. (See Chapter 5 for a discussion of these factors.)

FIGURE 7.2

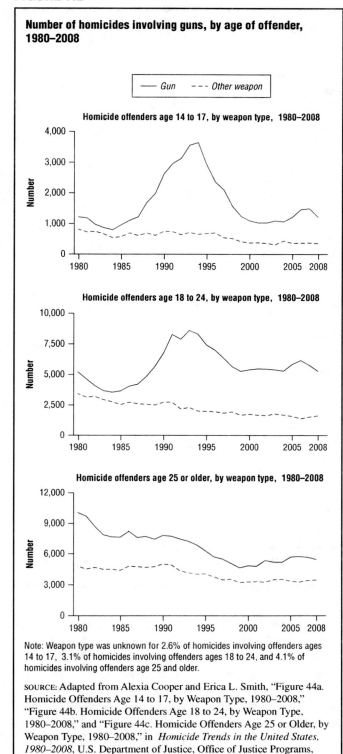

Number of homicides involving guns, by age of offender, 1980–2008

Homicide offenders age 14 to 17, by weapon type, 1980–2008

Homicide offenders age 18 to 24, by weapon type, 1980–2008

Homicide offenders age 25 or older, by weapon type, 1980–2008

Note: Weapon type was unknown for 2.6% of homicides involving offenders ages 14 to 17, 3.1% of homicides involving offenders ages 18 to 24, and 4.1% of homicides involving offenders age 25 and older.

SOURCE: Adapted from Alexia Cooper and Erica L. Smith, "Figure 44a. Homicide Offenders Age 14 to 17, by Weapon Type, 1980–2008," "Figure 44b. Homicide Offenders Age 18 to 24, by Weapon Type, 1980–2008," and "Figure 44c. Homicide Offenders Age 25 or Older, by Weapon Type, 1980–2008," in *Homicide Trends in the United States, 1980–2008*, U.S. Department of Justice, Office of Justice Programs, Bureau of Justice Statistics, November 2011, http://bjs.ojp.usdoj.gov/content/pub/pdf/htus8008.pdf (accessed August 28, 2012).

However, gun-related homicides began to rise again somewhat during the first decade of the 21st century. Why did this increase occur? Kevin Johnson reports in "Police Tie Jump in Crime to Juveniles" (*USA Today*, July 13, 2006) that officials from a variety of cities

FIGURE 7.3

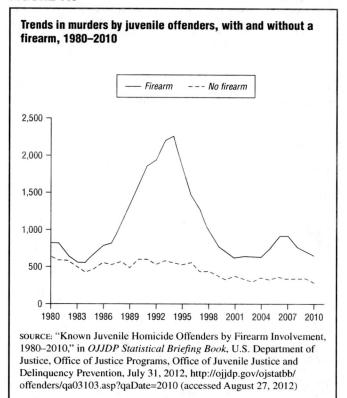

Trends in murders by juvenile offenders, with and without a firearm, 1980–2010

SOURCE: "Known Juvenile Homicide Offenders by Firearm Involvement, 1980–2010," in *OJJDP Statistical Briefing Book*, U.S. Department of Justice, Office of Justice Programs, Office of Juvenile Justice and Delinquency Prevention, July 31, 2012, http://ojjdp.gov/ojstatbb/offenders/qa03103.asp?qaDate=2010 (accessed August 27, 2012).

suggest that funding for police and community programs shifted to the War on Terror following the September 11, 2001, terrorist attacks against the United States. Thus, programs and police that worked to help thwart juvenile violent crime before September 2001 were no longer in place. In addition, gang leaders who were imprisoned during the early 1990s were being released. Following their release, they oftentimes returned to their old neighborhoods to reclaim turf and had young recruits carry weapons for them. This approach helped protect older gang members from weapons violations and a return to prison, but disputes among young gun-carrying gang members often resulted in firearm injuries and deaths.

JUVENILE ARRESTS SINCE 2000. Table 7.2 shows the estimated number of juvenile arrests in 2009 and the percent change in juvenile arrests over various time spans. Juvenile crime fell 17% overall from 2000 to 2009, and violent crime perpetrated by juveniles decreased by 13%. In particular, weapons-carrying arrests decreased by 7%; among teens under age 18 who were arrested for weapons offenses, 10% were female, 31% were younger than age 15, and 61% were white.

By 2009, however, the severe economic recession that was being experienced in the United States was also adding to an increase in the crime rate. In "U.S. Recession Fuels Crime Rise, Police Chiefs Say" (Reuters, January 27, 2009), Ross Colvin notes that the results of a survey conducted by the Police Executive Research Forum (PERF),

TABLE 7.2

Juvenile arrests, 2009, and percentage change, 2000–09

The number of arrests of juveniles in 2009 was 17% fewer than the number of arrests in 2000

Most serious offense	2009 estimated number of juvenile arrests	Percent of total juvenile arrests			Percent change		
		Female	Younger than 15	White	2000–2009	2005–2009	2008–2009
Total	1,906,600	30%	27%	66%	−17%	−11%	−9%
Violent crime index	85,890	18	26	47	−13	−10	−10
Murder and nonnegligent manslaughter	1,170	7	9	40	0	−7	−7
Forcible rape	3,100	2	32	65	−30	−22	−6
Robbery	31,700	10	18	31	15	9	−10
Aggravated assault	49,900	25	30	56	−24	−19	−11
Property crime index	417,700	38	28	64	−19	0	−4
Burglary	74,800	11	27	61	−21	−4	−10
Larceny-theft	317,700	45	28	65	−12	8	−1
Motor vehicle theft	19,900	17	20	54	−61	−47	−20
Arson	5,300	13	59	77	−37	−33	−17
Nonindex							
Other assaults	219,700	34	37	59	−6	−12	−5
Forgery and counterfeiting	2,100	30	13	67	−66	−49	−17
Fraud	6,200	35	17	62	−62	−21	−15
Embezzlement	600	42	7	64	−68	−47	−52
Stolen property (buying, receiving, possessing)	18,700	19	22	55	−28	−16	−10
Vandalism	90,500	14	39	79	−20	−13	−15
Weapons (carrying, possessing, etc.)	33,900	10	31	61	−7	−25	−15
Prostitution and commercialized vice	1,400	78	12	40	−4	−16	−8
Sex offense (except forcible rape and prostitution)	13,400	11	48	71	−23	−21	−7
Drug abuse violations	170,300	16	16	72	−14	−12	−5
Gambling	1,800	3	11	7	67	−13	9
Offenses against the family and children	4,500	36	28	74	−49	−21	−22
Driving under the influence	13,500	25	2	92	−37	−25	−15
Liquor laws	110,300	39	9	89	−15	−11	−15
Drunkenness	13,800	25	12	88	−37	−13	−11
Disorderly conduct	170,100	33	36	57	6	−17	−10
Vagrancy	2,700	28	24	72	−24	−29	−32
All other offenses (except traffic)	323,300	26	23	69	−17	−12	−10
Suspicion (not included in totals)	200	22	27	42	−82	−61	−20
Curfew and loitering	112,600	31	25	61	−27	−20	−15
Runaways	93,400	55	31	65	−34	−14	−14

Note: Detail may not add to totals because of rounding.

SOURCE: Charles Puzzanchera and Benjamin Adams, "The Number of Arrests of Juveniles in 2009 Was 17% Fewer Than the Number of Arrests in 2000," in *Juvenile Arrests 2009*, U.S. Department of Justice, Office of Justice Programs, Office of Juvenile Justice and Delinquency Prevention, December 2011, http://www.ojjdp.gov/pubs/236477.pdf (accessed August 27, 2012)

a law enforcement organization based in Washington, D.C., showed that 44% of police agencies surveyed attributed the rise in certain types of crime, such as robberies, burglaries, and thefts from vehicles, to the recession. In addition, 63% of police departments surveyed anticipated cuts in their funding, which would impede crime-fighting programs and reduce staffing funds. According to Colvin, Chuck Wexler, the executive director of the PERF, suggested that the survey results were "a wake-up call." Wexler, as well as criminologists, sociologists, and police chiefs interviewed by Colvin, expected that the overall crime rate would likely increase as the economic conditions worsened.

RACE AND GENDER. Young males, especially young African-American males, are involved in homicides as offenders out of proportion to their share of the population, which remained slightly over 1% from 1980 to 2008. (See Figure 7.4.) In addition, the proportion of homicide offenders in the African-American population of youth aged 14 to 24 years increased dramatically from 1985 to 1993. African-American males aged 14 to 24 years accounted for about 17% of all homicide offenders in 1985, compared with 34.6% of all homicide offenders in 1993. The proportion of young African-American males who were homicide offenders declined after 1993, reaching a low of 25.7% in 2002 before moving upward again after that time; in 2008 African-American males aged 14 to 24 comprised about 27% of homicide offenders.

The percentage of the population represented by white males aged 14 to 24 years declined from 9% in 1980 to 6% in 2008. (See Figure 7.4.) However, the proportion of homicide offenders among this group remained somewhat stable. White males aged 14 to 24 years represented between 15% and 20% of homicide offenders during the 28 years shown in Figure 7.4. Peaks in offending rates occurred in

FIGURE 7.4

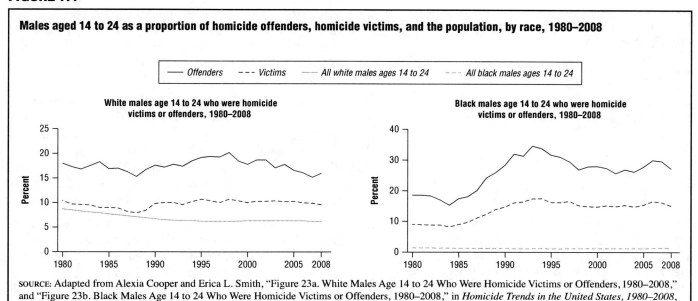

Males aged 14 to 24 as a proportion of homicide offenders, homicide victims, and the population, by race, 1980–2008

SOURCE: Adapted from Alexia Cooper and Erica L. Smith, "Figure 23a. White Males Age 14 to 24 Who Were Homicide Victims or Offenders, 1980–2008," and "Figure 23b. Black Males Age 14 to 24 Who Were Homicide Victims or Offenders, 1980–2008," in *Homicide Trends in the United States, 1980–2008*, U.S. Department of Justice, Office of Justice Programs, Bureau of Justice Statistics, November 2011, http://bjs.ojp.usdoj.gov/content/pub/pdf/htus8008.pdf (accessed August 28, 2012)

1984 at 18.3% and in 1998 at 20.1%; white males aged 14 to 24 years comprised 16% of homicide offenders in 2008.

Youthful Victims

Young people are often the targets of youth violent crimes. In "Age 14 Starts a Child's Increased Risk of Major Knife or Gun Injury in Washington, D.C." (*Journal of the National Medical Association*, vol. 96, no. 2, February 2004), Howard A. Freed et al. analyze trauma registry data at an inner-city trauma center over a period of eight years. The researchers find that the risk of a youth becoming a victim of a major gunshot wound or stabbing rose dramatically at age 14 and that this risk continued to rise sharply through age 18.

Figure 7.5 shows that between 1980 and 2008 more than three-quarters of homicide victims aged 16 to 22 years were killed with guns, with 17 years being the peak age for homicide by firearm (79% of 17-year-old homicide victims were killed with a gun). For purposes of comparison, note that less than half of homicide victims aged 63 years and older or aged 11 years and younger were killed with guns during the same period.

Young children are less frequently victims of gun violence than older children. Table 7.3 shows that the number of homicide firearm deaths of children aged 12 years and younger increased from 160 in 1999 to 175 in 2002 and then dropped to 121 in 2004 and 125 in 2005. The rate of homicide firearm deaths per 100,000 children aged 12 years and younger dropped from 0.31 per 100,000 in 1999 to a low of 0.23 per 100,000 in 2004. However, a dramatic increase occurred in 2006, raising both the number and the rate of homicide firearm deaths in children 12 years and younger

FIGURE 7.5

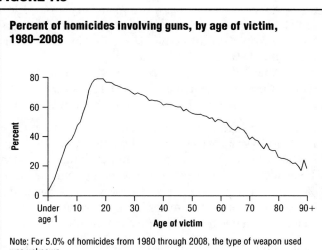

Percent of homicides involving guns, by age of victim, 1980–2008

Note: For 5.0% of homicides from 1980 through 2008, the type of weapon used was unknown.

SOURCE: Alexia Cooper and Erica L. Smith, "Figure 43. Homicides Involving Guns, by Age of Victim, 1980–2008," in *Homicide Trends in the United States, 1980–2008*, U.S. Department of Justice, Office of Justice Programs, Bureau of Justice Statistics, November 2011, http://bjs.ojp.usdoj.gov/content/pub/pdf/htus8008.pdf (accessed August 28, 2012)

back to the 1999 levels of 160 deaths and a rate of 0.30 per 100,000; thereafter, the number and rate of child firearm deaths remained steady, with 157 firearm homicides of children under age 12 in 2009 and a rate of 0.29 per 100,000 population.

RACE AND GENDER. Young males, especially young African-American males, are involved in homicides as victims out of proportion to their share in the population,

TABLE 7.3

Number and rate of homicide firearm deaths of children 12 and under, 1999–2009

Year	Deaths	Population	Rate
1999	160	51,936,751	0.31
2000	132	52,190,294	0.25
2001	166	52,416,972	0.32
2002	175	52,466,721	0.33
2003	146	52,354,607	0.28
2004	121	52,345,092	0.23
2005	126	52,407,866	0.24
2006	160	52,593,074	0.30
2007	156	52,993,768	0.29
2008	161	53,364,848	0.30
2009	157	53,753,412	0.29
Total	**1,660**		

SOURCE: "1999–2009, United States, Homicide Firearm Deaths and Rates per 100,000, All Races, Both Sexes, Ages 0 to 12," in *Web-Based Injury Statistics Query and Reporting System (WISQARS)*, U.S. Department of Health and Human Services, Centers for Disease Control and Prevention, National Center for Injury Prevention and Control, Office of Statistics and Programming, 2011, http://webappa.cdc.gov/sasweb/ncipc/mortrate10_us .html (accessed August 26, 2012)

which remained slightly over 1% from 1980 to 2008. (See Figure 7.4.) In addition, the proportion of homicide victims in the African-American population of youth aged 14 to 24 years increased dramatically from 1984 to 1994. African-American males aged 14 to 24 years accounted for 9% of all homicide victims in 1980, compared with 18% in 1994. The proportion of young African-American males who were homicide victims declined after 1994, reaching a low of 15% in 2000, then somewhat stabilizing through 2008 at about 16%.

The percentage of the population represented by white males 14 to 24 years of age declined from 9% in 1980 to about 6% in 2008. During the same period, however, the proportion of homicide victims in this population group remained near 10%. Thus, a gap appeared in recent years between the percentage of young white males in the population and their percentage as homicide victims. (See Figure 7.4.)

As reported by the BJS in data tables published together with *Homicide Trends in the United States: 1980–2008* (November 16, 2011, http://bjs.ojp.usdoj.gov/index.cfm?y= pbdetail&iid=2221), in 1980 the homicide victimization rate per 100,000 African-American males aged 18 to 24 years was 98.5 and fell during the following four years to a low of 71.8 in 1984. From that point, however, the rate began a dramatic increase; by 1993 African-American males in the 18 to 24 age group were homicide victims at a rate of 195.9 per 100,000. The rate declined to 97.8 per 100,000 in 2004 and then trended slightly upward again, averaging 106.7 per 100,000 from 2005 through 2007; the homicide victimization rate for black males aged 18 to 24 years fell to 91.1 per 100,000 in 2008.

Homicide victimization rates for African-American male teens aged 14 to 17 years, as reported by the BJS, decreased from 26.1 per 100,000 population in 1980 to a

low of 19.9 per 100,000 in 1984 before beginning a dramatic rise that peaked in 1993 at 79 per 100,000. The rate then fell steadily to a low of 24.1 in 2002 and remained between 26 and 35 per 100,000 between 2003 and 2008; the 2008 homicide victimization rate for black males aged 14 to 17 was 31.4 per 100,000.

The homicide victimization rate for white males in the 18-to-24 age group had its ups and downs from 1980 to 2008. As reported by the BJS, the rate increased from 16.8 per 100,000 population in 1980 to a high of 19.3 in 1991 and then began to fall; the 2008 rate of 11.4 per 100,000 was the lowest rate recorded during that period and reflected a return to rates not seen since the 1970s.

Homicide victimization rates for white male teens aged 14 to 17 years were lower than their older counterparts, as reported by the BJS. The rate increased from 5.4 per 100,000 population in 1980 to a high of 9.4 in both 1992 and 1993. The rate then fell steadily to a low of 3.8 in 2003 and leveled out at about 4.6 per 100,000 between 2004 and 2008; the 2008 homicide victimization rate for white males aged 14 to 17 was 4.5 per 100,000.

Homicide victimization rates for both white and African-American females declined in all age groups from 1980 to 2008, although the rates fluctuated over the years. The 2008 homicide victimization rate for white females aged 14 to 17 was 1.2 per 100,000 population; for white females aged 18 to 24, the 2008 rate was 2.6 per 100,000. For African-American females, like their male counterparts, the rates were higher. African-American females in the 14-to-17 age group experienced a rate of 4.6 per 100,000 in 2008; that year the homicide victimization rate was 12.2 per 100,000 for black females aged 18 to 24.

YOUNG, ARMED, AND DANGEROUS
Youth Gangs

Much of the violent activity among young people can be attributed to youth gangs, which tend to be concentrated in poor, inner-city neighborhoods. The Office of Juvenile Justice and Delinquency Prevention's National Youth Gang Center has surveyed law enforcement agencies annually since 1996 to determine the extent of gang problems nationwide and to investigate demographic and other gang-related data. The 2010 National Youth Gang Survey (NYGS; http:// www.nationalgangcenter.gov/Survey-Analysis) reveals that the prevalence of gang problems nationwide declined from 1996 to 2001 but rose again through 2007 and remained steady through 2010. To separate gang activity from broader crime data, the NYGS considers whether or not a group commits crimes together, has a leader or leaders, has a name, identifies itself using unique colors or symbols, and claims a particular territory. In 2010 the NYGS estimated there were 29,400 gangs in the United States with approximately 756,000 members.

In general, the larger a city is, the greater its gang problem. According to the 2010 NYGS, 86.1% of law enforcement agencies in larger cities reported having gang problems in 2010. In smaller cities (those with populations between 2,500 and 49,999) 33.6 % of law enforcement agencies reported gang problems, whereas only 14.1 % of law enforcement agencies in rural counties reported such difficulties. During the period 2006 through 2010, gang-related homicides reported in the survey averaged 2,000 annually. Of the 2,020 reported in 2010, 1,272 occurred in urban jurisdictions, 439 were reported by suburban counties, 209 were in cities with populations between 50,000 and 100,000, and 100 in rural areas or cities with populations below 50,000.

As reported by the NYGS, nearly three out of five (59.6%) known gang members in 2008 were age 18 or older, and 41.4% were younger. The age makeup of gangs had changed slightly since the survey began in the mid-1990s, when about half the known gang members were juveniles. The lowest point of known juvenile gang activity was in the 2002 survey, when two-thirds (66.8%) of gang members reported in the NYGS were age 18 or older, and only one-third (33.2%) were younger. The 2010 survey also notes that gang membership tends to be older in more populous cities and counties in which gangs are well established, whereas smaller cities and rural areas, where the development of gang problems may be more recent, are more likely to report a higher proportion of juvenile gang members. A gender breakdown in the 2009 survey reveals that at that time, 92.6% of gang members known to law enforcement were male, and 7.4% were female.

CRIMINALLY ACTIVE NONGANG GROUPS

Gangs are not always the source of gun violence, however, reports Anthony A. Braga of the Malcolm Wiener Center for Social Policy at Harvard University in *Gun Violence among Serious Young Offenders* (March 29, 2004, http://www.cops.usdoj.gov/pdf/pop/e01042199.pdf). In some cities criminally active nongang groups are major gun offenders.

Braga explains that gun violence and murders in gangs are usually related to rivalries among gangs; offenders often become victims and vice versa. Gun violence and murders in criminally active groups that are not gangs are usually related to "business interests," such as drug dealing. Murders tied to these groups usually occur in or near "street" drug markets, and many of the victims are part of the drug organization or criminal network.

In "Gun Carrying and Drug Selling among Young Incarcerated Men and Women" (*Journal of Urban Health*, vol. 83, no. 2, March 2006), Deborah Kacanek and David Hemenway study the correlation between illegal drug dealing and guns. Based on interviews with 204 state prison inmates between the ages of 18 and 25, the researchers find

that 45% of the incarcerated men and 16% of the women reported carrying a weapon in the 12 months prior to their arrest. Gun-ownership was more prevalent among the men (55%) than the women (16%). Two-thirds of the men (67%) and 28% of the women reported that they had been shot at. Of those who were shot at, 16% of the men and 6% of the women had been wounded. Kacanek and Hemenway conclude that survey participants who sold drugs were more likely to have carried a gun: 65% of men and 22% of women who sold crack cocaine reported carrying a gun, as did 49% of men and 27% of women who sold drugs but not crack, compared with just 16% of men and 3% of women who did not sell drugs at all.

How Do Young Offenders Acquire Guns?

Daniel W. Webster et al. of Johns Hopkins University interviewed 45 youths incarcerated in a juvenile justice facility to determine how they obtained guns. The researchers reported their findings in "How Delinquent Youths Acquire Guns: Initial versus Most Recent Gun Acquisitions" (*Journal of Urban Health*, vol. 79, no. 1, March 2002). Of the 45 youths, 30 had acquired at least one gun, and 22 had acquired multiple guns. Approximately 50% of their first guns were given to them by friends or family, or they found discarded guns. Those who acquired more than one gun usually got them from acquaintances or drug addicts. If they bought new guns, the youths generally purchased them from gun traffickers (people who are in the business of selling guns illegally). Webster et al. conclude that a way to reduce the number of guns in the hands of young offenders is to stop high-volume gun traffickers and recover discarded guns from areas in which illicit drug sales take place.

In "Source of Firearms Used by Students in School-Associated Violent Deaths—United States, 1992–1999" (*Morbidity and Mortality Weekly Report*, vol. 52, no. 9, March 7, 2003), the Centers for Disease Control and Prevention (CDC) investigates how students obtained firearms used in serious school-associated crimes such as homicide and suicide. Most students obtained guns from home (37.5%), with the next likely source being a friend or relative (23.4%). Only 7% of guns used in school-related crimes were purchased, and 5.5% were stolen.

TRACING JUVENILE CRIME GUNS

The Youth Crime Gun Interdiction Initiative, developed in 1996 by the Bureau of Alcohol, Tobacco, Firearms, and Explosives (ATF), was a voluntary project designed to reduce youth firearms violence. The initiative analyzed guns recovered from crimes and traced them to their original sources. According to the ATF, in *Crime Gun Trace Reports (2000): National Report* (July 2002), in 2000 there were a total of 88,570 crime firearms trace reports from 46 participating cities with populations exceeding 250,000. About 8% of crime guns were recovered from juveniles younger than

17 years old. About 33% of crime guns were recovered from young people between the ages of 18 and 24 years.

The ATF found that many recovered firearms moved rapidly from first retail sales at federally licensed gun dealers to the black market (a market where products are bought and sold illegally), which supplies juveniles with guns. When crime guns were recovered within three years from the time of sale, they were more easily traced to their illegal sources than older guns, which were more likely to have passed through many hands before entering the illegal market. According to the ATF, these "new" crime guns made up nearly one-third of all firearms recovered in 2000.

These data were the most recent national data available in 2012, and the ATF (http://www.atf.gov/publications/historical/) provided reports on the Youth Crime Gun Interdiction Initiative for years 1997 to 2000 only. Since 2003 the ATF has been prohibited by law from publishing firearms tracing statistics. (For more information on this restriction and efforts to change it, see Chapter 2.)

In "The Life Cycle of Crime Guns: A Description Based on Guns Recovered from Young People in California" (*Annals of Emergency Medicine*, vol. 43, no. 6, June 2004), Garen J. Wintemute et al. analyze data from ATF firearms tracing records to follow the life cycle of 2,121 crime guns recovered in California in 1999. The researchers make several interesting conclusions:

- Guns recovered from individuals younger than 18 years old were most often purchased by people aged 45 and older.

- Small-caliber handguns made up 41% of handguns recovered from this group.

- For 17.3% of crime guns recovered from teenagers, the median time from sale to recovery was less than three years, which indicates deliberate gun trafficking.

- A minority of retailers and straw purchasers (people buying guns for another) are disproportionately linked to the sale or transfer of crime guns.

A growing source for firearms is the Internet. Seung-Hui Cho (1984–2007), who killed 32 students and faculty members and injured 15 others at Virginia Polytechnic Institute and State University in April 2007, bought one of his guns online, and Steven Kazmierczak (1980–2008), who killed five students and injured 21 others at Northern Illinois University in February 2008, bought gun accessories online. However, long before these tragedies, Internet gun sales were known to be a problem. The Internet Gun Trafficking Act of 1999 was introduced in the U.S. House of Representatives and the U.S. Senate in an effort to ensure that people selling firearms on the Internet were licensed as firearm manufacturers, importers, or dealers and followed regulations regarding gun

sales. This bill was not enacted. In 2002 the Electronic Commerce Crime Prevention and Protection Act was introduced in the House. Its purpose was to require firearms, ammunition, and explosives purchases to be made in person. This bill was also not enacted. Regardless, every Internet gun purchase requires that the sale go through a federal firearms license holder. Laws in various states also regulate gun sales, including Internet sales.

STUDENTS AND GUNS

Since 1991 the CDC has been collecting information about risky behaviors among young people to determine how widespread the behaviors are and at what age the behaviors begin. The CDC surveys high school students nationwide to find out about drug and cigarette use, exercise and sexual habits, and weapons possession, among other things. Figure 7.6 shows the percentage of students by gender in grades nine to 12 who reported carrying a weapon anywhere and on school property according to the Youth Risk Behavior Surveys conducted from 1993 to 2009 and reported by Simone Robers, Jijun Zhang, and Jennifer Truman in *Indicators of School Crime and Safety: 2011* (February 2012, http://nces.ed.gov/programs/crimeindicators/crimeindicators2011/index.asp). Weapon-carrying prevalence anywhere and on school property declined overall from 1993 to 2009 for both males and females. The pattern of the decline was relatively smooth, often with stabilization or a slight increase in recent years, except for males carrying a weapon anywhere. Weapon-carrying prevalence anywhere for males declined through 1997, rose through 2001, declined through 2003, rose through 2005, and then declined once more through 2009.

Table 7.4 shows the percentage of high school students by race, ethnicity, and urbanicity who reported carrying a weapon anywhere and on school property according to the Youth Risk Behavior Surveys conducted from 1993 to 2009. In 1993 Native American or Alaskan Native students (34.2%) had the highest prevalence of weapon-carrying anywhere. Even though this figure dropped to 20.7% by 2009, it remained the highest. In 2007 Pacific Islander or Native Hawaiian students had a higher prevalence of weapon-carrying anywhere (25.5%) but dropped back below Native American or Alaskan Native students in 2009 (20.3%). By 2009 weapon-carrying prevalence anywhere for all ethnic groups had dropped from earlier levels. Asian-American students had the lowest prevalence (8.4%) of weapon-carrying anywhere in 2009. Among white, African-American, and Hispanic students, African-American students had the lowest weapon-carrying prevalence anywhere in 2009 (14.4%).

The situation was similar for weapon-carrying on school property. (See Table 7.4.) In 1993 Native American or Alaskan Native students (17.6%) had the highest prevalence of weapon-carrying on school property, although the

FIGURE 7.6

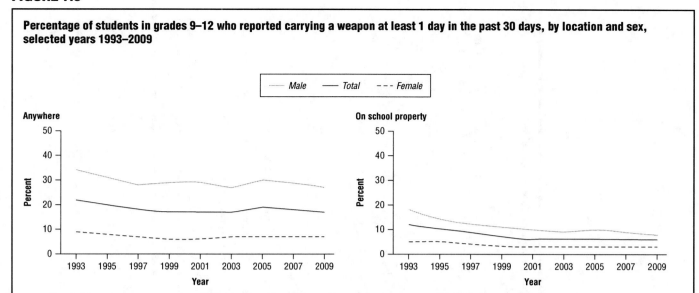

Percentage of students in grades 9–12 who reported carrying a weapon at least 1 day in the past 30 days, by location and sex, selected years 1993–2009

Note: "On school property" was not defined for survey respondents. The term "anywhere" was not used in the Youth Risk Behavior Surveillance questionnaire; students were simply asked how many days they carried a weapon during the past 30 days.

SOURCE: Simone Robers, Jijun Zhang, and Jennifer Truman, "Figure 14.1. Percentage of Students in Grades 9–12 Who Reported Carrying a Weapon at Least One Day during the Previous 30 Days, by Location and Sex: Various Years, 1993–2009," in *Indicators of School Crime and Safety: 2011*, U.S. Department of Education, National Center for Education Statistics, and U.S. Department of Justice, Bureau of Justice Statistics, February 2012, http://nces .ed.gov/programs/crimeindicators/crimeindicators2011/figures/figure_14_1.asp (accessed August 27, 2012)

data needed to be interpreted with caution. (Often this situation arises if the sample size is too small.) This figure dropped to 4.2% by 2009 (but the data were to be interpreted with caution), when it was the second lowest among the race and ethnicity groups, with Pacific Islander or Native Hawaiian students having the highest prevalence (9.8%) of weapon-carrying on school property. Weapon-carrying prevalence on school property had dropped for all ethnic groups during the period 1993 to 2009. Asian-American students had the lowest prevalence (3.6%) of weapon-carrying on school property in 2009. Among white, African-American, and Hispanic students, black students had the lowest weapon-carrying prevalence on school property in 2009 (5.3%). Figure 7.7 presents a visual interpretation of weapons-carrying among students by race/ethnicity and location.

As reported by Danice K. Eaton et al., in "Youth Risk Behavior Surveillance—United States, 2011" (*Morbidity and Mortality Weekly Report*, vol. 61, no. SS-4, June 8, 2012), about 16.6% of students in grades 9 through 12 reported carrying a weapon (such as a gun, knife, or club) on at least one day during the month preceding their participation in the 2011 survey. Table 7.5 shows that across all grades the prevalence of carrying a weapon decreased as grade increased, from 17.3% in the ninth grade to 15.8% in the 12th grade. Among those who reported carrying a gun, however, the decrease did not hold; of the four grades shown in the table, ninth-graders (4.7%) were the least likely to report carrying a gun in 2011. Overall, 5.1% of high school

students in grades 9 through 12 reported carrying a gun in 2011.

Gun carrying was much more prevalent among boys (8.6%) than among girls (1.4%) and was higher among African-American males (10.3%) than among white males (7.2%) or Hispanic males (9.2%) in 2011. African-American girls (1.7%) were slightly more likely than Hispanic girls (1.4%) or white girls (1.1%) to have carried a gun at least one day during the previous month in 2011. (See Table 7.5.) Eaton et al. find that the prevalence of gun carrying in 2011 was highest among 10th-graders (5.7%) and 11th-graders (5%). Female 12th-graders (1%) were the least likely demographic group to report having carried a gun on at least one day during the previous month in 2011.

Julie Ray of the Gallup Organization reports in *Growing up with Guns* (April 15, 2003, http://www.gallup.com/poll/ 8197/Growing-Guns.aspx), the most recent Gallup survey on this topic as of October 2012, that 42% of teens reported there was a gun at home in 2003. This percentage is comparable to the number of adults who claimed to keep a gun in the home in 2003 (43%) and in 2011 (45%). (See Table 7.6.) Ray notes that in 2003 teens with guns at home were more likely to live in the South and Midwest. White teens (51%) were more likely than Hispanic teens (27%) or African-American teens (20%) to have guns at home.

Student Reports of Threats or Injuries

Table 7.7 shows trend data on weapons threats and injuries on school property according to the Youth Risk

TABLE 7.4

Percentage of students in grades 9–12 who reported carrying a weapon at least 1 day in the past 30 days, by race/ethnicity and urbanicity, selected years 1993–2009

Student or school characteristic	Anywhere									On school property								
	1993	1995	1997	1999	2001	2003	2005	2007	2009	1993	1995	1997	1999	2001	2003	2005	2007	2009
Total	**22.1**	**20.0**	**18.3**	**17.3**	**17.4**	**17.1**	**18.5**	**18.0**	**17.5**	**11.8**	**9.8**	**8.5**	**6.9**	**6.4**	**6.1**	**6.5**	**5.9**	**5.6**
Race/ethnicity[a]																		
White	20.6	18.9	17.0	16.4	17.9	16.7	18.7	18.2	18.6	10.9	9.0	7.8	6.4	6.1	5.5	6.1	5.3	5.6
Black	28.5	21.8	21.7	17.2	15.2	17.3	16.4	17.2	14.4	15.0	10.3	9.2	5.0	6.3	6.9	5.1	6.0	5.3
Hispanic	24.4	24.7	23.3	18.7	16.5	16.5	19.0	18.5	17.2	13.3	14.1	10.4	7.9	6.4	6.0	8.2	7.3	5.8
Asian	—	—	—	13.0	10.6	11.6	7.0	7.8	8.4	—	—	—	6.5	7.2	6.6!	2.8!	4.1	3.6
American Indian/Alaska Native	34.2	32.0	26.2	21.8	31.2	29.3	25.6	20.6	20.7	17.6!	13.0!	15.9	11.6!	16.4	12.9	7.2	7.7	4.2
Pacific Islander/Native Hawaiian[b]	—	—	—	25.3	17.4	16.3!	20.0!	25.5	20.3	—	—	—	9.3	10.0!	4.9!	15.4!	9.5!	9.8
Two or more races[b]	—	—	—	22.2	25.2	29.8	26.7	19.0	17.9	—	—	—	11.4	13.2	13.3!	11.9	5.0	5.8
Urbanicity[c]																		
Urban	—	—	18.7	15.8	15.3	17.0	—	—	—	—	—	7.0	7.2	6.0	5.6	—	—	—
Suburban	—	—	16.8	17.0	17.4	16.5	—	—	—	—	—	8.7	6.2	6.3	6.4	—	—	—
Rural	—	—	22.3	22.3	23.0	18.9	—	—	—	—	—	11.2	9.6	8.3	6.3	—	—	—

—Not available.

! Interpret data with caution. The coefficient of variation (CV) for this estimate is 30 percent or greater.

Note: "On school property" was not defined for survey respondents. The term "anywhere" was not used in the Youth Risk Behavior Surveillance questionnaire; students were simply asked on how many days they carried a weapon during the past 30 days.

[a]Race categories exclude persons of Hispanic ethnicity.

[b]The response categories for race/ethnicity changed in 1999 making comparisons of some categories with earlier years problematic. In 1993, 1995, and 1997, Asian students and Pacific Islander students were not categorized separately and students were not given the option of choosing two or more races.

[c]Refers to the Standard Metropolitan Statistical Area (MSA) status of the respondent's household as defined in 2000 by the U.S. Census Bureau. Categories include "central city of an MSA (Urban)," "in MSA but not in central city (Suburban)," and "not in MSA (Rural)."

SOURCE: Adapted from Simone Robers, Jijun Zhang, and Jennifer Truman, "Table 14.1. Percentage of Students in Grades 9–12 Who Reported Carrying a Weapon at Least One Day during the Previous 30 Days, by Location and Selected Student or School Characteristics: Various Years, 1993–2009," in *Indicators of School Crime and Safety: 2011*, U.S. Department of Education, National Center for Education Statistics, and U.S. Department of Justice, Bureau of Justice Statistics, February 2012, http://nces.ed.gov/programs/crimeindicators2011/tables/table_14_1.asp (accessed August 27, 2012)

FIGURE 7.7

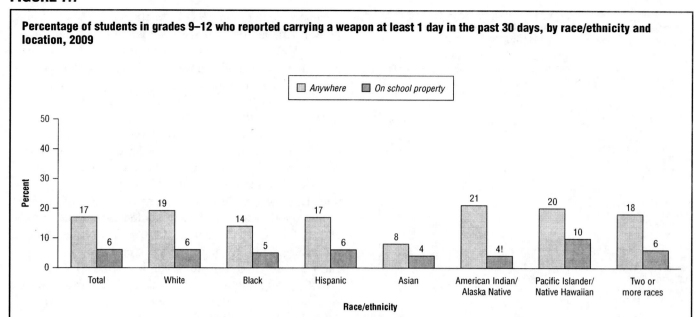

Percentage of students in grades 9–12 who reported carrying a weapon at least 1 day in the past 30 days, by race/ethnicity and location, 2009

Note: Interpret data with caution. The coefficient of variation (CV) for this estimate is 30 percent or greater. "On school property" was not defined for survey respondents. The term "anywhere" was not used in the Youth Risk Behavior Surveillance questionnaire; students were simply asked on how many days they carried a weapon during the past 30 days. Race categories exclude persons of Hispanic ethnicity.

SOURCE: Simone Robers, Jijun Zhang, and Jennifer Truman, "Figure 14.2. Percentage of Students in Grades 9–12 Who Reported Carrying a Weapon at Least One Day during the Previous 30 Days, by Race/Ethnicity and Location: 2009," in *Indicators of School Crime and Safety: 2011*, U.S. Department of Education, National Center for Education Statistics, and U.S. Department of Justice, Bureau of Justice Statistics, February 2012, http://nces.ed.gov/programs/crimeindicators/crimeindicators2011/figures/figure_14_2.asp (accessed August 27, 2012)

TABLE 7.5

Percentage of students who reported carrying a weapon[a, b] and who reported carrying a gun[b] at least 1 day in the past 30 days, by sex, race/ethnicity, and grade, 2011

	Carried a weapon			Carried a gun		
	Female	Male	Total	Female	Male	Total
Category	%	%	%	%	%	%
Race/ethnicity						
White[c]	6.2	27.2	17.0	1.1	7.2	4.3
Black[c]	7.5	21.0	14.2	1.7	10.3	6.1
Hispanic	7.5	24.5	16.2	1.4	9.2	5.5
Grade						
9	7.6	26.6	17.3	1.4	7.7	4.7
10	6.1	26.4	16.6	1.6	9.4	5.7
11	6.2	25.9	16.2	1.1	8.6	5.0
12	7.1	24.1	15.8	1.0	8.2	4.8
Total	**6.8**	**25.9**	**16.6**	**1.4**	**8.6**	**5.1**

[a]For example, a gun, knife, or club.
[b]On at least 1 day during the 30 days before the survey.
[c]Non-Hispanic.

SOURCE: Adapted from Danice K. Eaton et al., "Table 8. Percentage of High School Students Who Carried a Weapon and Who Carried a Gun, by Sex, Race/Ethnicity, and Grade—United States, Youth Risk Behavior Survey, 2011," in "Youth Risk Behavior Surveillance—United States, 2011," *Morbidity and Mortality Weekly Report*, vol. 61, no. SS-4, June 8, 2012, http://www.cdc.gov/MMWR/PDF/SS/SS6104.PDF (accessed August 28, 2012)

Behavior Surveys conducted from 1993 to 2009. The percentage of ninth- to 12th-graders who were threatened or injured with a weapon, such as a gun, knife, or club, on school property ranged from 7.3% in 1993 to 9.2% in 2003. As happened with other crime indicators, threat reports increased from 1993 (7.3%) to 1995 (8.4%). Threat reports dropped through 1997 (7.4%), rose again through 2003 (9.2%), and then decreased substantially

TABLE 7.6

Poll respondents' report on guns in their home and elsewhere on their property, selected years 1991–2011

DO YOU HAVE A GUN IN YOUR HOME? DO YOU HAVE A GUN ANYWHERE ELSE ON YOUR PROPERTY SUCH AS IN YOUR GARAGE, BARN, SHED OR IN YOUR CAR OR TRUCK? [COMBINED RESPONSES]

	Gun in home %	Gun elsewhere %	No gun %	No opinion %
2011 Oct 6–9	45	2	51	1
2010 Oct 7–10	39	2	57	2
2009 Oct 1–4	40	2	55	4
2008 Oct 3–5	42	1	55	1
2007 Oct 4–7	42	2	55	1
2005 Oct 13–16	40	2	57	1
2004 Oct 11–14	38	2	59	1
2003 Oct 6–8	43	2	54	1
2002 Oct 14–17	41	3	55	1
2000 Aug 29–Sep 5	39	2	58	1
1999 Feb 8–9	36	6	56	2
1996 Nov 21–24	44	1	53	2
1996 Jul 25–28	38	2	58	2
1993 Dec 17–21	49	5	45	*
1991 May 16–19	46	4	49	1

*Less than 0.5%

SOURCE: "Do You Have a Gun in Your Home? Do You Have a Gun Anywhere Else on Your Property Such As in Your Garage, Barn, Shed or in Your Car or Truck?" in *Guns*, The Gallup Organization, 2012, http://www.gallup.com/poll/1645/Guns.aspx (accessed August 27, 2012). Copyright © 2012 Gallup, Inc. All rights reserved. The content is used with permission; however, Gallup retains all rights of republication.

from 2003 to 2009 (7.7%). Males were more likely than females to be threatened or injured with a weapon. In 2009, for example, 9.6% of male students were threatened or injured with a weapon, compared with 5.5% of female students who had similar experiences. In all the survey years, students in lower grades were more likely to be threatened than students in higher grades. In 2009 the greatest percentage of threats or injuries with a weapon was directed toward Native American or Alaskan Native students.

Robers, Zhang, and Truman report in *Indicators of School Crime and Safety: 2011* that in 2009 most students (92.3%) had not been threatened or injured with a weapon on school property during the previous 12 months. Of those who had, 3.2% reported only one incident, whereas 1.9% of students had been threatened or injured at least two or three times, and 1.2% had been threatened or injured 12 times or more. (See Table 7.8.)

Students in the District of Columbia in both 2003 and 2005 experienced a greater percentage of threats or injuries with a weapon (12.7% and 12.1%, respectively) than did students in any state that had data available on this subject. (See Table 7.9.) In 2009 students in Arkansas (11.9%), Nevada (10.7%), and Alabama (10.4%) had the highest percentages of those experiencing threats or injuries with a weapon on school property. In 2009 other states with high

percentages of students being threatened or injured with a weapon were Louisiana (9.5%), Michigan (9.4%), Wyoming (9.4%), Arizona (9.3%), West Virginia (9.2%), and Maryland (9.1%). States with the lowest percentages of students being threatened or injured with a weapon on school property in 2009 were Oklahoma (5.6%) and Pennsylvania (5.8%).

Barring Guns from Schools

Table 7.10 shows the percentage of high school students who carried a gun in 2009 according to state and local surveys. The median for female students surveyed was 1.6%, which means that half the states reported more than 1.6% of female students carrying guns and half the states reported less. For male students, the median was 10.3%. The overall median was 6%. The states (among those surveyed) in which students were the most likely to carry a gun in 2011 were Wyoming (10.8%), Louisiana (10.4%), and South Carolina (10.2%). The states in which students were the least likely to carry a gun were Massachusetts (2.5%), Illinois (3.6%), Delaware (4.4%), and New York (4.5%). The area with the highest percentage of students carrying guns in 2011 was the District of Columbia (7.5%), followed by Duval County, Florida (7.1%) and Milwaukee, Wisconsin (7.1%).

The Gun-Free Schools Act of 1994 required states to pass laws forcing schools that receive funding under the Elementary and Secondary Education Act of 1965 to expel for at least one year any student who brings a firearm to school. The U.S. Department of Education reveals in *Report on the Implementation of the Gun-Free Schools Act of 1994 in the States and Outlying Areas: School Years 2005–06 and 2006–07* (September 2010, http://www2.ed.gov/about/reports/annual/gfsa/gfsarp100610.pdf) that 2,695 students were expelled from school during the 2006–07 academic year for carrying a firearm to school, a rate of 5.5 per 100,000 students. More than half (53%) of these students were expelled for carrying handguns, 10% were expelled for carrying rifles or shotguns to school, and the remaining 37% were expelled for carrying other types of firearms, such as bombs, grenades, and starter pistols.

The Department of Education also notes that the number of students expelled for carrying a firearm to school dropped by 22%, from 3,477 during the 1998–99 academic year to 2,695 during the 2006–07 academic year. Some states experienced reductions in the number of students expelled for carrying a firearm to school between the 2005–06 and the 2006–07 academic years. The states experiencing the greatest percentage of decreases in expulsions during this period were Delaware, Iowa, Kansas, New Hampshire, New Jersey, Rhode Island, and Wisconsin. The states that experienced the greatest percentage of increases in expulsions during this period were Idaho, Indiana, Louisiana, and Minnesota.

TABLE 7.7

Percentage of students in grades 9–12 who reported being threatened or injured with a weapon on school property during the last 12 months, by selected characteristics, selected years 1993–2009

Student or school characteristic	1993	1995	1997	1999	2001	2003	2005	2007	2009
Total	7.3	8.4	7.4	7.7	8.9	9.2	7.9	7.8	7.7
Sex									
Male	9.2	10.9	10.2	9.5	11.5	11.6	9.7	10.2	9.6
Female	5.4	5.8	4.0	5.8	6.5	6.5	6.1	5.4	5.5
Race/ethnicity[a]									
White	6.3	7.0	6.2	6.6	8.5	7.8	7.2	6.9	6.4
Black	11.2	11.0	9.9	7.6	9.3	10.9	8.1	9.7	9.4
Hispanic	8.6	12.4	9.0	9.8	8.9	9.4	9.8	8.7	9.1
Asian[b]	—	—	—	7.7	11.3	11.5	4.6	7.6!	5.5
American Indian/Alaska Native	11.7	11.4!	12.5!	13.2!	15.2!	22.1	9.8	5.9	16.5
Pacific Islander/Native Hawaiian[b]	—	—	—	15.6	24.8	16.3	14.5!	8.1!	12.5
Two or more races[b]	—	—	—	9.3	10.3	18.7	10.7	13.3	9.2
Grade									
9th	9.4	9.6	10.1	10.5	12.7	12.1	10.5	9.2	8.7
10th	7.3	9.6	7.9	8.2	9.1	9.2	8.8	8.4	8.4
11th	7.3	7.7	5.9	6.1	6.9	7.3	5.5	6.8	7.9
12th	5.5	6.7	5.8	5.1	5.3	6.3	5.8	6.3	5.2
Urbanicity[c]									
Urban	—	—	8.7	8.0	9.2	10.6	—	—	—
Suburban	—	—	7.0	7.4	9.0	8.8	—	—	—
Rural	—	—	5.6!	8.3	8.1	8.2	—	—	—

—Not available.

!Interpret data with caution. The coefficient of variation (CV) for this estimate is 30 percent or greater.

[a]Race categories exclude persons of Hispanic ethnicity.

[b]The response categories for race/ethnicity changed in 1999 making comparisons of some categories with earlier years problematic. In 1993, 1995, and 1997, Asian students and Pacific Islander students were not categorized separately and students were not given the option of choosing two or more races.

[c]Refers to the Standard Metropolitan Statistical Area (MSA) status of the respondent's household as defined in 2000 by the U.S. Census Bureau. Categories include "central city of an MSA (Urban)," "in MSA but not in central city (Suburban)," and "not MSA (Rural)."

Note: "On school property" was not defined for survey respondents.

SOURCE: Simone Robers, Jijun Zhang, and Jennifer Truman, "Table 4.1. Percentage of Students in Grades 9–12 Who Reported Being Threatened or Injured with a Weapon on School Property at Least One Time during the Previous 12 Months, by Selected Student or School Characteristics: Various Years, 1993–2009," in *Indicators of School Crime and Safety: 2011*, U.S. Department of Education, National Center for Education Statistics, and U.S. Department of Justice, Bureau of Justice Statistics, February 2012, http://nces.ed.gov/programs/crimeindicators/crimeindicators2011/tables/table_04_2.asp (accessed August 27, 2012)

SOME STUDENTS FEEL UNSAFE AT SCHOOL

In *Indicators of School Crime and Safety: 2011*, Robers, Zhang, and Truman report that the percentage of students who were afraid of being attacked at school decreased from 11.8% in 1995 to 4.2% in 2009. When the 2009 data were analyzed by race and ethnicity, 7% of African-American students and 4.9% of Hispanic students reported that they were afraid of being attacked at school, compared with only 3.3% of white students. In general, the percentage of students who were afraid of being attacked at school decreased as grade increased, from grade six (6.4%) to grade 12 (1.9%). A greater percentage of public school students (4.4%) were afraid of being attacked at school than private school students (1.9%).

Do students have a reason to be fearful? Table 7.4 shows that the percentage of students in grades nine to 12 who reported carrying a weapon such as a gun, knife, or club on school property declined from 11.8% in 1993 to 5.6% in 2009. In addition many schools had improved security in the post-Columbine era. Some schools limited building access, performed lockdown drills with students, and made door and classroom numbers visible from outside the building in order to enable first responders arriving on the scene in the event of a crisis. Robers, Zhang, and Truman report that by the 2009–10 academic year many public schools had implemented an array of security measures. Nearly all (99.3%) public schools required visitors to sign or check in at the office, and 91.7% controlled access to school buildings during school hours. Three out of five public schools (61.1%) used security cameras to monitor school areas in 2009–10, up from 19.4% in the 1999–2000 school year. Nearly half (46%) of schools controlled access to school grounds, and 63.1% had an electronic notification system for schoolwide emergencies. During the 2009–10 school year, however, only 1.4% of U.S. schools required students to pass through a metal detector daily.

SCHOOL SHOOTINGS

Americans were shocked by the rash of school shootings during the 1990s, and some parents were afraid to send their children to school. The Bipartisan Working Group on

TABLE 7.8

Percentage of students in grades 9–12 who reported being threatened or injured with a weapon on school property during the last 12 months, by number of times and selected student characteristics, 2009

Student characteristic	0 times	1 time	2 or 3 times	4 to 11 times	12 or more times
Total	92.3	3.2	1.9	1.4	1.2
Sex					
Male	90.4	3.7	2.2	1.9	1.8
Female	94.5	2.7	1.5	0.8	0.5
Race/ethnicity*					
White	93.6	2.9	1.7	1.0	0.8
Black	90.6	3.6	2.1	2.0	1.8
Hispanic	90.9	4.0	2.1	1.6	1.5
Asian	94.5	2.4!	1.5!	‡	1.3!
American Indian/ Alaska Native	83.5	8.1!	3.7!	‡	‡
Pacific Islander/ Native Hawaiian	87.5	2.5!	2.9!	3.7!	‡
Two or more races	90.8	2.6	2.8	2.1!	1.6!
Grade					
9th	91.3	4.1	2.0	1.4	1.2
10th	91.6	3.5	2.2	1.6	1.1
11th	92.1	3.2	1.8	1.6	1.3
12th	94.8	2.0	1.4	0.9	1.0

!Interpret data with caution. The coefficient of variation (CV) for this estimate is 30 percent or greater.
‡Reporting standards not met. Either there are too few cases or the coefficient of variation (CV) is 50 percent or greater.
*Race categories exclude persons of Hispanic ethnicity.
Note: "On school property" was not defined for survey respondents. Detail may not sum to totals because of rounding.

SOURCE: Simone Robers, Jijun Zhang, and Jennifer Truman, "Table 4.2. Percentage of Students in Grades 9–12 Who Reported Being Threatened or Injured with a Weapon on School Property during the Previous 12 Months, by Number of Times and Selected Student Characteristics: 2009," in *Indicators of School Crime and Safety: 2011*, U.S. Department of Education, National Center for Education Statistics, and U.S. Department of Justice, Bureau of Justice Statistics, February 2012, http://nces.ed.gov/programs/crimeindicators/crimeindicators2011/tables/table_04_2.asp (accessed August 27, 2012)

Youth Violence explores this issue in *Final Report: 106th Congress* (November 17, 1999, http://permanent.accessgpo.gov/lps65018/bipartisan_working_group_youth_violence_106th_final.pdf). It states that "while it is important to carefully review the circumstances surrounding these horrifying incidents so that we may learn from them, we must also be cautious about inappropriately creating a cloud of fear over every student in every classroom across the country. In the case of youth violence, it is important to note that, statistically speaking, schools are among the safest places for children to be."

In *Crime in Schools and Colleges: A Study of Offenders and Arrestees Reported via National Incident-Based Reporting System Data* (October 2007, http://www.fbi.gov/about-us/cjis/ucr/nibrs/crime-in-schools-and-colleges-pdf), the most recent report of this type on school violence released by the Federal Bureau of Investigation (FBI) as of 2012, James H. Noonan and Malissa C. Vavra of the FBI determine after a five-year study that only 3.3% of all

TABLE 7.9

Percentage of students in grades 9–12 who reported being threatened or injured with a weapon on school property during the last 12 months, by state, selected years 2003–09

State	2003	2005	2007	2009
Public school students				
United States	9.2	7.9	7.8	7.7
Alabama	7.2	10.6	—	10.4
Alaska	8.1	—	7.7	7.3
Arizona	9.7	10.7	11.2	9.3
Arkansas	—	9.6	9.1	11.9
California	—	—	—	—
Colorado	—	7.6	—	8.0
Connecticut	—	9.1	7.7	7.0
Delaware	7.7	6.2	5.6	7.8
District of Columbia	12.7	12.1	11.3	—
Florida	8.4	7.9	8.6	8.2
Georgia	8.2	8.3	8.1	8.2
Hawaii	—	6.8	6.4	7.7
Idaho	9.4	8.3	10.2	7.9
Illinois	—	—	7.8	8.8
Indiana	6.7	8.8	9.6	6.5
Iowa	—	7.8	7.1	—
Kansas	—	7.4	8.6	6.2
Kentucky	5.2	8.0	8.3	7.9
Louisiana	—	—	—	9.5
Maine	8.5	7.1	6.8	7.7
Maryland	—	11.7	9.6	9.1
Massachusetts	6.3	5.4	5.3	7.0
Michigan	9.7	8.6	8.1	9.4
Minnesota	—	—	—	—
Mississippi	6.6	—	8.3	8.0
Missouri	7.5	9.1	9.3	7.8
Montana	7.1	8.0	7.0	7.4
Nebraska	8.8	9.7	—	—
Nevada	6.0	8.1	7.8	10.7
New Hampshire	7.5	8.6	7.3	—
New Jersey	—	8.0	—	6.6
New Mexico	—	10.4	10.1	—
New York	7.2	7.2	7.3	7.5
North Carolina	7.2	7.9	6.6	6.8
North Dakota	5.9	6.6	5.2	—
Ohio	7.7	8.2	8.3	—
Oklahoma	7.4	6.0	7.0	5.8
Oregon	—	—	—	—
Pennsylvania	—	—	—	5.6
Rhode Island	8.2	8.7	8.3	6.5
South Carolina	—	10.1	9.8	8.8
South Dakota	6.5	8.1	5.9	6.8
Tennessee	8.4	7.4	7.3	7.0
Texas	—	9.3	8.7	7.2
Utah	7.3	9.8	11.4	7.7
Vermont	7.3	6.3	6.2	6.0
Virginia	—	—	—	—
Washington	—	—	—	—
West Virginia	8.5	8.0	9.7	9.2
Wisconsin	5.5	7.6	5.6	6.7
Wyoming	9.7	7.8	8.3	9.4

— Not available.

Note: "On school property" was not defined for survey respondents. National, state, territory, and local Youth Risk Behavior Surveillance data come from separate scientific samples of schools and students. With the exception of Ohio and South Dakota, state representative samples are drawn from public schools only for the state level data. U.S. total, Ohio and South Dakota include public and private schools.

SOURCE: Simone Robers, Jijun Zhang, and Jennifer Truman, "Table 4.3. Percentage of Public School Students in Grades 9–12 Who Reported Being Threatened or Injured with a Weapon on School Property at Least One Time during the Previous 12 Months, by State: Various Years, 2003–2009," in *Indicators of School Crime and Safety: 2011*, U.S. Department of Education, National Center for Education Statistics, and U.S. Department of Justice, Bureau of Justice Statistics, February 2012, http://nces.ed.gov/programs/crimeindicators/crimeindicators2011/tables/table_04_3.asp (accessed August 27, 2012)

TABLE 7.10

Percentage of students who reported carrying a weapon[a,b] and who reported carrying a gun[b] at least 1 day in the past 30 days, by sex and U.S. location, 2011

	Carried a weapon			Carried a gun		
	Female	Male	Total	Female	Male	Total
Site	%	%	%	%	%	%
State surveys						
Alabama	10.5	32.0	21.5	2.9	12.9	8.1
Alaska	10.5	27.0	19.0	1.6	7.7	4.8
Arizona	7.9	26.9	17.5	2.0	9.9	6.0
Arkansas	7.8	34.4	21.1	2.0	15.6	8.8
Colorado	6.9	23.4	15.5	—[c]	—	—
Connecticut	—	—	—	—	—	—
Delaware	6.6	20.3	13.5	1.3	7.3	4.4
Florida	7.9	22.9	15.6	—	—	—
Georgia	13.0	32.3	22.8	—	—	—
Hawaii	7.7	20.1	13.9	—	—	—
Idaho	9.4	35.3	22.8	—	—	—
Illinois	6.2	19.0	12.6	1.2	6.0	3.6
Indiana	5.4	28.0	17.0	1.0	8.1	4.6
Iowa	3.9	27.0	15.8	0.6	9.3	5.1
Kansas	—	—	—	—	—	—
Kentucky	8.9	36.4	22.8	2.2	14.7	8.6
Louisiana	11.5	32.9	22.2	2.9	17.9	10.4
Maine	—	—	—	—	—	—
Maryland	8.5	22.9	15.9	2.1	8.9	5.7
Massachusetts	4.4	19.9	12.3	0.2	4.7	2.5
Michigan	6.2	24.8	15.7	1.6	8.3	5.1
Mississippi	6.4	29.9	18.0	1.5	14.3	7.9
Montana	9.1	37.1	23.5	2.2	15.2	9.0
Nebraska	6.5	30.3	18.6	2.7	15.2	9.1
New Hampshire	6.0	22.2	14.5	—	—	—
New Jersey	4.7	14.3	9.6	—	—	—
New Mexico	11.9	33.3	22.8	3.3	13.6	8.5
New York	5.8	19.2	12.6	1.3	7.7	4.5
North Carolina	9.6	32.0	20.8	—	—	—
North Dakota	—	—	—	—	—	—
Ohio	7.2	24.5	16.4	—	—	—
Oklahoma	7.8	31.0	19.4	1.4	10.3	5.9
Rhode Island	4.7	17.4	11.2	—	—	—
South Carolina	8.6	37.8	23.4	1.3	19.0	10.2
South Dakota	—	—	—	—	—	—
Tennessee	7.4	34.4	21.1	1.2	11.6	6.5
Texas	7.5	27.3	17.6	1.6	10.3	6.0
Utah	5.6	27.2	16.8	2.1	9.3	5.9
Vermont	—	—	—	—	—	—
Virginia	9.5	31.2	20.4	4.4	13.6	9.1
West Virginia	6.0	35.0	20.7	1.2	9.8	5.6
Wisconsin	3.9	16.5	10.4	0.4	8.5	4.6
Wyoming	13.5	40.4	27.1	5.1	16.2	10.8
Median	7.5	27.3	17.6	1.6	10.3	6.0
Range	3.9–13.5	14.3–40.4	9.6–27.1	0.2–5.1	4.7–19.0	2.5–10.8
Large urban school district surveys						
Boston, MA	9.3	21.5	15.4	0.9	5.8	3.3
Broward County, FL	5.3	17.0	11.4	1.5	6.0	3.9
Charlotte-Mecklenburg, NC	7.5	24.4	15.9	1.7	8.9	5.4
Chicago, IL	12.5	21.1	16.5	2.0	9.5	5.8
Dallas, TX	6.8	22.4	14.4	1.0	9.1	5.0
Detroit, MI	8.0	18.2	13.2	1.4	7.3	4.4
District of Columbia	13.8	23.8	18.9	2.3	12.5	7.5
Duval County, FL	11.1	26.5	18.8	3.2	11.1	7.1
Houston, TX	6.2	21.5	13.9	1.2	9.1	5.3
Los Angeles, CA	5.7	18.5	12.5	1.6	6.7	4.4
Memphis, TN	6.5	16.5	11.4	1.3	9.6	5.5
Miami-Dade County, FL	6.4	15.9	11.1	2.0	7.5	4.8
Milwaukee, WI	8.0	21.7	14.9	1.4	12.7	7.1
New York City, NY	5.5	12.5	9.1	0.7	3.8	2.3
Orange County, FL	7.5	20.2	13.8	2.0	6.9	4.4
Palm Beach County, FL	7.9	20.4	14.2	3.0	7.0	5.1
Philadelphia, PA	10.2	20.7	15.6	1.5	9.0	5.4
San Bernardino, CA	6.4	19.8	13.1	0.9	7.4	4.2
San Diego, CA	6.2	17.9	12.2	0.8	6.6	3.9
San Francisco, CA	6.7	14.8	11.4	1.9	6.0	4.3

TABLE 7.10

Percentage of students who reported carrying a weapon[a, b] and who reported carrying a gun[b] at least 1 day in the past 30 days, by sex and U.S. location, 2011 [CONTINUED]

	Carried a weapon			Carried a gun		
	Female	Male	Total	Female	Male	Total
Site	%	%	%	%	%	%
Large urban school district surveys						
Seattle, WA	—	—	—	2.1	7.9	5.3
Median	7.1	20.3	13.8	1.5	7.5	5.0
Range	5.3–13.8	12.5–26.5	9.1–18.9	0.7–3.2	3.8–12.7	2.3–7.5

[a]For example, a gun, knife, or club.
[b]On at least 1 day during the 30 days before the survey.
[c]Not available.

SOURCE: Adapted from Danice K. Eaton et al., "Table 9. Percentage of High School Students Who Carried a Weapon, and Who Carried a Gun, by Sex— Selected U.S. Sites, Youth Risk Behavior Survey, 2011," in "Youth Risk Behavior Surveillance—United States, 2011," *Morbidity and Mortality Weekly Report*, vol. 61, no. SS-4, June 8, 2012, http://www.cdc.gov/MMWR/PDF/SS/SS6104.PDF (accessed August 28, 2012)

incidents reported through the National Incident-Based Reporting System occurred in schools. Most often, the perpetrator of the crime was a high school–aged white male. More than half of the offenses were for assaults or drug violations. Regardless, school violence occurs, and sometimes the violence is deadly.

The National School Safety and Security Services provides in "School Associated Violent Deaths and School Shootings" (2010, http://www.schoolsecurity.org/trends/ school_violence.html) data on school-related violent deaths for the academic years 1999–2000 to 2009–10. It indicates that during this period deaths due to school shootings in kindergarten to 12th grade ranged from a low of three in 2002–03 to a high of 24 in 2004–05. School stabbings are not as widely recognized in the media. Deaths due to school stabbings ranged from a low of one in 2001–02 to a high of 10 in 2003–04.

The following sections describe some of the better-known shooting incidents at U.S. high schools and universities in which multiple young people were shot. It should be noted that such incidents are not limited to the United States, however. Notable school shootings outside the United States include an incident in April 2009 at a university in Baku, Azerbaijan, in which a 29-year-old gunman killed 12 people and himself using a semiautomatic pistol. In another attack, an 18-year-old student in Jokela, Finland, outlined his plans in a YouTube video before killing eight people at his high school, wounding 12 others, and killing himself in November 2007; the .22-caliber pistol he used in the shootings had been legally obtained in the weeks prior to the spree.

SECONDARY SCHOOL SHOOTINGS
Thurston High School, Springfield, Oregon

MAY 21, 1998. Fifteen-year-old Kip Kinkel (1982–) walked into the crowded cafeteria at Thurston High School in Springfield, Oregon, and opened fire with a semiautomatic

rifle. The students Mikael Nickolauson and Ben Walker were killed, and 22 of their classmates were injured. Kinkel's parents were later found shot to death at their home. The year before, Kinkel's father had bought his son a Ruger .22-caliber semiautomatic rifle under the condition that he would use it only with adult supervision.

On September 24, 1999, as part of a plea agreement, Kinkel pleaded guilty to four counts of murder and 26 counts of attempted murder. On November 2, 1999, after a six-day sentencing hearing that included victims' statements and the testimony of psychiatrists and psychologists, Kinkel, by then aged 17, was sentenced to 111 years in prison without the possibility of parole.

Prompted by growing concerns over a rock-throwing incident that Kinkel had participated in and other behavioral problems, Faith Kinkel had taken her son to see a psychologist in January 1997, just over a year before the shootings. In this meeting the psychologist concluded that Kinkel was depressed, had difficulty managing his anger, and had shown a pattern of acting out his anger.

Columbine High School, Littleton, Colorado

APRIL 20, 1999. At 11:10 a.m., 18-year-old Eric Harris (1981–1999) arrived alone in the student parking lot at Columbine High School in Littleton, Colorado. Dylan Klebold (1982–1999), his 17-year-old classmate, arrived a short time later. Together, they walked to the school cafeteria carrying two large duffel bags, each concealing a 20-pound propane bomb set to detonate at exactly 11:17 a.m. After placing the duffel bags inconspicuously among hundreds of other backpacks and bags, Harris and Klebold returned to the parking lot to wait for the bombs to explode. As they waited, pipe bombs they had planted 3 miles (4.8 km) southwest of the high school exploded, resulting in a grass fire that was intended to divert the resources of the Littleton Fire Department and Jefferson County Sheriff's Office.

When their planted bombs failed to explode in the cafeteria, Harris and Klebold reentered the high school, this time via the west exterior steps, the highest point on campus with a view of the student parking lots and the cafeteria's entrances and exits. Both were wearing black trench coats that concealed 9mm semiautomatic weapons. They pulled out shotguns from a duffel bag and opened fire toward the west doors of the school, killing 17-year-old Rachel Scott. After entering the school, they killed 12 other victims, including a teacher, before finally killing themselves. Twenty-three more people were injured.

Within days, authorities had learned that three of the guns used in the massacre were purchased the year before by Klebold's girlfriend shortly after her 18th birthday. On May 3, felony charges were filed against 22-year-old Mark E. Manes for admittedly selling to Harris the TEC-DC9 semiautomatic handgun that he used in the shooting. On August 18, Manes pleaded guilty to the charge. The facts of this case as outlined came from *The Columbine High School Shootings: Jefferson County Sheriff Department's Investigation Report* (May 15, 2000).

THE COLUMBINE SHOOTERS. More than a year before the Columbine shootings, Harris and Klebold were arrested for breaking into a vehicle. In April 1998 both were placed in a juvenile diversion program and required to pay fines, attend anger management classes, and perform community service. Harris and Klebold successfully completed the diversion program and were released from it in February 1999 with their juvenile records cleared.

In the spring of 1998 Harris began to keep a diary, which was later recovered by authorities. In it he wrote of his desire to kill. In the only entry for 1999, Harris wrote of his and Klebold's preparations for what would become the Columbine massacre, including a detailed accounting of the weapons and bombs they intended to use.

After the Columbine shootings, Klebold's father, Tom Klebold, reported to investigators that his son had never showed any fascination with guns. The Klebolds told authorities that their son had been accepted by the University of Arizona, where he planned to major in computer science. Investigators who interviewed Klebold's friends and teachers heard him described as a nice, normal teenager.

Harris and Klebold left behind three videotapes documenting their plans and philosophies. The third videotape contained eight sessions taped from early April 1999 to the morning of the Columbine shootings on April 20, and showed some of their weapons and bombs, as well as recordings they had made of each other rehearsing for the shootings.

Red Lake High School, Red Lake, Minnesota

MARCH 21, 2005. The shooting that occurred at Red Lake High School was the nation's worst since the 1999 Columbine shooting. Red Lake High School is located on a Native American reservation in northern Minnesota. Jeffrey Weise (1988–2005), a 17-year-old junior, killed nine people and wounded seven in his shooting spree, and then shot and killed himself. Weise began his rampage by killing his grandfather—a tribal police officer—and his grandfather's female friend at their home, using a .22-caliber pistol of unknown origin. Weise then drove his grandfather's police cruiser to Red Lake High School. At the school, Weise used his grandfather's police-issued handguns and shotgun to kill a security guard, a teacher, and five students.

Weise came from a troubled background. He had lost his father to suicide in 1997. His mother was seriously brain-damaged in a car accident in 1999 and lived in a nursing home. Weise was thought to have posted messages on a neo-Nazi website. He called himself an "Angel of Death" and a "NativeNazi." He was often ridiculed and bullied by other students for his odd behavior.

Seven days after the shooting, Louis Jourdain, the son of the tribal chairman, was arrested and charged with conspiracy. It was believed that he helped plot Weise's actions. Jourdain was tried as a juvenile, and in January 2006 he received a sentence, which, because of his juvenile status, was not made public. In July 2006 families of those injured and killed settled a lawsuit with the school district for $1 million.

Millard South High School, Omaha, Nebraska

JANUARY 5, 2011. After being suspended for a trespassing incident in which he drove his car on the school athletic fields, Robert Butler Jr. (1993–2011), a senior at Millard South High School and the son of an Omaha, Nebraska, police detective, entered the school shortly before 1:00 p.m. and mortally wounded Assistant Principal Vicki Kaspar in what appeared to be a targeted shooting. Butler wounded Principal Curtis Case on his way out of Kaspar's office and was later found dead of an apparent self-inflicted gunshot. The .40-caliber Glock pistol used in the shootings was believed to be his father's service revolver. Shortly before the incident Butler posted on his Facebook: "ur gonna here about the evil sh** I did but that f***ing school drove me to this. I wont u guys to remember me for who I was b4 this ik. I greatly affected the lives of the families ruined but I'm sorry. goodbye."

Chardon High School, Chardon, Ohio

FEBRUARY 27, 2012. At about 7:30 a.m. on February 27, 2012, Thomas "T.J." Lane (1994–) opened fire with a .22-caliber semiautomatic Ruger handgun in the Chardon High School cafeteria as he and other students waited for bus transportation to other educational sites. Six students were hit by the gunfire; one died at the scene, and two other students died the following day from their wounds. As the incident happened, Lane was confronted by an unarmed football coach at the school and chased from the building. He was apprehended outside by law enforcement and detained in a juvenile facility as prosecutors sought to try him as an adult. At a hearing in June 2012 Lane registered a plea of not guilty by reason of insanity. He reportedly admitted to the shootings but told authorities that he did not know why he did it. The gun used in the case had been legally purchased by a relative and was allegedly stolen by Lane the night before the shootings. His trial is set for November 2012.

POSTSECONDARY SCHOOL SHOOTINGS

Virginia Polytechnic Institute and State University, Blacksburg, Virginia

APRIL 16, 2007. The Virginia Polytechnic Institute and State University (Virginia Tech) massacre was the deadliest shooting rampage by a single gunman in U.S. history. A Virginia judge had declared Seung-Hui Cho mentally ill. Nonetheless, this Virginia Tech student was able to purchase two handguns. On the morning of April 16, 2007, Cho entered a residence hall on campus, where he shot and killed a female student and a male resident assistant. Hours later, after returning to his dorm room to change out of his bloodied clothes and to delete various files from his computer, Cho entered a classroom building on campus and began shooting students and professors. When he finished, Cho had killed 32 students and faculty members and had injured 15 others. Cho committed suicide by shooting himself in the head.

Northern Illinois University, DeKalb, Illinois

FEBRUARY 14, 2008. The Northern Illinois University's (NIU) Department of Safety details in *The Report of the February 14, 2008, Shootings at Northern Illinois University* (March 2010, http://www.niu.edu/feb14report/Feb14report .pdf) the story of what happened on that deadly day in Cole Hall, where gunfire killed five students and wounded 21 others, including a professor. The shooter was Steven Kazmierczak (1980–2008), a once-successful student at NIU, who shot and killed himself when his rampage from the stage of an auditorium filled with oceanography students was over. The former NIU student first fired six rounds from a shotgun and then another 50 rounds from a 9mm Glock semiautomatic pistol; 55 unused rounds were found at the scene. Kazmierczak had a history of mental health problems and had chosen to discontinue his medication prior to the February 14 shootings. Officials could determine no motive for the killings other than his mental illness and suggested that Kazmierczak chose NIU as the site simply because he was a former student there and was familiar with the campus.

Oikos University, Oakland, California

APRIL 2, 2012. Seven people were killed and three others were wounded when One L. Goh (1968–) opened fire at about 10:30 a.m. on April 2, 2012, with a .45-caliber handgun in a nursing classroom at Oikos University in Oakland, California. The Korean-born Goh was identified as a former student at the private school, which was founded in 2004 and is affiliated with the Praise God Korean Church of Oakland. Officials at the school were unable to identify a motive in the shootings. Goh was in financial difficulty and had dropped out of the school, which is located in a tight-knit Korean-American community, but he had not been expelled. On the morning of the attack he attempted to meet with a school administrator, but when she was not in her office, he forced another worker at the school to accompany him into a classroom where he began shooting at the students. Goh left in a stolen vehicle and threw his gun, which he had purchased legally in California, into a nearby estuary before turning himself in to authorities that afternoon. As of October 2012, Goh's trial was on hold as his attorney sought a mental evaluation of his client.

WHEN ADULTS SHOOT SCHOOLCHILDREN

Even though most school shootings are carried out by students, school property occasionally becomes the site of gun violence perpetrated by adults against children. This was the case during the fall of 2006, when in just one week two schools were the scenes of violence involving adult males who entered school property intending to kill young female students. It was also the case in February 2010, when Littleton, Colorado, was once again the site of a school shooting, but this time it was an adult targeting middle school students. Just over two and a half years later, in December 2012, an elementary school in Newtown, Connecticut, was the site of a horrific attack that resulted in the deaths of 26 people, 20 of them children; the shooter also died.

Platte Canyon High School, Bailey, Colorado

SEPTEMBER 27, 2006. Fifty-three-year-old Duane Morrison (1952–2006) entered a second-floor classroom at Platte Canyon High School in Bailey, Colorado, with two handguns and a backpack that he claimed contained a bomb. Morrison, who had no apparent ties to the school, took six female students hostage, ordering the rest of the students out of the room. The students who were allowed to leave told police that Morrison seemed to choose blonde girls of small stature to keep as hostages. Several hours later, after Morrison had released four of the girls, police burst through the classroom door. One of the girls escaped unharmed, but before Morrison turned his gun on himself, he shot and killed 16-year-old Emily Keyes. Police were unsure of Morrison's motive, but the girls who had been held hostage confirmed that Morrison—who was described as a "drifter" with a record of minor criminal offenses—had sexually assaulted them during the standoff.

West Nickel Mines Amish School, Nickel Mines, Pennsylvania

OCTOBER 2, 2006. Less than one week after the incident in Bailey, Colorado, a 32-year-old milk truck driver entered a one-room Amish schoolhouse in Lancaster County, Pennsylvania. Armed with three guns, a stun gun, two knives, 600 rounds of ammunition, and a number of instruments believed to be intended for torture and sexual assault, the gunman ordered all male students and adult females to leave the building. He then lined up the remaining 10 children—all girls, aged six to 13—against the blackboard and bound their feet. After escaping, a teacher at the school ran to a farmhouse that had a telephone and called police. When the police arrived, the gunman shot all 10 girls and then himself. Five of the girls died.

Later identified as Charles C. Roberts IV (1973–2006), the gunman lived with his wife and children in Nickel Mines. Family and friends, including many of his Amish neighbors, were shocked by Roberts's actions, maintaining that he had appeared to be a devoted husband and father. Before taking his own life, Roberts called his wife and explained that he was plagued by guilt for having molested two young relatives when he was 12 years old and that he had recently experienced recurring dreams of molesting more girls. Police, however, were unable to confirm Roberts's story.

Reaction to the 2006 Shootings

The Nickel Mines school shooting was particularly shocking to most Americans because of the bucolic image typically associated with the Amish way of life. The one-room schoolhouse had no security system or even a telephone, unlike schools in much of the rest of the country, which have responded to school shootings by increasing security and holding regular drills to prepare students and staff for possible violent attacks. No one would have guessed, however, that the Amish could be the target of gun violence. The national consensus was that if it could happen there, no school was safe.

Some experts, however, maintain that the Platte Canyon and Nickel Mines shootings do demonstrate an important pattern. Gail Russell Chaddock and Mark Clayton note in "A Pattern in Rural School Shootings: Girls as Targets" (*Christian Science Monitor*, October 4, 2006) that even though the numbers of school shootings have gone down, the level of violence they involve has increased, and girls appear often to be the target of this violence. Still, determining patterns of why these events occur is not easy. Stuart Fox notes in "Why Do Adults Kill Children?" (*Live Science*, April 30, 2010) that "adults so rarely murder children that psychiatrists and law enforcement officials don't have enough data to draw any conclusions about possible similarities in the killers' motives." L. Thomas Kucharski, the chair of psychology at John Jay College of Criminal Justice, suggested to Fox that school shootings in which adults kill children are so rare, as are other situations in which adults kill children, that it is impossible to determine commonalities among cases. Kucharski discussed motives for murder in general, though, and noted that "the vast majority of murders occur as a result of revenge or anger between acquaintances,

or as an outgrowth of drug-related crime. The remaining murders are rooted in personal psychological problems or unique environmental conditions."

Deer Creek Middle School, Littleton, Colorado

FEBRUARY 23, 2010. As buses were leaving Deer Creek Middle School at the end of the school day, many students heard two shots ring out. Within seconds, 32-year-old Bruco Strongeagle Eastwood (1977?–) was tackled by a seventh-grade math teacher as Eastwood tried to reload his high-powered rifle. Lying wounded were eighth-graders Matt Thieu and Reagan Webber. Eastwood, a former student of Deer Creek Middle School, had previously visited the school and was seen inside the school shortly before the shooting. A student standing nearby the victims said that an adult approached and asked the students if they attended the school. When Thieu and Webber responded affirmatively, Eastwood shot them. Both students survived the shooting. Even though police revealed no motive for the shooting, they did note that Eastwood was apparently depressed about never graduating from high school and being unable to obtain a general equivalency diploma.

Sandy Hook Elementary School, Newtown, Connecticut

DECEMBER 14, 2012. Twenty-year-old Adam Lanza shot his mother to death at their home in Newtown and then proceeded to Sandy Hook Elementary School, where he shot his way inside. Armed with a variety of weapons, including two handguns and an assault rifle, he killed 20 children and six adult staff members before killing himself. The incident drew international media attention and prompted intense debate over the adequacy of the nation's gun-control regulations. On January 16, 2013, President Barack Obama (1961–) presented a plan to reduce mass gun violence that included 23 executive actions and proposals for four major pieces of legislation. Vowing to spend political capital in what would undoubtedly be difficult negotiations with the opponents of policy reform, Obama said, "I will put everything I've got into this."

CHILDREN INJURED AND KILLED BY GUNFIRE

The number of children whose lives have been lost to gun violence is calculated annually by the Children's Defense Fund (CDF), a charitable organization that focuses on the needs of poor and minority children and those with disabilities. Each year the CDF ranks the states according to how they measure up in terms of children's health. Besides death by gun violence, the CDF measures factors such as insurance coverage, low birth weight babies, prenatal care, infant mortality, and immunizations.

In *Protect Children, Not Guns 2012* (March 2012, http://www.childrensdefense.org/child-research-data-publications/data/protect-children-not-guns-2012.pdf), the CDF indicates that gunfire killed 2,947 American children and teens in 2008 and 2,793 in 2009. It states, "The 5,740 children and teens killed by guns in 2008 and 2009 would fill more than 229 public school classrooms of 25 students each [and] was greater than the number of U.S. military personnel killed in action in Iraq and Afghanistan (5,013)." Even though there was a decline in child gun deaths since the peak year of 1994—from nearly 16 deaths per day of children and teens by gunfire in 1994 to eight per day in 2008–09—116,385 children died from gun violence between 1979 and 2009. In addition, the CDF reports that 34,387 children and teens were injured by gunfire in 2008–09.

CHAPTER 8

PUBLIC ATTITUDES TOWARD GUN CONTROL

A DEEPLY PERSONAL ISSUE

During the past 50 years, gun control has been a prominent issue, fueled by firearm-related political assassinations, assassination attempts, and violent crimes that became top news stories. Americans mourned the deaths of President John F. Kennedy (1917–1963); his brother Senator Robert F. Kennedy (1925–1968); and the civil rights leader Martin Luther King Jr. (1929–1968). Presidents Gerald R. Ford (1913–2006) and Ronald Reagan (1911–2004) were victimized by would-be assassins, as were the presidential candidate George C. Wallace (1919–1998), the civil rights leader Vernon E. Jordan (1935–), and U.S. Representative Gabrielle Giffords (1970–).

The White House has been shot at on several occasions. In October 1994 Francisco Martin Duran (1968–), a convicted felon, fired 29 rounds at the White House from a Chinese-made assault rifle. Because of his felony conviction, Duran did not pass a background check when he tried to purchase a handgun, but no such check was required for the purchase of his rifle. Duran was convicted of the attempted assassination of President Bill Clinton (1946–). Robert W. Pickett (1953–), a former Internal Revenue Service auditor, fired shots at the White House in February 2001 and was subdued by Secret Service agents who shot him in the knee. Pickett had cleared an instant background check in Indiana to buy a handgun despite his history of mental illness. In August 2006 the former University of Maryland basketball star Lonny Baxter (1979–) was sentenced to two months in jail after he and Francis I. Martin (1971–) fired shots from a vehicle while driving near the White House. Nobody was injured.

However, political assassinations and assassination attempts are not the only events that bring gun control issues to the forefront of the collective American consciousness. In 2010, 56 law enforcement officers were shot and killed in the United States in the line of duty. (See Table 5.8 in Chapter 5.) From 1999 to 2009, 332,811 people were killed in the United States by firearms. (See Table 6.5 in Chapter 6.) Among those deaths were 1,660 children aged 12 years and younger. (See Table 7.3 in Chapter 7.)

THE DEBATE IS BITTER AND POLARIZING

Some Americans are convinced that more federal regulation of firearms is necessary to reduce the number of murders and injuries that are inflicted with guns and to ensure a safer, more civilized society. Others who support private ownership of guns insist that the right to bear arms is guaranteed by long-standing custom and by the Second Amendment to the U.S. Constitution. These gun rights advocates believe that no cyclical increase in crime, no mass killing, or any rash of political murders should lead the nation to violate the Constitution and the individual rights it guarantees. They also note that knives and other instruments are used to kill people and that there is no talk of regulating or banning them. Furthermore, they suggest that criminals are less likely to use a gun if they know that a gun may be used on them.

The National Rifle Association of America (NRA) generally believes that if more law-abiding citizens carried weapons, they would be better prepared to stop criminals from committing murders and other violent crimes. For example, in the aftermath of the Aurora, Colorado, theater massacre in July 2012, some gun rights advocates stated that innocent lives could have been saved if law-abiding citizens in the audience had been able to defend themselves with their own weapons.

Both supporters and opponents of gun control agree that some means should be found to keep guns out of the hands of criminals. Not surprisingly, the two sides approach this issue differently. The two different strategies for gun control involve deterrence (discouraging by instilling fear) and interdiction (legally forbidding the use of). Advocates of deterrence, most notably the Second Amendment Foundation and the NRA, recommend consistent enforcement of current laws and instituting tougher penalties to discourage individuals from using firearms in crimes. They maintain that interdiction will not have any effect on crime but will strip away the constitutional rights and privileges of law-abiding Americans by taking away their right to own guns.

Advocates of interdiction, led by organizations such as the Brady Center to Prevent Gun Violence, the Law Center to Prevent Gun Violence, and the Violence Policy Center, believe that controlling citizens' access to firearms will reduce crime. Therefore, they favor restrictions on public gun ownership.

EVALUATING PUBLIC OPINION POLLS

Public opinion polls, like all sources of information, must be used with care. Pollsters select sample populations because it is impossible to interview every American on a given question. The selection is usually performed randomly using computers. Most major pollsters interview between 1,000 and 2,000 people to establish a valid sample. Other pollsters may interview far fewer than 500, and the sample could be too small to fairly represent the opinions of all adult Americans. Generally, the larger the sample, the greater the chance for an adequate representation and a valid result.

The polling errors that concern most people are those caused by bias in the presentation of questions, which may influence the response. For example, is the question vague? Is it too long? Is it threatening? Is it leading? If the questions are asked in an in-person interview, was the interviewer too forceful or threatening? Did respondents provide answers they thought would please interviewers? Were respondents disqualified because of membership in gun control or gun rights organizations? What was the purpose of the poll? Who hired the polling organization, and what is its stance on the issue?

Respondents may be unwilling to candidly discuss their use of weapons. In addition, polling does not always determine how important a person considers an issue to be. The issue may be of absolutely no concern to the respondent, but when asked, the respondent then thinks about the topic and provides an answer. Five minutes after the question has been asked, the issue may completely disappear from his or her mind.

The polling organization might not include the number of times there was no response. If these "no replies" come predominantly from one group, they might influence the poll so that it does not truly represent the national opinion on a given issue. Pollsters are aware of these weaknesses, so they usually indicate how reliable they consider their polls to be. As a result, many polls indicate an accuracy rate of plus or minus ($+/-$) 2% to 4%.

IS GUN CONTROL AN IMPORTANT ISSUE?

The *Sourcebook of Criminal Justice Statistics* (2012, http://www.albany.edu/sourcebook/) is a document that is continually updated piecemeal as new information becomes available. Section 2 of the *Sourcebook* (http://www.albany.edu/sourcebook/pdf/section2.pdf) is titled "Public Attitudes toward Crime and Criminal Justice-Related Topics." The first table in Section 2 chronicles attitudes toward the most important problem facing the country as reported to Gallup Organization pollsters. As of October 2012, the most recent data included in this table spanned 1984 to 2004. In most of those years, few to no respondents mentioned guns or gun control spontaneously as the most important issue the government ought to be addressing. However, 1999 and 2000 saw a spike in interest, with 10% of respondents mentioning gun control as the most important issue in 1999 and 7% in 2000, possibly because of the spotlight placed on the gun control issue after the permanent provision of the Brady law went into effect in late 1998. (See Chapter 3.) Under "permanent Brady," the five-day waiting period for handgun purchasers was replaced by a national computerized criminal identification system that was designed to quickly screen purchasers of both handguns and long guns (rifles and shotguns). Great debate surrounded the elimination of the five-day waiting period to purchase firearms. In addition, controversy arose regarding how long records relating to background checks should be kept. After these and related issues died down, the percentages of poll respondents identifying gun control as the most important problem facing the country dropped to 1% in 2001 and was no longer on the list through 2004.

The second table in Section 2 of the *Sourcebook* chronicles attitudes toward the two most important problems that the government should address as reported to Harris Interactive pollsters. In most years only 1% or less of respondents mentioned gun control spontaneously. However, a spike of 4% was noted in 2000.

In October 2012 PollingReport.com (http://www.pollingreport.com/prioriti.htm) listed 24 national polls taken between June 2010 and September 2012 on what people believed was the most important issue facing the country or on what was the most important issue to them as they decided how to vote in the 2012 presidential election. Gun control was not cited as a top issue or as the most important issue that determined people's voting choices. Instead, the economy, jobs, health care, and the wars in Iraq and Afghanistan were the top priorities.

OPINION ON GUN CONTROL

Opinion on Stricter Gun Control Laws

The Gallup Organization conducted a poll in October 2011 to gauge public attitudes about gun control laws; it then compared the results with a similar poll it had conducted 20 years earlier in 1991. In general, the results show much less support in 2011 than in 1991 for increasing the level of strictness of gun control laws. In 2011, 43% of respondents favored stricter gun control laws, down from 68% in 1991. Table 8.1 shows a demographic breakdown of the percentage of adult respondents in the poll who believed that gun control laws should be stricter. A greater proportion of women (50%) than men (37%) favored stricter gun laws in 2011. Support for stricter firearms laws increased with age in the 2011 poll; a larger proportion of those aged 50 years and older (45%) favored stricter control of guns, compared with those aged 30 to 49 years (43%) and those aged 18 to 29 years (39%). A greater proportion of respondents living in the East favored stricter gun laws (54%) in 2011, more so than those in the Midwest (37%), the South (40%), or the West (44%). Democrats (64%) were more likely to favor a tightening of the gun laws in 2011 than independents (37%) or Republicans (31%).

In *Guns* (2012, http://www.gallup.com/poll/1645/Guns .aspx), the Gallup Organization indicates that it asked the question: "In general, do you feel that the laws covering the sale of firearms should be made more strict, less strict, or kept as they are now?" (See Figure 8.1.) Gallup then

TABLE 8.1

Poll respondents' views on whether gun laws should be stricter, by demographic characteristics, 1991, 2011, and percentage change

	1991 %	2011 %	Change (pct. pts.)
Men	59	37	−22
Women	76	50	−26
18 to 29 years	62	39	−23
30 to 49 years	69	43	−26
50+ years	71	45	−26
College	72	43	−29
No college	65	44	−21
East	77	54	−23
Midwest	72	37	−35
South	61	40	−21
West	63	44	−19
Democrat	74	64	−10
Independent	65	37	−28
Republican	66	31	−35
Gun in household	56	29	−27
No gun in household	78	57	−21

FIGURE 8.1

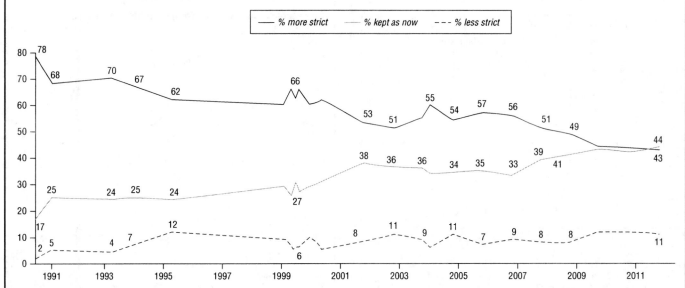

Poll respondents' views on stricter vs. less strict laws governing the sale of firearms, 1991–2012

IN GENERAL, DO YOU FEEL THAT THE LAWS COVERING THE SALE OF FIREARMS SHOULD BE MADE MORE STRICT, LESS STRICT, OR KEPT AS THEY ARE NOW?

— % more strict ⋯⋯ % kept as now - - - % less strict

compared responses to this question from 1991 to 2012. During this time span the percentage of those wanting stricter gun control laws declined considerably, whereas the percentage of those wanting gun control laws to be less strict or to remain the same rose. The result was that in 2012 the nation was evenly split on wanting gun laws that were stricter (44%) or wanting the laws to be kept as they were (43%); 11% wanted gun laws to be less strict.

The Pew Research Center for the People and the Press also polls Americans on this issue, but it asks a slightly different question: "What do you think is more important—to protect the right of Americans to own guns, or to control gun ownership?" In 1993 most respondents said it was best to control gun ownership (57%) rather than to protect the right of Americans to own guns (34%). (See Figure 8.2.) By 2010, however, the public was evenly divided: 46% were in favor of controlling gun ownership over protecting the rights of Americans to own guns, and 46% believed the opposite was best. In 2011 and 2012 the percentage of those in favor of protecting gun rights in the United States (49% both years) surpassed the percentage of those in favor of controlling gun ownership (46% in 2011 and 45% in 2012).

In *More Support for Gun Rights, Gay Marriage than in 2008, 2004* (April 25, 2012, http://www.people-press .org/files/legacy-pdf/4-25-12%20Social%20Issues.pdf) Andrew Kohut et al. of the Pew Research Center report that men and women have long been at odds on the issue. In 1993, 44% of men and 26% of women favored protecting gun rights over controlling gun ownership, and the gender disparity remained in 2012, when 60% of men and 39% of women thought it was more important to protect gun rights than to control gun ownership. (See Figure 8.3.)

Similarly, white people and Republicans were more likely to support the protection of gun rights, whereas African-Americans, Hispanics, and Democrats were more likely to support the control of gun ownership. Kohut et al. report in *More Support for Gun Rights, Gay Marriage than in 2008, 2004* that 57% of white respondents in 2012 favored gun rights over gun control, compared with 35% of African-Americans in the survey and 29% of Hispanics who were polled. (See Figure 8.4.) Nearly three-quarters (72%) of Republicans in the survey favored the protection of gun rights over gun control in 2012, whereas about one-quarter (27%) of Democrats took this position.

Harris Interactive has surveyed Americans on gun control since 1998. Responses to the question "In general, would you say you favor *stricter* gun control, or *less strict* gun control?" are shown in Table 8.2. The Harris results parallel the Gallup and Pew results, in that support for stricter gun control has decreased in recent years. In 1998, 69% of respondents favored stricter gun control, and 23% favored less-strict gun control. By 2010, 45% favored stricter gun control and 26% less strict control. It should be noted that in 2004 Harris pollsters began offering "neither" as a response when this choice had not been offered previously. The percentage of respondents noting "neither" in response to the question increased dramatically in 2004 through 2010,

FIGURE 8.2

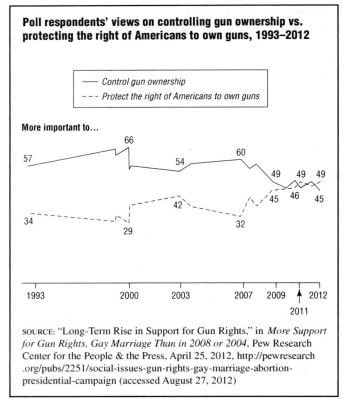

Poll respondents' views on controlling gun ownership vs. protecting the right of Americans to own guns, 1993–2012

SOURCE: "Long-Term Rise in Support for Gun Rights," in *More Support for Gun Rights, Gay Marriage Than in 2008 or 2004*, Pew Research Center for the People & the Press, April 25, 2012, http://pewresearch .org/pubs/2251/social-issues-gun-rights-gay-marriage-abortion-presidential-campaign (accessed August 27, 2012)

FIGURE 8.3

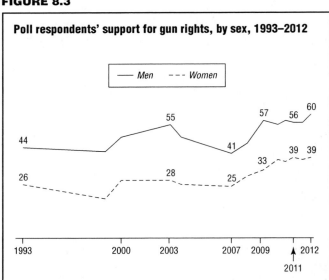

Poll respondents' support for gun rights, by sex, 1993–2012

SOURCE: "Gender Gap over Gun Rights," in *More Support for Gun Rights, Gay Marriage Than in 2008, 2004*, Pew Research Center for the People & the Press, April 25, 2012, http://www.people-press.org/files/ legacy-pdf/4-25-12%20Social%20Issues.pdf (accessed August 27, 2012)

which would affect the percentages choosing "stricter" or "less strict," but it is possible that the proportion of those responding "stricter" and "less strict" would remain the same. The Harris poll results for 2010 show that a greater percentage of Democrats (70%) than Republicans (22%) wanted stricter gun control, whereas a greater percentage of Republicans (42%) than Democrats (7%) wanted less-strict control of gun laws.

Opinion on Gun Bans

Jeffrey M. Jones of the Gallup Organization reports in *Record-Low 26% in U.S. Favor Handgun Ban* (October 26, 2011, http://www.gallup.com/poll/150341/Record-Low-Favor-Handgun-Ban.aspx) that from 1959 to 2011 the percentage of people who said there should be a law banning the possession of handguns except by police and other authorized people decreased dramatically. In 2011 only about one-quarter (26%) of poll respondents said handguns should be banned, whereas 60% said they should be banned in 1959.

In the 2011 Gallup poll, only one in five men (20%) and about one-third of women (31%) supported a handgun ban. (See Table 8.3.) Respondents in the 18- to 29-year-old age group were more likely to favor a handgun ban than their older counterparts; 23% of 30- to 49-year-olds and 25% of those aged 50 and older supported such a ban. A greater proportion of respondents living in the East favored a handgun ban (36%) in 2011, compared with those in the Midwest (25%), the South (21%), or the West (24%). Democrats (37%) were more likely to favor a handgun ban in 2011 than independents (23%) or Republicans (16%).

Even though support for banning handguns seemed to be dwindling, one survey found that there was support for banning gun use under certain conditions and for banning specialized weapons. In *Public Attitudes towards the Regulation of Firearms* (March 2007, http://www-news.uchicago.edu/releases/07/pdf/070410.guns.norc.pdf), Tom W. Smith of the National Opinion Research Center at the University of Chicago discusses the results of the 2006 General Social Survey (GSS), which show the levels of public support for various measures to regulate firearms. According to Smith, 91% of GSS respondents wanted gun use to be illegal for those under the influence of alcohol just as driving an automobile is illegal while under the influence. Eighty-five percent of respondents wanted sales of .50-caliber rifles to be restricted to the police and military. A similar proportion (82%) wanted sales of semiautomatic assault weapons to be limited to police and the military as well.

A Harris Interactive survey in 2010 indicates that Americans would strongly support prohibiting gun ownership of some weapons and would withhold the right to bear

FIGURE 8.4

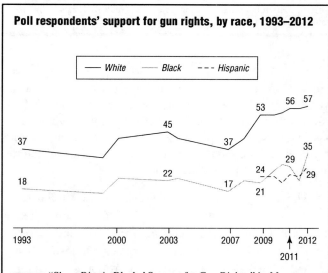

Poll respondents' support for gun rights, by race, 1993–2012

SOURCE: "Sharp Rise in Blacks' Support for Gun Rights," in *More Support for Gun Rights, Gay Marriage Than in 2008, 2004*, Pew Research Center for the People & the Press, April 25, 2012, http://www.people-press.org/files/legacy-pdf/4-25-12%20Social%20Issues.pdf (accessed August 27, 2012)

TABLE 8.2

Poll respondents' views on stricter or less strict gun control, 2010

"IN GENERAL, WOULD YOU SAY YOU FAVOR STRICTER GUN CONTROL, OR LESS STRICT GUN CONTROL?"

| | 1998 | 1999 | 2000 | 2004 | 2008 | 2010 | Political party | | | Own guns | |
| | | | | | | | Rep. | Dem. | Ind. | Yes | No |
	%	%	%	%	%	%	%	%	%	%	%
Stricter	69	63	63	52	49	45	22	70	37	29	59
Less strict	23	25	28	22	20	26	42	7	34	42	12
Neither*	7	10	6	20	21	20	27	14	23	24	18
Don't know/refused	1	2	4	7	10	10	9	9	7	5	11

*There is a change in the question in 2004. In the previous surveys "neither" was not offered as a possible response but was accepted if given. In this new survey it was offered as a possible response.
Note: Percentages may not add to 100% because of rounding

SOURCE: David Krane, "Table 2. Favor Stricter or Less Strict Gun Control," in *Americans Should Be Allowed to Have Guns, Say Large Majorities*, The Harris Poll, June 16, 2010, http://www.harrisinteractive.com/vault/HI-Harris-Poll-Gun-Control-2010-06-16.pdf (accessed August 27, 2012)

TABLE 8.3

Poll respondents' views on banning the possession of handguns, 1991 and 2011

	1991 %	2011 %	Change (pct. pts.)
Men	34	20	−14
Women	51	31	−20
18 to 29 years	39	32	−7
30 to 49 years	39	23	−16
50+ years	50	25	−25
College	44	24	−20
No college	42	28	−14
East	55	36	−19
Midwest	49	25	−24
South	34	21	−13
West	35	24	−11
Democrat	54	37	−17
Independent	40	23	−17
Republican	35	16	−19
Gun in household	24	12	−12
No gun in household	59	39	−20

SOURCE: Jeffrey M. Jones, "Percentage Favoring a Ban on Handguns, by Subgroup, 1991 and 2011 Gallup Polls," in *Record-Low 26% in U.S. Favor Handgun Ban*, The Gallup Organization, October 26, 2011, http://www.gallup.com/poll/150341/Record-Low-Favor-Handgun-Ban.aspx (accessed August 27, 2012). Copyright © 2011 Gallup, Inc. All rights reserved. The content is used with permission; however, Gallup retains all rights of republication.

TABLE 8.4

Poll respondents' views on the types of firearms that should be allowed, by current gun ownership, 2010

"DO YOU THINK AMERICANS SHOULD BE ALLOWED TO HAVE EACH OF THE FOLLOWING ITEMS?"

	Yes %	No %	Own guns (percent saying yes) Yes %	No %
Rifles/shotguns	80	20	91	71
Hand-guns	74	26	90	62
"Open carry", or unconcealed weapons	50	50	66	37
Concealed weapons	45	55	60	32
Unlimited number of guns	38	62	59	22
Semi-automatic weapons	30	70	45	17

Note: Percentages may not add to 100% because of rounding.

SOURCE: David Krane, "Table 5. Types of Weapons Allowed," in *Americans Should Be Allowed to Have Guns, Say Large Majorities*, The Harris Poll, June 16, 2010, http://www.harrisinteractive.com/vault/HI-Harris-Poll-Gun-Control-2010-06-16.pdf (accessed August 27, 2012)

arms from some individuals. For example, Harris found that 92% of those polled in 2010 would prohibit people on the FBI's "terrorist watch list" from buying guns, and 87% of respondents still would prohibit "watch list" individuals even if they were American citizens. Only 26% did not support the right of Americans to own handguns, but 70% did not think Americans should be allowed to own semi-automatic weapons. (See Table 8.4.)

Opinion on Open Carry Restrictions

"Open carry" means that a person is allowed to carry a firearm in plain view while in public. Many states and municipalities allow open carry. The Harris Interactive findings in Table 8.4 indicate that in 2010 half of Americans supported the right to carry unconcealed weapons and half did not. Some businesses located in jurisdictions that allow open carry have banned the practice in their establishments. Starbucks is one business that has not done that, and a few of its stores have become places where people congregate while wearing unloaded firearms. As a result, Starbucks has been criticized for allowing open carry. In the press release "Starbucks Position on Open Carry Gun Laws" (March 16, 2010,0http://news.starbucks.com/article_display.cfm?article_id=332), the company asserts that it will not ban law-abiding customers from its stores. Furthermore, it suggests that advocacy groups on both sides of the issue "have chosen to use Starbucks as a way to draw attention to their positions. . . . We comply with local laws and statutes in all the communities we serve. That means we abide by the laws that permit open carry in 43 U.S. states. Where these laws don't exist, openly carrying weapons in our stores is prohibited. The political, policy and legal debates around these issues belong in the legislatures and courts, not in our stores."

The Brady Campaign to Prevent Gun Violence, in conjunction with Lake Research Partners, conducted a survey on open carry policies in April 2010 and reported the results in "Poll: Most Americans Oppose Openly Carried Guns, Want Starbucks to Adopt a 'No Guns' Policy" (May 2010, http://www.bradycampaign.org/legislation/gunlobbybacked/opencarryguns). The Brady Campaign notes that 56% of those polled "favor Starbucks and other retail establishments establishing strict 'no guns' policies for their businesses—and far more gun owners support a 'no guns' policy for Starbucks than believe Starbucks and other businesses should allow firearms on their premises."

Figure 8.5 shows the Brady Campaign and Lake Research Partners results by gender, age category, education, and political affiliation when respondents were asked whether they favored or opposed the open carry of guns. Overall, a greater percentage of respondents (51%) opposed open carry than favored it (45%). Men (58%) and Republicans (60%) were more likely to favor open carry, whereas women (61%) and Democrats (68%) were more likely to oppose the practice. Younger respondents were divided: 47% opposed open carry, whereas 48% favored it. Older respondents were more likely to oppose it (55%) than support it (41%).

FIGURE 8.5

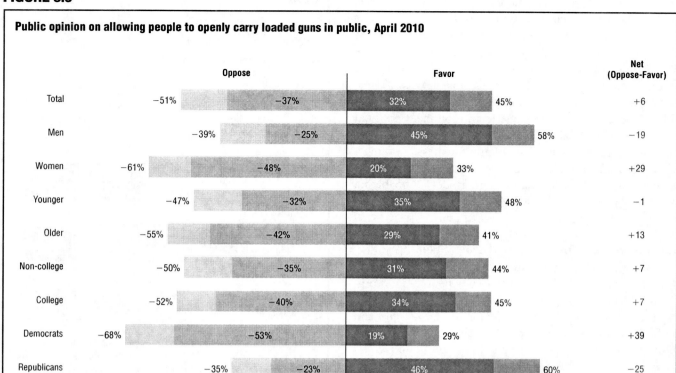

Public opinion on allowing people to openly carry loaded guns in public, April 2010

	Oppose	Favor	Net (Oppose-Favor)
Total	−51% −37%	32% 45%	+6
Men	−39% −25%	45% 58%	−19
Women	−61% −48%	20% 33%	+29
Younger	−47% −32%	35% 48%	−1
Older	−55% −42%	29% 41%	+13
Non-college	−50% −35%	31% 44%	+7
College	−52% −40%	34% 45%	+7
Democrats	−68% −53%	19% 29%	+39
Republicans	−35% −23%	46% 60%	−25
Independents	−50% −33%	33% 47%	+3

Note: The darker colors represent a stronger response and lighter colors a less strong response.

SOURCE: Celinda Lake, Joshua Ulibarri, and Christopher Panetta, "The political and demographic divide on this issue becomes pretty clear when it comes to allowing people to openly carry loaded guns in public. Women and Democrats drive the opposition while men and Republicans drive much of the support. Independents split down the middle," in *Findings from a National Survey of 600 Registered Voters April 26–28, 2010*, Brady Center to Prevent Gun Violence and Lake Research Partners, http://www.bradycampaign.org/xshare/bcam/legislation/open_carry/polling-overview-slides.ppt (accessed August 27, 2012)

OPINION ON GUN CONTROL FOLLOWING MAJOR SHOOTINGS

With gun crime trending downward after the 1990s and the national consciousness preoccupied with wars in Iraq and Afghanistan and the worldwide economic downturn that began in 2008, gun control legislation has languished during recent years. Calls for stricter gun laws have been made in the immediate aftermath of a notable incident of gun violence, but they seldom have a lasting impact on public opinion overall or bring about effective legislative responses.

Opinion on Gun Control after Tucson Shooting

In January 2011, after a shooting incident in Tucson, Arizona, in which six people were killed and 13 were wounded, including Representative Gabrielle Giffords (D-AZ), Gallup conducted a survey asking Americans what one or two things did they think could be done to help prevent mass shootings like the one that had just

occurred (January 24, 2011, http://www.gallup.com/poll/145757/Americans-Link-Gun-Laws-Mental-Health-Mass-Shootings.aspx). Respondents were able to formulate their own answers and were not instructed to pick from a list. The largest percentage (24%) suggested stricter gun control laws, followed by 15% who believed that better mental health screening and treatment would help prevent such violent incidents. Other answers in the Gallup survey included improved education about gun use and safety (9%), more thorough background checks for gun purchasers (8%), better security at public gatherings (6%), and banning either guns or bullets (5%).

In another approach to the topic, Gallup pollsters asked survey participants to rate six possible causes of the Tucson shooting specifically (asked of half of the group) or of recent U.S. mass shootings in general (asked of the other half). Of the group asked to place blame for the Tucson shooting, more than half (55%) said that a "great deal" of blame should be placed with the U.S.

mental health system that failed to identify dangerous individuals such as Jared Loughner (1988–), the shooter in the Giffords incident. Others placed a "great deal" of blame on the easy access to guns in the United States (43%), on drug use (37%), on violence in entertainment culture such as music, video games, and movies (31%), on extremist views that proliferate on the Internet (34%), and on "inflammatory language from prominent political commentators" (22%). In the responses of the group asked more generally to place blame for mass shootings, the causes ranked in the same order though with different percentages; 48% said that a "great deal" of blame should be placed with the U.S. mental health system, and 46% put blame on easy access to guns.

Opinion on Gun Control after Aurora Shooting

In "Views on Gun Laws Unchanged after Aurora Shooting" (July 30, 2012, http://www.people-press.org/012/07/30/views-on-gun-laws-unchanged-after-aurora-shooting/), the Pew Research Center for the People and the Press reports that there was "no significant change in public views on the issue of gun control and gun rights" following the shooting earlier that month at a movie theater in Aurora, Colorado, in which 12 people were killed and 58 others wounded. In July 2012, just after the Aurora theater massacre, two-thirds (67%) of those polled agreed that "shootings like this one are just the isolated acts of troubled individuals." Only 24% concurred that such incidents "reflect broader problems in American society." Figure 8.6 shows that there was little change in the proportion of Americans who favored either protecting the right to own guns or controling gun ownership in the aftermath of the Virginia Tech; Tucson, Arizona; and Aurora, Colorado, shooting incidents.

Opinion on Gun Control after Trayvon Martin Shooting

On the night of February 26, 2012, George Zimmerman (1983–), a neighborhood watch volunteer in Sanford, Florida, shot and killed Trayvon Martin (1995–2012), an unarmed teenager he said had attacked him. Zimmerman claimed that Martin had been suspiciously lurking in the gated community he patrolled and that when he approached Martin to investigate, the young man attacked him; he reported shooting Martin in self-defense with a 9mm semiautomatic pistol during the alleged altercation. Zimmerman possessed the gun legally and was a concealed-carry permit holder. He was taken into custody at the scene, interviewed by police, and released.

Soon public outcry over the death of the teenager led to a special investigation, and in June 2012 Zimmerman was charged with second degree murder (homicide that has not been planned or premeditated), despite a Florida law com-

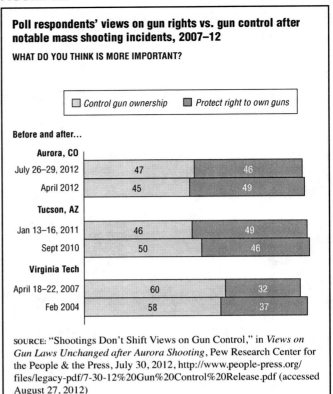

FIGURE 8.6

Poll respondents' views on gun rights vs. gun control after notable mass shooting incidents, 2007–12

WHAT DO YOU THINK IS MORE IMPORTANT?

☐ Control gun ownership ■ Protect right to own guns

Before and after...

Aurora, CO
July 26–29, 2012: 47 | 46
April 2012: 45 | 49

Tucson, AZ
Jan 13–16, 2011: 46 | 49
Sept 2010: 50 | 46

Virginia Tech
April 18–22, 2007: 60 | 32
Feb 2004: 58 | 37

SOURCE: "Shootings Don't Shift Views on Gun Control," in *Views on Gun Laws Unchanged after Aurora Shooting*, Pew Research Center for the People & the Press, July 30, 2012, http://www.people-press.org/files/legacy-pdf/7-30-12%20Gun%20Control%20Release.pdf (accessed August 27, 2012)

monly known as a "stand your ground" law, which protects the right of an individual to use deadly force in self-defense. Facing a sentence of up to 30 years in prison for killing Martin, Zimmerman pleaded not guilty and was seeking an acquittal. He posted bail and was released from jail on July 6, 2012, subject to travel and financial restrictions and wearing an electronic tether. Zimmerman's trial was set to take place in June 2013.

In an online poll of 1,922 people conducted in April 2012 as the case was unfolding (April 13, 2012, http://www.ipsos-na.com/download/pr.aspx?id=11545), Ipsos/Thomson Reuters finds that nearly nine out of 10 (88%) respondents supported laws that allowed "citizens to use deadly force to protect themselves from danger in their own home"; white respondents (91%) were more likely than African-Americans (79%) or Hispanics (83%) to support the legal use of deadly force within the home. About two-thirds (67%) of those surveyed supported laws that allowed "citizens to use deadly force to protect themselves from danger in public places"; white respondents (69%) and Hispanics (69%) were more likely than African-Americans (56%) to support the legal use of deadly force in self-defense in public places. Assessing the role of private citizens in helping to stop crime, 86% of respondents agreed that "police cannot stop all crime from happening" and 76% supported the idea that "regular people need to step up to help prevent crime from happening."

CHAPTER 9
THERE SHOULD BE STRICTER GUN CONTROL LAWS

This chapter presents a sample of the arguments used by the proponents of strong federal gun control to support their position. Chapter 10 provides arguments put forward by opponents of strong federal gun control.

EXCERPT OF STATEMENT OF REPRESENTATIVE EARL BLUMENAUER (1948–; D-OR), *CONGRESSIONAL RECORD*, U.S. HOUSE OF REPRESENTATIVES, SPEAKING ON GUN CONTROL, JULY 23, 2012

Imagine the headline, "Outbreak of Serious Illness Strikes; 12 People Killed, 58 Hospitalized," just like similar outbreaks, but the Federal Government prohibits the Centers for Disease Control from investigating.

Or another headline, "70 Trapped in a Collapsed Building, 20 Dead or Critically Injured," and your government makes it illegal for government organizations to collect data to study what could be done to solve it, to minimize this carnage in the future.

People would be justifiably outraged. They expect government to protect them and to help understand the nature of threats in the workplace, the marketplace, or in our homes. At some level, we want to know about why cars malfunction or if there are patterns of disease, illness, injury, or mechanical failure.

That is what our government is supposed to do. If food safety, mine safety, or TSA fails, there would be calls for accountability. Sadly, that's not what is happening as the Nation recoils in anguish at another outbreak of gun violence. The 70 killed or wounded are the latest in a pattern that happens repeatedly, predictably, with overall loss of life being in the tens of thousands over the years.

What is as appalling as the loss of life is the fact that we not only refuse to do anything about it, but we allow political bullies to intimidate us from even researching the facts.

Now, there's never been a threat in this country that sportsmen will not be able to hunt or target shoot, that false specter raised by the gun lobby so successfully that today there's virtually no gun protection. But that doesn't stop the number one gun advocacy group, the National Rifle Association [NRA], from making things up, creating phony threats to gun ownership. . . .

The NRA argues that all we need is for existing gun laws to be enforced, while they systematically set about to dismantle what laws we have and then defund even feeble government enforcement efforts.

Anyone who looks at the background of the recent so-called Fast and Furious controversy finds that, in part, the Bureau of Alcohol, Tobacco, and Firearms is dysfunctional because it's constantly under assault by the NRA for its most modest steps and most minimal budgets. We cannot even study gun violence, patterns, causes, and potential solutions.

While I didn't know anybody in Aurora, this most recent tragic, senseless rampage touches home for me. As I was growing up, a young man in a family that I was close to was killed by an act of random gun violence.

As I've followed the issues over the years, I continue to feel that there's no reason to permit armor-piercing, cop-killer bullets to be sold like Tic Tacs; that automatic weapons should be available over the counter with hundred-bullet magazines like the killer in Colorado had that facilitate such sprees. These things have no useful purpose in sports activities or target shooting.

I find it appalling that we, as citizens, have enabled Congress to act in a spineless fashion, to be taken over in the area of gun safety by the NRA; that we refuse to deal with something that has serious law enforcement implications so that we, alone, in the developed world are most at risk for random gun violence. Any time there's a mass killing spree, I hope against hope for a more enlightened reaction.

Perhaps the gun owners themselves, the majority of whom disagree with the NRA's extreme positions, will join with politicians, business, the health community to come together to deal with an epidemic of gun violence in the way we would treat any other threat to the safety of our families and our communities. We would study, we would work on solutions together, and we would act.

Sadly, we're still waiting.

STATEMENT OF SENATOR CARL LEVIN (1934–; D-MI), *CONGRESSIONAL RECORD*, U.S. SENATE, ON SCHOOL GUN VIOLENCE PROTECTION, MARCH 15, 2012

Mr. President, as news reports focus on yet another horrific shooting in an American school, we must again confront the simple and sad truth: tragedies like this are often preventable. On February 27, 17-year-old T.J. Lane [1994–] opened fire in his high school cafeteria in Chardon, OH, killing three of his classmates and wounding two other students.

This is a narrative we have heard over and over again. Lane is believed to have taken the gun from his grandfather's barn. Similar to what happened five days earlier in Port Orchard, WA, when a nine-year-old boy accidentally shot his classmate with a .45-caliber handgun he took from his mother's house. Or in 2009, when a 15-year-old boy was institutionalized after stealing three guns and hundreds of rounds of ammunition from his father as part of a plan to shoot other students at Pottstown High School in Philadelphia. Sadly, these are not rare circumstances. A 2000 study by the U.S. Secret Service found that in more than 65% of school shootings, the attacker got the gun from his or her own home or from a relative.

The guardians of these children never intended for their firearms to be used for harm. But they left their loaded guns without any measures to prevent their children—or anyone else—from using them irresponsibly. According to reports by the Legal Community Against Violence, in a nation where approximately one-third of households with minors have a firearm, studies have shown that 55% of these households store one or more of their guns unlocked. Another study showed that 22% of the parents who claimed their children had never handled their firearms were contradicted by their children. When it comes to gun safety, a young person's curiosity and recklessness can be a dangerous thing.

It is imperative that gun owners across the country safely store their weapons out of the reach of young people. But despite these troubling statistics, there are no Federal laws that prevent adults from leaving firearms easily accessible to children and minors. Some State and local governments around the Nation have adopted child firearm access prevention measures, and these laws work. From 1990 to 1994, in the 12 States where child access prevention laws had been in effect for at least one year, unintentional firearm deaths fell by 23% among children under the age of 15. Laws that encourage parents to keep their firearms locked and unloaded, to store their ammunition in a locked location separate from their firearms, and to educate their children on proper gun use and safety, would help prevent shootings involving children and teenagers.

We must not wait for the next Chardon High School or the next Virginia Tech or the next Columbine. Common-sense gun safety legislation protects our schools, our universities, our religious institutions, and our homes from gun violence. But despite this evidence, legislation has been introduced in this Congress to dismantle the few Federal gun safety provisions that protect the American people. I urge our colleagues to support sensible gun safety measures that could prevent tragedies like the one unfolding in Ohio.

EXCERPT OF STATEMENT OF REPRESENTATIVE LAURA RICHARDSON (1962–; D-CA), *CONGRESSIONAL RECORD*, U.S. HOUSE OF REPRESENTATIVES, IN OPPOSITION TO THE NATIONAL RIGHT-TO-CARRY RECIPROCITY ACT OF 2011 (H.R. 822), NOVEMBER 16, 2011

Mr. Chair, I rise today in strong opposition to H.R. 822, the proposed National Right-to-Carry Reciprocity Act of 2011. I call on my colleagues to join me in rejecting this ill-considered and unwise legislation which will effectively force all states to accept the lowest-common-standard in concealed carry laws. Passage of this bill is reckless and undeniably a threat to public safety.

This law would add an unnecessary burden on police officers who risk their lives every day in traffic stops and other risky situations. It would make it nearly impossible for them to be able to determine whether the guns they encounter are legal or not.

The very likely and viable threats posed to public safety if this legislation passes are egregious. This legislation will do away with the strict gun laws each state has established according to its constituent composition and needs and empower dangerous individuals to carry concealed, loaded guns in states where they would not qualify for a local permit.

California has one of the most stringent gun laws in the Nation, and there is a reason for that. California had the highest number of gun murders in the Nation last year, 1,257, which is 69% of all murders that year and equivalent to 3.37 per 100,000 people in the state.

A very real example of what this legislation will do is a person convicted of domestic violence and not allowed to possess, let alone carry a concealed weapon in California, can cross state lines into a state that does not have the same restrictions, receive a permit for a gun, then cross states lines back into California and exact revenge against his victim.

Proponents against gun laws and restrictions constantly chime, "Guns don't kill people. People kill people." That may be the case, but a person with a gun can kill another much more easily than a person without one. FBI crime statistics based on reports to FBI bureau and local law enforcement show that in 2010, the latest year for which detailed statistics are available, there were 12,996 murders in the U.S.; of those, 8,775 were caused by firearms. . . .

If ever you needed a concrete example of why this is such an ill-conceived and dangerous piece of legislation for both the public and law enforcement, consider the recent testimony of Philadelphia Police Commissioner Charles Ramsey before the House Judiciary Subcommittee on Crime, Terrorism, and Homeland Security. The Police Commissioner testified that in 2005, a man named Marqus Hill had his concealed carry permit revoked by Philadelphia Police after he had been charged with attempted murder. Mr. Hill later traveled to Florida, got a new permit despite his record, used his Florida permit to carry a loaded gun into Philadelphia, and later shot a teenager 13 times in the chest, killing him in the street.

Mr. Chair, the ramifications of such legislation do not stop there. It would also make it easier for gun traffickers to move loaded guns through urban city streets where police officers are already having a difficult time combating crime and violence. It will be nearly impossible for police to verify the validity of 49 different carry permits.

Policing our streets and confronting the risks inherent in even routine traffic stops is already perilous enough. Ambiguity as to the legality of firearm possession could lead to confusion among police officers that could result in catastrophic incidents. Congress should be working to make the job of law enforcement officers more, not less, safe.

Today, states establish standards for carrying concealed, loaded handguns in public places that include criteria beyond an applicant's ability to pass a federal background check. For example, at least 38 states prevent people convicted of certain violent crimes from obtaining carry permits, 14 states require applicants to demonstrate good character to obtain a carry permit, and about half of states grant law enforcement discretion to deny a permit. The National Right-to-Carry Reciprocity Act would gut these standards and empower dangerous individuals to carry concealed, loaded guns in states where they would not qualify for a local permit.

We see firsthand the tragedies that can unfold when guns end up in the hands of criminals, the seriously mentally ill, domestic violence offenders and other dangerous people. Let us not forget the tragedy earlier this year in Tucson, Arizona. Statistics show that every year, more than 12,000 gun murders are committed in big cities and small towns throughout the United States.

States and localities should have the right to determine who is eligible to carry firearms in their communities. It is essential that state, local and tribal governments maintain the ability to legislate concealed carry laws that best fit the needs of their communities.

EXCERPT OF STATEMENT OF REPRESENTATIVE LOUISE SLAUGHTER (1929–; D-NY), *CONGRESSIONAL RECORD*, U.S. HOUSE OF REPRESENTATIVES, IN OPPOSITION TO THE NATIONAL RIGHT-TO-CARRY RECIPROCITY ACT OF 2011 (H.R. 822), NOVEMBER 15, 2011

This is a serious piece of work for me today because less than a year ago, one of our colleagues [Representative Gabrielle Giffords (1970–)] from Arizona was shot in the head while she was trying to convene with her constituents outside a supermarket. The mayhem was awful. A little nine-year-old girl named Christina-Taylor Green [2001–2011], a baseball fan who just came to see her Congresswoman, was killed. And by all accounts, an extraordinary Federal judge named John Roll [1947–2011] died as well as some of Gabby's staff. Numbers of people were wounded. And yet the only person ever considered by this House would be the guy and his right to have that gun. What about the rights for the rest of us? Are we going to have to learn to dance up and down the street to try to escape the bullets? What happens to us? What about an amendment for us to ensure that we can be safe?

The statistics of people now being killed in places of worship, the rising number of people in law enforcement who face unspeakable and awful things because we won't do our job here to disarm people who are mentally ill.

. . . When are we going to reinstate in this House the automatic weapons ban, and why don't we outlaw guns that are so powerful that they serve no purpose at all in a civilized society? When will we allow the Federal authorities to computerize gun sale records so it is easier to hold guilty individuals responsible for their gun crimes?

In the age of iPhones and Androids, our police are tracing gun crimes with scraps of paper and handwritten notes. Surely that is a more important job for us to do here than what we're doing—to say you can carry a concealed weapon anywhere you want to go because that's who we are. Apparently, the Republican majority wants that.

Based on today's bill, they think it is more important to pass legislation that will make it easier to carry a gun to a public gathering, easier to carry a loaded weapon into NFL stadiums, easier to carry a gun to the grocery store on Saturday noon, or into your temple or your church. What in the world? How can we ever explain that to people who have had gun deaths in their family?

The horrible shooting of our colleague wouldn't have been stopped with the passage of today's bill, and no one is made safer by allowing guns into public space. And since last January, Congress hasn't considered a single piece of legislation that would make it harder for a mentally ill individual to get a gun. We have done nothing at all to make sure that another nightmare like the one in Tucson doesn't visit our country yet again, leaving innocent children, men, and women victims to a loaded gun. And yet the only person we care about here is the gun owner.

The only legislation we are considering will make it more convenient to carry your gun even in States that don't want it. Realizing this fact really puts the morality of this agenda into perspective...

This Congress should be considering legislation that will help the American people, not legislation that fulfills an ideological agenda, which is what we've been doing all year. I urge my colleagues to vigorously oppose today's legislation.

EXCERPT OF DISSENTING OPINION OF JUSTICE JOHN PAUL STEVENS (1920–), U.S. SUPREME COURT, IN *MCDONALD V. CHICAGO* (561 U.S. ___ [2010]), JUNE 28, 2010

Firearms have a fundamentally ambivalent relationship to liberty. Just as they can help homeowners defend their families and property from intruders, they can help thugs and insurrectionists murder innocent victims. The threat that firearms will be misused is far from hypothetical, for gun crime has devastated many of our communities. Amici [information briefs that are given to the court] calculate that approximately one million Americans have been wounded or killed by gunfire in the last decade. Urban areas such as Chicago suffer disproportionately from this epidemic of violence. Handguns contribute disproportionately to it. Just as some homeowners may prefer handguns because of their small size, light weight, and ease of operation, some criminals will value them for the same reasons.... In recent years, handguns were reportedly used in more than four-fifths of firearm murders and more than half of all murders nationwide.

Hence, in evaluating an asserted right to be free from particular gun-control regulations, liberty is on both sides of the equation. Guns may be useful for self-defense, as well as for hunting and sport, but they also have a unique potential to facilitate death and destruction and thereby to destabilize ordered liberty. Your interest in keeping and bearing a certain firearm may diminish my interest in being and feeling safe from armed violence. And while granting you the right to own a handgun might make you safer on any given day—assuming the handgun's marginal contribution to self-defense outweighs its marginal contribution to the risk of accident, suicide, and criminal mischief—it may make you and the community you live in less safe overall, owing to the increased number of handguns in circulation. It is at least reasonable for a democratically elected legislature to take such concerns into account in considering what sorts of regulations would best serve the public welfare.

The practical impact of various gun-control measures may be highly controversial, but this basic insight should not be. The idea that deadly weapons pose a distinctive threat to the social order—and that reasonable restrictions on their usage therefore impose an acceptable burden on one's personal liberty—is as old as the Republic. As the Chief Justice observed just the other day, it is a foundational premise of modern government that the State holds a monopoly on legitimate violence: "A basic step in organizing a civilized society is to take [the] sword out of private hands and turn it over to an organized government, acting on behalf of all the people."... The same holds true for the handgun. The power a man has in the state of nature "of doing whatsoever he thought fit for the preservation of himself and the rest of mankind, he gives up," to a significant extent, "to be regulated by laws made by the society."...

Limiting the federal constitutional right to keep and bear arms to the home complicates the analysis but does not dislodge this conclusion. Even though the Court has long afforded special solicitude for the privacy of the home, we have never understood that principle to "infring[e] upon" the authority of the States to proscribe certain inherently dangerous items, for "[i]n such cases, compelling reasons may exist for overriding the right of the individual to possess those materials."... And, of course, guns that start out in the home may not stay in the home. Even if the government has a weaker basis for restricting domestic possession of firearms as compared to public carriage—and even if a blanket, statewide prohibition on domestic possession might therefore be unconstitutional—the line between the two is a porous one. A state or local legislature may determine that a prophylactic ban on an especially portable weapon is necessary to police that line.

STATEMENT OF SENATOR FRANK R. LAUTENBERG (1924–; D-NJ), *CONGRESSIONAL RECORD*, U.S. SENATE, SPEAKING ON CLOSING THE GUN SHOW LOOPHOLE, APRIL 20, 2010

I rise because today marks 11 years since the massacre at Columbine High School in Littleton, CO, occurred. This is a painful recall of a horrible moment in our country that should remind us all of a condition that could easily happen again.

I and millions of other Americans watched in horror as young students hung out of windows in that schoolhouse to try to save their lives, while two of their schoolmates went on a rampage and killed 12 students and a teacher. Those images will forever be burned in our memory.

But here is what a lot of people do not know: All the firearms used by the shooters were bought by an underage friend [who was under the age of 21] at a gun show. That purchase was able to be made because of the gun show loophole. Because of the gun show loophole, they were bought with no questions asked, no background check, no questions about who you are, where you might live. The weapons were bought "cash and carry," without, again, any identifying questions being asked or being supplied. Those 13 people should never have died that day because those teenagers should not have had access to those guns. The young woman who bought the guns for the shooters said she would not have done it if a background check had been required.

Our laws require a background check for all gun sales by licensed dealers. But a special exemption allows anyone—including terrorists such as bin Laden, criminals, gun traffickers, and the severely mentally ill—to buy guns without a background check from so-called private sellers, who sell hundreds of guns every year at gun shows, fully exempt from any responsibility for those sales.

In 1999, I introduced legislation to close the gun show loophole and to keep guns from falling into the wrong hands. In the aftermath of Columbine, the Senate passed my legislation, with Vice President Al Gore casting the tiebreaking vote. It was a great victory but a short-lived one. The gun lobby stripped my legislation in conference with the House, and in the decade since then we have done absolutely nothing at the national level to close the gun show loophole. No wonder domestic terrorists frequently use gun shows to sell their firearms to fund their illegal activities....

Whether it is Virginia Tech, the recent shootings at the Pentagon, or Columbine, we are reminded over and over that our gun laws are not strong enough. Yet, while gunshots continue to ring out across this country, the silence from this Chamber is deafening....

Republican pollster Frank Luntz recently found that 69% of National Rifle Association members and...85% of other gun owners want us to close this loophole. After all, the vast majority of gun owners are law-abiding Americans who pass background checks and use their firearms responsibly. They know their lives and the lives of their children are in danger when a firearm is purchased by an unqualified buyer at a gun show, by someone who could never pass a background check at a neighborhood gun store. It is as easy as ever for criminals to buy guns—easier, in fact, than it is to get a library card.

We have an opportunity to save lives, and that is why I call on my colleagues to please join me and pass my bill to close the gun show loophole once and for all. Eleven years ago, we lost 12 students and a teacher to gun violence in Littleton, CO. One of the best ways to honor those who perished and those who have suffered is to make sure a tragedy like Columbine never happens again. We owe that and nothing less to the young people who died 11 years ago and the young people who count on us today. We have to step up to our responsibilities and ask all gun dealers to step up to their responsibilities.

EXCERPT OF STATEMENT OF SENATOR DIANNE FEINSTEIN (1933–; D-CA), *CONGRESSIONAL RECORD*, U.S. SENATE, IN SUPPORT OF RENEWING THE ASSAULT WEAPON BAN, MARCH 1, 2004

The issue of assault weapons is near and dear to my heart. It is not about politics or polls or interest groups. In my view, it is about real people and real lives. It is about the ability of working men and women and children to be safe from disgruntled employees or schoolmates who show up one day at a law firm or school or a place of business and fire away until the room becomes filled with dead and wounded colleagues.

Unfortunately, in this society, we are always going to have some people who are prone to grievance killing.

It is my belief the assault weapon, the military-style semiautomatic assault weapon, has become the weapon of choice for grievance killers.

It is about the ability of children to learn, play, and grow without the fear that someone such as Dylan Klebold or Eric Harris would show up at Columbine High School with assault weapons and fire until the school is literally littered with bodies—a dozen students and a teacher murdered, more than two dozen others injured.

It is about making sure our law enforcement officers can safely go about their duties and return home to their families at the end of the day, instead of finding themselves confronted, such as Officer James Guelff found himself in 1994, with assailants wearing body armor and firing from an arsenal of 2,000 rounds of ammunition and a cache of assault weapons.

The officer was gunned down after 10 years of service, and it took 150 police officers to equal the firepower of a gunman clad in Kevlar carrying assault weapons.

I first raised this issue in 1993, when I was a new senator. I was determined to try to pass the assault weapons legislation as an amendment to the crime bill. Members told me: Forget it; the gun owners around here have too much authority. We would never be able to enact assault weapons legislation. I was told the NRA was simply too strong. Senator Biden, then-chair of the Judiciary Committee, said it would be a good learning experience for me, and, in fact, it was.

It was the will of the American people, it turns out, that was stronger than any lobbying organization, even the National Rifle Association. And today, 77% of the American people and 66% of gun owners believe this legislation should be reauthorized.

CHAPTER 10
THERE SHOULD NOT BE STRICTER GUN CONTROL LAWS

This chapter presents a sample of the arguments used by the opponents of strong federal gun control to support their position. Chapter 9 provides arguments put forward by supporters of strong federal gun control.

EXCERPT OF SPEECH BY WAYNE LAPIERRE, EXECUTIVE VICE PRESIDENT OF THE NATIONAL RIFLE ASSOCIATION (NRA), AT THE CONSERVATIVE POLITICAL ACTION CONFERENCE, WASHINGTON, D.C., FEBRUARY 10, 2012

I've been leading the NRA—and our fight for freedom—for more than two decades now. We've had some tough fights. We've been through rough battles. But we've never backed down.

The NRA's four million members are among history's most committed, most active, and most politically savvy defenders of the fundamental freedom that separates us from every other nation on earth. The Second Amendment to the U.S. Constitution is the essence of what being an American is all about—living truly free as individual citizens.

No matter what other issues you may care about, it is the core principle of real freedom for each citizen that defines the uniqueness of our nation. There is no greater freedom than to own a firearm to protect your self, your family, your community, and your nation. Thus, Second Amendment freedom is, truly, the heart and soul of America.

EXCERPT OF STATEMENT OF REPRESENTATIVE RON KIND (1963–; R-WI), U.S. HOUSE OF REPRESENTATIVES, SPEAKING IN SUPPORT OF THE NATIONAL RIGHT-TO-CARRY ACT OF 2011 (H.R. 822), NOVEMBER 16, 2011

Mr. Chair, I rise today in strong support of the National Right-to-Carry Reciprocity Act, H.R. 822. Not only am I a proud cosponsor of this legislation but I am also a firm and committed supporter of Second Amendment rights. This

legislation will ensure further protection of this vital right by allowing law abiding citizens to carry concealed weapons across state lines.

On November 1st of this year, Wisconsin became the 49th state to implement a concealed carry law. The first day the law went into effect, the Wisconsin State Department of Justice website had 400,000 hits and residents had downloaded 83,000 applications. It is clear that Wisconsinites were eager to take advantage of this new law. Given the strong interest this law has garnered in my state and in other states throughout the country, I believe that it is only logical to extend this right across state lines.

The bill allows law-abiding gun owners with valid state-issued concealed firearm permits or licenses to carry a concealed firearm in any other state that also allows concealed carry. In all actuality, with all but one state allowing concealed carry, this legislation doesn't break that much new ground. In fact, for the majority of states that have had concealed carry laws on the books for some time now; they have been recognizing permits from other states for years. As can be the case, the state by state approach has caused confusion. This legislation will eliminate any uncertainty by putting in place simple and concise federal policy.

This is a widely supported bill with 245 bipartisan House cosponsors. Given the strong support here in Congress and the increased interest in states throughout the country, it is my hope that the Senate will follow our lead and pass this legislation. It would be a great victory to have this become law this year.

EXCERPT OF STATEMENTS OF REPRESENTATIVE RICH NUGENT (1951–; R-FL), U.S. HOUSE OF REPRESENTATIVES, SPEAKING IN SUPPORT OF THE NATIONAL RIGHT-TO-CARRY ACT OF 2011 (H.R. 822), NOVEMBER 15, 2011

Madam Speaker, until coming to this body 10 months ago, I had spent my entire career as a cop, the last 10 years as sheriff of Hernando County, Florida. During my 38 years in law enforcement, I found that disarming honest citizens does nothing to reduce crime. If anything, all it does is keep law-abiding citizens from being able to defend themselves from violent criminals. Although I know this just from my anecdotal experience, research backs up the claim.

For example, statistics indicate that citizens with carry permits are more law-abiding than the general public. In my home State of Florida, only 0.01% of nearly 1.2 million permits have been revoked because of firearm crimes committed by permit holders. Additionally, evidence indicates that crime declines in States with right-to-carry laws. Since Florida became a right-to-carry State in 1987, Florida's total violent crime and murder rates have dropped 32% and 58%, respectively.

Because of this evidence, as well as my firsthand experience, I am a proud defender of our Second Amendment right: ensuring "the right of the people to keep and bear arms shall not be infringed." My history as a law enforcement officer is also why I am a proud cosponsor of H.R. 822, the National Right-to-Carry Reciprocity Act of 2011.

H.R. 822 is a good, bipartisan bill, which enhances the constitutional rights of law-abiding gun owners. Today, if I drive from my home State of Florida into Georgia, Georgia recognizes that my Florida driver's license is still valid even once I cross the State line. H.R. 822 would require States to recognize each other's legally issued concealed carry permits in the same way. This legislation would take a comprehensive approach to helping law-abiding citizens navigate the patchwork of State concealed carry laws.

H.R. 822 does not—let me repeat—does not create a national concealed carry permit system nor does it establish any nationalized standard for a carry permit. H.R. 822 respects the States' abilities to create their own gun usage laws as well as their own permitting processes.

I am sure that we will hear arguments from my colleagues on the other side of the aisle saying that H.R. 822 somehow makes it easier for people to get a gun. Let me assure you that, again, this is not the case. This legislation does not mandate that anyone suddenly be given a gun nor does it relax any of a State's current permitting laws....

What it does is ensures that legal gun owners don't accidentally break a law simply because they brought their fully permitted gun into another State. This legislation gives peace of mind to Americans traveling across State lines with a legally registered, concealed firearm, knowing that they can practice their constitutional right to bear arms....

I believe that the Second Amendment is not a special interest group. I believe the Second Amendment needs to be protected at all costs....

Guns are dangerous tools that need to be treated with respect. Guns can be used by people to kill other people. However, what I saw in those 40 years as a cop is we

need to talk about these [issues] in broader terms. What we really need to do is talk about the difference between legal and illegal guns....

STATEMENT OF REPRESENTATIVE DENNIS REHBERG (1955–; R-MT), U.S. HOUSE OF REPRESENTATIVES, INTRODUCING THE FIREARMS FREEDOM ON FEDERAL LANDS ACT (H.R. 5523), JUNE 15, 2010

Mr. Speaker, too many people in Washington, D.C. are under the dangerous impression that the Second Amendment is obsolete and unnecessary. If they had their way, only criminals and agents of the State would be armed, while law-abiding Americans would be at their mercy.

While we can stop gun control in Congress, progressives and Washington, D.C. bureaucrats will use every tactic at their disposal to disarm the American public, including banning firearms on public lands.

That is why I have sponsored the Firearms Freedom on Federal Lands Act with Representatives Rob Bishop and Paul Broun. This legislation creates a statutory protection of gun rights, preventing land management agencies from restricting firearms on public lands, as they have done in the past.

The NRA has endorsed this measure, and I hope my colleagues will follow their lead and cosponsor this legislation.

STATEMENT OF SENATOR JOHN THUNE (1961–; R-SD), *CONGRESSIONAL RECORD*, U.S. SENATE, INTRODUCING AMENDMENT NO. 1618 TO AMEND CHAPTER 44 OF TITLE 18, UNITED STATES CODE, TO ALLOW CITIZENS WHO HAVE CONCEALED CARRY PERMITS FROM THE STATE IN WHICH THEY RESIDE TO CARRY CONCEALED FIREARMS IN ANOTHER STATE THAT GRANTS CONCEALED CARRY PERMITS, IF THE INDIVIDUAL COMPLIES WITH THE LAWS OF THE STATE, JULY 22, 2009

Amendment No. 1618 is a very simple amendment. It is tailored to allow individuals to protect themselves while at the same time protecting States rights.

My amendment would allow an individual to carry a concealed firearm across State lines if they either have a valid permit or if, under their State of residence, they are legally entitled to do so....

This carefully tailored amendment will ensure that a State's border is not a limit to an individual's fundamental right and will allow law-abiding individuals to travel, without complication, throughout the 48 States that currently permit some form of conceal and carry. Law-abiding individuals have the right to self-defense, especially because the Supreme Court has consistently found that police have no constitutional obligation to protect individuals from other individuals....

Responsible gun ownership by law-abiding individuals, however, provides a constitutional means by which individuals may do so, and responsible conceal and carry holders have repeatedly proven they are effective in protecting themselves and those around them.

Reliable, empirical research shows that States with concealed carry laws enjoy significantly lower crime and violent crime rates than those States that do not.

For example, for every year a State has a concealed carry law, the murder rate declines by 3%, rape by 2%, and robberies by over 2%.

Additionally, research shows that "minorities and women tend to be the ones with the most to gain from being allowed to protect themselves."

The benefits of conceal and carry extend to more than just the individuals who actually carry the firearms. Since criminals are unable to tell who is and who is not carrying a firearm just by looking at a potential victim, they are less likely to commit a crime when they fear they may come in direct contact with an individual who is armed.

This deterrent is so strong that a Department of Justice study found that 40% of felons had not committed crimes because they feared the prospective victims were armed. Additionally, research shows that when unrestricted conceal and carry laws are passed, not only does it benefit those who are armed, but it also benefits others around them such as children....

I believe this is something that is consistent with the constitutional right that citizens in this country have to keep and bear firearms. We have, as I said, 48 States currently today that have some form of concealed carry law that allows their individuals in their States, residents of their States, to carry. This simply extends that constitutional right across State lines, recognizing that the right to defend oneself and the right to exercise that basic second amendment constitutional right does not end at State borders or State lines.

STATEMENT OF SENATOR KAY BAILEY HUTCHISON (1943– ; R-TX), ON WASHINGTON, D.C., GUN BAN CASE BEFORE THE U.S. SUPREME COURT, MARCH 18, 2008

Today's oral arguments were a major step forward in the case that for the first time gives the Supreme Court a clear opportunity to establish the second amendment right as one of an individual to protect themselves in their home with possession of a gun. I was pleased to submit an amicus curiae brief to the Supreme Court with the most signatures of members of Congress ever obtained for a brief to the court. Our amicus brief, signed by 54 Senators, the Vice

President and 250 members of the House of Representatives firmly stated that every congressional act has assumed this second amendment to be one for individuals, not an organized militia. It is my hope that the Supreme Court will settle this clearly so that there will be no further attempts by gun control advocates to undermine this important right established by our Founding Fathers.

EXCERPT OF SPEECH BY SENATOR JOHN McCAIN (1936– ; R-AZ), AT THE NATIONAL RIFLE ASSOCIATION OF AMERICA'S CELEBRATION OF AMERICAN VALUES CONFERENCE, WASHINGTON, D.C., SEPTEMBER 21, 2007

For more than two decades, I've opposed the efforts of the anti-gun crowd to ban guns, ban ammunition, ban magazines and ban paint gun owners as some kind of fringe group—dangerous in "modern" America.

Some even call you extremists. My friends, gun owners are not extremists. You're the core of modern America. The Second Amendment is unique in the world and at the core of our constitutional freedoms. It guarantees an individual right to keep and bear arms. To argue anything else is to reject the clear meaning of our Founding Fathers.

But the clear meaning of the Second Amendment has not stopped those who want to punish firearm owners and those who want to make—and those who make and sell firearms for the actions of criminals. It seems like every time there's a particularly violent crime, the anti-gun crowd comes up with a plan to capitalize on tragedy and limit Second Amendment rights for all Americans.

I opposed the ban on so-called assault weapons, which was first proposed after a California schoolyard shooting. I thought it made no sense to ban a class of firearms based on cosmetic features. I opposed waiting periods for gun purchases. We lost on both in the short run, but it's worked out better in the long run. Fortunately, the gun ban sunsetted after 10 long years, and I was proud to vote against those who tried to extend it in 2004.

I also opposed efforts to cripple our firearms manufacturers by making them liable for the acts of violent criminals. This was a particularly devious effort, to use lawsuits to bankrupt our great gun manufacturers. A number of big city mayors decided it was more important to blame the manufacturers of a legal product than it was to control crime in their own cities. Fortunately—fortunately, we are able to protect manufacturers from...frivolous lawsuits....

In my years in Washington, I've seen what I call three myths used by politicians to excuse their support for gun control.

First is the big city myth, that it is acceptable, even necessary, to fight crime in big cities. If you have a crime problem, they say it's really a gun problem. So instead of increasing police patrols, instituting tough sentences for lawbreakers, and other measures that would actually address crime, we restrict ownership of guns and limit the rights of law-abiding citizens.

We're meeting today in a city that represents the worst of this myth. The citizens of the nation's capital do not enjoy the right to bear—to keep and bear arms. That's why I've co-sponsored legislation repealing the ban on firearms possession for law-abiding citizens in the District of Columbia. The Second Amendment is not just for rural Arizona; it's for all of America.

The second myth is that of the bad gun. This was at the core of the debate over the so-called assault weapons. Proponents of this myth argue that some kinds of guns are acceptable for now, but others are not if they have certain features like a pistol grip or an extended magazine. I will continue to oppose those who want to ration the Second Amendment based on their views of what guns it applies to.

Finally, there's the hunting myth. The hunting myth: If you show your bona fides by hunting ducks or varmints or quail, it makes up for support of gun control. This myth overlooks a fundamental truth: The Second Amendment is not about hunting, it's about freedom . . . .

Let's be clear. If the Democrat[ic] candidates were elected president, they will go after the rights of law-abiding gun owners just as Bill Clinton did when he was president. MoveOn.org, which seems to be calling the shots in the Democratic Party these days, will have more influence on gun control in the Oval Office, not John Dingell. These Democratic candidates voted to ban guns or ammunition or to allow gun-makers to be sued out of existence as senators. Think how much worse it would be if they had the power to appoint Supreme Court justices, name attorney generals and use the full power of the federal government.

TESTIMONY OF REPRESENTATIVE PHIL GINGREY (1942–; R-GA), ON H.R. 1384, FIREARMS COMMERCE MODERNIZATION ACT, COMMITTEE ON THE JUDICIARY, SUBCOMMITTEE ON CRIME, TERRORISM, AND HOMELAND SECURITY, MAY 3, 2006

Mr. Chairman and members of the subcommittee, thank you for the opportunity to testify today in support of my bill, H.R. 1384, the Firearms Commerce Modernization Act.

I introduced this legislation after I learned about some of the severe and, quite frankly, obsolete restrictions that Federal law imposes on businesses and individuals who want to sell firearms legally through our Nation's interstate economy.

In general, since 1968, it has been illegal for any person without a Federal firearms license to buy or sell handguns across State lines. Licensed dealers cannot sell firearms, except certain collectibles, at a gun show outside of their own State.

Even between dealers, who go through a thorough background check to get a dealer's license, the Bureau of Alcohol, Tobacco, Firearms, and Explosives does not allow face-to-face transfers. So dealers who agree on a sale must go back to their stores and ship the firearm.

Gun theft is a major source of the firearms used in crime, and it is senseless under current law to make a licensed dealer ship a firearm when they can make a legal and documented transaction at the time of purchase.

My bill would do three simple things, Mr. Chairman. Firstly, it would make it legal for a licensed dealer to sell a handgun to a resident of another State as long as they do the sale in person, and they obey the laws of both States as well as Federal law.

And secondly, it would allow dealers to do business at out-of-State gun shows. Again, they would have to obey the laws of the State they were visiting—this addresses Ranking Member Scott's concerns—as well as all the Federal laws and regulations they normally obey.

It would allow, thirdly, dealers to transfer firearms directly to one another, instead of risking theft or loss during shipment.

The reason we can make these changes today is really quite simple. It's based on technology. These restrictions were imposed in 1968, when the only way for a dealer to conduct a background check on an out-of-State buyer was by sending a certified letter to the police in the buyer's home State, waiting for a reply, and then waiting a week before making the sale. That was 1968 technology.

But today, dealers can request background checks with a phone call or online by either contacting the FBI directly or by contacting a State police agency that uses the FBI's database. They get an answer in seconds and with an exceptional degree of accuracy.

This routine applies one way or another to every gun sold by every dealer in every State . . . .

And we're going to improve this database with Representative McCarthy's bill. Just to show you how far the technology has come, any teenager can go online today and order a $500 laptop computer that carries more computing power than NASA carried on the first space shuttle 25 years ago. It costs less, and the teenager does not have to be a rocket scientist—no pun intended—to use it.

And if you bought a new cell phone in the last year, you're probably carrying more memory, programmability, and computing power in your pocket than AT&T had in all its long distance systems in the late 1960's.

So, with all of these advances, there is every reason to allow law-abiding individuals to buy handguns in other States, just as we currently allow for long guns. The key point is that anyone purchasing a firearm would, by Federal law, still have to go through the background check, and they would still have to obey the laws of their home State as well as the State where the sale takes place....

And that last point is very important because I know there are some arguments that this legislation bypasses strict or very strict certain State laws. And those arguments are just not true.

If you are from California or Massachusetts or New York, you would still have to obey your own State laws before you could buy a handgun at home or anywhere else. That would include licenses, waiting periods, bans on certain kinds of guns, or any other restrictions. And if a dealer is not confident he can comply with those laws, no one can force him or her to make the sale.

Mr. Chairman, I believe H.R. 1384 is a reasonable piece of legislation that helps get rid of some restrictions that we just do not need anymore and, frankly, can be downright dangerous. And I appreciate your time and effort in considering this legislation.

STATEMENT OF SENATOR DAVID VITTER (1961–; R-LA), *CONGRESSIONAL RECORD*, U.S. SENATE, INTRODUCING A BILL TO HELP SAFEGUARD AGAINST UNITED NATIONS' INFRINGEMENT ON SECOND AMENDMENT RIGHTS, JULY 27, 2005

Mr. President, I rise today to introduce a bill that would withhold United States contributions to the United Nations if the U.N. interferes with the second amendment rights guaranteed by our Constitution.

The U.N. has no business interfering with the second amendment rights guaranteed by our Constitution. That is why I am introducing legislation to safeguard our citizens against any potential infringement of their second amendment rights.

In July, 2001, the U.N. convened a conference, known as the "Conference on the Illicit Trade of Small Arms and Light Weapons in All Its Aspects in July 2001." One outcome of the conference was a resolution entitled, "The United Nations Program of Action to Prevent, Combat and Eradicate the Illicit Trade in Small Arms and Light Weapons in All Its Aspects." This resolution calls for actions that could abridge the second amendment rights of individuals in the United States, including: (1) national registries and tracking lists of legal firearms; (2) the establishment of an international tracking certificate, which could be used to ensure U.N. monitoring of the export, import, transit, stocking, and storage of legal small arms and light weapons; and (3) worldwide record keeping for an indefinite amount of time on the manufacture, holding, and transfer of small arms and light weapons.

The U.N. also wishes to establish a system for tracking small arms and light weapons. How would they do this? It would be done by forcing legal, licensed gun manufacturers to create identifiable marks for each nation. The gun manufacturer's lists would then be provided to international authorities on behalf of the U.N.

Who would maintain these intrusive lists? Would it be the World Customs Organization, which the U.N. has suggested as a possible vehicle? That organization counts Iran, Syria, China, and Cuba among its membership. Would all World Customs Organization members have access to such lists? In the event that those with access to such information abuse or misuse it, what would be the remedy? How would we prevent unauthorized persons, perhaps criminals and terrorists, from acquiring such information from rogue nations who have declared the United States an enemy?

Some at the U.N. have suggested that tracing certain financial transactions of a legal and law abiding gun industry could be a useful tool in tracking firearms. What would such tracing entail? Does the U.N. expect to receive private U.S. banking records of a legal and law abiding industry?

Furthermore, the U.N. has encouraged member States to integrate measures to control ammunition with regard to small arms, and some members have expressed a desire to tax international arms sales. The U.N. has no legal right or authority to collect a tax from American citizens to further any agenda, especially gun control measures.

The U.S. Constitution has guaranteed our citizens the right to keep and bear arms. I intend to help protect that right with this legislation. I urge my colleagues to support the Second Amendment Protection Act of 2005.

EXCERPT OF STATEMENT OF SENATOR JOHN CORNYN (1952–; R-TX), AGAINST THE PROTECTION OF LAWFUL COMMERCE IN ARMS ACT, PARTICULARLY CLOSING THE GUN-SHOW LOOPHOLE, MARCH 2, 2004

I believe it is absolutely imperative that, rather than focusing on and punishing law-abiding citizens who want nothing more than to provide for their families by engaging in a lawful enterprise and producing a legal product, we ought to focus our law enforcement efforts on the criminals. Indeed, we have found through programs such as Project Exile in Richmond, VA, and Texas Exile in my own State, we can have a real impact by punishing the convicted felons who illegally possess firearms and those who use firearms illegally to jeopardize our communities and threaten our communities, and that there is absolutely no benefit to be gained by passing additional laws, as the proponents of these amendments would do, that limit the rights of law-abiding citizens.

I would like to just mention in closing why I believe we do need to expand the role of instant background checks to all commercial gun sales, no matter where they occur. But as well-intentioned as the amendments proposed by Senator McCain and Senator Reed and Senator Lieberman and others are, the so-called closing the gun show loophole bill—as well-intentioned as they are, I think it misses the mark. I would like to work with them to try to bring the instant background check to all commercial gun sales in this country.

The problem is this amendment, as well-intentioned as it is, will have the effect, should there be a State attorney general who doesn't seek a 24-hour instant background check period, that there will be a default through a 3-day check period, which will essentially obliterate gun show sales.

It is important to point out that, currently, everybody who is a dealer in firearms is subject to the Federal firearms license. Indeed, there is no such thing as an unlicensed dealer. But what this amendment would seek to do would be to affect people who are not dealers in firearms, but are collectors, people who engage in sales to friends and family and others.... As long as they are lawful possessors of these firearms, I don't believe the full apparatus of the Federal Government ought to intrude on that ability to conduct a sale that is no threat to the people of this country.

APPENDIX: STATE CONSTITUTION ARTICLES CONCERNING WEAPONS

The Second Amendment of the Bill of Rights of the U.S. Constitution reads: "A well regulated militia, being necessary to the security of a free state, the right of the people to keep and bear arms, shall not be infringed."

Alabama: That every citizen has a right to bear arms in defense of himself and the state. Art. I, § 26 (enacted 1819).

Alaska: A well-regulated militia being necessary to the security of a free state, the right of the people to keep and bear arms shall not be infringed. The individual right to keep and bear arms shall not be denied or infringed by the State or a political subdivision of the State. Art. I, § 19 (first sentence was enacted in 1959; second sentence was added in 1994).

Arizona: The right of the individual citizen to bear arms in defense of himself or the State shall not be impaired, but nothing in this section shall be construed as authorizing individuals or corporations to organize, maintain, or employ an armed body of men. Art. II, § 26 (enacted in 1912).

Arkansas: The citizens of this State shall have the right to keep and bear arms, for their common defense. Art. II, § 5 (enacted in 1874).

California: No constitutional provision.

Colorado: The right of no person to keep and bear arms in defense of his home, person and property, or in aid of the civil power when thereto legally summoned, shall be called in question; but nothing herein contained shall be construed to justify the practice of carrying concealed weapons. Art. II, § 13 (enacted in 1876).

Connecticut: Every citizen has a right to bear arms in defense of himself and the state. Art. I, § 15 (enacted in 1818).

Delaware: A person has the right to keep and bear arms for the defense of self, family, home and State, and for hunting and recreational use. Art. I, § 20 (enacted in 1987).

Florida: (a) The right of the people to keep and bear arms in defense of themselves and of the lawful authority of the state shall not be infringed, except that the manner of bearing arms may be regulated by law. (b) There shall be a mandatory period of three days, excluding weekends and legal holidays, between the purchase and delivery at retail of any handgun. For the purposes of this section, "purchase" means the transfer of money or other valuable consideration to the retailer, and "handgun" means a firearm capable of being carried and used by one hand, such as a pistol or revolver. Holders of a concealed weapon permit as prescribed in Florida law shall not be subject to the provisions of this paragraph. (c) The legislature shall enact legislation implementing subsection (b) of this section, effective no later than December 31, 1991, which shall provide that anyone violating the provisions of subsection (b) shall be guilty of a felony. (d) This restriction shall not apply to a trade in of another handgun. Art. I, § 8 (sections (b) to (d) adopted in 1990).

Georgia: The right of the people to keep and bear arms shall not be infringed, but the General Assembly shall have power to prescribe the manner in which arms may be borne. Art. I, § 1, Paragraph VIII (enacted in 1877).

Hawaii: A well regulated militia being necessary to the security of a free state, the right of the people to keep and bear arms shall not be infringed. Art. I, § 17 (enacted in 1959).

Idaho: The people have the right to keep and bear arms, which right shall not be abridged; but this provision shall not prevent the passage of laws to govern the carrying of weapons concealed on the person nor prevent passage of legislation providing minimum sentences for crimes committed while in possession of a firearm, nor prevent the passage of legislation providing penalties for the possession of firearms by a convicted felon, nor prevent the passage of any legislation punishing the use of a firearm. No law shall impose licensure, registration or special taxation on the ownership or possession of firearms or ammunition. Nor shall any law permit the confiscation of firearms, except those actually used in the commission of a felony. Art. I, § 11 (enacted in 1890).

Illinois: Subject only to the police power, the right of the individual citizen to keep and bear arms shall not be infringed. Art. I, § 22 (enacted in 1970).

Indiana: The people shall have a right to bear arms, for the defense of themselves and the State. Art. I, § 32 (enacted in 1851).

Iowa: No constitutional provision.

Kansas: The people have the right to bear arms for their defense and security; but standing armies, in time of peace, are dangerous to liberty, and shall not be tolerated, and the military shall be in strict subordination to the civil power. Bill of Rights, § 4 (enacted in 1859).

Kentucky: All men are, by nature, free and equal, and have certain inherent and inalienable rights, among which may be reckoned:...The right to bear arms in defense of themselves and of the State, subject to the power of the General Assembly to enact laws to prevent persons from carrying concealed weapons. Bill of Rights, § 1 (enacted in 1891).

Louisiana: The right of each citizen to keep and bear arms shall not be abridged, but this provision shall not prevent the passage of laws to prohibit the carrying of weapons concealed on the person. Art. I, § 11 (enacted in 1974).

Maine: Every citizen has a right to keep and bear arms and this right shall never be questioned. Art. I, § 16 (enacted in 1820).

Maryland: No constitutional provision.

Massachusetts: The people have a right to keep and to bear arms for the common defence [*sic*]. And as, in time of peace, armies are dangerous to liberty, they ought not to be maintained without the consent of the legislature; and the military power shall always be held in an exact subordination to the civil authority, and be governed by it. Pt. I, Art. XVII (enacted in 1780).

Michigan: Every person has a right to keep and bear arms for the defense of himself and the state. Art. I, § 6 (enacted in 1963).

Minnesota: No constitutional provision.

Mississippi: The right of every citizen to keep and bear arms in defense of his home, person, or property, or in aid of the civil power when thereto legally summoned, shall not be called in question, but the legislature may

regulate or forbid carrying concealed weapons. Art. III, § 12 (enacted in 1890).

Missouri: That the right of every citizen to keep and bear arms in defense of his home, person and property, or when lawfully summoned in aid of the civil power, shall not be questioned; but this shall not justify the wearing of concealed weapons. Art. I, § 23 (enacted in 1875).

Montana: The right of any person to keep or bear arms in defense of his own home, person, and property, or in aid of the civil power when thereto legally summoned, shall not be called in question, but nothing herein contained shall be held to permit the carrying of concealed weapons. Art. II, § 12 (enacted in 1889).

Nebraska: All persons are by nature free and independent, and have certain inherent and inalienable rights; among these are life, liberty, the pursuit of happiness, and the right to keep and bear arms for security or defense of self, family, home, and others, and for lawful common defense, hunting, recreational use, and all other lawful purposes, and such rights shall not be denied or infringed by the state or any subdivision thereof. To secure these rights, and the protection of property, governments are instituted among people, deriving their just powers from the consent of the governed. Bill of Rights, Art. I, § 1 (right to keep and bear arms enacted in 1988).

Nevada: Every citizen has the right to keep and bear arms for security and defense, for lawful hunting and recreational use and for other lawful purposes. Art. I, § 11(1) (enacted in 1982).

New Hampshire: All persons have the right to keep and bear arms in defense of themselves, their families, their property and the state. Pt. I, Art. IIa (enacted in 1982).

New Jersey: No constitutional provision.

New Mexico: No law shall abridge the right of the citizen to keep and bear arms for security and defense, for lawful hunting and recreational use and for other lawful purposes, but nothing herein shall be held to permit the carrying of concealed weapons. No municipality or county shall regulate, in any way, an incident of the right to keep and bear arms. Art. II, § 6 (first sentence enacted in 1971; second sentence added in 1986).

New York: No constitutional provision.

North Carolina: A well regulated militia being necessary to the security of a free State, the right of the people to keep and bear arms shall not be infringed; and, as standing armies in time of peace are dangerous to liberty, they shall not be maintained, and the military shall be kept under strict subordination to, and governed by, the civil power. Nothing herein shall justify the practice of carrying concealed weapons, or prevent the General Assembly from enacting penal statutes against that practice. Art. I, § 30 (enacted in 1971).

North Dakota: All individuals are by nature equally free and independent and have certain inalienable rights, among which are those of enjoying and defending life and liberty; acquiring, possessing and protecting property and reputation; pursuing and obtaining safety and happiness; and to keep and bear arms for the defense of their person, family, property, and the state, and for lawful hunting, recreational, and other lawful purposes, which shall not be infringed. Art. I, § 1 (right to keep and bear arms enacted in 1984).

Ohio: The people have the right to bear arms for their defense and security; but standing armies, in time of peace, are dangerous to liberty, and shall not be kept up; and the military shall be in strict subordination to the civil power. Art. I, § 4 (enacted in 1851).

Oklahoma: The right of a citizen to keep and bear arms in defense of his home, person, or property, or in aid of the civil power, when thereunto legally summoned, shall never be prohibited; but nothing herein contained shall prevent the Legislature from regulating the carrying of weapons. Art. II, § 26 (enacted in 1907).

Oregon: The people shall have the right to bear arms for the defence [*sic*] of themselves, and the State, but the Military shall be kept in strict subordination to the civil power. Art. I, § 27 (enacted in 1857).

Pennsylvania: The right of the citizens to bear arms in defense of themselves and the State shall not be questioned. Art. I, § 21 (enacted in 1790).

Rhode Island: The right of the people to keep and bear arms shall not be infringed. Art. I, § 22 (enacted in 1843).

South Carolina: A well regulated militia being necessary to the security of a free State, the right of the people to keep and bear arms shall not be infringed. As, in times of peace, armies are dangerous to liberty, they shall not be maintained without the consent of the General Assembly. The military power of the State shall always be held in subordination to the civil authority and be governed by it. Art. I, § 20 (enacted in 1895).

South Dakota: The right of the citizens to bear arms in defense of themselves and the state shall not be denied. Art. VI, § 24 (enacted in 1889).

Tennessee: That the citizens of this State have a right to keep and to bear arms for their common defense; but

the Legislature shall have power, by law, to regulate the wearing of arms with a view to prevent crime. Art. I, § 26 (enacted in 1870).

Texas: Every citizen shall have the right to keep and bear arms in the lawful defense of himself or the State; but the Legislature shall have power, by law, to regulate the wearing of arms, with a view to prevent crime. Art. I, § 23 (enacted in 1876).

Utah: The individual right of the people to keep and bear arms for security and defense of self, family, others, property, or the state, as well as for other lawful purposes shall not be infringed; but nothing herein shall prevent the Legislature from defining the lawful use of arms. Art. I, § 6 (enacted in 1984).

Vermont: That the people have a right to bear arms for the defence [*sic*] of themselves and the State—and as standing armies in time of peace are dangerous to liberty, they ought not to be kept up; and that the military should be kept under strict subordination to and governed by the civil power. Ch. I, Art. XVI (enacted in 1777).

Virginia: That a well regulated militia, composed of the body of the people, trained to arms, is the proper, natural, and safe defense of a free state, therefore, the right of the people to keep and bear arms shall not be infringed; that standing armies, in time of peace, should be avoided as dangerous to liberty; and that in all cases the military should be under strict subordination to, and governed by, the civil power. Art. I, § 13 (enacted in 1971).

Washington: The right of the individual citizen to bear arms in defense of himself, or the state, shall not be impaired, but nothing in this section shall be construed as authorizing individuals or corporations to organize, maintain or employ an armed body of men. Art. I, § 24 (enacted in 1889).

West Virginia: A person has the right to keep and bear arms for the defense of self, family, home and state, and for lawful hunting and recreational use. Art. III, § 22 (enacted in 1986).

Wisconsin: The people have the right to keep and bear arms for security, defense, hunting, recreation or any other lawful purpose. Art. I, § 25 (enacted in 1998).

Wyoming: The right of citizens to bear arms in defense of themselves and of the state shall not be denied. Art. I, § 24 (enacted in 1889).

IMPORTANT NAMES
AND ADDRESSES

Americans for Responsible Solutions PAC
Po Box 15642
Washington, DC 20003-0642
URL: http://
americansforresponsiblesolutions.org/

Brady Campaign to Prevent Gun Violence
1225 Eye St. NW, Ste. 1100
Washington, DC 20005
(202) 898-0792
FAX: (202) 371-9615
URL: http://www.bradycampaign.org/

Brady Center to Prevent Gun Violence
1225 Eye St. NW, Ste. 1100
Washington, DC 20005
(202) 289-7319
FAX: (202) 408-1851
URL: http://bradycenter.org/

Bureau of Alcohol, Tobacco, Firearms, and Explosives
Public Affairs Division
99 New York Ave. NE
Room 5S 144
Washington, DC 20226
(202) 648-8500
URL: http://www.atf.gov/

Centers for Disease Control and Prevention
1600 Clifton Rd.
Atlanta, GA 30333
1-800-232-4636
E-mail: cdcinfo@cdc.gov
URL: http://www.cdc.gov/

Citizens Committee for the Right to Keep and Bear Arms
Liberty Park
12500 NE 10th Place
Bellevue, WA 98005
(425) 454-4911
1-800-486-6963
FAX: (425) 451-3959
E-mail: AdminForWeb@ccrkba.org
URL: http://www.ccrkba.org/

Coalition to Stop Gun Violence
1424 L St. NW, Ste. 2-1
Washington, DC 20005
(202) 408-0061
E-mail: csgv@csgv.org
URL: http://www.csgv.org/

Federal Bureau of Investigation
J. Edgar Hoover Bldg.
935 Pennsylvania Ave. NW
Washington, DC 20535-0001
(202) 324-3000
URL: http://www.fbi.gov/

Gun Owners of America
8001 Forbes Place, Ste. 102
Springfield, VA 22151
(703) 321-8585
FAX: (703) 321-8408
URL: http://www.gunowners.org/

Law Center to Prevent Gun Violence
268 Bush Street, Ste. 555
San Francisco, CA 94104
(415) 433-2062
FAX: (415) 433-3357
URL: http://smartgunlaws.org/

National Institute of Justice
810 Seventh St. NW
Washington, DC 20531
(202) 307-2942
URL: http://www.ojp.usdoj.gov/nij

National Rifle Association of America
11250 Waples Mill Rd.
Fairfax, VA 22030
1-800-672-3888
URL: http://www.nra.org/

National Safety Council
1121 Spring Lake Dr.
Itasca, IL 60143-3201
(630) 285-1121
1-800-621-7615
FAX: (630) 285-1315
info@nsc.org
URL: http://www.nsc.org/

Office of Juvenile Justice and Delinquency Prevention
810 Seventh St. NW
Washington, DC 20531
(202) 307-5911
URL: http://www.ojjdp.gov/

Second Amendment Foundation
James Madison Bldg.
12500 NE 10th Place
Bellevue, WA 98005
1-800-426-4302
(425) 454-7012
FAX: (425) 451-3959
E-mail: AdminForWeb@saf.org
URL: http://www.saf.org/

U.S. House of Representatives Committee on the Judiciary Subcommittee on Crime, Terrorism, and Homeland Security
B-370B Rayburn House Office Bldg.
Washington, DC 20515
(202) 225-5727
URL: http://judiciary.house.gov/about/subcrime.html

U.S. Senate Committee on the Judiciary Subcommittee on Crime and Terrorism
224 Dirksen Senate Office Bldg.
Washington, DC 20510
(202) 228-3740
URL: http://judiciary.senate.gov/about/subcommittees/crime.cfm

U.S. Supreme Court
1 First St. NE
Washington, DC 20543
(202) 479-3000
URL: http://www.supremecourtus.gov/

Violence Policy Center
1730 Rhode Island Ave. NW, Ste. 1014
Washington, DC 20036
(202) 822-8200
URL: http://www.vpc.org/

RESOURCES

The Bureau of Alcohol, Tobacco, Firearms, and Explosives (ATF) monitors the production and regulation of alcohol, tobacco, firearms, and explosives and is the major source for statistical and technical information on these categories. The annual *State Laws and Published Ordinances—Firearms* (http://www.atf.gov/publications/firearms/state-laws/30th-edition/index.html) provides a complete overview of firearms regulations of towns, cities, states, and the federal government. The ATF also publishes periodic press releases with vital information about licensing, domestic gun manufacturing, and exporting statistics. The ATF formerly provided information on importing statistics as well, but the International Trade Commission has taken over this function.

The Bureau of Justice Statistics (BJS) and the Federal Bureau of Investigation (FBI) maintain statistics on crime in the United States. The FBI's annual *Crime in the United States* (http://www.fbi.gov/about-us/cjis/ucr/crime-in-the-u.s/2010/crime-in-the-u.s.-2010) is based on crime statistics reported through its Uniform Crime Reports program. The FBI also publishes *Law Enforcement Officers Killed and Assaulted* (http://www.fbi.gov/about-us/cjis/ucr/leoka/leoka-2010).

The BJS's annual *Sourcebook of Criminal Justice Statistics* (http://www.albany.edu/sourcebook/) is the most complete source of statistical information published on crime and is updated as new information becomes available. The annual *Criminal Victimization in the United States* (http://bjs.ojp.usdoj.gov/index.cfm?ty=pbdetail&iid=1743) is based on periodic sampling surveys of about 45,000 U.S. households. Another report from the BJS is *Homicide Trends in the United States* (http://bjs.ojp.usdoj.gov/content/homicide/homtrnd.cfm), which provides information on handgun crime, handgun victimization, and weapons trends. In *Indicators of School Crime and Safety* (http://nces.ed.gov/programs/crimeindicators/crimeindicators2011/), the National Center for Education Statistics presents data on school violence.

Information on the National Instant Criminal Background Check System is available online at http://www.fbi.gov/hq/cjisd/nics.htm. Data on background checks for firearms transfers are available from the BJS at http://bjs.ojp.usdoj.gov/index.cfm?ty=pbdetail&iid=2214. The Centers for Disease Control and Prevention has published the results of several studies as part of its National Violent Death Reporting System in the *Morbidity and Mortality Weekly Report* (http://www.cdc.gov/mmwr/). The National Center for Health Statistics provides both national and international data on injury mortality.

Gale, Cengage Learning would like to express its continuing appreciation to the Gallup Organization for its kind permission to publish its surveys and to the National Opinion Research Center of the University of Chicago for use of its material. Thanks also goes to the Pew Research Center for the People and the Press and Harris Interactive for permission to publish material from their surveys. Gale, Cengage Learning would also like to thank the following organizations for permission to use information and tables from their Web postings, reports, and journals: the National Rifle Association of America and the Brady Campaign to Prevent Gun Violence.

INDEX

violent and property victimizations, by gender/race of victim, 80(t5.20)

violent victimizations by, 81t

weapon carrying by students by, 108, 109

of youthful homicide victims, 101, 106

General Social Survey (GSS)

on gun-carrying reasons, behaviors, demographics, 16, 18

on guns in the home, 14

public opinion on gun bans, 125

Geographical region

aggravated assaults, types of weapons used in, by region, 79t

gun ownership by, 15

law enforcement officers accidentally killed, by region, geographic division, state, 73t–74t

law enforcement officers killed, by type of weapon and region, 71t

police deaths/injuries by, 71

public opinion on gun bans by, 125

public opinion on stricter gun control laws by, 123

robbery, by type of weapon used/region, 78(t5.16)

Georgia, state constitution article, 141

Germany, firearms imports from, 11

Giffords, Gabrielle

assassination attempt on, 121

shooting of in Tucson, Arizona, 127, 131

Gingrey, Phil

bill introduced by, 23

gun control laws, argument against stricter, 138–139

Goh, One L., 118

Gonzales v. Raich, 47–48

Gore, Al, 133

Gorski, Gary, 43–44

Green, Christina-Taylor, 131

Grogan Investment Company, Robertson v., 56

Growing up with Guns (Ray), 109

GSS. *See* General Social Survey

Guelff, James, 133

Gun bans

assault weapon ban, Dianne Feinstein on renewal of, 133

in Chicago, court case on, 48

Morton Grove handgun ban, court case on, 53–54

poll respondents' views on banning possession of handguns, 126(t8.3)

public opinion on, 125–126

statement of Kay Bailey Hutchison on, 137

See also Assault weapons

Gun carrying

arguments for stricter gun control laws, 130–131

National Right-to-Carry Reciprocity Act of 2011, arguments for, 135–136

public opinion on open carry restrictions, 126, 127f

public opinion on personal safety if people carry guns openly in public, 20f

reasons, behaviors, demographics of, 16, 18

right-to-carry weapons laws, 19f

state concealed weapons permits, 37

state laws on open carry, 37–39

states allowing gun carrying, 18

"Gun Carrying and Drug Selling among Young Incarcerated Men and Women" (Kacanek & Hemenway), 107

Gun control

debate over, 121–122

modern debate over, 1, 4–7

as personal issue, 121

poll respondents' support for gun rights, by race, 125f

poll respondents' support for gun rights, by sex, 124(f8.3)

poll respondents' views on banning possession of handguns, 126(t8.3)

poll respondents' views on controlling gun ownership vs. protecting right of Americans to own guns, 124(f8.2)

poll respondents' views on gun rights vs. gun control after notable mass shooting incidents, 128f

poll respondents' views on stricter or less strict gun control, 125t

poll respondents' views on stricter vs. less strict laws governing sale of firearms, 123f

poll respondents' views on types of firearms that should be allowed, by current gun ownership, 126(t8.4)

poll respondents' views on whether gun laws should be stricter, by demographic characteristics, 123t

public opinion on after major shootings, 127–128

public opinion on allowing people to openly carry loaded guns in public, 127f

public opinion on gun bans, 125–126

public opinion on gun control as important issue, 122

public opinion on open carry restrictions, 126

public opinion on stricter laws, 123–125

public opinion polls, evaluation of, 122

Gun Control Act of 1968

efforts to amend, 22

Firearms Owners' Protection Act of 1986 and, 22–24

on imported firearms, 11

provisions of, 4, 21–22

Gun Control Act of 1986. *See* Firearms Owners' Protection Act of 1986

Gun control advocates

arguments for stricter gun control laws, 129–133

Brady provisions, controversies over, 32

gun control debate, 121–122

individual rights vs. collective rights, 41

U.S. v. Emerson and, 43

Gun control laws, arguments against stricter

Cornyn, John, 139–140

Gingrey, Phil 138–139

Hutchison, Kay Bailey, 137

Kind, Ron, 135

LaPierre, Wayne, 135

McCain, John, 137–138

Nugent, Rich, 135–136

Rehberg, Dennis, 136

Thune, John, 136–137

Vitter, David, 139

Gun control laws, arguments for stricter

Blumenauer, Earl, 129–130

Feinstein, Dianne, 133

Lautenberg, Frank R., 132–133

Levin, Carl, 130

Richardson, Laura, 130–131

Slaughter, Louise, 131–132

Stevens, John Paul, 132

Gun Control: Potential Effects of Next-Day Destruction of NICS Background Check Records (GAO), 32

Gun dealers

Firearms Commerce Modernization Act, 138–139

five-day waiting period with "interim Brady," 25–26

liability for purchaser's suicide, 56

responsibility for handgun deaths, 56

where criminals obtain firearms, 79–83, 85–86

Gun industry

American Shooting Sports Council, Inc. v. Attorney General, 50–51

liability for gunshot injuries, 56–58

responsibility for handgun deaths, 55–56

"Gun Industry Is Gaining Immunity from Suits" (Butterfield), 58

Gun manufacturers

liability for gunshot injuries, 56–58

liability of, 137

responsibility for handgun deaths, 55–56

"Gun Market Is Wide Open in America" (Sugarmann), 34

Gun Owners of America, 145

Gun ownership

by females, 18–20

gun carrying reasons, behaviors, demographics, 16, 18

gun in the home, trends in, 16f

gun in the home, trends in, by type of firearm/ownership, 16t

guns in the home, 14–15

Virginia Polytechnic Institute and State University
  gun control debate and shooting at, 1
  gun laws passed in response to shooting at, 35–36
  Internet purchase of gun by Seung-Hui Cho, 108
  shooting at, 69, 118
Virginia Tech. *See* Virginia Polytechnic Institute and State University
Virginia Youth Violence Project at the University of Virginia's Curry School of Education, 102
Vitter, David, 23, 139
Volk, Kristin, 19–20
Volokh, Eugene, 3

W

Wade, Roe v., 63
Waiting period
  Brady Handgun Violence Prevention Act and, 4
  elimination of, 31, 32
  five-day waiting period, 25–26
  with "permanent Brady," 122
  Printz v. United States, 46–47
  state firearms control laws, 37
Wal-Mart, 56
Wal-Mart Stores, Inc. v. Coker, 56
Walker, Ben, 116
Wallace, George C., 121
Warin, Francis J., 44
Warin, United States v., 44
Warren, Earl, 41
Warren, James, 51–52
Washington
  open carry law in, 37
  Renton, guns not permitted where alcohol is served, 53
  Seattle's gun ban, state law overrides, 55
  state constitution article, 143
Washington, D.C.
  constitutionality of handgun ban, 48
  Delahanty v. Hinckley, 58
  manufacturer liability issue, 58
  student reports of threats/injuries in, 112
"Weapon Use and Violent Crime" (Perkins), 97
Weapons
  aggravated assaults, types of weapons used in, by region, 79*t*
  assaults on federal officers, by extent of injury/type of weapon, 74(*t*5.10)
  guns, criminal advantages of, 67
  homicide circumstances by weapons used, 63
  homicides, by victim/offender relationship, weapon use, 102*f*
  homicides, by weapon type, 63(*f*5.2)

justifiable homicides, weapons used by law enforcement officers in, 80(*t*5.18)
justifiable homicides, weapons used by private citizens in, 80(*t*5.19)
law enforcement officers assaulted, by circumstance at scene of incident, type of weapon, 75(*t*5.11)
law enforcement officers killed, by type of weapon, region, 71*t*
murder, by state, type of weapon, 65*t*
murder circumstances, by weapon, 64*t*
personal crimes of violence, use of weapons in, by type of crime/victim-offender relationship, 77*t*
police deaths/injuries and, 71
robbery, by type of weapon used/region, 78(*t*5.16)
state constitution articles concerning weapons, 141–143
student reports of threats/injuries, 109, 111–112
students in grades 9–12 who reported being threatened or injured with weapon on school property during last 12 months, 113*t*
students in grades 9–12 who reported being threatened or injured with weapon on school property during last 12 months, by number of times/student characteristics, 114(*t*7.8)
students in grades 9–12 who reported being threatened or injured with weapon on school property during last 12 months, by state, 114(*t*7.9)
students in grades 9–12 who reported carrying weapon at least 1 day in past 30 days, by location/sex, 109*f*
students in grades 9–12 who reported carrying weapon at least 1 day in past 30 days, by race/ethnicity, urbanicity, 110*t*
students in grades 9–12 who reported carrying weapon at least 1 day in past 30 days, by race/ethnicity, location, 111*f*
students who carried a weapon, trends in, 108–109
students who reported carrying weapon, who reported carrying gun at least 1 day in past 30 days, by sex and U.S. location, 115*t*–116*t*
students who reported carrying weapon, who reported carrying gun at least 1 day in past 30 days, by sex, race/ethnicity, and grade, 111*t*
used for suicide, 90
used in aggravated assaults, 76, 79
used in armed robberies, 76
used in homicides, 63
used in justifiable homicides, 79
used in murder-suicides, 66–67
used in school assaults/shootings, 69

violent victimization by use of weapon/weapon type, 78(*t*5.14)
violent victimizations involving weapon, by type of crime/type of weapon, 78(*t*5.15)
youth homicide victims/offenders and, 101
Weapons offenses
  characteristics of weapons offenders, 87
  definition of, 86
  juvenile arrests for, 103–104
Web-Based Injury Statistics Query and Reporting System (WISQARS)
  on cost of firearm injuries, 96–97
  data on firearm fatalities, 90
  on nonfatal gunshot injuries, 89
  tracking of firearm-related injuries, 89
Webber, Reagan, 119
Weber, Joseph, 19–20
Webster, Daniel W., 107
Weise, Jeffrey, 117
West Hollywood, California, 55
West Nickel Mines Amish School, Nickel Mines, Pennsylvania, 118–119
West Virginia, state constitution article, 143
Wexler, Chuck, 103–104
When Men Murder Women: An Analysis of 2010 Homicide Data (Violence Policy Center), 66
Whirlpool Corporation, 51
White House, shooting incidents at, 121
Whites
  gun carrying by, 18
  public opinion on gun control after shooting of Trayvon Martin, 128
  public opinion on gun rights/ownership, 124
  students feeling unsafe at school, 113
  victimization, demographics of, 79
  weapon carrying by students, 108–109
  weapons offenders, 87
  youthful homicide offenders, 104–105
  youthful homicide victims, 106
Whitman, Coalition of New Jersey Sportsmen v., 51
"Why Do Adults Kill Children?" (Fox), 119
Wilchinski, Joseph, 50
Wilchinski, State v., 50
William III, King of England, 2
Williams, Daniel, 58
Williams Companies Inc., 51
Williams v. Beemiller, Inc., 58
Wintemute, Garen J., 108
Wisconsin
  concealed carry law of, 135
  state constitution article, 143
WISQARS. *See* Web-Based Injury Statistics Query and Reporting System
Women. *See* Females; Gender

CPSIA information can be obtained
at www.ICGtesting.com
Printed in the USA
FFOW021410280613
1326FF